THE DESIGN OF COMPETITION LAW INSTITUTIONS

LAW AND GLOBAL GOVERNANCE SERIES

Editors:
Andrew Hurrell, Benedict Kingsbury, and Richard B. Stewart

Global governance involves the exercise of power, beyond a single state, to influence behaviour, to generate resources, or to allocate authority. Regulatory structures, and law of all kinds, increasingly shape the nature, use, and effects of such power. These dynamic processes of ordering and governance blend the extra-national with the national, the public with the private, the political and economic with the social and cultural. Issues of effectiveness, justice, voice, and inequality in these processes are growing in importance. This series features exceptional works of original research and theory—both sector-specific and conceptual—that carry forward the serious understanding and evaluation of these processes of global governance and the role of law and institutions within them. Contributions from all disciplines are welcomed. The series aims especially to deepen scholarship and thinking in international law, international politics, comparative law and politics, and public and private global regulation. A major goal is to study governance globally, and to enrich the literature on law and the nature and effects of global governance beyond the North Atlantic region.

ALSO PUBLISHED IN THE SERIES

Governance by Indicators
Global Power through Quantification and Rankings
Edited by Kevin E. Davis, Angelina Fisher, Benedict Kingsbury, and Sally Engle Merry

The Design of Competition Law Institutions

Global Norms, Local Choices

Edited by
ELEANOR M. FOX
and
MICHAEL J. TREBILCOCK

OXFORD
UNIVERSITY PRESS

OXFORD
UNIVERSITY PRESS

Great Clarendon Street, Oxford, OX2 6DP,
United Kingdom

Oxford University Press is a department of the University of Oxford.
It furthers the University's objective of excellence in research, scholarship,
and education by publishing worldwide. Oxford is a registered trade mark of
Oxford University Press in the UK and in certain other countries

First Edition published in 2013

Published in the United States of America by Oxford University Press
198 Madison Avenue, New York, NY 10016, United States of America

British Library Cataloguing in Publication Data
Data available

Library of Congress Cataloging in Publication Data
Data available

ISBN 978–0–19–967004–8

Acknowledgments

We acknowledge with much gratitude the generous financial assistance of the International Development Research Centre of Ottawa, Canada, and the special help and advice of Susan Joekes, Senior Program Specialist at IDRC.

We acknowledge, also, the summer research support of the Filomen D'Agostino and Max E. Greenberg Foundation.

We owe many personal debts. Many thanks to Professors Richard Stewart and Benedict Kingsbury, founders of the project on Global Administrative Law, for sparking the GAL competition project and giving us inspiration and guidance throughout; to Megan Donaldson of NYU's Institute for International Law and Justice for her administration of the project; to NYU Law graduate students Marcos Exposto Jr., Kojiro Fujii, Shashank Gautum, and Tara Kelly for their excellent assistance at the various stages of the project; and of course to the whole GAL competition project team, the authors of the chapters from around the world, with whom we worked intensively to bring the project and book to fruition. Thanks also to our NYU assistant, Linda Smalls, for her tireless work on coordinating the many pieces.

Eleanor M. Fox
New York, New York
Michael J. Trebilcock
Toronto, Canada
May 2012

Contents

List of Contributors

Francisco Agüero is Director of the Center on Regulation and Competition in the Faculty of Law, University of Chile, and Secretary to the Expert Panel of the General Law of Electricity Services.

Arianna Andreangeli is the Lecturer in Competition Law at Edinburgh Law School, University of Edinburgh.

Amedeo Arena is Assistant Professor of International and European Union Law at the University of Naples "Federico II" School of Law.

Dennis Davis is a Judge of the High Court of South Africa, Judge President of the Competition Appeal Court of South Africa, and an Honorary Professor of Law at the University of Cape Town.

Harry First is Charles L. Denison Professor of Law at New York University School of Law, Director of the Law School's Competition, Innovation, and Information Law Program, and Co-Director of the Engelberg Center on Innovation Law and Policy.

Eleanor M. Fox is Walter J. Derenberg Professor of Trade Regulation at the New York University School of Law.

Lara Granville is an attorney at Norton Rose South Africa, Johannesburg.

Daniel E. Hemli is a partner at Bracewell & Giuliani LLP, New York.

Edward Iacobucci is the Osler Chair in Business Law in the Faculty of Law at the University of Toronto.

Ioannis Lianos is Reader in Competition Law and Economics at University College London, and Director of UCL's Centre for Law, Economics & Society.

Santiago Montt is a Senior Researcher at the Center on Regulation and Competition, Faculty of Law, University of Chile.

Simon Peart is an Associate at Freshfields Bruckhaus Deringer, London.

Tadashi Shiraishi is Professor of Competition Law in the Graduate Schools for Law and Politics at the University of Tokyo.

Jessica Su is a Postdoctoral Fellow at the Chinese Academy of Social Sciences.

Michael J. Trebilcock is University Professor and Professor of Law and Economics at the University of Toronto.

Xiaoye Wang is Distinguished Professor of Law at Hunan University and the Chinese Academy of Social Sciences, and Consultant Expert for the Anti-Monopoly Commission under the State Council of the People's Republic of China.

List of Abbreviations

AB	Appellate Body
ACCC	Australian Competition and Consumer Commission
ACT	Australian Competition Tribunal
AER	Australian Energy Regulator
ALJ (US)	administrative law judge
AMA (Japan)	Anti-Monopoly Act
AMC (China)	Anti-Monopoly Commission
AMEA (China)	Anti-Monopoly Enforcement Agencies
AML (China)	Anti-Monopoly Law
AMP (Can)	Administrative Monetary Penalties
AMSA (SA)	Arcelor Mittal South Africa
ANZ	Australia and New Zealand
ANZCERTA	Australia New Zealand Closer Economic Relations Trade Agreement
ASBP	abuse of a superior bargaining position
AUCL (China)	Anti-Unfair Competition Law
AUPMR (Japan)	Act against Unjustifiable Premiums and Misleading Representations
BIAC	Business and Industry Advisory Committee to the OECD
BRIC	Brazil, Russia, India, China
CAC (SA)	Competition Appeal Court
CADE (Brazil)	Administrative Council for Economic Defense
CCE (EU)	Chief Competition Economist
CCPB	Competition and Consumer Policies Branch of UNCTAD
CDPP (Aus)	Commonwealth Department of Public Prosecutions
CER (NZ)	Closer Economic Relations framework
COPAL	program of capacity building in Latin America
CRTC	Canadian Radio-television and Telecommunications Commission
CSRC (China)	China Securities Regulatory Commission
DG Comp (EU)	Directorate General for Competition
DOJ (US)	Department of Justice
DSU (US)	Dispute Settlement Understanding
DSB	Dispute Settlement Body
ECC	Economic Council of Canada
ECMR	EC Merger Regulation
ECSC	European Coal and Steel Community
FNE (Chile)	Fiscalía Nacional Ecónomica
FTC (US)	Federal Trade Commission
GAL	Global Administrative Law
GATS	General Agreement on Trade in Services
GATT (EU)	General Agreement on Tariffs and Trade
HSR (US)	Hart-Scott-Rodino Act
ICN	International Competition Network
JFTC	Japan Fair Trade Commission

MITI (Japan)	Ministry of International Trade and Industry
MOFCOM (China)	Ministry of Commerce
MOU (SA)	memorandum of understanding
NAAG	National Association of Attorneys General
NAFTA	North American Free Trade Agreement
NCA (EU)	National Competition Authorities
NCC (Aus)	National Competition Council
NDRC (China)	National Development and Reform Commission
NEP (Chile)	National Economic Prosecutor
NEPO (Chile)	National Economic Prosecutor's Office
NGA	Non-governmental advisor
NGO	Non-governmental organization
NPC (China)	National People's Congress
NZCC	New Zealand Commerce Commission
OECD	Organisation for Economic Co-operation and Development
OEEC	Organization for European Cooperation
PAIA (SA)	Promotion of Access to Information Act
PPO (Japan)	Public Prosecutors' Office
RCD	Regulated Conduct Defence
SA	South Africa
SADC (SA)	Southern African Development Community
SAFE (China)	State Administration of Foreign Exchange
SAIC (China)	State Administration for Industry and Commerce
SASAC (China)	State-Owned Assets Supervision and Administration Commission
SCA (SA)	Supreme Court of Appeal
SDE (Brazil)	Secretariat of Economic Law of the Ministry of Justice
SEAE (Brazil)	Secretariat of Economic Monitoring of the Ministry of Finance
SEM (ANZ)	Single Economic Market
SERNAC (Chile)	National Consumer Service
SII (Japan)	Structural Impediments Initiative
SIR (Can)	Supplementary Information Request
SME	Small- and medium-sized enterprises
SOE (China)	state-owned enterprises
STE	State Trading Enterprises
TAC (SA)	Treatment Action Campaign
TBT	Technical Barriers to Trade
TFEU	Treaty on the Functioning of the European Union
TRIMs	Agreement on Trade-Related Investment Measures
TRIPs	Agreement on Trade-Related Aspects of Intellectual Property Rights
TSO (NZ)	Telecommunications Services Obligation
UNCTAD	United Nations Conference on Trade and Development
VER	voluntary export restraints
VOIP	Voice Over Internet Protocol
WTO	World Trade Organization

1

Introduction

The GAL Competition Project: The Global Convergence of Process Norms

Eleanor M. Fox and Michael J. Trebilcock

I. The birth and evolution of the project

In 2004 New York University School of Law launched a project that has become a new area of law: Global Administrative Law, known in the literature as GAL. Professors Richard Stewart and Benedict Kingsbury developed this concept against the backdrop of globalization, the shrinking borders between nations, and the rise of international systems of governance.

Were these international systems of governance accountable and legitimate? Were the procedures and outputs fair? Transparent? Predictable? Were the decision-makers sufficiently expert? Were the systems efficient? How should they be assessed? Are there benchmarks by which the new institutions of governance can be evaluated?

Some scholars have engaged with the problem by invoking "global constitutionalism": rules from above. GAL attacks the problem from below.[1] GAL begins by reference to administrative law: requirements of accountability and legitimacy as informed by more specific norms such as transparency, reason-giving by decision-makers, and rights of review. Many of the GAL projects work from the ground up to uncover the process norms embedded in a system, to observe how the norms are formulated and applied, and how systems and their norms interact, with due respect to culture and context. This modus operandi does not presume a single best design or order. It reflects the aspiration, by knowledge, assessment, and increasing convergence of process norms and the institutional designs that reflect them, to improve global governance.

[1] *See* Benedict Kingsbury, Nico Krisch, Richard B. Stewart, and Jonathan B. Wiener, "Foreword: Global Governance as Administration—National and Transnational Approaches to Global Administrative Law," 68 Law and Contemporary Problems 1 (2005).

A description of the GAL project and links to numerous papers written under its aegis may be found at <http://www.iilj.org/GAL/GALNetwork.asp>.

During its first five years, participants in the GAL projects studied areas of law in which the global space was occupied by global institutions with powers of rule-making and adjudication, such as trade law and environmental law. In 2010, the project list expanded to include national law with intertwined international implications, and GAL launched this project on competition law. Although competition law is essentially national, the intense global nature of markets means that one nation's system affects its sister systems, and virtually every national system affects people and firms beyond its borders. Consider, for example, the proposed and aborted iron ore joint venture of Rio Tinto (UK) and BHP Billiton (Australia); or the practices of Microsoft, Intel, and Google; or the cartels in vitamins and lysene, all of which rippled around the world and were vetted in scores of nations.

In recognition of the deep interconnections, international institutions with a competition function have expanded their number and scope. The newest player is the International Competition Network, now comprising 120 competition authorities from 106 jurisdictions. An international law of competition was once on the World Trade Organization's notional agenda, and although it slipped from the agenda, it may resurface. In any event, WTO rules and initiatives deeply affect world competition, some more explicitly than others. The procedure/process/performance norms of the global institutions that bear on competition law affect all citizens of the world.

Fortuitously, quite separately from the GAL project, the subject of procedure and process norms in competition law has become a prominent issue in the world competition community in the last several years. Christine Varney gave a speech early in her tenure as US Assistant Attorney General in charge of Antitrust devoted to process norms, particularly transparency,[2] and she initiated a project on the subject at the Organisation for Economic Co-Operation and Development.[3] Meanwhile, in Europe, issues of fairness of process in the context of the EU administrative and inquisitorial model began to take a high profile, particularly with the advent of very high fines in cartel and abuse cases that were likened to criminal punishment. The Lisbon Treaty, with the promise of accession of the European Union to the European Convention on Human Rights, has influenced the debate on what protections a guarantee of fundamental rights demands. This

[2] Christine A. Varney, Assistant Attorney General, US Dep't of Justice, Coordinated Remedies: Convergence, Cooperation, and the Role of Transparency (February 15, 2010), <http://www.justice.gov/atr/public/speeches/255189.htm>. *See* Rachel Brandenburger, Special Advisor, International Antitrust Division, US Dep't of Justice, International Competition Policy and Practice: New Perspectives?, King's College, London (October 29, 2010), <http://www.justice.gov/atr/public/speeches/70980.htm>.

For some years Bill Kovacic, drawing on work of Douglass North and Hernando de Soto, has identified institutional and performance norms as crucial to the effectiveness of competition authorities. *See*, e.g., William E. Kovacic, "Rating the Competition Agencies: What Constitutes Good Performance?," 16 Geo. Mason L. Rev. 903 (2009); William E. Kovacic, "Getting Started: Creating New Competition Policy Institutions in Transition Economies," 23 Brook. J. Int'l L. 403 (1997).

The OECD, ICN, and UNCTAD have undertaken projects on agency effectiveness. Their projects express and reflect notional best practices for increasing agency effectiveness.

[3] *See* Procedural Fairness and Transparency—2012 (OECD), <http://www.oecd.org/document/20/0,3746,en_2649_37463_50235668_1_1_1_37463,00.html>, summarizing the OECD's three roundtable discussions on transparency and procedural fairness held during 2010 and 2011.

debate, and the policy-making and litigation surrounding it, are now a central focus of attention in Europe and elsewhere. As more jurisdictions, especially developing countries, adopt competition laws, and yet others modernize their laws, the subject has special and immediate practical importance. The GAL Competition Project is thus especially timely.

In 2010, the authors of this chapter became co-directors of the GAL Competition Project. We chose a representative selection of jurisdictions by continent or region and stages of economic development, assembled teams from these jurisdictions, and prepared a common research template.[4]

The jurisdictions/institutions represented in the study and the team members are:

Australia/New Zealand:	Simon Peart, Freshfields Bruckhaus Deringer, London
Canada:	Michael Trebilcock and Edward Iacobucci, University of Toronto
Chile:	Santiago Montt and Francisco Agüero, University of Chile
China:	Xiaoye Wang and Jessica Su, Chinese Academy of Social Sciences
Japan:	Harry First, New York University, and Tadashi Shiraishi, University of Tokyo
South Africa:	Dennis Davis, Competition Appeal Court, South Africa, and Lara Granville, Norton Rose, Johannesburg
United States:	Harry First and Eleanor Fox, New York University, and Daniel Hemli, Bracewell & Giuliani, New York
European Union:	Ioannis Lianos, University College London, and Arianna Andreangeli, University of Edinburgh
International institutions:	Eleanor Fox, NYU, and Amedeo Arena, University of Naples

Brazil and India, two notable fast-growing economies, are not included in the in-depth studies. The Brazilian competition system was reorganized after the country studies were complete, and India's law had seen virtually no enforcement at that time. Given the importance of these two jurisdictions, we include them in our country summaries, later in this chapter.

The members of the GAL Competition team drafted papers describing the institutional design of their country or jurisdiction, identifying the mandate of the competition authority therein, the norms embedded in the system for both rights of defense and institutional performance, and the trade-offs made (for example, more administrative efficiency versus more transparency or more rights of defense), and evaluating conformity with the list of notional norms in the template. For example, the due process norms in case-by-case decision-making include the opportunity to be heard and the open-mindedness of decision-makers;

[4] The relevant part of the template is set out in an appendix to this chapter.

institutional performance norms include timeliness, expertise, transparency, and accountability. The full list is set out in the research template appended to this chapter. The group met for a workshop at New York University School of Law in February 2011 to discuss draft papers. The workshop was joined by Stephen Harris, now of Baker & McKenzie, as China expert to stand in for Xiaoye Wang and Jessica Su, whose obligations required them to remain in China.

The papers were revised in the light of vigorous discussions at the workshop and thereafter. This volume presents the papers, each of which is deeply factual and contextual as well as evaluative. This introductory essay provides an overview of the major cross-cutting themes in the papers, including major points of convergence and divergence, as well as the major normative issues relating to institutional design and decision-making processes across the developed and developing world.

We can report that our country studies, and our study of the EU and the international bodies, demonstrate a remarkable degree of consensus on the basic procedural requirements and institutional performance norms of competition law institutions. Although the systems entail a range of approaches, we, as competition law scholars and lawyers, basically speak the same "language" and care about the same procedural/process values. There are some differences, which we are able to articulate within a common frame of reference. If the point of GAL is to take a ground-up approach towards revealing and nudging convergence of process norms, competition law globally seems well on its way to substantiating the project's hypothesis.

We note the limits as well as the breadth of the project. As explained, we selected eight national competition law systems, the European Union, and four international institutions as the database for study. Perhaps this study will inspire an enlargement of the sample. Scholars will have no dearth of attractive and diverse candidates from which to choose, including Brazil and India (for which we provide summaries but no separate studies), Egypt, Indonesia, Kenya, South Korea, Mexico, Russia, and Singapore, among many others.

As suggested, we conclude, albeit within our sample, that the procedure/process norms can be fulfilled within a number of institutional designs. At the end of this chapter we ask: if this is so, what relevance has this work to the project of convergence of competition laws? Our answer is, it has high relevance. In a world of more than 100 national competition law systems and thus potential for high costs of system clashes, the sympathy of national systems to one another is a compelling objective. Convergence of procedure/process norms, which we observe herein, no less than convergence of substantive law, enhances respect, regard, and legitimacy, and thus, the sympathy of nations.

II. Themes—A synthesis

We embarked upon this project without strong preconceptions of a best model for effective and procedurally fair systems. Fundamental design choices are, to an important extent, a function of a country's history and legal, political, and economic culture. We sought to identify specific shortfalls, on the one hand, and to identify choices likely to contribute to better performance and sense of legitimacy, on the other. In this spirit, we turn seriatim to institutional design, mandate of the agency, due process, and institutional performance.

A. Institutional design

At the start of the project we identified the three basic models: the bifurcated judicial model (the competition authority goes to court for enforcement), the bifurcated agency/tribunal model (the agency goes to a specialized tribunal for enforcement), and the integrated agency model (a commission within the agency makes the first-level adjudication). Among the nine national/regional jurisdictions studied there are examples or variants of each. Canada, South Africa, and Chile are examples of the bifurcated agency model; the EU, Japan, China, and US Federal Trade Commission are examples of the integrated agency model; and the US Antitrust Division of the Department of Justice (DOJ) exemplifies the bifurcated judicial model. India combines elements of the bifurcated agency model and integrated agency model. Australia and New Zealand combine elements of all three.

The studies reveal that, where courts are weak (as they are in many developing countries), the bifurcated or integrated agency/tribunal models have some significant advantages. On the other hand, where courts are strong, independent, honest, and efficient (as in the US), the bifurcated judicial model has some significant advantages. In jurisdictions adopting bifurcated agency/tribunal models, the South African, Chilean, and Canadian experiences reveal the importance of ensuring that the members of the adjudicative tribunal have substantial legal and economic expertise of a consistent and continuous nature. The Canadian experience demonstrates pitfalls of lack of such expertise.

Whichever model is chosen, cases go to court, whether immediately or ultimately. The studies reveal numerous problems with court systems including unacceptable delays and unknowledgeable jurists. In some jurisdictions, review of agency or tribunal determinations is de novo (South Africa) and in others review is deferential to fact-finding, at least normally and to some extent (European Union; US—appeals from the FTC). Concerns have arisen in both directions—too much intrusion by appellate courts (South Africa)[5] and too little examination by appellate courts (the European Union)[6]—thus underlining the observation that there are costs, benefits, and trade-offs of both approaches, and feasible solutions are particular to the context.

Design includes many other factors. Is competition law located in a common law or civil law system? Is enforcement civil only or also criminal? Is there one federal

[5] The South African law provides for de novo review of Tribunal decisions. This means that the Court of Appeal may substitute its judgment on facts for that of the Tribunal, and it often does. *See* South Africa country study, Chapter 7 *infra*.

[6] In the European Union, the General Court may set aside fact-finding by the European Commission only if the Commission has made manifest errors of assessment. Concerns of insufficient due process have led to proposals for more thorough appellate review.

enforcement body or more (as in China and the United States)? Is there a right of private enforcement, and how does private enforcement interact with public enforcement? The elements vary from jurisdiction to jurisdiction, with virtually all jurisdictions aspiring to efficient and effective enforcement subject to effective protection of rights, and subject to the context of the jurisdiction.

The status quo can include less-than-optimal institutions that may be politically difficult to dislodge. For example, observers of the US system note the jurisdictional overlaps of the Department of Justice Antitrust Division and the Federal Trade Commission, and some have emphasized attendant tensions.[7] Some reformers propose abolishing the competition arm of the FTC or consolidating merger review in either the FTC or DOJ. In Europe, concern focuses on the combination of the functions of investigator, prosecutor, and judge. Some reformers have proposed spinning-off the EU Competition Directorate to create an agency obliged to bring cases before an independent court, although current proposals with traction are more modest.

Dramatic changes may be difficult to execute especially at a mature stage of the institutions. Less dramatic adjustments may be the practical course, and might work better than a large reform whose own weaknesses may unfold only in time.[8] Yet sometimes major reform seems wise and achievable, as appears to be so in the case of consolidation in Brazil.

Some of the problems traceable to institutional design manifest themselves in due process and institutional performance, which we discuss below.

B. Mandate

The mandate of the competition authorities within our sample varies. All, of course, are charged with enforcing the competition law. Some authorities have consumer protection responsibilities (the US FTC, the Canadian Competition Bureau); others do not. Some function also as sector regulators (Australia). The Indian law prescribes a non-binding consultative mechanism between the Competition Commission and the sector regulators. Some systems authorize simultaneous competition and regulatory enforcement; some favor preemption by the regulatory

[7] *See*, e.g., Thomas Catan, "This Takeover Battle Pits Bureaucrat v. Bureaucrat," Wall Street J., April 12, 2011, quoting William Kovacic, then a Commissioner of the FTC. But compare US country study, Chapter 8 *infra*.

[8] *See* John Fingleton, when Chief Executive of the Office of Fair Trading of the UK, regarding the UK Government's proposed consolidation of the UK competition authorities: "The OFT has long recognised the potential benefits of a merger between the OFT and the Competition Commission (CC), particularly the opportunity for improved consistency, more efficient use of resources and greater flexibility. That said, the current regime is widely accepted as already being impactful and effective, and reforms should therefore build on these strengths."

"Big systemic changes should only be introduced where they will clearly contribute to the promotion of growth in the economy, given the potential risks and costs involved and the time needed to bed such changes in. Generally, incremental reform is preferable. . . . " J. Fingleton, "The future of the competition regime: increasing consumer welfare and economic growth," 25 May 2011, <http://www.oft.gov.uk/news-and-updates/speeches/2011/1011>.

The UK is, however, in the process of a major consolidation of agencies.

regime. Where preemption does not occur, jurisdictions differ as to the scope of competition law in regulated sectors.

With respect to the competition law mandate itself, degrees of consistency and predictability are influenced by the objectives of the law and how clearly they are articulated. A specific objective, such as consumer welfare or total welfare, constrains the discretion of the agency and tightens its focus, both in choosing priorities and evaluating particular practices and transactions. Regimes with a broader set of objectives, such as South Africa, China, and Japan in our project, face more daunting challenges in articulating clear and consistent rules of law.

C. Due process and rights of defense

In case-by-case decision-making, integrated agencies, such as the EU, Japan, China, and the US FTC in our project, raise systemic concerns that the integration of investigation, enforcement, and adjudicative functions create bias or lack of objectivity ("confirmation bias"),[9] or the appearance of it, in the discharge of the adjudicatory functions vested in the agencies. At least in perception, integration of these functions may render the agencies "judges in their own cause." There are avenues by which these concerns can be and have been addressed even within the integrated agency format. For example, the agency can sharply separate investigative and enforcement functions from the adjudicative functions through use of different personnel and through firewalls. The European system integrates prosecutor and adjudicator and applies a non-adversarial administrative tradition common in civil law jurisdictions. This approach trades off more rights of defense (for example, to cross-examine witnesses and to argue to decision-makers with no prior involvement in the case) for more efficiency and effectiveness in enforcement. The conformity of the system to notions of basic rights, especially as applied to high-stakes litigation, is being challenged in the European Union courts and may ultimately be taken to the European Court on Human Rights. The Human Rights Court thus far has upheld the consistency with human rights of systems featuring integrated agencies at least where the system offers robust appellate court review in cases that are not hard-core criminal cases.[10] Meanwhile, the European Commission has responded to concerns about systemic bias by strengthening the functions of the hearing officer, mandating transparency of intended fines and how they are calculated, and extending state-of-play meetings to cartel cases.[11] A pending

[9] Confirmation bias entails a person's readiness to accept the version of a story that confirms his or her pre-existing beliefs. *See* Wouter Wils, "The Combination of the Investigative and Prosecutorial Function and the Adjudicative Function," 27 World Competition L. & Econ. Rev. 202, 215 (2004).

[10] *See* A. Menarini Diagnostics, European Court of Human Rights, 27 September 2011; KME, Case C-272/09 P, European Court of Justice, 8 December 2011. *See* Wouter Wils, "EU Anti-trust Enforcement Powers and Procedural Rights and Guarantees: The Interplay between EU Law, National Law, the Charter of Fundamental Rights of the EU and the European Convention on Human Rights," 27 World Competition L. & Econ. Rev. 189, 203–6 (2011). *See* also the European Union study in this project, Chapter V *infra*.

[11] *See* Joaquín Almunia, Vice President of the European Commission responsible for Competition Policy, Fair process in EU competition enforcement, remarks at European Competition Day,

proposal would mandate more thorough rights of review in the European courts. Adversarial modes of adjudication may guarantee certain other rights of defense—such as the right to cross-examination of witnesses and the right to a full trial, which inquisitorial systems, common in civil law countries, do not normally offer.

We cannot conclude from our limited but fairly representative database that separation of prosecutorial and decisional functions, and the right to an adversarial trial including cross-examination, are currently global norms,[12] even if it may be argued that they should be.[13] We personally share the view that separation of functions is normally desirable, particularly in cases where much is at stake. Where separation is not practical, the tasks of investigation and prosecution, and the task of drafting the decision, might be assigned to different individuals in order better to preserve the right to argue to an open mind. The separation of functions and the right to cross-examination increase in importance as the consequences of the violation become more severe.

Certain more particular shortcomings emerge in a number of our studies, both in civil law and common law systems.

Our studies include instances of failure to notify investigation targets at an early stage of the substance of the issues being investigated and the evidence being relied upon, and the failure to provide opportunities for affected parties to address the issues and evidence in a timely way prior to formal adjudication of the issues. The jurisdictions generally agree that parties to a formal proceeding have the right to be fully apprised in a timely fashion of the allegations they face and the evidence being relied on to support them. What is full and what is timely is often a matter of debate.

In formal adjudicative proceedings, both inquisitorial and adversarial, there is consensus that decisions should be reasoned decisions and that these decisions should be made public, in the interests of transparency, predictability, and accountability. Courts may recognize different levels of robustness for rights of defense: a significant but comparatively lower level for civil/administrative cases, a higher level for cases imbued with some elements of a criminal action (for example, extremely high fines), and a very high level for unambiguously criminal prosecutions. There is consensus that formal settlements should be on the public record, along with supporting explanations or justifications. In a growing number of jurisdictions, provisional settlements are made public and interested parties have the opportunity to challenge the terms. If there is an outlying jurisdiction, it may be China; two of its three agencies need not publish their decisions (or judgments) determining adjudicated cases.

Budapest, 30 May 2011, <http://ec.europa.eu/competition/speeches/index_speeches_by_the_commissioner.html>.

[12] The authors of the European Union study in this volume express their view that the litigation system of the European Commission fails to satisfy appropriate standards for rights of defense.

[13] *See* European Union study, Chapter 9.

D. Agency performance

Various norms emerge across both inquisitorial and adversarial systems. These include timeliness of decision-making, predictability, expertise, transparency, independence, efficiency and effectiveness, and accountability. The jurisdictions embraced by our project exhibit a mix of strengths and weaknesses along these various dimensions. All appear to subscribe to the norms but some do not meet their aspirations. Again, China may be the outlier. The Chinese agencies are part of the state; independence is not to be expected; and the referent for consistency is party policy, not autonomous rules of competition law—even though most outcomes are consistent with international practice.

Excessive delays, lack of predictability, and lack of consistency in decision-making plague several systems. Lack of legal and economic expertise is a recurrent problem. Shortfalls in expertise are especially likely in younger and resource-starved jurisdictions, and also in small economies without a critical mass of competition cases. Some jurisdictions suffer from lack of reasoned decision-making, lack of publication of decisions, and lack of independence from political interference at some or all stages—investigative, enforcement, and adjudicative. Political interference varies from rare to pervasive. Institutional arrangements that tend to ensure public accountability of the agency on a regular basis are generally recognized as a virtue. The strengths and weaknesses in performance do not divide neatly by basic regime type. The studies display general agreement about what the appropriate norms are in evaluating these systemic performance qualities.

E. Trade-offs

Jurisdictions make many and different trade-offs. The US, in enforcement by the DOJ, generally prefers more expansive rights of defense to more expeditious investigations and prosecution. The EU, in the context of an inquisitorial rather than an adversarial system, strikes a different balance. The competition agencies in our sample all recognize rights of confidentiality, although in some jurisdictions attorney-client privilege is quite limited. Protection of confidential documents and other information can mean less transparency, less effective enforcement, and barriers to private enforcement.

F. Appeals: Appellate tribunals and courts

All jurisdictions we studied provide a right of appeal, which is one of the universal rights of defense. Some jurisdictions allow a series of yet higher appeals. In this subsection on appeals we make the following observations:

1. A right of appeal to a panel of decision-makers who can set aside decisions based on error is a recognized right of defense. So too is this function a recognized vehicle for obtaining more clarity and thus more predictability of the law. Scope of review of fact-finding differs, with some court reviews limited to manifest error and

others assigned de novo review. Particularly where there is a lack of separation of prosecutor and decision-maker, more in-depth review seems appropriate. On the other hand, an appeals process that entails in-depth review of all of the facts can lead to excessive delays and sometimes excessive reversals, and a rule of deference to an unbiased fact-finder who stays within a range of appreciation has merit.

2. In some jurisdictions, appeal lies to a specialized tribunal or court; in others to a general court. Our studies show that tribunals or courts denominated "specialized" are not necessarily composed of experts; that creation of a specialized tribunal or court does not ensure more expert decisions. Specialized tribunals or courts can add expertise, but they can also breed bias.[14] Our studies make the related observation that, in many smaller and younger jurisdictions, and even some larger, mature ones such as Japan and Canada, so few cases reach the specialized tribunals that the members of the tribunal develop virtually no expertise on the job. This is especially the case for part-time members. Our studies and dialogue revealed a worrying incidence of reviewing jurists who were not sufficiently conversant with competition law analysis.

3. In some jurisdictions the defendant has access to nearly endless appeals or other opportunities to tie up the case until the initial fact-finding is stale. In our workshop we discussed this phenomena as "undue process."[15] In South Africa, the potentially four-stage appeals process is too long. In Brazil, the Nestlé/Garota merger—prohibited by the competition tribunal, CADE, but consummated—has been on appeal for twelve years. Delay is a major concern in India, where the second and final appeal in competition cases lies with a notoriously overburdened court. In Mexico, defendants make liberal use of the amparo (habeas corpus-like injunction against an agency order), which can cause almost infinite delay. TelMex has escaped the Federal Competition Commission's authority for a quarter of a century. Its parent and sister corporations América Móvil and Telcel may be following a similar path.[16] Within our sample, there was also a worrying incidence of foot-dragging and delays in the courts.

4. In at least one case in our sample (South Africa), the Tribunal generally takes a teleological approach to the statute while the court takes a more technical lawyerly approach. The Tribunal has struck the balance in favor of more efficiency in performance (for example, in terms of length of argument, number of witness statements) as well as in favor of more economic opportunity for market players in its substantive interpretations. The Appeals Court and the yet higher court have struck a different balance: more rights of defense and a narrower interpretation of the proscriptions of law. Moreover, the Appeals Court reviews the Tribunal's fact-finding de novo. These factors have resulted in numerous reversals.

[14] The United States has a specialized appeals court for patent and trademark issues: The Court of Appeals for the Federal Circuit. These cases often involve antitrust issues. The Federal Circuit tends to place protection of patents higher in the hierarchy than protection of competition.

[15] *See* Adam Samaha, "Undue Process," 59 Stanford L. Rev. 601 (2006), for the coining of the term.

[16] *See* América Móvil obtiene amparo, México Noticias—3 October 2011, <http://legislaciones.item.org.uy/index?q=node/3335>.

5. As the foregoing paragraphs demonstrate, the courts can undo what the agencies and tribunals have done, for better or for worse. While reversals may sometimes be justified, it is common cause that agency decisions should never be compromised by excessive and unreasonable delay (see point 3), jurists who do not understand the case (see point 2), and even worse, corruption in the courts. Court ineffectiveness unravels agency effectiveness.

G. The international institutions

The international institutions do not fit neatly into our four categories for analysis, but the existence of and prospects for these organizations are central to competition law and its future; therefore design, process, and procedure are likewise critical as applied to these institutions. Indeed, as noted at the outset of this chapter, international institutions were the initial subject of the overarching GAL project, whose founders addressed the concern that international institutions were proliferating without normative checks on processes and procedures.

GAL itself, by co-founder Professor Richard Stewart, has examined the WTO in view of GAL normative benchmarks.[17]

We included the WTO in the GAL Competition Project because of its distinct relation to competition policy. The WTO may be seen as a node in the world competition network; indeed, a central connecting node. National competition law systems are conceptually and notionally linked to the WTO, which to an important extent prohibits its member states from doing what national law prohibits its private actors from doing (impairing trade and competition). The WTO bridges half the gap.[18]

In the WTO study in this volume, we found that adjudication and performance norms are moderately well met by the WTO's reformed dispute resolution system. However, case resolution in the WTO is slow; expertise varies among the individuals chosen as panel members; and predictability of outcomes is only moderate. Rights of defense to introduce evidence and be heard are not a problem, but there is a tilt toward the more powerful nations both because of bargaining power at the outset (the nations negotiate the rules) and in view of the greater difficulties facing weaker nations in calling violators to account. If competition law should in the future become an independent competence of the WTO, the intensity of fact finding, the lack of rules of evidence, and the inexperience of panels in dealing with competition evidence are problems that will need to be addressed.

The Organisation for Economic Co-operation and Development (OECD), the United Nations Conference on Trade and Development (UNCTAD), and the International Competition Network (ICN) are also bridging institutions. They

[17] *See* Richard Stewart and Michelle Ratton Sanchez Badin, "The World Trade Organization and Global Administrative Law" (2009), New York University Public Law and Legal Theory Working Paper 166, <http://lsr.nellco.org/nyu_plltwp/166>.

[18] The other half is not attended to. Private actors may, in most cases, restrain trade and competition if they hurt "only" foreigners, unless the victim nation has proscriptive law against these restraints (such as export cartels) and has practical power to catch them.

have no rule-making or decision-making power; therefore many of the problems of due process are not relevant. Yet we are acutely aware that less formal institutions are becoming generators of soft law that may harden into world law. Thus we would emphasize the importance of a norm of inclusiveness of all stakeholders in agenda-setting and in the development of best practices, rules, and standards.

The OECD caters to developed countries; it reaches out to developing countries with its Global Competition Forums. The UNCTAD caters to developing countries. It includes all UN member countries in its meetings and conferences. The ICN, which is uniquely composed of competition authorities, not states, recognizes a special responsibility to include in working groups and in agenda-setting the competition authorities of the developing countries.

III. Summaries of country/jurisdictional studies

In this section of our introductory chapter, we provide brief summaries of the studies of the competition law systems of eight nations, the European Union, and the relevant international institutions (drawn largely from summaries prepared by the authors of the chapters). It is divided into the four parts addressed by each study: 1) institutional structure, 2) mandate of the competition authority, 3) due process norms in case-by-case decision-making, and 4) institutional performance norms. We also provide brief comments on the new or consolidated competition law regimes in India and Brazil (which are not the subject of separate studies).

A. Institutional structure

1. Australia and New Zealand

The primary enforcement agencies for competition law in New Zealand and Australia are the Commerce Commission (NZCC) and the Australian Competition and Consumer Commission (ACCC), respectively. Both agencies are structurally independent of government and, although they report to government and are subject to government oversight, they carry out their statutory functions free from government influence.

The New Zealand and Australian models have elements of the integrated agency, bifurcated judicial, and (in the case of Australia) the bifurcated agency models. The agencies are responsible for a) investigating breaches of competition law, b) taking enforcement proceedings to the courts of general jurisdiction (the High Court in New Zealand and the Federal Court in Australia), and c) undertaking first instance adjudications in merger control proceedings and in a variety of regulatory matters (for example in the telecommunications and energy sectors). In relation to criminal cartel prosecutions, the ACCC shares responsibility with the Commonwealth Department of Public Prosecutions (CDPP). The ACCC undertakes criminal cartel investigations, and the CDPP prosecutes.

In New Zealand, enforcement proceedings (whether initiated by the NZCC or private parties) are heard by the High Court, often sitting with an economist as expert advisor. The High Court is also responsible for hearing appeals from NZCC determinations of merger control and regulatory matters. In Australia, enforcement proceedings (again, whether initiated by the ACCC or private parties) are heard in the federal courts but appeals from the ACCC's merger control and regulatory determinations are heard by the Australian Competition Tribunal—a specialist tribunal that sits in divisions comprising one federal court judge and two lay members. The Act specifies that the lay members' qualifications shall include expertise in economics, business, or public administration.

As a result of this hybrid structure, the investigative and enforcement functions are structurally independent from the adjudicative function in relation to enforcement proceedings, but the agencies combine investigative and adjudicative functions in relation to merger control and regulatory determinations.

Australia and New Zealand are common law countries with adversarial court systems. In New Zealand, the High Court is the trial court responsible for hearing competition matters, and two levels of appeal are available: to the Court of Appeal and then to the Supreme Court. In Australia, the Federal District Court is primarily responsible for competition matters,[19] again with two levels of appeal: to the Full Federal Court and then to the High Court of Australia. On appeal, the level of deference accorded to the agencies' first instance decisions varies depending on the nature of the decision challenged and the body hearing the appeal (for example, a court of general jurisdiction or the Australian Competition Tribunal). Generally speaking, the courts in both countries defer to the agencies' expertise in complex economic issues—particularly in regulatory determinations. However, the Australian Competition Tribunal—itself an expert body—accords less deference to the reasoning of the ACCC.

Private rights of action are available—for single damages and injunctions—and may be brought independently of (and before or after) agency-initiated proceedings. However, the agencies are the primary drivers of enforcement action due to the costs associated with private enforcement and the perceived effectiveness of the agencies' enforcement efforts.

2. *Brazil*

Brazil has recently released a new competition law (Law No. 12,529/2011), which brings important changes and developments for the enforcement of competition law in Brazil. The law came into force in May, 2012. We will address the old system and, where applicable, highlight the changes brought about by the new legislation.

Under the old competition law (Law No. 8,884/94), the institutional structure for competition enforcement in Brazil was based on a bifurcated agency model, and enforcement was carried out by three separate authorities. The Administrative

[19] Australia is a federal system, but responsibility for competition and trade practices matters lies primarily with the ACCC and federal courts.

Council for Economic Defense (CADE) was the enforcing authority, which had decision-making power regarding competition law matters. CADE was (and still is) structurally independent from other government bodies.

Investigations and case review prior to CADE's final decisions were handled by the Secretariat of Economic Law of the Ministry of Justice (SDE) and by the Secretariat of Economic Monitoring of the Ministry of Finance (SEAE). Formally, the competences of these agencies were somewhat overlapping but, through time, the competences were fine-tuned to promote the efficiency of the system as a whole: SDE focused on investigations of anticompetitive conduct and handled the Brazilian leniency program, and SEAE focused on the review of merger control filings. These agencies prepared non-binding technical opinions on cases which were then forwarded to CADE for a final decision.

The new competition law inaugurates an integrated agency model. CADE will now consist of three bodies: (1) a Tribunal, with decision-making powers on all competition law matters, as in the old CADE; (2) a General Superintendence, with the investigative authority previously allocated to the SDE and the SEAE; and (3) a Department of Economic Studies, an auxiliary division responsible for the elaboration of technical opinions on complex economic issues. The SDE's Antitrust Division was abolished (the SDE will retain competences related to consumer protection, which were handled by the Secretary through a separate division under the old law) and the SEAE's competences related to competition law is now limited to advocacy functions before other government bodies.

3. *Canada*

While having a history dating back to its first competition statute enacted in 1889, Canadian competition law was largely moribund for most of its first century. Apart from cartel prosecutions, very few cases were brought, and even fewer were successful. The lack of vigor was largely attributable to the institutional framework. Fear of intruding on provincial jurisdiction over property and civil rights led the Federal Government to criminalize all forms of antitrust offenses, including mergers and monopolies. The burden of proof in criminal cases was very difficult to surmount. Moreover, decision-making by inexpert criminal courts was widely seen as a further obstacle to the development of effective competition policy. In the late 1960s, the Economic Council of Canada recommended sweeping reforms, which culminated in the passage of the Competition Act 1986. Under this Act, the Competition Bureau, headed by the Commissioner of Competition, may investigate criminal matters (principally cartels). It remits prosecutions of criminal cases to the Federal Director of Public Prosecutions. Such cases are heard in ordinary criminal courts. The Competition Bureau is charged with investigating the wide range of civilly reviewable practices now recognized in the Competition Act, that is, refusals to deal, resale price maintenance, exclusive dealing, tying, exclusive territories, abuse of dominance, and mergers. The Bureau may, and frequently does, negotiate settlements, often in the form of consent agreements which assume the force of a court order by their mere registration with the Competition Tribunal created under the 1986 legislation. The Tribunal comprises judges from the Federal Court Trial Division and lay members. Contested civil matters are heard before the Tribunal, which may issue cease-and-desist orders and under recent amendments impose administrative monetary penalties for abuse of dominance. This reflects a version of the bifurcated agency model. Private parties may sue in the ordinary courts for single damages for breaches of the criminal provisions, which now focus mainly on price fixing.

Canada is a common law jurisdiction and it has an adversarial system. Appeals lie from Tribunal decisions to the Federal Court of Appeal on matters of law and with leave on matters of fact or mixed law and fact. Further appeals on matters of law lie to the Supreme Court of Canada, with leave.

4. Chile

In Chile, the competition law authority is the National Economic Prosecutor's Office (NEPO). This is an independent agency subject to the oversight of the President of the Republic through the Ministry of the Economy. The agency is headed by the National Economic Prosecutor (NEP), who is appointed by the President for a term of four years, renewable once. The NEP has broad powers to investigate competition law infringements. For enforcement, the NEP presents cases to the Competition Tribunal (thus, a bifurcated agency model). The Competition Tribunal was created in 2004 as a specialized, independent jurisdictional entity, subject to the oversight powers of the Supreme Court in appellate proceedings. Its members are appointed as the result of a public competition process. The Tribunal is composed of a president and four other members. The president must be a lawyer, two other members must be lawyers, and two must be economists. In addition to rendering decisions in the case of competition law infringements and mergers, the Tribunal may issue regulations, which are binding on private parties; may propose to the President of the Republic the amendment of any law or regulation that the Tribunal deems to be contrary to competition law; and may issue special reports to sectoral regulators in rate-setting proceedings regarding the competitive conditions in the sector. The Supreme Court hears appeals from Competition Tribunal decisions, and is generally deferential to the Tribunal's fact-finding. Private parties may also bring complaints before the Competition Tribunal. The NEPO and private parties may request an injunction from the Competition Tribunal. Successful NEPO and private plaintiffs may be awarded compensatory damages in civil tribunals. A private party may join a NEPO claim at the Competition Tribunal, and vice versa. Chile has a civil law model, but has increasingly withdrawn from an inquisitorial judicial system. However, the Competition Tribunal has retained some inquisitorial powers, which can be used both in competition law infringement cases and merger reviews. Enforcement and decision-making are split between the NEPO and the Competition Tribunal.

5. *China*

China's Anti-Monopoly Law (AML) became effective in 2008. Potential violations are investigated, adjudicated, and sanctioned by three different enforcement agencies. The National Development and Reform Commission (NDRC) is responsible for price-related infringements of the AML in the areas of restrictive agreements, abuse of dominance, and administrative monopoly (abuses by state and local governmental bodies, including provincial blockages of trade across borders). The State Administration for Industry and Commerce (SAIC) is responsible for non-price-related infringements of the AML in the areas of restrictive agreements, abuse of dominance, and administrative monopoly. It is noteworthy that, pursuant to Article 52 of the AML, the role of the NDRC and the SAIC in tackling administrative monopoly is marginal and is limited to making "suggestions" on the handling of the case to the relevant "superior authorities" of the alleged abusive governmental bodies. The Ministry of Commerce (MOFCOM) is responsible for enforcing the merger control regime. Above these three agencies is the Anti-Monopoly Commission (AMC), a high-level consultative and coordinating organ without law enforcement powers. The Office of the AMC has been formally set up within the MOFCOM. The AML provides that the enforcement agencies may authorize the corresponding organs at the provincial level to assume responsibility for anti-monopoly enforcement functions. The division of AML enforcement responsibilities among the three agencies, especially the division of price and non-price related matters between the NDRC and the SAIC, creates scope for frictions and conflicts. As well, the boundaries between the mandate of the NDRC, the SAIC, and the MOFCOM and sectoral regulators are unclear, especially in connection with regulated industries, wherein state-owned enterprises may be protected by sectoral regulations. The independence of these agencies is limited by the fact that the AMC and the three enforcement agencies all fall under the oversight of the State Council of China (the country's highest executive body). To date, the AMC's role and practices as a consultative and coordinating body are unclear and require further observation.

Contemporary China is a civil law country. The legislature has the power to interpret the Constitution and statutes. The court system is divided into four levels: the basic people's court, the intermediate people's court, the higher people's court, and the Supreme People's Court. The Communist Party of China formally introduced the principle of "rule by law" in 1997. The court procedure is usually inquisitorial and is not bound by precedent. A court case is usually heard at two levels (the first instance trial and the appellate trial). A judgment rendered by the appellate court is final and enforceable. However, if any party is dissatisfied with the final judgment and meets certain statutory criteria, the party may apply to invoke a retrial procedure. The AML entitles individuals and entities to bring private actions to challenge anticompetitive conduct and to claim damages. The scope for private actions under the AML is wide, and stand-alone and follow-on litigation are both permitted. Damages and injunctive relief are available to plaintiffs suffering loss from anticompetitive conduct. Further rules on private actions pursuant to the AML are in the drafting stage.

6. European Union

The competition law provisions of the European Treaty have remained unchanged since the Treaty of Rome was adopted in 1957. The Treaty is now called the Treaty on the Functioning of the European Union (TFEU). Article 101 prohibits agreements, concerted practices, and decisions of associations of undertakings that may affect trade between member states and that have as their object or effect restriction or distortion of competition. Article 101(3) contains a legal exception for otherwise unlawful practices where they contribute to improving the production or distribution of goods or promoting technical or economic progress while allowing consumers a fair share of the resulting benefit and do not impose on the undertakings concerned restrictions that are not indispensable to the attainment of these objectives, and do not afford the undertakings the possibility of eliminating competition in respect of a substantial part of the products in question. Article 102 prohibits the abuse of a dominant position and lists a number of illustrative practices constituting abuse. Merger review was established in 1989 by regulation and was substantially reformed in 2004.

The European Commission is the body primarily responsible for the enforcement of these provisions. Member-state courts and competition authorities may also enforce Articles 101 and 102.

The European Commission is composed of twenty-seven commissioners, each appointed by a member country. One commissioner holds the portfolio for competition. Competition matters reside in the Competition Directorate, which is headed by the Director General of Competition. The Directorate is subject to the oversight of the European Commission. Case teams in the Competition Directorate investigate potential violations and review mergers.

The European Commission, through the initiation of the Competition Directorate, investigates, enforces, and adjudicates all issues relating to competition law within its jurisdiction (hence, an integrated agency model). The case team writes the draft of the decision, albeit usually after a hearing and much vetting within the Competition directorate, Legal Service for the directorate, and a committee of member-state experts. The Commission does not sit as an adjudicating body. Appeal lies to the European General Court, and further to the European Court of Justice on matters of law.

Private actions cannot be brought within the European Union adjudication system, but EU law requires that the member states have effective vehicles for private enforcement. The European Commission is currently consulting with stakeholders on the possibility of a framework directive that would set standards for member-state private actions.

EU law melds civil and common law. The adjudication within the EU system is administrative and inquisitorial.

7. India

India has a common law legal system. Its competition regime is governed by the Competition Act. The Act was passed in 2002. The government constituted the Competition Commission in 2003.

The original form of the Act allowed the Commission to prosecute and decide cases and did not require the chairman to be a lawyer. This institutional arrangement was challenged as unconstitutional for lack of separation of powers, and during the pendency of this challenge the government proposed to amend the Act to address *inter alia* the issue of lack of separation of powers. Accordingly, the Competition (Amendment) bill was introduced into the Parliament in September 2007. This bill was enacted and is now the governing law.

The Competition Amendment Act of 2007 rewrote much of the original legislation. The amendment separated the Commission into two independent bodies—the Competition Commission of India (Commission), an expert administrative body, and the Competition Appellate Tribunal (Tribunal), an adjudicatory appellate body. The Commission may commence inquiries either on its own motion or on receipt of a complaint from any person, consumer, or their association or trade association or on reference from the central government or the state government or any other statutory body. The Commission is further assisted by the Director General of Investigation. The Office of the Director General is the investigative arm of the Commission. The Commission must refer all matters for investigation to the Director General. The Commission is not bound by the findings made by the Director General. The Commission may choose either to accept or reject the investigation report or issue fresh instructions to the Director General for carrying out further investigations.

The Commission consists of a chairperson and up to six other members who are required to have knowledge and professional experience of not less than fifteen years in the field of competition law and policy, economics, international trade, finance, commerce, etc. The appointment is made by the government on the basis of a recommendation made by a selection committee chaired by the Chief Justice of India.

The Tribunal discharges the appellate function. Any party aggrieved by an order of the Commission may appeal to the Tribunal. The Tribunal, after giving the parties an opportunity to of be heard, may modify or set aside the order of the Commission. Parties aggrieved by the Tribunal's order may make a final appeal to the Supreme Court of India. The Tribunal consists of a chairperson and two other members. Tribunal members are required to have knowledge and experience of not less than twenty-five years in competition matters including areas such as economics, business, commerce, and international trade.

Both the Commission and the Tribunal are structurally independent statutory bodies. However the Government may, subject to certain conditions laid down in the Act, (i) exempt a class of enterprises from the application of the Act, (ii) issue directions to the Commission, and (iii) supersede the Commission. These provisions are meant to be an exception; not the rule.

The structure of the Indian competition law system is a mix of a bifurcated agency model and the integrated agency model. The Commission is vested with inquisitorial, investigative, regulatory, adjudicatory, and, to a limited extent, advisory jurisdiction. The Tribunal has appellate jurisdiction over the orders passed by the Commission.

8. Japan

Japan's Anti-Monopoly Act (AMA) was originally enacted in 1947 at the prompting of US occupation authorities. The Japan Fair Trade Commission (JFTC), which investigates and enforces potential violations of the Act, was designed to follow the model of the US Federal Trade Commission. At least with regard to civil enforcement, the JFTC structure follows the integrated agency model. The Commission investigates violations of the Act, proposes remedial orders and/or administrative surcharges (a form of administrative fine), holds adversarial hearings in disputed cases, and decides whether there is sufficient evidence to support a finding of a violation and the entry of an order. Hearing officers are JFTC officials but must be independent from the investigators. JFTC decisions can be appealed twice, namely to the Tokyo High Court and the Supreme Court. On appeal, the courts defer to JFTC decisions under a substantial evidence rule which binds the courts' fact-findings to some extent. Certain violations of the AMA can be prosecuted criminally, although hard-core cartels (Unreasonable Restraint of Trade) are usually the only target. The JFTC has authority to investigate criminal violations, but not authority to prosecute. Where prosecutions are sought, cases are referred to the Public Prosecutor's office. Thus, for criminal enforcement, the JFTC reflects a version of the bifurcated judicial model. The JFTC is administratively attached to the Cabinet Office, rather than being part of a separate Ministry. Under the AMA, the JFTC is statutorily guaranteed independence; its chairman and four commissioners are appointed by the Prime Minister with the approval of both houses of the Diet; and the chairman and commissioners serve for fixed terms.

Private parties can obtain injunctive relief and single damages for violations of the AMA. Private damage suits under the AMA cannot be filed until the JFTC enters a final and binding cease-and-desist order. Private damage suits are tried by a special panel of the Tokyo High Court rather than by a court of general jurisdiction. Plaintiffs seeking damage recovery can avoid the procedural restrictions of the AMA, however, by filing suit under the general tort provisions of the Civil Code. Private injunction suits can be filed with a court of general jurisdiction without any order of the JFTC. There are few successful suits brought under the AMA; most successful suits challenging anticompetitive behavior are brought under the civil code or other statutes relating to bid rigging in government procurement. Reform proposals presently being debated in Japan would eliminate the right to a JFTC hearing in contested matters, and the Tokyo District Court would review JFTC orders de novo, moving the Japanese regime in the direction of the bifurcated judicial model.

9. South Africa

South Africa has a common law legal system. Its current competition regime is just over a decade old and is based on the Competition Act 1998, which is administered by three institutions: the Competition Commission, the Competition Tribunal, and the Competition Appeal Court. The Commission is the investigative and enforcement authority with respect to complaints alleging anti-competitive conduct, which it can refer to the Tribunal for a decision. Thus the investigation and enforcement functions are structurally independent from the first-level adjudication functions. The Commission has authority to approve or prohibit intermediary mergers and can recommend action on large mergers to the Competition Tribunal. The Commission is responsible for negotiating settlements with respondents in complaints proceedings, issuing advisory opinions, and granting exemptions from the Act such as for agreements that promote exports, small business, or the ability of historically disadvantaged persons to become competitive. The Competition Tribunal is an administrative tribunal composed of lay members drawn from a range of disciplines (economists, lawyers, accountants, but not judges). It is considered a tribunal of record, although not a formal court. The Tribunal is in effect the court of first instance in all competition matters. It adjudicates on, and provides remedies in respective complaints against prohibited practices, and assesses and adjudicates large mergers referred to it by the Commission. In some contexts, it acts as an appellate body in respect to issues over which the Commission has decision-making authority, such as the approval of intermediate mergers and the granting of exemptions from the Act. The Tribunal has extensive remedial powers, including prohibition of mergers, the imposition of injunctive relief, the levying of administrative penalties, and the ordering of divestiture.

Appeals from Tribunal decisions lie to a three-judge special competition panel of the Competition Appeal Court, which is a special division of the High Court. Only sitting judges may be appointed to the Court. Review proceedings may be instituted where there are alleged irregularities or improper conduct during the hearing process. The Competition Appeal Court also hears reviews. There is a possible further appeal to the Supreme Court of Appeal, and—if constitutional issues are raised—to the Constitutional Court. The appeal courts have not shied away from overturning the Tribunal's decisions, in respect of either fact-finding or legal issues.

Private enforcement actions (including actions for single damages, interim relief orders, and declarations) are available to complainants. An action for damages may be instituted once a right to such damages accrues, which is either on the date that the Tribunal makes a determination on the matter or on the date that any appeal process is concluded.

The South African model is thus a bifurcated agency model—a specialized investigation and enforcement authority that brings enforcement proceedings before a specialized competition tribunal for adjudication.

10. United States

The United States is a common law jurisdiction. The US enforcement system is complex. There are two major federal enforcement agencies and fifty state enforcement agencies, plus five federal districts or territories, and enforcement through private litigation. The state attorneys general can enforce federal antitrust law as well as state antitrust law when state residents are injured. The two US federal agencies are the Department of Justice Antitrust Division and the Federal Trade Commission. The former is a division of the executive branch; the latter is an independent regulatory agency. The Antitrust Division of the Department of Justice follows the bifurcated judicial model, investigating cases and bringing enforcement actions in federal courts of general jurisdiction. The Federal Trade Commission, consisting of five commissioners, follows the integrated agency model, with power to investigate and adjudicate cases internally, subject to subsequent appellate court review. The first level of adjudication within the agency occurs before an administrative law judge (ALJ). The ALJ's decision may be appealed to the Commission. The Commission's decision may be appealed to a federal appellate court. The appellate courts normally give deference to fact-finding by the Commission. They may overturn fact-finding that is clearly erroneous. Appellate courts have full power to decide questions of law, including issues of statutory interpretation. They may give deference to mixed fact-and-law conclusions; and they may be guided by interpretations by the specialized agency of the law that it is charged with applying.

If the Federal Trade Commission wishes to enjoin conduct or a merger pending proceedings in the Commission, it must seek the injunction in a federal district court. To this extent, the FTC procedures have elements of the bifurcated judicial model. The standard applicable to the FTC in seeking a preliminary injunction (serious questions on the merits is sufficient to shift the burden to the defendant to invoke equities) is lower than the standard applicable to the DOJ (reasonable probability of success and balance of the equities). This disparity has led to proposals to harmonize the standard. So, too, the significant level of overlap of jurisdiction of the two federal agencies, especially on mergers, has produced proposals for rationalization.

The Antitrust Division of the Department of Justice has power to prosecute criminal antitrust actions in federal courts of general jurisdiction. The FTC has only civil enforcement authority. State enforcement is handled by each state's attorney general and enforcement takes place exclusively through court litigation. Private antitrust suits for treble damages and injunctions may be brought in federal and state courts of general jurisdiction. The two federal antitrust agencies, which have overlapping formal jurisdiction in many areas of antitrust enforcement, notify each other of pending enforcement actions and have evolved informal agreements as to which agency should assume lead responsibility for reviewing mergers and non-criminal conduct cases in particular sectors or industries.

Appeals from federal appellate courts may be taken to the Supreme Court of the United States, but the Supreme Court has wide discretion to deny review. The

United States has an adversarial litigation system. In the Antitrust Division of the DOJ, the enforcement and decision-making functions are separated; in the FTC they are institutionally combined.

11. International

The international chapter deals with the following four institutions insofar as they are relevant to competition law: the World Trade Organization (WTO), the Organisation for Economic Co-operation and Development (OECD), the United Nations Conference on Trade and Development (UNCTAD), and the International Competition Network (ICN).

The agreements under the aegis of the World Trade Organization contain few antitrust law rules, although virtually all provisions relate to competition by limiting state measures that restrict trade (and thus usually competition). Adjudicative functions within the WTO are entrusted to the Dispute Settlement Body. Complaints are made by member nations. Consultations ensue. If matters are not resolved, the DSB refers the complaint to a panel. A party may appeal on matters of law from a panel report to the Appellate Body, a standing body composed of seven individuals, one each for broad geographic areas of the world.

The dispute resolution panels receive evidence and hear argument, both written and oral. The panel submits an interim report to the parties; after taking account of feedback from the parties, it submits a final report. If there is an appeal, parties have a right to a brief hearing before the Appellate Body and they submit written briefs. Appellate Body reports are adopted by the DSB and are final unless the DSB decides by consensus not to accept the report.

The structure of the OECD, UNCTAD, and ICN is less relevant because these organizations have no rule-making or dispute resolution authority. The OECD is composed mostly of developed nations. It operates through committees including the Competition Committee. It issues recommendations, sponsors peer reviews, and facilitates work product on common issues. Through its Global Forums, it reaches out to developing countries. UNCTAD is the principal arm of the United Nations General Assembly dealing with issues particularly relevant to developing countries. It maintains, and updates through commentary, a set of principles on competition policy that the UN nations originally adopted in 1980. Like the OECD, it sponsors peer reviews and it facilitates research projects. The ICN, unlike OECD and UNCTAD, is a roots-up virtual project on competition issues only; and its members are competition authorities, not nations. A number of private lawyers, economists, business people, and academics are non-governmental advisors and contribute to its work. ICN facilitates the sharing of knowledge on rules and processes of antitrust law and procedures; it derives and disseminates recommended practices, and it facilitates convergence of law and practice.

B. Mandate

1. Australia and New Zealand

The stated objective of the competition legislation in New Zealand is to "promote competition in markets for the long-term benefit of consumers within New Zealand." In Australia, the objective is to "enhance the welfare of Australians through the promotion of competition and fair trading and provision of consumer protection." Competition policy in Australia and New Zealand is influenced strongly by policy in the United States and, to a lesser extent, the European Union. As a result, the focus is primarily on competition as a means to achieving efficient output and lower prices to consumers.

Both the NZCC and ACCC are responsible not only for traditional *ex post* competition law enforcement but also important areas of *ex ante* economic regulation, specifically access pricing and more general forms of price control in industries that are structurally incapable of workable and effective competition (mainly utilities industries). In addition, both agencies are responsible for enforcing consumer protection and fair trading rules.

2. Brazil

Both the old and the new Brazilian competition laws state the mandate as follows: the prevention and repression of violations against the economic order, guided by constitutional principles of free enterprise, free competition, social role of property, consumer protection, and repression of the abuse of economic power. Despite the reference to other principles, the authority's focus is on competition policy and its goal can be understood as the enhancement of consumer welfare. Consumer protection and fair trading in Brazil are handled by separate statutes and fall outside of CADE's competences.

3. Canada

Section 1.1 of the Competition Act states (rather unhelpfully):

> The purpose of this Act is to maintain and encourage competition in Canada in order to promote the efficiency and adaptability of the Canadian economy, in order to expand opportunities for Canadian participation in world markets while at the same time recognizing the role of foreign competition in Canada, in order to ensure that small and medium-sized enterprises have an equitable opportunity to participate in the Canadian economy and in order to provide consumers with competitive prices and product choices.

In addition to enforcing competition laws, the Competition Bureau also has a statutory mandate to investigate and enforce prohibitions against unfair or misleading consumer advertising or related practices. It has no *ex ante* regulatory powers. Some sectoral exemptions exist for agricultural and fishing cooperatives, and labor unions. More generally, the courts have evolved a Regulated Conduct Defense, which provides immunity for parties acting pursuant to validly enacted provincial or federal legislation or regulation where the conduct in question might otherwise constitute a violation of the Competition Act. The precise parameters of this defense have not been clearly resolved in the case law. In addition, the Competition Bureau has overlapping jurisdiction with a number of sectoral regulators in areas such as banking, telecommunications, broadcasting, airlines, and railways, which has sometimes proven problematic, particularly with respect to merger review in these sectors, where the respective jurisdictions of the Competition Bureau and the sectoral regulators have not been clearly delineated.

4. *Chile*

The objective of Chile's competition law is "to promote and defend free competition in the markets." This objective has sometimes been criticized as vague and imprecise. Neither NEPO's nor the Competition Tribunal's mandates extend to consumer protection, which falls within the jurisdiction of a separate agency. There is potential for overlapping jurisdiction with sectoral regulators in a range of regulated sectors; sectoral regulators typically do not file claims or initiate consultations before the Competition Tribunal, except for energy and telecommunications issues.

5. *China*

The objectives of China's anti-monopoly law include promoting efficiency, encouraging free competition, safeguarding healthy development of a socialist market economy and the public interest, protecting the state-owned economy and small business, encouraging the expansion of domestic enterprises and scrutinizing foreign takeovers. No clear hierarchy has been established between these various objectives, and identification of broader non-competition goals may cause inconsistency in interpretation and enforcement of the AML. The AML also provides a statutory exclusion for the agricultural sector and sets out general exemptions for restrictive agreements. In addition, in relation to anticompetitive agreements, the AML also includes a sweeping clause that exempts "other circumstances as stipulated by law and the State Council." The boundaries between the jurisdiction of the three competition agencies and sectoral regulators are unclear.

6. *European Union*

The European Commission and major early decisions of the European Court of Justice have emphasized that the rationale for the competition provisions was the elimination of "distortions" within the internal market. Hence competition policy was historically conceived as advancing the goal of freedom of movement of goods, services, capital, and people within the European Union. Consumer or total-welfare rationales were not a central feature of the justifications for EU competition law. In recent years, EU treaty development has emphasized a range of economic and, more exceptionally, social objectives of the EU beyond completing the internal market, including protecting the competitive structure of the market, protecting the competition process, preserving and sometimes creating openness of markets and market access, and protecting the interests of consumers.

7. Japan

Japan's Anti-Monopoly Act aims to prevent anticompetitive conduct and thus to promote innovation and consumer welfare. It also regulates abuse of a superior bargaining position (ASBP), which provision in effect protects small- and medium-sized enterprises.

The JFTC formerly had power to enforce certain consumer protection legislation, but in 2009 this jurisdiction was ceded to the new Consumer Affairs Agency. The JFTC can apply the Anti-Monopoly Act to regulated industries absent explicit exemptions, of which there are relatively few. Rather strikingly (compared to other competition law jurisdictions), the JFTC also devotes considerable resources to policing low prices in Japan's economy, including bidding too low on public contracts. The JFTC provides expedited resolution of complaints of "unjust low sales prices" and provides formal and informal consultations for a high volume of cases in this context.

8. South Africa

The country's democratic transition from apartheid in the 1990s gave high priority to the redressing of economic inequality. The government chose competition law as one of the tools to achieve this. The new regime was mandated to use competition policy to address the failings of the old system and to promote the policy goals of employment and black empowerment. The Competition Act thus has an extensive and ambitious list of goals, which call on the authorities to balance both traditional competition concerns and public interest objectives. The Act embraces the goals of creating a free market and effective competition, but also incorporates uniquely South African elements, including addressing its exclusionary past by promoting participation of all citizens in the economy and promoting the fair distribution of ownership and control of markets among different racial groups. The preamble to the Act promotes the pursuit of "an efficient, competitive economic environment, balancing the interests of workers, owners, and consumers and focused on development." Marketing practices and consumer protection issues are not part of the jurisdiction of the competition authorities.

9. United States

The Sherman Act does not specify its purposes. It was applied for many years against loosely defined economic "power." It is interpreted today to prohibit conduct and transactions that increase or maintain market power and injure consumers.

In addition to its antitrust law enforcement agenda, the Department of Justice pursues an active competition advocacy role within the federal government, often providing its views to sectoral regulators. In some areas, the DOJ enjoys concurrent authority with sectoral regulators, and in some few other areas its enforcement authority is preempted by regulation. The Federal Trade Commission has a mandate to enforce the Federal Trade Commission Act. This is a broad mandate, which covers all of the anticompetitive conduct prohibited by the Sherman Act and the Clayton Act, and arguably a margin beyond (the FTC Act prohibits "unfair methods of competition"). The FTC also has a consumer-protection mandate—to prevent "unfair or deceptive acts or practices"—which is usually exercised quite separately from its competition authority.

10. India

The preamble of the Competition Act states that the statute has been enacted with a view towards the economic development of the country. The Commission is charged with preventing practices from having an adverse effect on competition, promoting and sustaining competition in markets, protecting the interests of consumers, and ensuring freedom of trade of participants in markets in India. According to the Supreme Court of India, "The main objective of the Competition Law is to promote economic efficiencies using competition as one of the means of assisting the creation of [a] market responsive to consumer preferences." The Act is applicable with equal force to government-owned enterprises and even government departments as well as private enterprises. The Act expressly excludes the sovereign functions of the government. There is potential for jurisdictional overlap between the Commission and sectoral regulators. The Act provides a non-obligatory reference mechanism, requiring the sector regulator and the Commission to make a reference to each other on matters of mutual concern. Consumer protection issues are not within the jurisdiction of the Commission. India has an exhaustive consumer protection law that includes unfair and restrictive trade practices in its ambit.

11. International institutions

The mandate of the WTO is to move increasingly towards lower barriers to trade and, in that spirit, to set the rules of world trade by the members' negotiation, by interpreting the rules, and by facilitating compliance with the rules. Compliance is triggered by member state complaints. Violations can be enforced by injured states, who may retaliate by imposing trade penalties on the violating state.

The mandates of the OECD, UNCTAD, and ICN are explained above in the section on Institutional Structure.

C. Due process norms in case-by-case decision-making

1. Australia and New Zealand

Competition law in Australia and New Zealand (with the recent exception of the criminalization of cartels in Australia) is predominantly civil in nature. Within the court system, principles of due process and rights of defense are similar to those applicable in the United Kingdom or the United States, reflecting Australia and New Zealand's position as commonwealth countries and former British colonies. In relation to agency determinations, issues of due process are generally framed in terms of judicial review principles of natural justice, which require agencies exercising public powers to exercise those powers in a procedurally fair manner. Typically, this mandates the right to be heard in relation to a matter affecting one's interests, and the right to have adequate notice of reasoning and evidence relied upon by the decision-maker. Reflecting these principles, almost all agency decision-making in Australia and New Zealand is attended by extremely rigorous consultation processes with affected parties requiring that agencies i) advise the affected party of the proposals they are considering, and the reasoning and evidence they have considered in formulating the proposals; ii) provide an opportunity to comment on these proposals as well as the reasoning and evidence; and iii) give genuine consideration, free of pre-determination, to the affected parties' submissions.

In relation to investigations, parties have on occasion complained that the agencies' use of their investigative powers is harsh and oppressive, imposing massive costs and unreasonable deadlines in a manner allegedly unjustified by the circumstances of the investigation. However, practitioners interviewed for this study agreed that the current chairpersons of the agencies have taken steps to promote greater efficiency, timeliness, and reasonableness in the investigative process. The institutional arrangements of competition law in both countries strongly support the independence of the commissioners from political interference in case-by-case decision-making. The legal principles governing penalties ensure proportionality of the penalty to the conduct by allowing courts to set penalties relative to a maximum figure based either on the commercial gain attributable to the infringement or the turnover of the infringer.

Rights of review and appeal vary, depending on the nature of the decision. Some practitioners and businesses in New Zealand have expressed dissatisfaction with the constraints on appeals from regulatory determinations, which exclude challenges to the merits of the agency's decision. With the recent criminalization of cartels in Australia, due process issues relating to rights of defense are likely to arise, given that the ACCC's investigative powers have traditionally been predicated on a civil rather than a criminal regime. For example, parties are not entitled to the privilege against self-incrimination in relation to testimony compelled by the ACCC, and thus the agency will have to determine how to use its powers in order to preserve the admissibility of evidence in subsequent criminal proceedings.

2. Brazil

Due process in competition law affairs is safeguarded in general by the Brazilian constitution and by principles of administrative law. Neither the old nor the new statute contains general due process rules. They do contain rules on practical matters such as deadlines pertaining specifically to procedures within the CADE.

The level of protection of constitutional rights applied to administrative and criminal procedures in general is very high. For example, parties cannot be required to produce evidence against themselves, even in administrative proceedings, and parties have the right of access to any information that may be used against them. In cartel investigations, this ultimately means that parties are often granted access to documents at an earlier stage than available in other jurisdictions.

In the context of cartel cases, some issues of due process and rights of defense have been raised by targets of investigations under the old law. Respondents have, for example, challenged the presumption of truthfulness attributed to a party's confession in leniency cases, it being claimed that such presumption violates the principle of presumption of innocence. Also, more technical issues have been raised, such as the validity of foreign documents and evidence in international cartel cases. Criticism has also been directed to the length of time taken in cartel investigations. Most of the cases in which such issues have been raised are yet to be decided.

3. Canada

With respect to criminal prosecutions for violations of the Competition Act (now principally cartel cases), general procedural protections for defendants are considered adequate, given that these matters are tried in the ordinary criminal courts and are subject to the due process protections in the Charter of Rights and Freedoms. In civil matters, there have been concerns in the recent past over the Bureau's utilization of Section 11 orders under the Competition Act, available by ex parte application to the Federal Court, demanding production of classes of documents named in these orders. Specifically, concerns have arisen as to the breadth of these demands, not only with respect to immediate parties to transactions but also with respect to competitors, suppliers, and customers. Supplemental Information Requests (SIR) have been introduced in recent amendments to the Competition Act (similar to Second Requests under the Hart-Scott-Rodino Act in the US). These may substitute for Section 11 applications in merger cases, and similar concerns about the potential for excessive frequency and scope of SIRs have been expressed.

Further concerns have been expressed relating to the inability or unwillingness of case officers within the Competition Bureau responsible for particular files or more senior officers to whom they report to isolate and communicate to the parties in a timely fashion the critical issues of concern to them in an investigation. Such early communication would permit the parties, again in a timely fashion, to address these concerns either by way of demonstrating that they are unwarranted or that remedial options may be available that effectively address them.

4. Chile

Enforcement action may be initiated before the Competition Tribunal at the request of the National Economic Prosecutor's Office, through a claim filed at the Competition Tribunal or by a lawsuit filed by a private individual. Once the Tribunal admits a complaint, it must notify the affected party, who may reply within a fifteen-day period or ask for an extension. After the term to reply to the claim has expired, the Tribunal may summon the parties to a conciliation hearing. If the Tribunal considers this not appropriate or if the conciliation procedure fails, it can set a twenty-day period for the submission of evidence. Once this period expires, the Tribunal must set the date and time of the public hearings, in which the parties' attorneys can submit pleadings. In the case of merger review, after the request for a merger review, the Tribunal opens the procedure with a decree published in the official gazette and on the internet website of the Tribunal. The decree must be notified to NEPO, public authorities who are directly affected, and economic agents who are related to the matter, so that they may provide information and economic evidence before the Tribunal. Once the period expires, parties may evaluate the recommendations that NEPO has made to the Tribunal and communicate their responses to it. After a period of fifteen days expires, the Tribunal may summon a public hearing so that those who provided information may express their opinion to the Tribunal. In all proceedings, decisions of the Tribunal, with the exception of the final ruling, are subject to challenge before the same Tribunal. All final rulings are subject to appeal to the Supreme Court, which hears such appeals in preference to other matters. While decisions of the Tribunal are not normally reversed by the Supreme Court, the Supreme Court's appellate jurisdiction is not entirely clear and its decisions are sometimes criticized as formalistic and unpredictable.

5. China

The Anti-Monopoly Law (AML) and the accompanying regulations have set up basic procedural rules for the National Development and Reform Commission (NDRC) and the State Administration for Industry and Commerce (SAIC). In December 2010, effective in February 2011, the NDRC and the SAIC issued further procedural rules relating to the leniency program and imposition of fines. The AML and the accompanying regulations do not require the NDRC and the SAIC to publish their enforcement decisions. To date, the NDRC and its local bureaus have made several decisions on cartels and abuse of dominance, but the NRDC has not published any decision in full; public announcements are made instead. These announcements contain only general descriptions of facts and of the sanctions imposed and do not provide any reasoning. In November 2011, the NDRC confirmed that it opened an investigation on China Telecom and

China Unicom, two giant state-owned telecom enterprises, in relation to their alleged abusive behavior of charging internet service providers discriminatory network access fees in order to squeeze out competitors. Until early 2011, no official enforcement action pursuant to the AML was reported to have been undertaken by the SAIC or its local bureaus. However, the SAIC stated that it had started to investigate complaints that it and its local bureaus had received and that it had investigated and prevented violations in seventy-nine cases involving restrictive competitive behavior in the first quarter of 2009 alone. Given the lack of published decisions or announcements, it remains unclear whether these cases were informally settled or closed under the SAIC's formal decision rules and whether the SAIC's decisional practices complied with the prescribed procedural rules. In January 2011, it was reported that a concrete manufacturers' association was penalized for market allocation by the SAIC's local bureau in Jiangsu province. In July 2011, the SAIC's local bureau in Guangdong province investigated and handled local governments' administrative monopoly conduct in relation to global positioning system services for motor vehicles.

The MOFCOM, which is responsible for the AML merger control regime, is subject to the same procedural rules as those applicable to the NDRC and the SAIC pursuant to the AML. In addition the MOFCOM is required to publish in a timely fashion decisions that prohibit or conditionally approve mergers, although publication of unconditional clearance decisions is left to the MOFCOM's discretion. By March 31, 2012, the MOFCOM had promulgated a series of AML implementing regulations in relation to merger control and had published thirteen merger decisions, including one prohibition decision (the Coco-Cola/Huiyan decision) and twelve conditional approvals. Although the MOFCOM has demonstrated its improved transparency by including more detailed facts in its merger decisions, to date, all of the MOFCOM's published decisions are still relatively light in the reasoning provided.

Although private enforcement is allowed under the AML, the AML does not contain any detailed rules of procedures for seeking damages, evidentiary rules, or guidelines for determining compensation. Apart from the generally applicable rules set out in the civil procedure law, China's courts have been carefully developing private litigation rules pursuant to the AML. Since 2009, the Supreme People's Court has been drafting judicial interpretations on private suits brought under the AML. It issued draft interpretations for public comment in April 2011. It is expected that the interpretations will be finalized shortly. Once issued, the interpretations are expected to provide more certainty and predictability to litigants and to enhance private enforcement of the AML. To date, a number of claims have been filed with the courts but in no case has the plaintiff won.

6. *European Union*

The issue of appropriate due process norms in case-by-case decision-making in EU competition law is currently a matter of vigorous debate. At its inception, competition law within the EU was largely conceived as an administrative function constituting one aspect of the larger executive functions vested in the European Commission by the Treaty of Rome. In many ways, this conception of the Commission's functions, in the competition area, was also consistent with the civilian traditions of the six original signatories to the Treaty of Rome. However, a concatenation of factors has cast due-process issues into sharp relief in recent years. First, the escalating level of fines imposed by the Commission in cartel and abuse cases has led some stakeholders and commentators to view Commission proceedings in these contexts as akin to criminal or quasi-criminal proceedings, warranting the kind of procedural protections associated with criminal proceedings. Second, the Treaty of Lisbon (2009), which last amended the Constitutive Treaties, adopted the protection of fundamental rights as one of its objectives, and the European Convention on Human Rights has been increasingly influential in European Court of Justice judgments on due process rights. The EU's candidacy for membership in the Convention reinforces this trend.

Several due-process issues have been raised. First, the nature of the Competition Directorate as an integrated agency that undertakes investigative, enforcement, and adjudicative functions has raised concerns of at least the perception of bias in adjudication. Second, EU competition law is not criminal law (despite possibilities of very high fines) and thus there is no right against self-incrimination. Moreover, lawyer–client privilege is defined by the civil law rule, which does not protect communications with in-house lawyers. Third, the hearing process is criticized. It follows civil law procedures, with the record resting primarily on written material submitted by the Commission, the parties, and interested third parties. The oral hearing is short, intended to clarify certain disputed matters. The proceeding is inquisitorial rather than adversarial and thus there is no right of the defense lawyers to cross-examine witnesses. The Commission has taken steps and proposes yet more steps to strengthen the independence and range of responsibilities of the Hearing Officer in these proceedings, but the Hearing Officer's role is still largely confined to ensuring procedural due process and otherwise resolving procedural issues. The Hearing Officer has no substantive decision-making authority. The Commissioners, who make the ultimate Commission decisions, do not attend the hearing.

The fourth concern regards the scope of appeal. Affected parties have rights of appeal from Commission decisions to the General Court. Fact-finding can be set aside if it is manifestly erroneous. In some cases the General Court appears to give a more thorough review of factual issues, but this is not mandated. The courts can and do interpret the law. Thus, appeals provide only limited ability to challenge substantive and technical aspects of Commission decisions. More robust court review has been suggested by the Commission. This proposal is pending.

Fifth, following the enactment of the Modernisation Regulation in 2003, enforcement of EU competition law was, to an important extent, decentralized, and powers devolved to national competition authorities (NCAs) of member states, subject to the possibility that the Commission itself might decide to pursue a matter. Much substantive and procedural convergence has occurred among the NCAs, but substantial differences persist. Due process rights accorded by different member NCAs may significantly diverge. Parties have asserted that a risk of double jeopardy may arise in the prosecution of complaints involving the same set of facts that are pursued simultaneously or sequentially by different NCAs and possibly by the Commission itself. However, care is usually taken to assess fines based only on effects within the court's own territory.

Many of the challenges to due process in the EU are made by individuals accustomed to the adversarial, common law system.

7. *India*

The Competition Act and the regulations made thereunder establish the framework for proceedings before the Competition Commission of India and the Competition Appellate Tribunal. The Act requires the Commission and Tribunal to follow the principles of natural justice. The Supreme Court has interpreted the doctrine of natural justice to include (1) no-one should be condemned or deprived of his right, even in quasi-judicial proceedings, unless he has been granted the right to be heard, (2) affected parties have the right of adequate notice, and (3) courts including quasi-judicial bodies are required to deliver reasoned orders.[20] The competition authorities are expected to ensure compliance with these principles. Article 14 of the Indian Constitution is considered the guardian of the principle of natural justice. Article 14 declares that "The State shall not deny any person equality before the law or the equal protection of the laws within the territory of India." The right of equality before law is a fundamental right under the Indian Constitution.

The Competition Act requires that the Commission shall, on receipt of reference or information or on its own knowledge, form an opinion whether or not there exists a prima facie case for issuance of a direction to the Director General of Investigation. At this stage the Commission is not required to issue a notice to either the informant or any other person. Once the Commission receives the report from the investigating authority, it must forward a copy of the report to all parties concerned with the investigation and must provide a right of hearing to the parties prior to arriving at any conclusion. Once the proceeding before the Commission is concluded, the parties have the right to appeal to the Tribunal, as long as the order is appealable under the Act. The Tribunal must give notice to the parties and thereafter conduct a hearing and, as it may deem fit, confirm, modify, or set aside the order of Commission. The final appeal from the order of the Tribunal lies with the Supreme Court of India.

In the cases concerning anticompetitive agreements or abuse of dominance, the Commission may issue a cease-and-desist order and impose a penalty not exceeding 10 percent of the average turnover during the preceding three years from the date of

[20] The concept of reasoned order/speaking order under the Indian legal system is similar to the provision contained in Section 8 of the Administrative Procedure Act. Section 8 of the said Act reads, "All decisions (including initial, recommended and tentative decisions) shall include a statement of findings and conclusions and the reasons or basis thereof, on all material issues of fact, law or discretion presented on the record."

the order. In cartel cases the Commission-imposed penalty can be the higher of either up to 10 percent of the turnover or three times the amount of profit derived from the cartel agreement. The Commission may also order the division of an enterprise in a dominant position if it has abused its dominance. In cases of combinations that are likely to have an appreciable adverse effect on competition in India, the Commission may either prohibit or condition the combination.

8. Japan

The JFTC has almost never issued an official order in connection with a merger case. Rather, through a system of informal pre-merger consultations, it is thought that the JFTC has deterred some mergers and achieved some restructuring in others to meet its competition concerns. Before a new framework for the merger review process took effect in July 2011, many stakeholders criticized the informal consultation system for lack of transparency and exclusion of third-party viewpoints. With respect to non-merger cases, the current investigatory system has been criticized for exclusion of attorneys for respondents at the interrogation phase of investigations and the lack of attorney-client privilege. As well, as noted above, there have been criticisms of the internal hearing processes conducted by the JFTC both for perceptions of biases, and proposals are under consideration to require hearings in contested matters before the Tokyo District Court.

As to proportionality of remedies, the JFTC's surcharge orders against cartels raise concerns about their constitutionality in light of the possibility of double jeopardy, given that a hard-core cartel may also be subject to a criminal fine. Because a surcharge is nondiscretionary in order to avoid unconstitutionality, the system has prevented the JFTC from exercising flexibility in penalty setting and enforcement. In addition, the surcharge must be linked to actual turnover in the relevant market. However, in the case of international market division agreements, where foreign companies promise not to sell in Japan, they may not have to pay a surcharge because they do not generate any actual turnover in the Japanese market, which may lead to under-deterrence.

9. South Africa

The South African Constitution states that "everyone has the right to administrative action that is lawful, reasonable and procedurally fair." However, balancing fair administrative action protections with the goals of the Competition Act has been a difficult challenge. The designers of the South African competition laws system wanted the institutions to reflect the goals of equality and accessibility espoused in the Act. In an attempt to avoid excessively legalizing the competition process, the Act enjoins the Tribunal to conduct itself informally. The Tribunal is not required to follow High Court procedures in its detailed rules regarding pleadings and evidence. The Tribunal is also granted inquisitorial powers. Nonetheless, competition law in South Africa has been largely "legalized" and lawyers expect competition proceedings to run like High Court proceedings. This results in a conflict of expectations—the Competition Tribunal is not bound by the formalities observed in court proceedings, and the competition authorities aim to achieve administrative efficiency. On the other hand, the firms involved in competition proceedings are centrally concerned with the fair procedure protections to which they are accustomed in standard civil litigation.

There has been significant dissatisfaction on the part of targets of investigation in relation to the procedures followed by the Competition Commission, including the initiation of industry-wide cartel investigations without identifying the particular targets of investigation ultimately named in the referral to the Tribunal. There have also been a number of court applications for the Commission to identify more clearly the conduct that forms the basis of the alleged contravention, and to make available documents evidencing the contraventions alleged in the referral.

In terms of proportionality of remedies to violations, under the Act a penalty may not exceed 10 percent of a firm's annual turnover in the preceding financial year, and the Act lists factors to be taken into account: the nature, duration, gravity, and extent of the contravention; the loss or damage suffered as a result of the contravention; the behavior of the respondent; the market circumstances in which the contravention took place; the level of profit derived from the contravention; the degree to which the respondent has cooperated with the Competition Commission and the Competition Tribunal; and whether the respondent has previously been found in contravention of the Act. Most penalties have been determined through the conclusion of Consent Agreements with the Commission rather than through the imposition of fines by the Tribunal. The Commission's approach to settlement is not entirely transparent and it has no fining guidelines.

10. United States

Parties are informed at a relatively early stage by either of the two federal antitrust agencies of their concerns and are afforded the opportunity to present their views. At the Department of Justice, the parties normally are granted the opportunity to meet with the reviewing officials at each successive stage of the investigation, except that, before criminal indictment, meeting with the Assistant Attorney General is rare. In criminal cases, the grand jury process imposes special rules of secrecy, preventing DOJ attorneys from sharing certain information with the parties. At the FTC, the parties meet with and are informed by the staff, and normally have a chance to meet with all commissioners.

For DOJ matters, and FTC matters before the courts, the parties receive all of the protections of federal courts, which are substantial. They have the right to introduce and contest evidence and the right of cross-examination, except that criminal defendants may not get full information as to informants in the interest of confidentiality. Criminal defendants are entitled to heightened protections, including the privilege against self-incrimination, the right to a speedy trial, and the right to proof beyond a reasonable doubt. For civil trials, speed varies. Complex monopoly cases have been known to take several years, although the very complex Microsoft trial took only five months.

At the FTC, in administrative proceedings, the respondent is entitled to discovery and to an evidentiary hearing with examination and cross-examination. The system has been criticized for unacceptable delays. To expedite matters, on occasion the FTC has appointed one of its own commissioners as administrative law judge, but this response has generated concerns about the appearance of partiality because the commissioners vote on whether proceedings should be brought in the first instance, and they later sit as judges in the case. Moreover, there is recurrent criticism that the integrated agency model is itself in tension with the right to an impartial decision-maker.

Remedies are generally proportional to the violation. Criminal remedies are keyed to the monetary harm caused by the violation, and are subject to the constraints of the federal Sentencing Guidelines.

11. International institutions

WTO procedural rules are relatively clear. There is transparency and fairness. The publication of reports has helped to transform the dispute settlement process from one of diplomatic facilitation to one of reasoned adjudication generally of a high quality.

There is in general adequate opportunity to be heard, full notice of the allegations, adequate notice of the evidence relied on, and time to prepare. There is a right of appeal to the Appellate Body (AB).

But panel members for dispute settlement are chosen from a large roster of experts, and also in view of the lack of *stare decisis*, expertise and predictability may vary.

Timeliness, also, is a problem. The dispute resolution process may take a considerable amount of time.

The insulation of decision-makers from external influence and their open-mindedness has been questioned. It has been alleged that panel members may be linked to or influenced by lobbies and special interests and that there may be discrimination against developing countries. The rules of conduct on dispute settlement attempt to prevent potential conflicts of interest; they require each panel and Appellate Body member to comply with a self-disclosure requirement and they contain a subsequent disclosure procedure.

The absence of rules of evidence in decision-making can be a problem, and it may become a more significant problem if competition law should become a WTO competence. The panels lack sophistication in handling and evaluating evidence. The DSU does not include any express rules concerning burden of proof, although the AB has clarified that the party that asserts a fact is responsible for proving it. As noted, lack of *stare decisis* may create problems of predictability. Still, well-reasoned reports are likely to be followed in subsequent similar cases, and reasoning contained in unappealed panel reports tends to provide guidance.

Implementation and remedies may be problematic. A successful complainant is not awarded compensation for harm or reimbursement of expenses; it must help itself by imposing retaliatory trade sanctions on the violator. Developed countries with big markets are at a distinct advantage, and effectiveness of sanctions is a special problem for less powerful members.

In the OECD, UNCTD, and ICN, there is no case-by-case decision-making.

D. Institutional performance norms

We focus here on systemic performance characteristics, such as timeliness of decision-making, expertise, predictability, transparency, and accountability.

1. Australia and New Zealand

There is a relative paucity of competition litigation in Australia and in New Zealand, and thus limited guidance from the case law on a range of important procedural and substantive questions. Moreover, traditionally, the NZCC and the ACCC did not articulate their interpretations of the law in the form of enforcement guidance or policy papers. Therefore it was difficult to know how the agencies would approach various kinds of trade practices and economic issues. More recently, the agencies have been more forthcoming with guidelines, both substantive and procedural. Concerns over predictability remain acute with respect to allegations of abuse of dominance.

With respect to timeliness, historically agency investigations and enforcement proceedings have been extremely protracted (especially in abuse of dominance cases), with some investigations dragging on for years with little apparent progress. The current chairpersons of the agencies have made this concern a priority, and the NZCC has committed itself to ensuring that investigations progress to proceedings or are closed within a year. Regulatory determinations are also extremely lengthy, in part because of the extensive and successive consultation procedures that are followed.

In terms of the other institutional performance norms investigated as part of this study—accountability, expertise, sufficiency of investigative and sanctioning powers, transparency, and public participation—the NZCC and ACCC perform at a high level. Both are viewed by practitioners and business as credible and generally high-performing agencies.

2. Brazil

Historically, timeliness has been one of the most serious problems in competition law enforcement in Brazil. Under the previous competition law, there was no pre-merger clearance, review was *ex post*, and the review often extended for long periods of time after the closing of a deal. This procedure impaired the effectiveness of the authority, as they had to deal with the issue of "unscrambling the eggs" in cases where remedies were required. Alternatively, the authorities issued injunctions imposing hold separate obligations on the merging parties. In any case, due to the extended review time frames, this imposed excessive costs on both the companies, which had to maintain separate structures and delay realization of synergies, and the authorities, which had to monitor compliance with complex obligations. The new pre-merger review system addresses these problems. The procedures limit the time frame available for merger review and make the proceeding more predictable as a whole. The new system will require more trained personnel and, generally, efficiency in vetting the mergers.

As to anticompetitive behavior, investigations have also tended to take a significant amount of time (often longer than four years), thus imposing costs on both investigated parties and the authority. It is yet to be seen whether the integrated agency model introduced by the new competition law will increase expedition in this area of enforcement. With respect to expertise in deciding merits, it is important to stress that CADE has come a long way since the enactment of Law No. 8,884/94. The authorities' repeated handling of similar questions has contributed to a positive learning curve over the years and officials now have a comparatively high level of expertise.

Certain procedures may require attention. An example is cartel settlements, a procedure introduced in 2007. There is a lack of consistent benchmarks for the negotiation of these agreements and a lack of consistency in the level of pecuniary contributions (in Brazil, amounts paid in the context of settlements cannot be regarded as fines). Thus, the outcome of these negotiations has been unpredictable, deterring potential settling parties from approaching the authority with a view to settlement. It is yet unclear how the new law might impact issues such as this, but the adoption of the new regime presents an opportunity for more guidance, clarity, and predictability.

3. Canada

A widely held concern in Canada relates to the current bifurcated Bureau-Tribunal structure. The Competition Tribunal, at least in contested cases, has often engaged in highly protracted adversarial proceedings, leading to most matters being settled within the Bureau. In addition, there are serious concerns as to whether the Tribunal has been able to bring substantial expertise to bear on its deliberations, given the mixed-to-weak quality of many lay member appointments, as well as the lack of specialized expertise on the part of most judicial members. Some commentators believe that these concerns can be most effectively addressed by creating a three- to five-member Competition Commission with full investigative, enforcement, and adjudicative authority (an integrated agency model), subject perhaps to an appeal on matters of law or mixed law and fact to the Federal Court of Appeal.

With respect to the Competition Bureau, its independence is not seriously questioned, although some commentators believe in this respect that it would be better constituted as a separate statutory agency rather than housed within a government department (Industry Canada).

With respect to accountability, there have been concerns in many quarters that the registration of Consent Agreements in merger cases with the Competition Tribunal, and enforcement thereof as orders of the Tribunal without review, is undesirable and that little public scrutiny of an agreement is possible given the skeletal nature of the agreements. This is exacerbated by a perception that the Bureau provides no or inadequate technical backgrounders or competitive impact assessments by which the broader public can evaluate the appropriateness of such orders or other settlement arrangements. The Bureau reports annually to Parliament on its past year's activities, current priorities, and future priorities.

With respect to expertise, concerns have been expressed regarding the lack of consistent input from senior experienced economists in the Bureau's investigative and enforcement activities.

With respect to timeliness of decision-making within the Bureau, concerns have been expressed as to the protracted nature of Bureau decision-making in many cases, and some observers favor legislated deadlines as opposed to merely internal service deadlines, in order to focus and discipline the Bureau's activities.

4. *Chile*

After the 2005 constitutional reforms that established as a norm the transparency of all state decisions, the right to information has been a key issue for competition law bodies; it has even been a hallmark of their behavior. NEPO has a website where some of its decisions are made public. The Competition Tribunal has created and improved its website, making accessible to the general public on a timely basis all its files and decisions.

NEPO has consulted with the public on some of its draft guidelines. The Competition Tribunal has also adopted a policy of public consultations with regard to some of its internal regulations, which must be observed by lawyers in litigating before the Tribunal.

A survey undertaken of users of the competition law system in Chile reveals that respondents consider that the performance of both NEPO and the Competition Tribunal have been improving with respect to issues such as transparency, expertise, public consultation, and predictability. Timeliness in concluding investigations within NEPO remains a concern, with some investigations dragging on for three years or more and some merger reviews taking a year or more.

With respect to expertise, the Competition Tribunal's mixed composition, jurisdiction, and appointment procedures have proven to be generally successful. Levels of expertise within NEPO seem somewhat more mixed and satisfactory levels may turn on which case officer has been assigned a given file.

The nature of the Supreme Court's appellate jurisdiction with respect to appeals from competition tribunals is somewhat unclear, and some concerns have arisen as to the level of expertise that members of the Court bring to competition appeals before it.

5. *China*

As noted earlier, neither the NDRC nor the SAIC is required to publish decisions or to provide reasons for its decisions. While the MOFCOM is required to publish its merger review decisions that prohibit or conditionally approve proposed mergers, it is not required to publish unconditional merger clearances or to provide detailed reasons for its decisions.

With respect to public accountability, the competition law regime reflects broader issues with China's current administrative law system because of the concentration of legislative, executive, and adjudicative functions. For example, as regards the enforcement of the anti-monopoly law, the budget allocated to the AML enforcement is not publicly available.

With respect to expertise in the three competition agencies, there appears to be very limited legal expertise and even less economic expertise among employees of the NDRC and the SAIC. The MOFCOM has recruited some PhD economists to its staff.

6. *European Union*

In order to enhance predictability and transparency in decision-making, the European Commission regularly publishes guidelines indicating its approach to various competition law issues, typically following a consultation process initiated by the release of draft guidelines. The Commission has established an informal "peer review" mechanism as a result of which panels of DG Competition and Legal Service officials oversee draft decisions. With respect to expertise, the Competition Directorate created the office of chief economist a decade ago. The chief economist and his team gives economic guidance to case teams from the early stages of proceedings, as well as to the Director General. The chief economist and the growing support group of economists have greatly enhanced the level of economic expertise of the Commission.

With respect to timeliness of decision-making, complaints have been made of protracted investigations in non-merger matters. The Commission recently adopted internal guidelines to address this concern.

As to external accountability, the Commission reports to the European Parliament every year on the outcomes of its competition policy and enforcement activities, thus providing a review of whether the objectives identified in the plan have been attained. An Advisory Committee on Restrictive Practices and Dominant Positions, composed of representatives of national competition authorities, is consulted on all draft decisions of the European Commission.

In addition, the Economic and Social Committee, an advisory body representing various social groups, such as employers, trade unions, consumers, and small and medium undertakings, comprises a specific section dealing with the single market, production, and consumption, including competition policy. The Committee may be consulted on legislative proposals by the Commission, the Council, and the European Parliament or may issue an opinion on its own initiative. The Committee also issues an opinion every year on the Commission's Annual Report on Competition Policy. Two committees at the European Parliament oversee the Commission's activities in the area of competition policy: the Committee on Internal Market and Consumer Protection and the Committee on Economic and Monetary Affairs. The European Parliament also adopts each year a resolution on the

Commission's Annual Report on Competition Policy and comments on all proposals of the European Commission.

The European Ombudsman is empowered to receive complaints on alleged instances of maladministration and to open an inquiry if the complainant has advanced sufficient evidence of facts that have not been or are not the subject of legal proceedings. On occasion, the ombudsman has noted concerns with aspects of the Commission's proceedings.

7. India

The Supreme Court of India has opined that "The scheme of the [Competition] Act and the Regulations framed thereunder clearly demonstrates the legislative intent that the investigations and inquiries under the . . . Act should be concluded as expeditiously as possible. The various provisions [of the Act] and the Regulations . . . direct conclusion of the investigation/inquiry or proceeding within [a] 'reasonable time.' The concept of 'reasonable time' thus has to be construed meaningfully, keeping in view the object of the Act and the larger interest of the domestic and international trade."[21]

The Supreme Court has directed that the Director General of Investigation should take not more than forty-five days to submit investigation reports to the Commission and in all the cases where the Commission exercises its jurisdiction to pass interim orders, the Commission must pass the order expeditiously and in all cases within sixty days. In the cases of mergers or combinations, the Act provides that a notifiable combination shall not come into effect until the earlier of (1) 210 days from the valid receipt of notification, or (2) the date the Commission approves the combination. However, under the Combination Regulations, the Commission has committed to endeavor to pass an order or issue a direction within 180 days. Further, the CCI shall, within thirty days of receiving valid notice, form a prima facie opinion as to whether or not the combination is likely to cause or has caused an appreciable adverse effect on competition within the relevant market in India.

Both the Commission and the Tribunal are required to publish their orders, which must be reasoned orders. The orders must appear on the website of the respective authorities. The Commission also publishes an annual report highlighting activities undertaken during the year under review. The Act empowers the Commission to make regulations consistent with the Act. The Commission has from time to time notified various regulations to carry out the purpose of the Act.

The Commission is accountable to the Parliament. The Commission is required to submit an annual report and statement of its activities to the Parliament. The Parliament may, on the receipt of a report, issue suitable directions to the Commission. The annual budget of Commission must be approved by the Parliament.

Indian competition law enforcement is relatively young and thus far only a limited number of cases have been dealt with by the Commission and the Tribunal.

[21] Writ Petition (civil) 490 of 2003; Brahm Dutt v. Union of India.

It is too early to make an objective assessment of issues such as transparency in the decision-making process or in policy formulation and elaboration.

8. Japan

The JFTC is a large agency roughly the size of comparable competition agencies in the US and EU. It appears to investigate most cases efficiently. It has, however, encountered more difficulties with international cartels, where cases can take from two to five years to complete. The JFTC's merger reviews depended heavily on pre-merger informal consultations. Although the Commission claimed to complete these consultations within the thirty-day period required by its operations manual, in practice they took far longer. As noted above, a new legal framework took effect in July 2011.

With respect to expertise, JFTC commissioners are not required to have expertise in competition law. Chairmen have generally been alumni of the Ministry of Finance. Usually one commissioner has been a former Secretary General of the JFTC. JFTC staff are career employees and are hired and retained on a seniority basis. Historically and currently, there have been few qualified lawyers or economists with advanced training at the JFTC.

With respect to transparency, the JFTC has issued guidelines in many areas, which have provided important guidance on its enforcement policies in the light of the lack of formal adjudications and case law.

With respect to accountability, the JFTC is accountable to the Diet in a number of ways: budget approval, appointments of commissioners, presentation of an annual report, and answering Diet member inquiries regarding specific enforcement decisions. The JFTC is also accountable to the courts, but the lack of formal decisions and the lack of party appeals to the courts have limited judicial review to minimal levels.

9. South Africa

With respect to timeliness of dispositions, the Commission has been relatively successful in concluding merger reviews expeditiously. It has also recently published new service standard commitments that reflect this policy. There is much more concern with the pace of decision-making in complaint proceedings in non-merger matters.

With respect to expertise, it has been a challenge for the Commission to attract and retain professional staff that can deal effectively with complex competition issues, given that their counterparts in the private sector are invariably well-paid and have a depth of experience. The Tribunal has the necessary expertise to perform its role and the permanent members of the Tribunal are well-respected. While the Competition Appeal Court is composed of sitting members of the provincial divisions of the courts, the judges volunteer to serve on this court because of a particular interest or expertise in competition law and therefore can be expected to be relatively well-qualified and to develop a greater expertise in the area over time.

With respect to predictability, the Commission's approach to its task is reasonably predictable in the sense that it must investigate all complaints lodged with it and analyze all mergers that are notified. Nevertheless, because of resource constraints it has had to prioritize certain aspects of its work. The Commission regularly communicates these priorities to the public. The breadth of the goals of competition policy in South Africa places inherent limits on predictability in the application of the law.

With respect to transparency in policy formulation or elaboration, there is a dearth of guidelines issued by the Commission indicating how it will apply the law. Indeed, it has issued no substantive enforcement guidelines.

With respect to public consultation and participation in policy formulation and elaboration, the Competition Tribunal has sought to encourage participation by interested stakeholders. For instance, merger rules require notifying the Minister of Trade and Industry[22] of the merger and the trade unions that represent a significant proportion of the employees of the merging parties. Interventions are generally encouraged by the Tribunal if the intervenor can demonstrate that it has a significant interest in the manner.

With respect with transparency of reasons for decisions, decision-making power is to a large extent *de facto* in the hands of the Commission, due to the large number of settlements in competition investigations. The Commission publicizes settlement agreements widely in the media and publishes press releases on its website. In addition, the settlement agreements themselves have to be confirmed by the Tribunal and are accessible on the Tribunal's website once confirmed. It is more difficult to obtain information regarding discontinuances, non-referrals, or decisions not to refer the matter.

With respect to public accountability, the Minister of Trade and Industry appoints the Commissioner and Deputy Commissioner based on qualifications and experience in law, economics, commerce, industry, or public affairs. The Commission has an annual performance agreement with the Department and is responsible to the Minister. Despite these links to the government, the decision-making independence of the Commission seems widely accepted. The Competition Act requires the Commissioner to prepare and submit an annual report to the Minister of Trade and Industry, including audited financial statements and a report of activities undertaken in terms of the functions set out in the Act, and a statement of progress achieved during the preceding year towards realization of the purposes of the Act. The Commissioner is periodically called on to report directly to Parliament.

The Competition Tribunal's members are nominated by the Minister of Trade and Industry and appointed by the President of South Africa. The members' tenure, like that of the Commissioner, is five years. The members of the Competition Appeal Court, who are High Court judges, are appointed by the President on

[22] Officially, the Competition Commission now falls under the jurisdiction of the Department of Economic Development.

the advice of the Judicial Service Commission, for a fixed but renewable term of ten years.

10. United States

Regarding operational efficiency, major issues center around merger review: first, the agencies must decide which one will review a given merger; second, both agencies face challenges in resisting excessive requests for documents and information from the parties to the transaction. The FTC faces challenges in timely decision-making in its administrative adjudication process. The FTC sought to address this problem in 2009 with rule changes that established tighter timetables. The adoption of case-management rules by the judiciary has substantially improved timeliness of judicial adjudication.

Both agencies rate well on expertise. They both employ and retain substantial staffs consisting of lawyers, economists, paralegals, and administrative personnel; they both employ a considerable number of PhD-level economists. The statutory provisions for appointing FTC commissioners and the head of the Antitrust Division do not specify qualifications. The quality of FTC commissioner appointments has sometimes attracted criticism. Despite the initial design of the FTC as an agency expert in the problems of business, economists and business executives have been sparsely represented among commissioners. Expertise of FTC administrative law judges has also been a concern because these initial decision-makers often have little or no expertise in areas of FTC enforcement. The DOJ relies on the courts, and the FTC does so to a lesser extent. Both agencies, state attorneys general, and private parties may litigate in courts, which are generalist courts. Although issues of judicial expertise on technical antitrust matters could in theory be a problem, this does not seem to be of acute concern in a US context.

Transparency in policy guidance and decision-making is high. Both agencies issue detailed public guidelines, policy statements, and reports that describe their approach to applications of the law. Both agencies have procedures for public comment on proposed settlement agreements. DOJ court settlements are also subject to judicial review before being entered as judicial decrees. When the agencies decide to take no action on notified mergers, they occasionally release closing statements.

Outcomes are predictable to a reasonable degree, given margins of discretion for both fact-finding and applications of law; and accountability to the relevant stakeholders is good.

11. International institutions

For *the WTO*, we refer to the International entry on Due Process Norms, above.

The OECD. Members have good access to agenda setting. Transparency is excellent. The output of the Competition Committee is evaluated by the members of the committee every other year; the budget allocated by the OECD is based on the output of the particular committee as compared with the output of other committees, thus tending to assure accountability. Responsiveness and level of activity have accelerated with the advent of the ICN into the circle of "competitor" institutions dealing with the issues of competition law in a global economy. Expertise, as reflected in reports and peer reviews, is very high. The level of research on cutting edge issues is impressive. Global Forums and other meetings, focused on issues of greatest importance to the members, provide an important venue for interaction and result in documentation that is a valuable resource.

The UNCTAD. The UNCTAD is largely secretariat-driven; the agenda is controlled by the secretariat. The work product increasingly reflects significant expertise. Recent peer reviews have been written by volunteers from member states who have substantial expertise. Significant work of the competition branch centers around the UN Set on Competition Policy, which dates back to the end of the 1970s (adopted in 1980). Its language is not entirely contemporary but cannot be changed without reopening a process for a new consensus. The gap is bridged by updating commentary on the principles of the Set. The competition branch of the UNCTAD sponsors cutting-edge research. It runs a well-received program of capacity building in Latin America, and is an important forum for convening developing (and developed) country competition officials and thus facilitating a developing country competition community.

The ICN. On all counts, performance and process are excellent. The ICN is engaged in a process of self-assessment to assure that it is responsive to its members' wants and needs and that it moves in directions desired by its members. If participation in agenda-setting and first-draft authorship fall mainly to individuals in the developed world (as it does), that is because the agencies in many developing nations have few human and monetary resources to devote to the ICN, given more urgent priorities.

IV. Concluding reflections

We can conclude, at a level of generality, that the jurisdictions studied in this volume aspire to achieve effectiveness in competition law enforcement while assuring fair process; they wish to be and to be perceived to be legitimate, and they strive to be accountable. All three of the institutional design models identified at the outset of this introductory chapter (the bifurcated judicial model, the bifurcated agency model, and the integrated agency model) can achieve these ends. The jurisdictions studied show variations, within a range, as to the specific requirements of due process. Jurisdictions strike different balances between agency effectiveness and rights of defense. Also, they achieve different levels of effectiveness. For example, several systems in our sample suffer from protractedness of proceedings and lack of sufficient expertise in decision-making, but most seem to aspire to a higher standard, and, in any event, increasing transparency of shortfalls through global competition journalism, published peer reviews, and word-of-mouth may produce gentle pressure to address the weaknesses.

We began this project with the notional norms in our template, reproduced in the Appendix to this chapter. As noted, the jurisdictional studies tend to confirm that these norms do exist within most competition law systems, although China may value independence and transparency differently from other jurisdictions in our study. Based on the limited sample of jurisdictions covered in this volume, we are comfortable in our tentative observation tending to verify as global the institutional and process norms identified in our template, while recognizing substantial scope for variation in institutional design choices bearing on their vindication. The variation reflects a complex set of context-specific factors—historical, cultural, political, and the forces of path dependency once a particular regime matures and becomes entrenched in a country's broader institutional matrix.[23] Thus, while we perceive the emerging outlines of a global consensus on certain core institutional and decision-making norms in competition law, local choices as to their instantiation will continue to exert significant influence and constrain the potential for full substantive and procedural convergence of competition law regimes.

In a world in which business transactions and practices increasingly transcend national borders in their scope and effect, there is obviously increasing potential for conflict among nations in applying their domestic competition laws.[24] Impressive progress has been made in promoting the convergence of competition law doctrines as they apply to the three major substantive pillars: arrangements among competitors, abuse of dominance (or monopolization), and mergers. Most recently, distinct progress has been made through the International Competition Network (ICN). Even so, as the legal realists taught us many decades ago, there will often be substantial divergence between law on the books and law on the ground. In the competition law context, one would predict that variations in the design of investigative, enforcement, adjudicative, and appellate institutions, and the decision-making processes that they employ, are likely to produce divergences in policy or decisional outcomes even if the substantive legal framework is largely congruent across jurisdictions. To date, most efforts at promoting convergence of competition laws across jurisdictions have focused on substantive doctrine. To a much lesser extent have they focused on differences in institutional design and decision-making processes.

Might our project on global process norms play a role in the larger project for convergence despite the fact that our conclusions do not suggest a need for convergence of institutional design in order to fulfill the procedure/process norms?[25] We think it does, for the following reasons.

[23] *See* Mariana Prado and Michael Trebilcock, "Path Dependence, Development, and the Dynamics of Institutional Reform," (2009) 59 U. Toronto L. J. 341.

[24] *See*, e.g., Richard Epstein and Michael Greve, eds, *Competition Laws in Conflict: Antitrust Jurisdiction in the Global Economy* (American Enterprise Institute, 2004).

[25] One exception is the view of some that the inquisitorial system does not fulfill due process norms particularly in cases that might result in very high fines. If the suggestion is that civil law systems should be converted into common law systems, we do not agree. But we do observe that the lively discussion of the due process issue within the European system has led to more convergent appreciation of the requirements of the norm of due process; the European Commission has implemented additional safeguards and has proposed yet others.

Transparency alone is a vital ingredient in attaining meaningful substantive convergence, in understanding and respecting substantive divergences, and in building bridges in the case of divergences. Moreover, the commonality of the procedure/process norms and the aspiration (or nudging) of nations to fulfill them is an important ingredient in the enterprise to maximize the sympathy of systems. The very fact of common process norms is likely to increase the respect of each nation and its people and firms for the decision-making of each other nation. Respect and regard[26] not only produce more harmony but are likely to work in the direction of more convergences.

Institutions and the decision-making processes that they employ are not cast in stone, and critical self-reflection on their adequacy, informed by insights from relevant comparative experience, hold significant promise for reducing the more severe or dysfunctional forms of conflicts between or among competition law regimes in a business environment where many transactions and arrangements tend to be less local and more global in their effects. Our hope is that this project will contribute to this process of self-reflection and comparative cross-fertilization. Thus, this project may be seen as a step towards redressing the imbalance between the study of substance and the study of procedure as we work towards greater sympathy among the competition systems of the world.

[26] *See* Christine Varney, note 2 *supra*; Rachel Brandenburger, note 2 *supra*.

APPENDIX

The Template—Outline of Elements Addressed in the Jurisdictional Studies

The following outline guided authors of the jurisdictional chapters.

History

Describe briefly the historical evolution of competition law institutions in your jurisdiction.

Structure

Briefly describe the contemporary structure of competition law institutions in your jurisdiction. We suggest reference to the three basic models: i) the bifurcated judicial model, where a specialized competition investigation and enforcement authority brings enforcement proceedings before the courts for adjudication; ii) the bifurcated agency model, where a specialized competition investigation and enforcement authority brings enforcement proceedings before a separate specialized competition tribunal for adjudication; and iii) the integrated agency model, where a single agency is responsible for investigation, enforcement, and adjudicative functions, normally with rights of review in the courts. Your jurisdiction may, of course, have variations on and mixtures of the above.

Mandate and boundaries of the competition authority

What is the mandate of the competition investigation and enforcement authority in your jurisdiction, both in terms of objectives and scope? (For example, as to scope: does the mandate extend to consumer protection? Regulated industries?) What are the stated objectives of competition policy? How are these objectives articulated? (For example, statutory recitals and text, guidelines, policy statements.) To what extent are there carve-outs or exceptions for particular industries or arrangements? To what extent is the authority also responsible for adjacent or flanking policies? (For example, intellectual property, foreign direct investment review, consumer protection, price regulation in monopolized industries.) Where industry-specific regulators also exist, how are the jurisdictional boundaries between the competition agency and these industry-specific regulators determined?

Procedural characteristics

To what extent do the procedural characteristics or practices of competition agencies in a selected jurisdiction reflect the following procedural norms?

1) **Due process norms in case-by-case decision-making**

For example:

a) In particular cases, the opportunity to be heard, timely and full notice of allegations, adequate notice of evidence relied on, adequate time to prepare a defense.
b) Independence of decision-makers from external influence or direction in the application of the law to particular parties or transactions.
c) Open-mindedness of first-level decision-makers on findings of fact based on sufficient evidence and free of incentives other than objective fact-finding.
d) Equality before the law: non-discrimination in the application of the law.
e) The rights to challenge critical agency determinations before an independent reviewing body or court.
f) Proportionality of remedies to violations.

2) **Institutional performance norms**

For example:

a) Timeliness of dispositions.
b) Expertise in determinations.
c) Sufficiency of investigative and sanctioning powers.
d) Reasonable predictability in application of law.
e) Transparency in policy formulation or elaboration (through, for example, enforcement guidelines).
f) Opportunities for public consultation and participation in policy formulation and elaboration.
g) Transparency of reasons for decisions including major settlements or discontinuances.
h) Public accountability mechanisms for general agency functioning, including personnel and budgetary decisions, and periodic reviews of appropriateness of legislative mandate and agency effectiveness.

Critical evaluation

Where, in your view, these norms have not been fully realized, is this because:

a) the norms are not recognized?;
b) the norms are recognized but trade-offs between or among norms have been made?;
c) the norms are recognized but agencies have exhibited certain deficiencies or faced particular impediments to their realization?

What are the options for improvement? What are your suggestions for improvement?

***

2

Australia and New Zealand

Their Competition Law Systems and the Countries' Norms

Simon Peart

I. Competition law enforcement and governance: Australia and New Zealand

A. History of Australian competition law

The Australian Industries Preservation Act 1906 marked Australia's first statutory foray into the field of competition law. Prior to this legislation, anticompetitive practices were addressed, if at all, through the common law doctrines of conspiracy and restraint of trade.[1] The AIPA was influenced by the Sherman Act, and prohibited, on the one hand, contracts or combinations in restraint of trade or commerce intended to injure Australian industry by unfair competition,[2] and on the other, monopolization or attempts to monopolize.[3] The prohibitions as originally drafted applied to commerce with other countries or between the Australian states (sections 4 and 7), and also to commerce within the Australian Commonwealth more generally (sections 5 and 8). However, an early decision of the High Court[4] deprived the Act of much of its force, holding that sections 5 and 8 exceeded the Australian Government's enumerated constitutional powers as they intruded into purely intrastate commerce.[5] In 1912 the Full High Court further limited the effect of the Act when it held that specific intent to injure the public was an element of the offences under sections 4 and 7.[6]

[1] David K. Round, Jeremy Tustin and Kerrie Round, *Australian Competition Law: History, Harmonisation, Issues and Lessons*, Paper delivered at Centre for Economic Policy Research Symposium, Competition Policy for International Development, Growth and Trade, Brussels, December 2005 at 28; S. G. Corones, *Competition Law in Australia* (5th edn Thomson, 2010) at 177–80.

[2] Australian Industries Preservation Act 1906 (Cth), sections 4 and 5.

[3] Australian Industries Preservation Act 1906 (Cth), sections 7 and 8.

[4] *Huddart Parker & Co Pty Ltd v Moorehead* (1909) 8 CLR 330.

[5] The Commonwealth of Australia is a federation of the several states and territories. Section 51 of the Australian Constitution grants enumerated legislative powers to the Commonwealth Parliament (heads of power). The remaining "residual powers" reside with the states.

[6] *Adelaide Steamship Company v Attorney-General of the Commonwealth* (1912) 15 CLR 65, upheld on appeal to the Privy Council in *Attorney-General of the Commonwealth v Adelaide Steamship Company* [1913] AC 781.

The AIPA remained on the statute books until 1965, but was largely ineffectual in preventing a proliferation of restrictive trade practices in Australian commerce during the 1930s and 1940s.[7] Rising dissatisfaction prompted the Commonwealth Attorney-General, Sir Garfield Barwick, to respond in December 1962, announcing a new proposal to address anticompetitive conduct.[8] The proposal was modeled on the administrative regime of the UK Restrictive Trade Practices Act 1956 and envisioned two lists: list A, comprising trade practices likely to be restrictive of competition but capable of justification in the public interest; and list B, comprising practices considered "inexcusable" in all circumstances.[9] Persons intending to engage in practices in list A could do so only after registering a document describing the intended practice in full, at which point they would be immunized from prosecution. A registrar, commission, and tribunal were to be established to institute and determine proceedings for deregistration of documents in cases where the described practice would "substantially reduce competition," unless one of a number of public benefit exceptions applied.[10]

The Barwick proposal was eventually enacted, although in a significantly modified form, as the Restrictive Trade Practices Act 1965. The Act required registration of instances of certain listed practices with the Commissioner of Trade Practices, whose role it was to examine such instances to ensure they were in the public interest, and consult with the parties involved if not. If consultation failed, the Commissioner referred the practices to the newly constituted Trade Practices Tribunal for a determination. The public interest criterion directed the Tribunal to apply a "balance sheet" assessment,[11] weighing the detriment from lessened competition against a variety of countervailing interests, including efficiency, overseas competitiveness, the interests of consumers, employees, producers, and other stakeholders in the supply chain, and the needs of small business.[12] Only two practices—collusive bidding and tendering—were prohibited outright.

The 1965 Act was invalidated on constitutional grounds[13] but promptly re-enacted on a different constitutional footing as the Trade Practices Act 1971. By 1973, however, the new Labour government had grown concerned that the scheme

[7] The Hon. Sir Garfield Barwick, "Trade Practices in a Developing Economy," G.L. Wood Memorial Lecture, (Government Printer 1963), at 2–3, 8–9. Sir Garfield's thesis was that the Great Depression of the 1930s and the economic regulation of World War II resulted in a highly rationalized and regulated economy which left little room for competition, eventually molding a business community that was unaccustomed to trading in a competitive way.

[8] Mr Freeth, Acting Attorney-General, Australian Parliamentary Debates, 6 December 1962, 3102–14.

[9] As an aside, and reflecting the shift in economic thinking over the past forty years, price fixing was included on list A, as potentially justifiable, whereas persistent price cutting at a loss was to be found in list B, and therefore considered inexcusable in all circumstances.

[10] Mr Freeth, Acting Attorney-General, Australian Parliamentary Debates, 6 December 1962, 3106. The public benefit exceptions included such goals as maintaining employment, promoting productive and allocative efficiency, and enhancing export trade amongst others.

[11] Maureen Brunt, "Legislation in search of an objective" in *Economic Essays on Australian and New Zealand Competition Law* (Kluwer, 2003) at 54.

[12] Ibid.

[13] *Strickland v Rocla Concrete Pipes Ltd* (1971) 124 CLR 468.

unfairly placed the onus of determining what forms of business conduct were unlawful on the Commission rather than on Parliament.[14] Moreover the administrative burden associated with assessing and consulting on thousands of individually registered practices rendered the Commission ineffective.[15]

The 1971 Act was accordingly repealed and replaced by the Trade Practices Act 1974, which ushered in the modern era of competition law and policy in Australia. Although significantly amended, the central provisions of the Trade Practices Act remain in force today. The central policy shift was towards a proscriptive approach to competition enforcement in place of the registration/examination scheme that preceded it. The Trade Practices Act prohibited a range of anticompetitive trade practices either on a per se basis (for example, cartel offences or misuse of market power), or subject to a competition test (for example, non-cartel agreements that lessen competition). It also introduced merger control into the Australian regulatory environment. In its original drafting, the Trade Practices Act borrowed language from the Sherman Act—for example section 45, which in its original form prohibited "contracts . . . in restraint of trade or commerce."[16] However, subsequent amendments have recast the prohibitions in the language of market power and lessened competition.

The Trade Practices Act established the foundations of the enforcement apparatus that continues to this day: the Trade Practices Commission (now the Australian Competition and Consumer Commission) and the Trade Practices Tribunal (now the Australian Competition Tribunal). The Commission's role is to enforce the Act's prohibitions through investigations and court proceedings, authorize restrictive trade practices where justified in the public interest, and clear mergers. The Tribunal is empowered to review determinations of the Commission.

The Trade Practices Act also introduced consumer protection provisions alongside the competition provisions, establishing the policy—which prevails in both New Zealand and Australia—that competition, economic regulation, and consumer protection should generally be the responsibility of a single integrated national regulatory body. Over time, the regulatory roles of the Commission have been added to; first with the addition of a regime to regulate access to essential facilities,[17] and then with industry-specific roles in areas such as telecommunications, electricity (in conjunction with the Australian Energy Regulator), postal services, shipping, aviation, and gas, amongst others.[18]

In 2011, the Trade Practices Act 1974 was renamed the Competition and Consumer Act 2010, although only minimal amendments were made to the

[14] Round et al., *supra* note 1, at 33; Australia, Senate 1973, DEBATES, 23 October, 2734.

[15] Round et al., *supra* note 1, at 32.

[16] Corones, *supra* note 1, at 185.

[17] A recommendation of the Hilmer Committee Report in 1993. *See* Independent Committee of Inquiry into Competition Policy in Australia, *National Competition Policy* (Australian Government Publishing Service, 1993).

[18] In some industries (i.e. telecommunications) the legislation specifically empowers the ACCC with a regulatory role; in other cases the ACCC has assumed jurisdiction under its access regime powers in Part IIIA, or its price surveillance powers under Part VIIA.

competition provisions. For simplicity all references to the prevailing regime are to the Competition and Consumer Act 2010 rather than the Trade Practices Act 1974, unless the context demands otherwise.

B. History of New Zealand competition law

Competition law in New Zealand has its genesis in three Acts promulgated between 1908 and 1919. The inaptly named Monopoly Prevention Act 1908 was in part an anti-dumping regime directed at overseas suppliers of agricultural equipment, and in remainder a price surveillance scheme for potatoes, wheat, and flour. Both elements of the Act were directed at the "competitive" price of the regulated goods.[19] The Act was too narrow in its application to be of lasting effect, however, and had fallen into disuse long before it was repealed in 1975.[20]

The Commercial Trusts Act 1910 was more recognizably a competition statute. With a stated purpose of repressing monopolies in trade and commerce,[21] the Act prohibited the use of discounts, refusals to deal, and discriminatory terms of trade as inducements for exclusive dealing or to join a commercial trust (defined as an association of persons with the object of controlling the supply of goods or prices, or maintaining a monopoly).[22] The Act also made it an offence for members of a commercial trust to fix prices unreasonably high, and defined an unreasonably high price as one that "produces or is calculated to produce more than a fair and reasonable rate of commercial profit" to the supplier.[23] However, like the Monopoly Prevention Act, the Commercial Trusts Act was aimed only at specified goods: agricultural implements, coal, meat, fish, flour, and oatmeal, petroleum products, sugar, and tobacco products.[24] Moreover, a 1927 Privy Council decision undermined the Act, holding that an adverse effect on public interest had to be shown in any prosecution under the Act.[25] It would of course have been open to the government to amend the Act in light of the Privy Council's decision. Donaldson suggests that the fact it did not do so can be viewed as reflecting a political preference in New Zealand at the time for centralized regulation over free markets.[26]

That regulatory instinct was evident in the third of these early competition statutes—the Board of Trade Act 1919. The Act established the Board of Trade to inquire into New Zealand industry and recommend to the Governor-General regulations for the prevention of "unfair or prejudicial" methods of competition, the suppression of monopolies, the establishment of fixed prices, the control of

[19] Rex J. Ahdar, *Competition Law and Policy in New Zealand* (Law Book Co., 1991) at 12.

[20] Ahdar, *supra* note 19, at 12; Stevenson, "The History of New Zealand's Competition Law," Department of Trade and Industry Monograph (1982) at 12.

[21] Commercial Trusts Act 1910 (NZ), Long Title.

[22] Commercial Trusts Act 1910 (NZ), section 2(1).

[23] Commercial Trusts Act 1910 (NZ), section 8.

[24] Commercial Trusts Act 1910 (NZ), section 2(2) and Schedule.

[25] *Crown Milling Co. Ltd. v R* [1927] AC 394; and *see* Ahdar, *supra* note 19, at 13.

[26] Ahdar, *supra* note 19, at 13.

differential prices, or for any other manner of regulation or control of industry.[27] In addition, the Act included general prohibitions against "profiteering" (defined in similar terms as "unreasonably high" prices under the Commercial Trusts Act) whether by an individual or through a cartel, and against hoarding or intentional destruction of goods to drive up prices.[28] The regulation-making powers of the Board of Trade Act were used primarily to control markets for particular goods and services through licensing or regulatory bodies—for example, the Cinematic Licensing Authority and the Wheat Committee.[29]

Through the 1930s and 1940s, administrative price control rather than competition was the dominant mode of economic regulation. The Board of Trade Act was supplemented by the Prevention of Profiteering Act 1936, and later the Control of Prices Act 1947 and the Economic Stabilisation Act 1948. These Acts empowered various forms of regulatory price control in an attempt to maintain a stable relationship between prices and wages.[30] The primary offences under this regulatory paradigm were accordingly profiteering, hoarding, and other forms of output limitation. The focus on direct regulation of prices relegated competition—as a means of enhancing consumer welfare—to a subordinate role.

In 1949 a change in government heralded a change in approach—the new national government indicating its desire to end price control as the primary means of economic regulation.[31] A 1954 inquiry by the Pricing Tribunal (established under the Control of Prices Act) determined that price control was unnecessary under conditions of competition, and should be reserved for industries in which there was inadequate supply or competition.[32] These observations served as the impetus for a law to address restrictive trade practices to ensure competition was not lessened in industries structurally capable of it.[33] The eventual result of this shift in policy was the Trade Practices Act 1958, modeled, like the Australian Trade Practices Act 1965, on the UK's Restrictive Trade Practices Act 1956.

The 1958 Act represented a compromise between *ex post* competition prohibitions and *ex ante* price control. Instances of enumerated restrictive trade practices were to be registered with the Commissioner of Trade Practices and Prices, and if found by that officer to injure the public interest by unreasonably increasing prices or limiting competition, referred to the Trade Practices and Prices Commission for determination. In parallel, the Commission was empowered to recommend that goods be made subject to price control in circumstances where orders restraining anticompetitive practices were insufficient to prevent monopoly.[34] The Commission's determinations were reviewable by the Trade Practices Appeal Authority. The 1958 Act was essentially folded, with some modifications, into the Commerce

27 Board of Trade Act 1919 (NZ), section 26.

28 Board of Trade Act 1919 (NZ), section 32.

29 Ahdar, *supra* note 19, at 13.

30 Ahdar, *supra* note 19, at 14.

31 Ahdar, *supra* note 19, at 15; Edwards, *Trade Regulations Overseas* (1966) at 600.

32 Round et al., *supra* note 1, at 37; Ahdar, *supra* note 19, at 15.

33 *See* Ahdar, *supra* note 19, at 15; Edwards, *supra* note 31, at 603.

34 Ahdar, *supra* note 19, at 16.

Act 1975, which also added a merger control regime and provisions for the breakup of monopolies.

Notwithstanding the competition provisions of the 1958 Act, the New Zealand economy up until 1984 was characterized by a high degree of centralized regulation and state ownership, and was widely viewed as inefficient and uncompetitive.[35] In 1984, the reforms introduced by the fourth Labour government fundamentally changed the New Zealand economy. The fourth Labour government sold the state telecommunications provider into private hands, reconstituted the electricity and postal services sectors as state-owned enterprises subject to commercial imperatives,[36] floated the New Zealand dollar, deregulated many trades and industries, and introduced competition into markets that had previously operated as state-run monopolies. The quid pro quo for deregulation was the introduction of a stronger *ex post* competition regime in the form of the Commerce Act 1986, which remains in force today. The 1986 Act was modeled on the Australian Trade Practices Act 1974, introducing similar substantive prohibitions and enforcement mechanisms. The Act prohibited certain restrictive trade practices on a per se basis—price fixing, resale price maintenance, and monopolization—and others subject to a competition test—for example, contracts, arrangements, and understandings that substantially lessen competition. The Act also provided for merger control, and for the imposition of price control in circumstances of limited competition. The Commerce Commission was empowered to enforce the Act's prohibitions through court proceedings, and to authorize restrictive trade practices and clear mergers. Where the New Zealand Act differed from its Australian cousin is in the absence of an equivalent to the Australian Competition Tribunal. Instead, determinations of the Commission were reviewable by the courts of general jurisdiction.

As in Australia, the Commerce Act envisions an integrated regulator with responsibility for competition, economic regulation, and consumer protection. Over time, the regulatory provisions of the Commerce Act have been strengthened—usually in response to perceived failings of the monopolization law to promote more competitive markets.[37] In 2006, a major review of the economic regulatory provisions of the Act was announced, culminating in the Commerce Amendment Act 2008, which established a regime for imposing price-quality regulation on markets with limited competition. Specific regimes were also introduced for electricity, gas pipelines, and airports.

[35] Richard J. Osborne, "Toward Prosperity? Some Aspects of Recent Economic Deregulation in New Zealand," 7 Pacific Basin L.J. 158 at 158–9, citing L. Bayliss, "Address to the Conference of Business Economists and Corporate Planners," The Labour Government's Economic Policies—An Appraisal (9 April 1987) at 1.

[36] Under section 4 of the State-Owned Enterprises Act 1986 (NZ), SOEs have the principal objective of operating as a successful business and, while they are 100 percent owned by the government, the government is afforded rights only slightly more extensive than those of ordinary shareholders.

[37] *See* Ian Gault et al., *Gault on Commercial Law*, (Thomson Reuters, 2010) at paragraph CA36.01.

C. Closer Economic Relations

The development of competition law and policy in New Zealand has proceeded with a conscious regard for the approach in Australia and, perhaps to a slightly lesser extent, the reverse is also true. While policy convergence is common in many areas due to the countries' shared colonial heritage and close trade, economic, and cultural ties, it has been particularly pronounced in the field of competition law due to the Australia New Zealand Closer Economic Relations Trade Agreement (ANZCERTA), signed in 1983. While ANZCERTA is primarily a bilateral free trade agreement, its recitals and objectives include a mandate to strengthen economic ties more generally, and to "develop trade between New Zealand and Australia under conditions of fair competition."[38] Integration is pursued through annual joint-Ministerial reviews which assess the operation of the Agreement and propose further integrative measures.[39] Article 22 of the Agreement specifically directed the Ministers to conduct a review in 1988 and to consider at that time "the need for changes in Government economic policies and practices, in such fields as . . . company law."

The result of these regular reviews has been a succession of memoranda of understanding on business law harmonization. The first, in 1988, recorded the intention of both governments to "examine the scope for harmonisation of business laws and regulatory practices" in, amongst other areas, "competition law, including in particular reliance on competition law to redress predatory trade between both countries."[40] The most immediate product of this engagement was the elimination of anti-dumping rules as between New Zealand and Australia in 1990, and their replacement with a trans-Tasman abuse of dominance offence.[41]

Successive memoranda have followed in 2000, 2006, and 2010. While the language of these later iterations has shifted to the "coordination" of business law rather than "harmonisation,"[42] the impetus for economic integration has remained. So, for instance, in 2001 the Commerce Act 1986 was amended to reflect more closely the language used in the Trade Practices Act 1974 in a conscious attempt to import the approach outlined in Australian case law into the New Zealand environment.[43]

In 2009, Closer Economic Relations received an additional boost when the two governments announced the "Single Economic Market" initiative.[44] SEM recasts

[38] Australia New Zealand Closer Economic Relations Trade Agreement, Recitals, Article 1.

[39] Australia New Zealand Closer Economic Relations Trade Agreement, Article 22.

[40] Memorandum of Understanding Between the Government of Australia and the Government of New Zealand on Harmonisation of Business Law, 1 July 1988.

[41] Commerce Act 1986 (NZ), section 36A; Competition and Consumer Act 2010 (Cth Aus), section 46A.

[42] Which is reflected in an acknowledgement in the operative provisions of the memoranda that there may be good reasons for differences between the Australian and New Zealand legal frameworks.

[43] Gault et al., *supra* note 37, at paragraphs CA36.04.

[44] Joint Statement of Prime Ministers Rudd and Key, 20 August 2009, <http://www.beehive.govt.nz/release/joint-statement-prime-ministers-rudd-and-key>.

business law coordination in terms of seven outcomes-based principles, including the following: (i) that persons in New Zealand and Australia should not have to engage in the same regulatory process twice, (ii) that regulation should deliver the same outcomes in both countries, (iii) that regulatory design should attempt to achieve economies of scale and scope as between the two countries, and (iv) that outcomes should seek to optimize net trans-Tasman benefit.[45] The ultimate ambition of SEM, where possible, is to develop trans-Tasman regulatory agencies with equivalent jurisdiction in both countries. Some such agencies already exist—for example, Food Standards Australia New Zealand—and some are in development, such as the Australia New Zealand Joint Therapeutic Products Authority. While no proposal has yet been made to combine the New Zealand Commerce Commission and the Australian Competition and Consumer Commission, SEM provides a framework to accomplish this should the two governments so desire.

II. Structure

A. Institutional arrangements

The frontline regulatory agencies in New Zealand and Australia are the Commerce Commission ("NZCC") and the Australian Competition and Consumer Commission ("ACCC") respectively. Both agencies serve dual roles of (i) enforcing competition and consumer protection rules through litigation in the general courts, and (ii) making first instance adjudicative determinations in the fields of merger control, authorization of restrictive trade practices, and various economic regulatory matters.

However, New Zealand's and Australia's institutional frameworks diverge once matters progress beyond the agencies. In New Zealand, appeals or reviews of NZCC determinations are decided by the general courts. In Australia, the Australian Competition Tribunal ("ACT") reviews adjudicative determinations made by the ACCC. Furthermore, the National Competition Council ("NCC") works in parallel to the ACCC, investigating and making recommendations to Ministers about the desirability of designating services under the Competition and Consumer Act's Part IIIA access regime. Finally, the Australian Energy Regulator ("AER"), a constituent part of the ACCC, has jurisdiction over certain regulatory matters pertaining to the electricity and gas sectors. So, whereas the New Zealand framework is a bifurcated judicial model, with jurisdiction allocated between an administrative agency and the courts of general jurisdiction, Australia's framework is a hybrid, with a bifurcated agency model (the ACCC and ACT) at its center, and a periphery of additional agencies with particular regulatory responsibilities.

[45] Memorandum of Understanding Between the Government of New Zealand and the Government of Australia on the Coordination of Business Law, 23 June 2010, para 8.

Figure 2.1 Structure of competition institutions in New Zealand and Australia

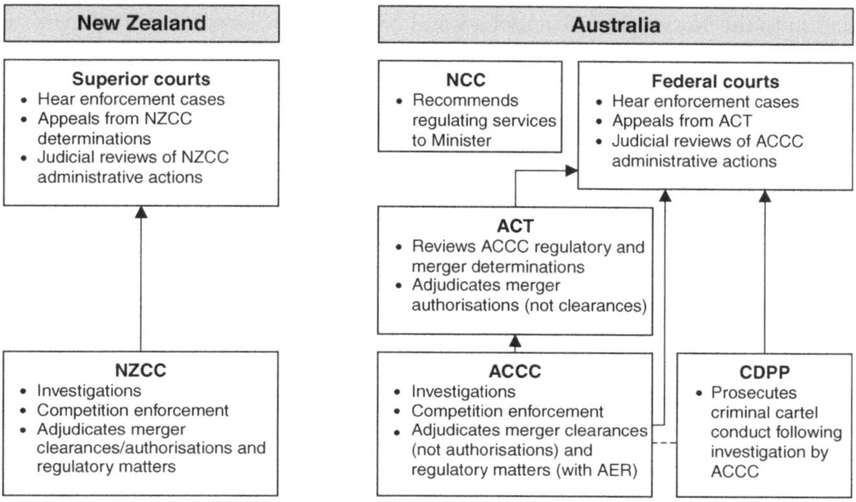

1. The NZCC and the ACCC

a) Constitution

The NZCC is a Crown Entity—an independent state agency constituted under the Crown Entities Act 2004 and the Commerce Act 1986.[46] The NZCC comprises a chairperson and four to six fellow commissioners, three to five of whom must be appointed by the Governor-General on the recommendation of the Minister of Commerce.[47] One of the members is separately appointed as the Telecommunications Commissioner with special responsibilities in relation to that sector.[48] The commissioners are appointed on the basis of their experience in industry, commerce, economics, law, accountancy, public administration, or consumer affairs.[49] They may only be removed before the expiry of their tenure for cause.[50]

The ACCC is similarly structured to the NZCC, and tasked with essentially the same role. The ACCC is established as a body corporate under Part II of the Competition and Consumer Act 2010,[51] is headed by a chairperson and includes as many fellow commissioners as the Attorney-General or responsible Minister sees fit to appoint.[52] Currently, the ACCC consists of the chairperson and deputy chair-

[46] Commerce Act 1986 (NZ), sections 8, 8A.
[47] Commerce Act 1986 (NZ), sections 9(1) and (2).
[48] Commerce Act 1986 (NZ), section 9(3); Telecommunications Act 2001 (NZ), section 9.
[49] Commerce Act 1986 (NZ), section 9(4).
[50] Commerce Act 1986 (NZ), section 13; Crown Entities Act 2004 (NZ), sections 39, 40.
[51] Competition and Consumer Act 2010 (Cth. Aus.), section 6A.
[52] Competition and Consumer Act 2010 (Cth. Aus.), section 7.

person, with four other members, and three associate members. The Australian Energy Regulator is a constituent part of the ACCC, with specific responsibilities in relation to the National Electricity Law and National Gas Law. Commissioners can be removed before their tenure expires only for cause.[53]

Both regulators are independent statutory authorities, although their level of independence from government influence differs slightly (in theory, if not significantly in practice). The NZCC's independence from external influence (including government) is confirmed by section 8 of the Commerce Act 1986. However, the NZCC is required to "have regard to the economic policies of the Government," which are communicated to the NZCC in writing from time to time and published in the *Gazette*.[54] Decisions of the NZCC and the High Court have held that "have regard to" means no more than that the NZCC must give such policy statements genuine attention and thought, and such weight as the NZCC considers appropriate.[55] Importantly, the NZCC considers that such policy statements are not able to influence or determine the decisions which the NZCC must make in specific cases.[56] The ACCC is also an independent entity, but section 29 of the Competition and Consumer Act allows the Minister to give the ACCC directions "connected with the performance of its functions or the exercise of its powers" under the Act. The Minister is prohibited from giving directions in relation to the access regime under Part IIIA, the restrictive trade practice provisions under Part IV, authorization and notifications, price surveillance, and the telecommunications competition and access regimes. However, that notwithstanding, the Minister's power of direction is stronger than the equivalent power in New Zealand. For example, in 1998 the Minister for Customs and Consumer Affairs directed the ACCC to initiate proceedings under section 51AC (unconscionable conduct) in order to establish legal precedent relevant to small business.[57]

Both agencies are also accountable to their responsible government ministries—the Ministry of Economic Development in the case of the NZCC and the Treasury in the case of the ACCC.

The powers of the NZCC and ACCC are exercised by the commissioners at periodic meetings for which the quorum is three members.[58] In addition, the agencies may sit in divisions, and in practice this is how most matters are dealt with.[59] For example, the ACCC is presently organized into five divisions—enforcement, mergers, communications, regulated industries, and adjudication—which then report to the full Commission.[60] The commissioners are supported by a

[53] Competition and Consumer Act 2010 (Cth. Aus.), section 14.

[54] Commerce Act 1986 (NZ), section 26.

[55] *NZ Co-op Dairy Co Ltd v Commerce Commission* [1992] 1 NZLR 601 at 612–13.

[56] *Re NZ Kiwifruit Exporters Association (Inc)/NZ Kiwifruit Coolstores Association (Inc)* (1989) 2 NZBLC (Com) 104,485 at 104,494. *See* also Gault et al., *supra* note 37, at paras CA26 and following.

[57] Russell V. Miller, *Miller's Annotated Trade Practices* (Lawbook Co, 2010), para 1.29.5.

[58] Commerce Act 1986 (NZ), section 15; Competition and Consumer Act 2010 (Cth. Aus.), section 18.

[59] Commerce Act 1986 (NZ), section 16.

[60] Miller, *supra* note 57, at para 1.19.10.

professional staff of public servants, including lawyers and economists, headed by a Chief Executive. Albeit the Commission staff undertake most of the day-to-day investigative and enforcement functions, all significant decisions in relation to any matter are made by the commissioners.

Australia is a federation of states, and hence the ACCC's empowering legislation also addresses the allocation of responsibility between state and federal authorities. The ACCC has a Commonwealth-wide jurisdiction, although the various States and Territories also have local authorities with competition law and regulatory responsibilities. Due to Constitutional limitations, the Competition and Consumer Act only applies to corporations. However, as part of the comprehensive reforms in 1995, the Commonwealth, State, and Territory governments agreed that the various States and Territories would extend the application of the competition provisions in Part IV of the Act to all "persons" within their jurisdiction.[61] The Competition Policy Reform Act 1995 thus established a new Part XIA of the Competition and Consumer Act—known as the Competition Code—which replicates Part IV and its ancillary operative provisions. Parallel legislation at the State and Territory level incorporates the Code into local law, and confers jurisdiction on the ACCC and other federal authorities to enforce the Code.[62]

b) Enforcement role

One of the agencies' central roles is enforcement of the competition provisions of their respective statutes. In both cases, enforcement takes place by way of litigation in generalist courts (the High Court in New Zealand, and the Federal District Court in Australia). Both agencies are entitled to proceed on their own initiative or on receipt of a complaint.

The competition provisions of the Commerce Act are in the main civil[63] and hence the NZCC takes proceedings relying on its own in-house counsel or on externally briefed barristers. Where the NZCC decides to proceed criminally[64] it involves the Crown solicitors—a network of law firms holding prosecution warrants issued by the Government. In Australia, hard-core cartel conduct has recently been criminalized and so in relation to cartels, the ACCC shares its enforcement role with the Commonwealth Director of Public Prosecutions ("CDPP"). The ACCC investigates cartels (with a view to establishing either civil or criminal liability, or both), collates the evidence, and then confers with the CDPP about the appropriateness of referring the matter to the CDPP for criminal prosecution.[65] The ACCC states that it will refer matters for criminal prosecution wherever the evidence indicates it is appropriate to do so. Accordingly, the ACCC refuses to

[61] Corones, *supra* note 1, at 246.

[62] *See*, for example, Competition Policy Reform (New South Wales) Act 1995, section 19.

[63] With the exception of criminal offences relating to obstructions of the NZCC's investigations and information disclosure regulations: Commerce Act 1986 (NZ), sections 86B, 103.

[64] Which it may do under the consumer protection provisions of the Fair Trading Act 1986 and the Credit Contracts and Consumer Finance Act 2003.

[65] ACCC, ACCC approach to cartel investigations, July 2009, <http://www.accc.gov.au/content/index.phtml/itemId/891982>.

negotiate for enhanced civil liability in exchange for refraining from referring a matter to the CDPP.[66]

The ACCC has entered into a memorandum of understanding with the CDPP that defines their respective roles.[67] The ACCC's civil enforcement jurisdiction is not extinguished when a criminal referral is made, and hence an investigation may result in both civil proceedings taken by the ACCC and criminal proceedings taken by the CDPP, often in reliance on the same evidence. The agencies recognize the potential for conflict. Accordingly, all investigations are treated as presumptively criminal until the agencies have determined that a criminal charge is not appropriate; and where both criminal and civil proceedings are intended, the agencies coordinate their respective proceedings in order to minimize the risk that one set of proceedings will prejudice the other.[68]

c) Adjudicative role

The agencies are empowered to make first-instance adjudicative decisions in relation to a variety of competition and regulatory matters. Their most visible adjudicative role is in the field of merger control. Notification of mergers and acquisitions in New Zealand and Australia is voluntary, but obtaining approval from the agency confers on the parties to the transaction immunity against future proceedings relating to the competition effects of the transaction.[69] Approval can be obtained in two ways:

1. *Clearance* is available if the agency finds that the transaction is not likely to substantially lessen competition.[70]
2. However, even if the transaction is likely to substantially lessen competition, the parties can apply for *authorization*[71] of the transaction if they can demonstrate that the transaction will result in such a benefit to the public that it should be permitted notwithstanding the effect on competition.[72]

In New Zealand, the NZCC is responsible for making first-instance decisions in relation to both clearances and authorizations. In Australia, the ACCC renders clearance decisions, but authorizations are the responsibility of the Australian Competition Tribunal.

[66] Ibid. at paras 38–39. And *see* Corones, *supra* note 1, at 867.

[67] Memorandum of Understanding between the Commonwealth Director of Public Prosecutions and the Australian Competition and Consumer Commission regarding Serious Cartel Conduct, 14 July 2009, <http://www.accc.gov.au/content/index.phtml/itemId/891982>.

[68] Ibid. at paragraph 6.2.

[69] Commerce Act 1986 (NZ), section 69; Competition and Consumer Act 2010 (Cth. Aus.), section 95AC.

[70] Commerce Act 1986 (NZ), section 66; Competition and Consumer Act 2010 (Cth. Aus.), section 95AC.

[71] As with clearance, authorization confers immunity on the transaction. The difference is the legal test that is applied.

[72] Commerce Act 1986 (NZ), section 67; Competition and Consumer Act 2010 (Cth. Aus.), section 95AT.

The New Zealand and Australian regimes also differ in the manner in which clearances are obtained in practice. In New Zealand, the formal clearance mechanism is frequently utilized. By contrast, Australia only introduced a formal clearance mechanism in 2006.[73] Prior to that, the only clearance option available was to seek a "no-action" letter from the ACCC on an informal basis (which technically does not confer immunity, but rather indicates the ACCC's inclination to take enforcement proceedings). What is more interesting is that the informal process continues to operate alongside the formal clearance process, and to date there have been no applications under the formal process—parties to mergers apparently prefer the informal process.[74] Part of the reason for this may be the degree of certainty that the informal process offers, notwithstanding the absence of statutory immunity—the ACCC has only departed from its no-action letters where the parties have provided misleading information.[75] The chairperson of the ACCC—Graeme Samuel—also suggested when interviewed that the greater scope for maintaining confidentiality in the informal process was an advantage to merger parties.

The NZCC is also open to approaches on an informal basis, and parties to mergers that are unlikely to raise substantive competition issues may approach the NZCC to explain the transaction and seek an indication from the NZCC that it is unlikely to initiate an investigation. However, this informal approach is generally limited to transactions that do not raise competition issues; where substantive issues do arise, the NZCC's strong preference is for the parties to proceed formally.

The NZCC and ACCC may also grant authorizations for some restrictive trade practices, including cartel conduct, but excluding monopolization.[76] Authorization is available only where the agency is satisfied that conduct is likely to result in a public benefit outweighing the harm to competition. Examples of authorization decisions include the player-contracting arrangements of the New Zealand Rugby Union,[77] the trading rulebook governing the wholesale electricity market,[78] and the joint marketing and sale of gas from the Pohokura gas field.[79]

Finally, the agencies are also responsible for making various *ex ante* economic regulatory determinations.[80]

d) Guidelines, policy, and advocacy

As a corollary of their enforcement and adjudicative roles, the agencies issue a number of guidelines and rulings. Guidelines may be non-legally binding indications of the agencies' analytical approach to an inquiry, or statutorily-mandated rulings. Examples of the former are the agencies' mergers and acquisitions guide-

[73] Trade Practices Act Amendment Act (No 1) 2006 (Cth. Aus.).

[74] Corones, *supra* note 1, at 407.

[75] Corones, *supra* note 1, at 413.

[76] Commerce Act 1986 (NZ), section 58; Competition and Consumer Act 2010 (Cth. Aus.), section 88; *NT Power Generation Pty Ltd v Power and Water Authority* (2004) 219 CLR 90 at 140.

[77] Commerce Commission, *Decision No. 580*, 2 June 2006.

[78] Commerce Commission, *Decision No. 473*, 30 September 2002.

[79] Commerce Commission, *Decision No. 505*, 1 September 2003. Later revoked in *Decision No. 581*, 2 June 2006.

[80] Discussed further *infra* at pages 70 to 74.

lines. An example of the latter is the NZCC's input methodologies, which set out the approach to calculating regulatory inputs such as cost of capital, asset valuation, tax treatment, and pricing methodologies.[81]

The agencies are also charged under their respective statutes with making available information with respect to their functions and competition policy generally.[82] Accordingly, the agencies publish a broad range of pamphlets, papers, and speeches aimed at educating the public and business community and promoting discussion of competition policy issues. All this material is available through their websites.

e) Investigative powers

The agencies are furnished with broad-ranging investigative powers to facilitate the discharge of their functions. Section 98 of the Commerce Act and section 155 of the Competition and Consumer Act allow the agencies to require any person to turn over documents, provide information (for example, in the form of responses to interrogatories), or appear before the agency to give evidence. The agencies' investigative powers are limited to information or documents relevant to their investigations. But the agencies have a broad discretion to determine what is relevant to the scope of their inquiry, subject to a limited power of review by the courts, and hence it is difficult for persons being investigated to withhold information on grounds of irrelevance.[83]

In addition to their powers to require production of documents and information, the agencies may obtain warrants to search premises.[84] Duly authorized officers of the agencies may use reasonable force in executing searches, and the ACCC may call on the assistance of the federal police if necessary.[85]

Persons subject to the agencies' investigative powers may not rely on the privilege against self-incrimination to avoid producing documents or giving evidence or information.[86] However, testimony obtained under compulsion cannot be admitted in subsequent criminal proceedings, with the exception of a criminal proceeding for refusing or failing to comply with the agencies' investigative powers.[87] Hence, the agencies could adduce evidence of a defendant's

[81] Commerce Act 1986 (NZ), section 52T; and *see* the Commission's website at: <http://www.comcom.govt.nz/input-methodologies/>.

[82] Commerce Act 1986 (NZ), section 25; Competition and Consumer Act 2010 (Cth. Aus.), section 28.

[83] *AstraZeneca Ltd v Commerce Commission* (2008) 12 TCLR 116; *Telecom Corporation of New Zealand Ltd v Commerce Commission* [1991] NZAR 155; *SA Brewing Holdings v Baxt* (1989) 23 FCR 357; *Kotan Holdings Pty Ltd v Trade Practices Commission* (1991) 30 FCR 511.

[84] Commerce Act 1986 (NZ), section 98A; Competition and Consumer Act 2010 (Cth. Aus.), section 154D and Division 4, Part XID.

[85] Commerce Act 1986 (NZ), section 98B; Competition and Consumer Act 2010 (Cth. Aus.), sections 154K, 154L.

[86] Commerce Act 1986 (NZ), section 106(4); Competition and Consumer Act 2010 (Cth. Aus.), sections 154R, 155, 159.

[87] Commerce Act 1986 (NZ), section 106(5), 106(6); Competition and Consumer Act 2010 (Cth. Aus.), sections 154R, 155, 159.

testimony obtained under compulsion in a subsequent prosecution for making a misleading statement.

In Australia, a tension is created by the new criminal cartel provisions as there is now the possibility that evidence of cartel activity obtained by the ACCC may be provided to the CDPP for the purposes of a criminal prosecution. As a result, testimony obtained under compulsion is quarantined from testimony obtained voluntarily and the former excluded from the criminal proceedings. In practice this has not proved a significant restraint on the effectiveness of the criminal regime as testimony is often obtained voluntarily through leniency applications. Moreover, documentary evidence obtained through dawn raids remains admissible in criminal prosecutions.

A further implication of the criminalization of the cartel process is that ACCC staff have had to train in criminal investigative procedures, including when and how to caution potential witnesses in order to preserve the admissibility of their voluntary testimony. In order to ensure that the ACCC's civil enforcement role and the CDPP's criminal enforcement role do not conflict, every cartel investigation is presumptively criminal in nature until the authorities determine that a criminal charge is not appropriate.

Persons subject to the agencies' investigative powers can rely on the privilege for legal advice, although the agencies may require the allegedly privileged documents to be placed before a judge so that the privilege claim can be assessed.[88]

Finally, both agencies can impose orders preventing any person from *disclosing* any documents or information.[89] The NZCC has used this power to prevent the disclosure of commercially sensitive information provided to counsel or commercial parties in the course of merger control or authorization inquiries. More recently, the NZCC has used such orders to prevent employees from disclosing to their employers the questions the NZCC has asked in interviews conducted as part of a cartel investigation.[90]

2. *Role of the courts and the Australian Competition Tribunal*

In New Zealand, enforcement proceedings taken by the NZCC are heard by the High Court. There is no specialist competition tribunal, nor is there a division of the High Court with particular responsibility for competition matters. However, there is provision for High Court judges to sit with a lay member—usually an economist—on competition law matters, and this provision is often utilized.[91] Lay members lend their expertise to the Court's consideration of the economic issues raised by the NZCC's determination. Usually the judge and lay member will issue a joint decision; however there have been occasions where the lay member has issued

[88] *Telecom Corporation of New Zealand Ltd v Commerce Commission* [1991] NZAR 155.

[89] Commerce Act 1986 (NZ), section 100; *Constantine v Trade Practices Commission* (1994) 48 FCR 141.

[90] *Air New Zealand v Commerce Commission* HC AK CIV 2008-404-008352 21 October 2009.

[91] Commerce Act 1986 (NZ), section 78.

a separate opinion.[92] Where the lay member and the judge disagree, the decision of the judge takes precedence.[93] In enforcement proceedings, the Court is empowered with a range of remedies, including injunctions, pecuniary penalties (which are quasi-criminal in nature), and compensatory damages.[94]

Appeals from NZCC first-instance determinations are also heard by the High Court (and then successively by the Court of Appeal and Supreme Court). The High Court may also be assisted by lay members when hearing appeals from NZCC determinations.[95]

In Australia, the judicial role in competition law matters is divided between the federal courts and the Australian Competition Tribunal ("ACT"). Enforcement proceedings taken by the ACCC are heard by the federal court, while appeals from first instance determinations of the ACCC are heard by the ACT (and then in turn by the federal court).

The ACT is made up of presidential members—who must be federal court judges—and non-presidential members who are appointed by the Governor-General by virtue of their expertise in industry, commerce, economics, law, or public administration.[96] Members of the ACT are appointed for fixed terms up to seven years, and may be removed on grounds of misbehavior, physical or mental incapacity, or bankruptcy.[97]

The ACT sits in divisions of three members, comprising one presidential member and two non-presidential members. Questions of law are determined by the presidential member alone, whereas all other questions are determined by a majority of the panel members.[98]

The ACT hears appeals from ACCC first-instance determinations in relation to authorizations of restrictive trade practices (whether granting, refusing, or modifying said authorizations), and appeals from determinations clearing (or declining to clear) merger clearances.[99] The ACT also hears originating applications for authorizations of mergers that would otherwise fail the competition test, but which the parties argue would result in public benefits justifying their authorization.[100] Finally, the ACT is responsible for reviewing certain decisions of the ACCC in relation to regulatory access determinations.

The ACT proceeds by way of rehearing and therefore has an unrestricted power to inquire into the merits of the ACCC's determination. For appeals from authorizations of restrictive trade practices, it hears the evidence afresh and is not required to proceed on the basis of the evidential record developed before the ACCC.[101] It is also entitled to exercise all the powers of the Commission, and may affirm, set aside,

[92] *See*, for example, *Commerce Commission v Port Nelson Ltd* (1995) 6 TCLR 406.
[93] Commerce Act 1986 (NZ), section 77(11).
[94] Commerce Act 1986 (NZ), sections 74AA, 80–84A, 86, 87, 87C.
[95] Commerce Act 1986 (NZ), section 77.
[96] Competition and Consumer Act 2010 (Cth. Aus.), section 31.
[97] Competition and Consumer Act 2010 (Cth. Aus.), section 35.
[98] Competition and Consumer Act 2010 (Cth. Aus.), section 37.
[99] Competition and Consumer Act 2010 (Cth. Aus.), Part IX.
[100] Competition and Consumer Act 2010 (Cth. Aus.), sections 95AT–95AZM.
[101] Competition and Consumer Act 2010 (Cth. Aus.), section 101(2).

or vary the ACCC's determination as it sees fit.[102] On reviews of merger clearances, the ACT may also inquire into the merits of the decision, but is required to proceed on the basis of the evidential record developed before the ACCC.[103]

Enforcement proceedings instituted by the ACCC for breach of the competition provisions of the Competition and Consumer Act are heard by the federal court—at first instance by a single federal court judge sitting alone, and then on appeal to the full federal court, comprising three judges. Unlike the High Court of New Zealand (and unlike the Australian Competition Tribunal), the federal court cannot sit with lay members. Hence a disadvantage of enforcement proceedings before the federal court is the lack of specialist competition economics expertise on the bench.

3. Private actions

Private actions are permitted under both the New Zealand and Australian regimes. In neither jurisdiction is there a requirement of standing to enforce the provisions of the Act through injunctions.[104] However, in order to recover damages, the complainant must establish that it has suffered loss.[105] Furthermore, only the agencies are entitled to apply for pecuniary penalties.[106]

The Competition and Consumer Act includes two additional provisions—absent from the Commerce Act—to facilitate the recovery of private damages. Under section 87(1B) the ACCC is entitled to bring a representative action on behalf of persons who have suffered damage. In addition, to assist private litigants, section 83 provides that a finding in proceedings brought by the ACCC serves as prima facie evidence of infringement for any follow-on damages action. However, unlike the damages regime in the United States, there is no entitlement to treble damages in either New Zealand or Australia.

The competition regimes in New Zealand and Australia are strongly regulator-led, and thus the practicing community works predominantly on the defense side. Private parties do bring competition litigation on their own account—for example, competitors of dominant industries occasionally bring actions attacking allegedly anticompetitive trade practices. But referring a complaint to the NZCC or ACCC is both straightforward and involves minimal cost, and given that the agencies are viewed as being vigorous proponents of their respective competition regimes, there is less of a need for private parties to resort to litigation themselves.

There is also a conspicuous absence, relative to the United States and Europe, of follow-on damages claims for cartel conduct, although (in Australia at least) this

[102] Competition and Consumer Act 2010 (Cth. Aus.), section 102(1).

[103] Competition and Consumer Act 2010 (Cth. Aus.), section 116.

[104] Gault, *supra* note 37, at para 75.03, *World Series Cricket Pty Ltd v Parish* (1977) 16 ALR 181.

[105] Gault, *supra* note 37, at para 75.03; Competition and Consumer Act 2010 (Cth. Aus.), sections 82, 87.

[106] Commerce Act 1986 (NZ), sections 80, 83, Competition and Consumer Act 2010 (Cth. Aus.), section 77.

form of private enforcement is slowly gathering steam.[107] For example, private actions have been instituted in relation to the Visy/Amcor packaging cartel, and the air cargo cartel. The follow-on provision in the Competition and Consumer Act is likely to be part of the reason, as are recent reforms in class-action procedures. Certainly, there is no equivalent follow-on provision in the Commerce Act in New Zealand, and no formal class-action procedure, and private cartel damages suits are essentially non-existent.

III. Mandate and central substantive provisions

A. Objects of the Acts

The stated purpose of the Commerce Act is to "promote competition in markets for the long-term benefit of consumers within New Zealand."[108] The object of the Competition and Consumer Act is to "enhance the welfare of Australians through the promotion of competition and fair trading and provision of consumer protection."[109]

B. *Ex post* competition prohibitions

Due to harmonization initiatives under CER, as well as a tradition of closely examining each other's legislation in law reform inquiries, the competition provisions of the Competition and Consumer Act and the Commerce Act are remarkably similar.

1. *Monopolization*

Section 36 of the Commerce Act and section 46 of the Competition and Consumer Act prohibit a firm with a substantial degree of market power from taking advantage of that market power for the purpose of eliminating a competitor, preventing entry, or deterring competitive conduct. A substantial degree of market power is evidenced by the ability of the firm in question to conduct itself largely free of competitive constraint.[110] Whether or not a firm has "taken advantage" of its market power is assessed under the "counterfactual test," which asks whether the firm in question would have conducted itself in a similar manner in the absence of its market power.[111] In recent years, Australia and New Zealand have diverged somewhat, with Australia applying a broader version of the counterfactual test

[107] S. Stuart Clark and C. Harris, "Class Actions in Australia: (Still) A Work in Progress," (2008) 31 Australian Bar Review 63.

[108] Commerce Act 1986 (NZ), section 1A.

[109] Competition and Consumer Act 2010 (Cth. Aus.), section 2.

[110] Competition and Consumer Act 2010 (Cth. Aus.), section 46(3).

[111] *Commerce Commission v Telecom Corporation of New Zealand Ltd* [2010] NZSC 111; *Queensland Wire Industries v BHP* (1989) 167 CLR 177.

which asks additionally whether the conduct was materially facilitated by, or occurred in reliance on, the firm's market power, or whether the conduct was otherwise related to the firm's market power.[112]

The monopolization offence covers conduct such as predatory pricing,[113] refusal to deal,[114] tying and bundling, leveraging, and price discrimination, and squeezes, although the boundaries of legitimate conduct in each case remain vague.[115]

2. *Contracts, arrangements, or understandings that affect competition*

Section 27 of the Commerce Act and section 45 of the Competition and Consumer Act contain generic provisions prohibiting contracts, arrangements, understandings, or covenants that substantially lessen competition, whatever the structure of the arrangement, and whatever the theory of competitive harm.[116] Both Acts also include sections prohibiting exclusionary provisions—defined as agreements that aim to limit the supply to, or acquisition from, third parties of goods or services, whether generally or subject to conditions.[117]

Whereas the Commerce Act relies chiefly on the broad prohibition in section 27 to prohibit multilateral or collusive conduct, the Competition and Consumer Act also prohibits separately a range of specific anticompetitive agreements: secondary boycotts (colluding with another for the purpose of preventing a third person from supplying to, or acquiring from, a fourth);[118] agreements with employees' organizations that exclude a customary supplier or customer of the firm;[119] and exclusive dealing arrangements that substantially lessen competition.[120]

Finally, both Acts separately prohibit resale price maintenance on a per se basis.[121]

3. *Cartels*

The Commerce Act prohibits cartel conduct under a combination of section 27 and section 30, which deems as likely to substantially lessen competition any

112 *Melway Publishing Pty Ltd v Robert Hicks Pty Ltd* (2001) 205 CLR 1; Competition and Consumer Act 2010 (Cth. Aus.), section 46(6A).

113 Recoupment is an element of the predatory pricing offence in New Zealand: *see* Carter Holt; but not in Australia: *see* Competition and Consumer Act 2010 (Cth. Aus.), sections 46(1AA) and 46 (1AAA).

114 *Queensland Wire Industries v BHP* (1989) 167 CLR 177; *Commerce Commission v Bay of Plenty Electricity Ltd* HC WN CIV 2001-485-917 13 December 2007.

115 *See* Gault, *supra* note 37, at paragraphs CA36 and following; and Corones, *supra* note 1, at chapter 8.

116 Commerce Act 1986 (NZ), sections 27, 28; Competition and Consumer Act 2010 (Cth. Aus.), sections 45, 45B.

117 Commerce Act 1986 (NZ), sections 29; Competition and Consumer Act 2010 (Cth. Aus.), sections 45, 4D.

118 Competition and Consumer Act 2010 (Cth. Aus.), section 45D.

119 Competition and Consumer Act 2010 (Cth. Aus.), section 45E.

120 Competition and Consumer Act 2010 (Cth. Aus.), section 47.

121 Commerce Act 1986 (NZ), section 37; Competition and Consumer Act 2010 (Cth. Aus.), section 48.

contract, arrangement, or understanding between competitors that fixes, controls, or maintains prices, or a component of prices. Hence, price fixing itself is per se illegal, but other aspects of cartel activity—market sharing, bid rigging, etc.—are subject to a competition test. In addition, cartel conduct in New Zealand results only in civil liability and pecuniary penalties, not criminal liability.

By contrast, the Competition and Consumer Act criminalizes entering into, or giving effect to, a cartel provision. A cartel provision is defined as a provision with the purpose or effect of fixing, controlling, or maintaining prices, or a component of prices, or the purpose of collusively limiting production, capacity, or supply, allocating customers, suppliers, or geographical markets, or bid rigging.[122] Furthermore, intentionally or knowingly entering into a cartel arrangement results in criminal liability.[123]

4. Mergers and acquisitions

As discussed earlier, the Competition and Consumer Act and Commerce Act prohibit anticompetitive mergers and acquisitions on almost an identical basis: any acquisition of assets or shares that would be likely to substantially lessen competition is prohibited.[124] Neither statute has an equivalent to the concepts of control or concentration in European merger control, and hence a narrower range of transactions is captured by merger control processes than is the case in the European Union and most EU member states. Apart from acquisitions of shares or assets, all other transactions that affect competition fall for consideration under the provisions that prohibit anticompetitive contracts, arrangements, or understandings.

Also, unlike the European Union, the United States, or Canada, there is no obligation to notify transactions to the NZCC or ACCC, irrespective of the likely competitive effects of those transactions. In order to enforce the prohibition against anticompetitive mergers, the authorities are obliged to initiate court proceedings. However, merger parties may voluntarily notify mergers to the NZCC, ACCC, or ACT in order to obtain clearance if the transaction is not likely to lessen competition, or authorization if the transaction is likely to lessen competition but will also result in such a benefit to the public that it should be permitted notwithstanding the effect on competition. Public benefit in this context refers to efficiencies, and hence the authorization inquiry requires a balancing of the competitive harm against the quantified and merger-specific efficiencies resulting from the transaction.[125] Merger clearances are routinely given, but authorizations are rarely applied for and generally much harder to obtain. For example, out of twenty-one applications in 2007 alone the NZCC granted seventeen clearances, with three applica-

[122] Competition and Consumer Act 2010 (Cth. Aus.), section 44ZZRD.

[123] Competition and Consumer Act 2010 (Cth. Aus.), section 44ZZRF, 44ZZRG.

[124] Commerce Act 1986 (NZ), section 47; Competition and Consumer Act 2010 (Cth. Aus.), section 50.

[125] Commerce Act 1986 (NZ), section 3A.

tions declined and one withdrawn.[126] By contrast, between 1992 and 2010 there were only fifteen applications for authorization, of which only a small number were authorized.[127]

Under both the New Zealand and Australian regimes, the parties can offer undertakings to remedy perceived competition issues.[128] Undertakings are most often structural, requiring divestments of assets, but on occasion the authorities have required behavioral undertakings as well.[129]

Lastly, both the NZCC and ACCC have published guidelines outlining the analytical approach they employ in their assessment of mergers. The guidelines reflect similar economic tools and theories of harm to those used by competition authorities in Europe and the United States.

5. Penalties

Since the Commerce Amendment Act 2001 in New Zealand, the penalty provisions of the Commerce Act and the Competition and Consumer Act have been aligned for most infringements. Corporate infringers of the restrictive trade practices provisions (under Part IV, Division 2 of the Competition and Consumer Act, and Part 2 of the Commerce Act) are subject to pecuniary penalties with a maximum of:

a) NZ$10 million; or
b) three times the commercial gain resulting from the infringement; or
c) if the commercial gain cannot be quantified, 10 percent of the turnover of the offender's corporate group in the preceding twelve months.[130]

Individuals are subject to a maximum pecuniary penalty of NZ$500,000,[131] and companies are prohibited from indemnifying their officers for their personal liability for infringements.[132]

In New Zealand, those maximum penalties apply to all restrictive trade practices infringements. There are separate maximum penalties for unlawful mergers (NZ$5 million for a corporate offender and NZ$500,000 for an individual).[133] In Australia, those maximum penalties apply to restrictive trade practices infringements

[126] The Commerce Commission's clearances register is available at: <http://www.comcom.govt.nz/clearances-register/>.

[127] The Commerce Commission's authorizations register is available at: <http://www.comcom.govt.nz/authorisations-register/>.

[128] Commerce Act 1986 (NZ), section 69A; Competition and Consumer Act 2010 (Cth. Aus.), section 87B.

[129] *See*, for example, the ACCC's decision in *Coca-Cola/Berri, Public Competition Assessment* (8 October 2003), in which the acquirer gave an undertaking not to tie or bundle certain products post-merger.

[130] Commerce Act 1986 (NZ), section 80; Competition and Consumer Act 2010 (Cth. Aus.), section 76.

[131] Ibid.

[132] Commerce Act 1986 (NZ), section 80A; Competition and Consumer Act 2010 (Cth. Aus.), section 77A.

[133] Commerce Act 1986 (NZ), section 83.

including mergers, except for certain forms of boycotts and exclusionary provisions, for which a maximum of AUS$750,000 applies.[134] However, in Australia individuals convicted of criminal cartel offences may additionally face terms of imprisonment of up to ten years. New Zealand does not presently criminalize cartel activity, although legislation will be introduced this year that, if passed, would result in criminal penalties for certain forms of cartel conduct.

New Zealand and Australian case law identifies deterrence as one of the primary objectives of pecuniary penalties. Hence, the penalty imposed should be sufficient to render the infringing conduct uneconomic.[135] Factors that are relevant to assessing the appropriate penalty include the nature and extent of the conduct, the damage caused, the size of the company, the level of management at which the conduct originated, and whether the company has a culture of compliance in general.[136]

As well as imposing pecuniary penalties, courts in New Zealand and Australia can impose compensatory damages, and disqualify individuals from serving as managers or directors of companies for a period of time.[137] Finally, there are a range of injunctions and mandatory orders that courts can impose to bring a halt to infringing conduct, and unwind anticompetitive arrangements, transactions, or mergers.

C. The role of regulation in competition policy

As the earlier discussion of the history of New Zealand competition law has shown, competition policy and economic regulation have always been closely intertwined in that country. The balance of policy has shifted regularly between favoring *ex ante* regulation as the dominant mode (for example, in the Board of Trade and Control of Prices Acts) to favoring *ex post* competition prohibitions (for example, in the Commerce Act as originally introduced in 1986). The fourth Labour government represented the high-water mark of free market economic policy in New Zealand, but since 1999 successive governments have progressively reintroduced economic regulation into the policy environment. Often the impetus for the promulgation of economic regulation has been the perceived failings of the competition regime to produce structurally more competitive markets. For example, the NZCC's failed monopolization litigation against Telecom in the 1990s[138] paved the way for the introduction of the Telecommunications Act 2001 which mandated wholesale

[134] The $750,000 maximum penalty applies to infringements of sections 45D, DB, E, and EA of the Competition and Consumer Act 2010 (Cth. Aus.).

[135] *TPC v CSR Ltd* (1991) ATPR 41-076; *Commerce Commission v Giltrap City Ltd [Penalty]* (2002) 10 TCLR 305; *Commerce Commission v Koppers Arch Wood Protection (NZ) Ltd* (2006) 11 TCLR 581. *See* also Ministry of Commerce (NZ), Penalties, remedies and court processes under the Commerce Act 1986 (1998).

[136] Ibid.

[137] Commerce Act 1986 (NZ), section 80C; Competition and Consumer Act 2010 (Cth. Aus.), section 86E.

[138] *See Telecom Corporation of New Zealand Ltd v Commerce Commission* [1992] 3 NZLR 429.

unbundling of Telecom's network services and then, in 2008, the operational split of Telecom into separate network, wholesale, and retail businesses.

In Australia, the Trade Practices Act 1974 was in its original drafting a reasonably narrowly drawn competition statute, with little in the way of economic regulation. However, it too has been the subject of a gradual but steady evolution towards a more regulated environment. The major shift came with the National Competition Policy Reforms of 1995, based on the report of the Hilmer Committee, which introduced the generic access regime in Part IIIA, and made the ACCC responsible for price surveillance under the Price Surveillance Act 1983.[139] In *Application by Chime Communications Pty Ltd* the ACT explained that the rationale for the access regime is to supplement competition law in natural monopoly industries.[140] There are now also industry-specific regimes for telecommunications,[141] electricity, and gas,[142] administered either by the ACCC or by the Australian Energy Regulator (a constituent part of the ACCC).

The current thinking in both New Zealand and Australia is that there is a place for both *ex post* competition and *ex ante* economic regulation as complementary elements of a balanced and integrated competition regime. In markets structurally capable of competition, traditional competition prohibitions ensure market participants do not undermine competition—either unilaterally or collusively. Where market structure prevents workable and effective competition, usually because of natural monopoly conditions, then economic regulation aims to reproduce the outcomes of a competitive market. Accordingly, because of the close relationship between competition and economic regulation, and in order to promote a more consistent and integrated approach to market regulation, both modes of regulation are the responsibility of a single agency.[143]

Along with their competition and regulatory roles, both the ACCC and the NZCC also have consumer protection responsibilities, covering deceptive trading, product quality and safety and disclosure requirements, amongst other matters.

1. Access regulation and price surveillance in Australia

Part IIIA of the Competition and Consumer Act establishes a generic access regime for essential facilities. The regime mandates access to "services" provided by means of a "facility," and gives as an example, infrastructure facilities such as roads or railway lines.[144] Part IIIA does not apply to the supply of goods, the use of intellectual property, or to production processes.[145] There are three ways in which access can be mandated.

[139] Competition Policy Reform Act 1995 (Cth. Aus.).
[140] *Application by Chime Communications Pty Ltd* [2008] ACompT 4.
[141] Competition and Consumer Act 2010 (Cth. Aus.), Part XIC.
[142] National Electricity Law, National Gas Law (Cth. Aus.).
[143] Corones, *supra* note 1, at 184.
[144] Competition and Consumer Act 2010 (Cth. Aus.), section 44B.
[145] Ibid.

First, the National Competition Council ("NCC") can recommend that a service be declared by the Minister. The NCC cannot make such a recommendation, and the Minister cannot declare the services, unless each is satisfied that:

a) access to the service would promote competition in a dependent market (for example, a downstream wholesale or resale market); and
b) it would be uneconomical for another person to develop an alternate facility to provide the same service; and
c) the facility is of national significance given its size or importance to commerce or to the national economy.[146]

The NCC and Minister must also consider the feasibility of allowing access and the public interest more generally. If the Minister decides to declare the service, the parties are obliged to negotiate terms of access. If they cannot agree, the ACCC is empowered to arbitrate their dispute. In conducting such an arbitration, the ACCC has to determine, amongst other things, the pricing model. In determining pricing, the ACCC must consider a number of criteria set out in section 44ZZCA—the most important of which (from the perspective of the access provider anyway) is that the expected revenue from access pricing must cover efficient costs and produce a return on investment commensurate with the risk involved in investing in the facility.

Second, if a State or Territory has promulgated an "effective" access regime, then the Minister must certify that regime, in which case the terms of access are as provided for in the State or Territory's regime.[147]

Third, a provider of a service may submit an undertaking to the ACCC regarding the terms on which it is willing to provide access, or an industry group may submit an access code. The ACCC may accept the undertaking or code if the service has not already been declared and it is appropriate to do so in light of, *inter alia*, the objects of the access regime, the pricing principles in section 44ZZCA, the legitimate interests of the access providers and those seeking access, and the public interest.[148] If the ACCC accepts the undertaking, then that determines the terms of access.

In addition to the generic access regime, through which a number of industries have been opened up to access, there are also industry-specific regimes for electricity and gas under the National Electricity Law and the National Gas Law. Those laws reflect a similar model to the negotiate/arbitrate model under Part IIIA,[149] as well as conferring rule-making powers for the electricity and gas markets on the Australian Energy Market Commission, and monitoring and enforcement powers on the Australian Energy Regulator ("AER"). There is also a separate access regime specifically for telecommunications in Part XIC of the Competition and Consumer Act administered by the ACCC.

[146] Competition and Consumer Act 2010 (Cth. Aus.), sections 44G, 44H.
[147] Ibid.
[148] Competition and Consumer Act 2010 (Cth. Aus.), section 44ZZA.
[149] Corones, *supra* note 1, at 741.

Finally, Part VIIA of the Competition and Consumer Act provides for price surveillance, monitoring, and control by the ACCC. Pursuant to section 95E, price surveillance is limited to those markets in which levels of competition are not sufficient to hold prices to efficient levels and protect consumers. Price surveillance, monitoring, and control can only be instituted by the responsible Minister, or by the ACCC at the Minister's direction.

2. Regulated goods and services in New Zealand

The regulatory regime in New Zealand is broader in its application than Part IIIA in Australia. Whereas the Australian regime only applies to essential facilities, Part 4 of the Commerce Act applies to any goods or services supplied in markets where there is little or no competition, and little likelihood of competition substantially increasing.[150] Furthermore, Part 4 provides for a hierarchy of different regulatory tools, depending on the nature and extent of the competitive problem at issue.

Regulation under Part 4 is triggered by an inquiry undertaken by the NZCC, at the conclusion of which the NZCC renders an opinion indicating whether the test of limited competition is met and, if so, what form of regulation should apply.[151] The Minister may then accept or reject the NZCC's recommendation, or recommend a modified form of regulation, which then forms the basis for an Order in Council imposing regulation in the terms recommended.[152] Responsibility then reverts to the NZCC to make determinations specifying how the forms of regulation imposed by the Order are to apply to suppliers in the market.[153]

The regulatory tools available to the NZCC are information disclosure, compulsory negotiate/arbitrate regulation, and price-quality regulation. Under the last of these, the NZCC can impose "default" price-quality paths, which establish a common set of prices and quality standards for all suppliers in the market, or the NZCC can impose individual price-quality paths on particular suppliers, either through accepting a proposal from a supplier, or by simply imposing an individual path on its own initiative.

In addition to this generic regulatory regime, Part 4 also includes specific regulatory regimes, based on a similar model, for electricity lines, gas pipeline services, and airport services.[154]

Apart from its regulatory responsibilities under the Commerce Act, the NZCC is also charged with regulating Telecom's network services under the Telecommunications Act 2001. That Act requires Telecom to offer certain unbundled wholesale network services to competitors on terms determined by the NZCC,[155] establishes the legal framework for Telecom's operational separation

[150] Commerce Act 1986 (NZ), section 52G.
[151] Commerce Act 1986 (NZ), section 52K.
[152] Commerce Act 1986 (NZ), sections 52M, 52N.
[153] Commerce Act 1986 (NZ), section 52P.
[154] Commerce Act 1986 (NZ), Part 4, subparts 9–11.
[155] Telecommunications Act 2001 (NZ), Part 2.

undertakings,[156] and empowers the NZCC to determine Telecom's remuneration from competing operators for providing a universal service to commercially non-viable customers.[157]

Finally, the NZCC also has a monitoring and enforcement role under the Dairy Industry Restructuring Act 2001, which established Fonterra—the New Zealand dairy export champion. The NZCC monitors and enforces regulations requiring Fonterra to disclose information, and to supply raw milk in the domestic market at regulated prices.

3. Consumer protection

Alongside their competition and economic regulation roles, the NZCC and ACCC are also responsible for enforcing wide-ranging consumer protection legislation addressing misleading and deceptive conduct in trade, product safety, and unfair contract terms.[158]

IV. Procedural characteristics[159]

A. Due process norms in case-by-case decision-making

1. The supervisory jurisdiction of the courts

The supervisory jurisdiction of the courts in New Zealand and Australia arises through two distinct mechanisms: appeal and judicial review. Rights of appeal reflect the role of the superior courts and courts of appeal in supervising the *judicial or quasi-judicial* decision-making of lower courts and tribunals. Judicial review, on the other hand, reflects the role of the superior courts in supervising the exercise of *administrative* functions and powers insofar as those functions and powers affect the rights or interests of those subject to the administrator's authority. Judicial review in New Zealand and Australia now has a legislative foundation in the Judicature Amendment Act 1972 and the Administrative Decisions (Judicial Review) Act 1977, respectively. But its historical basis is the jurisdiction developed by the

[156] Telecommunications Act 2001 (NZ), Part 2A.

[157] Telecommunications Act 2001 (NZ), Part 3. When Telecom was privatized, the quid pro quo was an ongoing obligation to continue supplying free local calling services to all New Zealanders at the same line-rental prices that prevailed pre-privatization, adjusted only for inflation (the Telecommunications Services Obligation). Because this entails supplying certain customers (generally small remote communities) at below-cost prices, the net cost of supplying such commercially non-viable customers is calculated and pro-rated amongst all telecommunications services providers, according to their market share. The NZCC calculates the net cost of the TSO annually.

[158] Fair Trading Act 1986 (NZ); Credit Contracts and Consumer Finance Act 2003 (NZ); Competition and Consumer Act 2010 (Cth. Aus.) (of which the Australian Consumer Law is a part).

[159] The following analysis of the procedural characteristics of the competition institutions in New Zealand and Australia is based on the author's research and practicing experiences, as well as interviews in 2010 with competition practitioners in New Zealand and Australia and the then chairpersons of the ACCC and NZCC, Graeme Samuel and Dr Mark Berry (still serving), respectively. Any errors are those of the author.

English Court of King's Bench in the 17th century to supervise the legality of administrative acts of public authorities through the prerogative writs of mandamus, prohibition, and certiorari.[160]

The grounds of review available under the judicial review jurisdiction are roughly equivalent to the concept of due process in American law. Those grounds were traditionally limited to procedural matters, on the theory that the judiciary was not constitutionally entitled to exercise the administrative powers of government (conferred either under statute or through the prerogative powers of the Crown) by substituting its own judgment for that of the administrator in question. The proper role of the courts was to ensure that administrative powers were exercised fairly and in a procedurally proper manner. Over time, the grounds of judicial review have periodically expanded and contracted, but in general they retain a procedural character. So for example, judicial review enables an applicant to challenge the fairness of the procedure adopted by the agency in making its decision, ask whether the agency has applied the correct legal test and taken into account all relevant considerations and excluded all irrelevant considerations, or allege that the agency has reached a decision that is totally unsupported by evidence,[161] or is so unreasonable or irrational that no reasonable decision-maker could have reached it.[162] However, an applicant for judicial review would not be permitted to allege simply that the decision was wrong or lacking in merit—that being the traditional preserve of the appellate function.

Because rights of appeal are conferred only by statute, and are usually only available for exercises of judicial or quasi-judicial power, judicial review is the primary means of challenging procedural errors committed by the ACCC or NZCC exercising their administrative powers. However, judicial review is not available for every action or decision of administrative bodies. In New Zealand, review is available for the exercise of a statutory power, which is defined as a power conferred by an Act to make rules or decisions affecting others, give directions, perform acts which but for the statutory authority would be a breach of a person's rights, or make any investigation or inquiry into a person's rights, powers, privileges, immunities, duties, or liabilities.[163] Essentially, therefore, judicial review is limited to actions or decisions taken pursuant to statute.[164] A similar situation prevails in Australia. Judicial review is available under the Administrative Decisions (Judicial Review) Act 1977 of decisions "of an administrative character" made under an Act.[165]

The relevance of this limitation is that not every decision or action performed by the NZCC or ACCC is made pursuant to an Act, and therefore amenable to judicial review. In Australia, the ACCC habitually clears transactions on an infor-

[160] Wade & Forsyth, *Administrative Law* (10th edn, Oxford University Press, 2009) at 12.

[161] *Edwards v Bairstow* [1956] AC 14.

[162] *Associated Provincial Picture Houses v Wednesbury Corporation* [1948] 1 KB 223.

[163] Judicature Amendment Act 1972 (NZ), section 3.

[164] For completeness, there is a residual, though not often used, power to judicially review non-statutory exercises of public power or duty affecting individuals rights or interests: *R v Panel on Takeovers and Mergers, Ex Parte Datafin* [1987] QB 815.

[165] Administrative Decisions (Judicial Review) Act 1977 (Cth. Aus.), section 3.

mal basis, without resort to the statutory clearance regime. Because clearance is not mandatory, and the mechanism for preventing anticompetitive mergers is court proceedings, informal "clearance" is simply an indication that the regulator will not pursue an injunction to block the transaction from proceeding. Such an indication is not made under or pursuant to the relevant legislation, but rather in the administrative discretion of the regulator, and therefore is not reviewable. The consequence is that parties subject to such informal non-statutory processes are not easily able to enforce due process norms applicable under judicial review.

The grounds of judicial review are set out in the Administrative Decisions (Judicial Review) Act, and articulated in the common law of Australia and New Zealand. The discussion in this study is limited to the principles of "natural justice"—a broad term that equates roughly to procedural propriety or fairness. What will be procedurally fair will depend on the circumstances of the case, but over time particular principles have emerged and hardened into rules that are applied to every administrative body unless expressly excluded by statute. The principles of natural justice most often called upon by applicants are the right to have sufficient notice of adverse facts and reasoning, and the right to be consulted or heard on a matter affecting one's interests (*audi alteram partem*).[166]

The remainder of this section discusses, first, due process issues arising in the context of the various phases of enforcement: commencing proceedings, conducting investigations, and settling or discontinuing proceedings; and second, specific due process norms and the extent to which they are recognized in the law and practice of the NZCC and ACCC.

2. *Commencing, settling, and discontinuing proceedings*

The ACCC and NZCC are independent administrative agencies, and as such are afforded broad discretion in the selection of cases and enforcement priorities, and the execution of their investigative and litigation functions. Neither the Competition and Consumer Act nor the Commerce Act obliges the regulators to take any particular steps in relation to a complaint that is made, nor do the Acts outline enforcement priorities for the regulators or compel them to take enforcement action under any circumstances. Furthermore, decisions to initiate investigations or enforcement action are presumptively unreviewable by the courts, with very few exceptions.[167] The courts refrain from intervening for two reasons: (i) an aggrieved

[166] Administrative Decisions (Judicial Review) Act 1977 (Cth. Aus.), section 5, *Daganayasi v Minister of Immigration* [1980] 2 NZLR 130, *Council of Civil Service Unions v Minister for the Civil Service* [1985] AC 374.

[167] *Clear Communications Ltd v Sky Network Television Ltd* HC WN CP 19/96 1 August 1997 (Gallen J and Dr M Brunt); *Visy Board Pty Ltd v Attorney-General of the Commonwealth of Australia* (1984) ATPR 40-448; *Electricity Supply Association of Australia Ltd v ACCC* (2001) 113 FCR 230. The exception is where the regulator has represented to a party that enforcement action will not be taken as a result of assurances given through, for example, an indemnity or leniency process: *Trade Practices Commission v CC (New South Wales) Pty Ltd* [1994] FCA 1368.

party is entitled to bring their own proceedings for breach of the Act;[168] and (ii) the decision whether to proceed or not is a complex one involving considerations of enforcement priorities, the strength of the evidence, and the availability of funds, all matters the courts are not well placed to second-guess.[169] The same principles apply to a decision to settle or discontinue proceedings, with the qualification that pecuniary penalties cannot be settled by the parties but rather must be imposed by the court.[170] However, this notwithstanding, there is no sense amongst practitioners that the regulators are insufficiently vigorous in their enforcement role. To the contrary, the independent enforcement discretion of the agencies is an essential mechanism to ensure that the regulators are free to discharge their enforcement role free of interference from government or third parties.

The high level of independence enjoyed by the regulators does mean that enforcement policy depends to a large extent on the personal style and priorities of the chairpersons of the agencies. So for example, Allan Fels (ACCC chairperson from 1995 to 2003) and Paula Rebstock (NZCC chairperson from 2003 to 2009) were both known as particularly activist and enforcement-focused commissioners who did a great deal to establish the reputation of their respective regulators amongst the business community. Both as a consequence faced very considerable criticism from the business community during their tenure.[171] This is not to say that other chairpersons have been overly friendly towards business interests during their tenure, but rather to emphasize the high level of influence that individual chairpersons have over the agencies and their role within the economy.

Any person may initiate a complaint by contacting the agencies by letter, telephone, or by filling out an online form on the agencies' websites.[172] There is no particular form in which complaints must be made, nor any minimum information requirements for submitting a complaint. The agencies aim to keep the complaints process as straightforward as possible, although obviously the more information the complainant is able to provide, the more likely the agencies are to pursue the matter. Both agencies receive thousands of complaints potentially falling within their jurisdiction every year. Initially, complaints are screened by staff, exercising the Commissioners' delegated authority, to eliminate those that are either not within the regulators' jurisdiction, do not on their face disclose conduct capable of constituting an infringement, or fall below a threshold of materiality.

After an initial screening, staff may conduct initial inquiries to substantiate the essential facts of the complaint in order to assist the Commissioners in deciding whether or not to pursue formal investigative action. The decision whether or not

[168] *Clear Communications Ltd v Sky Network Television Ltd* HC WN CP 19/96 1 August 1997 (Gallen J and Dr M Brunt).

[169] *Visy Board Pty Ltd v Attorney-General of the Commonwealth of Australia* (1984) ATPR 40-448.

[170] *Commerce Commission v Milk Corporation Ltd* [1994] 2 NZLR 730.

[171] *See*, for example, Grant David, "Do we still need a commerce commission?," NATIONAL BUSINESS REVIEW (March 16, 2009); Hugh Dillon, "Book review: Allan Fels: Portrait of Power," SYDNEY MORNING HERALD (October 11, 2003).

[172] *See* the NZCC and ACCC websites for general information on the complaints processes: <http://www.comcom.govt.nz/making-a-complaint>; <http://www.accc.gov.au/content/index.phtml/itemId/815322>.

to open an investigation is made in accordance with the agencies' enforcement guidelines, which are publicly available.[173]

The ACCC's guidelines note that the ACCC cannot pursue all the complaints it receives and, while all complaints are carefully considered, the ACCC exercises its discretion to direct resources to the investigation and resolution of matters that provide the greatest overall benefit for consumers and businesses. In making this assessment, the ACCC gives enforcement priority to matters that demonstrate one or more of the following factors:

- conduct of significant public interest or concern;
- conduct resulting in a significant consumer detriment;
- conduct demonstrating a blatant disregard for the law;
- conduct involving national or international issues;
- conduct detrimentally affecting disadvantaged or vulnerable consumer groups;
- conduct involving a significant new or emerging market issue;
- conduct that is industry-wide or is likely to become widespread if the ACCC does not intervene;
- whether the ACCC action is likely to have a worthwhile educative or deterrent effect; and/or
- the person, business, or industry has a history of previous contraventions of competition, consumer protection, and fair trading laws.[174]

The NZCC's enforcement criteria are to similar effect. The NZCC emphasizes that it must apply administrative discretion over a wide range of matters, including the strength of the NZCC's case, the availability of funds, competing claims on those funds by other cases, and assessments of the comparative importance of the various cases in which the Commission is involved. The enforcement criteria applied by the NZCC are:

- the extent of detriment—which includes the nature of the harm (physical, economic, or impaired choice), whether the consumers targeted are particularly vulnerable, the prevalence and persistence of the infringing conduct, and the effect on competition or output;
- the seriousness of the conduct—whether it is deliberate or reckless, repeated or ongoing, a serious departure from lawful commercial behavior, difficult to detect, or likely to infringe a per se provision;
- the public interest—including the level of public interest in the issue, whether public confidence would be undermined by a lack of enforcement action, the nature of aggravating and mitigating features, a need to clarify the law, and the timeliness of the enforcement action.[175]

[173] ACCC, Compliance and Enforcement Policy, <www.accc.gov.au>; NZCC, Enforcement Criteria, <http://www.comcom.govt.nz/enforcement-criteria>.

[174] Ibid. [175] Ibid.

The agencies' recent enforcement record suggests that cartels are their first priority—in part because they are viewed as the most egregious infringement of competition law, but likely also because they constitute low-hanging fruit for an agency with limited litigation resources. After cartels, per se violations (such as resale price maintenance), mergers and collusive conduct are significant enforcement priorities. Both agencies have had mixed experience with monopolization cases—although the ACCC has generally been more successful in its prosecution of monopolization cases due to the broader test for abusive conduct that applies in Australia.[176] Hence, while there have been a number of very high profile monopolization cases, the agencies will assess very carefully the facts of the complaint, the importance of the industry, and the likelihood of achieving either a successful litigation outcome (or at least a valuable precedent) before proceeding with a monopolization case.

If the agencies decide not to pursue a formal investigation, the complainant will be notified, but typically there will be no public statement of the decision. Where an investigation is undertaken but concluded without instituting proceedings or obtaining undertakings in lieu of proceedings the NZCC will usually announce the conclusion of the investigation, and its reasons for doing so, in a brief press release. The ACCC, by contrast, tends not to announce the closure of investigations that have not resulted in proceedings or undertakings. However, when an investigation does not result in proceedings, the agencies may take other steps in relation to complaints. For instance, they may provide information to the complainants to help them deal with the matter, postpone or cease the investigation with a view to returning to it later should more information come to light, encourage the parties to rectify minor or accidental breaches, or notify the parties of the agencies' concerns without taking formal action.[177]

If a case is taken to court, it may result ultimately in judgment, or more likely in an agreed settlement at some point during the proceedings. If the agency is seeking only an injunction or other behavioral undertaking to cease or modify conduct then the settlement need only be ratified by the court in accordance with the ordinary practice rules governing settlement of civil proceedings. However, only the court can impose pecuniary penalties, and hence if the agencies are seeking pecuniary penalties they will present an agreed submission and statement of facts to the court, which must then determine the appropriate penalty. Notwithstanding the court is free (within the bounds of the law) to impose whatever penalty it thinks appropriate; in practice the court seldom strays far from the penalty recommended by the parties.[178]

The agencies each have immunity and leniency policies for cartel conduct, and in practice most cartel proceedings are disposed of under these policies.[179] Immunity

[176] *Melway Publishing Pty Ltd v Robert Hicks Pty Ltd* (2001) 205 CLR 1.

[177] ACCC, Compliance and Enforcement Policy, <http://www.accc.gov.au>; NZCC, Enforcement Criteria, <http://www.comcom.govt.nz/enforcement-criteria>.

[178] *Commerce Commission v Milk Corporation Ltd* [1994] 2 NZLR 730.

[179] The policies are available at: <http://www.accc.gov.au/content/index.phtml/itemId/879795> and <http://www.comcom.govt.nz/cartel-leniency-policy-and-process-guidelines/>.

is available to the first participant in a cartel to admit their involvement and cooperate fully with the agency, with exceptions. In Australia, the exceptions are that the participant must not have coerced others to enter the cartel and must not be the prime mover. In New Zealand, the participant must not have coerced others, but immunity is still available to prime movers.[180]

Participants who are not first in line to admit their involvement will not be eligible for immunity, but the agencies will agree to a joint submission to the court recommending substantially reduced penalties in exchange for cooperation. Co-operation must, however, extend beyond mere compliance with the agencies' compulsory powers and therefore cartel participants seeking reduced penalties must proactively assist the agencies' investigation.[181]

3. Due process in investigations

As outlined earlier, the agencies have broad powers to require the production of documents and information and the giving of testimony, and may also conduct searches under warrant. Although the agencies' investigative powers increasingly resemble those of a criminal enforcement agency (and in Australia at least, the ACCC does now have a criminal investigatory role in relation to cartels), the basis for their statutory powers is a civil enforcement regime. Accordingly, ordinary rights of criminal defense do not necessarily apply, or apply to the same extent, which leads to a degree of tension around expectations of fairness in the investigatory process. Due process in investigations arises from express statutory protections in the empowering legislation and administrative law principles of natural justice.

A common cause of complaint amongst practitioners is the agencies' use of their document discovery powers. Although the process is similar to discovery in private civil litigation, the courts recognize that the power is necessary for the agencies' investigative role, and therefore the threshold for establishing relevance is very low. For example, the High Court of New Zealand has held in relation to the NZCC's section 98 power that the "primary right to decide as to relevance . . . reposes in the investigative body or officer but it is encumbent upon the investigative body or officer to show a degree of relevance bearing in mind that in an investigative situation and in the context of the section the onus must be a very easy one to discharge."[182] The breadth of the ACCC's latitude under its comparable provision—section 155—is slightly narrower,[183] but similar principles apply. The ACCC must demonstrate a "body of facts" that may constitute a contravention and a "reason to believe" that the person named in the section 155 notice is capable

180 Ibid.
181 Ibid.
182 *Telecom Corporation of New Zealand v Commerce Commission* [1991] NZAR 155.
183 Gault, *supra* note 37, at paragraph CA98.02.

of assisting the ACCC in relation to that potential contravention by providing information.[184]

Furthermore, failure to comply with section 98 or 155 notices by the stated deadline results in criminal liability. The result is that investigations can be extremely costly and burdensome for the parties involved, but more importantly that the parties may have limited time in which to review documents to exclude material outside the scope of the inquiry, or material subject to privilege.

On occasion, parties subject to investigations have sought judicial review of the ACCC's section 155 notices on the grounds they impose an unreasonable, harsh, and oppressive burden. The results illustrate the difficulty of persuading the courts to intervene in the regulators' investigative processes. In *Emirates v ACCC*,[185] the court agreed that the section 155 notice was objectively oppressive and harsh because of the expansive scope of Emirates' international operations; the information sought spanned a period of seven years and concerned surcharges applying to cargo shipped by Emirates from and to any destination in the world; the information sought applied to every individual charge levied; and Emirates was given only four to five weeks to comply. However, that conclusion notwithstanding, the court determined that it could not intervene because the ACCC had genuinely considered the burden it was imposing when it issued the notice, and had not imposed the burden in bad faith or for an improper purpose.

A number of practitioners suggested that both agencies had been guilty on occasion of using discovery notices as unfounded fishing expeditions, with no clear theory of liability evident in the information and documents requested. However, practitioners also agreed that both the ACCC under Graeme Samuel and the NZCC under Dr Mark Berry were making greater efforts to ensure that investigations were no more burdensome than necessary given the agencies' acknowledged need to identify evidence of infringements.

Reflecting the civil and administrative origins of competition enforcement in New Zealand and Australia, parties required to give testimony to the agencies are not entitled to rely on the privilege against self-incrimination.[186] However, the trade-off is that testimony obtained under compulsion is not admissible in court proceedings, other than proceedings for criminal failure to comply with an order to give testimony, or giving false or misleading testimony.[187] In New Zealand, this creates few problems as there are no criminal sanctions for breach of the substantive competition law provisions. In Australia, however, there is greater potential for testimony obtained under compulsion to contribute to a criminal cartel case under the new criminal regime. Mr Samuel indicated that the ACCC is alive to this risk, and hence its undertaking to treat every cartel investigation as presumptively criminal until the CDPP and ACCC have jointly determined that there is no

184 *SA Brewing Holdings v Baxt* (1989) 23 FCR 357; *Kotan Holdings Pty Ltd v Trade Practices Commission* (1991) 30 FCR 511.

185 [2009] FCA 312.

186 Commerce Act 1986 (NZ), section 106(4).

187 Commerce Act 1986 (NZ), sections 106(5); Competition and Consumer Act 2010 (Cth. Aus.), sections 154R, 155, 159.

basis for a prosecution. To this end, ACCC investigative staff have been trained in criminal investigative principles, including the need to caution witnesses and avoid tainting evidence. However, while Mr Samuel is very confident that the ACCC has had sufficient lead-in time to embed the appropriate procedural safeguards in its investigative practice, practitioners are less convinced and foresee a glut of admissibility litigation as the CDPP and ACCC bring the first criminal cartel prosecutions.

In Australia, the ACCC's compulsory investigative powers are extinguished at the point at which it commences court proceedings in relation to a matter.[188] Thus, from the point at which it commences proceedings, the ACCC is forced to rely on ordinary powers of civil discovery. This places additional time pressure on the ACCC when conducting investigations as it must complete the investigation before statutory limitation periods compel it to file its statement of claim. In New Zealand, by contrast, the NZCC can continue to exercise its investigative powers notwithstanding it has commenced proceedings, with the proviso that the courts may deem a subsequent radical amendment to its causes of action as a fresh filing, and therefore out of time if the applicable limitation period has already elapsed.[189]

However, the relationship between the investigative and litigation phases in enforcement proceedings in New Zealand has recently given rise to a substantial point of contention relating to section 100 suppression orders. These orders allow the NZCC to prevent parties subject to an investigation from disclosing or publishing any information or document that has been provided to the NZCC during an investigation. The intent behind the provision is to preserve the integrity of the NZCC's ongoing investigations. During the course of the NZCC's air cargo cartel investigations, the NZCC interviewed employees of Air New Zealand, showed them documents that allegedly supported the existence of the cartel, and asked them to comment. Subsequently, the NZCC made section 100 orders preventing those employees from disclosing to their employer the details of the interviews. The NZCC moreover asserted that the orders applied even after it had commenced proceedings against Air New Zealand. Air New Zealand applied to the High Court to have the section 100 orders struck out, arguing that preventing it from speaking to its employees about the NZCC's interviews prejudiced its rights of defense. The High Court ruled in favor of Air New Zealand, holding that the section 100 orders expired at the point that proceedings were commenced.[190] The NZCC appealed the decision to the Court of Appeal, which overturned the High Court, ruling that nothing in the Commerce Act suggested the NZCC's jurisdiction to make section 100 orders expired at the point proceedings were commenced.[191]

The Competition and Consumer Act has no equivalent to section 100, but the courts in Australia have accepted that the ACCC has the power to require a person appearing before it not to disclose any matters raised in the examination for "a

[188] Competition and Consumer Act 2010 (Cth. Aus.), section 155(4).
[189] Commerce Act (NZ), section 98G.
[190] *Air New Zealand v Commerce Commission* HC AK CIV 2008-404-008352 21 October 2009.
[191] *Commerce Commission v Air New Zealand* [2011] NZCA 64.

reasonable time."[192] The courts have not indicated whether a reasonable time extends beyond the commencement of proceedings, but the ACCC in its guidelines accepts that the non-disclosure obligation would not extend beyond the institution of proceedings.[193]

4. *Right to be heard*

The right to be heard in relation to an exercise of administrative power affecting one's interests (and conversely, the obligation of the decision-maker to consult interested parties) is the strongest of the due process norms in New Zealand and Australian administrative law, and the one most often called upon. The essence of the rule is that, whenever a statute confers a power upon an administrative decision-maker to destroy, defeat, or prejudice a person's rights, interests, or legitimate expectations, the rules of natural justice, including the right to be heard in relation to the matter, regulate the exercise of that power unless they are clearly excluded by the words of the statute.[194]

The obligation to consult is not satisfied upon the granting of a mere opportunity to make a submission. The decision-maker must outline to interested parties the relevant proposals (which must be not yet finally decided upon), listen to what affected parties have to say, genuinely consider their responses, and then decide what will be done.[195] The duty to consult implies that the decision-maker will approach the parties' submissions with an open mind. However, this is not to say that the decision-maker must approach the consultation with a blank mind—it is permissible for the decision-maker to have preliminary views, as long as the decision-maker remains open to being persuaded otherwise.[196] Furthermore, the decision-maker is not obliged to adopt the views of interested parties. The obligation is only to genuinely consider those views. As a practical matter, therefore, all the decision-maker need show is that he or she provided an opportunity for interested parties to comment, and that his or her subsequent conduct was not inconsistent with a genuine open-minded consideration. Put another way, if the opportunity to be heard has been afforded, a complainant has to surmount a substantial evidential hurdle to prove that the decision-maker did not adequately consider the complainant's views.

The extent of the obligation to consult also varies depending on the circumstances of the decision. The consultation required with well-informed, knowledgeable, and sophisticated consultees is less exacting than is expected when uninformed members of the public are being consulted.[197] Accordingly, the obligations on a

[192] *Constantine v Trade Practices Commission* (1994) 48 FCR 141.

[193] ACCC, Section 155 of the Trade Practices Act, March 2008, <http://www.accc.gov.au/content/index.phtml/itemId/263816>.

[194] *Annetts v McCann* (1990) 170 CLR 596.

[195] *Wellington International Airport v Air New Zealand Ltd* [1993] 1 NZLR 671.

[196] *Auckland City Council v Auckland Electric Power Board* HC AK CP26/93 16 August 1993.

[197] *Darling Casino Ltd v Minister for Planning and Sydney Harbour Casino Ltd* (1995) 86 LGERA 186; *Powerco Ltd v Commerce Commission* HC WN CIV 2005-485-1066 24 December 2007.

regulator when consulting with industry are arguably less onerous than those that would fall upon, for instance, the Minister of Immigration when consulting with a foreign national subject to a deportation notice.[198] In practice, however, the greater litigation risk posed by sophisticated commercial parties usually prompts the agencies to adopt a more than necessarily rigorous standard of consultation.

Even where legislation is silent as to obligations to consult, the rules of natural justice apply. However, the Commerce Act and the Competition and Consumer Act also impose substantial obligations of consultation on the agencies when exercising their adjudicative function. A typical example is section 52V of the Commerce Act, which establishes the process for the NZCC's determination of regulatory input methodologies, and provides in part as follows:

52V Commission process for determining input methodologies

(1) When the Commission begins work on an input methodology, it must publish a notice of intention to do so that—
   (a) outlines the process that will be followed; and
   (b) sets out the proposed time frames.
(2) During the course of its work on an input methodology, the Commission—
   (a) must publish a draft methodology; and
   (b) must give interested persons a reasonable opportunity to give their views on that draft methodology; and
   (c) may hold 1 or more conferences; and
   (d) must have regard to any views received from interested persons within any time frames set.

The agencies have also tended to establish formal consultation procedures where the legislation is silent on consultation. For example, in relation to merger clearances, the agencies have published guidelines setting out the processes they will follow, and the opportunities for merger parties to comment on the regulators' reasoning and preliminary conclusions. The ACCC seeks comment from merger parties (i) following its preliminary assessment having reviewed the application for clearance, (ii) after the ACCC has conducted market inquiries, and (iii) in relation to the publicly disclosed statement of issues.[199] The NZCC affords an opportunity for comment (i) after the Statement of Preliminary Issues is published on its website, (ii) following the transmission of the Letter of Issues (in cases with more significant competition issues) to the merger parties, and (iii) after transmitting the Letter of Unresolved Issues, which occurs late in the process if the NZCC and parties have been unable to resolve competition issues identified earlier in the process.[200]

In practice, therefore, both agencies engage in extensive consultation in almost every exercise of their adjudicative powers, and thus there should be minimal scope

[198] *Daganayasi v Minister of Immigration* [1980] 2 NZLR 130.

[199] ACCC, Merger Review Process Guidelines, July 2006, <http://www.accc.gov.au/content/index.phtml/itemId/740765>.

[200] NZCC, Mergers and Acquisitions Clearance Process Guidelines, July 2010, <http://www.comcom.govt.nz/clearances/>.

for complaints in practice. Where parties do complain that they have not been adequately heard, the allegation is usually that the quality of the consultation has not met the required standard, rather than that there has been no consultation at all. For example, Powerco complained about a lack of consultation in relation to the NZCC's 2006 imposition of price control over gas pipelines.[201] Amongst other failures, Powerco alleged that the Minister, who was required to make the final decision, did not properly consider Powerco's submissions because he simply referred them to the NZCC for its comment and accepted the NZCC's response that the submissions contained nothing new. The court held that the Minister's approach was an obvious practical step given the NZCC had already engaged in substantial and lengthy consultation on the same issues. Given the NZCC's extensive consultation, the Minister was entitled to restrict his own consultation process to new matters.

In the Australian context, Telstra complained about the ACCC's determination granting access to its local loop infrastructure on the basis, *inter alia*, that the ACCC had failed to consider the cost model that Telstra had provided with its submissions.[202] The facts were that the cost model had been supplied in the form of two spreadsheets entitled "Summary of cost model." The ACCC reviewed the spreadsheets and in its final decision preferred its own cost model to that of Telstra, noting that Telstra had only provided a "summary" of its cost model and not the complete version that would have enabled the ACCC to understand the basis upon which it had been prepared. Telstra alleged that the ACCC had failed to appreciate that the spreadsheets entitled "Summary" were in fact the complete cost model, and that the ACCC's comments indicated that it had failed to give the model proper weight as a result, thus denying Telstra procedural fairness. Telstra further submitted that, to the extent the ACCC was expecting an additional "complete" cost model, it should have contacted Telstra to request it. The court ruled against Telstra, holding that the ACCC had given adequate consideration to its cost model. Moreover, the court held that the failure to request the "complete" cost model was irrelevant because, had the ACCC made the request as Telstra contended, this would simply have confirmed that the ACCC had already received all the material Telstra intended to provide.

Mr Samuel and Dr Berry, when interviewed, took the position that if anything the administrative law requirements in Australia and New Zealand have resulted in too much consultation, which results in unnecessary delay. In many cases, and particularly in regulatory determinations, the submissions of industry participants are either predictable, repeatedly rehash the same points, or consist of broad unsupported assertions. Accordingly, Mr Samuel and Dr Berry were of the view that often the decision-making process did not significantly benefit from multiple rounds of consultation.

[201] *Powerco Ltd v Commerce Commission* HC WN CIV 2005-485-1066 24 December 2007.
[202] *Telstra Corporation Ltd v ACCC* [2008] FCA 1436.

5. *Adequate notice of evidence and reasoning*

The right to receive adequate notice of the decision-maker's reasoning and the evidence relied upon is closely related to the right to be heard. In order for parties to be able to effectively exercise their right to be heard, the decision-maker must disclose to them (i) "the substance of material that is significant, relevant, credible and obtained from a source other than that party";[203] and (ii) the options the decision-maker is considering and the major points of reasoning supporting those options.[204]

The first of those limbs is implicated in a developing debate in Australia over disclosure of third-party submissions in the informal merger clearance process. At present, the ACCC does not disclose to the merger parties submissions it receives from third parties regarding the merger. Accordingly, while the merger parties are able to comment on the issues that the ACCC raises in its statement of issues, they are unable to comment on the underlying submissions that may be influencing the ACCC's thinking. Practitioners interviewed indicated that this prevents the parties from correcting potentially incorrect factual statements, or rebutting unfounded arguments that may be influencing the ACCC's thinking but are not expressly disclosed in the statement of issues.

In response to this concern, Mr Samuel stated that the position of the ACCC was that merger parties did have an opportunity to comment on third-party submissions, just not at the informal clearance stage. If the parties received an adverse decision from the ACCC it was open to them to indicate their intention to proceed with the transaction, at which point the ACCC would institute proceedings for an injunction blocking the transaction. Third party submissions relevant to the matter would then be disclosed through the ordinary discovery processes of the court. Alternatively, it was open to merger parties to proceed under the formal clearance process set out in the Competition and Consumer Act, in which case this issue would not arise.

As yet, the point has not been raised before the courts, and so there is no conclusive answer on whether the ACCC is breaching its natural justice obligations by declining to disclose adverse third-party submissions.

A similar concern was raised by practitioners in the New Zealand context, also in relation to merger control. Although the NZCC provides the merger parties with a succession of issues statements, it does not produce a draft determination showing in detail the factual/economic basis for the NZCC's reasoning. Accordingly, it is only on appeal to the courts that the parties have an opportunity to respond to the evidence underlying the NZCC's decision. In the attempted Woolworths acquisition of the Warehouse's grocery business, the NZCC commissioned substantial volumes of detailed econometric analysis that was only disclosed to the parties in

[203] *Telstra Corporation Ltd v ACCC* [2008] FCA 1436, citing *Kioa v West* (1985) 159 CLR 550 and *Applicant VEAL of 2002 v Minister for Immigration and Multicultural and Indigenous Affairs* (2005) 225 CLR 88.

[204] *Contact Energy v Electricity Commission* HC WN CIV 2005-485-624 29 August 2005.

the final determination. Accordingly, on appeal, Woolworths requested leave to adduce expert evidence in reply. The High Court gave leave, accepting that it was appropriate that Woolworths have the opportunity now to respond to the NZCC's economic evidence.[205] On further appeal, however, the Court of Appeal criticized the High Court for admitting the further evidence, holding that the proper appellate function of the High Court was limited to the evidential record developed by the Commission.[206] The result is that, as the law stands, parties to contested merger cases have limited opportunities to engage with the evidence that the NZCC relies on in making its first instance decision.

The second limb of the "adequate notice" right is founded on the principle that, for consultation to be meaningful, there must be available to the affected parties sufficient information (whether by means of a statement of proposal or draft determination) to enable them to make intelligent and useful responses.[207] The regulator must also be alert to ensure that the draft determination is not undermined by what occurs thereafter. If a matter of substance emerges after the draft is issued, which is likely to be material to the final determination, an opportunity must be afforded to the affected parties to comment further.[208]

That principle formed the basis for a successful challenge to a regulatory determination by the Electricity Commission (whose responsibilities have since been folded into the NZCC) in *Contact Energy v Electricity Commission*.[209] There, all the draft material presented to Contact and Meridian (two of the major generator/retailers) prior to the issue of the final determination had indicated that charges for the HVDC link[210] would be distributed amongst North and South Island generators. When the final determination was issued, it transpired that the Commission had elected to impose the cost of the HVDC link solely on existing South Island generators. Contact and Meridian sought judicial review, alleging that the consultation process had miscarried. They had not made any submissions on the appropriate means of recovering HVDC charges as the draft proposal reflected their preferred outcome. They were not aware that the Commission was considering an alternative option and therefore argued they had not been afforded an adequate opportunity to comment. The court agreed that the Commission had failed to satisfy its obligation to consult. When it decided to change its view on the HVDC pricing methodology it was obliged to notify the affected parties and seek further comment.

The test posed in *Contact Energy* was: was the option or proposal eventually adopted "on the table" at the time when the affected parties were afforded the opportunity to comment? That is a question of fact, and turns on a detailed examination of the consultation process and the materials released. In this case

205 *Woolworths Ltd v Commerce Commission* HC WN CIV 2007-485-1255 12 September 2007.
206 *Commerce Commission v Woolworths Ltd* [2008] NZCA 276.
207 *Wellington International Airport Ltd v Air New Zealand Ltd* [1993] 1 NZLR 671.
208 *New Zealand Co-operative Dairy Co Ltd v Commerce Commission* [1992] 1 NZLR 601 at 637.
209 HC WN CIV 2005-485-624 29 August 2005.
210 The High Voltage Direct Current electricity transmission link between the North and South Islands of New Zealand.

the court was satisfied the final HVDC pricing principle was not "on the table" because, whereas the Commission had stated in its draft a number of options for other elements of the proposal, only one option was stated for HVDC pricing. Accordingly, when the Commission subsequently put the alternative pricing principle "on the table," it was obliged to reconsult.

6. *Independence of decision-makers*

An administrative decision-maker should be independent in two ways: free from political interference, and free from bias born of personal conflict of interest.

The institutional structure of competition law in New Zealand and Australia is intended to ensure independence from political interference.[211] The ACCC and NZCC are structurally independent from their respective governments and political systems in terms of the three axes identified in the United Nations' Model Law on Competition:[212]

1. Independence in decision-making: the agencies are empowered by legislation rather than by government fiat, and are afforded a largely unreviewable discretion under their empowering legislation to enforce the Acts. The Australian and New Zealand governments have no ability to influence the day-to-day decision-making of the agencies. Rather, the role of the governments is one of supervision and policy direction.
2. Budgetary independence: the agencies are funded by Parliamentary appropriation and, while their budgets are overseen by Parliamentary officials, the agencies take responsibility for expenditure within their overall appropriation. While the Australian and New Zealand governments would theoretically be able to limit the effectiveness of the agencies by restricting their overall appropriation, the general sense amongst practitioners and the chairpersons of the agencies is that their operations are adequately funded, and that funding is not manipulated for political ends.
3. Personnel independence: the commissioners are appointed through a political process. However, once appointed, they are afforded security of tenure. The staff of the agencies are appointed by the commissioners (or more accurately, by the general manager exercising a delegated authority under the commissioners). The principle of public service political neutrality protects the commissioners and their staff from political direction or interference.[213]

[211] Subject to the limited power of policy direction the Australian and New Zealand governments are afforded under the Commerce Act and Competition and Consumer Act: *see infra* at 12–13.

[212] United Nations Conference on Trade and Development, Model Law on Competition (revised 2010), chapter IX.

[213] Cabinet Office, Department of the Prime Minister and Cabinet, Cabinet Manual 2008 (Cabinet Office 2008), paragraph 3.51; Public Service Act 1999 (Cth. Aus.), sections 3, 10 and 19; Australian Public Service Commission, Values in the Australian Public Service (2nd edn 2002).

The theory is also reflected in practice. Practitioners interviewed agreed that the agencies are genuinely free from political interference. In fact, if anything, complaints in the past have been about "rogue" behavior by the regulators suggesting a need for stricter oversight, rather than about the politicization of the competition law regime.[214]

Australia and New Zealand are comparatively small markets, and hence there is also a constant risk of personal conflicts of interest arising. Both agencies are subject to guidelines for managing conflicts of interest through the public service codes of conduct. In addition, legislation requires members of the agencies to disclose financial interests on a register to ensure transparency. The principle governing conflicts of interest in both New Zealand and Australia is that public officials must ensure not only that they avoid actual conflicts of interest, but also the appearance of conflict that would undermine public confidence in the agency.

Both agencies have been reasonably vigilant about managing personal conflicts of interest (with one notable exception). For example, in August 2010 Mr Samuel recused himself from further involvement in the review of NAB's proposed merger with AXA because he is a key investor in a property development company that is currently in crisis talks over substantial debts owed to NAB.[215] Similarly, in 2006 the NZCC replaced a member of a panel appointed to review its draft guidelines on estimating the cost of capital. The member was a senior consultant with CRA International, who was at the same time advising a number of industry participants on cost of capital issues in New Zealand. CRA complained that the appointment of one of its consultants to the panel raised a risk of actual or perceived conflict of interest with CRA's clients. After discussions, the NZCC agreed that the member would step down.[216]

A notable failure occurred in relation to Donal Curtin—deputy chairperson of the NZCC—who failed to adequately disclose his involvement as chairman of the investment committee of a finance company that the NZCC was investigating for consumer protection breaches. Mr Curtin disclosed only the parent company's name, rather than the subsidiary that was under investigation. When the nature of his interest in the subsidiary emerged, Mr Curtin was stood down pending an independent investigation. The investigation found that Mr Curtin's inadequate disclosure was unintentional, and that the Ministry of Economic Development's vetting process was also at fault as the Ministry had given only "cursory scrutiny" to Mr Curtin's disclosure form.[217] The result has been a heightened focus at the NZCC, and in the New Zealand public service more generally, on the potential for

[214] *See*, for example, Grant David, "Do we still need a commerce commission?," NATIONAL BUSINESS REVIEW (March 16, 2009); Hugh Dillon, "Book review: Allan Fels: Portrait of Power," SYDNEY MORNING HERALD (October 11, 2003).

[215] ACCC, press release, "Samuels recuses from NAB/AXA decision" (August 18, 2010), <http://www.accc.gov.au>.

[216] NZCC, press release, "Replacement member appointed to cost of capital panel" (December 13, 2006), <http://www.comcom.govt.nz>.

[217] NZCC, press release, "Commerce Commission initiates disclosure of interests inquiry" (September 12, 2008), <http://www.comcom.govt.nz>; NATIONAL BUSINESS REVIEW, "Curtin report divides the blame" (March 16, 2009), <http://www.nbr.co.nz>.

conflicts of interest to arise as a result of officials' past or present employment in the field in which they now operate as a regulator.

7. Proportionality of sanctions

Proportionality is a well-accepted principle in the context of penalties imposed on violators of competition law.

The maximum penalties for corporate infringements in New Zealand and Australia are: (a) AUS/NZ$10 million, or (b) three times the commercial gain derived from the infringing conduct, or (c) if the commercial gain cannot be calculated, 10 percent of the turnover of the corporate group within the twelve months preceding the infringing conduct. The reason for the floating maximum penalties under (b) and (c) is to reflect the wide variation in economic and financial strength of corporate offenders and to enable the courts to impose a penalty that is proportionate to either the conduct (under (b)) or to the financial strength of the company (under (c)) if the value of the infringing conduct cannot be determined. The preference of the agencies is to proceed under (b) in the first instance. However, it is often not possible to calculate with any precision the commercial gain attributable to the infringing conduct. For example, in the context of a cartel, the commercial gain is the overcharge attributable to the cartel, and hence an econometric comparison must be made of actual prices against the likely prices that would have prevailed in the absence of the infringing conduct. That in turn requires the agencies to control for other variables that affect price—such as changes in input costs and the prevailing level of competition in the market absent the cartel.

These are maximum penalties, and hence the appropriate penalty will fall somewhere below these maxima (which are notionally reserved for the most egregious examples of infringing conduct). In assessing the appropriate penalty, a range of factors must be taken into account. These factors are intended to ensure that the penalty imposed is proportionate to the nature and circumstances of the infringing conduct:

1. The nature and extent of the contravening conduct;
2. The amount of loss or damage caused;
3. The circumstances in which the conduct took place;
4. The size of the contravening company;
5. The degree of power it has, as evidenced by its market share and ease of entry into the market;
6. The deliberateness of the contravention and the period over which it extended;
7. Whether the contravention arose out of the conduct of senior management or at a lower level;

8. Whether the company has a corporate culture conducive to compliance with the Act, as evidenced by educational programs and disciplinary or other corrective measures in response to an acknowledged contravention;
9. Whether the company has shown a disposition to cooperate with the authorities responsible for the enforcement of the Act in relation to the contravention.[218]

Whether or not the offender has applied under the NZCC's or ACCC's leniency policy is also relevant to the assessment of penalty. Both agencies offer immunity to the first cartel participant to come forward, and gradated concessions on penalty to subsequent participants who admit the conduct and cooperate with the investigation.[219]

The primary goal of penalties in New Zealand and Australia is to deter similar conduct in the future—both by the instant offender and by other market participants more generally.[220] To that end, the penalty imposed must be at least sufficient to eliminate the commercial gain attributable to the conduct.[221] The court is entitled to impose a separate penalty for each instance of infringing conduct, but subject to the "totality principle." The totality principle states that the overall penalty imposed must be appropriate to the conduct, and that the imposition of penalties for several contraventions must not result in the overall penalty exceeding what is proper having regard to the "totality of the contravening conduct involved."[222]

Penalties are most frequently imposed in cartel cases and, because of the success of leniency programs in Australia and New Zealand, they are usually imposed as part of an agreed settlement procedure rather than at the conclusion of a contested case. Because the responsibility for imposing penalties reposes in the court, the procedure involves the submission of an agreed statement of facts and a joint submission as to the appropriate penalty. The courts have been careful to note that they are not bound to accept the joint submission, but in practice they have seldom strayed from the recommendation of the parties.[223] The attitude of the courts is that:

> ... so long as a negotiated sum is not outside the range within which a court would fix a penalty, there is no good reason why parties should not be at liberty to reach an agreement about what will be submitted to the court. If they were to attempt to go outside the range, the purposes of the law would be in danger of frustration, and it would be incumbent upon

[218] *Trade Practices Commission v CSR* (1991) 13 ATPR 41-076; adopted widely in the Australian and New Zealand jurisprudence.

[219] The agencies' leniency policies are available at: <http://www.accc.gov.au/content/index.phtml/itemId/879795> and <http://www.comcom.govt.nz/cartel-leniency-policy-and-process-guidelines/>.

[220] *Commerce Commission v BP Oil NZ Ltd* [1992] 1 NZLR 377; *Trade Practices Commission v Mobil Oil Australia* (1984) 4 FCR 296; *NW Frozen Foods Pty Ltd v ACCC* (1996) 71 FCR 285.

[221] *Commerce Commission v BP Oil NZ Ltd* [1992] 1 NZLR 377.

[222] *ACCC v Australian Safeway Stores Pty Ltd* (1997) 75 FCR 238.

[223] An exception is *ACCC v NZ Frozen Foods Pty Ltd* (1996) ATPR 41-515 where the court rejected the agreed figure and imposed a higher penalty, holding that the agreed position did not adequately reflect the seriousness of the conduct.

the court to insist upon its function of determining the matter, irrespective of the agreement of the parties.[224]

One result of the prevalence of negotiated settlements, however, is that the development of the legal principles for assessing quantum has arguably stalled. In both New Zealand and Australia the current maximum penalties are relatively recent legislative developments, but there are very few contested cases in which the courts have been required to rule on the principles for assessing quantum. This risks undermining the legitimacy of the penalty regime overall, and also deprives parties to settlement negotiations from recourse to a foundation of court-enunciated quantum principles.

This state of affairs is exacerbated in New Zealand, where it is not yet clear whether contesting the NZCC's position on penalty constitutes non-cooperation within the terms of the leniency policy, thus potentially removing concessions the NZCC would otherwise grant. Hence, parties to cartel proceedings are loath to take a disagreement over penalties to the court. In Australia, the court has held that disagreeing with the ACCC on the magnitude of the appropriate penalty cannot constitute non-cooperation.[225]

8. *Rights of appeal and review*

Recourse to review or appeal varies depending on the nature of the decision that is challenged. As explained earlier,[226] there are two mechanisms for challenging agency decisions:

1. Appeal—rights of appeal from exercises of judicial or quasi-judicial power are granted under statute, either under the competition legislation specifically, or under the legislation governing the superior courts in New Zealand and Australia. The breadth of the right of appeal is set out in the relevant statutory provision and varies from full de novo appeals (in which the court or tribunal is entitled to draw its own conclusions on factual and legal questions, and has a free hand to determine the merits of the issue) through to more restricted appeals (for example, on questions of law only).
2. Judicial review—judicial review is available to challenge administrative decision-making (whether of a judicial/quasi-judicial character or otherwise) in both New Zealand and Australia through the Judicature Amendment Act 1972 and the Administrative Decisions (Judicial Review) Act 1977 respectively. Judicial review is notionally limited to procedural matters, but the extant grounds of judicial review provide some scope to challenge the substance of the regulators' decision. For example, the merits of a decision of an agency can be challenged on the grounds that there is a total lack of

[224] *Trade Practices Commission v TNT Australia Pty Ltd* (1995) ATPR 41-375.
[225] *Trade Practices Commission v Axive* (1994) ATPR 41-368.
[226] *See supra* at pages 74 to 76.

evidence in support of the decision,[227] or that decision is so unreasonable or irrational that no reasonable decision-maker could have made it.[228]

a) Enforcement proceedings

In both New Zealand and Australia, enforcement proceedings take place by way of litigation through the courts of general jurisdiction. Accordingly, all the ordinary appellate rights apply. As a general rule, appeals in the superior courts in New Zealand and Australia are by way of rehearing, and therefore the appellate court is free to substitute its own findings on both the law and the evidence and decide the merits of the case for itself, subject to a margin of appreciation afforded to the first instance decision-maker who has had the opportunity to hear the evidence first hand.

b) Merger decisions

In New Zealand, merger clearance or authorization decisions are appealable to the High Court. As in enforcement proceedings, the appeal proceeds by way of rehearing, entitling the court to inquire into the facts, law, and merits of the NZCC's decision. However, as noted earlier, the Court of Appeal's decision in *Commerce Commission v Woolworths* has limited the scope for the High Court to accept new evidence from the merger parties.[229] Because the NZCC does not provide the parties with a draft decision that fully outlines the economic evidence relied upon, the Court of Appeal's ruling means that the ability of merger parties to challenge the NZCC's expert evidence on appeal is severely restricted.

If the allegation is that the NZCC has erred procedurally rather than in the merits of its decision, then it is also open to the parties to proceed by way of judicial review rather than appeal.

In Australia, rights of appeal or review depend on whether the merger parties have proceeded using the formal merger clearance process in the Competition and Consumer Act, or under the informal process. Under the former, the parties may appeal the ACCC's decision to the Australian Competition Tribunal, which then assesses the merits of the clearance application afresh, or apply to the courts for judicial review if the ACCC has erred procedurally. However, to date no applicants have utilized the formal clearance mechanism. If the parties proceed under the informal process, then their recourse to appeal or judicial review is severely curtailed. There is no scope for either appeal or judicial review because there is no statutory power implicated in the ACCC's decision to informally clear the merger.[230] The only way to access the courts if the parties are dissatisfied with the outcome of the informal process is to indicate to the ACCC their intention to proceed with the transaction notwithstanding the ACCC's adverse decision. The

[227] *Edwards v Bairstow* [1956] AC 14.

[228] Administrative Decisions (Judicial Review) Act 1977 (Cth. Aus.), section 5(2)(g); *Associated Provincial Picture Houses v Wednesbury Corporation* [1948] 1 KB 223.

[229] *Commerce Commission v Woolworths Ltd* [2008] NZCA 276.

[230] *See supra* at pages 75 to 76.

ACCC will then apply to the court for an injunction to block the merger, which provides an avenue for the merger parties to challenge the ACCC's view that the merger will substantially lessen competition.

c) Regulatory determinations

Parties subject to regulatory determinations in Australia can either appeal the determination to the Australian Competition Tribunal (exercising a full merits-based jurisdiction), and then onwards to the federal courts, or they can apply for judicial review of the ACCC's decision in the federal court.

In New Zealand, the availability of appellate rights from regulatory determinations varies significantly. For instance, in relation to the calculation of the telecommunications service obligation under the Telecommunications Act 2001,[231] appeal is limited to a question of law arising from the determination. Where the appeal is limited to a question of law, the parties must rely on one of the following three limited grounds to challenge the substance of the decision:

1. The court applied a wrong legal test;
2. The court failed to take into account relevant matters, or took into account irrelevant matters;
3. The court came to a view unsupported by evidence (or a view to which, on the evidence, it could not reasonably have come).[232]

Alternatively, the parties may apply for judicial review, in which case they must either allege a procedural flaw, or rely on the limited substantive grounds that are available under judicial review—for example, that the decision is so unreasonable that no reasonable decision-maker could have made it. This is a deliberately high threshold for intervention.[233]

The result is that, in relation to a number of regulatory determinations, there is no effective way to challenge the merits of the NZCC's decision, even where there is a clear substantive error in the reasoning or conclusions of the NZCC.

Dissatisfaction with this situation led to a compromise approach when Parts 4 and 4A of the Commerce Act were amended to afford the NZCC new powers to regulate goods and services. Parties affected by the input methodologies the NZCC is required to establish under Part 4 can appeal on the ground that a substitute methodology would be "materially better" in meeting the purposes of the Act than that established by the NZCC. Appeals are presently underway which will determine how the courts will apply the "materially better" threshold for appellate intervention.

[231] Telecommunications Act 2001 (NZ), sections 60, 100.

[232] *Vodafone New Zealand Ltd v Telecom New Zealand Ltd* HC WN CIV-2007-485-826 18 December 2007.

[233] *Associated Provincial Picture Houses v Wednesbury Corporation* [1948] 1 KB 223.

B. Institutional performance norms

1. *Public accountability*

The NZCC and ACCC are subject to a wide range of accountability mechanisms that allow government and the public to monitor their performance and ensure they exercise their powers within the bounds of their empowering statutes. That said, the central design principle of the ACCC and NZCC is independence, and hence these oversight mechanisms do not allow third parties (private or public) to interfere in the agencies' decision-making in individual cases.

a) Tribunals and courts

The most obvious mechanisms for public accountability are the courts and tribunals exercising jurisdiction over the agencies. The roles of the courts and the Australian Competition Tribunal have already been discussed.

b) Parliament and governmental departments

Parliament, and in Australia the Senate Estimates Committee, exercise budgetary oversight over the agencies.

The agencies are also subject to governmental oversight from the Ministry of Economic Development and the Treasury. The agencies are required to produce business plans in consultation with those governmental departments. The agencies are required to publish an annual report, which reports against the objectives outlined in the business plan, as well as commenting in detail on the agencies' activities for the previous year.[234]

c) Ombudsman

The office of the Ombudsman provides an additional avenue for persons aggrieved by the actions or decisions of the agencies to complain.[235] The Ombudsman is an independent officer empowered to investigate complaints that agencies have behaved in a manner that is unjust, unlawful, discriminatory, or unfair. The Ombudsman also has a role in ensuring official information is disclosed in the manner that the law required.

The Ombudsman utilizes an informal process, and can only make recommendations as to corrective measures. The office is intended to provide a straightforward avenue of complaint for individuals who would otherwise lack the resources to complain through more formal mechanisms, and hence the Ombudsman is infrequently involved in NZCC or ACCC matters as the most active participants in those processes are well-resourced companies.

[234] Crown Entities Act 2004 (NZ); Public Service Act 1999 (Cth. Aus.).
[235] Ombudsman Act 1976 (Cth. Aus.); Ombudsmen Act 1975 (NZ).

d) Media

Finally, ACCC and NZCC activities are widely reported on the media. Media attention therefore provides a significant source of accountability for the agencies' activities.

2. Timeliness

The agencies have historically been criticized for a lack of timeliness in discharging their functions. However, the current chairpersons have placed considerable emphasis on improving the performance of their respective agencies in this regard.

a) Enforcement proceedings

Enforcement proceedings are divided into the investigative phase and the litigation phase. The overall time frame for an enforcement proceeding—from initial investigation to final disposition in court proceedings—is extremely protracted. To take just one example, the NZCC initiated a monopolization investigation against Telecom in 1999, which only resulted in a final disposition from the Supreme Court in June 2010. The investigation and subsequent proceedings related to Telecom's method for calculating termination charges applied to rival operators seeking to access its network as part of their provision of dial-up internet services to their customers. By the time the Supreme Court rendered its decision, not only had the business practice at issue long expired, but the industry had moved on entirely from the technology and network infrastructure that had formed the basis of the dispute.[236]

That said, once court proceedings are commenced, the market participants who are the subject of the agency's attention are usually motivated to slow the process down and hence the agencies alone cannot be blamed for the slow progress of the case. Accordingly, the length of the investigative phase is a better test of the agency's performance in enforcement matters.

The only legislative time limit that controls the length of investigations is the need to file court proceedings before statutory limitation periods expire. However, as limitation periods are numbered in the years, this is not a constraint that translates into timely disposition of proceedings. Practitioners interviewed indicated that historically the agencies had tended to maintain some active investigations for years without any apparent progress being made.

Dr Berry and Mr Samuel both confirmed that increasing the timeliness of enforcement proceedings was a key focus of their tenure. To that end, the NZCC has appointed a General Manager of Enforcement whose role is to oversee all active enforcement matters and to ensure that investigations are advanced through to proceedings or otherwise completed. Dr Berry stated his intention, by the end of 2010, to arrive at a position where no active investigation is more

[236] *Commerce Commission v Telecom Corporation of New Zealand Ltd* [2010] NZSC 111.

than twelve months old. Mr Samuel indicated that, while in his view the performance of the ACCC was improving, an added challenge was its disaggregated enforcement network, which made it more difficult to effect changes to the agency's institutional culture.

While there is a still a prevailing sense amongst practitioners that investigations drag on unduly, a recent review of the performance of the agencies tends to confirm that the timeliness of the investigative process is improving (see Table 2.1):

Table 2.1 Duration of investigations

	ACCC			NZCC		
	2008	2010	2011	2008	2010	2011
Average length of dominance investigation	15 months	11.6 months	No info	36 months	19 months	10 months
Average length of cartel investigation	36 months	24.9 months	No info	26 months	10.5 months (cases closed)	5.3 months (cases closed)
					19.5 months (litigation)	10.6 months (litigation)
Longest running investigation	91 months	21 months	17 months	96 months	22 months	No info

Source: Global Competition Review, Rating Enforcement 2008, Rating Enforcement 2010, Rating Enforcement 2011.[237]

b) Mergers

The Commerce Act provides that the NZCC has only ten working days to issue a decision either clearing or declining to clear a merger.[238] However, the parties can agree to extend the deadline and, in practice, they inevitably do so because the alternative is that the NZCC simply refuses to report within the ten working days and the application is deemed to have been declined.[239] Accordingly, the ten working-day deadline in the legislation has long been considered a fiction.

The NZCC's guidelines (see Table 2.2)[240] provide the following indicative timetable which practitioners indicate is generally adhered to:

[237] Available at: <http://www.globalcompetitionreview.com/surveys/>.

[238] Commerce Act 1986 (NZ), section 66(3).

[239] Commerce Act 1986 (NZ), section 66(4).

[240] Commerce Commission, Mergers and Acquisitions Clearance Process Guidelines (July 2008), <http://www.comcom.govt.nz/clearances/>.

Table 2.2 NZCC indicative merger control timetable

Day 1	Application for clearance registered.
Day 10	Commission provides a draft timeline for the assessment of the application for clearance based on likely complexity and resources. Commission seeks an extension based on the draft timeline.
Day 15	Commission publishes a Statement of Preliminary Issues on its website.
Day 25	Commission gives clearance (for straightforward applications) or sends a Letter of Issues.
Day 30	Meeting with applicant and provision of an updated tentative timeline.
Day 40	Commission gives, or declines to give, clearance in less complex applications. For more complex applications, the process continues.
Day 45	Meeting with applicant on Letter of Unresolved Issues and provision of updated tentative timeline.
Day 60 +	Commission gives a final decision.

The Competition and Consumer Act imposes a deadline of forty working days for the ACCC to make a decision under the formal merger review process, with the possibility of the parties agreeing to extend it.[241] As with the NZCC, the ACCC is deemed to have declined if it fails to make a decision within this time frame, and hence parties proceeding under the formal process (and as yet there have been none) are likely to agree to extensions as a matter of course. The ACCC's guidelines on the formal process do not elaborate any further than the statutory test;[242] however, it is reasonable to expect that reviews under the formal process would take somewhat longer than under the informal process due to the additional formal procedural requirements under the Competition and Consumer Act.

No deadlines are imposed on the ACCC under the informal merger review process. When parties apply under the informal process, the ACCC will produce an indicative timetable tailored to the circumstances of that case, which will outline the steps the ACCC plans to take, as well as the likely decision date.[243] In addition, the ACCC's guidelines outline roughly the timetable that parties should expect for cases of various levels of complexity:[244]

Table 2.3 ACCC Informal timetable for merger control

No market inquiries needed	Two to three weeks
One round of market inquiries	Approximately five weeks
Second round of market inquiries needed	Approximately twelve weeks

241 Trade Practices Act (Cth. Aus.), section 95AO.

242 ACCC, Formal Merger Review Process Guidelines (June 2008), <http://www.accc.gov.au>.

243 ACCC, Merger Review Process Guidelines (July 2006), <http://www.accc.gov.au>.

244 Ibid.

Again, practitioners said that the ACCC adhered closely to its indicative timetables. In fact, the ACCC's informal merger review process is widely seen as being a model of efficient decision-making, which in Mr Samuel's view was a contributing factor to the lack of interest in the formal merger review process.

c) Regulatory determinations

The greatest dissatisfaction expressed by practitioners and the chairpersons of the two agencies as regards timeliness was in relation to regulatory determinations. All parties agree that the regulatory regimes are overly complex and as a result extremely protracted, taking years to complete.

In part, the sheer complexity of the regulatory function is to blame for the length of the processes. For example, the annual calculation of the telecommunications service obligation in New Zealand results in a dense econometric report of several hundred pages. However, Dr Berry and Mr Samuel were also of the view that the extensive consultation obligations and requirements to produce multiple drafts at every stage of the process added needless delay to regulatory determinations. Seldom if ever, in their experience, did repeat rounds of consultation produce substantial new information or insight from the submitting parties.

3. *Expertise*

The expertise of both agencies is rated highly by practitioners in Australia and New Zealand. Both agencies are considered relatively prestigious and high-caliber work places, and therefore they do not tend to suffer the same difficulties recruiting staff as other less well-regarded public service agencies. Both agencies have also successfully recruited at an international level, and have therefore been able to import international best-practice to enhance their performance.

The balance of professional qualifications between the two agencies differs somewhat, as Table 2.4 demonstrates. A much higher percentage of the ACCC's staff are lawyers or economists, with the NZCC utilizing a greater proportion of non-legal or economic personnel to carry out its activities. That said, the NZCC's legal and economic expertise is highly regarded notwithstanding its different mix of staff. The NZCC also employs substantially lower proportions of legal and economic personnel than the United States Department of Justice, the UK Office of Fair Trading, and the European Union's Directorate-General of Competition.

The one area where the ACCC and NZCC clearly fall short in comparison to those agencies is in the number of economics PhDs at their disposal: one at the ACCC and none at the NZCC against thirteen at the OFT, thirty-two at DG Comp, and fifty-five at the DOJ.

Table 2.4 Balance of professional staff

	ACCC	NZCC	US DOJ	UK OFT	EU DG Comp
Total staff	819	170	774	556	764
percent lawyers	51 percent	21 percent	87 percent	38 percent	55 percent
percent economists	20 percent	6 percent	13 percent	22 percent	32 percent
Standalone economics unit?	Yes	No	Yes	Yes	Yes
No. of staff with PhDs in economics	1	0	55	13	32

Source: Global Competition Review, Rating Enforcement 2011.[245]

It is perhaps not surprising, therefore, that practitioners indicated that the regulatory function is where the most concerns about expertise have arisen. When the NZCC was first given significant regulatory responsibilities in the early 2000s, it had to quickly reorient itself from a solely *ex post* competition enforcement agency to a mixed *ex post* competition and *ex ante* economic regulatory agency. This resulted in some teething problems while the NZCC developed the internal expertise to accompany its new responsibilities. The general sense amongst practitioners is that the NZCC is now performing at a high level in its regulatory sphere.

Dr Berry stated that, where the NZCC is unable to recruit the required expertise on a permanent basis, it will often contract international experts for specific roles. For instance, the NZCC is currently engaged in a substantial but short-term work program developing input methodologies for its new regulatory functions. The NZCC requested and received additional funding appropriations to allow it to contract international experts to assist in developing those methodologies.

Competition law and economics expertise also varies in the courts. Neither New Zealand nor Australia utilizes specialist divisions of the courts to handle competition matters, and so the expertise of the judge depends on his or her previous practicing or judicial experience in the area (which may be none). That said, in New Zealand High Court judges are assisted by a lay member (usually an expert economist) in competition law proceedings. The federal court in Australia is not entitled to sit with an economist, but the existence of the Australian Competition Tribunal as the first appellate stage in merger and regulatory matters (but not enforcement matters) goes some way towards compensating for the lack of specialist assistance for the federal court bench.

245 <http://www.globalcompetitionreview.com/surveys/>.

4. Sufficiency of investigative and sanctioning powers

The ACCC's and NZCC's investigative powers, and the limits on those powers, are outlined above.[246] Dr Berry and Mr Samuel stated that in their view their agency's investigative powers were sufficient for their purposes, and they did not see a need for additional or enhanced powers.

The maximum penalties in section 76 of the Competition and Consumer Act and section 80 of the Commerce Act were increased to their present level in 2000 and 2001 respectively, reflecting a perceived need for stronger deterrence.[247] Those amendments also introduced the concept of a floating maximum based on commercial gain or turnover. As a result, in the past few years the penalties imposed for breaches of the law, and particularly for hard-core cartel conduct, have increased significantly.

In 2009 criminal penalties of up to ten years' imprisonment were introduced for hard-core cartel conduct in Australia. As yet, no terms of imprisonment have been imposed. In January 2010 the New Zealand Ministry of Economic Development published a discussion document exploring the options for, and desirability of, introducing a criminal regime in New Zealand. In addition, the government has announced its intention to release a draft bill in 2012. Given the tendency for New Zealand policy-makers to follow the lead of Australia in this area, it is likely that criminalization will be a feature of the New Zealand competition law regime within the next five years.

5. Reasonable predictability

a) Procedure

In the regulatory arena, the processes for making determinations are generally set out in legislation, and hence there is a high degree of predictability regarding the process to be followed. Where the legislation is silent as to certain procedural aspects of regulatory determinations, both agencies have generally indicated to interested parties well in advance the approach they tend to take. Enforcement is conducted through the courts, and so here again the relevant legislation dictates the processes that the agencies follow.

In other areas the legislation provides either minimal or no guidance on process. In relation to merger control, in the past the agencies generally followed a similar approach from one case to the next (and this was well understood by practitioners familiar with merger control), but this was more a matter of habit than stated intention. However, since 2006 (in Australia)[248] and 2008 (in New Zealand),[249]

[246] *See supra* at pages 62 to 63.

[247] Gault, *supra* note 37, at paragraph CA 80.01.

[248] ACCC, Formal Merger Review Process Guidelines (June 2008), <http://www.accc.gov.au>; ACCC, Merger Review Process Guidelines (July 2006), <http://www.accc.gov.au>.

[249] Commerce Commission, Mergers and Acquisitions Clearance Process Guidelines (July 2008), <http://www.comcom.govt.nz/clearances/>.

the agencies have published process guidelines that outline the information required for notifications and the processes the agencies will follow in assessing the merger. As a result, merger control procedure, and particularly the timing for decisions, is now reasonably predictable and well understood by the practicing and business community.

Investigations remain highly unpredictable. In part this is a necessary incident of the investigative function as the agencies have a legitimate interest in preserving flexibility in how they approach an investigation, and also a degree of secrecy about the progress of the investigation and its likely direction. However, practitioners in both New Zealand and Australia said they had been dissatisfied in the past with the length and opacity of investigations. Mr Samuel and Dr Berry were aware that their respective agencies had been criticized for the manner in which they conducted investigations in the past and have taken steps to improve the timeliness and transparency of their respective agencies' investigations; for example, establishing a General Manager of Enforcement within the NZCC to ensure investigations progress or are discontinued in a timely manner.

b) Enforcement

The agencies each publish enforcement policies that indicate the circumstances under which they will take enforcement action, as well as the likely form that enforcement action will take.[250] Moreover, both agencies publish guidance on their websites indicating what conduct will be considered a breach of the various competition rules they are charged to enforce. Traditionally, this guidance was of a very superficial nature, but increasingly both agencies (although the ACCC is more advanced on this front) are publishing detailed guidance documents that elaborate on the agencies' interpretation of the law, and thus indicate how the agencies are likely to respond to various forms of conduct.[251] As a consequence, the agencies' attitude towards specific instances of potentially anticompetitive conduct is now much more predictable than it has been in the past—both what the agencies will consider a breach of the law, and the likely enforcement response given the magnitude of the breach and its effects on the market.

One area of enforcement which remains highly unpredictable (perhaps unsurprisingly) is monopolization cases. As with many jurisdictions, both the agencies and the practicing and business communities have expressed dissatisfaction with the state of the law. The Commerce Act and Competition and Consumer Act have been repeatedly amended to attempt to bring clarity to the monopolization offence, with mixed success. In addition, both agencies have pursued litigation strategies that have resulted in a complex and ambiguous jurisprudence which provides little

[250] ACCC, Compliance and Enforcement Policy, <www.accc.gov.au>; NZCC, Enforcement Criteria, <http://www.comcom.govt.nz/enforcement-criteria>.

[251] *See* the ACCC's website at: <http://www.accc.gov.au/content/index.phtml/itemId/816373>; and the NZCC's website at: <http://www.comcom.govt.nz/anti-competitive-practices/>.

predictive value except perhaps to a small minority of highly specialized competition counsel.

The NZCC was until recently engaged in monopolization litigation with Telecom—the former monopolist telecommunications provider—which the NZCC expected would result in a clearer (and more regulator-friendly) precedent. Dr Berry stated that the NZCC, relying on that expectation, had begun work on a guidance document for the monopolization offence which would have outlined the NZCC's interpretation of the law and approach to enforcement. In the event, the Supreme Court's decision in the *0867* case purported to develop the law in the direction the NZCC had hoped, but on closer reading appeared to endorse the test that had previously applied.[252] As a result, the NZCC abandoned work on its guidance and Dr Berry said the NZCC will instead seek legislative change, after which it will publish guidance.

c) Merger control

Merger control—both its procedural and substantive aspects—are highly predictable as a result of the guidance material the agencies have developed. The frequency of merger inquiries (in comparison to, say, monopolization litigation) means that the practicing community and the agencies have a clear and common understanding of the issues that are likely to arise in any given case. One consequence of this, according to practitioners, is that they feel reasonably comfortable self-assessing mergers, which in turn means that parties can limit applications to cases that raise genuinely difficult issues.

d) Regulatory determinations

As discussed above, the procedure for regulatory determinations is highly predictable due to the detailed legislative requirements. The substantive outcome of regulatory determinations is, however, necessarily unpredictable due to the range of variables that must be taken into consideration. However, the agencies go through multiple rounds of draft determinations in most regulatory exercises, and therefore the parties are kept apprised of the agencies' developing thinking on both methodologies and likely outcomes. Hence, the final determination is very seldom a surprise.

6. *Transparency*

Both agencies have a reasonably strong culture of transparency within the limits posed by commercial confidentiality and the need to protect the integrity of ongoing investigations. However, practitioners in both jurisdictions agree that the agencies are more forthcoming about decisions or events that further their regulatory objectives than those that go against them.

[252] *Commerce Commission v Telecom Corporation of New Zealand Ltd* [2010] NZSC 111.

There are a number of mechanisms to promote transparency:

a) Both agencies produce extensive annual reports that outline their financial performance, performance against business plan objectives and activities during the previous year. In addition, the agencies regularly report to Parliamentary select committees and Senate committees, as well as to their respective government departments (the Treasury in Australia and the Ministry of Economic Development in New Zealand). With only a few exceptions, those reports are publicly available.

b) Both agencies publish press releases about significant decisions or events through their websites, including receipt of applications for clearances or authorization, the initiation of investigations, and the commencement of enforcement proceedings. Generally speaking the agencies will also publicize decisions to settle or discontinue proceedings, and often a public statement will be one of the conditions of settlement, though the level of detail of these releases varies. On the other hand, the agencies are less thorough in their coverage of court decisions that go against them, or decisions to close investigations that have not produced sufficient evidence to warrant enforcement proceedings.

c) Both the ACCC and the NZCC publish on their websites registers of merger decisions, authorizations of restrictive trade practices, and regulatory determinations. The ACCC generally only publishes short summaries of their decisions in relation to mergers that have been informally cleared without a statement of issues or undertakings having been given. If a statement of issues is produced, undertakings accepted, or the ACCC declines to clear the merger, then it will usually publish the full text of the decision, subject to withholding commercially/competitively sensitive information. The NZCC publishes the full text of all decisions, whether the merger/trade practice is cleared or not, but again subject to withholding commercially/competitive sensitive information. Both agencies publish the full text of authorizations of restrictive trade practices and regulatory determinations.

d) The ACCC and NZCC are subject to freedom of official information legislation, which obliges the agencies to publish information within their possession and relating to their functions, subject to a variety of exceptions.[253] Disclosure of official information can be required by any member of the public by written request to the agency. If the obligation to disclose is disputed, then the Australian Information Commissioner (Australia) and the Ombudsman (New Zealand) have jurisdiction to determine whether the information ought to be disclosed.

e) The agencies publish a great deal of general information on their websites, including discussion documents, speeches, working papers and articles, competition advocacy materials, consumer-oriented brochures, and court judgments of interest. The websites are regularly updated.

[253] Freedom of Information Act 1982 (Cth. Aus.); Official Information Act 1982 (NZ).

7. Public consultation and participation

The public are afforded a number of opportunities for consultation and participation:

a) Legislation: the legislative process affords multiple opportunities for the public to comment on draft bills amending the competition legislation. In addition, the government departments responsible for competition policy will frequently issue discussion documents at the outset of the policy-development process (that is, well in advance of draft legislation) to seek a broad range of views on the proposed policy options.[254]

b) Agency guidelines: both agencies periodically update their guidelines and produce new guidelines on emerging issues. During that process they will usually publish draft versions of the guidelines for public comment.

c) Mergers: with the exception of occasional confidential merger reviews, the details of merger inquiries are published on the agencies' websites for interested parties to comment on. As the inquiry develops, the agencies will progressively make available statements of issues, working papers, draft undertakings, and so on.

d) Regulatory exercises: in addition to making draft determinations publicly available, the agencies also actively seek consultation opportunities on working papers and input methodologies that define the agencies' approaches to various common regulatory tools. For example, the NZCC has for some years been working on a methodology for calculating cost of capital, with the intention that the NZCC will then use the same methodology in all exercises in the future. Multiple rounds of drafts and discussion documents have been issued for public comment, and the views of experts and key regulatory stakeholders have been actively sought out.

e) Enforcement: enforcement is conducted using a private litigation model, and therefore the public is not invited to participate in the agencies' enforcement processes. However, court processes in New Zealand and Australia generally occur in the public domain, and genuinely interested parties can apply to the court to intervene or join the proceedings.

V. Critical evaluation

A. Influences

New Zealand and Australia strongly influence each other's competition regimes as a result of their close economic, political, and cultural ties; although in practical terms

[254] *See*, for example, Ministry of Economic Development, Cartel Criminalisation: Discussion Document (January 2010), <http://www.med.govt.nz/templates/MultipageDocumentTOC_42186.aspx>.

New Zealand is more often than not the junior partner in the relationship. The special relationship between the two countries is given an institutional form through the Closer Economic Relations framework. CER mandates harmonization of competition law policy and competition law institutions, and provides the institutional structure for politicians and officials to engage on policy development and identify opportunities to reconcile regulatory processes and eliminate duplication. The results of CER are evident in the similar institutional structure and substantive competition law and policy of the two regimes. In the future, the pace of CER harmonization is expected to accelerate through the Single Economic Market initiative. Officials in both governments are already looking for opportunities to eliminate regulatory duplication through enhanced mutual recognition regimes or the establishment of joint agencies with equivalent jurisdiction in both countries. While the NZCC and ACCC have not been publicly announced as candidates for such coordination, the current high level of harmonization would make them an obvious choice.

More generally, Australia and New Zealand are both strongly outward looking countries and champions of multilateralism. Accordingly, both countries look to developments overseas as part of the process of formulating new policy. The European Union, the United States, and the United Kingdom are influential sources, but both countries borrow liberally from a wide variety of different competition regimes. The result is a unique blend that is neither wholly European nor American in its policy and institutions, but draws extensively on both. In turn, New Zealand and Australia influence (or attempt to influence, at any rate) the development of competition law in the Asia Pacific region. As export-led economies, their primary foreign policy objective is to open up the markets of their trading partners. Recognizing that competition law facilitates access to foreign markets, both New Zealand and Australia advocate the implementation of competition law as part of their trade negotiations.

New Zealand and Australia also draw extensively on international expertise. Both the agencies and the practicing community regularly utilize overseas experts, particularly economists from the major international consultancies. Indeed, a brief review of trial judgments in New Zealand and Australia reads as a "Who's who" of internationally recognized competition economists. In fact, the influence of overseas economists has sometimes been so pervasive that it has resulted in a policy backlash. For example, the efficient component pricing rule developed by Professors Baumol and Willig became so firmly entrenched in New Zealand's monopolization jurisprudence that the government expressly outlawed it in the Telecommunications Act 2001 as a means of calculating wholesale prices for Telecom's unbundled network services.[255]

[255] *See* clause 2, Schedule 1 to the Telecommunications Act 2001 (NZ): "(1) To avoid doubt, the Baumol-Willig rule does not apply in respect of any applicable initial pricing principle or any applicable final pricing principle that provides for a forward-looking cost-based pricing method as a possible pricing principle. (2) For the purposes of subclause (1), the Baumol-Willig rule means the pricing rule known as the Baumol-Willig rule as referred to in *Telecom Corporation of New Zealand Ltd v Clear Communications Ltd* (1994) 6 TCLR 138, PC."

Finally, the trend in the New Zealand and Australia since the late 1980s/early 1990s has been in favor of regulation rather than deregulation. In fact, in New Zealand the trend has been one of *re*-regulation after the rapid and extensive deregulatory push of the fourth Labour government of the mid to late 1980s. Hence, the ACCC and NZCC have steadily acquired more powers and responsibilities, and where they have been unable to achieve their competition policy objectives through litigation, they have generally achieved legislative change either amending the competition provisions of their respective Acts, or introducing new *ex ante* regulatory powers.

B. Design choices and performance

The foregoing discussion of procedural characteristics demonstrates that the NZCC and ACCC are sophisticated agencies that generally perform at a high level across a broad range of due process and institutional performance norms. This overall impression was confirmed by practitioners interviewed during the preparation of this chapter. Both agencies demonstrate a high degree of awareness of due process norms, and practitioners tend to be satisfied with the agencies' performance as a whole. To the extent that practitioners have raised issues about due process or agency performance, they have stressed that those issues are at the margins.

That said, both regimes demonstrate two very pronounced design choices: independence over accountability, and due process over administrative efficiency. The ACCC and NZCC are afforded a high degree of independence from political oversight and the commissioners have an essentially unfettered latitude to set the agency's priorities and determine the agency's direction within the overarching statutory framework. On the other hand, this high degree of independence is attended by extensive due process obligations, particularly in relation to consultation on decision-making. The result is that the decision-making process—particularly in relation to regulatory determinations—is frequently extremely protracted.

These design trade-offs are reflected in the one significant complaint raised by most practitioners: the duration and cost of regulatory determinations and investigations. In relation to regulatory determinations, it is clear that the Australian and New Zealand legislatures have consciously traded timeliness and efficiency in favor of due process rights for interested parties. The legislation mandates multiple rounds of drafts and consultations, giving interested parties a number of opportunities to engage with the agencies, but at great cost and delay. In addition, because of the difficulty of challenging the merits of agency determinations under the judicial review jurisprudence in New Zealand and Australia, the litigation strategy for aggrieved parties hinges on complaints about procedure. Accordingly, the agencies' best protection against challenge is to ensure that the process is unimpeachable from a due process perspective, which further exacerbates delay. The irony is that both the chairpersons of the agencies and practitioners indicated that the status quo was unsatisfactory, suggesting that, if the scope for procedural challenge could be reined in, regulatory processes could be streamlined to the overall benefit of both the agencies and regulated businesses.

Cost and delay in relation to investigations is at least in part a function of the latitude afforded the agencies in the manner in which they conduct investigations, and the lack of scrutiny of the investigative process. The view of practitioners was that the agencies were insufficiently aware (and/or uncaring) of the level of cost they imposed on business through investigative orders, and that the agencies did not do enough to advance or close investigations. There is no reason in principle why this should be so, and the chairpersons of the agencies have acknowledged as much through their efforts to promote timeliness in investigations and ensure that they do not degenerate into elongated fishing expeditions. However, it is important that the agencies be afforded a degree of latitude in their investigative functions to ensure that anticompetitive practices are brought to light.

Both the ACCC and the NZCC have enjoyed strong and effective leadership through the tenures of the past several chairpersons, which has led to an increasingly sophisticated approach to decision-making. A good example of this is the increasing reliance on detailed guidelines (which are a key element of European competition policy) to spell out the agency's approach to common competition/regulatory issues like the estimation of cost of capital, the criteria for failing firms, and the identification and assessment of efficiencies in merger control processes. Given the relative paucity of competition litigation as a means of explicating competition policy, guidelines provide much needed clarity for practitioners and businesses and facilitate the implementation of new economic concepts.

The clarity that results from the use of guidelines has benefits for the performance of the agencies. As the practicing community has come to understand the agencies' thinking better, there has been increased scope for self-assessment of mergers and business practices, and hence less need for the agencies to be involved in more straightforward matters. Where the agencies do become involved, the engagement between practitioners and agency staff is more likely to focus quickly on the key issues and points of evidence. The result is that the agencies' resources are deployed more effectively.

Finally, the ACCC's performance in the criminal arena has yet to be tested, and most practitioners agreed that there will almost certainly be a round of procedural litigation as the first criminal cartel prosecutions commence. However, given the recent experiences of the UK's Office of Fair Trading, the ACCC is alive to the challenge it faces, and through careful preparation has given itself the best possible chance of a smooth transition to criminal enforcement. While New Zealand has not yet criminalized cartels, it is likely only a matter of time, and hence the NZCC will also have to confront the procedural difficulties of parallel civil and criminal enforcement regimes.

3

Canada
The Competition Law System and the Country's Norms

*Edward Iacobucci and Michael J. Trebilcock**

I. History

A. The early history of Canadian competition law

The powerful influence of institutions on substantive competition law and policy is clearly demonstrated by the Canadian example. The history of competition policy in Canada began in the late 19th century when the dominance of railway companies, the rise of department stores, and mail-order houses, and the emergence of unprecedented firm size in areas such as meat packing, agricultural machinery, and flour milling began to change the face of business in both the US and in Canada.[1] By the late 1880s in Canada, examples of abuses of economic power—typically in the form of industry-wide combines—were found in the watch, retail grocery, coal-dealing, and other businesses, leading to widespread public criticism.[2] These abuses provided the impetus for regulation, and in 1889 the *Anti-Combines Act* was enacted, the first post-industrial revolution antitrust law in the world.[3] The *Anti-Combines Act* imposed prohibitions of a criminal law nature on conspiracies and in 1910 extended them to include monopolies and mergers. The associated criminal law burden of proof on the Crown, along with the highly nebulous nature of the prohibitions in the case of mergers and monopolies where the Crown was required to prove that they were operating or were likely to operate to the public detriment, meant that

* We are grateful to Emma Costante for invaluable research assistance and to interviewees identified herein for their time and thoughtful insights.

[1] Alfred D. Chandler, *The Visible Hand: The managerial revolution in American business* (Cambridge, MA: Belknap Press of Harvard University Press, 1977).

[2] Jamie Benedickson, "The Combines Problem in Canadian Legal Thought 1867–1920" (1993) 43 U. Toronto L.J. 799 at 820.

[3] Michael J. Trebilcock, "The Supreme Court and Strengthening the Conditions for Effective Competition in the Canadian Economy" (2001) The Canadian Bar Review: Commemorative Edition on the 125th Anniversary of the Supreme Court of Canada 542 at 586.

in the early years of Canadian competition law enforcement efforts were sporadic at best.[4]

Recognizing the limitations of a criminal law approach to potentially anti-competitive practices, the federal government introduced the *Board of Commerce Act* and the *Combines and Fair Prices Act* in 1919 that contemplated a more regulatory or administrative approach to competition issues. However, two years later, the Privy Council found both these acts to be *ultra vires* the federal government because they infringed on the provinces' exclusive domain over property and civil rights.[5] The implication of this decision was that the constitutional validity of federal competition law would henceforth have to rest solely on the federal government's criminal law powers.[6] Reinforcing this position in 1935, the Supreme Court of Canada struck down the *Dominion Trade and Industry Commission Act* which established a commission to administer the *Combines Investigation Act*. Following the Privy Council's earlier decision, the court held that the Act exceeded the legislative authority of Parliament.[7]

The implications of these constitutional holdings for the evolution of Canadian competition policy were little short of disastrous. While a steady trickle of price-fixing conspiracies were successfully prosecuted under the criminal conspiracy provisions of the *Combines Investigation Act*, only a tiny handful of prosecutions were brought with respect to mergers and monopolization and almost all failed.[8]

Throughout the 1960s and 1970s a series of court decisions further limited the efficacy of the Act culminating in the Supreme Court of Canada's decision in *K.C. Irving Limited*.[9] In *K.C. Irving* the court ruled that even where an entire industry was controlled by one firm as a result of mergers this did not necessarily imply an unlawful combine. Detriment to the public was essential for a conviction and the court held that this could not be presumed even when one firm controlled an industry completely.[10]

B. The reform process and recent history of Canadian competition law

By the mid-1960s, the trend of court decisions on competition issues coupled with the fact that only one monopoly and no mergers had ever been found to be detrimental to the public interest resulted in the government's acknowledgement that reform was needed. To this end, the government commissioned the Economic Council of Canada (ECC) to study and recommend changes to the Act—a process

[4] Ibid.

[5] *Re Board of Commerce Act and Combines and Fair Prices Act of 1919* (1920), 60 S.C.R. 456.

[6] Trebilcock, "Conditions for Effective Competition," *supra* note 3 at 586.

[7] *Reference re Dominion Trade and Industry Commission Act, 1935,* [1936] S.C.R. 379.

[8] Trebilcock, "Conditions for Effective Competition" *supra* note 3 at 587.

[9] Michael Trebilcock, Ralph Winter, Paul Collins and Edward Iacobucci, *The Law and Economics of Canadian Competition Policy* (University of Toronto Press, 2003) at 16–17.

[10] *R. v. K.C. Irving Ltd.*, [1978] 1 S.C.R. 408.

which would eventually culminate in the 1976 and 1986 amendments and establish competition policy in Canada as we know it today.[11]

In 1969, the ECC released its recommendations for competition law in Canada, proposing that collusive arrangements to fix prices, allocate markets, or prevent entry, as well as resale price maintenance and misleading advertising, all be subject to criminal sanctions. The ECC also recommended that mergers and monopolies as well as business practices such as refusal to deal, exclusive dealing, and tying arrangements become matters for review by a civil tribunal.[12] The acknowledgement that the criminal law was not an effective method of regulating complex economic activity was the catalyst for the two-track criminal and civil model that now prevails in Canada.

In 1971, the government proposed dramatic revisions to the *Combines Investigation Act* in response to the ECC's recommendations. However, the amendments were promptly withdrawn due to pressures from the business community which believed that the new bill would be burdensome and intrusive.[13] In the light of these criticisms, the government decided to split the bill into two stages. The first contained the less controversial aspects of the ECC report including the extension of competition policy into services, the creation of bid rigging as a per se offence, as well as the inclusion of a number of reviewable practices such as refusal to deal, consignment selling, exclusive dealing, tied selling, and market restrictions, to be civilly reviewable by the Restrictive Trade Practices Commission. These amendments, passed in 1975, also permitted private rights of action for violations of the criminal provisions of the Act. The constitutionality of the private rights of action provisions was challenged in *General Motors Canada v. City National Leasing* et al. The Supreme Court of Canada ruled that the private right of action did not impinge on the rights of the provinces given that the provision was part of an integrated scheme of economic regulation and fell within the federal government's general trade and commerce power.[14]

From 1977 to 1986, efforts were made to address the problematic regulation of monopolies and mergers as well as the ECC's recommendation to establish a tribunal consisting of non-judicial experts to review civil cases.[15] Accordingly, in 1986 the *Competition Act* replaced the *Combines Investigation Act*.[16] The *Competition Act* continued to treat agreements which unduly lessened competition, resale price maintenance, bid rigging, price discrimination, promotional allowances, and predatory pricing, as criminal offences tried in the regular court system as they had been under the *Combines Investigation Act*. It further classified abuse of dominant

[11] Bruce Dunlop, David McQueen, and Michael Trebilcock, *Canadian Competition Policy: A Legal and Economic Analysis* (Toronto: Canada Law Book Inc., 1987) at 50.

[12] Economic Council of Canada, Interim Report on Competition Policy (Queen's Printer, 1969).

[13] W.T. Stanbury, *Business Interests and the Reform of Canadian Competition Law* (Methuen Press, 1977) at 45.

[14] *General Motors of Canada v. City National Leasing* et al. (1989), 58 D.L.R. (4th) 255 [*City National Leasing*].

[15] Ian Clark, "Legislative Reform and the Policy Process: The Case of the Competition Act" in Khemani and Stanbury, eds, Historical Perspectives at 232.

[16] The Competition Act, R.S.C. 1985, c.19.

position, mergers which substantially lessened competition, registration of specialization agreements, refusal to deal, consignment selling, tied selling, exclusive dealing, exclusive territories, and delivered pricing as civilly reviewable procedures to be adjudicated by the newly constituted Competition Tribunal.[17]

The *Competition Act* has since been subject to minor amendments by Parliament in 1992, 1999, 2000, 2002, and most recently in 2009. However, the basic structure has remained as it was in 1986.

II. Structure

A. Institutional arrangements

The institutional framework of Canada's current competition policy is embodied in the federal *Competition Act* and the federal *Competition Tribunal Act*, both enacted in 1986. All potential violations of the *Competition Act* (the Act) are investigated by the Competition Bureau, and enforcement action may entail referral to the Attorney-General for criminal prosecutions in the ordinary courts or application by the Bureau for civil review to the Competition Tribunal. In this sense, the adjudication of competition laws in Canada is effectuated through a two-track system.

1. The Commissioner of Competition and the Competition Bureau

The Competition Bureau is headed by the Commissioner of Competition, appointed by the Governor in Council of Canada (the Governor General acting on the advice of the federal Cabinet). It is the Commissioner's responsibility to investigate any conduct that may be contrary to the Act. Any six persons who are residents of Canada over the age of eighteen with reason to believe that the Act has been contravened may apply to the Commissioner of Competition to initiate an inquiry. The Commissioner may also begin an inquiry if she is instructed to do so by the Minister of Industry or if she has any reason to believe that the Act has been contravened.[18] Any investigation undertaken by the Competition Bureau can be terminated if it is found that the matter does not justify further inquiry. The decision to discontinue must be reported to the Minister or, if the inquiry was started by six residents, to them. If the inquiry was requested by six citizens or the Minister, the Minister may instruct the Commissioner to make further inquiry even after reasons for termination are given.[19] Once an inquiry is completed and an assessment has been made, the Commissioner will conclude whether there is a likely contravention of the Act. Where the Commissioner concludes such a contravention is likely, she brings the matter either to the Competition Tribunal for the adjudication of civil matters or she refers it to the Attorney General for

[17] The Competition Tribunal Act, R.S.C. 1985, c.19, s.1.
[18] The Competition Act § 9–10. [19] *Id.* § 22.

prosecution in the provincial superior courts of criminal jurisdiction for criminal matters.[20]

2. *The Competition Tribunal and the bifurcated agency model*

Civilly reviewable practices follow a bifurcated agency model where one agency, the Competition Bureau, carries out investigations and another, the Competition Tribunal, undertakes adjudication. The Tribunal is a hybrid body, comprised of both judges and expert lay members. Only judicial members may determine matters of law, while both judicial and lay members may adjudicate issues of mixed law and fact or fact alone.[21] The Tribunal is chaired by a judicial member as are the three member panels in individual cases.[22] It is supported by the Registry of the Competition Tribunal, which provides administrative support to the Tribunal for the hearing and disposition of all applications.[23] The Competition Tribunal, similar to the superior courts, has the power to examine witnesses, enforce its orders, make rules, award costs, and issue a variety of prohibitions and remedial orders.[24] Breach of a Tribunal order is punishable either by contempt proceedings before a judicial member of the Tribunal or by prosecution in the courts by summary conviction or indictment. Decisions by the Tribunal may be appealed to the Federal Court of Appeal as of right for questions of law or mixed law and fact, and with leave for questions of fact alone. Decisions of the Federal Court of Appeal can be appealed with leave to the Supreme Court of Canada.[25]

Since its establishment in 1986, the Competition Tribunal has adjudicated only six contested merger cases, and only two since 2006.[26] This has resulted in 99 percent or more of merger cases being resolved in the Bureau either through approval, modification, monitoring, undertakings, or abandonment.[27] The abuse of dominant position provisions of the Act have only been contested before, and adjudicated by, the Tribunal on five occasions since 1986.[28] In 2008, the Tribunal held fourteen proceedings, only seven of which were contested. Of those, two were deceptive marketing cases,

[20] Brian A. Facey and Dany H. Assaf, *Competition and Antitrust Law: Canada and the United States,* (3rd edn 2006) at 31.

[21] The Competition Tribunal Act § 12.

[22] Competition Tribunal, "Tribunal Members," December 2008. <http://www.ct-tc.gc.ca/Tribunal/Members-eng.asp>.

[23] Competition Tribunal, "Registry Staff," December 2008. <http://www.ct-tc.gc.ca/Registry-Greffe/RegistryStaff-eng.asp>.

[24] The Competition Tribunal Act § 8(2), 16, (8.1), 9(5).

[25] *Id.* § 13.

[26] *Canada (Director of Investigation and Research) v. Hillsdown Holdings (Canada) Ltd.* (1992), 41 C.P.R. (3d) 289 (Comp. Trib.) [*Hillsdown*]; *Canada (Director of Investigation and Research) v. Southam Inc.* (1992), 4 C.P.R. (3d) 261 (Comp. Trib.); *Canada (Commissioner of Competition) v. Superior Propane Inc.* (2000), 7 C.P.R. (4th) 385 (Comp. Trib.); *Canada (Commissioner of Competition) v. Canadian Waste Services Holdings Inc. et al.* (2001), 11 C.P.R. (4th) 425 (Comp. Trib.); *Canada (Commissioner of Competition) v. Labatt Brewing Co.* [2007] C.C.T.D. No. 5 (Comp. Trib.); *The Commissioner of Competition v. CCS Corporation et al.*, 2012 Comp. Trib. 14.

[27] Michael J. Trebilcock and Edward M. Iacobucci, "Designing Competition Law Institutions" (2002) 25:3 World Competition 361 at 374.

[28] Trebilcock et al., *The Law and Economics of Canadian Competition Policy, supra* note 9 at 24–5; *Canada (Commissioner of Competition) v. Canada Pipe Co.*2006, D.L.R. (4th) 193 FCA.

leaving only five contested competition cases, all of which dealt with leave applications by private parties under the refusal to deal or exclusive dealing provisions and only one of which was granted.[29]

3. The Courts and the bifurcated judicial model

Once the Competition Bureau has found that there has been a likely contravention of the criminal provisions of the Act, the Commissioner must refer the case to the federal Attorney General for prosecution. Cases are then brought to a provincial superior court of criminal jurisdiction.[30] The decision to lay charges ultimately rests with the Attorney General, but in practice the Attorney General generally follows the recommendations made by the Commissioner either to prosecute or to grant immunity to parties due to their cooperation in the detection or investigation of criminal offences.[31] Since investigations are undertaken by an independent agency and criminal matters are adjudicated through the courts, this regime can be described as a bifurcated judicial model.

The potential consequences of violating a criminal provision of the Act range from fines to imprisonment. Maximum fines for criminal conspiracies have been increased from C$10million to $25 million and maximum terms of imprisonment have been increased from five to fourteen years in the most recent amendments to the Act in 2009.[32]

As with other criminal offences in Canada, questions of law can be appealed as of right from the provincial superior courts to the respective provincial courts of appeal either by the accused or the prosecution. Questions of fact or mixed fact and law may be appealed with leave to the provincial Court of Appeal if initiated by the accused.[33] Most cases can then be appealed to the Supreme Court of Canada with leave. For convictions resulting in imprisonment over one year (indictable offences) an appeal as of right lies if one of the judges on the Court of Appeal dissented on a question of law or if a court of appeal reversed an acquittal.[34]

4. Private actions

Canadian competition laws provide only a limited scope for private actions unlike the US with its strong history of private action promoted by treble damages,

[29] Calvin S. Goldman and Navin Joneja, "The Institutional Design of Canadian Competition Law: The Evolving Role of the Commissioner" (Spring 2010) 41:3 Loyola University Chicago Law Journal 535 at 548.

[30] The Competition Act § 23.

[31] Goldman and Joneja, *supra* note 29 at 543.

[32] Davies Ward Phillips & Vineberg, "Amendments to the Competition Act: What do they mean for you?" (2009). <http://www.dwpv.com/en/17620_23426.aspx>.

[33] Nora Rock and Valarie Hoag, *Foundations of Criminal and Civil Law in Canada* (Toronto: Edmond Montgomery Publishers, 2006) at 116.

[34] Supreme Court of Canada, "Filing an Application for Leave to Appeal: Frequently Asked Questions" (June 2009). <http://www.scc-csc.gc.ca/faq/ala-daa/index-eng.asp>.

contingency fees, one-way cost rules, and liberal class-action procedures. In 1976, the right to private actions was enacted in section 36 of what is now the *Competition Act*. This section allows private actors who have suffered loss or damage as a result of the violation of a criminal provision of the *Competition Act*, or due to a party's failure to comply with an order of the Tribunal or of a court, to sue for an amount equal to the loss or damage proved to have been suffered, together with any additional amount the court may allow not exceeding the full cost of any investigation in connection with the matter.[35] Between the Supreme Court's 1989 decision in *City National Leasing* and 1996, there was only one reported case on section 36. More recently however, private enforcement of criminal competition law has increased significantly through more liberal class action procedures enacted by most provinces.[36] Since 2004, twenty-four class actions for criminal competition matters have been filed in Canada.[37]

Prior to 2002, there were no private rights of action for conduct contrary to the civilly reviewable provisions of the Act. Amendments to the *Competition Act* in that year created section 103.1 which established a limited right of private access to the Tribunal for remedial orders (although not damages) with respect to refusal to deal, exclusive dealing, tied selling, and market restrictions. Price maintenance was added to this list with the most recent amendments in 2009.[38] To pursue a private action based on sections 75, 76, or 77, applicants require leave of the Tribunal and they must also submit an application for leave to the Commissioner. The Tribunal may choose whether or not to hear the case only after obtaining the Commissioner's certification that there is no ongoing inquiry into the matter and that there has been no prior inquiry which was discontinued due to settlement. If the Commissioner's certification is received and the Tribunal chooses to accept the case, and providing that the applicant has adequate standing as being directly affected by the alleged offending practice, then the case may proceed and the applicant may attempt to obtain remedial orders. Since 2002 there have been nineteen applications for leave brought to the Tribunal, five of which were granted and one that was withdrawn.[39]

In addition to statutory rights, private parties may also have recourse to common law actions such as the torts of conspiracy, inducing breach of contract, and unlawful interference with economic relations.[40] Beyond sections 36 and 103.1 of the Act only the Competition Bureau has the power to investigate violations and determine whether a case should be brought.[41]

[35] The Competition Act § 36.

[36] K. Roach and M. Trebilcock, "Private Enforcement of Competition Laws" (1996) 4:3 Osgoode Hall Law Journal 461 at 470.

[37] Data supplied by Charles River International (CRI), Toronto office, July 28, 2010.

[38] The Competition Act § 103.1.

[39] CRI, *supra* note 37.

[40] Facey and Assaf, *supra* note 20 at 484–5.

[41] Goldman and Joneja, *supra* note 29 at 545.

B. Central substantive provisions

The central substantive provisions of the *Competition Act* are outlined in parts VI through VIII of the Act and cover a wide variety of horizontal and vertical anti-competitive practices.

1. Horizontal practices

Historically, all horizontal practices were addressed through the criminal provisions of the Act. Prior to 2010, section 45 of the *Competition Act* provided that all agreements which unduly lessened competition or unreasonably enhanced the price of a product were subject to criminal sanctions.[42] However, since the 2009 amendments, Canada now takes a "two-track" approach to the enforcement of agreements and arrangements between competitors.[43]

Agreements and arrangements are now set out in section 90.1 as civilly reviewable practices. Existing or proposed agreements or arrangements between two or more competitors which prevent or lessen or which are likely to prevent or lessen competition substantially may be subject to a remedial order by the Tribunal on application by the Commissioner. There is no possibility of fines or private damages.[44] There are exceptions to this provision where the agreement or arrangement creates efficiency gains which offset the competitive losses, where the companies are affiliates, where the agreement relates only to the export of goods from Canada, or where a federal Minister has certified the agreement with the Commissioner. There are also exceptions for a range of agreements between federal financial institutions including loans made outside of Canada, exchange of statistics and research, restrictions on advertising, and the underwriting of securities.[45]

Hard-core cartels that fix prices, allocate sales, territories, customers, and markets, or fix production or supply are subject to criminal sanctions which render them per se illegal.[46] These strict criminal laws are partially balanced by a new defense which places the burden on the accused to prove, on a balance of probabilities, that the agreement in question is ancillary to a broader or separate principal agreement which includes the same parties and is "reasonably necessary" for the implementation of the principal agreement.[47] As is the case for civil sanctions on agreements and arrangements, the criminal provision contains exceptions for export cartels as well as certain agreements between federal financial institutions.[48]

Bid rigging is another horizontal practice which, like hard-core cartels, is a per se criminal offence. Unless the person calling for bids is notified of the agreement in

[42] Trebilcock et al., *The Law and Economics of Canadian Competition Policy, supra* note 9 at 29.
[43] Goldman and Joneja, *supra* note 29 at 544.
[44] The Competition Act § 90.1.
[45] *Id.* § 90.1(4), (7), (8), (9).
[46] Davies Ward Phillips & Vineberg, *supra* note 32.
[47] Ibid.
[48] The Competition Act §45, 49.

advance, any agreement knowingly entered into between bidders who are not affiliates before the submission of bids is a criminal offence.[49]

2. *Abuse of dominance and restrictive practices*

The 1986 Act replaced the criminal offence of monopolization with civil review of abuse of a dominant position.[50] To violate these provisions, a defendant must control wholly or substantially a class or species of business and be shown to have engaged in anticompetitive practices the effect of which must be to substantially lessen competition in the market. If these conditions are met, the Tribunal can order remedial measures that are reasonable and necessary to overcome the effects of the practice. As a result of the recent 2009 amendments, the Tribunal can also impose Administrative Monetary Penalties (AMPs) of up to C$10 million dollars (C$15 million dollars for repeat offenders) in addition to the other remedies.[51] The Act outlines eight practices considered abuses of a dominant position in a non-exhaustive list. The practices include squeezing by a vertically integrated supplier, vertical integration with the intent to eliminate competition, freight equalization for the purposes of preventing entry, use of "fighting brands," purchasing products to prevent price erosion, and selling articles at a price lower than acquisition cost for the purposes of disciplining or eliminating a competitor.[52] It also contains an exception for acts engaged in pursuant to copyright, trademark, or patent laws.[53]

Other vertical practices are set out in sections 75 to 77, and are civilly reviewable and not subject to AMPs. Refusal to deal is reviewable where a person is substantially affected in his or her business due to an inability to obtain adequate supplies resulting from insufficient competition, where that person is willing and able to meet usual trade terms, and where the product is in ample supply (s.75).[54] Price maintenance occurs when by agreement, threat, promise, or any like means, a person influences upward or discourages the reduction of the price at which his customer offers to sell or advertise a product within Canada (s.76). A refusal to supply a product to, or otherwise discriminate against, any person engaged in business in Canada because of that person's low pricing policy may amount to a form of price maintenance.[55]

Section 77 deals with three related practices. Firstly, exclusive dealing occurs when a major supplier induces a downstream provider to deal only with them and the practice impedes entry or expansion of a firm or product or has some other exclusionary effect in the market. An exception permits the practice if it is engaged in for a reasonable period of time only to facilitate entry of a new supplier or new product into a market.[56] Secondly, market restrictions involve arrangements between a major upstream seller and its downstream dealer which allocate customers

[49] *Id.* § 47. [50] *Id.* § 79.
[51] Goldman and Joneja, *supra* note 29 at 558.
[52] The Competition Act § 78.
[53] *Id.* § 79. [54] *Id.* § 75.
[55] *Id.* § 76. [56] *Id.* § 77.

by class or geographic area so that a downstream dealer may sell a product only in a defined market as a condition of the supply of that product. As is the case with exclusive dealing, there is an exception if the practice is carried on for a reasonable time only in order to facilitate entry of a new supplier or a new product into the market.[57] Lastly, tied-selling arrangements exist where a major supplier only sells a product (the "tying good") on the condition that a buyer purchases a second product (the "tied good"), or offers inducements for a buyer to buy two products from the same firm.[58]

Proceedings based on sections 75, 76, and 77 may be initiated before the Tribunal by the Commissioner as of right or by a private party with leave and if they are found to have had an adverse effect on competition, the Competition Tribunal may make an order prohibiting a person from continuing to engage in the practice.[59]

3. *Mergers*

While many mergers are not detrimental to competition, some mergers may increase the propensity to collude or potentially lead to abuses of dominance. Instead of waiting for one of these prohibited practices to occur, Canada, like many other jurisdictions, has chosen to adopt pre-emptive policies.

Pre-merger notification procedures apply where the combined size of the parties and their respective affiliates as well as the size of the business being acquired are above a certain threshold. In such cases, the completion of the transaction must be delayed an initial thirty days followed by a possible demand for information. Amendments in 2009 altered this process so that the demand for information is now made at the Commissioner's discretion through the issuance of a more detailed Supplementary Information Request (SIR). Parties are not permitted to close a transaction until thirty days after compliance with an SIR, and the Commissioner retains the ability to seek an injunction to prevent closing. In addition, the Tribunal has the power to extend the review period beyond that time up to an additional sixty days if the Bureau requires more time to investigate due to circumstances beyond the control of the Commissioner.[60]

If, on application by the Commissioner, the Tribunal finds that any proposed merger lessens or is likely to prevent or lessen competition substantially, it can prohibit the merger or order divestiture or dissolution.[61] However, this is subject to an efficiency defense in section 96 of the Act which provides that even when competition is substantially lessened, if the efficiencies likely to be realized by the merger more than offset the losses which would be brought about by the decreased competition, the Tribunal may not prohibit the merger.[62] Furthermore, joint ventures are not subject to these provisions if two firms have agreed to undertake

[57] *Id.* [58] *Id.* [59] *Id.* § 75–77, 81.
[60] Goldman and Joneja, *supra* note 29 at 543, 555; The Competition Act § 100(7).
[61] The Competition Act § 92.
[62] *Id.* § 96.

a specific project or program which would not otherwise occur and if competition is not lessened to a greater degree than is necessitated by the joint venture.[63] There is also an exemption to these provisions for mergers certified to the Commissioner by the Minister of Finance in the case of bank mergers or the Minister of Transport for transactions that involve a transportation undertaking related to section 53.2(7) of the *Canada Transportation Act*.[64]

III. Mandate

A. Objectives of the Competition Act

The objectives of Canadian competition policy are found in s.1.1 of the Competition Act which reads:

> 1.1 The purpose of this Act is to maintain and encourage competition in Canada in order to promote the efficiency and adaptability of the Canadian economy, in order to expand opportunities for Canadian participation in world markets while at the same time recognizing the role of foreign competition in Canada, in order to ensure that small and medium-sized enterprises have an equitable opportunity to participate in the Canadian economy, and in order to provide consumers with competitive prices and product choices.[65]

The objectives outlined above are ambiguous and potentially conflicting. For example, encouraging small businesses to participate in the Canadian economy is not always economically efficient.[66] These ambiguities are likely the residue of an ambivalent history in which various competing economic and social ideologies vied for dominance in Canada.[67]

Until the turn of the millennium the fundamental goal of contemporary Canadian competition policy was widely thought to be economic efficiency.[68] Perhaps reflecting such an emphasis, Canada's competition policy has been touted as the most economically literate competition law in the world.[69] Since then, the claim that efficiency is the most important goal of competition has become contestable. Case law, especially *Canada (Commissioner of Competition) v. Superior Propane Inc.*, has emphasized distributive objectives of competition policy, and this has led to questions regarding the priority of economic efficiency in Canadian competition policy.[70] In this case, the Tribunal found that the merger substantially lessened

[63] *Id.* § 95. [64] *Id.* § 94. [65] *Id.* § 1.1.

[66] Michael Trebilcock, "The Great Efficiencies Debate in Canadian Merger Policy" (2004) 10:4 New Zealand Business Law Quarterly 298.

[67] Michael Trebilcock et al., *The Law and Economics of Canadian Competition Policy, supra* note 9 at 31.

[68] William T. Stanbury, "Competition Policy in Canada: Evolution, Effectiveness and the Changing Context of Competition" (October 1997) Policy Options. <http://www.irpp.org/po/archive/oct97/stanbury.pdf>.

[69] Trebilcock, "The Great Efficiencies Debate" *supra* note 66.

[70] Ibid.; *Canada (Commissioner of Competition) v. Superior Propane Inc.* (C.A.), 2003 FCA 53, [2003] 3 F.C. 529 [*Superior final appeal*].

competition and created a dead-weight loss of $3 million per annum. However, Superior Propane raised the section 96 efficiency defense, which allows mergers where the efficiencies are greater than and offset the anticompetitive effects of those mergers. Superior Propane argued that under the Total Surplus standard efficiencies of roughly $30 million per annum were realized by the transaction, outweighing the anticompetitive effects of the merger. The Total Surplus standard, which was adopted by the Competition Bureau in its Merger Enforcement Guidelines in 1991, allows mergers where they increase the sum of consumer and producer surplus.[71] The Tribunal applied this standard in its initial decision in the *Superior Propane* case and would have allowed the merger; the $40 million per annum wealth transfer from consumers to producers was considered neutral and disregarded in applying the efficiencies defense.[72]

The Commissioner appealed this decision to the Federal Court of Appeal, arguing that the efficiencies defense should be reformulated so as to put greater weight on consumer than producer surplus by assigning a negative value to the wealth transfer from consumers to producers. The Federal Court of Appeal endorsed a Balancing Weights approach and remitted the case to the Tribunal. Under the Balancing Weights approach, the Tribunal is required to exercise its discretion to determine how negative the wealth transfer should be viewed in the particular circumstances of the merger in question.[73] If, for example, consumers of the product in question are relatively poor, there would be greater reason for the Tribunal to treat the transfer as a factor against allowing the merger. In the redetermination of *Superior Propane* by the Tribunal, it found that even under a Balancing Weights approach the merger should be allowed. The Competition Bureau argued that a Consumer Surplus approach to efficiency should be taken which would allow the merger to proceed only if the gains in efficiency outweighed the loss in consumer surplus. This argument was rejected by the Tribunal and its position was affirmed by the Federal Court of Appeal.[74] The Balancing Weights approach has since become the standard for evaluating efficiency under section 96.[75]

B. International application of Canadian competition law[76]

In a small, open economy like Canada's, it would be plainly incomplete to think of competition law and policy as involving only domestic interests. Canadian compe-

[71] *Commissioner of Competition v Superior Propane Inc.* (2000), 7 CPR (4th) 385 (Comp Trib) [*Superior initial decision*]; Competition Bureau, Merger Enforcement Guidelines (Government of Canada, 1991). <http://strategis.ic.gc.ca/pics/ct/meg_executive.pdf>.

[72] *Superior initial decision, supra* note 71.

[73] *The Commissioner of Competition v Superior Propane Inc* (2001), 11 CPR (4th) 289 (FCA).

[74] *The Commissioner of Competition v Superior Propane Inc.* (2002), 18 CPR (4th) 417 (Comp Trib); *Superior final appeal, supra* note 70.

[75] Competition Bureau, Merger Enforcement Guidelines, (Government of Canada, September 2004).

[76] This section was largely drawn from Edward Iacobucci, "The International Reach of Canadian Competition Law" in Andrew Guzman, ed., *Cooperation Comity and Competition.*

tition law also has some important international implications. Several provisions in the *Competition Act*, including the purpose clause, section 1.1, that make reference to Canadian markets, are concerned with preserving competition in Canada. It thus appears that, while no cases have been litigated expressly on the matter, Canadian competition laws assume jurisdiction over foreign conduct that has an impact on Canadian markets. However, even where Canada does have jurisdiction, it may decline to assume jurisdiction on the grounds of international comity, which includes specific comity provisions in bilateral competition agreements that Canada has entered into with many of its trading partners. Canada's most important trade relationship is with the United States. The two countries have many bilateral agreements including a comity agreement on competition which was signed in 1995, and the Mutual Legal Assistance Treaty of 1990 which facilitates cooperation in criminal investigations including criminal competition investigations.[77] Canada also has bilateral competition agreements with the European Union, Mexico, Australia, New Zealand, Costa Rica, Chile, Japan, and the UK.

C. Explicit exceptions

Certain activities are explicitly excluded from the Competition Act. Combinations or activities of workmen or employees for their own reasonable protection are exempt. Also exempt are contracts, agreements or arrangements among fishermen or associations of fishermen.[78] Contracts, agreements, or arrangements between or among two or more employers in a trade, industry, or profession where collective bargaining with employees in respect of salary or wages and terms and conditions of employment is involved are also exempt. There is a limitation on the collective bargaining exception where an employer contracts to withhold any product from any person or to refrain from acquiring from any person any product other than the services of workmen or employees, in which case the Act applies.[79]

The conspiracy provisions of the Act do not apply in respect of an agreement or arrangement between underwriters, defined as people who ordinarily engage in the business of dealing in securities, or in the case of arrangements between underwriters and the issuer or vendor of a specific security.[80] Also, the Act does not apply in respect of agreements or arrangements between or among teams, clubs, and leagues pertaining to participation in amateur sport which is defined as sport where the participants receive no remuneration for their services as participants.[81]

D. The interface between regulation and Canadian competition policy

Regulation plays an important role in sectors ranging from network industries like telecommunications and transportation to health care. National competition laws

[77] Competition Bureau, Speaking Notes for Konrad von Finckenstein, Q.C., Director of Investigation and Research, August 1998. <http://www.competitionbureau.gc.ca/eic/site/cb-bc.nsf/eng/00907.html>.
[78] The Competition Act, § 4.
[79] *Id.* [80] *Id.*, § 5. [81] *Id.*, § 6.

cannot be interpreted as overriding or displacing all these forms of regulation, but must take all or most of them as given. Thus, regulation places a number of limitations on the scope of Canadian competition law.

1. The Regulated Conduct Defence (RCD)

Where regulatory regimes and competition policy conflict, the RCD has evolved through case law to provide implicit exceptions to the Competition Act. This evolution began with a series of agricultural marketing board decisions such as *Cherry v. The King ex rel. Wood* in which the Saskatchewan Court of Appeal in 1938 declared that acts of a regulatory board either specifically legislated or ancillary to provincial regulatory schemes are exempt from Canadian competition laws as they are by definition in the public interest.[82] Later cases including *R. v. Independent Order of Foresters,*[83] *Waterloo Law Association v. Canada (Attorney General),*[84] and *Garland v. Consumers Gas Co.*[85] held that individuals who are part of regulated industries are not necessarily immune from the application of competition policy. They are only exempt insofar as there is a direction or authorization to perform the prohibited act.[86] Thus, in *Waterloo Law Assn.*, a group of lawyers were not excused from voluntarily agreeing to fix prices for their services in violation of the Competition Act simply because the legal profession is regulated in certain respects in Ontario.[87]

The RCD, as currently interpreted, exempts conduct from competition scrutiny where: (1) a legislature has conferred regulatory power on a commission or board or other authority; (2) the conduct in question falls within the scope of the legislation and is ordered or authorized by the legislation; (3) the regulatory power has been exercised; and (4) the impugned conduct has not hindered or prevented the regulatory body from effectively exercising its powers.[88]

Although the application of this defense was fairly straightforward in both *Cherry* and *Waterloo Law Assn.* discussed above, it is less clear in cases which fall between these extremes.[89] In *Jabour*, for example, the Law Society of British Columbia argued that its decision to ban certain forms of advertising was not in violation of the *Combines Investigation Act* (*CIA*) because the society was established under the *Legal Professions Act* (*LPA*). The *LPA* gave the law society wide-ranging powers to

[82] *Cherry v. The King ex rel. Wood,* [1938] 1 D.L.R. at 144 [*Cherry*]. This holding was upheld under the 1986 Competition Act by *Industrial Milk Producers Assn v. British Columbia (Milk Board)* (1988), 47 D.L.R. (4th) 710, 21 C.P.R. (3d) 33, [1989] 1 F.C. 463 (T.D.).

[83] *R. v. Independent Order of Foresters* (1998), 26 C.P.R. (3d) 229, 32 O.A.C. 278 (C.A.) [*Foresters*].

[84] *Waterloo Law Association v. Canada (Attorney General)* (1986), 58 O.R. (2d) 27, 35 D.L.R. (4th) 751 (H.C.J.) [*Waterloo Law Assn.*].

[85] *Garland v. Consumer Gas Co.*, [2004] 1 S.C.R. 629, 237 D.L.R. (4th) 385 [*Garland*].

[86] Ibid.; *Foresters, supra* note 83; *Waterloo Law Assn., supra* note 84.

[87] *Waterloo Law Assn., supra* note 84.

[88] Michael Trebilcock and Edward Iacobucci, "Appendix D-4: The Design of Regulatory Institutions for the Canadian Telecommunications Sector" in *Bell Canada's Submission to the Telecommunications Policy Review Panel* at para. 43.

[89] Michael Trebilcock, "Regulated Conduct and the Competition Act" (2005) 41 Canadian Business Law Journal 492 at 495.

decide if conduct was "unbecoming a lawyer," whereas the *CIA* arguably prohibited collective advertising bans. The Supreme Court of Canada deferred to the provincial regulation, holding that the advertising ban was *intra vires* the provincial government.[90]

Recently, the Competition Bureau has released a Technical Bulletin indicating its willingness to test the boundaries of the RCD.[91] In the bulletin, the Bureau acknowledges that there is a lack of clarity surrounding the defense and expresses the hope that case law will help to clarify the RCD in the near future. If no cases are brought forward, the Bureau is open to potentially exploring a legislative resolution of the issue.[92]

2. *Regulation and forbearance*

Regulation has been pervasive in Canada since the birth of the nation. In recent years, however, there has been a trend towards deregulation propelled in part by technological changes that have undermined economies of scale in many regulated industries. This has been characterized by a move from command-based regulation and natural monopoly models towards increased market governance monitored by competition policy.[93] An example of this type of transitional industry in Canada is telecommunications, where the Canadian Radio-television and Telecommunications Commission (CRTC) has forborne from regulation in both the long-distance and wireless sectors on the grounds that they are effectively competitive, but continues to regulate local telephone services in some areas.[94]

Where a regulator forbears completely, competition policy regains its jurisdiction over the sector. The Competition Bureau recognizes that the success of regulatory forbearance will depend, in part, upon the effectiveness of competition law as a deterrent to potentially anticompetitive behavior.[95] One potential issue with complete forbearance and to a greater extent conditional forbearance is a lack of oversight. Where a regulator decides to forbear in certain aspects of an industry but competition authorities are prevented by the RCD from monitoring the transition in the light of the residual or contingent regulatory authority vested in the industry-specific regulator, a regulatory lacuna may arise.[96] The Competition Bureau seeks

[90] *Canada (Attorney General) v. Law Society of British Columbia,* [1982] 2 S.C.R. 307, 137 D.L.R. (3d) 1, 66 C.P.R. (2d) 1.

[91] Mark Katz and Charles Tingley, "The 'Regulated Conduct Defence' in Canada" (2006) 11:2 Competition Law 730 at 734. <http://www.dwpv.com/images/Competition_Law_Article_-_Regulated_Conduct_-_Vol_11_No_2_-_May_2007.pdf#page=1&zoom=100>.

[92] Competition Bureau, Draft Technical Bulletin on "Regulated" Conduct, (2009). <http://www.competitionbureau.gc.ca/eic/site/cb-bc.nsf/eng/01993.html>.

[93] Margaret Sanderson and Michael Trebilcock, "Merger Review in Regulated Industries" (September 2005) 42:2 The Canadian Business Law Journal 157 at 157.

[94] Edward Iacobucci, Michael Trebilcock, and Ralph A. Winter, "The Canadian Experience with Deregulation" (2006) 56 U Toronto L.J. 1 at 10.

[95] André Lafond, "Evolution of the Regulatory Process 'The Impact of Deregulation' for the Competition Bureau", March 2010. <http://www.competitionbureau.gc.ca/eic/site/cb-bc.nsf/eng/00902.html>.

[96] Trebilcock et al., *The Law and Economics of Canadian Competition, supra* note 9 at 706.

to minimize this problem through cooperation and coordination with regulators throughout the process of deregulation.[97]

3. *Regulators implementing competition policy*

Where regulators do not forbear, they are responsible for monitoring the sector to ensure that participants are acting in the public interest. Regulators play an important role in ensuring that prices are not excessive, as this cannot always be effectively dealt with by competition policy.[98] However, regulators have also sought to maintain jurisdiction over certain matters which are best understood as competition policy matters. For example, the CRTC attempted to regulate Voice Over Internet Protocol (VOIP) citing the potential for predatory pricing as the rationale for its intervention.[99] This raises at least two issues. Firstly, many economists see predatory pricing as a rare phenomenon: it is "rarely tried and even more rarely successful."[100] Secondly, the CRTC's position on predatory pricing was out of step with economic thinking given that the conditions that would make predatory pricing rational (a dominant position in the market with high barriers to entry) did not exist in the VOIP market. In the end, Cabinet stepped in to overrule the CRTC's decision to impose regulation.[101]

Regulators such as the CRTC have also scrutinized price discrimination practices. For example, the CRTC has disallowed incumbent telephone service providers from targeting low prices to customers who recently switched carriers. Again, the CRTC is out of step with conventional thinking on this issue given that the consensus among economists is that price discrimination is mostly benign; indeed, price discrimination was recently removed from the Competition Act as a specific offence or reviewable practice.[102] Targeted pricing is likely to result in lower prices, and can be interpreted as symptomatic of increased competition in the market. The federal Cabinet ordered the CRTC to cease imposing blanket restrictions on promotions including such "win-backs" in April 2007.[103]

[97] Lafond, *supra* note 95.

[98] Edward Iacobucci and Michael Trebilcock, "The Design of Regulatory Institutions for the Canadian Telecommunications Sector" (June 2007) 33:2 CANADIAN PUBLIC POLICY 127 at 131.

[99] Ibid. at 134–5.

[100] *Matsushita Electric Industrial Co., Ltd.* et al.*v. Zenith Radio Corp* et al. 1986. 475 US 574.

[101] Canadian Radio-television and Telecommunications Commission, "Regulatory Framework for Voice Communication Services Using Internet Protocol" (2005) Telecom Decision CRTC 2005–28. Available at <http://www.crtc.gc.ca/archive/ENG/Decisions/2005/dt2005-28.htm>; Government of Canada, "Order Issuing a Direction to the CRTC on Implementing the Canadian Telecommunications Policy Objectives" (2006a) Part II 140:26 CANADA GAZETTE. SOR/2006-355. <http://canadagazette.gc.ca/partII/2006/20061227/html/sor355-e.html>.

[102] Iacobucci and Trebilcock, "The Design of Regulatory Institutions for the Canadian Telecommunications Sector," *supra* note 98 at 136; The Competition Act § 75–81.

[103] Telecommunications Policy Review Panel, Telecommunications Policy Review Panel Final Report 2006. Ottawa: Public Works and Government Services Canada; Government of Canada, "Order Requiring the CRTC to Report to the Governor in Council on Consumer Complaints." PC 2007-533, 4 April. <http://canadagazette.gc.ca/partI/2007/20070526/html/decret-e.html>.

4. Duplication and uncertainty: mergers

As industries evolve through the deregulation process and the boundaries between competition policy and regulation shift, problems of concurrent jurisdiction can arise just as easily as an absence of effective oversight.[104] Overlapping jurisdiction is problematic because it leads to unnecessary duplication as well as overly strict regulation.[105] One example of such duplication is merger review.

In regulated sectors such as telecommunications, airlines, railways, banking, and electrical utilities, there is (to varying extents) duplication in the merger review processes between industry-specific regulators and the Competition Bureau.[106] Although regulators and the Bureau typically have different foci in their reviews, the processes can be duplicative and less commonly but more seriously, conflicting. This creates confusion and uncertainty within the industry which can lead to a chilling effect on efficient mergers.[107] In the case of conflicting regulation, overlap can also induce a lack of confidence in the law.

The Competition Bureau, in conjunction with various sector regulators, has taken some steps to resolve the issue of overlap. In industries such as banking and airlines, the Bureau and sector regulators have come to an arrangement to govern the merger review process. The Bureau provides the regulators with a report on the competitive aspects of the merger. The regulators then consider whether the proposed merger should be allowed within their broader public interest mandate.[108] In other sectors, the Bureau and regulators have come to different arrangements in order to minimize overlap. Despite these efforts there is still potential for conflicts although to date the instances of direct conflicts have remained few. Issues which remain unresolved require further policy development.[109]

IV. Procedural characteristics

A. Due process norms in case-by-case decision-making

1. The Competition Bureau

The Commissioner of Competition has the power to decide which sections of the *Competition Act* should be the subject of an inquiry, the overall scope of an inquiry, what enforcement proceedings should occur as a result of a civil inquiry, and to an increasing extent, the terms of resolution.[110] All inquiries must be conducted in

[104] Trebilcock et al. *The Law and Economics of Canadian Competition Policy, supra* note 9 at 706.

[105] Iacobucci and Trebilcock, "The Design of Regulatory Institutions for the Canadian Telecommunications Sector," *supra* note 98 at 137.

[106] Sanderson and Trebilcock, "Merger Review in Regulated Industries," *supra* note 93.

[107] Ibid. at 190.

[108] Ibid. at 174, 178.

[109] For potential options on policy strategies, *see* Sanderson and Trebilcock, ibid.

[110] Goldman and Joneja, *supra* note 29 at 540.

private, without notice to the public.[111] The Commissioner shall inform a person subject to inquiry under the Act as to the progress of the inquiry only at that person's request and otherwise she has no duty to inform the subject that an inquiry is taking place.[112] During an investigation, the Commissioner may apply to a judge for an order to have a person attend and be examined on oath or solemn affirmation if he has or is likely to have information relevant to the inquiry. Such persons may also be requested to produce a record or certified true copy of a document to the Commissioner, or make and deliver a written oath.[113] Any person examined pursuant to such an order and any person whose conduct is being inquired into has the right to representation by counsel.[114] In most circumstances the target of an investigation is entitled to attend examinations which form a part of the inquiry against them unless their presence would be prejudicial to the effective conduct of the examination or result in the disclosure of confidential commercial information.[115]

If a judge finds that there are reasonable grounds to believe that a person has contravened the Act and there are reasonable grounds to believe that there is on any premises any record or other thing that will afford evidence with respect to the alleged infringement, the judge may issue a warrant authorizing the Commissioner or any other person named in the warrant to enter the premises, subject to such conditions as may be specified in the warrant. They may search the premises for any such record or other thing and copy it or seize it for examination or copying.[116] It is the duty of the Bureau to reasonably preserve and return all items seized in search within sixty days after they were produced unless the person agrees to further detention or a judge authorizes further detention.[117]

The Bureau's powers of search and seizure are wide relative to other investigatory bodies in Canada and some critics believe them to be excessive and potentially unconstitutional given the search and seizure provisions of the *Canadian Charter of Rights and Freedoms*.[118] Others believe that such expansive powers are necessary in order to investigate effectively anticompetitive acts such as price fixing, an activity which is covert, making evidence difficult to uncover.[119]

Until recently, the vast majority of ex parte applications under section 11 for production of documents were approved by the Federal Court of Canada without

[111] The Competition Act, § 10(3).

[112] *Id.* § 10(2); Competition Bureau, "Remarks of Harry Chandler Deputy Director of Investigation and Research (Criminal Matters)" in *Criminal Investigations: Process and Procedure* The Canadian Bar Association Competition Law Annual Fall Conference, Ottawa, Ontario, September 1998. <http://www.competitionbureau.gc.ca/eic/site/cb-bc.nsf/eng/00912.html>.

[113] The Competition Act § 11.

[114] *Id.* § 12(3).

[115] *Id.* § 12(4).

[116] *Id.* § 15.

[117] *Id.* § 18.

[118] James D. Sutton, "Investigations Under the Competition Act: Recent Issues" in *Competition Law and Competitive Business Practices* (The Canadian Institute, 1996) at 21.

[119] Neil Finkelstein, "Competition Tribunal and the Constitutionality of Certain Investigative Procedures under the New Competition Act" (February 1987) 7:4 ADVOCATES' QUARTERLY 459 at 466–8.

question. However, in 2008 in *Canada v. Labatt Brewing*,[120] the Federal Court adopted a different approach to the powers of the Bureau. While investigating a proposed merger between Labatt and Lakeport breweries, the Commissioner obtained orders through ex parte applications for the production of documents which resulted in the delivery of a significant amount of information to the Bureau. In February of 2007, Labatt alone produced nearly 140,000 pages. Nine months later, the Commissioner obtained additional orders which were promptly challenged by Labatt and Moosehead. The challengers argued that the requested documents represented a substantial duplication with prior orders sought by the Commissioner and, moreover, that much of the additional information and documentation requested was not relevant in the circumstances. Justice McTavish agreed and chastised the Commissioner, describing the applications for orders being sought by the Commissioner as inadequate, inaccurate and misleading. Justice McTavish stated that she had not been informed of the substantial amount of documentation which had previously been requested and obtained by the Commissioner and that there was a substantial amount of overlap and duplication in the items requested.[121] This ruling prompted the Competition Bureau to initiate an internal review procedure in which all proposed section 11 applications are first approved by a three-member review committee composed of the Assistant Deputy Commissioner responsible for the case, a Senior Counsel, and the Special Economic Advisor to the Commissioner. The Bureau and the Department of Justice also commissioned a review of s.11 of the *Competition Act* by Brian Gover of Stockwoods Barristers. In his review, Gover found that many of the criticisms regarding the Bureau's s.11 powers were directed to the existence of s.11 rather than its application. Mr Gover concluded that the existence of s.11 was necessary in order to effectively administer and enforce the Competition Act and made several recommendations to enhance the efficacy of s.11 applications and reduce the burden on respondents. He recommended that the Bureau continue their internal review process, that s.11 orders be made in person by counsel as opposed to in written form, and that the Bureau engage in dialogue with respondents both pre-application and post-service where possible. In his recommendations, Gover also noted that courts, in assessing applications for s.11 orders, should resist the urge to read in requirements not present in the Act which requires only that a s.10 investigation has commenced and that a person has or is likely to have information relevant to the inquiry.[122]

If the Bureau finds there has been a likely contravention of the Act then an application may be made to the Competition Tribunal for civilly reviewable matters and to the Attorney General for prosecution in the provincial courts of criminal jurisdiction for criminal matters. This two-track system results in an

[120] *Canada (Commissioner of Competition) v. Labatt Brewing Co. Ltd.*, 2008 FC 59, [2008] 2 F.C.R. D-6 [*Labatt*].

[121] Ibid.

[122] Brian Gover, *Report on s.11 of the Competition Act*, August 2008. <http://www.competitionbureau.gc.ca/eic/site/cb-bc.nsf/eng/02709.html>.

asymmetry in the right to challenge decisions made by the Bureau. Parties may always challenge a Bureau determination that conduct is anticompetitive either in the court or the Tribunal but, given limited private rights of action, if the Bureau determines that a matter such as a merger is not problematic from a competition perspective, private parties have no right to challenge that determination.[123]

2. *The provincial courts and criminal competition sanctions*

The prosecution of alleged violations of the criminal sanctions of the *Competition Act* is undertaken by the Attorney General of Canada.[124] Those accused of criminal acts under Canadian competition laws are generally granted the same procedural fairness rights as other criminal accuseds including the right to be informed of the specific offence without unreasonable delay, the right to a trial within a reasonable time, the right to be considered innocent until guilt is proved by the Crown beyond a reasonable doubt, and the right to a fair and public hearing before an independent and impartial tribunal.[125] Under the *Competition Act* an accused individual has a right to elect to be tried by jury, except where the provisions of the *Criminal Code* require a trial by judge without jury. However, corporations only have the right to trial by judge alone.[126] The independence and impartiality of the Canadian court system as well as its ability to provide equality before the law is well accepted. There have been no expressions of concern about external influence or direction in the application of the law to particular parties.[127]

Punishments for criminal convictions under the *Competition Act* can range from fines to imprisonment. Violations of the criminal provisions of the *Competition Act* can result in a maximum fine of C$25 million and a maximum term of imprisonment of fourteen years and there is no specified minimum.[128] The appeal process, as in other criminal proceedings, allows questions of law to be appealed by either the accused or the prosecution to the respective provincial court of appeal by right. Questions of fact, or mixed fact and law may be appealed with leave to the provincial Court of Appeal if initiated by the accused.[129] Most cases may then be appealed to the Supreme Court of Canada with leave. Convictions resulting in imprisonment over one year may be appealed to the Supreme Court of Canada as of right if one of the judges on the Court of Appeal dissents on a question of law or if a court of appeal reverses an acquittal.[130]

[123] The Competition Act § 10, 22. [124] *Id.*, § 23.

[125] *The Canadian Charter of Rights and Freedoms,* Part I of the *Constitution Act, 1982* being Schedule B to the *Canada Act 1982* (UK), 1982, c.11 § 11.

[126] The Competition Act § 67.

[127] Fabien Gélinas, "Judicial Independence in Canada: A critical overview" forthcoming in *Judicial Independence in Transition—Strengthening the Rule of Law in the SCE Region,* Anja Seibert-Fohr, ed., Max Planck Institut Series "Beitraege zum auslaendischen oeffentilichen Recht und Voelkerrecht" (Heidelberg: Springer, 2010).

[128] The Competition Act, §45(2), 47(2).

[129] Rock and Hoag, *supra* note 33 at 116.

[130] Supreme Court of Canada, "Filing an Application for Leave to Appeal: Frequently Asked Questions," *supra* note 34.

3. The Competition Tribunal

The Competition Tribunal has its own procedures separate and distinct from those of the provincial courts. With respect to attendance, the swearing in and examination of witnesses, the production and inspection of documents, the enforcement of its orders, and other matters necessary or proper for the due exercise of its jurisdiction, it has all such powers, rights, and privileges as are vested in a superior court of record.[131] However, the Tribunal also has the power to make its own set of rules, subject to the approval of the Governor in Council and provided those rules are not inconsistent with the *Competition Act* or the *Competition Tribunal Act.*[132]

The Tribunal may create rules in order to regulate its own practice and procedure, for carrying out the work of the Tribunal, as well as for the management of its internal affairs and the duties of its officers and employees.[133] The Tribunal has adopted detailed rules for the filing of applications, intervention, admissions, discovery, access to documents, pre-hearing disclosure, evidence at the hearing, and witness panels akin to those of Canadian courts.[134] Furthermore, the procedural rules of the Tribunal may be supplemented by the Federal Court Rules where they are incomplete.[135] It is important to note that these rules are not binding on the Tribunal. In fact, section 9(2) of the *Competition Tribunal Act* states that "these rules may be dispensed with, varied or supplemented in order to deal with all matters as expeditiously and informally as the circumstances and considerations of fairness permit."[136]

Tribunal hearings are open to the public except when a person requests an *in camera* hearing for commercially sensitive evidence. *In camera* hearings will be granted if the Tribunal finds that direct harm would result from conducting the hearing or a portion of the hearing in public.[137]

The remedial powers of the Tribunal are quite broad and include the ability to order such actions as are reasonable and necessary to overcome the effects of anticompetitive practices.[138] The Tribunal may dissolve mergers or order divestitures and, as a result of the 2009 amendments, impose Administrative Monetary Penalties of up to $10 million on corporations for violations of the abuse of dominance provisions.[139]

Decisions of the Tribunal may be appealed to the Federal Court of Appeal.[140] However, this process is constrained by the doctrine of deference, which requires deference by appellate courts to specialized administrative tribunals.[141] Deference does not apply equally across all tribunals or tribunal decisions, and the subject

[131] The Competition Tribunal Act § 8. [132] *Id.* § 16(1).
[133] *Id.* [134] *Id.* § 6–30, 36–80. [135] *Id.* § 34.
[136] *Id.* § 9(2). [137] *Id.* § 29, 30. [138] *Id.*, § 79(2).
[139] Goldman and Joneja, *supra* note 29 at 542.
[140] Gélinas, *supra* note 127.
[141] Donald B. Houston and Jeanne L. Pratt, "The Marginalization of the Competition Tribunal" for the *CBA National Competition Law Conference* (Gatineau, QC: Fraser Milner Casgrain LLP, 2005). <http://www.fmc-law.com/upload/en/publications/20052006/3074814_Marginalization_of_the_Comp_Tribunal_D_Houston.pdf>.

matter of the decision will be relevant to the level of deference.[142] In 1997 a unanimous Supreme Court decision in the case of *Canada v. Southam Inc.* concluded that curial deference was owed to the Tribunal as an expert body on a question of mixed law and fact.[143] In *Superior Propane,* in contrast, the Federal Court of Appeal concluded that no deference was owed the tribunal on a pure question of law involving the interpretation of a statute, in part on the basis that such questions are to be decided exclusively by judges on the Tribunal. Whether or not increased levels of deference towards the decisions of the Competition Tribunal even on pure questions of law are appropriate is a matter of debate in Canada.[144]

B. Institutional performance norms

1. Dyadic values in institutional decision-making

The normative criteria or values for evaluating competition law institutions are likely to be relatively uncontroversial. However, each value implies an obverse value and indeed interactions with other values, thus rendering the weighting of, or trade-offs among, values a quintessential polycentric and highly contestable exercise. The key dyadic values are listed below.[145]

a) Independence—accountability

On the one hand, competition law institutions should be free from day-to-day political interference. Independence serves to depoliticize enforcement decisions, reduce the risk of perceived bias, and provide consistency from one political administration to the next.[146] On the other hand, at least in a representative democracy, it is difficult to defend institutional independence without some form of accountability; for example, with respect to appointments, budgetary allocations, financial expenditures, periodic mandate, and performance review.

b) Expertise—detachment

Competition law matters typically require high levels of expertise in their resolution—expertise with respect to particular industries, expertise in marshalling and interpreting empirical data, and expertise in industrial organization theory. How-

[142] Neil Campbell, Hudson N. Janisch, and Michael Trebilcock, "Rethinking the Role of the Competition Tribunal" (1997) 76:3 The Canadian Bar Review 298 at 316.

[143] *Canada (Director of Investigation and Research) v. Southam,* [1995] 3 F.C. 557 (F.C.A.), rev'd (1997), 209 N.R. 20 (S.C.C.); *Dunsmuir v. New Brunswick,* [2008] 1 S.C.R. 190, 2008 SCC 9; note that a 2008 ruling by the Supreme Court of Canada on *Dunsmuir* has overruled the categories for deference laid out in *Southam* but not the level of deference which *Southam* dictated should be granted to the Competition Tribunal by appellate courts.

[144] Campbell, Janisch, and Trebilcock, "Rethinking the Role of the Competition Tribunal," *supra* note 142 at 328.

[145] The identification and explanation of dyadic values is largely drawn from a previous paper, Michael Trebilcock and Edward Iacobucci "Designing Competition Law Institutions" (Spring 2010) 41:3 Loyola University Chicago Law Journal 455 at 457–9.

[146] Competition Bureau, Options for the Internationalization of Competition Policy (August 2009), <http://www.competitionbureau.gc.ca/eic/site/cb-bc.nsf/eng/01646.html>.

ever, too close an involvement in the industry in question or excessively doctrinaire commitments to particular theoretical paradigms may compromise detachment in evaluating or adjudicating novel arrangements or evolving economic or theoretical environments.

c) Transparency—confidentiality

In order to enhance the public credibility of competition laws, high levels of transparency in performing investigative, enforcement, and adjudicative functions are desirable. However, much of the information that a competition law agency is required to evaluate from the immediate parties involved and from competitors, suppliers, and customers is commercially highly sensitive; and public disclosure may be seriously damaging to legitimate business interests. The ideal degree of transparency therefore varies depending on the type of decision being made. For example, formal adjudications are normally on-the-record public proceedings whereas many interim or procedural matters may be determined in a much less open manner.[147]

d) Administrative efficiency—due process

Competing concerns also exist between administrative efficiency and due process protections. Many matters with which a competition law agency may be seized are time-sensitive (for example, merger review). However, timeliness in disposition is in tension with the value of due process in providing all affected or interested parties a right to be heard, to adduce evidence, and to contest the position of parties adverse in interest.

e) Predictability—flexibility

In a legal system based on the rule of law, significant value is placed on the predictability and consistency with which laws are applied. In such a legal system, affected parties can order their affairs with a fairly high level of confidence in the nature of the rules that govern those affairs. But the value of predictability is in tension with the obverse value of flexibility where the evolution of economic theory and the idiosyncrasies of particular industries, transactions, or practices may require re-evaluation and refinement of pre-existing rules, policy positions, or adjudicative decisions. This often leaves a large domain of uncertainty in the application of competition laws.

In balancing these values, a complex, subjective, and inevitably highly contentious optimizing calculus is involved. Moreover, the complexity of this calculus is, in fact, greater than the primary dyadic value tensions identified above in that many of the values interact with one another in polycentric, mutually reinforcing, or antithetical ways. These values and the trade-offs they entail need to be kept in mind when analyzing the institutional performance of competition bodies.

[147] Andrew Neil Campbell, *The Review of Anti-Competitive Mergers,* thesis for the Degree of Doctor of Juridical Science, Faculty of Law, University of Toronto, 1993 at 78–9.

2. *The operation of institutional performance norms in Canadian competition bodies*

Evaluating the institutional performance of all aspects of Canadian competition policy would entail an in depth analysis of the Competition Bureau, the Competition Tribunal, as well as Canada's entire criminal court system. However, the institutional performance of Canada's criminal courts is tangential to the central goal of identifying the performance norms for competition policy and therefore beyond the scope of this paper. This section instead will analyze the operation of institutional performance norms in the Competition Bureau and the Competition Tribunal.

a) Timeliness of dispositions

i. The Competition Bureau

There are very few formal limitations on the amount of time the Bureau can take to initiate or conduct an investigation. Merger review is the exception to this as it is particularly time sensitive. Section 97 of the *Competition Act* states that an application to the Tribunal for merger review must be made within one year after the merger has been substantially completed.[148] Once a merger investigation has been initiated, the Act places further restrictions on waiting periods and specifies an inquiry length of forty-two days.[149] However, the Bureau has adopted service standards which allow investigations to take up to five months.[150] This inconsistency was brought to light in the *Labatt* merger case.[151] The Tribunal ruled that the Bureau should attempt to adhere to the statutory time limits despite its service standards. Since the Bureau did not meet those limits, the Tribunal allowed the merger to proceed under a hold-separate agreement. Furthermore, the Tribunal ruled that interim orders which allow the Bureau to prolong investigations would be granted only in exceptional circumstances.[152] This decision may encourage shorter time frames for merger review. In May 2010, the Bureau released a Draft for Consultation Regarding Fee and Service Standards Handbook for Merger Related Matters which seeks to reduce service standard investigation periods for mergers. In particular, the service standard for very complex mergers such as *Labatt*

[148] The Competition Act § 97.

[149] *Id.*, § 100.

[150] Competition Bureau, Competition Bureau Fee and Service Standards Policy, March 2003. <http://www.competitionbureau.gc.ca/eic/site/cb-bc.nsf/eng/01388.html>. Service standards are articulated in a handbook created by the Bureau and available to the public. In 1997 the Bureau established fees for services including statutory merger notification filings, ARC requests, advisory opinions, and photocopies. The handbook was later created to serve as a point of reference for parties using the above services and for the Bureau as guidance in its determination of the complexity of proposed transactions or business conduct.

[151] *Labatt, supra* note 120.

[152] Law Times, "Labatt Ruling Means Mergers Will Happen Faster" April 2007. <http://www.lawtimesnews.com/200704131703/Headline-News/Labatt-ruling-means-mergers-will-happen-faster>; Shawn Neylan and Michael Kilby, "Commissioner Swallows Defeat in Beer Battle," February 2008, *Stikeman Elliott.* <http://www.stikeman.com/cps/rde/xchg/se-en/hs.xsl/10661.htm>.

would be reduced from five months to 120 days.[153] This Draft has now been finalized.

During a Bureau investigation, procedural rules govern the submission of documents, orders for oral examination and production of documents, warrants for entry of premises, the presentation of evidence, and the discontinuance of investigations. The function of each of these procedures is to ensure fairness and due process; however such procedures also limit the efficacy of inquiries and hamper the timeliness of dispositions.[154] The Bureau has a wide mandate which includes the enforcement of the *Textile Labelling Act*, the *Consumer Packaging and Labelling Act*, the *Precious Metals Marking Act*, and the misleading advertising provisions of the *Competition Act*, in addition to the Bureau's primary role in enforcing the competition provisions of the *Competition Act*.[155] Despite these responsibilities, the Bureau manages to process an extremely large and growing caseload.[156]

ii. The Competition Tribunal

The Tribunal's constituting act provides that "all proceedings before the Tribunal shall be dealt with as informally and expeditiously as the circumstances and considerations of fairness permit."[157] Despite this statutory direction the Tribunal has often focused on due process requirements at the expense of achieving administrative efficiency, resulting in higher costs and longer delays than were anticipated when the Tribunal was first created.[158]

The Tribunal is working to alter the balance between due process and timeliness by treating time limits for pleadings as mandatory, issuing scheduling orders which timetable the major pre-hearing steps and hearing date near the beginning of each proceeding, and refusing to grant extensions of time limits or adjournments of scheduled hearings unless persuasive reasons are offered.[159] The Tribunal has also attempted to reduce the disruption and delay resulting from third party interventions in three major ways. Firstly, all applications to intervene (and notices of intervention by provincial attorneys general) must be made within sixty days after filing the notice of application.[160] Secondly, a prospective intervenor must indicate the matters at issue which affect it and the competitive consequences arising from those matters.[161] Lastly, there is a presumption that intervenors (including provincial attorneys general) will be limited to attending and making submissions and

[153] Competition Bureau, Fee and Service Standard Handbook for Merger Related Matters: Draft for Consultation—May 2010.

[154] Campbell, *The Review of Anti-Competitive Mergers, supra* note 147 at 58.

[155] Thomas Ross, "Viewpoint: Canadian Competition Policy: Progress and Prospects" (2004) 37:2 Canadian Journal of Economics 243 at 259.

[156] Trebilcock and Iacobucci, "Designing Competition Law Institutions," 2010, *supra* note 145 at 462; Goldman and Joneja, *supra* note 29 at 541.

[157] Competition Tribunal Act § 9(2).

[158] Trebilcock and Iacobucci, "Designing Competition Law Institutions," 2010, *supra* note 145 at 462; Campbell, Janisch, and Trebilcock, *supra* note 142 at 306.

[159] Campbell, Janisch and Trebilcock, *supra* note 142 at 306.

[160] Competition Tribunal Rules § 37, 38, 42, 50.

[161] *Id.* § 43.

motions at pre-hearing conferences and the main hearing unless broader participation is authorized by the Tribunal.[162]

In recent years, the Tribunal, under the chairmanship of Justice Sandra Simpson, has taken significant steps to expedite its decision-making processes, rendering prompt decisions in urgent applications, adopting a "chess clock" rule in contested matters that imposes a total time envelope on both parties in contested hearings, adopting new rules requiring pre-filing of all witnesses' evidence (eliminating examination-in-chief), and providing for many procedural issues to be resolved informally by letter rather than formal motions.

As of 2002, the average length of merger cases from the notice of application to the Tribunal by the Commissioner to the Tribunal's decision (including that on remedies) was almost twenty months in fully-contested merger cases and about twenty-seven months from initial notification of the merger to the Bureau.[163] Since then there have been only two contested merger cases. *Commissioner of Competition v. Saskatchewan Wheat Pool* lasted 20 months from the date when the notice of application was filed until the case was dropped by the Commissioner, matching the average trial length from 2002.[164] The *Labatt* case on the other hand lasted only eight days. This was not a typical contested merger case but rather a hearing to contest the Commissioner's application for an interim order under section 100, which was successful.[165]

b) Expertise in determinations

i. The Competition Bureau

The economic expertise of the Bureau has been questioned as it has a relatively low number of economists per staff member compared to many other countries with competition agencies.[166] Only one branch of the Bureau (the Economic Policy and Enforcement Branch) requires staff to have economic expertise.[167] However, the Bureau may also retain outside experts. These experts are most commonly economists, industry experts, and accountants. Experts usually assist in the design of the investigation and the evaluation of information which is gathered by Bureau staff. They may also become witnesses if a matter proceeds to the Tribunal or the courts.[168]

162 Campbell, Janisch, and Trebilcock, *supra* note 142 at 310.

163 Trebilcock and Iacobucci, "Designing Competition Law Institutions," 2010, *supra* note 145 at 463.

164 Competition Tribunal, "Case Details: CT-2005-009" December 2008. <http://www.ct-tc.gc.ca/CasesAffaires/CasesDetails-eng.asp?CaseID=263>.

165 Competition Tribunal, "Case Details: CT-2007-003" December 2008. <http://www.ct-tc.gc.ca/CasesAffaires/CasesDetails-eng.asp?CaseID=282>.

166 Ross, *supra* note 155 at 263. Note that in Canada the definition of an economist requires that the person hold a doctoral degree in economics whereas the definition of economist in other countries may only require some lower educational attainment. Also note that this study took place in the year 2000 and has not since been updated.

167 Competition Bureau, Annual Report of the Commissioner of Competition for the Year Ending March 31 2008. <http://www.competitionbureau.gc.ca/eic/site/cb-bc.nsf/eng/03114.html>.

168 Andrew Neil Campbell, *Merger Law and Practice: The regulation of mergers under the Competition Act* (Carswell Thompson Canada Limited, 1997) at 214.

ii. The Competition Tribunal

The goal of having both expert lay members and judicial members on the Tribunal was to create an expert body with the independence and detachment of a court.[169] However, not all Tribunal members have equal authority. Only judicial members may adjudicate questions of law whereas all members may adjudicate questions of fact or mixed fact and law. Also, a judicial member must preside over each panel.[170] The large role for judicial members has led many to question whether the Tribunal possesses the necessary expertise to adjudicate complex competition matters.[171] Further adding to this scepticism is the fact that the Tribunal hears very few competition cases. In any given year, no more than one or two contested competition cases are heard by the Tribunal. Most of its docket consists of deceptive marketing practices, applications for leave (most of which are denied), and consent order proceedings (many of which orders it is now required to register without review).[172] As a result, there have been limited opportunities for Tribunal members to develop expertise on the job.

c) Investigative and sanctioning powers

i. The Competition Bureau

According to the Bureau's enabling statute, "the Commissioner shall cause an inquiry to be made into all such matters as the Commissioner considers necessary to inquire into with the view of determining the facts [of a potentially anti-competitive acts]."[173] These broad investigatory powers are internally limited by the Bureau's rules for due process and fairness.[174] As an external check, the Bureau is overseen by the federal Minister of Industry. The Minister has the power to review inquiries, discontinue them, or instruct the Commissioner to make further inquiries. The Minister does not directly oversee competition investigations and ultimately the Commissioner is responsible for the administration and enforcement of the Act.[175]

The Bureau itself does not sanction parties but it has the power to bring cases to the appropriate reviewing body if it finds there has been a likely contravention of the Act. The Bureau has the power to apply a flexible array of dispositions. For example, at the conclusion of a merger investigation, the Bureau issues a binding advance ruling certificate, continues to monitor the industry in borderline situations, applies to the Tribunal for an interim order, or brings the case to the Tribunal for adjudication.[176]

[169] Michael J. Trebilcock and Lisa Austin, "The Limits of the Full Court Press: Of Blood and Mergers," (1998) 48 U. Toronto L. J. 1 at 15.

[170] The Competition Tribunal Act § 4(1), 10(2), 12(1).

[171] Campbell, Janisch, and Trebilcock, *supra* note 142 at 305.

[172] Competition Tribunal, "Cases by Date Decided," in COMPETITION TRIBUNAL, June 30, 2010. <http://www.ct-tc.gc.ca/CasesAffaires/CasesDateDecided-eng.asp>.

[173] The Competition Act § 10(1).

[174] *See* "B.2.a)i) *The Competition Bureau*" above.

[175] Goldman and Joneja, *supra* note 29 at 540; The Competition Act § 10(c), 22(1), 22(4).

[176] Campbell, *Merger Law and Practice, supra* note 168 at 469; The Competition Act §100.

ii. The Competition Tribunal

The Tribunal has no investigative powers, which reside in the Competition Bureau. However, it does have the ability to sanction parties who appear before it. The *Competition Act* outlines the types of remedies that the Tribunal may issue for violations, including financial penalties with maximum limits. For example, the Tribunal has the power to decide whether or not a merger violates the *Competition Act* and if it does, it may prohibit the merger, or order divestiture or dissolution.[177] Where the Tribunal finds there has been an abuse of dominance which substantially reduces competition, it may order any remedial measures that are reasonable and necessary to overcome the effects of the practice. In addition, it may also impose an Administrative Monetary Penalty of up to C$10 million and C$15 million for repeat offenders.[178]

d) Reasonable predictability in application of law

i. The Competition Bureau

The breadth of investigatory power and the amount of flexibility granted to the Bureau has raised questions regarding the predictability of Bureau processes.[179] The Bureau has attempted to promote predictability through an enhanced focus on communication to consumers and businesses. Examples of these efforts include the release of warnings as well as information bulletins, some of which explain how the Bureau reaches its decisions and others which address ways that the *Competition Act* will adapt to new challenges such as representations on the internet.[180] The Bureau has also released enforcement guidelines on a number of topics. Those pertinent to competition issues are listed in Table 3.1.

Table 3.1 Enforcement Guidelines on Competition Issues[181]

Application of the *Competition Act* to the Representations on the Internet
Competitor Collaboration Guidelines
Merger Review Process Guidelines
Enforcement Guidelines on the Abuse of Dominance Provisions
Predatory Pricing Enforcement Guidelines
Merger Enforcement Guidelines
The Merger Enforcement Guidelines as Applied to a Bank Merger
The Abuse of Dominance Provisions as Applied to the Retail Grocery Industry
Notifiable Transactions under Part IX of the *Competition Act* Interpretation Guidelines
Notifiable Transactions and Advance Ruling Certificates Under the *Competition Act:* Procedures Guide

[177] The Competition Act § 99. [178] *Id.* § 79(2), 79(3.1).

[179] Campbell, *Merger Law and Practice, supra* note 169.

[180] Competition Bureau, "Competition Bureau Releases Information Bulletin on the Application of the *Competition Act* to Representations on the Internet" February 2003, <http://www.bureau-delaconcurrence.gc.ca/eic/site/cb-bc.nsf/%20eng/00348.html>; Competition Bureau, Annual Report of the Commissioner of Competition for the Year Ending March 31 2008, *supra* note 167.

[181] Competition Bureau, Enforcement Guidelines. (March 2010), <http://www.competitionbureau.gc.ca/eic/site/cb-bc.nsf/eng/h_00168.html>.

ii. The Competition Tribunal

The paucity of litigation before the Tribunal has prevented the development of a significant body of precedent which in turn has resulted in some degree of unpredictability about Tribunal decisions.[182]

e) Transparency in policy formulation and elaboration

i. The Competition Bureau

The policy formulation process of the Bureau is fairly transparent. The Bureau publicly releases drafts of guidelines and information bulletins for comment before publishing final versions.[183] Furthermore, the information bulletins and enforcement guidelines discussed above provide a detailed account of the Bureau's policies regarding specific practices. All of these documents are displayed on the Bureau's website and there is a physical information centre in Gatineau, Quebec with a toll-free phone line which increases access to this information.

ii. The Competition Tribunal

The Tribunal is an adjudicative body and therefore like a court it adjudicates particular cases and does not formulate general policies. As mentioned above, the Tribunal has had some difficulty generating a significant body of precedents due to its small case load. The precedents which are established are available in the form of Competition Tribunal decisions and are posted on the Tribunal's website.[184]

f) Opportunities for public consultation and participation in policy formulation

i. The Competition Bureau

Many of the Bureau's efforts to increase transparency in policy formulation have also improved public consultation and participation. As previously mentioned, guidelines and information bulletins are first released in draft form. The Bureau then asks for feedback from the public which is collected and considered before the publication of the final guidelines or bulletins.[185] In addition, the Commissioner of Competition hosts a number of open dialogue sessions with consumer and business groups across Canada each year. These meetings provide the Bureau with an opportunity to outline its work and mandate. They also provide consumers and businesses with an opportunity to communicate their concerns.[186]

182 Campbell, Janisch, and Trebilcock, *supra* note 142 at 315.

183 The Canadian Bar Association, RE: Draft Bulletin on Corporate Compliance Programs (January 2006), <http://www.cb-bc.gc.ca/eic/site/cb-bc.nsf/vwapj/CanadianBarAssociation.pdf/$file/CanadianBarAssociation.pdf>.

184 Competition Tribunal, Cases by Date Decided, *supra* note 172.

185 Competition Bureau, Annual Report of the Commissioner of Competition for the Year Ending March 31, 2007 at 41–5. <http://www.competitionbureau.gc.ca/eic/site/cb-bc.nsf/vwapj/Annual-Report-2006-2007-eng.pdf/$FILE/Annual-Report-2006-2007-eng.pdf>.

186 Competition Bureau, Annual Report of the Commissioner of Competition for the Year Ending March 31 2008, *supra* note 167.

ii. The Competition Tribunal

As the Tribunal does not formulate policy, there is no opportunity for public consultation or participation in that sense. However, through the expanded doctrines of standing, intervention, and private rights of action, the public may participate in hearings and in doing so help to create precedent.[187] In 2002 the doctrine of standing was expanded such that the Tribunal must provide "any person directly affected by the interim order with a full opportunity to present evidence and make representations before the Tribunal."[188] As noted above, while the Tribunal has significant discretion to allow interventions, in the interest of timeliness it has recently limited the role that interveners play in hearings, restricting them to making submissions. Private parties may also initiate proceedings before the Tribunal with the introduction of limited private rights of action in section 103.1 in 2002.

g) Transparency of reasons for decisions

i. The Competition Bureau

The Bureau places a strong emphasis on confidentiality in its proceedings which critics have claimed reduces transparency.[189] To increase transparency, the Bureau has employed four principal case-specific disclosure techniques: annual report listings of dispositions of cases receiving Significant Assessments (an investigation of more than two days), press releases to announce decisions in high-profile cases, annual and quarterly report summaries of selected cases, and backgrounders to provide detailed commentary on the competition issues and analysis in particularly important cases.[190]

Statutory confidentiality restrictions create a significant barrier to greater transparency.[191] Statutory confidentiality restrictions[192] grant discretion to the Bureau or a judge to conduct parts of an investigation or hearing in private in order to prevent the disclosure of confidential commercial information or to protect witnesses and instigators of investigations who might otherwise fear repercussions.[193]

ii. The Competition Tribunal

In contrast to Bureau investigations, Tribunal proceedings are usually open to the public, except where *in camera* proceedings and restrictions on access to documents

[187] Campbell, *The Review of Anti-Competitive Mergers, supra* note 147 at 74–5; Roach and Trebilcock, *supra* note 36 at 473.

[188] Canada Parliament "Bill C-23" *37th Parliament 1st Session January 29 2001–September 16 2002,* <http://www2.parl.gc.ca/HousePublications/Publication.aspx?DocId=2330907&Language=e&Mode=1&File=72>.

[189] Trebilcock and Iacobucci, "Designing Competition Law Institutions," 2002, *supra* note 27 at 374.

[190] Campbell, *Merger Law and Practice, supra* note 168 at 477.

[191] Ibid. at 479–80; Competition Bureau, *Communication of Confidential Information under the Competition Act,* (May 2010). <http://www.bureaudelaconcurrence.gc.ca/eic/site/cb-bc.nsf/%20eng/01277.html>.

[192] The Competition Act § 10(3), 12(4), 19, 29.

[193] The Competition Act § 12.

are necessary to protect commercially sensitive material.[194] Reasons accompany all Tribunal decisions even for basic consent orders. All of these decisions and many case documents are available to the public on the Tribunal's website.[195]

h) Public accountability mechanisms for general agency functioning

i. The Competition Bureau

The Bureau remains subject to limited oversight by the Ministry of Industry. Examples of this oversight include the requirement that the Bureau submit reasons to the Minister for the discontinuation of an investigation, as well as the Minister's authority to review such decisions and instruct the Commissioner to make further inquiry if the circumstances warrant.[196] The Minister may also at any time require the Commissioner to submit an interim report with respect to any inquiry stating the actions taken, the evidence obtained, and the Commissioner's opinion as to the effect of the evidence.[197]

Funding for the Bureau is determined by Parliament and provided through the Ministry of Industry.[198] The budget is periodically re-evaluated by the Treasury Board. There have been increasing demands on the Bureau's resources particularly following the 2009 amendments that established a supplementary information request process for mergers. To complete such reviews in an informed manner without unduly delaying proposed mergers may require more resources for the Mergers Branch of the Bureau.[199]

The content of the Bureau's mandate and its effectiveness are internally evaluated each year in the Annual Report of the Commissioner to the Minister of Industry (and Parliament). Ad hoc reviews may also occur, as with the *Competition Policy Review Panel* which was constituted in 2007 with the mandate to undertake a review of Canada's competition policies.[200] The Bureau's mandate is subject to modification by Parliament via statutory amendment.

ii. The Competition Tribunal

The appeal process holds the Tribunal accountable for its decisions but there is no oversight of general agency functioning akin to the Minister of Industry's role in overseeing the Bureau. The Tribunal is financially accountable to the Treasury Board of Canada through its budget as well as the Management Accountability Framework which engages in periodic assessments of Tribunal funding with the

[194] Campbell, *The Review of Anti-Competitive Mergers, supra* note 147 at 405.

[195] Competition Tribunal, Cases by Date Decided, *supra* note 172.

[196] The Competition Act § 22.

[197] *Id.* § 28.

[198] W.T. Stanbury, "Expanding Responsibilities and Declining Resources: The strategic responses of the Competition Bureau 1986–1996" (1998) 13 Journal of Industrial Organization 205 at 236.

[199] Goldman and Joneja, *supra* note 29 at 541.

[200] Competition Policy Review Panel, Terms of Reference, June 2008. <http://www.ic.gc.ca/eic/site/cprp-gepmc.nsf/eng/h_00004.html>; Competition Bureau, Annual Report of the Commissioner of Competition for the Year Ending March 31 2008, *supra* note 167.

Registry of the Competition Tribunal, the Tribunal's administrative branch.[201] Like the Bureau, the mandate of the Tribunal is subject to review and change through statutory amendment.

V. Critical reflections on institutional design issues in Canadian competition policy

A. Introduction

Over the period August to October 2010, we interviewed, either in person or by conference calls lasting from forty-five minutes to an hour, all former Commissioners of Competition over the almost twenty-five year period since the current institutional arrangements were implemented in the round of reforms reflected in the *Competition Act* of 1986: in sequence, Lawson Hunter, Calvin Goldman, Howard Wetston, George Addy, Konrad von Finckenstein, and Sheridan Scott.[202] Some former Commissioners have gone on to chair major sector-specific regulatory bodies, while others have become leading members of the Canadian competition bar. In addition, we interviewed Madam Justice Sandra Simpson, Federal Court Judge and Chair of the Competition Tribunal since 2003, and Lilla Csorgo, economist lay member of the Competition Tribunal from 2005 to 2007 and Senior Economic Advisor to the Commissioner of Competition and TD MacDonald Chair holder at the Competition Bureau from 2007 to 2009, to provide the perspective of an economist on current institutional arrangements. We posed the following four sets of questions to each interviewee:

1. Does the current bifurcated Competition Bureau-Competition Tribunal structure work well? Can it be improved? Is more radical reform called for, such as integrating all investigative and adjudicative functions within a single agency, or replacing the Competition Tribunal with, for example, the Federal Court in contested civilly reviewable matters?
2. Does the mandate of the Competition Bureau require re-evaluation with respect to explicit or implicit exemptions or exceptions, such as the regulated conduct defense, and overlapping jurisdiction between the Bureau and sector-specific regulators (such as the Canadian Radio-television and Telecommunications Commission or the Canadian Transportation Agency)?
3. With respect to case-by-case decision-making by either the Bureau or Tribunal, are appropriate protections in place to ensure: full and timely notice of allegations, notice of evidence relied on, appropriately constrained investigative powers, an effective right to challenge Bureau determinations before either the Tribunal or a court, and proportionality of remedies to violations?

201 Treasury Board of Canada Secretariat, MAF Assessment: Registry of the Competition Tribunal—2007, March 2009, <http://www.tbs-sct.gc.ca/maf-crg/assessments-evaluations/2007/rct/rct-eng.asp>.

202 The current Commissioner declined our invitation to comment.

4. With respect to institutional performance norms, in the case of both the Bureau and the Tribunal, are appropriate standards adhered to in terms of the following values: timeliness; expertise; predictability; transparency about decisions; public consultation; public accountability; and independence?

We review the responses of our interviewees below, indicating where, on the one hand, substantial consensus exists or where, on the other hand, substantial dissensus prevails.

B. Structure

Most interviewees agreed that the current bifurcated structure has not worked well. The Competition Tribunal, at least in contested cases, has often engaged in highly protracted, adversarial proceedings. The Tribunal's record in this respect has significantly improved recently. The adoption of a "chess clock" rule for allocating time envelopes to each party in contested matters seems to hold out some promise of disciplining contested hearings, as do rule changes requiring all witness statements to be pre-filed in full (avoiding examination in chief). The consensus, however, is that timeliness of disposition is still a major concern with Tribunal proceedings, at least in contested cases. A number of interviewees argued that there was a strong case for legislating timelines for decision-making by the Competition Tribunal, from the date of application by the Commissioner or a private party to final disposition, as is already the case with decision-making by the Canadian International Trade Tribunal in trade remedy cases and is also already the case in merger review by the European Commission.

Beyond issues of timeliness, most interviewees were highly skeptical that the Tribunal has been able to bring substantial expertise to bear on its deliberations, noting the mixed to weak quality of most lay member appointments, as well as the lack of specialized expertise on the part of most judicial members. One interviewee noted that the idea that lay expertise is sought with current appointments is undermined by the selection of lawyers (and not competition lawyers) for positions with the Tribunal. Not only does this lack of expertise affect the quality of ultimate determinations but it was suggested that it also affects the ability of the Tribunal to engage in aggressive case management by judicial members who lack the expertise and confidence to discipline the advocacy strategies of the parties to contested proceedings.

Interviewees noted that there is a feedback effect from the lack of expertise: the very light case load of the Tribunal since its creation has inhibited the development of a specialized body of expertise, which in turn has inhibited hearings before the Tribunal. Most interviewees were skeptical that the case load is likely to increase in the future. In the case of mergers, which are typically extremely time sensitive, it is difficult to conceive of many contested merger cases ever coming before the Tribunal, but rather are likely to be resolved in the Commissioner's office (albeit with much attenuated due process and transparency relative to the Tribunal).

In light of these perceived shortcomings, different reforms were suggested by the interviewees. One suggestion would be to reform the Competition Tribunal with panels of perhaps two Federal Court judges and one economist. The economist would be a full decision-maker, unlike under the status quo in which the lay members (who may not be economists) cannot make decisions of law; the consensus among interviewees was that this restriction lacks a justification. One possibility is that this reconstituted Tribunal would review matters of law or matters of mixed law and fact based on the Commission's own evidentiary record, rather than hearing all evidence de novo, with a remand power in the event of evidentiary inadequacies. This option has some appealing qualities, but interviewees noted that given the Tribunal's light case load it may be difficult to justify a full-time appointment of an economist. This may argue for the appointment by order-in-council of a roster of economists from whom one would be chosen on a case-by-case basis by the Chair of the Tribunal to serve as a member of an adjudicative panel. Interviewees noted that this seemed a more desirable arrangement than the current practice at the Tribunal of appointing ad hoc staff economists to advise Tribunal members informally on particular cases where their role and inputs are not transparent.

For many interviewees, the Competition Tribunal, at least in anything resembling its present form, is "unsalvageable." Interviewees taking this view tended, by substantial consensus, to favor reconstituting the Competition Bureau as a Commission with a body of three to five commissioners, including a Chair of the Commission, recognizing that as a practical matter most competition policy decisions will be made in the Bureau in settlement discussions with the parties and that these decisions should not be dependent entirely on the views and mindset of a single Commissioner. With such a structure, the general view was that at least one of the commissioners should be a senior industrial organization economist with full co-decision-making responsibilities.

There were different views on the authority that would be vested in this Commission. Many believed that the Commission should not have responsibility for both investigating and adjudicating because of a concern about bias, or perceived bias, from such dual roles. Others were less concerned about such matters, citing the Ontario Securities Commission and the Federal Trade Commission as examples. The primary perceived strength of overlapping adjudication and investigation is the increased expertise that the commissioners, as both adjudicators and investigators, would develop. The alternative is that the commissioners would only investigate, and engage in settlement discussions with parties, but would not ultimately adjudicate. Rather, any matter in dispute would be referred either to a reconstituted Tribunal or possibly the Federal Court.

However, the proposal to create a true competition Commission elicited several potential concerns. First, there was a concern that political considerations may militate in favor of ensuring representation of major regions, language, ethnic, and gender groups, leading to an excessively large Commission with highly variable expertise. Second, concerns were expressed over the proper division of responsibility between the Commission and an independent adjudicative body. Even those that supported the idea of an integrated body responsible for both investigation and adjudication agreed that there would still need to be some external form of check and balance on decisions taken by such a multi-member Commission, but in this respect there was much less consensus on what form this external check or balance should take.

This is clearly an important issue where reasonable people can disagree on the most desirable option. One option is to abolish the Competition Tribunal and simply replace it with the Federal Court Trial Division, where a single judge, perhaps drawn from a sub-set of Federal Trial Court judges that are prepared to commit to developing expertise in competition matters, would perform the adjudicative functions presently performed by the Competition Tribunal, subject to further appeals to the Federal Court of Appeal (as at present, in the case of decisions of the Competition Tribunal). However, other interviewees were of the view that Federal Trial Court judges would, in many cases, lack even the expertise of members of the Competition Tribunal, and that this option would exacerbate the concerns over lack of expertise in external adjudicative bodies. Moreover, this option would not address timeliness issues if proceedings before the Federal Court were to involve de novo hearing of the evidence. Another concern about vesting authority in the Federal Court was that it would be difficult for that body to accommodate competition policy-specific procedures within an otherwise general adjudicative framework.

In order to address the timeliness question before the Federal Court, one suggestion would be that the Commission would develop an evidentiary record and appeals to the Federal Court Trial Division would be limited to matters of law or mixed law and fact, with the possibility of remand to the Commission in the event of factual or evidentiary inadequacies in its record. These concerns in turn raise questions as to how a multi-member Commission would develop an evidentiary record which could be reviewable on appeal. One possibility is to contemplate a highly inquisitorial process before the Commission in contested cases. For example, the investigative staff of the Commission and the private parties involved could submit competitive impact assessments to the Commission, along with supporting written expert opinions, perhaps subject to written interrogatories by parties adverse in interest, with a highly truncated oral hearing before the Commission, followed by a written reasoned decision. If the Commission's decision-making processes, at least in contested cases, were structured in this fashion, a yet further option would be to provide for appeals not to the Federal Court Trial Division but to the Federal Court of Appeal, although this option again would raise questions of relevant expertise of members of the Federal Court of Appeals in competition matters.

C. Mandate

Most interviewees were of the view that the current scope and boundaries of the regulated conduct defense are highly unclear, and a majority of interviewees favored a legislative amendment to the *Competition Act* to clarify this scope and increase predictability for all affected parties.

With respect to overlapping jurisdiction of the Competition Bureau and sector-specific regulators, especially with respect to merger review, the consensus of interviewees was that no special merger review regime is required in the case of airline and rail mergers, and political oversight of mergers in these two sectors, as at present, is unwarranted. Most interviewees also were of the view that there is no case for a special merger review regime in the telecommunications sector, while recognizing that in both the banking and broadcasting sector financial stability and cultural concerns may warrant special review procedures that recognize considerations specific to these two sectors. However, even in these two cases, the consensus amongst interviewees was that the Competition Bureau should undertake the initial assessment of the competitive implications of a proposed merger and make public its findings and recommendations, while leaving sector-specific regulators free to reach other findings and recommendations. Other regulators would be disciplined, however, by the requirement of providing a public document setting out their reasons for diverging from the views of the Competition Bureau, thus ensuring adequate levels of transparency in decision-making between the two affected agencies.

Similarly, while some expressed concern about the Bureau's lack of expertise in certain dynamic regulated sectors like telecoms, the consensus was that where a sector-specific regulator purports to apply competition principles, for example, with respect to predatory pricing, it should defer to the Bureau in making an initial assessment of the issues at hand and follow a procedure similar to that proposed for merger reviews in such a sector in the event of diverging from the Bureau's views of the relevant competition policy concerns.

D. Due process protections

Most interviewees were of the view that with respect to criminal prosecutions for violations of the *Competition Act*, there are adequate general procedural protections for defendants, given that these matters are tried in the ordinary criminal courts and are subject to the application of the Charter of Rights and Freedoms. In civil matters, there have been concerns in the recent past over the Bureau's utilization of section 11 orders, available by ex parte application to the Federal Court, demanding production of classes of documents named in these orders. Specifically, concerns have arisen as to the breadth of these demands, not only with respect to immediate parties to transactions, but competitors, suppliers, and customers. Most of the interviewees were of the view that the two-stage internal decision-making process in the Bureau for seeking section 11 orders has been an appropriate response to disciplining applications by the Bureau for section 11 orders. However, it has not always been the case that a senior economist is involved in these reviews, with the ability to shape the focus of the information being sought, nor is it entirely clear whether this two-tier process continues to function as originally contemplated. Some interviewees also favored providing notice to affected parties in ex parte applications for section 11 order in civil matters (but not, for obvious reasons, in criminal matters); others were concerned that publicity about competition investigations may create unwarranted reputational costs for firms who may not ultimately have done anything anticompetitive. Some interviewees were of the view that Supplemental Information Requests (SIRs) introduced in recent amendments to the *Competition Act* (similar to Second Requests under the *Hart-Scott-Rodino Act* in the US) will substitute for section 11 applications, and similar concerns about the potential for excessive frequency and scope of SIRs will arise.

A further concern expressed to us by some interviewees relates to the inability or unwillingness of Bureau case officers responsible for particular files or more senior officials to whom they report to isolate and communicate to the parties in a timely fashion the critical issues of concern to them in an investigation. Such early communication would permit the parties, again in a timely fashion, to address these concerns either by way of demonstrating that they are unwarranted or that remedial options may be available that effectively address them. Some interviewees were of the view that this delay reflects, at least in some cases, lack of experience by case officers along with a hesitancy on their part to communicate to the parties views that their superiors might disagree with, or alternatively a litigation mentality that one should hold one's cards close to one's chest in the event of an investigation leading to litigation.

E. Systemic performance qualities of the Competition Bureau

In this respect, most interviews focused on three issues pertaining to the institutional performance of the Bureau: independence, accountability, and expertise, with some mention being made of a fourth factor, timeliness of decision-making.

With respect to independence, interviewees were unanimously of the view that their decisions as Commissioners in particular cases had never been influenced by the Minister or his or her political staff, and indeed that no such efforts had been attempted. However, the majority of interviewees were of the view that the Bureau, which is currently constituted as a statutory agency within Industry Canada, would be better assured of institutional independence, in a systemic sense, if the head of the Bureau held the status of Deputy Head and the Bureau received its own parliamentary budget allocation separate from Industry Canada, thus avoiding the need for the Commissioner to negotiate or curry favors with the Deputy Minister of Industry in securing budgetary allocations (and indirectly the Minister). A minority of interviewees were of the view that the Bureau's systemic independence would be better assured if it were removed from Industry Canada and constituted as a separate statutory agency (similar to the CRTC). This would have the virtue of completely detaching the Bureau from current policy concerns of Industry Canada, which may not always be entirely consistent with the objectives of competition policy, while at the same time entailing the vice of removing the Bureau from at least the potential of providing inputs into general areas of government economic policy-making—a vice that some interviewees felt to be of little consequence, because the Bureau is rarely consulted on such matters now.

With respect to accountability, a number of interviewees expressed concern that amendments to the *Competition Act* that provide for the registration of consent agreements in merger cases with the Competition Tribunal, and automatic enforcement thereof as orders of the Tribunal, without review by the Tribunal, has been an undesirable development in that little public scrutiny of the agreement is possible given the skeletal nature of the agreements. This is exacerbated by the fact that the Bureau provides no or inadequate technical backgrounders or competitive impact assessments by which the broader public can evaluate the appropriateness of such orders, or other settlement arrangements. By extension, some interviewees also expressed concerns that the Bureau inadequately utilizes technical backgrounders to explain its decisions in major cases to discontinue or settle a matter, thus rendering its decision-making processes less than adequately transparent. Some interviewees also expressed concern that there is very little retrospective examination of the ultimate market results following orders in particular cases.

With respect to expertise, most of the interviewees were of the view that while the Bureau has had some success in recruiting case officers with MAs in economics, it has been less successful in recruiting and retaining suitably qualified PhD economists. In addition, concerns were expressed that often PhD economists are either unwilling or not encouraged to involve themselves heavily in particular investigative or enforcement files, but rather operate in corners of the Bureau focusing on theoretical/technical issues. To address the perceived lack of economic input, some interviewees favor the appointment of a Senior Economic Advisor to the Commissioner to advise on broader policy matters, while with respect to particular cases under investigation, there could be a requirement that the economists on such a team prepare a written assessment of the economic issues at stake in the case and submit this report not only to the case officer but to the head of division to whom the case officer reports. While many interviewees noted the lack of consistent input from senior experienced economists in the Bureau's activities (as with the Competition Tribunal), they also noted that the Canadian academy currently produces very few economists with the industrial organization and applied skill sets required in regulatory environments such as the Competition Bureau (but also in other areas of economic policy making, such as energy policy).

With respect to timeliness of decision-making within the Bureau, some interviewees were critical of the protracted nature of Bureau decision-making in many cases, and argued for legislated deadlines, as opposed to merely internal service deadlines, in order to focus and discipline the Bureau's efforts.

VI. Conclusion

We have reviewed the central institutions in Canadian competition policy, as well as reflections on the performance of these institutions from observers who are uniquely positioned to provide insight: every past Competition Commissioner, the Chair of the Competition Tribunal, and an economist who has served both on the Tribunal and with the Bureau. In our view what emerges from this canvass is that the core institutional question confronting Canadian competition policy, particularly with respect to civil matters, is how best to structure the institutional relationship between investigation and adjudication.

As we have argued in the past,[203] perceived shortcomings of the performance of the current institutional framework stem in large part from the existing structure. Concerns have been expressed about timeliness, expertise, and public accountability of both the Bureau and the Tribunal. Some causes of this concern are exogenous to institutional structure; for example, if relatively few industrial organization economists are being trained in Canada, this has nothing to do with the Bureau and the Tribunal. But others we believe relate intimately to the institutional set-up. For example, timeliness at the Tribunal may relate to the lack of expertise at the Tribunal, which in turn relates to the small case load that it hears. Relatively inexpert adjudicators on the Tribunal cannot develop such expertise on the job because of the rarity of cases, which in turn contributes to the rarity of cases. Timeliness at the Bureau may also depend ultimately on the challenges that parties face in considering litigation before the Tribunal. The Tribunal has, for all practical purposes, ceased to provide an external check on the Bureau's decision-making. Parties, especially in mergers, thus effectively require the Bureau's approval because they are not in a position to threaten credibly to take disagreements to the Tribunal. Moreover, third parties have limited rights to bring complaints before the Tribunal. This allows the Bureau considerable leverage both in conducting its inquiries and in reaching settlements with the parties. While there is no reason to suppose that officers at the Bureau would act unprofessionally, there is little discipline on their discretion, which may contribute to delay as risk-averse case officers probe every possible competition angle in a case. Accountability also relates obviously to the institutional framework. With public adjudication at the Tribunal occurring only rarely, the Bureau can enforce the law with relatively little public oversight. Settlement discussions behind closed doors are the norm and publicity the exception.

Given the connection between the central criticisms of current institutional performance and the current institutional structure, we believe that this structure deserves thorough review and reform. The difficulty for reform is that while there is a consensus on the shortcomings of the status quo, there is no such agreement over fundamental aspects of reform. In particular, while our interviews suggest that there is general support for the idea of a multi-person Commission, there is division over its particular role, as well as the institutional framework for review of its decisions.

As we have written in the past,[204] we are drawn to greater de jure integration of the adjudicative function within the Competition Commission. We understand the concerns about bias that arise from such integration, but believe that the gains from increasing expertise, timeliness, and accountability in the adjudication process justify the risk of bias. At present, adjudication, when it arises (which is very rarely), involves adjudicators for the most part without considerable expertise in the

[203] *See* Trebilcock and Iacobucci, *supra* note 145. [204] Ibid.

competition policy sphere. By bringing greater adjudicative responsibilities within the Commission, the decision-makers will be fully immersed in the field and the expertise, timeliness, and accountability problems will be mitigated considerably. While there are interaction effects of a number of kinds, the core reason to integrate investigation and adjudication is that expert adjudicators are better able to provide timely decisions, which will increase formal adjudication, which will increase accountability.

There are four responses to concerns about bias, which clearly do not individually or collectively eliminate these concerns, but do diminish the role such concerns should play in shaping institutional reform. First, under the status quo, there is de facto integration of investigation and adjudication within the Bureau. Parties are very wary of litigation before the Tribunal, which grants considerable power to the Bureau to extract settlements. Investigators are de facto, and with consent agreements to some extent de jure, already adjudicators under the status quo, yet there is very little publicity about the inputs into and bases for their decisions. Formalizing adjudication within the Bureau would have the advantage of potentially rendering certain features of the process more transparent. The Bureau could be required to produce reasons for its decisions, for example. In short, concerns about bias cannot be invoked to reject proposed reforms in favor of the status quo.

Second, concerns about bias can be addressed within the reform. Reform could take advantage of the multi-person Commission, for example, by ensuring that Commissioners vested with decision-making authority in any given case are not involved in the investigation associated with that particular case.

Third, in our view it is essential in contemplating reform not to treat concerns about bias as a kind of trump card. In civil matters, the typical remedy is a cease-and-desist order. The mildness of the remedy, which could even be institutionalized by eliminating Administrative Monetary Penalties if the Commission adjudicates a matter, undermines concerns about bias. Moreover, while concerns about bias are relatively weak under the status quo, concerns about expertise, accountability, and timeliness are widespread and strong. Allowing residual concerns about bias to exist within an institutional framework may well be appropriate in light of the potential gains to be had on these other dimensions.

Fourth, we are open to persuasion that appeals should lie to the Federal Court of Appeal on matters of law, mixed law and fact, and fact (with leave) from Commission decisions (as is the case currently with decisions of the Tribunal), although this option comes at a cost—lack of timeliness and expertise in decision-making. The latter concern would be mitigated if the Federal Court of Appeal were to show more deference to decisions of an expert Commission than it has to decisions of the Tribunal.

In conclusion, while we recognize that the integration of adjudication and investigation at other competition bodies, such as the FTC and the European Commission, has invited controversy over bias, we believe that these concerns, while legitimate, should not stand in the way of a reconstitution of Canadian institutions to address an unsatisfactory status quo.

4

Chile
The Competition Law System and the Country's Norms[1]

Francisco Agüero[*] *and Santiago Montt*[**]

I. Introduction

Assessing how competition law enforcement and governance has developed in a country such as Chile demands looking first at how the competition legislation has evolved and why it has been amended. The task of evaluating our competition institutions also compels us to review the decisions and critical literature in this field of law. But this assessment also requires asking operators of the competition law system—typically, antitrust lawyers—how they assess the existing institutions and legal rules, and how well they have been working since their enactment. Therefore, this country study will use several tools in order to take a broad and in-depth look at the institutional governance of competition law bodies. In the following pages we describe briefly the recent history and institutional setting for competition agencies in Chile, followed by the evidence we gathered in our study and the conclusions arising from this information.

In this process we attempt to critically assess a common assertion about the Chilean antitrust system: that there is mistrust in its institutional design.[2] Is this mistrust real, or is it a myth? Certainly, part of this assertion is based on the absence of sufficient scholarship in competition law.[3] The absence of analysis is most likely

[1] We gratefully acknowledge the valuable and helpful collaboration of Nader Mufdi in the research, design, and application of the interviews and survey for this chapter; Claudia Perez with translations; Barbara Woessner; and the valuable comments of Michael Trebilcock, and of the participants in a Global Administrative Law Competition project workshop at New York University.

[*] Assistant Professor, University of Chile; Director, Center on Regulation and Competition, RegCom, University of Chile. In some of the cases mentioned in this chapter, Mr Agüero was the attorney for some parties. The cases are *Constructora e Inmobiliaria Independencia v. Aguas Nuevo Sur, Maule* (for Aguas Nuevo Sur, Maule); *FNE v. Telefónica Móviles de Chile SA* (for Claro Chile SA); and *Telmex Servicios Empresariales SA v. Compañía de Telecomunicaciones de Chile SA* (for Telmex).

[**] Academic, Public Law Department, University of Chile; Former Director, Center on Regulation and Competition, RegCom, University of Chile (December 2009 to March 2011).

[2] Elina Cruz and Sebastián Zarate, "Building trust in antitrust: the Chilean case," *Competition Law and Policy in Latin America*, Eleanor M. Fox and D. Daniel Sokol, eds (Hart Publishing, 2009) 157.

[3] Craig Beaker, *Chilean Competition Act of 2009: A new age in prosecuting Collusion?*, 2010.

a result of the practitioner status of most of the lawyers who operate in the competition system, who fear reprimand or a misuse of their academic writings during trials. This is caused also by the fact that Chilean competition law academics are usually also antitrust lawyers, so the fear to publish writings that criticize competition bodies' decisions is reinforced.[4] This deficiency has been addressed only in the last decade, with more literature dedicated mostly to the substantive analysis of competition law, and only recently to the critical assessment of decisions affecting certain industries, such as retail.[5]

In order to evaluate the arrangement of competition law institutions in Chile and their governance, we have to bear in mind that the design of each country's regulatory institutions will reflect its institutional endowments. We can measure regulators' efficiency by looking at the transparency and predictability of their decisions. Following North,[6] Levy and Spiller place emphasis on the formal accountability of regulators; that is, the design of legal frameworks and the formal structures of systems.[7] This emphasis looks mostly at *how* the law and institutions were conceived and designed. Consequently, we have tried to use six different defined fields in order to assess the regulatory or institutional governance. These issues have been organized into two groups. The first three aspects are grouped under the institutional design: roles and objectives, autonomy (independence), and accountability. The second group refers to informal accountability, regulatory process, and practices, consisting of participation, transparency, and predictability. Meanwhile, other authors place emphasis on informal accountability: the country's customs and informal, broadly accepted norms of behavior, and the character of contending social interests within that society.[8]

Undertaking a detailed review of the practical aspects of governance and enforcement in competition law's institutions in Chile may well serve us to improve the outcome of the existing administrative and judicial bodies. In order to do so, we used public reports or statements of existing competition institutions, judicial decisions, international peer-reviews, specialized literature, and interviews and surveys of operators of the competition law system. The methodology and questions used in the surveys and interviews are included as an annex to this chapter.

Daniel Sokol recently encouraged us to start rating antitrust agencies the way restaurant guides do.[9] However, rating agencies as if all served similar or the same dishes can be mischievous. Making international comparisons can be unpleasant,

[4] Exceptions to this observation are the creation of at least two legal centers of competition law analysis in renowned universities since 2006 and 2010.

[5] Paulo Montt and Nicole Nehme, *Libre Competencia y Retail. Un Análisis Crítico* (Abeledo Perrot, 2010).

[6] Douglass North, *Institutions, Institutional Change and Economic Performance*, 1990.

[7] Brian Levy and Pablo Spiller, "The Institutional Foundation of Regulatory Commitment: A Regulatory Analysis of Telecommunications Regulation," Journal of Law, Economics and Organization, 10 (2) (1994).

[8] Jon Stern and Stuart Holder, "Regulatory governance: criteria for assessing the performance of regulatory systems: An application to infrastructure industries in the developing countries of Asia," Utilities Policy, 8(1), 33–50 (1999).

[9] D. Daniel Sokol, *Designing Antitrust Agencies for More Effective Outcomes: What Antitrust Can Learn from Restaurant Guides* (2010).

especially in an environment of cooperation between agencies. In that sense, this assessment can be helpful for the national institutions. Thus, periodical reviews of previous evaluations may certainly be useful. But efforts to compare substantive law have been undertaken successfully in international networks, such as the OECD and the International Competition Network (ICN). Therefore, we should also ask *how* well competition law systems have arranged their institutions.

Following Sokol's analogy, in this work we went further and assessed the competition agencies not only based on the opinion of "regular customers" of the "Chilean restaurants" (antitrust lawyers), but also on the expert opinion of frequent customers (top Chilean competition practitioners, selected by international rankings), foreign restaurant critics (international peer reviews), and even their own menus (self-assessments). As expected, and as we show, opinions vary. Some owners, the *restaurateurs,* are tempted to enthusiastically promote their own dishes, even though customers may complain about the owner's ability and cooking skills. Using these methods, we consider we now have an overall appraisal of the governance of Chilean agencies. The evaluation has just started. We have just proposed which questions should be asked, and we take a look at the results. Analysis of the surveyed data should certainly continue.

Despite the fact that we surveyed many lawyers in order to make this evaluation—and considering the amount of cases the Competition Tribunal has heard in the last seven years—this study is far from being a census. Since we were *rating restaurants,* we also mixed the empirical results with statements from their *owners*; that is, the Competition Tribunal and National Economic Prosecutor's Office, some *food critics* (academics), and when relevant, decisions by the Chilean Supreme Court (sorry, no analogy!).

II. History

A. The early years: 1959–1973

The first Chilean competition act, Title V of Statute No. 13.305 (Antitrust Law) was enacted in 1959, in a miscellaneous law addressing several financial issues.[10] This act created the Antitrust Commission, constituted by one Supreme Court Justice, and two chief financial regulators. Only in 1963, after a legal reform was approved by Congress, was the National Economic Prosecutor (NEP) established. This public officer was hired by the Antitrust Commission, and his role was, amongst others, to represent the general interest of the economic community before the courts of justice.

Prior to the enactment of Statute No. 13.305, the Klein-Sacks Mission, an American consultancy firm hired by the Chilean ministry of finance and economy, recommended substituting for price controls a public policy based on freedom of prices, competition law, and the possibility to adjust trade tariffs when internal

[10] The competition regulation was restricted to the fifth section of Law No. 13.305.

prices grew excessively.[11] Since price controls continued to be massively used in the Chilean economy after the former recommendations, Statute No. 13.305 had very little influence on the Chilean economy. Besides, in its early years the NEP did not have an active role in the prosecution of anticompetitive conducts.[12]

B. Decree-Law 211: 1973–2003

Until 1973, the Chilean economic regime severely restricted international trade, through high import tariffs, a dominant role for state-owned enterprises, and thousands of prices regulated and controlled by the State. In addition, both the Antitrust Commission and the NEP lacked financial means to enforce competition law on a national level.[13] In 1973, only a couple of weeks after the military *coup d'état*, the new government enacted Decree-Law 211, which established the current foundations of competition law in Chile.[14] The military government had adopted as a guideline on economic issues an anonymous book called "*El Ladrillo*" ("The Brick"), prepared by Chilean economists—mostly *Chicago Boys*—after their graduate studies at the University of Chicago. This economic program favored the elimination of price control regulations, limiting them to natural monopoly industries, and encouraged the use of competition law as a means to attack cartels.[15] Accordingly, the decision to reinforce competition law came promptly.

Decree-Law 211 created two different levels of institutions: on a regional level, the Central and Regional Preventive Commissions (thirteen in total), whose main function was to be consultative bodies, in order to push the heavily regulated economy towards a more liberalized market economy. This role was crucial in the early years of the enactment of Decree-Law 211, a period of transition towards competitive markets.[16] Indeed, the Central Preventive Commission continued to be an active institution until its dissolution in 2003. A higher level body was the Resolutive Commission, composed of one Supreme Court Justice, two civil service officers, one professor of law, and one professor of economics. Members of both the Preventive and Resolutive Commissions worked *ad honorem*, and none of the commissions had a budget. Until 2003, a separate physical area at NEP offices (NEPO) in Santiago served as the secretariat for both the Resolutive and Central Preventive Commissions, which reflected the lack of independence of both commissions in those days.[17]

Despite the fact that these bodies did not fulfill the minimum requirements of independence, specialization, dedication, and human and budgetary resources, they

[11] Ricardo Paredes Molina, "Jurisprudencia de las Comisiones Antimonopolios en Chile," Estudios Públicos, No. 58, (1995), 229.

[12] OECD—Inter American Development Bank, *Exámenes inter-pares de la política y del derecho de la competencia en América Latina: Un seguimiento. Argentina, Brasil, Chile, México y Perú*, 2007, 15.

[13] Radoslav Depolo, *El sistema chileno de defensa de la competencia*, 1997, 2.

[14] This law had its foundations in Law 13.305.

[15] Centro de Estudios Públicos (ed.), *El Ladrillo: Bases de la Política Económica del Gobierno Militar Chileno*, Santiago, 1992, 89.

[16] Presidential Bill of Law which creates a Competition Tribunal, Bulletin N° 2944-03, 2002.

[17] OECD-IADB, *Chile—Peer Review of Competition Law and Policy*, 2004, 28.

accomplished their tasks successfully during the first thirty years of Decree-Law 211. However, after almost three decades, both a more globalized economy and comments from the private sector demanded regulatory reform, making way for a new institutional framework for competition law in Chile.[18]

C. Statute No. 19.911 and the creation of the Competition Tribunal: 2003–2009

Since 1973, Decree-Law 211 has been amended on several occasions. However, the more significant reforms occurred in 2003 (Statute No. 19.911) and 2009 (Statute No. 20.361). In 2003, Statute No. 19.911 created the Competition Tribunal, which replaced the existing bodies established in 1973.[19]

The Competition Tribunal is a special tribunal constituted by three lawyers and two economists with competition policy experience, with separate proceedings for consultations (including mergers and acquisitions) and competition law infringement cases. Besides the creation of the Competition Tribunal, Statute No. 19.911 established different procedures to select the members of the Competition Tribunal, with the participation of institutions such as the President, the Supreme Court, and/or the Central Bank.[20] The 2003 reform enabled the creation of a bifurcated model, having on the one hand the NEPO, a specialized competition investigative body filing claims, and on the other, the Competition Tribunal, a specialized competition law court which decides the claims and lawsuits brought for its decision.

D. Statute No. 20.361: rethinking the cartel offense: leniency and dawn raids

Decree-Law 211 was most recently amended by Statute No. 20.361, enacted in 2009, which gave strong investigative powers to the NEPO, allowing wire-tapping, dawn raids, and leniency in cartel cases. It also introduced new grounds for recusation for the members of the Competition Tribunal, strengthened the standards for ensuring independence, improved the protection of confidentiality of the information gathered in investigations, increased the amount of fines, and established procedural reforms regarding the number of witnesses that could testify in competition infringement proceeding. It seems too early to tell if those powers have been used wisely or not. Only in 2010 did the NEPO file its first complaint using information gathered after a leniency application by a member of an international cartel that was part of a cartel claim brought by the Brazilian competition authorities.[21]

18 Presidential Bill of Law which creates a Competition Tribunal, Bulletin No 2944-03, 2002.

19 That is the Resolutive Commission and the Regional and Central Preventive Commissions.

20 Other purposes of the 2003 reform were a new wording for the antitrust offenses, procedural modernization, enhancing the independence of the Competition Tribunal from the NEPO, ending the *ad honorem* regime of wages, and decriminalization of antitrust infringements.

21 NEPO, *Requerimiento en contra de Whirpool SA y Tecumseh do Brasil Ltda,* July 29, 2010.

E. Recriminalizing cartels?

In 2003, the general criminal antitrust offense was abrogated by Decree-Law 211. In the thirty year period, no criminal prosecution existed for antitrust offenses. Then, in 2009, after a *pseudo*-leniency case (a settlement approved by the Competition Tribunal between a private drugstore chain—charged with cartel behavior—and the NEPO before Statute No. 20.361 came into force), the discussion of the applicability to cartels of an old and general offense contained in the Criminal Code resurfaced.[22] After the drugstore cartel case was brought by the NEPO in 2008, and one of the alleged members of the cartel confessed and settled at the Competition Tribunal, several Bills were discussed in the Chilean Congress in order to recriminalize cartels.

Although most competition lawyers would argue that the abrogation of the criminal antitrust offense done in 2003 was general to the Chilean legal system and that no offense contained in the Criminal Code is still applicable to cartels, criminal lawyers argue otherwise. As a consequence of the debate, the question of whether a cartel can still be considered a criminal offense depends on the final decision of criminal tribunals.[23] In March 2011, a criminal tribunal accepted the petition of the public prosecution in order to hear a case against several offenders in the drugstore cartel case.[24] This proceeding reveals that the previous uncertainty has been partially clarified, with the understanding that the Criminal Code offense has—so far—superseded the 2003 Competition Law amendment.

III. Structure and procedure

A. National Economic Prosecutor's Office (NEPO)

The National Economic Prosecutor's Office (*Fiscalía Nacional Económica, FNE*) is a decentralized public service, with legal personality and assets of its own, independent, and subject to the oversight of the President of the Republic, through the Ministry of Economy, Development and Tourism. The NEPO is headed by the National Economic Prosecutor (NEP), who is appointed by the President of the Republic following a selection process for senior public officers. The NEP can remain in office for four years, and his appointment may only be renewed once. Since 2009, the NEP can only be removed as ordered by the President of the Republic, for cause, with the approval of the Supreme Court, upon request of the Ministry of Economy, Development and Tourism.[25]

22 Art. 385, Criminal Code punishes those who through fraud modify the natural price of goods, shares, and public or private rents.

23 Estrategia "Las Falencias que Hacen Inaplicable la Delación Compensada en Chile," <http://www.estrategia.cl/detalle_cifras.php?cod=4303>.

24 Poder Judicial, *Séptimo juzgado de garantía de Santiago ordena firma mensual para ejecutivos de laboratorios y farmacias*, <http://www.poderjudicial.cl/modulos/Home/Noticias/PRE_noticias.php?cod=2974&opc_menu=0>.

25 Decree-Law 211, Art. 33.

In exercising his functions, the NEP is independent from authorities and tribunals. Therefore, he must exercise the authority entrusted to him in the manner he finds consistent with law, according to his own appreciations.[26] The NEP's principal powers consist of initiating investigations which he finds necessary to prove violations of the law and notifying the affected party; acting as a party, representing the general interest of the economic community before the Competition Tribunal and the courts of justice; requiring from the Competition Tribunal the exercise of any of its powers and the adoption of preventive measures in investigations that the NEPO is executing; overseeing compliance with decisions, rulings, and instructions made by the Competition Tribunal or the courts of justice; issuing reports requested by the Competition Tribunal on those cases where the NEP is not acting as a party; and negotiating extrajudicial agreements or settlements with agents involved in investigations in order to protect competition in the markets.[27]

The NEPO must investigate accusations brought by private individuals regarding acts and contracts that could imply a violation of Decree-Law 211. In order to determine if the accusations should be investigated or dismissed, the NEPO may request information from private individuals, as well as summoning any person to testify who could have information of the alleged fact.[28] In investigative procedures, the NEPO has the broadest powers, and is able to request from individuals information and documents it considers necessary in relation to the investigations being conducted; ask for the collaboration of any officer from public entities and administrations, from municipalities or state-owned enterprises; call to testify, or request written testimony, of legal representatives, administrators, advisors, and workers of the firms or individuals who could have knowledge about acts or agreements that are the object of investigations.[29] Regarding investigations, the NEPO must generally notify the affected parties that an investigation is being conducted against them, although only a general description of the facts may be provided.[30]

Since the 2009 legal reform, in cartel investigations the NEP also has the power—with prior approval of the Competition Tribunal—to request authorization from a judge of the Court of Appeals, through a substantiated petition, that the police or the judicial investigations police, under the guidance of an officer of the NEPO, proceed to, enter public or private premises, and if necessary, force entry and break in (dawn raids); search and seize all kinds of objects and documents that prove the existence of a violation; authorize interception of all types of communications, and order any company that supplies telecommunication services to provide copies and records of communications transmitted or received by them.[31] Rules of the Criminal Procedure Code are to be applied as a complement to Decree-Law 211's regulations on cartel investigation techniques.

[26] Decree-Law 211, Art. 39.
[27] *See* Decree-Law 211, Art. 39.
[28] Decree-Law 211, Art. 41.
[29] Decree-Law 211, Art. 39.
[30] Decree-Law 211, Art. 39 § a.
[31] Decree-Law 211, Art. 39, n.

B. Competition Tribunal

The Competition Tribunal (*Tribunal de Defensa de la Libre Competencia*) is a specialized, independent jurisdictional entity—a court that does not strictly belong to the Judicial Branch—which decides cases under the directional and correctional supervision of the Supreme Court, whose purpose is to prevent, correct, and punish infringements of competition law. The Competition Tribunal was created in 2004, after the enactment of Law 19.911. Since 2004, the Competition Tribunal operates in offices separate from the NEPO.[32]

All the Tribunal's judges are appointed following an open and public competition. Additionally, the Competition Tribunal's judges come from two professional backgrounds: two lawyers, experts in competition matters; two economists;[33] and the President of the Tribunal (also a lawyer), appointed by the President of the Republic from a list of candidates designated by the Supreme Court also after a public contest. In this competition, candidates must show a distinguished professional or academic career in the area of competition, or in commercial or economic law. The Tribunal also has two alternate or substitute members, one economist and one lawyer.[34] The Competition Tribunal has a professional staff of one secretary of the tribunal (lawyer), three court clerks, and two economists. In addition, temporary staff may be hired by the Tribunal, if required, after approval by the Government Budget Office.[35]

The Competition Tribunal's budget is annually approved according to the Public Sector Budget Law. According to this law, resources necessary for the functioning of the Competition Tribunal must be annually assessed in a comprehensive manner. For these purposes, the President of the Tribunal must communicate the budgetary needs of the Tribunal to the Minister of Finance.[36]

Apart from adversarial and non-adversarial litigation at the Competition Tribunal, this court has other powers contained in Decree-Law 211. For instance, the Competition Tribunal has the power to issue general regulations (*instructions*), which must be observed by private individuals executing or entering into acts or contracts that are related to or that could infringe free competition.[37] This has been the case in waste disposal management auctions, medicine pricing, electricity

[32] Prior to the 2003 reform, the predecessors of the TDLC (Resolutive and Central Preventive Commissions) used the facilities of the FNE in their duties.

[33] In the case of remaining judges, they are selected in two ways: two of the members, one from each professional area, are appointed by the Council of the Central Bank, after a public contest. The other two members, also one from each professional area, are appointed by the President of the Republic, from two lists of three applicants, one list for each appointment, elaborated by the Council of the Central Bank, also after a public contest process. The public contests are based on objective conditions, which are public, transparent, and non-discriminatory. Decree-Law 211, Art. 6.

[34] Decree-Law 211, Art. 6.

[35] Decree-Law 211, Art. 13.

[36] Decree-Law 211, Art. 17.

[37] Decree-Law 211, Art. 18, No 3.

auctions, etc., where general regulations have been discussed and issued by the Competition Tribunal or its predecessor.[38]

The Competition Tribunal can also propose to the President of the Republic, through the relevant Minister, the amendment or derogation of any statute or regulation which the Tribunal deems contrary to competition law, or the enactment of statute or regulations deemed necessary for promoting competition or regulating certain economic activities that are provided in non-competitive conditions.[39] Since 2004, the Tribunal has proposed thirteen legal or regulatory amendments.[40]

1. Damages and class actions

Damages are not awarded by the Competition Tribunal. A damage claim that may result from the anticompetitive conduct sanctioned by a final ruling of the Competition Tribunal must be individually filed before the competent civil court. These damages claims must be handled according to proceedings established by the Civil Procedure Code and, when ruling on the damages claims, the civil court must base its ruling on the conduct, actions, and legal classification established by the decision of the Competition Tribunal.[41] As a result, civil courts cannot establish themselves whether the Decree-Law 211 was infringed and cannot deviate from the Competition Tribunal's decision regarding the antitrust violation, although the civil court has broad powers to establish the nature and amount of damages.[42] Finally, according to the statute of limitations, civil actions derived from competition law infringements cannot be initiated after four years from the time that the Competition Tribunal rendered its final decision.[43] To our knowledge, since the enactment of Law 19.911, only two civil lawsuits have been filed asking for anticompetitive damages.[44]

Class actions or collective claims are not provided for antitrust law infringements.[45] However, one class action was filed in 2009 in a civil court against several drugstores which the NEPO had previously charged with cartel behavior. In October 2009, the civil court declined its jurisdiction to deal with the class action.[46]

38 The list of general instructions issued by the Competition Tribunal and its predecessors can be found at <http://www.fne.cl/?content=notes&db=jurispru&view=2fdd44beb2bd68188425733e005e052c>.

39 Decree-Law 211, Art. 18, No 4.

40 The complete list of proposals can be checked at: <http://www.tdlc.cl/Portal.Base/Web/VerContenido.aspx?ID=2420&IDI=1318>.

41 Decree-Law 211, Art. 30.

42 Montt and Mordoj, "Chile, The Private Competition Enforcement Review," Ilene Knable Gotts (ed.), 3rd edn, *Law Business Research*, 2010, 3132.

43 Decree-Law 211, Art. 20.

44 Montt and Mordoj. 31. In January 2011 a new damages suit was filed in Talca: *Constructora Independencia y otros v. Nuevo Sur.*

45 P. Montt and B. Mordoj, 36.

46 P. Montt and B. Mordoj, 36.

2. *Public and private litigation at the Competition Tribunal*

If the NEPO chooses not to dismiss a complaint, it must file a claim before the Competition Tribunal (a so-called *requerimiento*), arguing violations of competition law.[47] Private litigation at the Competition Tribunal has a broad scope. Decree-Law 211 allows the Tribunal to hear, upon request by *any party* or by the NEPO, cases that could constitute violations of competition law. After a private lawsuit has been brought at the Competition Tribunal, the NEPO may join the claim,[48] and vice versa.[49] In those cases, the Competition Tribunal has been flexible in allowing third parties to participate in proceedings, even if they could not prove specific or economic interests in the claim.[50] Once a private individual has filed a lawsuit, the NEPO is invited by the Tribunal to file a report or a claim to the case.[51]

The Chilean system considers private antitrust litigation, combining both a plaintiff and a defense bar which have litigated antitrust cases at the Competition Tribunal, and, in increasing numbers, unfair competition cases at civil courts. The growing number of lawyers related to competition law cases—for our survey we asked almost 300 lawyers whom had participated in competition law cases since 2004—reflects a growing epistemological community. This community has started to gather annually, in meetings organized by the NEPO (*Competition Day*), and conferences organized by the two academic centers devoted to competition law analysis.

Lawsuits can be brought not only by the affected parties and the NEPO, but also by competitors, non-governmental organizations (NGO), foundations, etc., although only if they are able to show a legitimate interest.[52] In 2010, the Competition Tribunal and the Supreme Court ruled repeatedly that a non-governmental organization lacked a legitimate interest when filing a lawsuit against a telecommunications company, and lacked standing, due to the fact that the NGO did not prove a direct interest in punishing the defendant.[53] The courts clarified that the role of representing the general economic interest belongs strictly to the NEPO.

As noted, civil society has participated actively in several cases, both adversarial and non-adversarial. As early as 2004 a first claim of cartelization against a banking business organization was brought by a consumer association.[54] In 2005, a

[47] Decree-Law 211, Art. 18, No. 1.

[48] Montt and Mordoj, 32, quoting *FNE v. Almacenes Paris y Falabella,* Case No. C 103–106, TDLC, Decision 63, April 10, 2008.

[49] *Constructora e Inmobiliaria Independencia v. Aguas Nuevo Sur, Maule,* Case No. C 79-05, TDLC, Decision 85/2009.

[50] Montt and Mordoj, 34, quoting *FNE v. Farmacias Ahumada SA, Farmacias Cruz Verde SA y Salcobrand SA,* Case No. c 184–08, TDLC.

[51] Decree-Law 211, Art. 20.

[52] Decree-Law 211, Art. 18, No. 1.

[53] Montt and Mordoj, *id.*, TDLC: *Fundación Chile Ciudadano y Otro v. VTR BA Chile SA,* Decision No. 98, March 18, 2010, Cause No. C 168-08, and Supreme Court, Cause No. 2680, September 22, 2010.

[54] *Conadecus v. Asociación de Bancos e Instituciones Financieras A.G.,* TDLC, Decision No. 15/2005.

consumer NGO filed a claim against a financial services company, accusing it of infringing competition and information transparency rules.[55] Even environmental organizations have filed claims against energy firms at the Competition Tribunal, charging them with monopolizing water rights for a controversial hydroelectric project in Patagonia.[56] Finally, in January 2011, and after an amendment to Decree-Law 211, a consumer association was allowed to request a full review of a proposed international merger between two airlines (LAN and TAM),[57] impeding a consent decree between the NEPO and the Chilean airline, LAN.

In merger and other non-adversarial procedures, any party who has a *legitimate interest*, and the NEPO, may request the Competition Tribunal to review issues of a non-adversarial nature that could violate the provisions of Decree-Law 211, regarding existing acts, agreements, or contracts or those pending completion, for which purpose the Tribunal may set the conditions to be met by these acts or contracts.[58] The parties that submit their acts, agreements, or contracts to the conditions imposed by the Competition Tribunal are granted immunity from future antitrust claims from the NEPO or third parties, unless the market or regulatory conditions change. In such cases, the Competition Tribunal must modify its decisions before imposing fines or sanctions to those that acted relying upon them.

3. *Settlements*

Until 2009, there was a limited scope for negotiating and settling a dispute between the NEPO and a private party, despite the text of Decree-Law 211 on the topic. Settlements were usually restricted in time only to proceedings at the Competition Tribunal, requiring the Tribunal to give its approval, provided that it did not infringe competition law.[59] However, as Montt and Mordoj note, even the Supreme Court has encouraged settlements between parties in adversarial proceedings.[60]

After the enactment of Law 20.361, the NEPO has the power to settle cases with private parties during the investigative phase, in order to protect competition policy. Settlements require the subsequent approval of the Competition Tribunal. During the first year of application of this rule, the NEPO has settled with two firms.[61] An appeal against the Competition Tribunal's approval decision on settlements can be filed by third parties who were not party to such agreements.[62]

[55] *Fundación Chile Ciudadano v Car S.A.*, TDLC, Decision No. 41/2006.
[56] *Conservación Patagónica Chile S.A.*et al. *v. Endesa S.A.* et al., TDLC, Decision No. 109/2011.
[57] *Conadecus, LAN Airlines S.A. and TAM Linhas Aéreas S.A.* TDLC, Case NC 388-11, 2011.
[58] Decree-Law 211, Art. 18, No. 2.
[59] Decree-Law 211, Art. 22.
[60] Montt and Mordoj, 38, and *FNE v. D&S and Cencosud*, Case No. 2998-2008, Supreme Court, Decision of July 24, 2008.
[61] Montt and Mordoj, 39.
[62] Decree-Law 211, Art. 22 and Art. 39.

IV. Mandate and boundaries of the Competition Authority

A. Competition law mandate: Decree-Law 211, jurisprudence, and the Chile–USA Free Trade Agreement

Decree-Law 211 states that the objective of the law is *to promote and defend free competition in the markets,*[63] although this objective has been considered imprecise and vague by academic commentators.[64] However, the Resolutive Commission declared that the mandate of competition law was not only to take care of consumer interests, but to also consider the economic freedom of all participants in economic activities (producers, entrepreneurs, and consumers), in order to benefit society as a whole. Accordingly, the Resolutive Commission has repeatedly stated that "the purpose of competition law is the interest of society in producing more and better goods, at lower prices, which can be achieved by ensuring liberty of all participants in economic activities."[65]

The Free Trade Agreement between the US and Chile, in force since 2004, incorporated an explicit definition of the competition law policy objective for each country: promoting economic efficiency and consumer welfare.[66] Consequently, it can be argued that the purpose of competition law in Chile is reflected at a supranational law level, despite reasonable arguments on the non-enforceable effects of the competition law chapters envisaged in free trade agreements.[67]

B. Consumer protection, regulated industries, and unfair competition practices

Neither the NEPO's nor the Competition Tribunal's mandates formally extend to consumer protection. In consumer issues, a separate body, the National Consumer Service (SERNAC), is in charge of consumer protection,[68] an area of law with a special regulation since 1996.[69] Although the SERNAC cannot sanction infringements to consumer policy, it can enforce and prosecute Consumer Law infringements through civil courts. The NEPO and SERNAC have carried out joint initiatives on some occasions, such as a merger case regarding supermarkets and retailers filed in 2007 at the Competition Tribunal.[70]

[63] Decree-Law 211, Art. 1.

[64] Francisco Agüero, "Nuevos elementos para el debate sobre el bien jurídico libre competencia," Boletín Latinoamericano de Competencia (2004).

[65] Ruling 90, §. 17, Ruling 93, § 12, Ruling 171, § 15, and Ruling 368, § 2, Resolutive Commission.

[66] Chile–U.S. Free Trade Agreement, Article 16.1: Anticompetitive Business Conduct.

[67] D. Daniel Sokol, *Order without (Enforceable) Law: Why Countries Enter into Non-Enforceable Competition Policy Chapters in Free Trade Agreements,* 2007.

[68] Created by Law No. 18.959.

[69] Law No. 19.496.

[70] OECD, Directorate for Financial and Enterprise Affairs Competition Committee, Global Forum on Competition, *The Interface Between Competition And Consumer Policies, Contribution from Chile*, 2008, § 12.

Specialized industry regulators exist in different areas of the Chilean economy, such as telecommunications, energy, water and sewage, financial markets, the banking sector, private health insurers, pension funds, etc. In general, regulators do not have in their respective acts rules regarding competition law or competition policy mandates. However, in some cases (banking, electricity, water and sewage) special rules apply to mergers or integration between regulated firms.[71] Regulators usually do not file claims or initiate consultation procedures before the Competition Tribunal. The exception to this has been in energy and telecommunications issues, where several competition procedures have taken place in the last decades promoted by utilities regulators.[72] Only, by exception—a rare one, indeed, not familiar to many practitioners in Chile—certain insurance transactions are exempted from antitrust laws.[73]

The Competition Tribunal has, within its scope, regulated industries such as telecommunications, electricity, water and sewage, and natural gas utilities. Within those industries it has to inform administrative regulators whether price controls should be adopted in those areas, if the markets do not meet competitive conditions. Accordingly, the Competition Tribunal may inform an administrative agency that price controls should be terminated when conditions in that market ensure competitive outcomes. In broadcasting and ports, the Tribunal has jurisdiction also in concession transfers or tendering for new port infrastructure.

Article 3, section c, Decree-Law 211 states that unfair competition practices, carried out with the purpose of attaining, maintaining, or increasing a dominant position, are deemed competition law infringements. In unfair trade matters, Statute No. 20.169, enacted in 2007, establishes the right of private parties alleging unfair competition from agents to sue in civil courts, whether these agents attain market power or not. After the unfair competition decision is awarded against the sued party, the civil court has to send the file to the NEPO, who may or may not bring a corresponding claim before the Competition Tribunal. In that case, and in contradiction of Decree-Law 211's fining rules, the fine cannot exceed US$75,000. In both cases, that is, unfair competition practices and competition law infringements, private parties may recover damages after the judicial decision that establishes the legal infringement.

C. Public administration, regulators, and state-owned enterprises

The Decree-Law 211 does not limit the scope of competition law to private entities. Thus the Competition Tribunal has declared that it can decide cases regarding state-owned enterprises and even administrative bodies, such as government ministries when they are acting as regulators.[74] Therefore the Competition Tribunal

[71] *See* General Electric Services Law, Art. 46, General Water and Sanitation Law, Arts 62 and 65, et al.

[72] Where specialized regulators exist, competition agencies tend to interfere in the industry-specific regulation, especially in telecoms and energy issues.

[73] Decree-Law 3057, of 1977, Art. 5.

[74] OECD-IADB, *Chile—Peer Review of Competition Law and Policy*, 2004, p. 33.

has decided repeatedly that it has a *broad mandate* to evaluate potential situations that may affect competition, such as rules and regulations, tender offer rules, public bids, and other administrative acts of government that may be deemed anti-competitive.

Surprisingly, especially considering the institutional setting before 2003, major successes were achieved in the first thirty years since the enactment of Decree-Law 211 in areas of privatized firms or network industries, where the NEPO or competition commissions focused their attention and enforcement efforts, although those achievements diminished enforcement activities in non-regulated markets.[75]

In the last couple of years, the Competition Tribunal has ruled against sector regulators' decisions or activities in cases affecting public works franchising,[76] broadband public subsidies and public policy,[77] and telecommunication services previously characterized as illegal by the regulator (firms that provided those allegedly illegal services won a margin-squeeze claim against one of the incumbent firm before the Competition Tribunal).[78]

In these decisions, sector-specific regulation has not been a full defense for the defendants.[79] Nevertheless, only one Competition Tribunal decision concerning regulators or the Administration fined the condemned defendants, and in the one case the fine was small.[80] However, the Supreme Court has reversed several decisions concerning and affecting public policy and local councils.[81] All in all, and notwithstanding the fact that utility or sector specific regulators and the NEPO are administrative bodies, there has been some conflict or lack of convergence in certain sectors, such as telecommunications.[82]

D. Enforcement priorities

In Chile, priorities in competition law enforcement and its reform have been issued publicly by presidential candidates in their government programs, and in their annual reports to Congress while serving as presidents. In 1999, for the first time, a presidential government program considered some policy recommendations about competition law,[83] regarding the need for reform of its institutions. In 2005,

[75] OECD—Inter American Development Bank, *Exámenes inter-pares de la política y del derecho de la competencia en América Latina: Un seguimiento. Argentina, Brasil, Chile, México y Perú*, 2007, 19.

[76] *Nutripro SA v. Puerto Terrestre Los Andes Sociedad Concesionaria S.A. y Fisco*, Case No. C 127-07, July 21, 2010, Decision 100, TDLC.

[77] *Netland Chile SA v. Ministerio de Transportes y Telecomunicaciones*, Decision 105, October 22, 2010, TDLC.

[78] *OPS et al. v. Telefónica Móviles*, October 10, 2009, Decision 88, TDLC.

[79] Montt and Mordoj, *id.*, 38.

[80] *FNE v. Municipalidad de Curicó*, November 4th, 2008, case No. C 137-07, Decision 77 TDLC.

[81] Case No. 396-2004, July 15, 2007, Decision Supreme Court, and Case No. 4797-2008, January 27, 2009.

[82] OECD, Directorate for Financial and Enterprise Affairs Competition Committee, *Latin American Competition Forum, Session IV: Competition Issues in Telecommunications, Contribution from Chile (FNE)*, 2009, § 7 and § 21.

[83] Ricardo Lagos, *Para crecer con igualdad*, October 1999, 5.

Michelle Bachelet's government program devoted several pages to competition law and its application, in issues such as cartel prosecution, leniency, fines, institutional reforms, and damages awards.[84] This was a clear shift from previous governments. More recently, competition policy has appeared as a key issue in the annual presidential reports to the Chilean Congress. That was the case in 2009, when the president, through the presidential public report, promoted the criminalization of cartels, submitting a bill to Congress on the subject.[85] In 2010, the annual presidential report argued in favor of a competition policy prosecutor for the agriculture sector.[86] Subsequently, the NEPO created a specialized agriculture unit in 2010.

Enforcement priorities are made explicit by the NEP in its annual reports, competition day speeches (*Día de la Competencia*), and in the NEPO's annual reports, reflecting the concern of the NEP to catch and prosecute cartels.[87] For instance, Competition Day 2008 focused its agenda on bid rigging in public procurement,[88] while activities for 2007[89] and 2009[90] were devoted to cartel prosecution and leniency programs. In 2010, the priorities shifted to cartels and business organizations, issuing in January 2011 a guideline regarding business organizations and competition law.

Consequently, these public policy statements have been reflected both in guidelines and in claims filed at the Competition Tribunal. Although the data reveal that since 2004 the NEPO has brought thirty-five claims before the Competition Tribunal, and only fourteen of them are cartel cases, since 2008 the number of dominance and cartel filings has evened out. Since 2009, cartel prosecutions by the NEPO have become predominant, leaving monopolization cases to private litigation. These results show that the explicit change in enforcement policies has actually been reflected in more cartel prosecutions.

V. Procedural norms

In the following section we describe briefly the procedural regulations regarding both competition law infringements and non-adversarial or consultation matters. These two general procedures have in common that the process at the Competition Tribunal is written, with the exception of the hearing of the case, and that parties must be represented by lawyers before the Competition Tribunal.[91]

[84] Michelle Bachelet, *Estoy contigo, Programa de Gobierno 2006–2010,* Santiago, October 2005, 42–4.
[85] Michelle Bachelet, *Mensaje Presidencial 21 de mayo de 2009.*
[86] Sebastián Piñera, *Mensaje Presidencial 21 de mayo de 2010.*
[87] NEPO, *Informe Anual 2007*, and NEPO, *Informe Anual 2009,* March 2010.
[88] NEPO, *Día de la Competencia 2008*, Programa, 2008.
[89] NEPO, *Día de la Competencia 2008*, Programa, 2008.
[90] NEPO, *Día de la Competencia 2009*, Programa, 2009.
[91] Decree-Law 211, Art. 20.

A. Procedure in adversarial issues (competition law infringements)

In the case of competition law infringements, the procedure may be initiated at the request of the NEP, through a claim filed at the Competition Tribunal, or by a lawsuit filed by a private individual. Private lawsuits must be immediately conveyed to the NEPO. The complaint or lawsuit must contain a clear and precise account of the facts, acts, or agreements that may infringe competition law, and indicate the market or markets that may be affected by the presumed violation. Where the complaint or lawsuit does not fulfill the aforementioned requirements, the Competition Tribunal must grant the plaintiff or petitioner a term of three days to rectify the mentioned omissions. After this term has expired without rectifying the omissions, the Tribunal may reject the lawsuit or request for proceedings. Once the Competition Tribunal admits a complaint or request, it must notify it to the affected party, which may reply within a fifteen-day period or ask for an extension period established by the Tribunal, which may not exceed thirty days.[92] Since 2004,[93] a total of 216 competition law infringement cases have been filed before the Competition Tribunal. Among all final decisions, the Competition Tribunal has issued 105 decisions that formally adjudicate the dispute and 55 decisions that close the case without doing so.[94]

After the time to reply to a claim has expired, the Competition Tribunal may summon the parties to a conciliation hearing. If the Tribunal does not deem it pertinent, or if the conciliation procedure fails, the Competition Tribunal can set a twenty-day period for the submission of evidence, if relevant, pertinent, and contradictory factual issues need to be proved.[95]

General evidence is admissible in accordance with the general rules set forth in the Civil Procedure Code (that is, witness testimony, expert testimony, documents, personal inspection, party admissions, etc.). It is also admissible evidence any indication or background information that, in the opinion of the Competition Tribunal, is suitable for establishing the facts. The Competition Tribunal may investigate *ex-officio* at any stage of the case, and even after the hearing, when it considers it indispensable for clarifying facts or evidence that still appear to be obscure and doubtful.[96]

Regarding witnesses, declarations are limited to three witnesses designated by each party for each of the relevant "points to be proved" decreed by the Competition Tribunal, except that the latter, upon request made by a party when submitting its list of witnesses, increases the said limit. Evidentiary proceedings are performed before one of the members of the Competition Tribunal, who may ask the witnesses or experts any questions he deems suitable,[97] exclude statements

[92] Decree-Law 211, Art. 20.

[93] May 2004–December 2010.

[94] Those decisions vary from conciliations, settlements, archiving the case after a long time with no procedural activity, etc.

[95] Decree-Law 211, Art. 22.

[96] Decree-Law 211, Art. 22.

[97] These proceedings are audio recorded by the Competition Tribunal.

and questions of the parties that relate to irrelevant or inadmissible matters, and resolve objections.[98] Once the evidence period expires, the Competition Tribunal must set the date and time for the public hearing, where the parties' attorneys may file pleadings, if requested by any of them.[99]

The Competition Tribunal assesses the evidence according to the rules of logic and acquired knowledge. The final ruling must be substantiated, and must state fact, law, and economic reasons on which it is based. Minority votes, if any, must be expressed.[100]

In its judgment, the Competition Tribunal may adopt measures such as modifying or terminating acts, contracts, agreements, systems, or pacts that are contrary to the provisions of Decree-Law 211; ordering the modification or dissolution of companies and corporations and other private entities involved in competition law infringements; imposing fines up to an amount equivalent to US$17.5 million, and in the case of sanctioning cartels, up to an amount of US$26.5 million. When imposing a fine, the Competition Tribunal may consider circumstances such as the economic benefit obtained from the infringement, the seriousness of the behavior, the fact of being a recidivist, and the cooperation provided to the NEPO before or during the investigation.[101]

The Competition Tribunal can, at any stage of the trial or prior to its commencement, decree preliminary injunctions or temporary restraining orders that may be needed to avoid the negative effects of the conduct that is the subject of the complaint and to safeguard the common interest, for the time being. The adoption of these measures must be notified to the parties, who may challenge them.[102] The petitioner must attach background information that constitutes at least a serious presumption of the right claimed and of the facts reported. The Tribunal may require collateral from the particular actor to assure payment of the damages caused.

Decisions awarded by the Competition Tribunal, except for the final ruling, can be challenged before the same Tribunal (*reposición*). The final ruling is subject to a special recourse before the Supreme Court (*recurso de reclamación*). This recourse in competition matters before the Supreme Court is heard with preference to other matters within the jurisdiction of that court and the filing of this recourse does not suspend the execution of the decision, except in relation to the payment of fines.[103]

Finally, according to Decree-Law 211, the Civil Procedure Code is supplementary to the special procedure contained in Decree-Law 211 regarding all that is compatible with it.[104] Nevertheless, and demonstrating the complexity of competition law infringement procedures, the Criminal Procedure Code is applicable partially in the use of intrusive techniques regarding investigations of cartels, even though it is unusual in Chilean law to mix criminal and civil procedural laws in the same court.

[98] Decree-Law 211, Art. 22.
[99] Decree-Law 211, Art. 23.
[100] Decree-Law 211, Art. 26.
[101] Decree-Law 211, Art. 26.
[102] Decree-Law 211, Art. 25.
[103] Decree-Law 211, Art. 27.
[104] Decree-Law 211, Art. 29.

B. Procedure in non-adversarial issues

All non-adversarial matters—which include merger review, rulemaking, law reform proposals, and sectoral law reports—follow the same procedure rules, which differ from the adversarial ones previously explained.

After the request for a report or merger review, the Competition Tribunal opens the procedure with a decree published in the Official Gazette and on the website of the Tribunal. This decree must be notified to the NEPO, to the public authorities who are directly affected, and to the economic agents who, in the Tribunal's judgment, are related to the matter, so that they and those who have a legitimate interest can contribute any relevant information during a period of no less than fifteen days. Once the period expires, those who have filed a request may evaluate the recommendations that the NEPO made during the information period and communicate in writing their agreement with them to the Tribunal. After the period of no less than fifteen days expires, the Competition Tribunal must convene a public hearing, so that those who contributed information may express their opinions. The Tribunal may obtain information *ex-officio* or upon petition by the interested party, and receive information it deems pertinent.

Decisions and reports issued by the Competition Tribunal on non-adversarial issues can be challenged before the same Tribunal (*reposición*). The final resolutions, regardless of whether or not they set conditions or remedies, may only be challenged before the Supreme Court. This special recourse may be filed by the petitioners, the NEPO, or any of the third parties that have contributed information to the procedure (*recurso de reclamación*).[105] This does not apply to administrative reports issued by the Competition Tribunal which are required by sectoral laws in administrative proceedings, such as telecommunications, electricity, gas, water and sanitation, ports, etc. In those cases, there is no recourse before the Supreme Court. Until December 2010, the Competition Tribunal had issued thirty-two non-adversarial decisions, fifteen decisions different from a judgment that put an end to the proceeding, and seven special reports required by sectoral regulations.

C. Due process norms

The Chilean Constitution (1980) provides in article 19, No. 3 that citizens have the right to a rational and fair process of law, but does not set out with precision the minimum requirements for a due process of law, leaving to decision-makers certain autonomy in defining such elements. The Constitutional Court has filled the gap, clarifying that due process of law consists in timely knowledge of the claim or lawsuit, application of bilateral hearing (*audi alteram pars*), possibility to provide evidence, and a right to challenge the decision before an impartial and qualified court, established earlier by law (Decisions 481 and 1202). The Constitutional

[105] Until recently, parties did not have the right to appeal a negative decision in merger cases.

Court has also concluded that due process of law also imposes the right to a rational and fair legal process, which includes the publicity of jurisdictional decisions and the right to have an adequate legal defense, with lawyers (Decision 1432). As we have noted, Decree-Law 211 contains several rules that define the elements of due process before the Competition Tribunal. In this section, we assess how these rules are *really* appraised by operators of the system, with respect to their legal wording.

1. *Due process and effective defense*

In this area, there is a growing importance of the investigative proceedings handled by the NEPO. In those proceedings, the Competition Tribunal has decided that the Administrative Procedure Act applies to cases investigated by the NEPO.[106] Therefore, minimal rules regarding investigations and evidence apply, besides the rules contained in Decree-Law 211. The Administrative Procedure Act explicitly has an appeal and revision system for administrative procedures.

More than 70 percent of the answers in our survey consider that the NEPO's decisions in investigative proceedings (for example, summoning witnesses, request for documents, filing the case) are not effectively reviewable, whether internally or externally. The lawyers who were interviewed added that when they had attempted, those requests of revision to the NEP were generally dismissed. They also mentioned that the use and examination of evidence provided in this phase was uncertain, since the argumentation of the NEPO's final decision was not supported by the evidence.

Critics argue that there is secrecy and disorder in administrative files, which complicates potential collaboration with the NEPO and with the legal right of defense. More recently, since the Transparency Statute was enacted (Statute No. 20.285, and Art. 8 of the Constitution), if someone requires a copy of a complaint, NEPO has demanded the requestor to invoke the Statute on Transparency. In all cases, it has refused to answer and give copies, according to an interviewed lawyer. This means that the complainant is always being consulted and is always refusing to answer. As such, the only recourse left is to resort to the *Consejo para la Transparencia* (Transparency Agency). By doing so, the NEPO remits the decision to another entity. The procedure to obtain copies of the NEPO files, prior to 2009, was simpler, although it did not usually require the approval of the parties. Since the enactment of this statute, the NEPO has emphasized that transparency in their actions, files, and documents are limited to the exceptions detailed in Statute No. 20.285.[107]

[106] Case No. C 132-07, September 13, 2007, Decision TDLC, and decision in case No. 77-05, April 13, 2006.

[107] NEPO and Competition Tribunal. *Working Party No. 3 on Co-operation and Enforcement, Procedural Fairness Issues in Civil and Administrative Enforcement (OECD Working Paper)* <http://www.oecd.org/competition/mergers/48825133.pdf>.

Regarding due process before the Competition Tribunal, the survey's results indicate that more than 85 percent of the answers consider that defendants are informed in a timely manner of the complaints brought against them before the Tribunal. In general, more than 75 percent of the answers agreed with statements regarding due process of law, in topics such as hearing rights, procedural issues (avoiding surprises, unexpected procedural events, or deadlines that cannot be reasonably complied with), right to provide evidence at trial, rights to cross-examine expert and non-expert witnesses, and counterparts, etc. However, some opinions consider that procedural rights of the parties may vary substantially if the decision adopted during the trial was taken by judges of the Competition Tribunal who are lawyers or by members who are economists.[108]

2. *Independence and non-discrimination*

One of the criteria for assessing the institutions of the competition system is independence from external interference in the application of the law to particular parties. In a recent joint opinion, the Competition Tribunal and the NEPO pointed out that they act independently from each other, a circumstance that is facilitated by the clear roles of each body as stated in Decree-Law 211.[109]

In this sense, NEPO values the 2009 reform of Decree-Law 211, specifically in the appointment and removal mechanisms for the NEP.[110] After Law 20.361 was passed, the Tribunal noted that the introduction of new grounds of recusation for judges strengthened the standards for ensuring independence, and also facilitates the pursuit of excellence. New incompatibilities defined in the Statute also allow professionals to combine their work as substitute judges with restricted professional activities, providing guarantees of impartiality.[111] In a comprehensive assessment of the Chilean system and institutional arrangements, the Competition Tribunal stated that "the existence of a dual authority, constituted by the NEPO, who investigates and files claims, and the independence of the decision-making body [the Competition Tribunal] answers well to the need of separation between the investigative and decision-making phases."[112]

In general, our survey showed that the NEPO was considered to act independently from public pressures or inappropriate private influence in judicial proceedings, both at the Competition Tribunal and the Supreme Court. In broad terms, lawyers agreed that NEPO acts independently. A similar result appeared in the case of administrative investigations undertaken by the NEPO. When asked about the

[108] This is a consequence of the fact that witnesses are examined with the presence of only one judge of the Competition Tribunal, a role that may be assumed by both economists and lawyers.

[109] NEPO and Competition Tribunal. *Working Party No. 3 on Co-operation and Enforcement, Procedural Fairness Issues in Civil and Administrative Enforcement (Documento para la OCDE)*, 2.

[110] NEPO, *Informe Anual 2009*, 13.

[111] Competition Tribunal, *Quinta Cuenta Pública del Presidente del Tribunal de Defensa de la Libre Competencia Don Eduardo Jara Miranda*, 2009, 19.

[112] Competition Tribunal, *Segunda Cuenta Pública del Presidente del Tribunal de Defensa de la Libre Competencia Don Eduardo Jara Miranda*, 2006, 3.

possibility that the NEPO could initiate investigations or complaints for pure publicity or political purposes, and without a technical basis, a large majority of the interviewees rejected that possibility (69 percent).

The interviews we conducted show that practitioners see slight differences in the way the NEPO relates to the administration, in comparison to the way it relates to private parties. A risk is perceived in the administrative relationship between the Ministry of Economy and the NEP, since the ministerial agenda may influence the prosecutorial conduct of the NEPO. Nevertheless, the fact that the Competition Tribunal could mount cases against the administration, regulators, and other public bodies when their behavior affects the competitive process may prove to be problematic for the NEPO if it has a favorable bias towards the public administration. This has been the case when the NEPO has investigated or informed the Competition Tribunal of a case where the defendant is a public body. For instance, in a recent case tried before the Tribunal, the NEPO did not issue a report requested by the Competition Tribunal during the whole extension of the case (three years).[113] However, it must be noted that the NEPO has filed claims against the Civil Aeronautics Board (an administrative body) and several local councils for infringements of competition law.[114]

The opinion about the independence of the Competition Tribunal is very favorable, both by interviewed and surveyed lawyers. More than 80 percent of the latter consider this tribunal to act independently, both from private and public interference. The prohibitions, incompatibilities, and asset declaration regulations established by statute are considered to operate in practice in such a way that the Competition Tribunal members can work with independence.

The Tribunal must also be independent from the prosecutorial body, the NEPO. In that sense, the Competition Tribunal has rejected and sanctioned the use of the NEPO's investigative powers during trials,[115] declaring void the evidence brought by the NEPO to the process.[116] Another example of independence has been the order given by the Competition Tribunal to the NEPO to act in good faith during the trial, limiting the number of possible witnesses it had presented (757 possible witnesses, when the law at the time allowed only three witnesses per "point to be proved" and only three of those points had been decreed in the case), considering that this behavior looked like a procedural strategy affecting the due process between parties.[117]

Discrimination does not seem to be an issue of concern in the system, and it can be reviewed with the independence of the institutions. The fear is that one agency could favor certain parties. In this order, the NEPO has stated that after submitting

[113] *See Nutripro SA v. Puerto Terrestre Los Andes Sociedad Concesionaria SA and Fisco*, Case No. C 127-07, July 21, 2010, Decision 100, TDLC.

[114] *FNE v. Junta de Aeronáutica Civil*, Case No. C 148-07, January 16, 2009, Decision 82, TDLC; *FNE v. Municipalidad de Antofagasta*, Case No. C 172-08, December 29, 2009, Decision 92, TDLC; *FNE v. Municipalidad de Curicó*, Case No. C 137-07, November 4, 2008, Decision 77, TDLC.

[115] TDLC decision in case No. 79-05, July 7, 2007.

[116] TDLC decision in case No. 79-05, April 8, 2008.

[117] TDLC decision in case No. 79-05, April 19, 2007.

its claim to the Competition Tribunal, "[the Tribunal] *prosecutes the case (. . .) in equivalent terms as any other party, with no particular procedural privileges.*"[118]

The NEPO considers that publishing NEP's agenda online on a daily basis is not only an improvement in transparency but also is a tool that has "allowed the creation of citizen trust in the impartiality and non-discrimination [of the NEPO] when dealing with economic agents and private parties."[119] In addition to this statement, the Competition Tribunal has also ordered the NEPO to act and require information from investigated agents in a non-discriminatory way when exercising investigative powers.[120]

The interviewed practitioners agreed, and dismissed possible allegations of discrimination by the NEPO. Consistently, a large majority of the answers to our survey dismissed the possibility of discrimination based on nationality, wealth, notoriety, or social class of the parties, both during administrative investigations (75 percent +) and judicial proceedings before the Competition Tribunal and Supreme Court (almost 80 percent).

Finally, wages of the tribunal members and officers are said to be high enough to safeguard their impartiality. In general, the survey reflects the view that the Supreme Court is considered to be independent from public and private influence.

3. *Investigative powers*

The NEPO has declared that the new powers obtained through Statute No. 20.361 are consistent with international best practices in prosecuting cartels.[121] An overwhelming majority (75 percent) of the surveyed lawyers, and the majority of the interviewed lawyers, believes that the new powers NEPO acquired in 2009 are more than sufficient. Only the institution of an undercover agent is absent in the legal system. In the case of the Competition Tribunal, almost 90 percent of the lawyers we surveyed say that the power to impose sanctions and remedies is sufficient.

4. *Confidentiality of sensitive data*

Information provided by economic agents during investigations or judicial procedures in competition cases can be highly sensitive, and may include commercial and trade secrets. Therefore, commercial data should be made public only in limited cases, in order not to affect the competitive advantages of the parties. The relevance of confidential information in competition litigation is key, in order to provide confidently any data to the NEPO during an investigation. If the information is revealed or disclosed to rivals, business and the economy can seriously be affected.

118 OECD, 2010, § 2.1.
119 NEPO. *Informe Anual 2008*, 2008, 25.
120 TDLC, Decision in case *Solicitud de Telefónica Móviles de Chile SA*, November 7, 2006.
121 NEPO, *Balance Cuatrienio 2006–2010*, 2010, 21.

In Chile, both the NEPO—during the investigation—and the Competition Tribunal—during trials—attempt to balance the rights of defense with the need to protect data confidentiality, by making available public versions of sensitive confidential information.[122] Parties must provide public (sanitized) versions of secret or confidential files. The public (sanitized) version must have sufficient information available to allow an adequate legal defense. The Competition Tribunal can decide whether the provided public version is sufficient. If it is not sufficient, it can declare that information must be made available to the parties.[123]

In the course of investigative procedures before the NEPO, it can be declared *ex officio* or on request of a party that certain information is confidential.[124] The NEPO has become conscious of the risks and effects of disclosure of confidential or commercial information. NEPO's current policy is to protect as much as possible the confidentiality and reputation of the investigated agents. However, the protection of confidentiality must be balanced and should not interfere with NEPO's duty to investigate and prosecute.[125] Decree-Law 211 allows investigations initiated by the NEPO not to be communicated to the affected party, pending the authorization of the Competition Tribunal.[126]

Despite the fact that the NEPO has issued an internal guideline for investigations, the real procedure applied to investigations at that office remains unclear. However, the General Administrative Procedure Act can be applied to investigation proceedings, as has been established in several rulings issued by the Competition Tribunal.[127] The 2009 statutory reform allowed the NEP to dismiss *in limine* investigations requested by private parties to the NEPO when lacking any basis or relevance.

The Competition Tribunal has recognized that information gathered by the NEPO during investigative procedures may have a confidential and strategic character, and therefore cannot be accessed by rivals nor disclosed to the public.[128]

There is consensus amongst surveyed lawyers—more than 80 percent agree, moderately or strongly—that during NEPO's administrative investigations, economic agents can rely on the effective guarantee that any confidential information remains subject to strict confidentiality. This understanding is similar for the interviewed lawyers. To their knowledge, they did not know of any infringement of the secrecy of the information.[129]

[122] OECD, 2010, § 11.

[123] OECD, 2010, § 12. *See* also, Competition Tribunal's Internal Regulation No. 11/2008.

[124] Decree-Law 211, Art. 39 § a, and OECD, 2010, § 14.

[125] OECD, 2010, § 19.

[126] Decree-Law 211, Art. 39 § a.

[127] Competition Tribunal, rulings 5/24/2006, in file No. C 60-05; 4/13/2006, in file No. C 77-05; 13/9/2007, in file No. C 132-07; 5/29/2007, in file No. C 79-05.

[128] Competition Tribunal ruling April 13, 2006, Case No. C 77/2005, § 18º, § 19º and § 20º.

[129] However, one of the authors of this chapter, as a practitioner, saw in a NEPO investigative file, provided as evidence to a Competition Tribunal case, confidential commercial data from a firm that was not supposed to have been disclosed to rival firms.

For the Competition Tribunal, more than 85 percent of the lawyers consider that the confidentiality of information provided during judicial proceedings is effectively safeguarded from competitors and third parties.

5. Proportionality of remedies

Regarding the proportionality of the remedies imposed by the Competition Tribunal and requested by the NEPO, the survey results showed that almost 45 percent of the answers consider that the fines, remedies, and sanctions requested by the NEPO to the Competition Tribunal are not proportional to the facts and law of the case. We received several comments that the NEPO has a tendency to request the maximum amount of fines established in Decree-Law 211, with no proportion between the demanded fines and the infringement. In contrast with those results, the interview group emphasized that the NEPO is prudent when requesting the Competition Tribunal impose fines. The fines are considered relatively low in comparison to other jurisdictions. Other practitioners believe that there is a signaling or deterrent rationale in NEPO's requests for fines.

On the other hand, more than half of the surveyed lawyers thought that sanctions and remedies imposed by the Competition Tribunal were proportionate. Similar results were obtained for the Supreme Court. The interviewed practitioners consider that sanctions and remedies imposed by the Competition Tribunal are proportionate to the facts and law involved in each case.

On this issue, the Supreme Court has reasoned that the enumerated circumstances in which Decree-Law 211 requires the court to consider when to impose sanctions and remedies are merely examples (that is, a non-exhaustive list). The Competition Tribunal, according to the Supreme Court, must exercise its sanctioning power with prudence. In any case, it must state the reasons that explain why it decided to impose one sanction or another, and in case of fines, state the reasons that explain the amount imposed on the defendant.[130] Thus, this discretionary power entails the obligation to provide precise reasons and circumstances about the parameters used in order to set a fine. Communicating and clarifying this reasoning is necessary in order to ensure a due process of law, in its formal or substantive form.[131]

6. Right to challenge agency decisions

All final decisions taken by the Competition Tribunal can be challenged before the Supreme Court. In its review, the Supreme Court assesses *a quo* Tribunal decisions in broad terms; evaluating due process, jurisdiction, factual bases of the ruling, and the reasonableness of the sanctions or remedies imposed.[132] The nature of the special recourse (*recurso de reclamación*) and the powers/standard of review of the

[130] Supreme Court, July 7, 2010, Decision Case No. 8077-2009.
[131] Case No. 2339-2008, August 13, 2008, Decision Supreme Court.
[132] OECD, 2010, § 33.

Court have been the subject of discussion by experts. Cruz and Zárate have argued that the review powers the Supreme Court has are unclear and ill-defined. In their view, this has had consequences in the deference and scope of review of the Competition Tribunal's decisions. In the institutional design created after the 2003 reform, they criticize the absence of discussion of the nature and scope of review of the *recurso de reclamación*. They argue that there was no awareness of the powers granted to the Supreme Court. Therefore, according to these authors, the Supreme Court became the "*ultimate decision-maker in competition policy,*" having a non-deferential attitude towards the Competition Tribunal, and delving into technical issues in its decisions. Thus, the Supreme Court has based its review on its expertise and experience in civil and criminal law instead of antitrust law and economics.[133] Consequently, they reason, in order to quash a Competition Tribunal decision, attorneys must argue in civil and criminal law terms.

The Supreme Court recently stated that the legal history of the 2003 competition law reform allows the court to review in full the reasoning behind the Competition Tribunal's decision. Certainly, this includes both the legal and economic analysis made by the Competition Tribunal. For the Supreme Court, the *reclamación* does not seem to limit its jurisdictional activity and powers when reviewing a decision from the Competition Tribunal.[134]

On the issue of the special recourse to challenge decisions before the Supreme Court (*recurso de reclamación*), the opinion is split. We find answers form attorneys that range from a total disapproval of the review undertaken by the Supreme Court, to approval on procedural grounds. The lack of economic expertise of the Supreme Court judges is not troublesome for some of the lawyers we surveyed. For other practitioners, the quality of review of the Supreme Court did not match that of the Tribunal's decisions. All in all, almost 75 percent of the answers of the survey consider that the proceedings before the Supreme Court guarantee due process of law. Interviewed practitioners also agree on the uncertainty of the extension of the *reclamación* to the Supreme Court. As a matter of fact, each and every one of the interviewed lawyers had different proposals regarding this topic.

Contrary to Cruz and Zárate's opinion, the NEPO has recognized that the Supreme Court shows a high level of deference to the Competition Tribunal's rulings. From a statistical perspective, decisions are not normally reversed by the Supreme Court. However, the Supreme Court has quashed decisions that affect administrative bodies when decisions invade the field of competence of regulators. In general, we may observe, deference has been a "happy accident"—that is, a situation where the Supreme Court non-deferential decision coincides with the decisions adopted by the Competition Tribunal—where the Supreme Court has rarely reviewed decisions and their economic and legal reasoning, with the exception of decisions that affect administrative bodies, and on occasion where the Competition Tribunal has issued split decisions (notably, cartel cases with no hard evidence).

[133] Cruz and Zarate, 159.

[134] Supreme Court, Decision in case No. 4797-2008, January 1, 2009.

Finally, the amount of the fines imposed by the Supreme Court is frequently reduced and rarely raised.[135] On the issue of the *reclamación,* the Competition Tribunal acknowledged in 2006 that, although the Supreme Court can review both evidence and legal issues, a careful reading of its decisions shows that it has concentrated its reviews on substantive and procedural law while supporting the economic analysis and technical considerations regarding the markets adopted by the Competition Tribunal.[136]

The members of the Supreme Court are not provided with any formal training in antitrust economics or applied industrial organization in order to prepare them for deciding recourses filed against the Competition Tribunal's decisions. The survey results show that lawyers assess the Court as deferential towards the Competition Tribunal.

D. Institutional performance norms

After describing how the competition law institutions are established in the Chilean competition legislation, with some references to the case law and the application of due process rules, we now examine the *modus operandi* behind the rules contained in Decree-Law 211, in connection to institutional performance.

1. Expertise in the decision-making process

The Competition Tribunal recently revealed how it elaborates its decisions, stating that its decisions are based exclusively on the work of its judges and *staff.*[137] In competition law infringements decisions, both counterfactual evidence and alternative scenarios are considered by the Competition Tribunal.[138] The Tribunal bases its judgment exclusively on the evidence gathered in the process, filed and produced according to due process of law.[139] When discussing and drafting a decision, the Tribunal says its members study OECD and ICN guidelines, along with relevant legal and economic literature.[140] Also, the Tribunal considers that international fora of competition law provide its judges and officials the opportunity to train and acquire the experience of their peers, as a complement to the work they perform every day in their functions.[141] These revelations are certainly

[135] OECD, 2010, § 33. *FNE v Cia. Chilena de Fósforos SA,* Case No. 277-2010, June 2, 2010, Supreme Court Decision and *FNE v. Transportes Central Ltda.* et al., Case No. 1746-2010, December 29, 2010, Supreme Court Decision.

[136] Competition Tribunal, *Segunda Cuenta Pública del Presidente del Tribunal de Defensa de la Libre Competencia Don Eduardo Jara Miranda,* 2006, 10.

[137] OECD, Directorate for Financial and Enterprise Affairs Competition Committee, *Procedural Fairness Issues in Civil and Administrative Enforcement,* Chile, 15 June 2010, § 6. It has to be noted that the abovementioned report "represent[s] the joint opinion of both the FNE and the TDLC unless otherwise stated." Ibid., § 4.

[138] OECD, 2010, § 5.

[139] OECD, 2010, § 8.

[140] OECD, 2010, § 10.

[141] Competition Tribunal, *Quinta Cuenta Pública del Presidente del Tribunal de Defensa de la Libre Competencia Don Eduardo Jara Miranda,* 2009, 21.

unusual for Chilean courts, which are not accustomed to disclosing decision-making processes.

Regarding the recruitment and development of its staff, NEPO has declared that training of its officials is a key tool for achieving its aims and moving towards better analysis. Therefore, the NEP has promoted staff dialogue within the NEPO, which permits it to take a look at various aspects of institutional management. From this effort, a human resources policy has been established, in addition to induction courses, training and performance evaluation.[142]

The survey reveals that civil servants working at the NEPO are considered experts in their field, applying with criteria their knowledge in cases handled by them (according to 77 percent of the surveyed practitioners and 68 percent of the interviewed ones). However, spontaneous comments affirmed that there were uneven levels of knowledge and variations between civil servants employed by the NEPO. The interviews reflected the fact that there is an overall favorable opinion of the NEPO as an economic prosecutor. There is a broad opinion that there is a clear tendency to incorporate better trained personnel.

In the case of the Competition Tribunal, answers were even more favorable. Almost 80 percent of the surveyed lawyers agree that judges and officers are experts in their respective fields of expertise. In the case of the decisions and rulings of the tribunal, more than 70 percent considered them to have solid economic bases. Similar results were reflected from our interviews. The expertise of the Competition Tribunal has been recognized even by the Supreme Court, noting that "the [Tribunal] was created as a high professional level tribunal and expert in [competition law issues]."[143]

Our survey reflects that 67 percent of the lawyers hold the view that the Supreme Court decisions regarding competition law do not have a solid economic base. However, there is a sense of deference by the Supreme Court towards the Competition Tribunal, and that the Court reviews with good sense and good criteria competition law decisions (47 percent). When asked specifically about the economic deference of the Supreme Court towards the Competition Tribunal, 37 percent moderately agree with that statement, and another 38 percent more than agree with the statement. Cases usually mentioned by experts and practitioners in which the Supreme Court has not had a solid economic reasoning have been few. Respondents commonly cited the *James Hardie* case (in which the Supreme Court quashed a predatory-pricing decision, allowing such an allegation in the absence of market power), and several cartel cases (in which the Supreme Court reversed decisions taken by the Competition Tribunal).

Most of the interviewed lawyers consider that the judges of the specialized chamber of the Supreme Court that review the Competition Tribunal's decisions were not experts in competition law, but had a reasonable understanding of the

[142] NEPO. *Balance Cuatrienio 2006–2010*, 2010, 29.

[143] Case No. 4332-2005, January 10, 2006, Decision Supreme Court. A similar reasoning in Supreme Court Decision No. 4862-2007, December 26, 2007, § 9.

field. However, they noted that notwithstanding that fact, they were good specialists in public law (that is, constitutional and administrative law), and in recent times an increased interest has been observed in attending competition law courses (we were not able to verify which courses they had attended, although they have recently started quoting competition law textbooks, both Chilean and foreign, but only in Spanish).[144] Asked about the economic reasoning of those decisions, most of the practitioners replied that in broad terms the Supreme Court is reluctant to express opinions on economic issues addressed in the Competition Tribunal's decisions. Therefore, most of the topics discussed are centered on essentially legal topics and not on economic ones.

2. Transparency in policy formulation and decision-making

In 2005, the Chilean Constitution was amended and in its article 8 a new value or right was embedded: transparency of acts and decisions of public bodies. Accordingly, acts and decisions of all bodies of the State are public, as are their procedures and reasoning, subject to limited exceptions to protect; for example, human rights, national security, and other national interest.

In a recent report elaborated by the NEPO, which assessed the 2006–2010 quadrennial, transparency was identified as one of the two aims of the economic prosecutor. In order to enhance the efficiency of its investigations, NEPO oriented itself towards two issues: "[to] improve the management of investigative processes and [to] increase transparency in [administrative] procedures,"[145] especially in investigations conducted by NEPO. For the prosecutorial agency, the need to regulate and keep its investigations transparent aims to "instruct [...] NEPO staff on the basis, major grounds and methods of analysis of anti-competitive practices, according to best practices of foreign agencies and, on the other hand, grant certainties, to both economic operators and citizens in general, in the way the NEPO fulfills its mission."[146]

Evidence of this commitment, according to the NEPO, can be found in its decision to undertake public consultations of its merger and leniency program and internal investigation guidelines. First drafts of these guidelines received comments from the public and specialized agencies, both national and foreign. Such comments and inputs, in the case of the leniency guide, "upgraded the draft guide and established a methodological tool that provides certainty to participants in the system."[147] In 2009, due to the need to implement its leniency powers in cartel investigations, the NEPO publicly consulted about its leniency guidelines and even asked the Chilean Bar Association for comments to its draft.[148] The final text

[144] Supreme Court Decision No. 3344-2009, August 31, 2009; Supreme Court Decision No. 96-2009, April 16, 2009; Supreme Court Decision No. 4797-2008, January 27, 2009.

[145] NEPO, *Balance Cuatrienio 2006–2010*, 2010, 7.

[146] Ibid., 9.

[147] Ibid., 24.

[148] Colegio de Abogados de Chile, Oficio No. 81, September 21, 2009.

adopted some of the recommendations made by third parties[149] and stated its gratitude for the comments and observations made by third parties (law firms and academia).[150] As a consequence of the guidelines and the certainty it has brought to parties, in 2010 the NEPO filed its first claim before the Competition Tribunal using information obtained from a leniency applicant.[151]

Also, since 2007 some investigations opened by the NEPO and decisions related to investigations and mergers are published on the NEPO's website, but only in cases where this disclosure does not involve the disclosure of classified information. However, NEPO has stated that it is not legally bound to provide the whole reasons that justify its decisions.[152] NEPO also noted the publication of the agenda of the national economic prosecutor, which the public can access on the institutional website. This tool reveals the meetings and other activities of both the chief and sub-chief of the NEPO.[153]

Our survey showed that 56 percent of the lawyers who operate within the Chilean antitrust system are less than "moderately satisfied" of the NEPO's manner of formulating decisions (such as filing a complaint before the Competition Tribunal, and the reasons that justify that decision). Answering a similar question, now regarding the criteria used by the NEPO on how and when to exercise its powers conferred by law, more than 65 percent of the surveyed lawyers said that they were not fully known to the public. Specific and spontaneous answers diverged about the transparency of the role of the NEPO in cases of merger reviews and dominance investigations. In the latter, litigants could appreciate greater transparency in procedures involving the control of mergers and acquisitions than in the investigation of competition law infringements, where secrecy reigned. Interviewed lawyers also expressed worries about the lack of transparency in the NEPO's final decisions. When asked, competition law specialists do not demand full transparency from the NEPO: they agree that excessive information may lead to unsatisfactory and unfair decisions in investigative procedures. Our set of interviewed competition law practitioners had a unanimous opinion regarding the significant advances made in this area by the NEPO, especially in the last few years. The elaboration and diffusion of guidelines and internal decisions has been helpful, but there are still actions to be taken in favor of transparency. The Competition Tribunal has considered that the merger guidelines are only NEPO internal regulations and have no binding effect for economic agents, administrative bodies, or tribunals.[154]

[149] NEPO, *Guía interna sobre beneficios de exención y reducción de multas en casos de colusión,* October 2009.

[150] Competition Tribunal, "TDLC dictó Auto Acordado que establece la información que deben proporcionar las empresas que solicitan su aprobación para una operación de concentración" (3/23/2009). <http://www.tdlc.cl/Portal.Base/Web/VerContenido.aspx?ID=1929&GUID>.

[151] NEPO, *Requerimiento en contra de Whirpool SA y Tecumseh do Brasil Ltda,* July 29, 2010.

[152] NEPO, *Working Party No. 3 on Co-operation and Enforcement, Transparency Issues in Civil and Administrative Proceedings (OECD Working Paper),* 4.

[153] NEPO, *Informe Anual 2008,* 25.

[154] Competition Tribunal ruling in Case No. 101-06, July 27, 2006.

The Competition Tribunal has publicly stated its belief that "transparency has been installed as a hallmark of this Tribunal and that it is a prerequisite for safeguarding its operation independent from any interest different than the general interest of the society."[155] Consequently, the Tribunal has pointed out that one of its concerns has always been transparency and access to information. In this sense, in 2010 the Competition Tribunal emphasized that, since its creation, it had made consistent efforts to gradually make available to the public the work of those who "operate the system," allowing public scrutiny of the grounds of its decisions. Therefore, the public may assess the strength of the economic analysis of the parties and the Tribunal.[156] Also, the agenda and the daily schedule of its President are posted permanently on the Tribunal's website and may be consulted in detail for the previous months. This publicity—rarely seen in Chilean tribunals—aims to avoid any improper interference and limits the space for lobbying.[157] Finally, last year the Competition Tribunal announced its commitment that its website would have in the near future the complete historical records for cases and economic reports presented by parties to the Tribunal, with the databases on which those reports were based, unless they contain confidential commercial information, which should be qualified on a case-by-case basis.[158]

Concerning the Competition Tribunal, it has a very useful and easily accessible website (mostly for practitioners, but also for journalists and media), where the current status of cases handled by that tribunal can be visited, by case and decision. On the website all decisions and rules are published on a daily basis. As a matter of fact, rulings in each case are published online the same day the decision has been issued (in Chile, civil procedure law makes decisions known to the public the day after). Files in general, complaints and lawsuits, legal presentations, economic reports, etc. can be viewed online by the public. This full access to the files dates back to 2007.[159] A critic of this system claims that there is a probable *excess* of transparency. Thus, in some cases complaints that have not been legally notified to the parties can be seen on the website even by third parties. That could be *imprudent*, a practitioner argued, and may affect the due process of law.

The survey's results suggest that the Competition Tribunal has a high level of clarity and coherence in its reasoning, and about how and when it will exercise its non-jurisdictional powers, granted by Decree-Law 211. Nevertheless, after more than 130 decisions (judgments), concepts such as "abuse of dominant position" are still unclear and undefined. Also, the Competition Tribunal has not stated explicitly which test it uses to approve or reject a merger, nor the criteria to establish the amount of the fines. The interviewed practitioners were critical about the coherence

[155] Competition Tribunal, *Sexta Cuenta Pública del Presidente del Tribunal de Defensa de la Libre Competencia Don Eduardo Jara Miranda*, 2010, 8.

[156] Ibid.

[157] Ibid.

[158] Ibid.

[159] Competition Tribunal, "Tribunal potencia sitio web para facilitar acceso a información sobre las causas y favorecer el escrutinio público," <http://www.tdlc.cl/Portal.Base/Web/VerContenido.aspx?ID=1080&GUID>.

of the Competition Tribunal's decisions: therefore, they would like more consistency between different decisions, in order to obtain a more consistent jurisprudence. In a rare decision, when a party requested the Competition Tribunal database and files used in order to calculate the final fine it had imposed, arguing a constitutional right to know the procedures and methodology used, the Tribunal rejected the petition based on the argument that the calculations were self-explanatory, and were elaborated using information provided by the parties.[160]

The Competition Tribunal has also adopted the policy of publicly consulting some of its procedural regulations (*autos acordados*), which must be applied by lawyers that litigate before the Tribunal. In 2009, it consulted a draft of its merger filing requirements guidelines.[161] This practice is not known to any other Chilean tribunal.

Related to this issue, since 2004, *Fundación de la Prensa* and Diego Portales University (Chile) elaborates a survey in which they asked journalists about access to information (*Barómetro de Acceso a la Información*) in several institutions, such as the central bank, administration, legislative branch, sectoral regulators, judiciary, public utilities, and other relevant national organizations (Catholic church, political parties, etc.). In that study, on a national level, the Competition Tribunal has shifted from the fortieth place (2005), to second place in the ranking in 2007,[162] to third in 2008, and to ninth in 2009.[163] In 2010, the Competition Tribunal ranked tenth in the overall ranking.[164] The Supreme Court has moved from the forty-ninth place (2005) to the twelfth (2010).[165] Unfortunately, no information is available for the NEPO in those reports. Decree-Law 211 does not require the NEPO or the Competition Tribunal to provide annual reports on their activities to the public. Nevertheless, since 2005, in the case of the Competition Tribunal, and since 2006, in the case of the NEPO, these institutions have publicly reported their activities in annual reports. These reports can be found on their websites.

On the inclusive review of this issue, the practitioners have a clear appreciation that the Competition Tribunal has much higher practices of transparency than ordinary tribunals in Chile.

3. *Timeliness and opportunity of decisions*

The NEPO has noted that in order to improve the handling of investigations it proposed to reduce deadlines that could delay inquiries. In that sense, over 75 percent of cases have a duration of less than twelve months, and only more complex cases justify longer analysis.[166] Nevertheless, the NEPO has pointed out that while

[160] Competition Tribunal decision, Case No. 79-05, July 8, 2009.

[161] Competition Tribunal Internal Regulation No. 12/2009, regarding the relevant information for the preventive control of mergers.

[162] Fundación de la Prensa—UDP—KAS, *IV Barómetro de Acceso a Información*, Santiago, 2007.

[163] Fundación de la Prensa—UDP, *Barómetro de Acceso a Información 2009*, Santiago, 2009.

[164] Fundación de la Prensa—UDP, *Barómetro de Acceso a Información 2009*, Santiago, 2010.

[165] Fundación de la Prensa—UDP, *Barómetro de Acceso a Información 2009*, Santiago, 2010.

[166] NEPO, *Balance Cuatrienio 2006–2010, 2010,* 7.

Decree-Law 211 does not set a deadline for investigations, the law has stated implicit ones, such as the statute of limitations for collusion (five years) and abuse of dominance (three years).[167] The data gathered by the Competition Tribunal reflects the fact that, on average, from the time the claim is filed to the issuing of the final decision by the Tribunal, the duration is of 396 days for adversarial cases, and of 204 days for non-adversarial cases.[168]

On this issue, the survey we conducted shows that more than 50 percent of the surveyed lawyers considered that the NEPO's actions were efficient and timely when prosecuting infringements, and when responding to public and private complaints (80 percent). The answers obtained also reflect that there is a wide impression among lawyers that the NEPO adapts promptly to legal reforms and economic changes in different industries (more than 75 percent). Most of the interviewed lawyers agreed that the NEPO answers both effectively and in a timely fashion to prosecution of infringements and to requests by public and private parties.

Although most surveyed practitioners have a moderately positive impression of the time and duration the NEPO takes to investigate competition law, considering the complexity of the cases, some disagree. For instance, the duration of investigations and cases at the NEPO is uncertain. Some argue that the prosecutor takes too much time in the process, longer than what is legally acceptable. Certain investigations are perceived to be paralyzed for several months, without receiving notice of the NEPO's actions. An example of this arose recently, after two Competition Tribunal decisions revealed that the NEPO had been investigating two soft-drink firms for more than two years, without any complaint being filed before the tribunal.[169]

In the case of the Competition Tribunal, 70 percent of the answers given by surveyed attorneys suggested that it acts in a timely and efficient way, punishing antitrust violations, imposing measures and conditions, and reaching final decisions on complaints by the NEPO or private litigants. A similar percentage of favorable answers appear regarding the question of the amount of time the Competition Tribunal takes in deciding a case, considering its complexity. However, in non-adversarial cases, that is, merger review, some opinions consider those proceedings too lengthy. Most of the interviewed lawyers concur that the Competition Tribunal acts in a timely manner, although on occasions the decision takes more time than expected. However, complaints exist about the excessive duration of merger review cases, which may last for several months at the Supreme Court. In the largest proposed merger since 2005, *Falabella-D&S*, the decision not to challenge the

[167] NEPO, *Working Party No. 3 on Co-operation and Enforcement, Transparency Issues in Civil and Administrative Proceedings (Documento para la OCDE)*, <http://www.fne.gob.cl/wp-content/uploads/2011/08/oecd_0007_2010.pdf>.

[168] Competition Tribunal, *Sexta Cuenta Pública del Presidente del Tribunal de Defensa de la Libre Competencia Don Eduardo Jara Miranda*, 2010, 13.

[169] *Coca-Cola Embonor SA*, November 9, 2010, Decision TDLC and *Coca-Cola Polar SA*, November 9, 2010, Decision TDLC.

rejection by the Competition Tribunal considered amongst others the uncertainty of the results and the intention to not affect the companies' business plans.[170] In the case of requests for preliminary injunctions and discovery, the Competition Tribunal is seen as reluctant to order such measures.[171]

In the case of the Supreme Court, more than half of the surveyed lawyers consider that the court responds in an efficient and timely manner when reviewing a case decided previously by the Competition Tribunal.

4. *Predictability in decisions*

As we have noted earlier, the NEPO investigates probable antitrust infringements and mergers and acquisitions, before deciding whether to file a claim at the Competition Tribunal or in cases of reports required by that tribunal in judicial proceedings. The results of our study found that almost 45 percent of the surveyed lawyers disagreed with the statement that NEPO investigations were always predictable or foreseeable. Several interviewed attorneys stated that there was no uniform criterion; "it all depends on the person in charge of the investigation and his expertise," said one attorney. Nevertheless, procedural decisions by the NEPO are foreseeable. Also, the reasons for the decision to file an investigation by the NEPO are not stated explicitly enough. Some question a lack of uniformity in the criteria and background used by the economic prosecutor. Nevertheless, the decisions issued by NEPO have been improving, said the surveyed practitioners.

An investigated party or a party filing a claim before the NEPO can request reconsideration by the NEP. Although the NEPO states that this right is not established in Decree-Law 211, and considering that it applies in theory as a general rule to all public entities,[172] our research has not found relevant reconsiderations by the NEP. Moreover, during investigations, a party can request the Competition Tribunal to limit, condition, or invalidate the NEPO's request for information. In order to do so, the party must argue that the request of information may cause damage to their interests or those of third parties.[173] Until recently, the Competition Tribunal's decisions in this field were not public. Evidence suggests that the judicial remedy to limit requests of information has been partially successful.[174]

In civil law countries, such as Chile, judicial precedents are not binding in future cases. A clear example of this is the Chilean Civil Code, which explicitly states that court decisions do not have a binding effect except in the specific case concerned.[175] Decree-Law 211 does not alter this rule, but competition case law is

170 José Troncoso, "Controladores de Falabella y D&S ponen punto final a su acuerdo de fusión," *El Mercurio*, Santiago, March 4, 2008, <http://diario.elmercurio.cl/detalle/index.asp?id={717ec3d8-f846-43b8-833a-3404165e099d>.

171 *See* also Montt and Mordoj, 35.

172 OECD, 2010, § 24.

173 Decree-Law 211, Art. 39 h.

174 Francisco Agüero and Luis-Eduardo Toro, "Límites a la potestad inspectora de la Administración: El caso de la Fiscalía Nacional Económica," Revista de Derecho Económico (2010).

175 Civil Code, Art. 3.

viewed by the legal community as a relevant and useful tool for predicting the behavior of the Competition Tribunal.[176] Even the Competition Tribunal has started to refer to previous decisions when deciding adversarial cases, which has happened in topics such as refusal to deal,[177] sham litigation,[178] vertical restrictions,[179] etc. On the contrary, in excessive pricing litigation (especially in the unregulated areas of electricity, water and sanitation, and public works franchising pricing), so far no clear pattern has been set by the Competition Tribunal. For instance, in a two-year period different criteria have appeared in several decisions from the same tribunal.[180]

In conciliations and settlements, although there is no explicit NEPO policy,[181] this agency has recently stated that Decree-Law 211's provisions allow settling cases with all or only some of the defendants in collective infringements (cartels), and with the defendant in unilateral cases, with or without the consent of private plaintiffs.[182] The Competition Tribunal has power to actively encourage the parties to settle, although there is no policy regarding this. Usually, the Tribunal summons the parties to a conciliation hearing to discuss the possibilities of a settlement after the period has expired.[183] In one case, the Supreme Court allowed a settlement while deciding a special recourse filed against a Competition Tribunal's decision.[184]

The rulings and decisions of the Competition Tribunal were assessed as not always predictable or foreseeable by the lawyers we surveyed. The results are the same for the Supreme Court. The interviews reflect the opinion that there is a reasonable level of predictability in the Tribunal's decisions, something that is related to the coherence between different decisions. Some of the practitioners agree on the issue that the Competition Tribunal dislikes procedural discussions during trials.

In general, the interviewed lawyers agree that the Supreme Court's decisions, although not always predictable, always contain sound legal reasons and grounds. An individual opinion remarked that predictability depends on the type of proceeding. That is, if the Supreme Court is deciding a cartel case, the review will most

[176] Cruz and Zarate, 159.

[177] *FNE v. Telefónica Móviles de Chile SA* et al., Case No. C 139-07, Decision 104, September 13, 2010, TDLC.

[178] *Telmex Servicios Empresariales SA v. Compañía de Telecomunicaciones de Chile SA*, Case No. C 155-08, January 31, 2009, TDLC; *FNE v. Cia. Chilena de Fósforos SA,* Case No. C 165-08, December 14, 2009, Decision 90, TDLC; *FNE v. Telefónica Móviles de Chile SA* et al., Case No. C 139-07, Decision 104, September 13, 2010, TDLC.

[179] *FNE v. Cia. Chilena de Fósforos SA,* Case No. C 165-08, December 14, 2009, Decision 90, TDLC.

[180] *Constructora e Inmobiliaria Independencia v. Aguas Nuevo Sur, Maule*, Case No. C 79-05, TDLC, Decision 85/2009; *FNE v. Empresa Eléctrica Atacama SA*, Case No. 183-08, January 6, 2010, Decision 93, TDLC; *Nutripro SA v. Puerto Terrestre Los Andes Sociedad Concesionaria S.A. y Fisco,* Case No. C 127-07, July 21, 2010, Decision 100, TDLC.

[181] OECD, 2010, § 30.

[182] OECD, 2010, § 29.

[183] Decree-Law 211, Art. 22 and OECD, 2010, § 30 and § 31.

[184] OECD, 2010, § 31.

likely be on evidentiary issues. On the other hand, on economic issues the Supreme Court is more predictable, said the same practitioner.

A recent report that studied the predictability and regularity of the Supreme Court when hearing a Competition Tribunal's decision has shown 22 percent of the cases brought before the Court have been withdrawn or amended, of which 12 percent were adversarial decisions. Of the quashed decisions, the study considers that 8.9 percent of them (four cases) were amended due to considerations regarding evidentiary issues, 17.8 percent of the decisions (eight cases) were revoked because of discrepancies regarding issues of law, and only two cases—that is, 4.4 percent—had reduced the fines imposed by the Competition Tribunal.[185]

VI. Critical evaluation

We started this chapter with the intention of reviewing the hypothesis of distrust in the institutional design of the Chilean competition law system. Mistrust affects the governance of the institutions and may have consequences for reforms of the legislation.

After hearing and reading the results of the users of the competition law system, that is, attorneys who regularly use the existing institutions, this hypothesis seems to be rebutted. It appears that lawyers do have complaints, but the general assessment looks much better than what it would have been in 2003. Users consider that the standards of the Competition Tribunal and the NEPO have been improving in areas such as transparency, expertise of their members, participation, and predictability. An overall evaluation shows a general good result of the dual system created with Law 19.911 in 2003.

The mixed composition of the Competition Tribunal, its jurisdiction, and the selection method used to appoint its members have proved to be successful. As a consequence of this, in 2009 the Executive branch submitted to Congress a bill that pursued the reform of the environmental jurisdiction, and the model it was proposing was almost identical to the Competition Tribunal.[186] It must be noted that the interviews we conducted exposed that the presence of professionals in the tribunal with no legal training, such as economists, may imply different or contradictory decisions during the trials, especially if some of them have a decision-making role in evidentiary matters. This raises issues on procedural debates and decisions during trials that could affect the final outcome.

After several years of implementation of the institutional design of the competition law bodies, discussion about the lack of independence between the NEPO and the Competition Tribunal looks significantly different from what an impartial observer could have described in 2003, at the beginning of the reform. Certainly, the separation of roles stated in Decree-Law 211 has made this transition easier and

[185] Teodoro Wigodski, "Regularidades en los Fallos de la Corte Suprema sobre Libre Competencia," Documentos de Trabajo, No. 122, Serie Gestión, April 2010.

[186] Bill that creates an Environmental Tribunal, 2009.

favored independence. From a geographical and logistical dependence in 2003, we have moved towards two bodies that can differ in procedures, decisions, and even amend each other's mistaken decisions. Thus, the bifurcated model has operated in an autonomous manner, promoting the creation of expert organizations, with good operating criteria.

Independence has been enhanced since the 2009 reform, for both the NEPO and the Competition Tribunal. The NEPO appears also as an independent prosecutor, despite being part of the administration. However, this autonomy may be less clear when the NEPO has to deal with or investigate administrative regulators. Independence was also gained by the Competition Tribunal from administrative bodies, and more and more often decisions affecting public bodies have been issued by the Tribunal. Nevertheless, the increasing role of the Competition Tribunal in areas covered by sector-specific regulators, and in topics such as public policy, state-aids, state-owned enterprises, public procurement, and regulations has lacked a comprehensive analysis. In this field, the jurisprudence from the Supreme Court has conflicted with the opinion of the Tribunal, quashing several decisions.

The opinion of practitioners shows that the professionals of the NEPO and the Competition Tribunal appear to be experts in their fields, law and economics. The opinion differs in the case of the Supreme Court. However, there is a growing recognition by the Court of the need to address this issue, and decisions have started to use specialized literature in the field. The lack of proper training may be replaced with considerations about the level of deference to the Competition Tribunal, specifically in the economic reasoning of decisions. As said, the problem seems to be the Supreme Court's extension of review of the Competition Tribunal's decisions; apparent deference may be more a "happy accident"—that is, a situation where the Supreme Court non-deferential decision coincides with the decisions adopted by the Competition Tribunal—than real deference.

The role of transparency, so as to reveal the reasons behind decisions and help with the predictability of decisions, has increased. In this area the two institutions have different evaluations. The NEPO has promoted transparency in its procedures, but users still consider that the investigations are uncertain and unclear in their results. Not only are the decisions not reviewable, but attorneys consider that any evidence they could provide may have an uncertain destiny, in the sense that they have no proof that the evidence provided has been taken into account. Some opinions complain about the secrecy and disorder of the cases in which they have been involved. The NEPO has also made significant efforts to promote access to information and participation of stakeholders in rulemaking (guidelines), but nonetheless agents still consider that the investigations are secret and obscure. This uneven evaluation is most likely because of the unclear implementation of the Administrative Procedure Act, a law that contains complementary regulations to Decree-Law 211. Whether it must be applied fully in investigative procedures or only in a limited way is a matter yet to be addressed by the NEPO. A probable consequence of the former is that the survey revealed that lawyers were unsatisfied with the predictability of investigations handled by the NEPO. Operators of the system said that there was no uniform criterion. Nevertheless, efforts to make corrections have been observed. The information we have gathered for this study reveals that legal practitioners would expect and promote reform specifically in investigative procedures handled by the NEPO.

The uncertainty in the operation of the NEPO can also be appreciated when requesting the imposition of a fine to the Competition Tribunal. In comparison, the Competition Tribunal has deepened its reasoning behind the fines it imposes, moving towards more proportionate remedies. This Tribunal has even revealed which inputs it uses in its decisions, which is an unusual step for the Chilean judiciary, not accustomed to disclose their decision-making process.

The Competition Tribunal has been a strong promoter of transparency in its proceedings. Consequently, claims, evidence, and decisions are not only public but also can be browsed on its website the same day they are issued, exceeding the requirements of the procedural rules. Some have criticized this as an excess of transparency, which in some cases may eventually affect the due process of law.

However, even promoting transparency may be insufficient. Rulings and decisions by the Competition Tribunal were assessed as not always predictable or foreseeable for the lawyers we surveyed. More significantly, results did not vary considerably from those obtained on the Supreme Court. Practitioners would expect that after more than 130 decisions, essential concepts in competition law such as abuse of dominant position would not remain unclear and undefined. Even though the NEPO has issued merger guidelines, it does not bind the Competition Tribunal, so practitioners find no clarity in merger analysis before the Tribunal. Therefore, a question remains unanswered about the real consequences of having guidelines only applied in the administrative phase but not enforceable in the judicial phase at the Competition Tribunal.

Annex

I. General methodological aspects

The study adopts a mixed methodology that incorporates different qualitative and quantitative methodological elements. We opted for this methodological alternative as a result of the range of tools it offers, and to obtain a broader study perspective, favoring the development of an analysis that comprises the multiplicity of forms found within relevant information for this evaluation.

Regarding the qualitative methodological tools, this investigation used interview techniques and document analysis. Through interviews, we gained access to the opinions of the most relevant competition law agents in Chile. Through the analysis of documents, we incorporated the most transcendent decisions of Chilean competition bodies, as well as the official documents containing institutional information from the NEPO and the Competition Tribunal.

In terms of the quantitative methodological techniques, this investigation incorporates information obtained from a survey answered by attorneys who habitually participate in competition law proceedings, whether at the NEPO or at the Competition Court.

II. Qualitative methodology techniques: Interviews and document analysis

II.1. Interviews

As mentioned above, this study incorporates the opinions of the most relevant agents in the area of competition in Chile. The group of interviewees was composed of former members of the Competition Tribunal, former National Economic Prosecutors, and five attorneys with the greatest level of expertise in the field of competition in Chile.

To determine the five attorneys with the greatest competition expertise we resorted to different criteria, including said expert's volume of participation in competition proceedings, the frequency of appearances in the highest professional rankings (*Global Competition Review, Who's Who Legal, Practical Law Company*, etc.), and the permanent development of academic activities related to competition law.

It is noteworthy to mention that not all of the selected experts agreed to participate. The interviewees were questioned by the modality of an interview of a holistic or intensive approach, and semi-structured.

The questionnaire used was similar to that employed in the survey, and was comprised of diverse, specific questions, grouped by the generic themes addressed in this study. For the purpose of preserving unbiased answers, the section on questions regarding the Competition

Tribunal was not allotted to the former members of the TDLC. The former National Economic Prosecutors also did not respond to questions referring to the performance of the NEPO.

The combination of answers from the interviews was compiled and synthesized into one sole document, from which all references to the authors of each declaration were deleted. This modality was adopted to ensure the confidentiality of the interviewees and their candor in answering the questions.

II.2. Document analysis

The technique of document analysis was used in the exploration of two different sources: the most relevant decisions of the Competition Tribunal and the Supreme Court chamber that hears appeals from the Competition Tribunal, and the official documents of the NEPO and the Competition Tribunal reflecting their opinions regarding diverse aspects of their own performance.

Analysis of decisions

By analyzing decisions we intended to access the assessment of those bodies that review challenges to the decisions issued by the bodies here evaluated with respect to the different aspects addressed in this study. The purpose of this tool of analysis was to learn how the reviewing bodies respond to eventual vices related to institutional or procedural aspects of the NEPO and the Competition Tribunal.

Analysis of other official documents of the NEPO and the Competition Tribunal

The purpose of accessing these documents was to contrast the viewpoints the NEPO and the Competition Tribunal have regarding their own performance methods, with other sources of information to which this study resorts. At the core of this tool is the diligence to evaluate the level of perception said bodies have with respect to their own institutional flaws.

These methods of analysis were unable to be applied to the performance of the Supreme Court specialized chamber that hears competition law appeals, given the fact that their decisions are unappealable, and it is uncommon to publish information related to the competition law's institutions.

III. Quantitative methodology technique: Survey

Through the development of a survey we intended to access the perceptions habitual users of the NEPO and the TDLC have regarding the observance in the performance of said bodies concerning the topics that guide this study.

The survey universe comprised all attorneys admitted to practice law in Chile and that have habitually participated in competition proceedings since 2004 (the year in which the current institution commenced operation).

The total number of individuals that compose the population was impossible to determine (neither the Competition Tribunal nor the NEPO have the statistics thereof).

The invitation to participate in the survey was extended to 193 attorneys; previously, 96 professionals were excluded because they did not comply with the requirement of having participated habitually in competition proceedings (at least three participations).[187] Finally, the survey was answered by seventy-six attorneys. In certain answers one can observe a slightly lower level of participation, given that those polled are attorneys for the NEPO, the reason for which they were excluded from answering questions referring to the performance of said legal body. Moreover, a smaller group of those polled omitted certain questions.

The questionnaire consisted of ninety-three assertions referring to the different performance areas of the NEPO, the Competition Tribunal, and the specialized chamber of the Supreme Court that hears competition law appeals. Each surveyed individual was asked to assess on a scale of one to ten how much they agreed with each one of these assertions. Additionally, we provided text space so that each person could express his or her appraisals when deemed pertinent.

Survey: "Institutional evaluation for competition-related matters"

We ran an internet-based survey, applied to the NEPO, the Competition Tribunal, and the specialized chamber of the Supreme Court that hears appeals from the Competition Tribunal. For space reasons, we have eliminated the questions regarding the Supreme Court, although they are similar to those regarding the Competition Tribunal. In total, the survey had ninety-three questions.

I. National Economic Prosecutor's Office (NEPO)

1. Transparency

1.1 The criteria used by the NEPO to make decisions (for example, initiate or file an investigation, file a complaint), are fully known to the public.

1.2 There is a high level of transparency regarding the information that justifies the complaint the NEPO files before the Competition Tribunal/Supreme Court.

1.3 The criteria used by the NEPO regarding how and when to exercise the powers conferred to it by law are fully known to the public.

1.4 The NEPO publishes in a timely manner institutional information relevant to economic agents and citizens in general (its achievements and plans of action, its adherence to a determined manner of interpreting a legal provision, the general guidelines of its role, within a determined period of time, etc.).

2. Independence

2.1 In proceedings before the Competition Tribunal/Supreme Court, the NEPO is completely independent from influences stemming from public powers.

2.2 In proceedings before the Competition Tribunal/Supreme Court, the NEPO is completely independent from inappropriate influence by private parties.

[187] Initially, there was a list of 289 attorneys that originally complied with the requirements established to define the population. Subsequently, it was determined that 96 of them did not comply with the "habitual" requirement, and were therefore excluded from the study. The initial list was drawn up based on the verification of documents in which representation was delegated in the different proceedings the [TDLC] publishes on its website.

2.3 The administrative investigations brought by the NEPO are free from any external influence by public authorities or private parties.

3. Accountability

3.1 In the case of official public positions not selected through the Senior Public Office Authority, the application, evaluation, and appointment processes of NEPO officers are subject to rigorous criteria of selection, control, and notification.

3.2 In the case of official public positions selected through the Senior Public Office Authority (including the National Prosecutor), the processes of application, evaluation, and appointment for NEPO officers are subject to rigorous criteria of selection, control, and notification.

3.3 The NEPO never initiates investigations or files complaints for pure publicity or political purposes, and never without a technical basis.

4. Predictability

4.1 The results of the NEPO's investigations are always predictable or foreseeable.

4.2 The procedural decisions adopted by the NEPO during judicial proceedings are always within the framework of expected alternatives.

5. Proportionality

5.1 The fines, measures, and sanctions the NEPO requests the [Antitrust Court] to apply in its complaints are proportional to the factual and legal circumstances of the case (in accordance with the last paragraph of article 26 of Law Decree 211).

6. No discrimination

6.1 The NEPO does not arbitrarily discriminate based on the nationality, wealth, notoriety, or social class of the affected party in its administrative and judicial proceedings.

7. Capacity for responding

7.1 The NEPO responds in an efficient and timely manner in prosecuting illegal acts against fair competition.

7.2 The NEPO responds in an efficient and timely manner to the complaints filed by public and private agents in its area of expertise.

7.3 The NEPO, within its organization and performance, adapts to legal modifications in a timely fashion.

7.4 The NEPO is aware of and responds in a timely manner to the economic changes the country's various industries face.

8. Expertise of the officers

8.1 The NEPO officers are experts in their respective areas of expertise.

8.2 The NEPO officers apply with criteria their knowledge in their respectively assigned cases.

9. Reviewability of decisions

9.1 The decisions adopted by the NEPO in its investigative proceedings (for example, summoning witnesses, request for documents, filing the case, etc.) are internally re-examinable through an effective system of reviewability.

9.2 The decisions adopted by the NEPO in its investigative proceedings (for example, summoning witnesses, request for documents, filing the case, etc.) are externally re-examinable through an effective system of reviewability.

10. Complying with deadlines

10.1 The duration of the investigative proceedings conducted by the NEPO is reasonable considering the complexity of the case.

11. Defense

11.1 The agents investigated by the NEPO are informed in timely manner of the accusations brought against them.

11.2 During the NEPO's investigative proceedings, the investigated agents count on the effective procedural guarantee to provide information that can distort possible illicit conducts.

11.3 During the NEPO's investigations, requests for copies of information are resolved within a reasonable period.

12. Sufficiency of investigative competence

12.1 The investigative competence of the NEPO is sufficient and effective to discover and prosecute unfair competition actions.

13. Confidentiality

13.1 During the NEPO's administrative investigations, economic agents can rely on the effective guarantee that, in the matter of handling confidential information, it remains under strict confidentiality.

14. Satisfying criteria on filing an investigation

14.1 The NEPO's decision to file information originating from an administrative investigation is always justified by objective and well-founded criteria.

II. Competition Tribunal

1. Transparency

1.1 The criteria used by the Competition Tribunal to make administrative decisions (for example, selection processes, incentives, and evaluations of its officers, self-regulation guidelines, etc.) are fully known to the public.

1.2 There is a high level of clarity and coherence in the reasoning of the Competition Tribunal's jurisdictional decisions.

1.3 The criteria used by the Competition Tribunal regarding how and when to exercise its special powers (rule-making powers, informative powers, inquisitive powers, etc.) are fully known to the public.

1.4 The Competition Tribunal publishes in timely fashion institutional information relevant to economic agents and citizens in general (its achievements and plans of action, decisions, statistics, self-regulation guidelines, etc.).

2. Independence

2.1 The Competition Tribunal is completely independent from influences stemming from public powers.

2.2 The Competition Tribunal is completely independent from inappropriate influences by private parties.

2.3 The conflicts, prohibition, incompetence, and asset declaration system established by law operates in practice in such a way that the Competition Tribunal members can conduct their functions with complete independence.

2.4 The wages of the Competition Tribunal judges and officers are sufficiently high in order to effectively safeguard their independence.

3. Accountability

3.1 The application, evaluation, and appointment processes for Competition Tribunal officers are subject to rigorous criteria of selection, control, and notification.

3.2 The Competition Tribunal is subject to an effective regime of control and responsibility in matters of budgetary administration.

3.3 The processes for the application, evaluation, and appointment of the Competition Tribunal's judges are developed subject to rigorous criteria of selection, control, and notification.

4. Predictability

4.1 The Competition Tribunal's decisions are always predictable or foreseeable.

4.2 The Competition Tribunal's intermediate resolutions are always predictable or foreseeable.

5. Proportionality

5.1 The fines, measures, and sanctions issued by the Competition Tribunal in its decisions are proportional to the factual and legal circumstances of the case (in accordance with the last paragraph of article 26 of Law Decree 211).

6. No discrimination

6.1 The Competition Tribunal does not arbitrarily discriminate based on the nationality, wealth, notoriety, or social class of the affected party in its administrative and judicial proceedings.

7. Capacity for responding

7.1 The Competition Tribunal responds in an efficient and timely manner, punishing illicit acts against fair competition.

7.2 The Competition Tribunal responds in an efficient and timely manner to petitions made requesting precautionary and prejudicial measures.

7.3 The Competition Tribunal responds in an efficient and timely manner to complaints filed by public and private agents.

7.4 The Competition Tribunal, within its organization and performance, adapts to legal modifications in a timely fashion.

7.5 The Competition Tribunal is aware of and responds in a timely manner to the economic changes the country's various industries face.

8. Expertise of judges and officers

8.1 The Competition Tribunal's judges are experts in their respective fields of expertise.

8.2 The Competition Tribunal's officers are experts in their respective fields of expertise.

8.3 The Competition Tribunal's judges apply with criteria their knowledge in their respectively assigned cases.

8.4 The lack of specialized chambers in the Competition Tribunal regarding regulated markets and deregulated markets is not detrimental to the quality of its decisions.

8.5 The reasoning behind the jurisdictional decisions issued by the Competition Tribunal has a solid economic base.

9. Reviewability of the decisions

9.1 The complaint recourse against the Competition Tribunal's decisions filed before the Supreme Court constitutes an excellent system for jurisdictional reviewability.

10. Complying with deadlines

10.1 The duration of the proceedings before the Competition Tribunal is reasonable considering the complexity of the case.

10.2 The amount of time it takes the Competition Tribunal to resolve matters once they are in "*a decision-issuing stage,*" is proportional to the complexity of the subject.

11. Defense

11.1 The defendants or respondents before the Competition Tribunal are informed in a timely fashion of the accusations brought against them.

11.2 The proceedings before the Competition Tribunal are fully guaranteed the fundamental principle of a bilateral hearing.

11.3 The proceedings before the Competition Tribunal guarantee the full procedural exercise of rights by avoiding surprises, unexpected procedural events, or deadlines that cannot be reasonably complied with.

11.4 The proceedings before the Competition Tribunal guarantee the full exercise of the right to prove the alleged facts.

11.5 The proceedings before the Competition Tribunal guarantee the full exercise of the right to cross-examine expert and non-expert witnesses, and counterparts.

11.6 It is easy and expeditious to obtain copies of the Competition Tribunal's files.

11.7 The institution of substitute members does not imply a violation of due process or the independence of the Competition Tribunal.

12. Sufficiency of competence for sanctioning

12.1 The Competition Tribunal possesses sufficient competence to determine and sanction actions contrary to fair competition.

13. Confidentiality

13.1 The institutions of confidentiality and reserve, regulated by the Competition Tribunal Resolution No.11/2008, effectively safeguard "sensitive" information that is provided by the parties, intervenors, or providers of background information in proceedings heard by the Competition Tribunal.

5

China
The Competition Law System and the Country's Norms

*Jessica Su and Xiaoye Wang**

I. History

A. Brief history of China's competition legislation

China had a socialist centrally-planned economy from 1949 to 1978.[1] Since the late 1970s, China has been in a transition from a planned economy to a market economy. In 1978, the Third Plenary Session of the Eleventh Central Committee of the Communist Party of China (CPC) heralded an era of economic reform.[2] The reform has since then delivered more efficiency, unlocked the people's potential, and changed the traditionally hostile attitude toward competition. By opening up the market, accepting private wealth, and allowing competition, China has become one of the world's most promising emerging economies.

Chinese competition law was conceived in the 1980s, soon after China adopted an open-door policy. The *Interim Provisions for Promoting and Protecting Competition in the Socialist Economy*, issued by the State Council on October 17, 1980, was the first normative document to protect competition and regulate government monopolies in China.[3] The Interim Provisions stipulated that "in economic

* Jessica Su, PhD (London), Postdoctoral Fellow, Institute of Law, Chinese Academy of Social Sciences; Xiaoye Wang, Dr iur (Hamburg), Distinguished Professor of Law at Hunan University and the Chinese Academy of Social Sciences, and Consultant Expert for the Anti-Monopoly Commission under the State Council of the People's Republic of China.

The authors are grateful to Professor Eleanor Fox of New York University, Professor Michael Trebilcock of University of Toronto, and Mr Stephen Harris of Baker & McKenzie for invaluable comments and insights on the revision of this chapter. The law is stated as at March 31, 2012. The laws and regulations of the People's Republic of China cited in this chapter are authentic in Chinese. English translation is provided for reference only.

[1] For the purpose of this chapter, "China" refers to the mainland of the People's Republic of China, excluding the Hong Kong Special Administrative Region (SAR), the Macao SAR, and the Taiwan region.

[2] Background information about the Third Plenary Session of the Eleventh Central Committee of the CPC is available at: <http://www.bjreview.com.cn/nation/txt/2009-05/26/content_197538.htm>.

[3] *See* Interim Provisions for Promoting and Protecting Competition in the Socialist Economy, promulgated by the State Council on October 17, 1980 and repealed October 6, 2001, available at OFFICIAL GAZETTE OF THE STATE COUNCIL, No. 487.

activities, with the exception of products exclusively managed by state-designated departments and organisations, monopolization or exclusive dealing is not allowed." Economic reform has accelerated since 1992 following the Fourteenth National Congress of the CPC. In 1993, the Second Amendment to China's *Constitution 1982* (Constitution) declared that "the State implements socialist market economy."[4] Under these conditions, China is well on the way to establish a mechanism that tackles restrictive behavior and monopolization, provides a level playing field, and protects free and fair competition.

Prior to 2008, China dealt with competition-related issues through a series of laws and regulations. The enactment of the *Anti-Unfair Competition Law 1993* (AUCL) was the first major step forward in establishing a Chinese competition law system. The AUCL incorporated provisions that address unfair trading practices and certain types of restrictive agreements, abuse of dominance, and administrative monopoly.[5] The *Price Law 1997* (Price Law), mainly as a price control instrument, also prohibits "unfair pricing activities," including collusion to control market price, selling products below cost in order to eliminate competitors or monopolize the market, and offering the same products or services at discriminatory prices.[6] The *Provisions on Mergers and Acquisitions of Domestic Enterprises by Foreign Investors 2006* (hereinafter M&A Rules 2006) provide a basic regulatory framework for

[4] *See* Constitution, Art. 15. The Constitution was promulgated by the 5th National People's Congress (NPC) on December 4, 1982, effective the same day, and amended 1988, 1993, 1999, and 2004. English translation of the Constitution is available at <http://english.gov.cn/2005-08/05/content_20813.htm>. It should be noted that the concept of "socialist market economy" was devised by Deng Xiaoping, the former CPC leader. When answering the question of whether there is a latent contradiction between a market economy and the socialist system, Deng stated that: "[t]here is no fundamental contradiction between socialism and a market economy. The problem is how to develop the productive forces more effectively. We used to have a planned economy, but our experience over the years has proved that having a totally planned economy hampers the development of the productive forces. If we combine a planned economy with a market economy, we shall be in a better position to liberate the productive forces and speed up economic growth. . . ." *See* Excerpts from an Interview on October 23, 1985 between Deng Xiaoping and a Delegation Consisting of Senior Journalists and Entrepreneurs, Organized by the Time Inc., <www.china.org.cn/english/features/dengxiaoping/103358.htm>. Later, in a speech delivered during his famous southern tour in 1992, Deng noted that: "[w]e should be bolder than before in conducting reform and opening to the outside and have the courage to experiment . . . The proportion of planning to market forces is not the essential difference between socialism and capitalism. A planned economy is not equivalent to socialism, because there is planning under capitalism too; a market economy is not capitalism, because there are markets under socialism too. Planning and market forces are both means of controlling economic activity . . . We shall push ahead along the road to Chinese-style socialism." *See* Deng Xiaoping, *Excerpts from Talks Given in Wuchang, Shenzhen, Zhuhai and Shanghai (January 18–February 21, 1992)* in *Selected Works of Deng Xiaoping, Vol.* 3 (1982–1992) 360, 361, & 370 (China Foreign Languages Press 1994).

[5] *See* AUCL, Arts 6 and 23 regarding forced transactions by public utilities; Arts 7 and 30 regarding administrative monopoly; Art. 11 regarding below-cost sales; Art. 12 regarding tying; and Arts 15 and 27 regarding bid rigging. The AUCL was promulgated by the Standing Committee of the 8th NPC on September 2, 1993 and effective December 1, 1993, English translation available at: <http://en.chinacourt.org/public/detail.php?id=3306>.

[6] *See* Price Law, Art. 14(1), (2) & (5). The Price Law was promulgated by the Standing Committee of the 8th NPC on December 29, 1997 and effective May 1, 1998, English translation available at: <http://www.fdi.gov.cn/pub/FDI_EN/Laws/GeneralLawsandRegulations/BasicLaws/P020060620320511406803.pdf>.

mergers and acquisitions of domestic enterprises by foreign investors and incorporate four articles devoted to anti-monopoly scrutiny of mergers and acquisitions.[7] The AUCL, the Price Law, the M&A Rules and other competition-related laws and regulations have been separately enforced by the State Administration for Industry and Commerce (SAIC), the National Development and Reform Commission (NDRC), and the Ministry of Commerce (MOFCOM). However, to some extent, the three agencies' roles in regulating competition overlap.[8] Most of these competition-related laws and regulations are still effective post 2008.

The piecemeal competition legislation created fragmented and discriminatory provisions, insufficient remedies, and weak enforcement authorities. For example, bid rigging is prohibited under the AUCL and the *Bidding Law 1993* (Bidding Law) but with different level of penalties.[9] In addition, bid rigging can be prosecuted under the *Criminal Law 1997* (Criminal Law) if the circumstances are serious, where conviction could lead to fines, detention, and up to three years imprisonment.[10] The M&A Rules 2006 regulate mergers or acquisitions of domestic enterprises by foreign investors but do not apply to mergers among domestic enterprises. Moreover, the AUCL and the Price Law mix provisions concerning unfair trading practices and price control with provisions aimed at protecting competition. These conflicting objectives of the law blurred the scope and boundaries of lawful behavior. Regarding remedy design, for example, the maximum administrative fine for designated transactions by public utilities is only Chinese Yuan (CNY) 200,000, which does not provide the AUCL with tools of effective deterrence.[11] In addition, a major side-effect of the lack of a unified anti-monopoly

[7] *See* M&A Rules 2006, Arts 51–54; also *see* M&A Rules 2006 Arts 1 and 3 that stipulated the principle of the protection of fair competition and the prohibition of transactions causing excessively concentrated markets and thus eliminating or restricting competition. The M&A Rules 2006 were jointly issued by the Ministry of Commerce (MOFCOM), the State-Owned Assets Supervision and Administration Commission (SASAC), the State Administration of Taxation (SAT), the State Administration for Industry and Commerce (SAIC), the China Securities Regulatory Commission (CSRC) and the State Administration of Foreign Exchange (SAFE) in August 2006. English translation of the M&A Rules 2006 is available at: <http://www.fdi.gov.cn/pub/FDI_EN/Laws/law_en_info.jsp?docid=66925>. It should be noted that the Chinese merger control regime was first introduced in 2003, as part of the *Interim Provisions on Mergers and Acquisitions of Domestic Enterprises by Foreign Investors 2003* (hereinafter Interim M&A Rules). *See* Interim M&A Rules, Arts 1, 3, and 19–22. The Interim M&A Rules were jointly issued by the former Ministry of Foreign Trade and Economic Cooperation, the SAT, the SAIC, and the SAFE in March 2003. English translation of the Interim M&A Rules is available at: <http://www.fdi.gov.cn/pub/FDI_EN/Laws/law_en_info.jsp?docid=51173>.

[8] For example, under the Interim M&A Rules and the M&A Rules 2006, the MOFCOM and the SAIC had concurrent powers to conduct anti-monopoly review of mergers and acquisitions of domestic enterprises by foreign investors.

[9] *See* AUCL, *supra* note 5, Arts 15 and 27; also *see* Bidding Law, Arts 32 and 53. The Bidding Law was promulgated by the Standing Committee of the 9th NPC on August 30, 1999 and effective January 1, 2000, English translation available at: <http://www.fdi.gov.cn/pub/FDI_EN/Laws/law_en_info.jsp?docid=50918>.

[10] *See* Criminal Law, Art. 223. The Criminal Law was promulgated by the 8th NPC on March 4, 1997, effective October 1, 1997 and amended 1999, 2001, 2002, 2005, 2006, 2009, and 2011, English translation available at: <http://www.npc.gov.cn/englishnpc/Law/Frameset-page6.html>.

[11] *See* AUCL, *supra* note 5, Art. 23.

law was that China also lacked a centralized and independent anti-monopoly enforcement authority with sufficient mandate to enforce the law.

Following the promulgation of the AUCL in 1993, an anti-monopoly law, envisaged as a principal pillar of Chinese competition law, was placed on the legislative agenda of the 8th, the 9th, and the 10th National People's Congress (NPC). The legislative history had witnessed intense debates on the necessity and suitability of an anti-monopoly law, with rivalry between agencies to gain enforcement powers, warnings about the potential damage the law could have on the state-owned economy and on foreign investment, and complaints about foreign control and real or perceived threats of anticompetitive behavior of multinational corporations in the Chinese market. In 2004, the MOFCOM, as the drafting agency, submitted a draft anti-monopoly law to the Legislative Affairs Office of the State Council. After another two years of consideration and consultation, the State Council submitted a draft to the Standing Committee of the 10th NPC in June 2006. The draft was reviewed and revised three times in June 2006, June 2007, and August 2007. China's *Anti-Monopoly Law 2007* (AML) was finally promulgated by the Standing Committee of the 10th NPC on August 30, 2007 and became effective on August 1, 2008.[12]

The AML does not explicitly repeal competition-related provisions existing in other laws and regulations, and therefore coexists with many pertinent provisions in prior legislation.[13] This has caused uncertainties as to which law will prevail in case of conflict although the general principles of hierarchy of Chinese law may provide some guidance.[14] Similar to other major competition law regimes, the AML covers three main areas: anticompetitive agreements, abuse of dominance, and merger control. The AML also covers a fourth area, namely, abuse of administrative powers to eliminate or restrict competition by "administrative agencies" and "organizations empowered by laws or regulations with responsibilities for public affairs adminis-

[12] English translation of the AML is available at: <http://www.fdi.gov.cn/pub/FDI_EN/Laws/law_en_info.jsp?docid=85714>. Another source of unofficial English translation is available as an appendix to Nathan Bush, "The PRC Antimonopoly Law: Unanswered Questions and Challenges Ahead," ANTITRUST SOURCE, October 2007, <http://apps.americanbar.org/antitrust/at-committees/at-ic/pdf/spring/08/03-26-08-Bush.pdf>.

[13] It should be noted that the SAIC is responsible for drafting the amendments of the AUCL in order to align the AUCL and the AML. In addition, to be consistent with the AML, the M&A Rules 2006 were further amended in June 2009 by MOFCOM (hereinafter the M&A Rules 2009). The M&A Rules 2009 repealed the anti-monopoly review provisions, expressly referred to the AML, and become a pure instrument of investment law governing takeovers of domestic enterprises by foreign companies. English translation of the M&A Rules 2009 is available at <http://www.fdi.gov.cn/pub/FDI_EN/Laws/law_en_info.jsp?docid=108906>.

[14] Based on the general principles of hierarchy of laws in accordance with China's Legislation Law, in the case of contradictions, laws prevail over regulations, new laws prevail over previous laws, and special laws prevail over general laws. Therefore, in principle, the AML as a more recent economy-wide legislation should take precedence over previous economy-wide laws and economy-wide or sector-specific regulations in cases of conflict. Prior legislation also applies to the extent that they do not contradict the AML. *See* Legislation Law (promulgated by the 9th NPC on March 15, 2000 and effective July 1, 2000), Arts 79 & 83, English translation available at: <http://www.npc.gov.cn/englishnpc/Law/2007-12/11/content_1383554.htm>.

tration."[15] This type of behavior is widely referred to as "administrative monopoly." Most AML provisions broadly conform to international norms and are comparable to competition laws in the European Union, the United States and elsewhere, although some of the provisions have notable Chinese characteristics.

Focusing on undertakings' competitive behavior in the marketplace and based on the rationale that competition delivers lower prices, better quality, and more choices, the AML directly affects business operators and is expected to improve consumer and social welfare in China. Furthermore, the AML affects governmental agencies at all levels through the prohibition of administrative monopoly. The AML indicates that China has chosen the market as a fundamental mechanism to allocate resources instead of the previous system of administrative dictates. It reflects the success of a three-decade reform process and promotes the establishment of a competition culture in China. Therefore, the enactment of the AML is deemed as a landmark event in China's legal and economic developments.[16]

The AML has been in force for over three years. A series of AML implementing regulations have been issued or are under consideration.[17] Most implementing regulations have been published for comment before enactment and the enforcement agencies have embraced opinions from domestic and foreign interested parties. These implementing regulations are welcome and encouraging because they amplify the AML provisions and codify the enforcement agencies' practices; thus they significantly increase transparency and predictability.

[15] *See* AML, *supra* note 12, Arts 8, 32–37.

[16] Xiaoye Wang, "Highlights of China's New Anti-Monopoly Law," 75 Antitrust L.J. 133, 144–5 (2008); Xiaoye Wang, "The New Chinese Anti-Monopoly Law: A Survey of a Work in Progress," 54 Antitrust Bull. 579, 584–98, 618–19 (2009).

[17] The published AML implementing regulations to date include, for example, (1) the NDRC *Measures on the Prohibition of Price Monopoly* (promulgated by the NDRC on December 9, 2010 and effective February 1, 2011, official Chinese version available at: <http://jjs.ndrc.gov.cn/zcfg/t20110104_389399.htm>), (2) the NDRC *Measures on the Administrative Enforcement Procedures of the Prohibition of Price Monopoly* (promulgated by the NDRC on December 9, 2010 and effective February 1, 2011, official Chinese version available at: <http://jjs.ndrc.gov.cn/zcfg/t20110104_389401.htm>), (3) the SAIC *Measures on the Prohibition of Monopoly Agreements* (promulgated by the SAIC on December 31, 2010 and effective February 1, 2011, official Chinese version available at: <http://www.saic.gov.cn/fldyfbzdjz/zcfg/zcfg/201101/t20110107_103378.html>), (4) the SAIC *Measures on the Prohibition of Abuse of Dominant Market Position* (promulgated by the SAIC on December 31, 2010 and effective February 1, 2011, official Chinese version available at: <http://www.saic.gov.cn/fldyfbzdjz/zcfg/zcfg/201101/t20110107_103379.html>), (5) the SAIC *Measures on the Procedures for Investigation and Handling Cases of Monopoly Agreements and Abuse of Market Dominant Position* (promulgated by the SAIC on June 10, 2009 and effective July 1, 2009, official Chinese version available at: <http://www.saic.gov.cn/fldyfbzdjz/zcfg/zcfg/200910/t20091013_71551.html>), (6) the MOFCOM *Measures on the Notification of Concentrations of Undertakings* (promulgated by the MOFCOM on July 15, 2009 and effective January 1, 2010, official Chinese version available at: <http://fldj.mofcom.gov.cn/aarticle/c/200911/20091106639149.html>), (7) the MOFCOM *Measures on the Review of Concentrations of Undertakings* (promulgated by the MOFCOM on July 15, 2009 and effective January 1, 2010, official Chinese version available at: <http://fldj.mofcom.gov.cn/aarticle/c/200911/20091106639145.html>), (8) the State Council *Rules on the Notification Thresholds for Concentrations of Undertakings* (promulgated by the State Council on August 1, 2008 and effective August 3, 2008, official Chinese version available at: <http://fldj.mofcom.gov.cn/aarticle/c/200811/20081105917434.html>), etc. English translation of these implementing regulations is available by subscription at <http://www.chinalawinfo.com>.

B. Development of China's competition enforcement agencies

Prior to 2008, competition enforcement responsibilities were divided mainly among three ministries pursuant to the AUCL, the Price Law, and the M&A Rules. This arrangement was marked by overlapping, ambiguous, and decentralized powers, a low level of enforcement authority, insufficient specialized staff, and lack of independence.

The NDRC is a ministry-level macro-economic regulatory body with broad authorities over national industrial and economic policies. The NDRC's role as a competition enforcement agency to handle price-related competition cases derived from the Price Law. The Price Law gives enforcement powers to the "price authority under the State Council" and "price authorities above the county level"—referring to the former State Bureau of Commodity Prices, which later became the NDRC Price Supervision Department, and local price bureaus.[18]

The SAIC is a ministry-level agency under the State Council to be responsible for the administration of industry and commerce, such as enterprise registration, consumer protection, and trademark protection. The SAIC's role as a competition enforcement agency derived from the AUCL, which vests enforcement powers in the SAIC and its local bureaus above the county level.[19] The SAIC also shared merger review authority with the MOFCOM pursuant to the M&A Rules 2006.[20] Compared to the MOFCOM's active role under the M&A Rules 2006, the SAIC's approach was much more passive. It did not conduct substantive review of transactions. Parties were required to notify the SAIC of their transactions only for registration purposes. Within the SAIC, the Anti-Unfair Competition Bureau was granted relevant authority under the AUCL and the M&A Rules 2006.

The MOFCOM was created in 2003 when the former Ministry of Foreign Trade and Economic Cooperation consolidated part of the functions of the State Economy and Trade Commission. It is an agency under the State Council to be mainly responsible for negotiating bilateral and multilateral trade agreements and regulating domestic and foreign trade and investment. The Department of Treaty and Law was vested with powers to review mergers and acquisitions of domestic enterprises by foreign investors on anti-monopoly grounds pursuant to the M&A Rules 2006.[21] In 2004, the Anti-Monopoly Investigation Office was established. This office took over the role of the Department of Treaty and Law under the M&A Rules 2006.[22] It was reported that, by the end of 2007, the MOFCOM had reviewed more than 400 notified mergers and acquisitions of domestic enterprises by foreign investors.[23]

[18] *See* Price Law, *supra* note 6, Art. 5.

[19] *See* AUCL, *supra* note 5, Art. 3.

[20] *See* M&A Rules 2006, *supra* note 7, Arts 51–54.

[21] *Id.*

[22] The MOFCOM Anti-Monopoly Investigation Office was renamed the Anti-Monopoly Bureau in 2008.

[23] *See* Yi Dong, "Will China Say No to Microsoft?," China Economy, April 3, 2008, Chinese version available at: <http://finance.ce.cn/law/home/right/msjf/200804/03/t20080403_12907429.shtml>.

The design of the anti-monopoly enforcement mechanism was the most heavily debated issue in the AML's legislative process, and a single enforcement authority had been considered or perceived as politically impossible.[24] The pre-existing enforcement structure remained but minor changes to enforcement agencies did occur after the AML entered into force. Headed by the Vice Prime Minister and comprised of senior officials from fifteen ministries, the Anti-Monopoly Commission (AMC), a high-level consultative organization, was established pursuant to the AML in August 2008 to be responsible for developing general policy and policy guidelines, assessing the overall market conditions, and coordinating the AML enforcement by the Anti-Monopoly Enforcement Agencies (AMEAs). The AMC established a working office within the MOFCOM. The AMEAs, empowered with concrete enforcement functions pursuant to the AML, have a triumvirate structure that includes three departments under the MOFCOM, the SAIC, and the NDRC respectively. Based on the three agencies' pre-existing competition-related enforcement authorities, the MOFCOM Anti-Monopoly Bureau alone is responsible for merger control, the SAIC Anti-Monopoly and Anti-Unfair Competition Enforcement Bureau (hereinafter "SAIC Competition Enforcement Bureau") is responsible for regulating non-price-related monopoly conduct, and the NDRC Price Supervision and Anti-Monopoly Bureau is responsible for regulating price-related monopoly conduct.

Since the AML entered into force, the MOFCOM has become the most active among the three enforcers and has published twelve conditional clearance decisions and one prohibition decision to date.[25] Local bureaus of the NDRC in Guangxi province have taken the first official action in early 2010 against a price fixing cartel initiated by local rice noodle producers.[26] In July 2010, the NDRC announced that its local bureaus have made three decisions in relation to price collusion in the markets for green beans and garlic and imposed fines on a large number of domestic agricultural trading companies.[27] No official enforcement action pursuant to the AML was reported to have been undertaken by the SAIC and its local bureaus until early 2011. However, the SAIC made a statement that it had started to verify complaints that the SAIC and its local bureaus had received and that it had already investigated and prevented seventy-six cases involving restrictive competitive be-

[24] Zhenguo Wu, "Perspectives on the Chinese Anti-Monopoly Law," 75 Antitrust L.J. 73, 103–5 (2008); also *see* Wang, *supra* note 16, antitrust bull., 587–92.

[25] The twelve conditional clearance decisions include the *InBev/Anheuser Busch, Mitsubishi Rayon/Lucite, Pfizer/Wyeth, GM/Delphi, Sanyo/Panasonic, Novartis/Alcon, Uralkali/Silvinit, Alpha V/Savio, GE China/China Shenhua JV, Seagate/Samsung Hard Disk Drive Business, Henkel Hong Kong/Tiande Chemical JV*, and *Western Digital/Hitachi Hard Disk Drive Business* decisions and the prohibition decision involves the *Coca-Cola/Huiyuan* transaction. Official Chinese versions of these decisions are available at <http://fldj.mofcom.gov.cn/ztxx/ztxx.html>.

[26] *See* NDRC, *Heavy Penalties Imposed on Rice Noodle Producers in Nanning and Liuzhou for Price Collusion,* March 31, 2010, Chinese version available at <http://jjs.ndrc.gov.cn/fjgld/t20100331_338262.htm>.

[27] *See* NDRC, *NDRC, MOFCOM and SAIC Press Release Regarding the Investigation and Handling of Hoarding to Increase Prices of Agricultural Products*, July 2, 2010, Chinese version available at <http://jjs.ndrc.gov.cn/gzdt/t20100702_358457.htm>.

havior in the first quarter of 2009 alone.[28] In January 2011, it was reported that a concrete manufacturer association was penalized by the SAIC's local bureau in Jiangsu province for market allocation.[29] The relatively lax enforcement of the AML by the NDRC and the SAIC may signal the tension between competition policy and industrial policy arising out of China's unique political and economic conditions. For example, the NDRC itself is a powerful agency responsible for price control and other macroeconomic and industrial policy.

C. Evolution of private enforcement

The right to private actions was established by the AUCL, the Price Law, and the Bidding Law in 1993, 1997, and 1999 respectively, pursuant to which injured parties are entitled to bring actions to the courts and to seek damages.[30]

Prior to the enactment of the AML, companies in China were actively seeking a legal basis within the existing framework, for example, by relying on the AUCL and the contract law, to challenge alleged monopoly conduct. High-profile cases include *Sichuan Dexian v. Shanghai Sony Guangdian Electronics* (hereinafter "*Dexian v. Sony*") on leverage effects and bundling of consumables in the aftermarket and *Dongjin v. Intel* on bundling and intellectual property disputes.[31] At the same time, Chinese judges had written decisions that were consistent with the AML legislation based on broad principles in existing statutes. In *Dexian v. Sony*, the court held that the plaintiff failed to proffer convincing evidence that Sony applied digital recognition code on Sony digital cameras and camcorders as well as the bundled batteries and, by doing so, abused its intellectual property rights so as to restrict competition from non-Sony batteries. In *Dongjin v. Intel*, the parties reached a settlement and the plaintiff withdrew the compliant.[32]

Article 50 of the AML entitles individuals and entities to bring private actions in respect of monopoly conduct, including restrictive agreements, abuse of dominance, and anti-competitive mergers, and to claim damages. The scope for private actions under the AML is wide, and stand-alone and follow-on litigation are both allowed. The procedural aspects of private antitrust litigation are governed by China's *Civil Procedure Law 1991* (Civil Procedure Law), according to which

[28] *See* SAIC, Keynote Speech Delivered by Mr Zhou Bohua, Head of SAIC, at the BRIC Competition Conference, September 3, 2009, Chinese version available at <http://www.saic.gov.cn/ywdt/gjjl/200909/t20090911_70416.html>.

[29] Xinhua News Agency, Trade Association Allocated Market Share; Jiangsu Completed the First Anti-Monopoly Investigation, January 21, 2011, Chinese version available at <http://www.js.xinhua.org/xin_wen_zhong_xin/2011-01/21/content_21923072.htm>.

[30] *See* AUCL, *supra* note 5, Art. 20; Price Law, *supra* note 6, Art. 41; Bidding Law, *supra* note 9, Art. 53.

[31] Zhihong Hou, "Sichuan Dexian Sued Sony in Shanghai for Monopolizing Behaviour" (in Chinese), China Securities Daily, June 30, 2006; People's Daily Online, Review: Causes and Consequences of Dongjin's Counterclaim against Intel, July 24, 2006, Chinese version available at <http://it.people.com.cn/GB/8219/68399/68409/4621379.html>.

[32] Xiangjun Kong & Zhonglin He, "Establishing China's Anti-Monopoly Civil Litigation Regime" (in Chinese), in Report on Competition Law and Policy of China (2010) 24–5, 28–9 (China Society for World Trade Organization Studies ed., China Law Press 2010).

multiple claimants can bring representative actions to the courts.[33] China's Supreme People's Court is finalizing the judicial interpretations in relation to civil litigation brought under the AML that will provide detailed guidance on private antitrust litigation in China.[34] The draft interpretations cover issues such as the scope of claims, jurisdiction, qualified plaintiffs, remedies, the finding of monopoly conduct, the relationship of administrative enforcement and private enforcement, the relationship of the protection of intellectual property and antitrust, etc. Judges of the Supreme People's Court have emphasized that rules of evidence, especially the standard of proof and the burden of proof, are particular challenges and require further consideration.[35] The Supreme People's Court issued the draft judicial interpretations for public comments in April 2011. It is expected that the judicial interpretations will be finalized before long. Once issued, the interpretations will provide more certainty and predictability to litigants and are expected to enhance private enforcement of the AML.

II. Structure

A. Institutional arrangements under the AML

The institutional framework of the AML was determined by the State Council in 2008. Potential violations of the AML are investigated, adjudicated, and sanctioned by the AMEAs, which currently includes three departments under the NDRC, the SAIC, and the MOFCOM. Enforcement actions may entail administrative reconsideration or judicial review. Thus, the current institutional structure of the AML may be categorized as a "variant" of an "integrated agency model."

1. The AMC

The AMC is a consultative and coordinating organization and its authorities and responsibilities include: (1) formulating competition policy; (2) organizing the investigation and assessment of the overall competition conditions and generating evaluation reports; (3) formulating and publishing anti-monopoly guidelines; (4) coordinating the anti-monopoly law enforcement work by the enforcement agencies; and, (5) other responsibilities stipulated by the State Council.[36]

The day-to-day work of the AMC has been assigned to MOFCOM instead of a separate organ. The AMC is currently chaired by China's Vice Premier Wang

[33] *See* Civil Procedure Law (promulgated by the 7th NPC on April 9, 1991 and amended 2007), English translation available at <http://www.npc.gov.cn/englishnpc/Law/2007-12/12/content_1383880.htm>.

[34] China's court (called the "people's court") system is divided into four levels: the basic people's court (at district level or county level), the intermediate people's court (at the prefectures level, or at capital cities of provinces), the higher people's court (at the provinces, autonomous regions and centrally administered municipalities), and the Supreme People's Court (the highest court in China).

[35] *See* Kong & He, *supra* note 32, 35–41.

[36] *See* AML, *supra* note 12, Art. 9.

Qishan. It has four vice chairpersons (the heads of the MOFCOM, the NDRC, the SAIC, and a deputy secretary-general of the State Council) and consists of fourteen commissioners (the incumbent deputy heads of fourteen ministries and institutions under the State Council). These ministries and institutions include: (1) the NDRC, (2) the SAIC, (3) the MOFCOM, (4) the State-owned Assets Supervision and Administration Commission, (5) the Ministry of Industry and Information Technology, (6) the Ministry of Transport, (7) the Ministry of Finance, (8) the Ministry of Supervision, (9) the State Intellectual Property Office, (10) the China Banking Regulatory Commission, (11) the China Securities Regulatory Commission, (12) the China Insurance Regulatory Commission, (13) the State Electricity Regulatory Commission, and (14) the Legislative Affairs Office of the State Council.[37]

2. *The NDRC*

As one of China's three AMEAs, the NDRC is responsible for price-related infringements of the AML in the areas of restrictive agreements, abuse of dominance, and administrative monopoly. The responsible unit within the NDRC is the Price Supervision and Anti-Monopoly Bureau (formerly the Price Supervision Department), which also has other regulatory roles pursuant to the Price Law.[38] The NDRC Price Supervision and Anti-Monopoly Bureau currently has nine divisions, among which the Price Monopoly Investigation Division I, the Price Monopoly Investigation Division II, and the Competition Policy and International Cooperation Division are the functioning units responsible for the NDRC's role of the AML enforcement.

3. *The SAIC*

As one of China's three AMEAs, the SAIC is responsible for non-price-related infringements of the AML in the areas of restrictive agreements, abuse of dominance, and administrative monopoly. The responsible unit within the SAIC is the Competition Enforcement Bureau (formerly the Anti-Unfair Competition Bureau).[39] The Competition Enforcement Bureau currently has five divisions, including (1) the Comprehensive Division, (2) the Anti-Monopoly Enforcement Division, (3) the Anti-Monopoly Legislative Affairs Division, (4) the Anti-Unfair Competition Division, and (5) the Case Supervision and Coordination Division. The Anti-Monopoly Enforcement Division and the Anti-Monopoly Legislative

[37] *See* General Office of the State Council, Notice of the Main Responsibilities and Members of the Anti-Monopoly Commission of the State Council, Guo Ban Fa [2008] No. 104, July 28, 2008, available at <http://www.pkulaw.cn/fulltext_form.aspx?db=chl&gid=109404> (subscription required).

[38] *See* NDRC, Main Functions of the NDRC, <http://en.ndrc.gov.cn/mfndrc/default.htm> and Main Functions of the NDRC Price Supervision and Anti-Monopoly Bureau (in Chinese), <http://jjs.ndrc.gov.cn/jgsz/default.html>.

[39] *See* SAIC, Mission of the SAIC, <http://www.saic.gov.cn/english/aboutus/Mission/> and Information of the SAIC Competition Enforcement Bureau (in Chinese), <http://www.saic.gov.cn/zzjg/zyzz/>.

Affairs Division are the functioning units responsible for the SAIC's role of the AML enforcement.

4. The MOFCOM

As one of China's three AMEAs, the MOFCOM is responsible for enforcing the merger control regime under the AML. The responsible unit within the MOFCOM is the Anti-Monopoly Bureau (formerly the Anti-Monopoly Investigation Office), which currently has six divisions, including (1) the General Office, (2) the Competition Policy Division, (3) the Consultation Division, (4) the Legal Division, (5) the Economics Division, and (6) the Supervision and Enforcement Division.[40] The MOFCOM Anti-Monopoly Bureau also has authority to coordinate bilateral and multilateral cooperation in competition policy, coordinate overseas antitrust litigation involving Chinese enterprises, etc.

5. The Enforcement Agencies' local bureaus

The AML provides that, based on the enforcement needs, the AMEAs may authorize their corresponding organs at the provincial level to be in charge of the anti-monopoly enforcement work.[41] The SAIC *Measures on the Procedures for Investigation and Handling Cases of Monopoly Agreements and Abuse of Market Dominant Position* further provide that SAIC may authorize its local bureaus at the provincial level to investigate and handle monopoly conduct occurring or mainly occurring within their corresponding administrative regions. Such authorization should be decided on a case-by-case basis and the authorized local bureaus should not re-delegate the cases to lower-level bureaus.[42]

6. Appeals of the AML enforcement decisions and the role of the courts

Decisions made by the AMEAs are binding on the undertakings to whom they are addressed. According to the AML, parties who disagree with a decision made by the NDRC or the SAIC on restrictive agreements or abuse of dominant position can choose to apply for administrative reconsideration, or directly challenge the decision by bringing an action before a people's court.[43]

[40] *See* MOFCOM, Mission of the MOFCOM, <http://english.mofcom.gov.cn/column/mission2010.shtml> and Information of the MOFCOM Anti-Monopoly Bureau (in Chinese), <http://fldj.mofcom.gov.cn/aarticle/gywm/200811/20081105873785.html>.

[41] *See* AML, *supra* note 12, Art. 10, para 2.

[42] *See* SAIC Measures on the Procedures for Investigation and Handling Cases of Monopoly Agreements and Abuse of Market Dominant Position, *supra* note 17, Art. 3.

[43] *See* AML, *supra* note 12, Art. 53, para 1. "Administrative reconsideration" refers to the situation where individuals, legal persons, and other organizations request for administrative organs to reconsider the legality and/or appropriateness of specific administrative actions; *see* Administrative Reconsideration Law (promulgated by the Standing Committee of the 9th NPC on April 29, 1999 and effective October 1, 1999), Art. 2, English translation available at <http://www.npc.gov.cn/englishnpc/Law/2007-12/11/content_1383562.htm>.

Dissatisfied parties who wish to contest a merger review decision made by the MOFCOM must appeal to the MOFCOM for administrative reconsideration in the first instance. If the parties are still not satisfied with the outcome of the administrative reconsideration, they can then bring an action to challenge the decision before a people's court.[44] Thus, administrative reconsideration is a prerequisite for challenging the MOFCOM's merger review decisions, but is not a prerequisite for administrative decisions made by the NDRC and the SAIC pursuant to the AML.

Although administrative litigation is provided as a statutory remedy for dissatisfied parties to challenge decisions made by the AMEAs, the AML does not provide any further information on jurisdiction, standing, time limit, etc. In an informal statement, an anonymous judge in charge of the Administrative Tribunal of the Supreme People's Court confirmed that general principles set out in the Administrative Litigation Law 1999 (Administrative Litigation Law) are applicable to administrative lawsuits brought against decisions made by the AMEAs.[45] The judge also confirmed that, considering the complex nature of anti-monopoly cases, the people's courts will further study the application of laws and strengthen the role of judicial review.[46]

The concept of "specific administrative actions" refers to administrative actions that address specific individuals, legal persons, or other organizations, and affect these counterparties' interests, rights, and obligations. The Administrative Litigation Law specifies eight types of specific administrative actions that are judicially reviewable. Among these the first three categories are relevant to the AML enforcement, including (1) administrative sanctions, such as detention, fines, revocation of business licenses or permits, orders to suspend production or business, confiscation of properties, etc.; (2) coercive administrative measures, such as seizing or freezing properties; and (3) interfering with legitimate autonomous rights of business.[47] In contrast, abstract administrative actions refer to administrative regulations, ministerial rules, decisions and orders, and other normative documents adopted by administrative organs that are binding on the general public. Abstract administrative actions are not judicially reviewable pursuant to the Administrative Litigation Law.[48]

Under the AML, decisions imposed by the AMEAs are specific administrative actions and are thus subject to administrative reconsideration and/or administrative

[44] *See* AML, *supra* note 12, Art. 53, para 2.

[45] *See* Administrative Litigation Law, also translated as "Administrative Procedure Law" (promulgated by the 7th NPC on April 4, 1989 and effective on October 1, 1990), English translation available at <http://www.npc.gov.cn/englishnpc/Law/2007-12/12/content_1383912.htm>.

[46] "Strengthen anti-monopoly judicial review and protecting fair competition—an interview with the judge in charge of the Administrative Tribunal of the Supreme People's Court," People's Court Daily, November 3, 2008, Chinese version available at <http://rmfyb.chinacourt.org/public/detail.php?id=123368>. The interview also covers topics including standing, scope of review, evidentiary rules, etc.

[47] *See* Administrative Litigation Law, *supra* note 45, Art. 11(1)–(3).

[48] *See* Administrative Litigation Law, *supra* note 45, Art. 12(2); also *see* Administrative Reconsideration Law, *supra* note 43, Art. 7.

litigation. On the other hand, the AML prohibits administrative organs from abusing their administrative powers by promulgating rules containing provisions that eliminate or restrict competition. The rule-setting function, categorized as "abstractive administrative actions," is, however, beyond the court's jurisdiction through administrative litigation.[49]

The Administrative Litigation Law provides that seven circumstances may cause a specific administrative action to be revoked, partially revoked, or modified by the courts. The courts may also order the administrative organ to perform a new specific administrative action or fulfill its legal responsibilities. These circumstances are: (1) the administrative organ relied upon inadequate principal evidence; (2) the administrative organ applied the laws incorrectly; (3) the administrative organ failed to follow the legally prescribed procedures; (4) the administrative organ exceeded its powers; (5) the administrative organ abused its powers; (6) the administrative penalties are obviously unfair; and, (7) the administrative organ failed to fulfill or fulfill in a timely manner its legal responsibilities.[50]

Judicial review may, however, play a limited role, given that private parties often have a continuing "client" relationship with the AMEAs and there would be risk of upsetting future relations by seeking judicial review. To date, no actions challenging decisions made by the AMEAs have been reported. It thus remains to be seen to what extent the court would play a role in the judicial review of administrative decisions made by the AMEAs.

B. Private enforcement of the AML

The Supreme People's Court has confirmed that, if the party who brings civil litigation pursuant to the AML meets the criteria set out in Article 108 of the Civil Procedure Law, the people's courts should accept the case.[51] These criteria include: (1) the plaintiff must be a natural person, a legal person, or any other organization that has direct interest in the disputed matter; (2) the identity of the defendant is definite; (3) the claim, facts and reasons are concrete; and (4) the claim is within the jurisdiction of the court.[52] The Supreme People's Court is considering how direct interest should be defined when determining who has standing to bring civil competition litigation.[53] In addition, the Supreme People's Court has promulgated the *Amendments to the Provisions on Causes of Actions in Civil Cases* (hereinafter "Amended Provisions on Causes of Actions") on February 18, 2011. In particular, the Amended Provisions on Causes of Actions classify competition disputes as Class

[49] *See* AML, *supra* note 12, Art. 37.

[50] *See* Administrative Litigation Law, *supra* note 45, Art. 54.

[51] *See* Supreme People's Court, Notice on the Study and Implementation of the Anti-Monopoly Law, July 28, 2008, Chinese version available at <http://vip.chinalawinfo.com/newlaw2002/SLC/slc.asp?db=chl&gid=107282>.

[52] *See* Civil Procedure Law, *supra* note 33, Art. 108.

[53] Zhonglin He & Li Zhu, "Principal Questions of Civil Anti-Monopoly Litigation: Report of the Consultation Meeting of Civil Anti-Monopoly Litigation and Judicial Interpretation," People's Court Daily, August 6, 2009, 6, Chinese version available at <http://rmfyb.chinacourt.org/public/detail.php?id=130778>.

I causes of actions and non-exhaustively specify the causes of actions based on monopoly conduct pursuant to the AML. Specified causes of actions under the AML include disputes relating to: (1) horizontal monopoly agreements, (2) vertical monopoly agreements, (3) monopoly pricing, (4) predatory pricing, (5) refusal to deal, (6) designated transactions, (7) bundling transactions, (8) discriminatory treatment, and (9) concentrations of undertakings.[54]

It has been reported that, by May 2010, at least ten private lawsuits have been brought under the AML. All were stand-alone claims. Among these cases, nine challenged alleged abuse of dominant market positions and one involved an alleged monopoly agreement; half of the cases involved new technologies; around one-third of cases were settled or withdrawn. Among the ten cases, the Beijing court accepted six cases, two of which were referred to the Zhejiang court. The Shanghai court accepted one case while the Chongqing court accepted two cases, and the Zhejiang court accepted one case and two referrals.[55] In cases where judgments were rendered, the claims were all dismissed because the plaintiffs failed to prove the relevant markets, the defendants' dominant position, that the defendants abused dominant positions, or on statute of limitation grounds.

For example, in *Beijing Zhaoxin v. the General Administration of Quality Supervision, Inspection and Quarantine* (AQSIQ), the plaintiff, a competitor in the supply of inspection services, alleged that AQSIQ, a state department that certifies the quality of inspection services, had abused its administrative powers to restrict competition by requiring companies to purchase services from a company related to AQSIQ. The court held that the short statute runs from the start of the abusive conduct and dismissed the case on statute of limitations grounds.[56]

In *Zhou Ze v. China Mobile*, Zhou Ze, a customer of China Mobile, accused China Mobile of abusing its dominant position by imposing discriminatory tariffs to existing and new customers of mobile phones. The case was settled in October 2009 and China Mobile gave Zhou Ze a prize of CNY1,000 for his help in improving China Mobile's services.[57]

In *Tangshan Renren Information Service Ltd.* (Renren) *v. Baidu, Inc.* (Baidu), the court for the first time conducted substantive analyses on the market definition, the presumption of dominance, and the evidentiary standards required for a finding of an abuse of dominance. Renren operates a medical information website while Baidu is a leading search engine provider in China. Renren accused Baidu of abusing its dominant position in the search engine market by blocking Renren's website after Renren reduced payment for listing in Baidu's search results. Renren claimed damages of CNY1.106 million and sought an order for Baidu to cease its

[54] *See* Supreme People's Court, Amended Provisions on the Causes of Actions of Civil Cases, March 20, 2011, official Chinese version available at <http://www.court.gov.cn/xwzx/fyxw/zgrmfyxw/201103/t20110320_18959.htm>.

[55] *See* Kong & He, *supra* note 32, at 30–5.

[56] Peter Wang, H. Steve Harris and Mark Allen Cohen, "PRC Courts Beginning to Establish Procedural Framework for Anti-Monopoly Litigation," available at <www.mondaq.com>.

[57] China Daily, China Mobile "Monopoly Case" Settled; Plaintiff Awarded a "Prize" of CNY 1,000, Chinese version available at: <http://www.chinadaily.com.cn/zgzx/2009-10/28/content_8860663.htm>.

conduct. Baidu denied that it held a dominant position in China's search engine market but admitted that it had blocked Renren's website. However, Baidu argued that the blocking measures were taken indiscriminately pursuant to Baidu's policy of banning websites with junk links. The court dismissed the plaintiff's claim, holding that (i) Renren failed to adduce sufficient evidence to establish Baidu's dominance, and (ii) Baidu's measures against Renren were justified.[58]

C. Brief review of substantive provisions of the AML

1. Monopoly agreements

The AML adopts the term "monopoly agreements" and defines it as "agreements, decisions or other concerted actions that eliminate or restrict competition,"[59] which broadly accords with the concept of restrictive agreements that prevent, restrict, or distort competition under EU competition law.[60] The AML provides an illustrative list of prohibited horizontal monopoly agreements, according to which competing undertakings are prohibited from price fixing, output restriction, market sharing, restriction of products or technology developments, and joint boycott.[61] The AML further provides a separate article that prohibits non-competing undertakings from fixing resale price and restricting minimum resale price.[62] Industry associations are specifically prohibited from organizing undertakings to engage in monopoly agreements.[63] In addition, the AMEAs are empowered by the AML to determine "other monopoly agreements" and "other abuses of dominant market position" that are not explicitly prohibited by the AML.[64]

The AML establishes a general exemption mechanism stipulating that the prohibition on horizontal and vertical monopoly agreements shall not apply if the undertakings involved can prove that the agreements in question fall under one of the following circumstances: (1) researching and developing new product with a view to improving technology; (2) unifying specifications and standards of products with a view to upgrading product quality, reducing cost, and enhancing efficiency; (3) improving operational efficiency and enhancing competitiveness of small and medium-sized undertakings; (4) realizing social public interests such as energy saving, environment protection, disaster relief, etc.; (5) moderating serious sales decreases or production surpluses in periods of economic depression; (6) ensuring legitimate interests in foreign trade and economic cooperation; and (7) other circumstances specified by laws and the State Council.[65]

[58] Wenbo Wang, The Baidu Case Heard Today, April 22, 2009, Chinese version available at: <http://bj1zy.chinacourt.org/public/detail.php?id=612>; Qinghui Yang, Judgment of the First Monopoly Case in Beijing Delivered, December 23, 2009, Chinese version available at: <http://bj1zy.chinacourt.org/public/detail.php?id=675>.

[59] *See* AML, *supra* note 12, Art. 13.

[60] *See* Treaty on the Functioning of the European Union, Art. 101.

[61] *See* AML, *supra* note 12, Art. 13.

[62] *See id.* Art. 14. [63] *See id.* Art. 16.

[64] *See id.* Arts 13(6), 14(3), and 17(7).

[65] *See id.* Art. 15, para 1.

For agreements that fall under the circumstances set out in (1) to (5) above, the undertakings involved are further required to prove that the agreements (a) will not substantially eliminate competition in the relevant market; and (b) can enable consumers to share the benefits derived from the agreement.[66] The sweeping clause that exempts "other circumstances as stipulated by law and the State Council" implies more discretionary space for the AMEAs and provides leeway for particular sectors and special interest groups. As indicated by the statutory text, the exemption mechanism envisaged by the AML has chosen multi-layer and non-exhaustive standards which mix considerations of efficiencies, trade and industrial policy, and public interest.

The AML does not provide a mechanism for undertakings to seek a monopoly agreement exemption. It is thus unclear as to whether the exemption must be obtained in advance or can be invoked as a defense *ex post*. Early drafts of the AML provided a notification mechanism which was ultimately abandoned. It seems that the Chinese legislators have learned from the previous European Commission and German experience. However, without further delineation of the AML exemption mechanism, the self-assessment required by Article 15 may leave open a wide range of possible outcomes from strict to lax application to hard-core cartels and other restrictive agreements, and thus would create difficulties and uncertainty for undertakings.

Infringement of the AML prohibition on restrictive agreements that do not meet the criteria for exemption may lead to investigation and penalties by the AMEAs. Penalties for the infringement include orders to cease the conduct, confiscation of illegal gains, and fines in amounts between 1 and 10 percent of the undertaking's previous annual turnover. For non-implemented monopoly agreements, a fine of up to CNY500,000 may be imposed.[67] The AMEAs may reduce or exempt sanctions for undertakings that voluntarily report important information and evidence concerning monopoly agreements.[68] In addition to administrative sanctions, offenders are liable for damages to injured parties.[69]

2. *Abuse of dominance*

Under the AML, a dominant undertaking is understood as an undertaking having a market position that enables it to control prices, quantities, or other trading conditions in the relevant market, or to restrict or affect market entries in the relevant market.[70] Dominant undertakings are prohibited from abusing their dominant positions to eliminate or restrict competition.[71]

The AML does not prohibit attempts to acquire or acquisition of a dominant position, but only actual abuse of a dominant position. The AML does not define the concept of "abuse" but provides a list of categorized abusive behavior. The specifically prohibited behavior is illustrative and includes both exploitative and exclusionary conduct. Dominant undertakings are prohibited, without valid justi-

[66] *See id.* Art. 15, para 2.
[67] *See id.* Art. 46, para 1.
[68] *See id.* Art. 46, para 2.
[69] *See id.* Art. 50.
[70] *See id.* Art. 17, para 2.
[71] *See id.* Art. 6.

fications, from carrying out excessive pricing, below-cost sales, refusals to deal, exclusive or designated dealing, tying or imposing other unreasonable transactional terms, and discriminatory treatment.[72] In addition, the AMEAs have a general power to determine and penalize "other abuses of dominant market position" that are not explicitly prohibited by the AML.[73]

Penalties for the infringement of the AML prohibition of abuse of dominance include orders to cease the conduct, confiscation of illegal gains, and fines in amounts between 1 and 10 percent of the undertaking's previous annual turnover.[74] In addition, offenders are liable for damages to injured parties.[75]

3. *Merger control*

The main provisions of merger control are set out in Chapter IV of the AML. In addition, the AML provides, as a basic principle, that "undertakings may implement concentrations in accordance with the law through fair competition and voluntary combination to expand business scope and enhance market competitiveness."[76]

The AML defines concentrations of undertakings as: (1) mergers of undertakings, (2) acquisitions of control of other undertakings through the purchase of shares or assets, and (3) acquisition of control of other undertakings, or of the ability to exercise decisive influence on other undertakings, through contract or other means.[77] First, concentrations that meet the notification thresholds stipulated in the State Council Rules on the Thresholds for the Notifications of Concentrations of Undertakings must be notified to the MOFCOM. With a preliminary (Phase I) review of thirty days following the notification, the MOFCOM may either decide to open an investigation for further (Phase II) review, or decide not to conduct further investigation. There is no extension to the thirty-day time limit for the preliminary review. If the MOFCOM fails to reach a decision within the time limit, the proposed concentration is deemed to be cleared.[78] A notifiable concentration cannot be implemented before the MOFCOM decides that no further review will be conducted unless the preliminary review period has expired. The time limit for further review is ninety days which can be extended up to another sixty days under one of the circumstances specified by the AML and with the MOFCOM's written notice to the undertakings involved. These circumstances are (1) the undertakings concerned agree to extend the time limit; (2) documents submitted by the undertakings concerned are inaccurate and need further verification; and (3) relevant circumstances have significantly changed following the notification.[79] During the course of the further review, if the MOFCOM reaches a conclusion that the proposed concentration may eliminate or restrict competition and the undertaking concerned cannot prove either that the pro-competitive effect of the proposed concentration obviously outweighs its anti-competitive effect, or

[72] *See id.* Art. 17, para 1(1)–(6). [73] *See id.* Art. 17, para 2.
[74] *See id.* Art. 47. [75] *See id.* Art. 50.
[76] *See id.* Art. 5. [77] *See id.* Art. 20.
[78] *See id.* Art. 25. [79] *See id.* Art. 26.

that the proposed concentration is in accordance with the public interest, the MOFCOM should adopt a decision to prohibit the concentration; otherwise the concentration should be cleared. The clearance may be subject to conditions imposed by the MOFCOM.[80]

Penalties for the infringement of the AML merger control rules include orders to cease the implementation of the concentration, to dispose of shares or assets, to transfer business within a given time limit, or to adopt other necessary measures to restore the market situation before the concentration. A fine up to CNY500,000 may also be imposed.[81]

4. Abuse of administrative powers to eliminate or restrict competition

"Monopoly conduct," a concept covering restrictive agreements, abuse of dominance, and anti-competitive mergers, is the principal subject matter of the AML. The AML also prohibits "administrative monopoly," that is, the abuse of administrative powers by the government to exclude or restrict competition, as distinct from restrictive agreements and abuse of dominance. The AML prohibits administrative agencies and "organizations empowered by laws or regulations with responsibilities for public affairs administration" from abusing their administrative powers by participating in designated transactions, hindering free movement of goods among regions, restricting non-local undertakings' bidding activities in the local market, restricting non-local undertakings' investment and establishment of subsidiaries in the local market, forcing undertakings to engage in monopoly conduct, or promulgating anti-competitive rules.[82]

Although the AML generally prohibits administrative monopoly, the AMEAs have not secured substantial jurisdiction over administrative monopoly. Under the AML, where a public authority engages in administrative monopoly conduct, its superior agency shall order the public authority to make a correction, and the persons directly in charge and others directly responsible shall be subject to disciplinary sanctions in accordance with law. The AMEAs may make proposals on the handling of administrative monopoly to the relevant superior agency of the public authority.[83] Thus the enforcement mechanism vis-à-vis administrative monopoly is weak and cannot provide sufficient deterrence.

III. Mandate and boundaries of the Anti-Monopoly Enforcement Agencies

A. Objectives of the AML

Objectives of China's AML are prescribed or implied in Articles 1, 4, 5, 7, 15, 27, 28, and 31 of the AML. These include promoting efficiency, encouraging free

[80] *See id.* Art. 30.
[81] *See id.* Art. 48.
[82] *See id.* Arts 32–37.
[83] *See id.* Art. 51.

competition, safeguarding healthy development of socialist market economy and the public interest, protecting the state-owned economy and small business, encouraging the expansion of domestic enterprises, and scrutinizing foreign takeovers. No clear hierarchy has been established between these various objectives, and the influx of broader, non-competition goals may cause inconsistencies in interpretation and enforcement.

The AML was designed to serve both economic and non-economic objectives, and it has both direct and ultimate goals.[84] Article 1 provides that "[t]his Law is enacted for the purposes of preventing and prohibiting monopoly conduct, protecting fair market competition, improving efficiency of economic operation, safeguarding the consumer interest and the public interest, and promoting the healthy development of the socialist market economy." Article 4 provides that "the State formulates and implements competition rules compatible with the socialist economy, improves macro regulation and control, and strengthens a unified, open, competitive and orderly market system." The economic and direct objectives of the AML include prohibiting monopoly conduct and protecting competition and consumer welfare. The sociopolitical and ultimate objectives of the AML include protecting the public interest and promoting the healthy development of the socialist market economy. The AML does not establish a clear hierarchy between these various objectives and the task of reconciling these objectives in implementing the AML has been left to the AMEAs.

The sociopolitical objectives have been considered "structural shortcomings" from which the AML suffers.[85] The public interest approach to competition law and policy might have provided for a somewhat clearer and more predictable formulation within which to balance different economic, social, and political objectives. Articles 15(4) and 28 further provide that monopoly agreements may be exempted from the AML or concentrations may be approved if the undertakings involved can prove that the agreements or transactions are for the purpose of achieving "public interest." However, the independence of competition law administration may become curbed, since what constitutes the "public interest" is questionable. In many situations, perception of the "public interest" can be widely divergent, and what might be desirable to one party may be seen as less important or even immaterial by another.[86] As regards the "healthy development of the socialist market economy," what conduct could be categorized as "healthy" or "unhealthy" is subject to the decision-makers' preference and the "socialist market economy" is an ideologically involving concept. The generality of these sociopolitical objectives could cause uncertainty in interpretation and application of the law, and may produce conflicts with other objectives if regarded as operational

[84] Wang, *supra* note 16, at 584–7.

[85] Fei Deng, Adrian Emch, & Gregory Leonard, "A Hard Landing in the Soft Drink Market—MOFCOM's Veto of the Coca-Cola & Huiyuan Deal," Global Competition Policy (April 2009), <https://www.competitionpolicyinternational.com/a-hard-landing-in-the-soft-drink-market-mofcoms-veto-of-the-coca-cola–huiyuan-deal/>.

[86] C.D. Ehlermann & L.L. Laudati eds, *European Competition Law Annual 1997: Objectives of Competition Policy 58* (Hart Publishing 1998).

objectives to determine the lawfulness of specific conduct in particular cases. As illustrated in the *Coca-Cola/Huiyuan* decision, the inclusion of industrial policy goals and other sociopolitical grounds may facilitate input from other government agencies and stakeholders with conflicting interests and may blur the AMEAs' analysis in individual cases.

Apart from Articles 1, 4, 15, and 28, several articles may also imply the AML's industrial policy considerations. For example, Article 7 provides that the state shall protect the legitimate operating activities of industries dominated by the state-owned economy and which are vital to the Chinese national economy or national security or both. This article has led some to believe that special treatment under the AML will be given to large state-owned enterprises (SOEs) that operate effectively as monopolies in industries such as telecommunications and energy.[87] Article 15 (3), on the other hand, allows exemptions of monopoly agreements if they are aimed at improving operational efficiency and competitiveness of small and medium enterprises (SMEs).

In regard to merger control, Article 5 provides that undertakings may, through fair competition and voluntary combination, implement concentrations to expand business scale and improve market competitiveness. During the AML legislative process, stakeholders had argued that the AML should pay attention to the situation of China's economic development; that is, many Chinese enterprises have insufficient scale and low competitiveness. Therefore, although the AML should prevent over-concentration and monopoly, it should also "encourage domestic enterprises to consolidate lawfully in order to become big and strong, realize economies of scale, increase industry concentration, and increase competitiveness."[88] Thus, Article 5 was added by the Standing Committee of the 10th NPC as a result of industrial policy considerations to encourage the expansion of domestic enterprises, although the draft AML submitted by the State Council to the NPC for reading did not include this article.[89]

In addition, Article 27 lists various factors that the MOFCOM will take into account when conducting merger reviews. Most of these factors relate to market competition conditions and align with the main aspects of merger assessment of the EU and US.[90] However, one of the factors listed in Article 27 is the effect that the proposed concentration may have on the national economic development and "other factors" the MOFCOM may regard as relevant. Some have questioned whether such considerations could encourage the MOFCOM to prohibit transactions simply based on industrial policy considerations because the proposed trans-

[87] Bruce M. Owen, Su Sun, & Wentong Zheng, "China's Competition Policy Reforms: the Anti-Monopoly Law and Beyond," 75 Antitrust L.J. 231, 244–7 (2008); also *see* Wu, *supra* note 24, 98–100.

[88] Wu, *supra* note 24, at 97.

[89] *Id.*

[90] These factors include (1) market shares of undertakings to the concentration as well as their ability to control the market, (2) the degree of concentration in the relevant market, (3) the effect of the concentration on market entry and technological progress, and (4) the effect of the concentration on consumers and other undertakings; *see* AML, *supra* note 12, Art 27(1)–(4).

actions may be capable of adversely impacting domestic Chinese companies or the development of Chinese industry.[91]

Article 31 is also significant and has triggered concerns of whether the AML contains any inherent bias against foreign firms. It provides that mergers and acquisitions of domestic enterprises by foreign investors or other forms of concentrations involving foreign investors, if they are deemed to raise national security concerns, must go through both anti-monopoly review and national security review in accordance with the relevant provisions of the State. Senior officials of the MOFCOM have publicly stated that domestic and foreign business operators are treated equally under the AML merger control regime, both from a procedural and substantive review perspective.[92] However, Western governments and multinational corporations are concerned that China may use the AML to block non-domestic competitors' access to the lucrative Chinese market as well as to justify the government's heavy market intervention under the name of "national security." Recent overseas investments by Chinese enterprises and sovereign wealth funds have caused many to believe that the AML may reflect the fact that an increasingly prosperous China no longer needs foreign investment as badly as before, and that Beijing is therefore using its national security review to discourage foreign investment.[93]

On February 12, 2011, the General Office of the State Council promulgated the *Notice on Establishing a Mechanism of Security Review of Mergers and Acquisitions of Domestic Enterprises by Foreign Investors* (hereinafter "National Security Review Notice"). Promulgated to guide the orderly development of foreign takeovers of domestic enterprises and to safeguard national security, the National Security Review Notice sets out the scope, content, review mechanism, and procedures of the national security review system. An Inter-Ministerial Joint Committee has been established under the State Council. It is to be responsible for the national security review which is to be led by the NDRC and the MOFCOM.[94] Private practitioners disclosed that they have started to notify transactions on behalf of their clients pursuant to Article 31 of the AML and the National Security Review Notice. It is understood that the definition of national security in China may be effectively extended to cover "national economic security" rather than just matters of national defense and thus may reflect China's intention of retaining national control over key economic sectors.[95] Indeed, it is observed that Article 31 of the AML overlaps

[91] *See* Deng, Emch, & Leonard, *supra* note 85.

[92] Haitao Du, "Four Main Points of the Anti-Monopoly Law: An Interview with Shang Ming," People's Daily, August 31, 2007, Chinese version available at <http://news.xinhuanet.com/politics/2007-08/31/content_6635548.htm>.

[93] Michael Han & Jessica Su, "China's Antimonopoly Law: Status Quo and Outlook, Global Competition Policy," August 2008, <https://www.competitionpolicyinternational.com/chinas-antimonopoly-law-status-quo-and-outlook/>.

[94] *See* National Security Review Notice, English translation available at: <http://www.fdi.gov.cn/pub/FDI_EN/Laws/law_en_info.jsp?docid=130963>.

[95] Hannah C. L. Ha, John M. Hichin, and Gerry P. O'Brien, China's Anti-Monopoly Law Merger Control Regime—10 Key Questions Answered (Part I), MONDAQ (March 11, 2010), <http://www.mondaq.com>.

with the M&A Rules 2009, which provide for special review of inbound merger and acquisitions that may affect "key industrial sectors," the "national economy security," or involve "well-known trademarks or traditional brands" of China.[96]

B. Statutory exclusion for the agriculture sector

The AML provides a statutory exclusion for agricultural producers by declaring that it will not apply to alliances or concerted actions among agricultural producers and rural economic organizations in operational activities, such as the production, processing, sales, transportation, and storage of agricultural products.[97] It is noteworthy that this is not a general exemption for the agricultural sector. For example, the NDRC announced in July 2010 that several local price agencies have made three decisions in relation to price collusion and manipulation of green beans and garlic. A number of agricultural trade associations and trading companies had been subject to fines and warnings.[98] Except for alliances or concerted actions among agricultural producers, the AML is in principle a piece of economy-wide legislation that applies to all sectors.

C. Investigation and adjudication powers of the Anti-Monopoly Enforcement Agencies

A principal feature of the AML administrative enforcement is the combination of investigative, adjudicative, and prosecutorial functions. The AML authorizes the enforcement agencies with substantial powers to investigate suspected monopoly conduct. Such powers include: (1) inspecting business premises or any relevant places of undertakings under investigation, (2) interviewing undertakings under investigation or other relevant individuals or undertakings, (3) inspecting and copying relevant documents and materials such as agreements, accounting books, business correspondence, and electronic data, (4) seizing and retaining relevant evidence, and (5) inquiring into bank accounts of undertakings under investigation.[99]

D. The division of AML enforcement responsibilities

The AML lacks an independent enforcement agency with sufficient authority. Under the current institutional arrangement, coordination between the NDRC, the SAIC, and the MOFCOM will be one of the key challenges to the successful enforcement of the AML. However, achieving effective inter-government agency coordination has proved to be relatively difficult in the past, and attempts have

[96] Qian Hu, "National Security Review Considered by the Legislator," Caijing, August 30, 2007, Chinese version available at <http://www.caijing.com.cn/2007-08-30/100028567.html>; also *see* M&A Rules 2009, *supra* note 13, Art. 12.

[97] *See* AML, *supra* note 12, Art. 56.

[98] *See* NDRC, *supra* note 27.

[99] *See* AML, *supra* note 12, Art. 39.

often been hampered by excessive bureaucracy. The division of enforcement responsibilities with respect to the AML may already have created a scope for friction or conflict between the three agencies, which have different degrees of experience in handling competition-related cases and vary in their access to resources. What is more problematic is the division of jurisdiction between the NDRC and the SAIC along the line of price-related or non-price-related violations. What happens when a case involves both of these elements? For instance, an output restriction cartel can be characterized as a "non-price-related" violation, on the one hand, because it does not directly fix the price, while on the other hand, it can be well argued as a "price-related" violation, given its impact on the price.

E. Concurrent mandates and authorities of the Anti-Monopoly Enforcement Agencies

It is clear that in order for the AMEAs to carry out their statutory functions effectively, they should have sufficient independence and authority. However, in addition to the role of enforcing the AML, all three agencies have concurrent mandates and authorities to implement industrial, trade, and wider economic and public policies with different policy agenda and political constituency. These include the MOFCOM's role of regulating foreign trade and investment, the SAIC's role of consumer protection and regulating unfair trade practice, and the NDRC's role of price control and formulating macro-economic and industrial policies. Thus, in addition to the conflicting objectives of the AML, the current institutional design itself may give rise to problematic situations where industrial policy considerations may override competition policy.

F. The interface between industrial policy, sectoral regulations, and the AML

China's sectoral regulations include certain competition-related rules, which have resulted in concurrent jurisdictions between the AMEAs and sectoral regulators. Pursuant to a variety of sectoral regulations, a number of sectoral regulators, such as the General Administration of Civil Aviation, the Ministry of Industry and Information Technology, the People's Bank of China, and the Ministry of Justice, are vested with authority to regulate anti-competitive behavior falling within their remit.[100] The boundaries between the power of the AMEAs and sectoral regulators are by no means clear, especially in connection with regulated industries where

[100] Sectoral regulations that contain provisions on restrictive behavior include, for example, (1) the Provisions to Prohibit Unfair Competition in Civil Aviation Transportation Market (promulgated by the General Administration of Civil Aviation on February 27, 1996), (2) the Telecommunications Regulations (promulgated by the State Council on September 25, 2000), (3) the Provisions for Countering Unfair Competition Conduct by Lawyers (promulgated by the Ministry of Justice on 20 February 1995), and, (4) the Provisions on Prohibitions of Unfair Competition in Savings Service (promulgated by the People's Bank of China on February 14, 1996).

SOEs may be protected by sectoral regulations and Article 7 of the AML.[101] However, the AMEAs' recent enforcement activities have indicated that SOEs are not granted a general exemption under the AML. For example, in November 2011, the NDRC confirmed that it had opened an investigation on China Telecom and China Unicom, two giant state-owned telecom enterprises, in relation to their alleged abusive behavior of charging internet service providers discriminatory network access fees in order to squeeze out competitors.[102]

IV. Procedural characteristics

A. Due process norms in case-by-case decision-making

This section further describes the investigation and adjudication powers, the procedural rules, and the decisional practices of the AMEAs. The recognition of and trade-offs involving due process norms are noted.

1. The NDRC and the SAIC

The NDRC and the SAIC can open administrative proceedings pursuant to the AML on their own initiative or after receiving complaints; if a complaint is submitted with the relevant facts and evidence, the NDRC and the SAIC are obliged to open an investigation.[103] The expansive powers of the NDRC and the SAIC to investigate suspect monopoly conduct are discussed above.[104]

The investigations are required to be carried out by at least two enforcement officials who are required to present their enforcement credentials. The officials must keep a written record of the inspection that must be signed by the undertakings or individuals being investigated.[105] The enforcement agencies and their officials are required to maintain confidentiality of business secrets obtained during the investigation and the identities of informants.[106] Details of the investigating powers of the NDRC and the SAIC are further stipulated in the SAIC *Measures on the Procedures for Investigation and Handling Cases of Monopoly Agreements and Abuse of Market Dominant Position* and the NDRC *Measures on the Administrative Enforcement Procedures of the Prohibition of Price Monopoly*.[107]

[101] For an analysis of the relationship between the AML and the regulated industries and statutory monopoly, *see* Yong Huang, "Pursuing the Second Best: the History, Momentum, and Remaining Issues of China's Anti-Monopoly Law," 75 ANTITRUST L.J. 126–8 (2008).

[102] For latest developments of the NDRC's investigation on China Telecom and China Unicom, *see* China Competition Research Centre, "Update on the National Development and Reform Commission's Anti-Monopoly Investigation of China Telecom and China Unicom," CHINA COMPETITION BULLETIN, Edition 18, March 2012, 3, available at: <http://www.anzsog.edu.au/research/publications/the-china-competition-bulletin>.

[103] *See* AML, *supra* note 12, Art. 38.

[104] *See* discussion at III. C, above.

[105] *See* AML, *supra* note 12, Art. 40.

[106] *See id.*, Art. 41 and Art. 38, para 2.

[107] *See supra* note 17.

Apart from the wide and substantial investigating powers established by the AML, the NDRC and the SAIC also have powers to accept commitments and reopen proceedings, find infringements, adopt decisions, and impose fines and other penalties.[108] For example, the AML provides for the adoption of decisions by the AMEAs whereby the undertakings under investigation are committed to implementing specific measures to eliminate consequences of monopoly conduct within a prescribed time. The enforcement agencies may decide to suspend the investigation without making a finding as to whether there has been an infringement of the AML.[109] The AMEAs must monitor the performance of the commitments and may terminate the investigation upon fulfillment of the commitments.[110] The AMEAs are authorized to resume the investigations if (1) the undertakings fail to perform the commitments; (2) material changes have occurred with respect to the facts based on which the decision to suspend the investigation was made; and (3) the decision to suspend the investigation was made based on incomplete or false information provided by the undertakings.[111]

In regards to the right of defense, the AML provides that undertakings under investigation have the right to state their opinions. The enforcement agencies are required to verify the facts, justifications, and evidence presented by the undertakings.[112] It should be noted that the AMEAs' decisional practice must also follow the procedural rules set out in the *Administrative Penalty Law 1996* (Administrative Penalty Law). Pursuant to the Administrative Penalty Law, administrative organs are required to ascertain facts of the violations and not to impose penalties if the facts are unclear. Before deciding to impose administrative penalties, administrative organs are required to notify parties of the facts, grounds, and basis on which the administrative penalties are based and must notify the parties of their legitimate right to state their case and defend themselves. Administrative organs must fully hear the opinions of the parties, reexamine the facts and evidence put forward, and accept the facts and evidence should they be established.[113]

The AML also establishes a leniency mechanism to detect and combat cartels. Pursuant to the AML, where undertakings involved in monopoly agreements, on their own initiative, report important evidence relating to the conclusion of monopoly agreements to the enforcement agencies, the undertakings may be given a mitigated punishment or be exempted from punishment at the agencies' discretion.[114] To increase the effectiveness of the leniency mechanism and legal certainty to "whistle-blowers," the relevant AML implementing regulations contain specific provisions that provide further guidance on leniency. For example, the

[108] *See* AML, *supra* note 12, Arts 44–49.

[109] *See id.* Art. 45, para 1.

[110] *See id.* Art. 45, para 2.

[111] *See id.* Art. 45, para 3.

[112] *See id.* Art. 43.

[113] *See* Administrative Penalty Law, Arts 30–32. The Administrative Penalty Law was promulgated by the 8th NPC on March 17, 1996, effective October 1, 1996 and amended 2009, English translation available at: <http://www.npc.gov.cn/englishnpc/Law/2007-12/11/content_1383613.htm>.

[114] *See* AML, *supra* note 12, Art. 46, para 2.

SAIC Measures on the Prohibition of Monopoly Agreements define "important evidence" as "evidence that can enable the initiation of the investigation or that plays a key role in the determination of monopoly agreements, such as the parties to the agreements, the product scope involved, the way such agreements are reached, the implementation of such agreements, etc."[115] For the undertaking which is the first to voluntarily report the relevant information and material evidence and offer comprehensive and voluntary cooperation during investigations, the undertaking shall be exempted from the penalty; for other undertakings voluntarily reporting relevant information with material evidence, penalties may be reduced by the enforcement agencies by taking the circumstances into consideration.[116] As can be seen in the above description, the AML and accompanying implementing regulations have set up basic procedural rules for the NDRC and the SAIC. Further procedural rules, such as more systematic and administrable rules for the leniency program and imposition of fines, are expected to be formulated in the future.

To date, the NDRC local price bureaus have made several decisions on cartels and abuse of dominance. Thus far NDRC has not published any decision in full but has made public announcements instead. These announcements contain only general descriptions of facts and of the sanctions imposed. For example, in July 2010, the NDRC announced three decisions made by local price bureaus in Inner Mongolia, and provinces of Shandong, Henan, and Guangdong in relation to price collusion and manipulation of the markets for green beans and garlic. According to the announcement, Jilin Corn Centre Wholesale Company was fined CNY1 million, the severest fine since the AML came into force. The trading company was alleged to have led and cooperated with other companies, through meetings and other means, to fabricate and disseminate information on price increases and to collude to increase the price of green beans. Several cooperating companies were fined CNY500,000 each. Another 109 agricultural trading companies alleged to have joined the collusion received warnings. The alleged trade associations and trading companies in Henan and Shandong provinces that colluded to increase the price of garlic were fined between CNY80,000 and CNY100,000. The NDRC further stated that the government will strengthen the measures on price supervision in order to protect market supply and safeguard the legitimate interests of agricultural producers, consumers, and business operators. The announcement did not mention which law and procedures were used to investigate the offenders and to reach the decisions.[117]

Following the announcement, it was reported that two trading companies, each fined CNY500,000 by local price bureaus for price collusion in green beans, had decided to apply for administrative reconsideration of the decision. However, the companies found themselves in a difficult situation to retain lawyers. The companies said they had contacted lawyers and started to prepare documents. The lawyers later decided to stop representing the companies after local bar associations

[115] *See* SAIC *Measures on the Prohibition of Monopoly Agreements*, *supra* note 17, Art. 11.
[116] *See id.* Art. 12.
[117] *See* NDRC, *supra* note 27.

warned them that "the decision concerns state policy and lawyers should be careful to act." The bar associations in question have not confirmed the facts of the news report.[118] The difficulties faced by the two companies indicate that it is difficult to assess whether the enforcement agencies comply with the prescribed procedural rules and it can be difficult for parties to rely on their procedural rights.

Since the AML entered into force, the SAIC's decisional practice seems less active than that of the MOFCOM and the NDRC. Given the lack of published decisions or announcements it remains unclear whether the restrictive cases mentioned by the SAIC were informally settled or closed under the SAIC's formal decisions, and whether the SAIC's decisional practices complied with the prescribed procedural rules. It is expected that the SAIC will be more active and transparent because the relevant AML implementing regulations concerning the SAIC's role and procedures were finalized and implemented in January 2011.

2. The MOFCOM

As the enforcement agency solely responsible for the AML merger control regime, the MOFCOM enjoys expansive investigation and adjudication powers and is obliged to comply with the same prescribed procedural rules as those that apply to the NDRC and the SAIC. Given the specific features of merger control, the AML and the relevant implementing regulations provide further procedural rules for the MOFCOM. For example, regarding the opportunity to be heard, the MOFCOM *Measures on the Review of Concentrations of Undertakings* (hereinafter "Concentration Review Measures") provide rules on hearings, including initiation of hearings, hearing attendees, confidentiality, and procedures.[119]

Regarding the rights of effective defense and adequate time to prepare a defense, the Concentration Review Measures affirm the parties' rights to submit written statements and to defend their interests in the review process. The MOFCOM is required to issue a statement of objections to the parties if it finds that the proposed transaction has or may have the effect of eliminating or restricting competition, and to set a reasonable time limit for the parties to submit their written defense.[120] However, since the MOFCOM does not publish the statement of objections or publicly announce that a statement of objections has been issued and the reasons for it, it is unclear whether MOFCOM is able to provide timely and full notice of allegations with the evidence upon which it relied.

Under the AML, a concentration must not be implemented until clearance has been obtained from the MOFCOM. The MOFCOM has the power to block a concentration or impose remedies before clearing the concentration. To enhance

[118] Yu Gu, Two Green Bean Dealers Face Obstacles When Seeking Reviews of the NDRC Decision, Experts Support the Heavy Penalties, July 14, 2010, Chinese version available at <http://money.163.com/10/0714/17/6BINQDQ3002526O3.html>.

[119] *See* MOFCOM *Measures on the Review of Concentrations of Undertakings*, *supra* note 17, Arts 6–8, English translation available at <http://www.fdi.gov.cn/pub/FDI_EN/Laws/law_en_info.jsp?docid=115886>.

[120] *See id.* Art. 10.

the transparency and predictability and to formalize its divestiture policy, the MOFCOM promulgated the *Interim Measures on the Divestiture of Assets or Businesses when Implementing Concentration of Undertakings* (hereinafter "Interim Measures on Divestiture") in July 2010, which are primarily concerned with procedural issues. According to the Interim Measures on Divestiture, potential buyers of the divested assets must be independent from the parties to the transaction and must have adequate resources to develop the divested business. The merging parties are required to hold separate and independent the business to be divested, pending its sale to a third party buyer. The merging parties are required to appoint a "supervisory trustee" to monitor the process and report to the MOFCOM on the steps taken to implement the divestiture. If the merging parties fail to find a suitable buyer for the assets or businesses to be divested within the time period stated in the MOFCOM's decision, a "divestiture trustee" is to be appointed to effectuate the sale.[121] The Interim Measures on Divestures reflect the MOFCOM's decisional practice. It is reported that the MOFCOM is considering substantive issues involved in merger remedies such as basic conditions for acceptable commitments, appropriateness of different types of remedies, and so on.

However, the MOFCOM's decisional practice to date may raise issues of the proportionality of remedies and also its wisdom in view of the interests of competition. For example, in the *Novartis/Alcon* decision, the MOFCOM found that the ophthalmic anti-infective and anti-inflammatory compounds constitute a relevant market and the parties overlap in China with a combined market share of more than 60 percent, although Novartis held less than one percent market share. It is unclear from the MOFCOM's decision whether Novartis had a foothold and appeared to be growing, and thus was the only real challenger of Alcon. Although Novartis stated that it would strategically exit the market globally after the transaction, the MOFCOM seemed concerned with such *de minimis* market share increment and required Novartis to cease all sales of its product of ophthalmic anti-infective and anti-inflammatory compounds in China by the end of 2010, to refrain from re-entering the Chinese market for ophthalmic anti-infective and anti-inflammatory compounds for five years from the date of the decision, and to cease supplying the relevant products currently sold outside of China to the Chinese market for five years.[122]

Pursuant to the AML, the MOFCOM is required to timely publish decisions that prohibit or conditionally approve concentrations, thus producing a public record of blocked and conditionally cleared deals.[123] However, publication of unconditional clearance decisions is left to the MOFCOM's discretion. The MOFCOM is required to provide the parties with a written confirmation of

121 *See* Interim Measures on Divestiture, Arts 3, 5, 7, & 12, Official China version available at: <http://fldj.mofcom.gov.cn/aarticle/zcfb/201007/20100707012000.html>.

122 *See* MOFCOM, Announcement of the *Novartis/Alcon* Decision, Chinese version available at <http://fldj.mofcom.gov.cn/aarticle/ztxx/201008/20100807080639.html>.

123 *See* AML, *supra* note 12, Art. 30.

approval if it decides to clear a transaction unconditionally.[124] To date, the MOFCOM's published decisions are all relatively light on reasoning.

Regarding the principle of non-discrimination, it is rumored that Chinese lawyers advising on merger transactions normally advise that purely domestic transactions do not need to be notified. Due to the lack of a full statistical profile of enforcement activities, a factual question is whether purely domestic merger transactions have ever been notified to the MOFCOM pursuant to the AML. It is interesting to note, however, that China-based international antitrust lawyers have commented that the enforcement of the AML thus far should allay fears that the AML would be enforced disproportionately against foreign businesses. Although it is still too early to predict how the enforcement of the AML will evolve, it appears that the Chinese enforcers have adopted a fairly conservative approach to the AML enforcement, with the law not being used solely against foreign multinationals. The lawyers further noted that, of the more than 140 merger cases reviewed by the MOFCOM to date, a good number involved only domestic firms, including some transactions between large state-owned enterprises. Non-merger enforcement has largely consisted of actions taken against domestic price-fixing cartels. Moreover, nearly all the private lawsuits to date have been filed by Chinese complainants against Chinese companies.[125]

B. Institutional performance norms

This section describes the recognition and trade-offs of institutional performance norms observed through the AMEAs' decisional practice, policy formulation, advocacy, and other activities.

1. *Timeliness of disposition*

The AML and its implementing regulations to date do not provide time limits for the delivery of decisions regarding monopoly agreements and abuse of dominance. This implies more discretion of the authorities and results in legal uncertainty because it is unclear how quickly the NDRC and the SAIC will act pursuant to the AML. In the *Rice Noodles Cartel* and the *Tableware Sanitizing Industry Cartel*, local price bureaus appeared to be quite swift in rendering decisions. The *Rice Noodles Cartel* decision was made within three months after the collusion was reported by the media, and the local price bureau ordered the tableware sanitizing enterprises to terminate the collusive behavior within one month after the collusion was reported by the media.[126] In the *Garlic and Green Beans Cartels*, the NDRC announced the

[124] *See* MOFCOM *Measures on the Review of Concentrations of Undertakings*, *supra* note 17, Art. 14.

[125] Peter Wang & Sébastien Evrara, "Life after China's Antimonopoly Law," Wall Street Journal, October 20, 2010.

[126] *See* NDRC, *supra* note 26; also *see* NDRC, Collusion to Increase Prices by the Tableware Sanitizing Industry in Xiamen was Timely Prohibited, April 30, 2010, Chinese versions available at <http://jjs.ndrc.gov.cn/fjgld/t20100430_344632.htm>.

three decisions made by local price bureaus in July 2010 regarding cartels that had started in October 2009. It is unclear when the local price bureaus became aware of the cartels.[127]

In contrast, the AML merger control regime provides clear time limit rules as discussed at section II.C.3 above. Table 5.1 below lists the length of the MOFCOM's review period in the seven decisions published to date, which indicates that, in principle, the MOFCOM has been able to complete merger reviews within prescribed time limits.[128]

2. Transparency of reasons for decisions and reasonable predictability in application of law

Pursuant to the AML, the MOFCOM is required to publish its decisions that prohibit or conditionally approve the proposed concentrations but is not required to publish unconditional merger clearances.[129] For monopoly agreements and abuse of dominance, the AML provides that the enforcement agencies "may publish the decisions," which means that the publication of decisions is at the discretion of the NDRC and the SAIC.[130] With this obvious structural shortcoming of the AML, the transparency of reasons for decisions and reasonable predictability in application of law are open to doubt.

For example, although the lack of a publicly available notification registration system and the lack of transparency in unconditional clearance decisions do not contradict the MOFCOM's obligations under the AML, publishing notification information and unconditional clearance certainly would increase transparency and enhance public credibility of the AML administration. In addition, the practice of not publishing unconditional clearance decisions undervalues the cases that do not raise significant competition concerns. Publication of the relevant decisions would provide guidance on enforcement practice and thus improve business predictability. It is encouraging that the MOFCOM appears to realize the problem. In a press conference held in August 2010, Mr Shang Ming, Director General of the MOFCOM Anti-Monopoly Bureau, stated that the MOFCOM had been considering how much and what types of information about unconditional clearances would be publishable.[131] Furthermore, although criticized for brevity of decisions and lack of detail when assessing competition concerns, the MOFCOM should be applauded for its efforts on improving the transparency of reasons for decisions. First, analysis in and reasoning of the MOFCOM's merger decisions have been improving steadily. One notes that many more details have been provided if one compares the more recent decisions, such as *Pfizer/Wyeth* and *Panasonic/Sanyo*, with

[127] *See* NDRC, *supra* note 27.

[128] *See supra* note 25.

[129] *See* AML, *supra* note 12, Art. 30.

[130] *See id.* Art. 44.

[131] *See* MOFCOM, MOFCOM Held Press Conference regarding the Enforcement of the Anti-Monopoly Law, August 12, 2010, Chinese version available at <http://www.mofcom.gov.cn/aarticle/ae/ai/201008/20100807078063.html>.

Table 5.1 MOFCOM's review period for mergers since the AML took effect

Merger	Decision date	Outcome	Length of Phase I review (calendar days)	Length of Phase II review (calendar days)
Coca-Cola/Huiyuan	18 March 2009	Prohibited	30	88
InBev/Anheuser Busch	18 November 2008	Conditionally cleared	22	n/a
Mitsubishi Rayon/Lucite	24 April 2009	Conditionally cleared	30	66
GM/Delphi	28 September 2009	Conditionally cleared	28	n/a
Pfizer/Wyeth	29 September 2009	Conditionally cleared	30	76
Panasonic/Sanyo	30 October 2009	Conditionally cleared	30	147 (Phase II plus an extension)
Novartis/Alcon	13 August 2010	Conditionally cleared	27	89
Uralkali/Silvinit	2 June 2011	Conditionally cleared	30	51
Alpha V/Savio	31 October 2011	Conditionally cleared	26	31
GE China/China Shenhua JV	10 November 2011	Conditionally cleared	30	149 (Phase II plus an extension)
Seagate/Samsung Hard Disk Drive Business	12 December 2011	Conditionally cleared	30	150 (Phase II plus an extension)
Henkel Hong Kong/Tiande Chemical JV	10 February 2012	Conditionally cleared	30	109
Western Digital/Hitachi Hard Disk Drive Business	2 March 2012	Conditionally cleared (1st notification withdrawn by the parties before the expiry date of the extended Phase II review period)	1st notification: 30 2nd notification: 30	1st notification: 146 (Phase II plus an extension) 2nd notification: 87

the earlier decisions, such as *InBev/Anheuser Busch* and *Coca-Cola/Huiyuan*. Second, Chinese administrative and judicial decisions are notable for their formulaic, perfunctory, and conclusory style and lack of reasoning. Compared to the decisional practice of other administrative agencies in China, the MOFCOM's decisional practice in merger review has already become one of the best in terms of transparency and clarity of reasoning.

The NDRC and the SAIC certainly need to do more work to improve transparency and predictability considering that they are not obliged to publish any decisions under the AML. The structural shortcoming of the AML may be rectified by promulgating implementing regulations.

3. Transparency in policy formulation and opportunities for public consultation and participation in policy formulation

The formulation of AML implementing regulations began after the AML took effect and the NDRC, the SAIC, and the MOFCOM were designated as the AMEAs in 2008. To date, most published regulations have gone through consultation procedures and the public have been given opportunities to participate in the policy formulation process.

The current practice is as follows: the AMEAs first invite comments on draft regulations from a small circle of experts, including scholars, lawyers, in-house counsel, bar associations, and other stakeholders within and outside of China. When the draft regulations are in a more advanced shape, the AMEAs publish the draft and invite comments from the public. The drafting of three sets of merger regulations provides the latest example. From July 21–24, 2010, the MOFCOM invited legal scholars and practitioners to a seminar to discuss three sets of draft measures on merger control that were unavailable to the public. These draft measures include the *Measures on the Definition of Undertakings Participating in Concentrations*, the *Guidance on the Assessment of the Eliminative or Restrictive Effects of Horizontal Concentration of Undertakings*, and the *Measures on the Imposition of Restrictive Conditions on Concentration of Undertakings*.[132] Two problems may be observed from the current practice. One is that the public consultation period is normally short. For example, only twelve days were given for submission of comments when the SAIC invited public comments on its three draft measures concerning monopoly agreements, abuse of dominance, and administrative monopoly in May 2010.[133] Secondly, it is difficult to judge the effectiveness of consultation because the submitted comments are normally not publicly available.

[132] MOFCOM, MOFCOM Held Legislative Seminar, July 27, 2010, Chinese version available at <http://fldj.mofcom.gov.cn/aarticle/xxfb/201007/20100707045197.html>.

[133] SAIC, SAIC Invites Comments on Three Sets of Anti-Monopoly Law Implementing Regulations, Chinese version available at <http://www.saic.gov.cn/gzhd/fldf/201005/t20100525_85719.html>.

4. *Sufficiency of investigative and sanctioning powers*

As described above, the AMEAs have expansive investigative and sanctioning powers regarding monopoly agreements, abuse of dominance, and mergers. The generality of the statutory language has been clarified by the AML implementing regulations to some extent, such as the *SAIC Measures on Procedures for Investigating and Handling Cases of Monopoly Agreements and Abuse of Market Dominance.*[134] However, the effective use of the investigative and sanctioning powers may be compromised because of the lack of human resources.

Regarding administrative monopoly conducted by public authorities, the AML empowers the relevant superior agencies to take corrective action, and the AMEAs may only make proposals on the handling of the cases to the relevant superior agencies.[135] Although this rule seems effectively to deprive the AMEAs of jurisdiction over administrative monopoly, the AMEAs have started to play a positive role in tackling administrative monopoly. For example, in July 2011, the SAIC's local bureau in Guangdong province investigated and handled local government's administrative monopoly conduct in relation to global positioning system services for motor vehicles.[136]

5. *Expertise of key decision-makers and staff*

At the time of writing, the NDRC Price Supervision and Anti-Monopoly Bureau has less than twenty and the SAIC Competition Enforcement Bureau has less than ten officials responsible for the AML enforcement. The MOFCOM Anti-Monopoly Bureau has approximately thirty officials in total.[137] It is noted that MOFCOM has become the most active AML enforcer and the primary interlocutor in inter-agency exchanges on competition policy with the support of the personnel from the Anti-Monopoly Bureau. Most of these officials hold advanced degrees in law or economics, and all have obtained specially designed or ad hoc on-the-job training in competition law and economics.

6. *Public accountability for general agency functioning*

An insufficient degree of public accountability is a problem with China's current administrative system in part because of the concentration of the legislative, executive, and judicial powers. For example, there is lack of transparency in relation

[134] *See supra* note 17.

[135] *See* AML, *supra* note 12, Art. 51.

[136] *See* China Competition Research Centre, "The Administration for Industry and Commerce of Guangdong Province Investigated and Handled Local Government's Administrative Monopoly Conduct," China Competition Bulletin, Edition 12, August 2011, 3, available at: <http://www.anzsog.edu.au/research/publications/the-china-competition-bulletin>.

[137] The staff composition information of the AMEAs is publicly unavailable and the information provided here is obtained from the authors' informal contact with officials of the AMEAs or from the officials' presentations at academic seminars.

to government budgets, although the central government is acting to improve the situation.[138] The NDRC, the SAIC, and the MOFCOM published their budget information for 2010, but the data are general and budget information for each division is publicly unavailable.[139] Therefore, it is unclear how much of the budget is allocated to the AML enforcement. However, the perceived scarcity of financial and human resources appears to constitute a significant obstacle to establishing an effective AML enforcement system, and human resource constraints might also lead to lax enforcement by the NDRC and the SAIC.

To date, the AMEAs have not conducted systematic and periodic reviews of performance of their legislative mandate and agency effectiveness. The MOFCOM has provided periodic overviews of its performance regarding AML merger control through press releases.

7. Efficacy of enforcement to achieve goals

The conflicting objectives expressed or implied by the AML may compromise the efficacy of enforcement. For example, for the generally agreed objective of "protecting competition," the efficacy of the AML enforcement is sometimes questionable as illustrated by the *Novartis/Alcon* decision discussed above. In this case, the MOFCOM required Novartis to exit from the relevant market for five years, although Novartis held less than one percent market share. This remedy actually reduced the choices available to consumer and the MOFCOM might rather have required Novartis to divest the business to a competitor. Moreover, monitoring Novartis' performance of the remedy can be very costly.

V. Critical evaluation

Although the current AML institutional framework may cause inter-agency conflicts and uncertainty, the design of AML enforcement agencies is "driven" by "politics, and political and economic context" and is a child of political compromise. It was made either because it "best fit the context" or because it was "the best that the thoughtful policymakers could obtain in the context, and at the time."[140] It has been noted that "[c]lose attention to the underlying conditions and attitudes that will drive Chinese antitrust enforcement may yield more insight than comparing the text of the AML with that of U.S. and European statutes and court

[138] Xinhua News Agency, Chinese Premier Promises Transparency in Government Budgets, September 19, 2010, <http://english.peopledaily.com.cn/90001/90776/90785/7145338.html>.

[139] General budget information of NDRC, SAIC and MOFCOM for 2010 (in Chinese) is available at: <http://www.saic.gov.cn/zwgk/zyfb/bmys/201004/t20100407_81528.html>, <http://politics.people.com.cn/GB/1027/11331533.html>, and <http://file.mofcom.gov.cn/moffile/search/pages/detail.jsp?seqno=15555>.

[140] Eleanor Fox, "Antitrust and Institutions: Design and Change," 41 Loy. U. Chi. L.J. 473–4, 476–7 (2010); also *see* Huang, *supra* note 101, at 117.

decisions."[141] "Context informs design"—the current institutional design may call for incremental or significant changes depending on "changes in environment, new learning or appreciation, and recurrent flaws and insufficiencies."[142]

A. Suitability of norms

1. The procedural norms that are recognized

As described in Section IV above, the procedural norms that are recognized include basic due process rules, judicial review as the last check, confidentiality, right of defense, etc.

2. The procedural norms that are recognized but with trade-offs

Transparency in decision-making and policy-making and clarity of reasoning have improved but are still insufficient in the AMEAs' decisional practice. To date, the published decisions seem not fully or accurately to provide the underlying reasoning, and the enforcement agencies need to improve their ability to handle cases in ways that are procedurally sound and render decisions that are substantively meritorious.

3. The procedural norms that are not recognized

The procedural norms that are not recognized include but are not limited to the following.

- Accessibility of case information. The unavailability of record information of (1) merger cases notified and unconditionally cleared, and (2) investigations of restrictive agreements and abuse of dominance compromises the transparency of the AML enforcement. In the merger control area, it is desirable to establish a case record system, such as has been done by the European Commission Competition Directorate-General. A publically available case record system improves transparency and can serve the AMEAs' education and advocacy functions.
- Articulation of the applicable laws and procedure. The failure to identify the procedures and applicable laws used to investigate and sanction cartels as indicated by the *Garlic and Green Beans Cartel* compromises the predictability of the AML enforcement.
- The failure to set clear enforcement priorities and to inform the public of such priorities.

[141] R. Hewitt Pate, "What I Heard in the Great Hall of the People—Realistic Expectations of Chinese Antitrust," 75 ANTITRUST L.J. 195, 211 (2008).

[142] *See* Fox, *supra* note 140, at 485.

- The lack of competition advocacy and the need to reinforce cooperation and create collective memory between the NDRC, the SAIC, and the MOFCOM.
- The failure to set up *ex post* evaluations both case-specific and process-based.

B. Evaluation and suggestions for improvement

Competition law and policy cannot be separated from the context in which it is set up.[143] While the enactment of the AML is a major step in establishing a competition policy system consistent with international norms, it is just the beginning of a prolonged, conflict-driven, and interest-oriented process.[144] Nevertheless, China has been making further efforts to nurture a competition culture, to reform its political regime, and to facilitate its transition to a modern market economy.

1. *The competing goals of the AML and the tensions between the anti-monopoly enforcement agencies and other regulators*

The issue of legislative objectives is relevant for recognizing legislators' motivation to adopt competition law in a particular jurisdiction. Furthermore, the issue of competition policy objectives is significant because the approaches by which objectives are expressed affect the way in which they are conceived and understood.[145] Clear objectives inform the implementation of the law and policy by helping to identify and explain differences in legal standards and outcomes in specific cases. Such implementation makes the rationales for decision-making explicit and thus increases transparency and certainty. Moreover, although economic theory and empirical techniques provide a set of tools with which to assess the relative merits of competing economic hypotheses, the hypotheses the decision-makers and practitioners should seek to test are implicitly related to the objectives of a particular system of competition policy.[146]

It is noteworthy that the expressed objectives of competition policy are much broader in developing and transitional countries than in developed countries and competition policy in developing countries often takes a more regulatory approach. The reason for such divergence is understandable. Competition policy does not live in a vacuum. Embedded in a specific order, competition policy functions as an indication of contemporary values and goals of a particular society, and may evolve as political ideas in general evolve. In such countries there is less consensus among officials and politicians about the desirability of competition policy; also, the economic, legal, social, or political frameworks are less developed for the proper functioning of a free market economy. However, commentators suggest that

[143] *Id.* at 474.

[144] *See* Wang, *supra* note 16, ANTITRUST BULL., at 619.

[145] David J. Gerber, "Constructing Competition Law in China: the Potential Value of European and U.S. Experience," 3 WASH. U. GLOBAL STUD. L. REV. 325–9 (2004).

[146] Simon Bishop & Mike Walker, *Economics of EC Competition Law: Concepts, Application and Measurement* 3–6 (2nd edn Sweet and Maxwell, 2003).

objectives should not be mixed because, by so doing, competition policy would be burdened with innumerable objectives for direct application, and the criteria for the assessment of individual cases would be unclear.[147]

The inclusion of non-competition goals in the AML and the existence of competing enforcement institutions raise concerns about whether the AML will be used primarily to protect competition and consumer welfare, or whether it will be used as a protectionist instrument to favor SOEs and other interest groups in China. Other jurisdictions are no strangers to the inclusion of broader non-competition goals in competition policy. As illustrated by the cases of the EU, the USA, and Germany, it is difficult to completely avoid the conflict between competition policy and industrial policy. Nevertheless, pure competition/efficiency goals have been given a superior position in these advanced economies' competition laws. Therefore, the key question is to what extent competition law and industrial policy are compatible with each other, or to what extent industrial policy is aligned with competition law in a given jurisdiction, at a given time. Moreover, a cautious design of the enforcement mechanism certainly helps to avoid problematic situations where one agency is required to simultaneously balance conflicting goals and considerations in individual cases.

The case of China is more complicated, as less attention has been paid to competition policy, and compromise may be inevitable when there are conflicting industrial policy considerations. The conflict between competition law and industrial policy has been and will continue to be unavoidable in China. Ideally, the AMEAs should create a countervailing force to traditional regulators who are more likely to rely on command-and-control regulatory tools and may cause government restrictions on competition.

2. *The disequilibrium between the development of competition policy institutions and the current status of China's administrative law and regulatory practices*

The effectiveness of China's administrative law is less than optimal in terms of controlling government actions, in part because of the legacy of the centrally planned economy and the concentrations of powers. The institutional and systemic obstacles include a weak legislature and judiciary, fewer checks on administrative powers, and corruption.

The AML lacks an independent enforcement agency with clear and sufficient authority for enforcement. However, the recognized procedural norms, the AMEAs' activities, and the increased private enforcement actions have indicated a rapid development of competition policy institutions in China. Such rapid development of competition policy institutions in China goes beyond, but is inevitably constrained by, the status quo of China's administrative law and regulatory practice. The AMEAs, notably the MOFCOM, are pioneers in the process of China's

[147] *See* Ehlermann & Laudati, *supra* note 86, at 9.

reform of its administrative system. Furthermore, the symbolic role of the AML should not be undervalued and competition policy may act as a catalyst for China's further transition to a modern market economy and accountable governance.

3. *The proposed "truly integrated agency model" and the incremental development toward the model*

Institutional arrangements should be designed to match institutional mandates and to limit duplication. Based on the analysis of the underlying conditions and context that drive China's competition policy, we argue that a "truly integrated agency model," namely, a commission model, would be a sensible choice for the institutional design of China's competition policy in the future. The principal features of a "truly integrated agency model" include administrative control and the combination of investigative, prosecutorial, and adjudicative functions in a specialized administrative agency, subject to the separation of the individuals involved in each of the three functions and to judicial checks. Creating such a model should entail a cautious design of institutions to avoid problematic situations where one agency is required to simultaneously balance conflicting goals and considerations in individual cases. For example, China may establish a ministry-level commission with concrete enforcement powers directly under the State Council in the future as envisaged by a previous draft of the AML, or integrate all anti-monopoly enforcement powers in the MOFCOM Anti-Monopoly Bureau.

Currently, the incentives for establishing a "truly integrated agency mode" seem low and the practical and political difficulties for reallocating authorities and other constraints imbedded in the context are obvious. The reform may be achieved through incremental changes to establish a "truly integrated agency model" step by step in China. From an institutional capacity perspective, there is a need to increase financial and human resources. From a structural perspective, there is a need to limit overlaps, duplications, and inefficiencies, and to improve dialogues and create collective know-how among the AMEAs.

6

Japan
The Competition Law System and the Country's Norms

*Harry First and Tadashi Shiraishi**

I. History of antitrust enforcement

A. Japan Fair Trade Commission

Japan's Antimonopoly Act (AMA) was passed in 1947 at the prodding of US occupation authorities.[1] The Act combined various aspects of US antitrust law, including provisions relating to unreasonable restraints of trade, monopolization, and mergers, as well as a provision condemning specified "unfair methods of competition." The Act also established Japan's Fair Trade Commission (JFTC), modeling the Commission after the US Federal Trade Commission and giving it similar powers.

At the time the AMA was enacted, Japan's governmental structure lacked analogues to US independent regulatory agencies. Japan's government negotiators originally wanted the JFTC to be placed within the Ministry of Justice, and subject to that Ministry's control, but the US occupation authorities objected, seeking greater independence for the Commission.[2] A Cabinet vote was necessary to approve the provision that eventually was enacted, placing the JFTC administratively within the Prime Minister's Office and giving the Commissioners fixed terms and protection from removal except for cause.[3]

Although early enforcement of the Act was rather vigorous, JFTC enforcement efforts began to wane in the early 1950s when the end of the Korean War procurement boom led to pressure on the JFTC to approve output-limiting

* The authors thank Kojiro Fujii (New York University School of Law, Trade Regulation LL.M., 2011) for his invaluable research assistance.

[1] *See* Harry First, "Antitrust In Japan: The Original Intent," 9 Pac. Rim L. & Pol'y J. 1 (2000) (reviewing drafting history of original Antimonopoly Act) (hereinafter *Original Intent*). The initial draft of the AMA was prepared by an antitrust attorney working for the US occupation forces. *See id.* at 35.

[2] US negotiators feared that the Justice Ministry lacked "sympathy" for antitrust legislation and was "unduly conservative, tradition bound, [and] legalistic." *Id.* at 58.

[3] *See id.*

cartels.[4] After the JFTC disagreed with some of MITI's (the Ministry of International Trade and Industry) efforts to approve these cartels, MITI backed amendments to the AMA that were approved by the Diet in 1953.[5]

The 1953 amendments made some important changes to the 1947 Act. For example, the 1953 amendments eliminated a provision making certain horizontal agreements "per se" violations of the Act, allowed resale price maintenance under certain circumstances,[6] and permitted the JFTC to authorize depression and rationalization cartels. Nevertheless, the basic structure of the original legislation was retained, with the amended statute continuing to forbid unreasonable restraints of trade, Private Monopolization, mergers with anticompetitive effects, and designated Unfair Trade Practices, including the "unjust use" of bargaining power.[7]

The JFTC's enforcement efforts were revived during the 1960s and 1970s, spurred in part by rising consumer prices, and then again in the late 1980s. The latter increase in enforcement came when Japan's government was under pressure from the United States over barriers to import trade. One aspect of the US effort was the Structural Impediments Initiative ("SII") talks in which the United States pressed for increased antitrust enforcement as a way to open Japan's markets to greater competition from imports from the United States.[8] The JFTC responded by increasing its enforcement efforts, although with little apparent impact on import competition. Enforcement efforts have continued since that time, backed, in part, by support from political leaders.[9]

One area of particular enforcement focus has been cartel activities. In 1977 the AMA was amended to require the Commission to impose administrative "surcharges" (a form of administrative fine) on firms that have engaged in unreasonable restraints of trade affecting the price of goods or services.[10] The surcharge was originally set at between 0.5 to 2 percent of sales during the price-raising period, but was increased in 1991 to 1 to 6 percent (although the period covered was limited to the three years prior to the conclusion of the firm's participation in the cartel).[11] In 2005 the amounts were raised again (to between 2 and 10 percent) and the surcharge was broadened to include "Private Monopolization by Control" (that

[4] For early enforcement, *see* Harry First, "Antitrust Enforcement in Japan," 64 ANTITRUST L.J. 137, 148–56 (1995) (hereinafter "Antitrust Enforcement in Japan").

[5] *See id.* at 156–7. For the basic outlines of the 1953 amendment, *see* Harry First, "Japan's Antitrust Policy: Impact on Import Competition," in FRAGILE INTERDEPENDENCE: ECONOMIC ISSUES IN THE U.S.-JAPANESE TRADE AND INVESTMENT 64 (1986) (hereinafter "Import Competition").

[6] *See infra* note 61 and accompanying text.

[7] *See infra* notes 50–54 and accompanying text.

[8] *See* "Antitrust Enforcement in Japan," *supra* note 4, at 158–73. For further discussion of SII, *see* Mitsuo Matsushita, "The Structural Impediments Initiative: An Example of Bilateral Trade Negotiation," 12 MICH. J. INT'L LAW 436 (1991).

[9] For example, in his first parliamentary policy speech on May 7, 2001, Prime Minister Koizumi said: "We will strengthen the structure of the Fair Trade Commission, which should serve as the guardian of the market, thereby establishing competition policies appropriate for the 21st century." 80 BNA ANTITRUST & TRADE REGULATION REPORT 473 (May 18, 2001).

[10] For discussion of the political dynamics leading to the 1977 amendments, *see* "Import Competition," *supra* note 5, at 65.

[11] *See* Art. 7-2. The amount of surcharge varied (from highest to lowest) depending on whether the firm was a manufacturer, retailer, or wholesaler.

is, monopolistic restrictions that control the conduct of other firms).[12] In addition, the 2005 amendments added leniency provisions that require the Commission either to eliminate or to reduce the surcharges imposed on the first three firms that submit information about the violation to the JFTC.[13] In 2009 the surcharge provision was further expanded to include "Private Monopolization by Exclusion"[14] and certain types of Unfair Trade Practices.[15] Surcharges were further increased if the firm was a repeat offender or a cartel ringmaster (or both).[16]

B. Criminal enforcement

The Antimonopoly Act provides criminal penalties for monopolization and unreasonable restraints of trade (but not for Unfair Trade Practices) and permits the prosecution of both individuals and business firms.[17] The Act does not give the JFTC power to bring criminal prosecutions directly. Rather, criminal violations of the Act are prosecuted by the Public Prosecutors' Office (PPO) but only after the JFTC files a formal accusation with the PPO.[18] The provision also requires the PPO to provide written reasons in the event that the PPO declines to bring a prosecution.[19]

The first significant criminal prosecution was not brought until 1974, when prosecutions were brought against the Petroleum Industry Federation and the major Japanese oil companies and their officers for output restrictions and price fixing. Criminal prosecutions continue to be rare.[20] Even after the 2005 amendments improved criminal investigations and introduced a leniency program,[21] the Commission made few criminal referrals to the PPO (only four from 2006 to April 2012).[22] No individual has ever served time in jail for a violation of the Antimonopoly Act.[23]

[12] Art. 7-2 (2).

[13] Art. 7-2 (7)–(9) (in original; now 7-2 (10)–(12)). *See infra* notes 74–79 and accompanying text.

[14] Art. 7-2 (4).

[15] *See* Arts 20-2–20-6.

[16] Art. 7 (7)–(9). For firms falling in one category the increase is 50 percent; for firms falling in both categories the increase is 100 percent. The repeat offender increase was introduced by the 2005 amendment, while the cartel ringmaster increase was added by the 2009 amendment.

[17] Art 89. For corporate liability, *see* Art. 95.

[18] Although the draft originally prepared by US authorities would have given the JFTC the power to bring criminal prosecutions, Japan's government objected. The current structure is the result of a compromise between the US and Japan. *See* "Original Intent," *supra* note 1, at 57–8. The US also originally proposed that all provisions of the Act carry criminal penalties and that criminal prosecutions be pursued before civil remedies. *See id.* at 49 Table 7.

[19] Art. 74(3).

[20] *See* "Antitrust Enforcement in Japan," *supra* note 4, at 157. Prior to the oil cartel cases there had been only four other criminal prosecutions. *See id.* The convictions of the oil companies and their officers were affirmed by the Supreme Court in 1984. *Id.* at 157 n.93.

[21] *See infra* notes 69–79 and accompanying text.

[22] *See* <http://www.jftc.go.jp/en/pressreleases/> (press releases for years 2006–2012; the 2005 amendment took effect in 2006). For discussion of criminal referrals during the SII period, *see* "Antitrust Enforcement in Japan," *supra* note 4, at 167–8 (three referrals from 1991 through 1995).

[23] As of March 2011, all jail sentences have been suspended.

Despite the lack of criminal prosecutions, the Diet has several times increased the maximum penalties under the AMA. The ¥50,000 fine for corporations originally provided in the 1947 Act was increased to ¥500,000 in 1949, ¥5 million in 1977, ¥100 million in 1992, and then raised to ¥500 million in 2002.[24] In 2009 the maximum term of imprisonment was raised from the original three years to five years (although the fine for individuals remains at ¥5 million since 1977).

C. Private enforcement

The Antimonopoly Act provides for private damages suits.[25] The original US draft had proposed treble-damages plus attorney's fees, as under the Sherman Act, but Japan's government was opposed. The final version reduced damages to the actual amount of injury, although it also provided that damages can be awarded without regard to whether the defendant was willful or negligent.[26] The Act also makes private suits under the AMA contingent on a prior JFTC finding that the defendant has violated the Act.[27]

Private suits for violating the AMA can only be heard by a special panel of judges in the Tokyo High Court, rather than by a court of general jurisdiction.[28] This provision was adopted in the original Act as a result of a compromise between the US occupation negotiators, who wanted a separate antitrust court, and Japan's government, which wanted the suits heard in regular courts of general jurisdiction.[29] Subsequent experience with this procedure indicates that the special panel has not developed into a court with any particular antitrust expertise[30] and litigants have often avoided the Tokyo High Court by bringing suit in a local court under general tort law. Indeed, to the extent that litigants have had success in pursuing private remedies for anticompetitive behavior, they have done so under either general tort law or other statutes rather than under the Antimonopoly Act.[31]

[24] Arts 89, 95. If a company commits two or more crimes within a course of conduct, it may face consolidated punishment (The Penal Code Article 45), which could result in a fine in excess of ¥500 million. This was the result in the Steel Bridge case, where some companies were ordered to pay more than ¥500 million. *See* Tokyo District Court Decision on November 10, 2006, Shinketsushu vol. 53, 1133 and Tokyo District Court Decision on September 21, 2007, Shinketsushu vol. 54, 773.

[25] *See* Art. 25.

[26] Under general principles of Japanese tort law, either proof of negligence or willfulness is required for a plaintiff to recover. *See* Civil Code Art. 709.

[27] *See* Art. 26(1). The JFTC's order must be "final and binding."

[28] *See* Arts 85, 87.

[29] *See* "Original Intent," *supra* note 1, at 57.

[30] *See infra* text accompanying note 106.

[31] *See infra* notes 45–46 and accompanying text.

II. Institutional structure

A. JFTC

The JFTC consists of one Chairman and four Commissioners,[32] with the General Secretariat attached to the Commission.[33] The Commission is guaranteed independence and the Prime Minister has the authority to appoint its members.[34] Although from 2001 to 2003 the JFTC was formally placed under the jurisdiction of the Ministry of Internal Affairs and Communications (MIC), it is now formally placed under the jurisdiction of the Cabinet Office.[35] The officials of the General Secretariat, antitrust professionals led by the Secretary General, have substantial involvement in antitrust policy making, although it is the Commission itself that has the legal power to authorize them to act.[36]

In civil matters the JFTC currently follows the "integrated agency model."[37] The JFTC investigates alleged violations, issues orders, and gives adjudicative reviews of them. The JFTC orders addressees to cease and desist and to pay an administrative surcharge, depending on whether the case satisfies statutory requirements. Only after the JFTC makes its own adjudicative review can the addressee of the order ask for court review.[38] This review is done on the record made before the JFTC, with no de novo presentation of evidence to the court.[39]

With respect to criminal enforcement, the Japanese system belongs to a limited version of the "bifurcated judicial model." The JFTC has jurisdiction to investigate criminal violations of the AMA[40] but it has no power to bring criminal prosecutions. Instead, the JFTC must make a criminal referral to the Public Prosecutors' Office (PPO),[41] and the decision on whether to prosecute is legally up to the PPO and not the JFTC. Nevertheless, the referral carries great weight and the PPO and the JFTC have established a process for consulting on criminal referrals prior to their being formally made.[42]

B. Private enforcement

The AMA permits private parties to seek injunctive relief as well as damages for violations of the Act.[43] Victims can also seek damages recovery alternatively under

[32] Art. 29.

[33] Art. 35. *See* "JFTC—Organizational Chart (as of April, 2010)", <http://www.jftc.go.jp/en/about_jftc/pdf/JFTC_organizational_chart_2010.pdf>.

[34] Arts 28, 29.

[35] *See* Cabinet Office Organization Act Arts 4(3), 64.

[36] *See* Arts 27, 34.

[37] If the 2010 Bill is enacted, however, the JFTC would become a hybrid, combining aspects of the integrated agency model and the bifurcated judicial model. The 2010 Bill is discussed *infra* notes 99–105 and accompanying text.

[38] Art. 77(3).

[39] *See* Arts 80 (substantial evidence rule), 81(3) (new evidence can be submitted only on remand to the Commission).

[40] *See* Arts 101–118.

[41] *See* Arts 73, 96.

[42] *See infra* note 73 and accompanying text.

[43] *See* Arts 24, 25.

the general tort provision of the Civil Code Article 709. It is well established that "unlawful conduct" under the meaning of Article 709 includes antitrust violations. This interpretation enables injured persons to take legal action in cases where the JFTC has not rendered a formal enforcement decision, which is a requirement before a private action can be brought under the Antimonopoly Act.[44] The Civil Code and other civil statutes provide many other channels for arguments based on competition law, including the argument that anticompetitive contract clauses are void.

Many commentators have complained that the courts facing competition law arguments are hostile to victims. The record of very few successful cases seemed to support those complaints. Recently, however, one can find many successful cases where bid rigging victims, for example, national or local governments or residents, recover damages, although most of these cases have been brought under the Civil Code.[45] This shows that the historically small number of cases was not necessarily the result of plaintiff-unfriendly legal doctrine or enforcement attitude, but more likely the result of legitimate legal difficulties with the cases that were brought to the courts.[46]

Turning to other categories than bid rigging, one can observe few successful cases, probably caused by the small number of good cases that are available. It is also important to note the small number of plaintiff's lawyers, the lack of competition law expertise on the part of judges, and the lack of a class action mechanism. Although the number of competition lawyers has increased recently, most of them tend to represent alleged targets of the JFTC rather than injured plaintiffs.

III. Mandate

A. Competition policy

The objectives of the Antimonopoly Act are described at the beginning of the Act:

Article 1 The purpose of this Act is, by prohibiting private monopolization, unreasonable restraint of trade and unfair trade practices, by preventing excessive concentration of economic power and by eliminating unreasonable restraint of production, sale, price, technology, etc., and all other unjust restriction on business activities through combinations, agreements, etc., to promote fair and free competition, to stimulate the creative initiative of entrepreneurs, to encourage business activities, to heighten the level of employment and actual national income, and thereby to promote the democratic and wholesome development of the national economy as well as to assure the interests of general consumers.

[44] Art. 26(1).

[45] For an intensive overview, *see* Simon Vande Walle, "Private Enforcement of Antitrust Law in Japan: An Empirical Analysis," 8 Competition Law Review 7 (2011).

[46] The landmark case illustrating these legal problems is the Tsuruoka Oil case (Supreme Court Judgment of December 8, 1989, Minshu vol. 43, no. 11, p. 1259). This was a very difficult case for the plaintiffs for two reasons: economic fluctuations caused by the Oil Shock in the 1970s made it difficult to assess causation and the plaintiffs were indirect purchasers. Recent successful lawsuits against bid rigging have not faced either of these difficulties.

The Supreme Court has made clear that this Article emphasizes the importance of a free competition process. But the Court at the same time has admitted that conduct which brings a benefit offsetting the anticompetitive effect should not be deemed illegal. The Court pointed out that such an interpretation is pursuant to the "ultimate objectives" showed in Article 1: "thereby to promote the democratic and wholesome development of the national economy as well as to assure the interests of general consumers."[47]

The AMA gives the JFTC jurisdiction over a wide range of conduct. Non-merger competition law provisions are threefold: Private Monopolization (Articles 2 (5) and 3), Unreasonable Restraint of Trade (Articles 2 (6) and 3), and Unfair Trade Practices (Articles 2 (9) and 19). Horizontal agreements are covered only by Unreasonable Restraint of Trade, while vertical agreements and exclusionary conduct are covered by both Unfair Trade Practices and Private Monopolization.[48]

In 1947 when the AMA was enacted, Private Monopolization was based on US Sherman Act Section 2, Unreasonable Restraint of Trade based on US Sherman Act Section 1, and Unfair Trade Practices (then called Unfair Methods of Competition) based on US FTC Act Section 5. Combining jurisdiction over collusive trade restraints, monopoly, and unfair trade practices into a single statute, enforced by a single agency, created problems of statutory overlap that Japanese negotiators of the original statute found confusing and that US negotiators did not fully appreciate.[49] Although Japan's negotiators originally wanted to limit Unfair Methods of Competition to those that lessen competition, and not include conduct that only affects particular customers or competitors, the final bill took the broader approach, enumerating a variety of practices that restrained "relations" between contracting parties.[50] The 1953 amendments added an explicit provision forbidding the "unjust use of bargaining power," or "Abuse of Superior Bargaining Position" (ASBP) as it is now commonly called. The result is a very broad mandate for the JFTC that permits it to go beyond conduct that has anticompetitive effect. The JFTC and scholars have tended to justify the redundant overlap by emphasizing the "incipiency doctrine" for Unfair Trade Practices, that is, the coverage of trade practices "at the early stage" where harmful competitive effects start to be felt, "thereby preventing the possibility of developing into substantial competition restrictions."[51]

[47] Oil Cartel Criminal Case, February 24, 1984, Keishu vol. 38, no. 4, 1287. Although the Supreme Court assumed it was possible that the anticompetitive price fixing could have mitigated the huge effect that the Oil Shock brought, the Court found that, in fact, the conduct of the Japanese oil companies did not mitigate the Oil Shock's price-raising effects.

[48] Because Article 2 (9) defining Unfair Trade Practices is prescribed not to include horizontal agreements (with the exception of group boycott), such conduct is solely covered by Unreasonable Restraint of Trade.

[49] *See* "Original Intent," *supra* note 1, at 50–1 (Japanese negotiators' questions about meaning of unfair methods of competition).

[50] These provisions were drafted on the Japanese side. *See id.* at n. 225 and accompanying text, nn. 278–80, and accompanying text.

[51] *Microsoft NAP*, JFTC Decision on September 16, 2008, Shinketsushu vol. 55, 380.

The AMA was amended in 2009 to impose an administrative surcharge on ASBP.[52] According to JFTC guidelines and decisions, as well as court cases, one aspect of having a "superior bargaining position" is that the victim cannot switch to another seller (or another buyer, if the victim is a seller).[53] This could mean that the alleged violator is in a dominant position in EU-type terminology, at least if one defines the relevant market from the perspective of the victims. Taking this approach would make the ASBP regulation into a kind of exploitative abuse regulation similar to abuse of a dominant position under Article 102 TFEU. Many commentators, however, regard ASBP's victim-protective approach as being unique to Japan, and the JFTC's Guidelines state that a firm need not have a "market-dominant position" to violate this provision of the AMA.[54]

Turning to merger regulation, Chapter 4 of the AMA (Articles 9–18) is a hybrid of two categories: normal competition law merger regulation and regulations focusing on "excessive concentration of economic power." The latter, Articles 9 and 11, are the descendant of post-war concern over Zaibatsu control of companies in diverse markets.[55] It may still be an important matter for some huge groups in their routine notification practices, but the competition law community does not pay much attention to its substantive provisions. With the exception of Articles 9 and 11, the merger regulation of the AMA is similar to other jurisdictions in focusing on anticompetitive effect in relevant markets.

The JFTC can apply the AMA to regulated industries absent explicit exemptions. Explicit exemptions are exceptional and are narrowly limited in their substance.[56] For example, Article 21 of the AMA provides that exercise of intellectual property rights is exempt, but JFTC Guidelines narrowly interpret this exemption.[57] As a matter of practice, however, there appear to be some "implicit" exemptions from the Act. Although it is difficult to describe their scope,[58] there are times when the JFTC will not enforce the AMA but will cooperate with the regulatory agencies by several methods, including competition consultation.[59]

52 Articles 2 (9) (v) and 20–6.

53 *See* JFTC Guidelines Concerning Abuse of Superior Bargaining Position under the Antimonopoly Act, II.2 (Note 7) (2010), <http://www.jftc.go.jp/en/legislation_guidelines/ama/pdf/101130GL.pdf>.

54 *See id.* II.1 (one party needs only to have a "relatively superior bargaining position" over the other party).

55 Until the 1997 amendment, Article 9 squarely banned holding companies. The amendment lifted the ban to make Article 9 prohibit only those holding companies with "excessive concentration of economic power." After the 2002 amendment, the range of Article 9 was broadened from holding companies to companies in general, where there is an "excessive concentration of economic power," thereby integrating the function of former Article 9-2, which had regulated shareholdings by large companies.

56 Regulation of certain "natural monopoly" industries was exempt under the AMA from 1947 until the repeal of the exemption provision in 2000.

57 Japan Fair Trade Commission, "Guidelines for the Use of Intellectual Property under the Antimonopoly Act" (September 28, 2007), <http://www.jftc.go.jp/en/legislation_guidelines/ama/pdf/070928_IP_Guideline.pdf>.

58 For further discussion, *see* Harry First & Tadashi Shiraishi, "Concentrated Power: The Paradox of Antitrust in Japan," in *Law In Japan: A Turning Point* 526–8 (Daniel H. Foote, ed., 2007).

59 For example, the JFTC made a proposal for improvement of air freight regulation on April 17, 2009. Such proposals are based on the Act Establishing the Cabinet Office Article 58, although they are not binding on the regulatory agencies.

On the other hand, when the regulatory agency is interested in promoting competition using its regulatory power, the JFTC sometimes makes joint guidelines.[60]

The only robust exemption under the AMA is for resale price maintenance of "copyrighted works."[61] It was inserted in the AMA in 1953. The concept of "copyrighted works" has been interpreted to cover only those which existed in 1953: the "copyrighted works" thus include only newspapers, books, magazines, and music CDs (as a successor of analog phonograph records).

B. Consumer protection

Unfair Trade Practices under the AMA includes a consumer protection functionality; that is, regulation of deceptive misrepresentation, among others. But the main coverage of deceptive consumer behavior is the Act against Unjustifiable Premiums and Misleading Representations (AUPMR), which is a more convenient tool for an enforcer to regulate deceptive misrepresentation exhibited to end consumers. Prior to 2009 the JFTC was responsible for enforcing the AUPMR, but jurisdiction over the Act has now been given to the new Consumer Affairs Agency (CAA). It is now unlikely that the JFTC will enforce the general consumer protection provisions in the AMA, given the CAA's jurisdiction over the AUPMR.[62]

IV. Procedural characteristics of Japan's enforcement system

A. Case-by-case decision-making: due process norms[63]

1. Pre-order procedure

a) Non-merger cases

i. Overview

The JFTC detects potentially illegal conduct using many channels, including reports from "any person" (Article 45) and/or leniency applications from violators (Article 7-2 (10)–(12)). If the JFTC finds a case, it then decides which course to select, non-criminal or criminal. If non-criminal, the JFTC assigns the case to an

[60] *See* Guidelines for Proper Electric Power Trade with the METI (1999), <http://www.jftc.go.jp/en/legislation_guidelines/ama/pdf/electric.pdf>; Guidelines for Proper Gas Trade with the METI (2000), <http://www.jftc.go.jp/en/legislation_guidelines/ama/pdf/guidelines_gas.pdf>; Guidelines for Promotion of Competition in the Telecommunications Business Field with the MIC (2001), <http://www.jftc.go.jp/en/legislation_guidelines/ama/pdf/telecom.pdf>. METI stands for Ministry of Economy, Trade and Industry, formerly MITI (*see supra* text accompanying note 5). MIC stands for Ministry of Internal Affairs and Communications.

[61] Art. 23.

[62] The AUPMR admits that the CAA may ask the JFTC to execute some power provided in the Act (AUPMR Article 12 (2)). But it seems to be a minor point in that the JFTC's task would be limited to investigation of local cases outside Tokyo, because the CAA does not have branches outside Tokyo.

[63] For another source written in English, Kozo Kawai, Futaba Hirano & Kojiro Fujii, "Japan," in *The Public Competition Enforcement Review* (Shaun Goodman, ed., 2nd edn, 2009)(hereinafter "Kawai Hirano Fujii Japan Chapter").

administrative investigation section. If criminal, the JFTC assigns it to a criminal investigation section. When the criminal investigation section finds a violation, the JFTC refers it to the PPO and then reassigns the case also to an administrative investigation section.

Besides formal enforcement described below, a company may seek a pre-conduct consultation from the JFTC. Although the JFTC has established a written framework for such consultations,[64] it seems that the framework is rarely used. Instead, companies seem to mostly use a more informal approach, called "General Consultation." This informal approach lacks process requirements, however, such as obtaining third-party views.[65]

ii. Administrative investigation

The JFTC can investigate by using dawn raids, interrogation, and orders to parties to submit documents (Article 47). Dawn raids do not need court permission.[66] Because the investigation is a civil one, the ordered person can be criminally charged if he or she does not obey (Article 94).[67] It appears that during the investigation parties under investigation and/or their representatives may have some informal contact with investigators and that some may be able to undertake negotiations with regard to their case.[68]

iii. Criminal investigation

The 2005 amendment introduced the system of criminal investigation within the JFTC (Articles 101–118). Under this regime, the JFTC, with court permission, can directly force the persons to obey its investigative orders.[69] With respect to interrogation, the ordered person can refuse to reply without fear of criminal charge. By those points, the system of criminal investigation has escaped from possible unconstitutionality claims when the collected information and evidence is utilized for a criminal prosecution.[70]

Thanks to such a constitutional system, the PPO can coordinate with the JFTC's criminal investigation section during the investigation, providing its criminal

[64] Fair Trade Commission, "Prior Consultation System For Activities Of Businesses, etc." (October 1, 2001), <http://www.jftc.go.jp/en/legislation_guidelines/ama/pdf/priorconsultationsystem.pdf>.

[65] In the case of Google/Yahoo Japan, the JFTC gave a green light without hearing views of third parties including Microsoft. Japan Fair Trade Commission, "Yahoo Japan's Use of Technological Service Such As Search Engine Provided by Google (Tentative translation)" (December 2, 2010), <http://www.jftc.go.jp/en/pressreleases/archives/individual-000002.html>.

[66] The Supreme Court has made clear in a tax procedure case that such a framework is not unconstitutional. *Kawasaki Minsho*, November 22, 1972, Keishu vol. 26 no. 9 554.

[67] *See id.* (procedure not unconstitutional). For detailed rules for investigations, *see* Rules on Administrative Investigations by the Fair Trade Commission (2005), <http://www.jftc.go.jp/en/legislation_guidelines/ama/pdf/investigations.pdf>.

[68] *See*, e.g., "Shinshun Zadankai: Kosei Torihiki Iinnkai no Shoraizo" (Roundtable Discussion: The Future Image of the JFTC), Kousei Torihki (Fair Trade) No. 723 (2011) (hereinafter "Roundtable Discussion"), 40–1 (comment by Kozo Kawai).

[69] Orders in administrative investigations are described to be "indirect" in the sense that the ordered persons can refuse, although they have to fear being criminally charged for their refusal.

[70] It follows that the JFTC is required to make a firewall between its administrative investigation sections and criminal investigation sections.

prosecutorial expertise to the JFTC. Moreover, where the PPO has started an original investigation, it is possible for the PPO to urge the JFTC to join its investigation. Other criminal investigations may be initiated by other means including leniency applications.

Every AMA criminal prosecution of a cartel, the only category criminally prosecuted so far, must be preceded by a criminal referral by the JFTC (Article 96).[71] Receiving a criminal referral from the JFTC, the PPO decides whether to bring a criminal proceeding before a district court.[72] The PPO statutorily has prosecutorial discretion, but it has to report the reason to the Prime Minister when it does not prosecute after the JFTC's referral (Article 74(3)). This provision seems to make the prosecutors feel obliged to prosecute when the JFTC refers.[73] That seems to be why the PPO has established the system of the Meeting on Criminal Referral with the JFTC. The Meeting is said to choose those cases where the PPO feels it is most likely to win in court: in other words, it works for deterring the JFTC from bringing difficult cases with less probative evidence.

iv. Leniency program[74]

The 2005 amendment introduced a leniency program to Japan. It can be the starting point for either administrative or criminal investigations, although its legal effect is statutorily limited to administrative surcharges and it does not technically apply to criminal fines nor does it affect private damages suits (Article 7-2 (10)–(12)).[75] The first leniency applicant, if the application was before the dawn raid, can be exempted from any administrative surcharge. The second applicant, if it was before the dawn raid, can get 50 percent discount. Other applicants, before or after dawn raids, if any, can get 30 percent discount. The number of total applicants cannot exceed five violators.[76] The leniency program does not apply to surcharges imposed on Private Monopolization and Unfair Trade Practices, but only to Unreasonable Trade Restraint which deals with hard-core cartels.

[71] The JFTC has officially announced that it will refer "vicious and serious" cartels and repeated violations. Fair Trade Commission, "The Fair Trade Commission's Policy on Criminal Accusation and Compulsory Investigation of Criminal Cases Regarding Antimonopoly Violations" (October 7, 2005) (hereinafter "JFTC Policy on Criminal Accusation"), <http://www.jftc.go.jp/en/legislation_guidelines/ama/pdf/policy_on_criminalaccusation.pdf>.

[72] Before the 2005 amendment, the first instance for an AMA criminal litigation had to be the "specialized" panel at Tokyo High Court, the same organization as that for judicial review of JFTC decisions (*see infra* note 106 and accompanying text). The PPO was clever enough to earlier abandon the idealist system in 2005. It has enabled the PPO to allocate AMA criminal cases to district prosecutors' offices, especially Tokyo, Osaka, and Nagoya.

[73] e.g., Toshikazu Ochiai & Toshio Adachi, "Dokkinho Ihan Jiken no Keiji Kokuhatsu wo meguru Shomondai (Topics on Criminal Referral for AMA Violations)," SHIHO KENSHUJO RONSHU no. 88, 1 (1992) at 44.

[74] For another source written in English describing the program, *see* Hideto Ishida, Shigeyoshi Ezaki, Yusuke Nakano & Koya Uemura, "Japan," in: Kevin J. Arquit & Jacques Buhart (ed.), *Leniency Regimes: Jurisdictional Comparisons* (3rd edn, European Lawyer Reference, 2010).

[75] Article 7-2 (7)–(9), the initial provisions inserted by the 2005 amendment, moved to Art. 7-2 (10)–(12) at the time of the 2009 amendment.

[76] Before the 2009 amendment, it was three.

The program does not statutorily cover cease-and-desist orders, probably because they are not penalties in a narrow sense. But the JFTC, in its actual practice, makes it a rule not to issue cease-and-desist orders to those violators that applied before the dawn raid.

The reason why the leniency program does not statutorily cover criminal prosecutions and private lawsuits is probably because it was not so easy for the JFTC to take an initiative that would change the grand framework of the civil and criminal law, which is the responsibility of another agency, the Ministry of Justice. Nevertheless, the JFTC has made clear that it will not refer the first before-dawn-raid applicant and its employees to the PPO.[77] During the Diet session for the 2005 amendment, a high official of the Ministry of Justice answered that if the JFTC declined to make a criminal referral as to certain violators, the PPO would respect that decision so that the leniency program would work effectively.[78]

The detailed procedures with respect to the leniency program have not been fully revealed. The process seems to have been structured in a closed room among the Leniency Officer, the JFTC official in charge of the leniency program, and leniency applicants and their representatives. The first Leniency Officer published books to explain the framework of the program, but these books do not deal with deep details.[79] These details are shared only by a limited number of JFTC officials and lawyers.

b) Merger cases

i. Pre-merger notification and consultation

The AMA's pre-merger notification requirements vary depending on the type of merger involved, that is, stock acquisition, merger in a narrower sense, demerger, share transfer, and acquisition of business.[80] Amendments to the AMA in 2009 dramatically changed notification thresholds and the timing for notifying stock acquisitions.[81] Mergers without any obligation for notification might still violate the statute, but such situations are believed to be exceptional.

[77] *See* JFTC Policy on Criminal Accusation.

[78] March 11, 2005 at the House of Representatives and April 19, 2005 at the House of Councillors. Generally, if the JFTC refers only some participants in a cartel case, the PPO is statutorily allowed to bring a criminal prosecution even against those whom the JFTC did not refer. *See* Code of Criminal Procedure Art. 238 (2).

[79] Takeshi Shinagawa, the first Leniency Officer, published a book just before the 2005 amendment took effect (Takeshi Shinagawa & Hiroo Iwanari, Kachokin Genmen Seido To no Kaisetsu (Fair Trade Institute 2005)). The book was revised when the 2009 amendment took effect (Takeshi Shinagawa & Hiroo Iwanari, Dokusenkinshiho ni okeru Kachokin Genmen Seido (Fair Trade Institute 2010)).

[80] *See* Arts 10 (2)–(10), 15 (2)(3), 15-2 (2)–(4), 15-3 (2)(3), and 16 (2)(3)).

[81] One aspect of the change in thresholds for notification was from asset size to domestic turnover. The other aspect was the change of the definition of company group. Pre-2009, the basic threshold was aggregate asset values of the merging company A, A's parent, and A's subsidiaries. Post-2009, it is aggregate domestic turnover of the whole group consisting of all companies which have parent-subsidiary linkages, direct or indirect, with the merging company A. Stock acquisition notification was changed from *ex post* to *ex ante* and the thresholds of voting shares were simplified, from "10 percent, 25 percent, and 50 percent" to "20 percent and 50 percent."

The JFTC, however, has almost never issued an official order to stop or unwind a merger. Although the Commission has the statutory power to do so under Article 17-2 if it finds a merger proposal illegal in light of Chapter 4 of the AMA, its only official orders in a merger case came in 1969 and 1973.[82]

The lack of actual cases does not mean that the JFTC's merger regulation does not function at all. Most major merger plans are said to have been self-reported to the JFTC for informal consultation prior to the required notification pursuant to the AMA. Through a system of informal pre-notification consultations, the JFTC deterred some mergers and achieved some restructuring in others to meet its competition concerns. This informal consultation system was undertaken pursuant to procedural guidelines promulgated by the JFTC. These procedures called for "Phase 1" and "Phase 2" of the consultation.[83] Phase 1 was supposed to end within thirty days after the complete submission of documents, with some exceptions, and Phase 2 should have ended within ninety days, again with some exceptions. When the process moved to Phase 2, the merger proposal had to be made public to collect public comments. Criticisms attacked the fact that the JFTC was usually unwilling to get into Phase 1, claiming that the submitted documents were incomplete and thereby engaging in what some term "Phase 0" of the investigation.[84]

ii. Modification of the pre-merger process

Facing the criticisms above, the JFTC made substantial change in the merger review process, which took effect on July 1, 2011.[85] Informal consultation being abolished,[86] the new merger review process is much more under the statutory framework. A new Phase 1 review ("Primary review") is undertaken during the

[82] Yahata Steel/Fuji Steel, JFTC Consent Decision on October 30, 1969, Shinketsushu vol. 16, 46; Hiroshima Electric Railway, JFTC Recommendation Decision on July 17, 1973, Shinketsushu vol. 20, 62.

[83] Fair Trade Commission, "Policies dealing with prior consultation regarding enterprise combination plans" (December 11, 2002). It should be noted that these two phases are totally different from those in the United States and the EU in the sense that the Japanese two phases are for pre-notification consultation. *See* also *infra* notes 85–87 and accompanying text.

[84] Kozo Kawai, "Kotorii no Kigyoketsugo Shinsa no Kadai (Topics on JFTC Merger Reviews)," Kosei Torihiki no. 711 (2010). More moderately as an ex-JFTC-official, Yusuke Kashiwagi, "Kyosoho ni okeru Kihan no Junshu (Compliance in the Area of Competition Law," SOFT LAW KENKYU no. 16 (2010).

[85] Japan Fair Trade Commission, "Partial Amendment, etc. of the Fair Trade Commission Rules Associated with Reviews of Business Combination Regulations (Investigation Procedures and Criteria)," June 14, 2011, <http://www.jftc.go.jp/en/pressreleases/archives/individual-000432.html>. The core document for the new merger review process is: Japan Fair Trade Commission, "Policies Concerning Procedures of Review of Business Combination," June 14, 2011 (hereinafter "JFTC Policies on Merger Review Procedures"), <http://www.jftc.go.jp/en/legislation_guidelines/ama/pdf/pcbr.pdf>. As of March 2011, three mergers have been cleared after getting into Secondary reviews under the new framework. Nippon Steel/Sumitomo Metal, JFTC press release on December 14, 2012, <http://www.jftc.go.jp/en/pressreleases/uploads/2011_Dec_14.pdf>; Seagate/Samsung and Western Digital/Hitachi, JFTC press release on December 28, 2012, <http://www.jftc.go.jp/en/pressreleases/uploads/2011_Dec_28.pdf>.

[86] "Consultation Prior to Notification" which is described in JFTC Policies on Merger Review Procedures, Section 2, seems to be just for formalities in filling out the notification form. Exceptional informal consultations include those mergers without statutory obligation of notification. JFTC Policies on Merger Review Procedures, Section 7.

statutory waiting period prescribed by Article 10(8)[87] (usually lasting for thirty days). A Phase 2 review ("Secondary review") would then be undertaken if the JFTC requests the merging firms to submit more documents, called "reports" (Article 10 (9)). By statute, the JFTC must initiate a proceeding for a cease-and-desist order within ninety days after the complete submission of reports (Article 10 (9)). These two new phases, unlike those in the framework of informal pre-notification consultation, are equivalent of those two phases in the United States and the EU.

The 2011 modification of merger review process has apparently taken care of the two major criticisms of the informal consultation process: uncertainty of time and opacity of legal perspectives.

As for certainty of time, under the new regime, although it is usually still up to the JFTC when the thirty- or ninety-day period starts,[88] notifying parties can rely on Administrative Procedure Act.[89] The Act prescribes that "acceptance" of notification or reports in AMA Article 10(8)(9) should be the time of their "arrival," provided that they are without formalistic errors (Administrative Procedure Act Article 7). It may not be easy for the notifying parties to prove that their reports are free from errors, in the sense that the reports fully respond to JFTC requests, but the fact that the JFTC is under the rule of Administrative Procedure Act is expected to improve the JFTC's behavior.

With respect to legal transparency, the JFTC "will explain the current issues" when the notifying parties ask the JFTC to clarify its concern about the proposed merger or the JFTC itself finds the need to do so.[90] Also for legal transparency, a JFTC request for notifying parties' reports pursuant to Article 10(9) to initiate Phase 2 should be furnished with "points" or legal perspectives as described by the JFTC.[91]

2. *Decision and adjudication*

a) Introduction

The JFTC has the discretion to issue formal orders, to take informal measures (such as warnings or cautions[92]), or to do nothing. This section examines the process for

[87] Art.10 (8)(9), prescribed literally for stock acquisition, applies mutatis mutandis to merger in a narrower sense, demerger, share transfer, and acquisition of business. *See* Arts 15 (3), 15-2 (4), 15-3 (3) and 16 (3).

[88] The JFTC delivers a "receipt" of notification or reports pursuant to "Rules on Applications for Approval, Reporting, Notification, etc. Pursuant to the Provisions of Articles 9 to 16 of the Act on Prohibition of Private Monopolization and Maintenance of Fair Trade" (hereinafter "JFTC Rules on Merger Notification"), Arts 7, 8(2). The clock is usually assumed to start at the date recorded on those receipts.

[89] It is probable that the JFTC insisted the Act would not be applied to informal consultation.

[90] JFTC Policies on Merger Review Procedures, Section 4.

[91] JFTC Rules on Merger Notification Art. 8(1). Also in JFTC Policies on Merger Review Procedures, Section 6 (1). Transparency for third parties is secured by a public release at the time of the JFTC request for reports. Interested third parties can submit opinions within 30 days after the publication. JFTC Policies on Merger Review Procedures, Section 6 (1)(2). This is unchanged compared to the regime of informal consultation.

[92] There are two kinds of informal measures that the JFTC can take, "Keikoku" (warnings) and "Chui" (cautions). The difference between warnings and cautions is that a warning needs a "suspicion of violation," while a caution just indicates the "possibility of future violation." Every keikoku has to be

issuing formal orders and making decisions in cases that the JFTC has decided to bring. In 2005, after fifty-eight years, the original framework for decision and adjudication was changed substantially. Another drastic change was proposed in 2010, but has not yet been adopted. We go through the procedures in chronological order.

b) Pre-2005

i. Cease-and-desist order

The feature of the pre-2005 framework was "pre-order quasi-judicial hearing" held by the JFTC. After the JFTC concluded its investigation, if it decided to make a formal order it would issue a "recommendation decision." If the proposed addressee admitted the JFTC recommendation, the JFTC issued a cease-and-desist order (pre-2005 Article 48). If the proposed addressee refused, the JFTC issued a formal complaint signed by the Chairman and the Commissioners (pre-2005 Article 50). The Commission almost always used JFTC Hearing Examiners to conduct the hearing on the complaint (pre-2005 Article 51-2). Before the Examiners, both the defendant and the JFTC investigators had a full adversary procedure (pre-2005 Articles 51-3 and 52). This process is similar to that of the US FTC, on which the JFTC was originally based.

If the defendant wanted to end the hearing process and obey, the JFTC issued a Consent Decision (pre-2005 Article 53-3). If the defendant and the investigators concluded the adversary procedure, the Hearing Examiners rendered a draft decision after which the JFTC issued a formal decision (pre-2005 Article 54). Formal decisions usually just cited the draft decisions made by the Hearing Examiners without any corrections and additions. The defendant had a right to present views to the Commission—the Chairman and the Commissioners—(pre-2005 Article 53-2-2), but the hearing was believed to be just a formality.

ii. Administrative surcharge

Only after the process for issuing a cease-and-desist order could the JFTC begin the process for an administrative surcharge (pre-2005 Article 48-2 (1)). This approach was taken probably because the JFTC did not have a sufficient reputation for due process at the time of the 1977 amendment which first introduced the administrative surcharge. Originally administrative surcharges were imposed only for hard-core cartels (pre-2005 Article 7-2).

Differently from a cease-and-desist order, the JFTC issued a payment order no matter whether the addressee admitted it or not (pre-2005 Article 48-2). When the addressee was not satisfied, the JFTC held a quasi-judicial hearing (pre-2005 Article 50). It is similar to that of post-2005 procedure of ordering an administrative

publicly announced with the real name of the addressee, due to an undertaking of the Japanese Government with the United States during the Structural Impediment Initiative (SII)(*see supra* note 8 for the SII talks). Every keikoku has to be preceded by an *ex ante* procedure allowing the would-be addressee to submit evidence and express opinions, pursuant to the "Rules on Administrative Investigations by the Fair Trade Commission" Art. 31, which was added in 2009.

surcharge. But the important difference between pre-2005 and post-2005 procedures is that pre-2005 contested payment order was made void once a hearing was requested (pre-2005 Article 49 (3)) and the addressee(s) did not have to pay the surcharge until the JFTC's formal decision entering a de novo payment order (pre-2005 Article 54-2). In this sense, the adjudication process of an administrative surcharge, as well as that of a cease-and-desist order, belonged to the framework of "pre-order quasi-judicial hearing" held by the JFTC.

c) Post-2005

After the Structural Impediments Initiative (SII) around 1990, the JFTC had become gradually empowered politically and bureaucratically.[93] The JFTC planned an amendment which would improve the defects of the long-used pre-2005 framework. One of the defects was that the JFTC could not issue cease-and-desist orders quickly; another was that the entry of a valid administrative surcharge order was so late that the addressees were given incentive for delay.[94]

The solution was threefold: (1) the JFTC would issue a cease-and-desist order before holding a quasi-judicial hearing (Article 49), like the pre-2005 framework for administrative surcharges; (2) the JFTC would be able to get into an administrative surcharge proceeding at the same time as a cease-and-desist order (Article 50, without a clause like similar one in pre-2005 Article 48-2 (1));[95] (3) unlike the pre-2005 framework, an initial administrative surcharge order would not be made void even when the addressee requested a quasi-judicial hearing (removal of pre-2005 Article 49 (3)).[96]

Although JFTC orders are issued without a quasi-judicial hearing, would-be addressees are provided with some *ex ante* procedural protections. They must be furnished with the tentative content of the cease-and-desist order, setting out the facts and the relevant law, and be allowed to look at the evidence that the JFTC investigators choose to disclose. They are also allowed to submit their own evidence and present their views in writing.[97]

If the addressee does not agree with the cease-and-desist order, it cannot appeal directly to a court (Article 77 (3)), even though the cease-and-desist order goes into immediate effect (Articles 49 (2)).[98] Rather, the addressee must request a quasi-judicial hearing before the JFTC (Articles 49 and 50). The proceeding itself is much the same as the pre-order quasi-judicial hearings under the pre-2005 proced-

[93] *See supra* notes 8–9 and accompanying text.

[94] For details of the thoughts of the JFTC officials who drafted the 2005 amendment, Sadaaki Suwazono (ed.), Heisei 17 Nen Kaisei Dokusenkinshiho (Shojihomu, 2005).

[95] As a result of (2), most hard-core cartel cases post-2005 have delivered cease-and-desist orders and administrative surcharge orders at the same time.

[96] It means that the addressee, even when it requests a quasi-judicial proceeding, has to pay interest (Article 70-9). Of course the addressee can "pay and contest" without interest.

[97] Articles 49 (3)–(5) and 50 (6), and the JFTC Rule for Administrative Investigation Articles 24–27 and 29.

[98] The addressee can seek a stay of the cease-and-desist order from the Tokyo High Court by depositing money (Article 70-6). Such stays appear to be granted routinely. The JFTC could decide on its own to stay its order (Article 54), but such stays have not been reported.

ures. A hearing is initiated (Article 52), in which the Commission almost always uses Hearing Examiners (Article 56), and the investigators and the respondent engage in a full adversary proceeding (Articles 58 and 59). The JFTC then issues a decision as to whether to rescind the contested orders or not (Article 66). These decisions, however, usually just cite the draft decision made by the Hearing Examiners without any corrections and additions. The respondent has a right to present its views to the Commission (Article 63), but this is just a formality.

d) The 2010 Bill[99]

i. Overview and background

On March 12, 2010, the Cabinet submitted its proposed amendment of the AMA (2010 Bill) to abolish the post-order quasi-judicial JFTC hearing system completely, enabling addressees of cease-and-desist orders and surcharge orders to appeal directly to court. The 2010 Bill would strengthen the pre-order hearing system as well. Moreover, the 2010 Bill made clear that the next issue should be due process in investigation (Article 16 of the Annex to the 2010 Bill).

Those proposed changes were supported by most of the business community and competition lawyers, with Nippon Keidanren (Japan Business Federation) a leader in the effort.[100] Most competition lawyers in Japan usually represent defendants against the JFTC, being well-informed of the defects of current regime.[101] In brief, the defects from their viewpoints are lack of impartiality and lack of transparency.

ii. Improvement of pre-order hearing

The 2010 Bill would improve the due process of the pre-order hearing.[102] The JFTC would be required to nominate a neutral Hearing Officer (proposed Article 53), and allow the would-be addressee to get photocopies of some types of evidence (proposed Article 52).

iii. Abolition of post-order quasi-judicial hearing

The 2010 Bill would abolish the JFTC post-order quasi-judicial hearing and allow addressees to appeal directly to court. The first instance for those lawsuits would be

[99] The Diet review of the proposed bill is currently stuck due to political turbulence (as of March 2012).

[100] Nippon Keidanren (Japan Business Federation), "Proposal for Comprehensive Amendments to the Antimonopoly Act—To Establish International Parity in the Investigation and Appeals Process" (November 20, 2007).

[101] Kyosoho Forum (Japan Competition Law Forum), the most organized competition lawyers' association in Japan, has released some documents suggesting various reforms. *See* Kyosoho Forum, "Shinsa Tetsuduki ni kansuru Teigensho" (Proposal for better investigation procedure) (November 10, 2009); Kyosoho Forum, "Shinpan Seido ni kansuru Iken" (Opinion on Quasi-judicial Hearing) (January 28, 2010); Kyosoho Forum, "Shinpan Seido ni kansuru Iken (Dokusenkinshiho Kaiseihoan ni tsuite" (Opinion on Quasi-judicial Hearing—After Taking a Look at the Cabinet's Proposal) (May 10, 2010). For a good discussion of the controversy and differing viewpoints on the proposals, *see* Mitsuo Matsushita, "Reforming the Enforcement of the Japanese Antimonopoly Law," 41 Loyola U. Chicago L.J. 521 (2010).

[102] For current regime, *see supra* note 97 and accompanying text.

the Tokyo District Court (proposed Article 85), instead of the Tokyo High Court.[103] In non-competition-law cases, district court procedures are usually handled by single-judge panels (Court Act Article 26), but AMA lawsuits would have three judges (proposed Article 86).[104] Judgments by the Tokyo District Court could be appealed to the Tokyo High Court. The number of judges in a panel would be three, pursuant to the general law for High Courts (Court Act Article 18 (2)).[105]

3. Appeal to the courts

Under the current version of the AMA, an addressee of a JFTC Decision can sue to rescind it in the courts. The first instance is the "specialized" panel of five judges at the Tokyo High Court.[106] This provision was a part of the effort in the original 1947 Act to assure expertise in competition matters once a case was reviewed in court. As a practical matter, however, the judicial system cannot afford to allocate five judges solely to competition law—there are not that many competition law cases appealed to the courts. The solution to the problem has been an interpretation of Article 87. Article 87 provides as follows: "A panel of judges invested with the authority to hear exclusively the cases listed in Article 85 and cases listed in the preceding Article shall be established within the Tokyo High Court." Most readers might think the "judges" should be "invested" with authority, but the provision has been interpreted that "a panel" should be "invested" with authority. Thus the Tokyo High Court collects five judges from various panels that are busy in non-competition law litigation and appoints them to a virtual and instant competition-law panel, which "exclusively" handles AMA litigation. It seems that the Tokyo High Court collects a different set of five judges from case to case. It is doubtful whether this kind of "specialized" panel can be really equipped with enough time and expertise.

The Tokyo High Court reviews cases without de novo presentation of evidence. The JFTC findings of fact are binding on the Court if they are supported by "substantial evidence" (Article 80). The Tokyo High Court can reject unreasonable findings by the JFTC, but cannot reject reasonable findings even when the Court

[103] Along with the change, the first instance for damage recovery lawsuits using the AMA Article 25 would be changed from Tokyo High Court to Tokyo District Court (proposed Article 85-2).

[104] Proposed Article 86 further allows the possibility of five-judge panel. It is probably a formal descendant of the current provision (*see* Art. 87). Taking account of the shortage of judges, it would not be likely that we would observe a five-judge AMA panel very often.

[105] Confusingly enough, proposed Article 87 only prescribes that five-judge panels are allowed, without mentioning a three-judge panel. This is because, if a special Act does not change a norm provided by a more general Act, the special Act is silent. With respect to court matters, the AMA is a special Act of the Court Act. That is why proposed Article 86 explicitly mentions three-judge panel as to Tokyo District Court. Anyway, it would not be so likely that we would very often observe a five-judge panel at Tokyo High Court.

[106] *See* Arts 85, 87.

believes that different findings would be more reasonable.[107] Judgments by the Tokyo High Court are subject to review by the Supreme Court.

4. Equality and non-discrimination

Some critics in the past have viewed the AMA, as enforced by the JFTC, to be protectionist. The symbol was the Commission's review of international contracts. Under Article 6 a victim who is a party to an anticompetitive contract can also be a "violator" of the AMA and the JFTC can then order the "violator" to abandon the anticompetitive contractual clauses, without giving any due process to the foreign party to the contract.[108] Further, because parties were required to notify the Commission within thirty days of entering into an international agreement, the Commission was given an opportunity to guide parties to rewrite objectionable provisions. This protectionist approach found expression in JFTC guidelines on international licensing agreements.[109]

Currently, Article 6 sagas are just old tales. Notification obligations were mitigated by the 1982 amendment and abolished by the 1997 amendment. The old guidelines were totally replaced in 1989.[110] The 2008 Intellectual Property Guidelines do not make any special mention of international trade,[111] which is of particular importance because much of the criticism of the JFTC centered around international intellectual property licensing agreements. Although it is still possible that the JFTC could "order" a Japanese firm not to comply with an international agreement, and leave the international party without a remedy, there have been no cases like this for many years.

More generally, it is hard to find clear evidence of protectionist or discriminatory applications in current enforcement. There are, of course, some recent cases in which the JFTC has investigated non-Japanese firms at the behest of or with the cooperation of firms based in Japan. For example, in the Microsoft NAP case,

[107] *Wakodo*, Supreme Court Judgment on July 10, 1975, Minshu vol. 29, no. 6, p.888. The Tokyo High Court can reject unreasonable findings. Examples include *Omori Kogyo*, Tokyo High Court Judgment on June 24, 2011, available in Japanese at: <http://snk.jftc.go.jp/JDSWeb/jds/dc/DC005.do?documentKey = H230624H22G09000006_>. Tokyo High Court reviewed the JFTC's fact-findings from every aspect and determined they were unreasonable enough to be reversed. The JFTC reportedly did not appeal to the Supreme Court.

[108] The landmark case is Novo/Amano case, Supreme Court Judgment on November 28, 1975, Minshu vol. 29, no. 10, 1592. Novo, a Danish pharmaceutical company, licensed its intellectual property to a Japanese pharmaceutical company, Amano. The licensing contract contained a non-competition clause after the contract terminated. The JFTC ordered Amano, not Novo, to abandon the clause, a good result for Amano although not for Novo. Novo tried to rescind the JFTC order, but the Supreme Court denied standing for Novo, because Novo was not the addressee itself and Novo was still free to argue the validity of the contract in private litigation against Amano in a Japanese court.

[109] The Fair Trade Commission, "Kokusaiteki Gijutsu Donyu Keiyaku nikansuru Nintei Kijun" (Guidelines for International Licensing Agreements) (May 24, 1968).

[110] The Executive Office of the Fair Trade Commission, "Tokyo-Knowhow License Keiyaku niokeru Fukousei na Torihikihoho no Kisei nikansuru Unyo Kijun To" (Guidelines on Unfair Trade Practices in Patent and Know-how Licensing Agreements), February 15, 1989.

[111] Japan Fair Trade Commission, "Guidelines for the Use of Intellectual Property under the Antimonopoly Act," September 28, 2007.

which involved Microsoft's imposition of a non-assertion of patents clause in its Windows licensing agreements with Japanese PC manufacturers, some Japanese companies cooperated in the JFTC's investigation.[112] Another example is the BHP Billiton/Rio Tinto merger cases in 2008 and 2010, where Japanese steel manufacturers, buyers of iron ore and other products, persuaded the JFTC to engage in an intensive investigation.[113] But those facts alone would not provide basis for protectionist claims: it is not surprising that domestic companies that believe they have been hurt by an antitrust violation would urge their own competition authority to act.

5. *Proportionality of remedies*

One can observe the steady expansion of the administrative surcharge, both in amounts and coverage. Amounts have always been statutorily determined as a fixed percentage of the violator's real turnover in the relevant market. This percentage has been increased from 2 percent in 1977, to 6 percent in 1989, to 10 percent in 2005 (Article 7-2 (1) by each amendment). The 2005 and 2009 amendments also introduced a 50 percent increase to repeat violators and cartel ringmasters (current Article 7-2 (7)–(9)). Those two amendments also expanded the surcharge coverage from Unreasonable Trade Restraints (hard-core cartels) to Private Monopolization (Article 7-2 (2) and (4)) and certain categories of Unfair Trade Practices including abuse of superior bargaining position (ASBP) (Articles from 20–2 to 20–6).[114] The leniency program reduces or eliminates surcharges on a statutorily determined basis which seem appropriately calibrated to fault-based criteria arising from a willingness to confess to illegal behavior.

With respect to international cartel cases, however, the JFTC does not impose administrative surcharges on foreign companies that have agreed not to sell to Japanese purchasers, because the surcharge calculation is based on actual sales in the

[112] *Microsoft NAP*, JFTC Decision on September 16, 2008, Shinketsushu vol. 55, 380.

[113] Japan Fair Trade Commission, "The JFTC closes its investigation into BHP Billiton's proposed acquisition of Rio Tinto's shares" (December 3, 2008), <http://www.jftc.go.jp/en/pressreleases/archives/individual-000067.html>; Japan Fair Trade Commission, "The JFTC closed its prior consultation's review on the proposed joint venture for iron ore production between BHP Billiton and Rio Tinto" (October 18, 2010), <http://www.jftc.go.jp/en/pressreleases/archives/individual-000016.html>. In the 2008 case, because the proposed stock acquisition did not need notification to the JFTC pursuant to pre-2009 regime, the JFTC tried to make BHP Billiton submit documents by an order to report prescribed by Art. 47. After the company, based in Australia, refused to voluntarily receive the order, the JFTC "delivered" the order using a public notification process, by posting on the notice board in front of the JFTC building in Tokyo (Article 70-18).

[114] From constitutional or administrative law viewpoints, the adjustment system introduced by the 2005 amendment may be interesting. Because the AMA could impose both administrative surcharge and criminal penalties to a single violation, there have been constitutional disputes. The Supreme Court has denied unconstitutionality (Supreme Court Decision on October 13, 1998, Shinketsushu vol. 45, 339), but some still argue that the combination of surcharge and criminal fine results in a lack of proportionality and could be a support to unconstitutionality. Pursuant to the provisions introduced by the 2005 amendment, when an administrative and criminal fine is imposed on a violator, half the criminal fine would be deducted from the administrative surcharge (current Article 7-2 (19)–(21) and Article 51). Examples include Forest Resource Institute case and Hot Dip Galvanizing case.

relevant market; that is, the market for Japanese purchasers.[115] This is in contrast to the EU's practice of basing fines on worldwide sales, among other factors, in a case where a violator had no turnover in the European Economic Area.[116]

With respect to the statutory expansion of the administrative surcharge to cover additional types of anticompetitive conduct, no-one can yet persuasively estimate whether the surcharges will be disproportional. The 2005 amendment added administrative surcharges for "Private Monopolization by Control" (Articles 2 (5) and 7–2 (2)), which mainly covers vertical restraints. It took effect in January 2006, but there have been no cases reported as of March 2012. The 2009 amendment added "Private Monopolization by Exclusion" (Articles 2 (5) and 7–2 (4)) and ASBP (Articles 2 (9) (v) and 20–6) to violations for which an administrative surcharge must be imposed. This provision took effect in January 2010 and there have been no cases for Private Monopolization and only three for ASBP as of March 2012.[117]

Private Monopolization by "Exclusion" and ASBP do not have clear-cut illegality criteria like hard-core cartels and this may be why there have been no cases yet brought for administrative surcharges in these areas. Another reason may be difficulties in calculating amounts. The AMA obliges the JFTC to calculate without discretion, apparently in order to escape the constitutional argument of double jeopardy.[118] Exclusion and ASBP cases would require the JFTC to make much more surcharge-tuned fact-findings than before. It is possible that the continual expansion of the coverage of administrative surcharges has had unintended consequences, resulting in chilled enforcement due to the perceptions among JFTC investigators that such cases will now be difficult to bring.

B. Institutional performance norms

1. *Operational efficiency*

a) Size and organization

The JFTC is a large agency. It has its main office in Tokyo and eight branch offices around Japan.[119] In terms of number of personnel, the JFTC is roughly the size of comparable competition authorities in the United States and the EU.[120]

[115] The good illustration is *Marine Hose*, JFTC Order on February 20, 2008, <http://www.jftc.go.jp/en/pressreleases/archives/individual-000147.html> (English summary). The JFTC ordered cease and desist but did not order the foreign violators to pay administrative surcharge.

[116] *See* Case T-133/07 *Mitsubishi Electric Corp. v. European Commission* and Case T–113/07 *Toshiba Corp. v. European Commission* (July 13, 2011) (the General Court nullified the Commission's fine orders on a different ground).

[117] *Sanyo Marunaka*, JFTC Order on June 22, 2011, <http://www.jftc.go.jp/pressrelease/11.june/110622marunaka.pdf> (in Japanese); *Toys 'R Us-Japan*, JFTC Order on December 13, 2011, available at: <http://www.jftc.go.jp/en/pressreleases/uploads/2011-Dec-13.pdf>; *Edion*, JFTC Order on February 16, 2012, <http://www.jftc.go.jp/en/pressreleases/uploads/2012_Feb_16.pdf>.

[118] The Supreme Court requires administrative measures to be "administrative" in the sense that the enforcement agency has very limited discretion whether to impose orders and how to calculate the amounts. *Kotobukiya*, Supreme Court Judgment of April 30, 1958, Minshu vol. 12, no. 6, 938.

[119] *See supra* note 33.

[120] *See id.* at 26.

b) Non-merger enforcement

i. Overview

In FY 2009 the JFTC completed investigations in 130 cases.[121] The JFTC adopted formal legal measures in twenty-six cases (this does not include informal measures like warnings or cautions).[122] The average investigation period of the twenty-six cases was about twelve months.[123]

Taking a look at non-merger pre-conduct consultations,[124] in FY 2009, the JFTC provided consultations in 3,000 cases, all of which was done informally.[125] More than two-thirds of the cases (2335) involved distribution system and business practices; 352 cases involved trade association activities; 112 cases involved collaborative conduct; 66 cases involved patent and know-how licenses; 24 cases involved joint research and development. The remaining 111 cases involved other activities by enterprises.[126] Of these 3,000 consultations the JFTC selected and published the content of twelve that it believed would be useful for other enterprises and trade associations (although the Commission does not include identifying names of the parties or the industry in this review).[127]

ii. International cartels

Two of the cases investigated in FY 2009 were international cases; the investigation periods for those cases were about twenty-three months.[128] The JFTC explained that the longer investigation period was due to the burden of interviewing relevant persons and collecting evidence related to foreign entities.[129] In this regard, the 2009 amendment extended the statute of limitations for cease-and-desist orders and administrative surcharges from three years to five years. Competent JFTC officials explained that part of reason for this extension was the longer investigation period required for international cartels.[130] In addition, the JFTC established a permanent staff of investigators specialized in international cartels on April 1, 2010, to more efficiently collect evidence and coordinate with foreign competition authorities.[131]

[121] "Heisei 22 Nendo no Seisaku Hyoka (Heisei 21 Nendo ni Jisshi Shita Shisaku no Hyoka) ni Tsuite" (hereinafter "JFTC Policy Review FY 2009") (July 28, 2010), Appendix 2, 7. This number does not include the cases in which the JFTC issued cautions ("Chui") in the special expedited procedure against "Unjust Low Price Sales" that violate Article 19 of the AMA.

[122] Ibid.

[123] Ibid., 9.

[124] *See supra* notes 64 and 65 and accompanying text.

[125] Japan Fair Trade Commission General Secretariat, "Dokusen Kinshiho ni kansuru Sodan Jireishu (Heisei 21 Nendo)" (July, 2010), Preface.

[126] Ibid.

[127] Ibid.

[128] Ibid.

[129] Ibid.

[130] The Secretary General of the JFTC explained at a news conference on April 7, 2010, that this extension aimed to fill the gap between the JFTC and other major competition authorities, such as DOJ and the European Commission, which are able to take measures against cartels by the time five to ten years after the cartels ceased (*see* <http://www.jftc.go.jp/teirei/h22/kaikenkiroku100407.html#k100407_2>).

[131] *See* statements of the Secretary General of the JFTC at a news conference on April 7, 2010, <http://www.jftc.go.jp/teirei/h22/kaikenkiroku100407.html#k100407_2>.

iii. Protection of small or medium sized enterprises

The JFTC has recently emphasized the desirability of promoting fair trade to protect small and medium sized enterprises, which are vulnerable to unfair practices by large corporations in the economic depression. As part of this enforcement program, the JFTC established the "Abuse of Superior Bargaining Position (ASBP) Case Task Force." This led to two formal legal measures (cease-and-desist orders), two warnings, and twenty-two cautions involving ASBP in FY 2009. In the same year, the JFTC also vigorously acted against violations of the Subcontract Act with the Small and Medium-Size Enterprise Agency, issuing recommendations ("Kankoku") and instructions ("Shidou"), in 3605 cases.[132] Similarly, the JFTC took a large number of expedited actions (cautions "Chui") against Unjust Low Price Sales to wholesalers and retailers of liquor, petroleum products, and household electrical products (3225 cases).[133] The JFTC thus seems to have allocated substantial resources to protecting small or medium sized enterprises.

iv. Quasi-judicial hearing

As for quasi-judicial hearing under the JFTC, it took two years on average to adjudicate cease-and-desist order cases between FY 2002 to FY 2004 under the pre-2005 regime (which required a quasi-judicial hearing prior to entering a cease-and-desist order).[134] For cases adjudicated in FY 2009, it took about four to five years to adjudicate cease-and-desist order cases that were pending under pre-2005 regime.[135] To take one prominent example, in the Unfair Trade Practices proceeding against Microsoft for its non-assertion of patent licensing provision, it took the JFTC nearly four years from commencement of the hearing to rendering the decision that Microsoft had violated the AMA and should be ordered to cease and desist from the violation. Under the post-2005 regime (where the quasi-judicial hearing is held after entering the cease-and-desist order), it is pointed out that it still takes a long time to adjudicate cases.[136] In fact, it took about two to three years for most of the cases adjudicated in FY 2008 and FY 2009.[137] It is difficult to draw firm conclusions from these data as to whether the JFTC operates efficiently, however, because the data do not reflect the complexity of the proceedings. Thus, it is difficult to say whether the JFTC is taking "too long" or "too short" a time to decide cases.

[132] "Heisei 21 Nendo Kosei Torihiki Iinnkai Nenji Hokoku" (2010)(hereinafter "JFTC Annual Report FY 2009"), Part 2, Chapter 9.

[133] Ibid., Part 2, Chapter 8.

[134] *See* "Dokusen Kinshihou Kihon Mondai Kondankai Siryou (Dai 11 kai)" (material prepared by the JFTC for discussion regarding the basic issues of the AMA) (April 21, 2006), <http://www8.cao.go.jp/chosei/dokkin/kaisaijokyo/mtng_11th/mtng_11-1.pdf>.

[135] JFTC Annual Report FY 2009, Part 2 Chapter 3.

[136] Kimitoshi Yabuki, "Dokusen Kinshi Hou no Kaisei to Sinpann Seido" *Tokyo Daigaku Houka Daigakuinn Law Review* vol. 3 (2008.9) p. 272.

[137] JFTC Annual Report FY 2009, and "Heisei 20 Nendo Kosei Torihiki Iinnkai Nenji Hokoku" (The JFTC's annual report for FY 2008), Part II Chapter 3.

c) Merger enforcement

As the 2011 merger review process has too short a history since July 2011, only the statistics of former informal regime are available, as discussed below.[138]

The JFTC handled 24 informal consultations cases in FY 2009.[139] All of the informal prior consultation cases that the JFTC answered in FY 2009 ended in former Phase 1.[140] The JFTC reported that all cases ended within the thirty-day period set in the JFTC's manual and the average review period between the initiation and termination of Phase 1 was 21.3 days (16 cases).[141] However, these data cannot be taken at face value. For one, they do not include cases where the merging parties voluntarily asked the JFTC to extend the review period.[142] For another, the JFTC was criticized for sometimes conducting lengthy investigations before former Phase 1 begins ("Phase 0") by requesting detailed information from the merging parties and conducting interviews with relevant parties, including customers and competitors of the merging parties.[143]

2. *Expertise*

a) JFTC commissioners

The Chairman and the four Commissioners are statutorily required to have "knowledge and experience in law or economics."[144] They are not required to have expertise in competition law and policy, however. The Chairman, Kazuhiko Takeshima (as of March 2012), is an alumnus of the Ministry of Finance, as have been most Chairmen of the JFTC. He has served as the Chairman since 2002. Commissioners as of March 2012 are Seisui Kamigaki, an alumnus of the Public Prosecutors Office; Michiyo Hamada, a law professor specializing in commercial and corporate law; Kiyoshi Hosokawa, a former judge; and Hiroyuki Odagiri, a professor of economics specialized in industrial organization. Historically, one Commissioner has usually been a former Secretary General of the JFTC, a career JFTC officer with strong expertise in competition law and policy. In this regard, the current JFTC is an exception.

b) Executive leadership: General Secretariat

The Secretary General and most of the executives of the General Secretariat are usually career officials of the JFTC, with the exception of some hearing examiners and other lawyers discussed below. They are supposed to train themselves to obtain expertise in competition law and policy over the course of their careers.

[138] For the old and new regimes, *see supra* notes 80–91 and accompanying text.
[139] JFTC Policy Review FY 2009, Appendix 1, 4.
[140] Ibid.
[141] JFTC Policy Review FY 2009, Appendix 1, 4.
[142] *Id.*
[143] *See supra* note 84 and accompanying text.
[144] Art. 29 (2).

c) JFTC staff

The AMA requires that the General Secretariat include "[a] public prosecutor, an attorney practicing at the time of the appointment or a person qualified to be an attorney."[145] This language has been in the AMA since its passage in 1947, reflecting the US concern that the JFTC should have the capability to enforce its orders in court proceedings and not be thwarted in its enforcement efforts by the Ministry of Justice. Despite this provision, however, there have historically been very few admitted lawyers on the staff of the JFTC. Most of the JFTC staff are career employees without professional legal qualifications or advanced training in economics. The JFTC has recently recognized the importance of strengthening the expertise of the staff. As of February 2012, it hired seventeen qualified lawyers and three economists who will stay at the JFTC for limited terms.[146]

d) Hearing examiners

There are now six hearing examiners engaging in the quasi-judicial hearings under the AMA. Four are qualified legal professionals, such as lawyers and judges; the other two are JFTC employees. In the past when there were seven hearing examiners, the Secretary General had expressed the view that the body of seven examiners consisting of four legal professionals and three JFTC career employees was appropriately balanced.[147] In order to assure neutrality, no person who has performed duties of an investigator of a case or who has otherwise been involved in the examination of a case may be designated as a hearing examiner for the same case.[148]

3. Transparency

a) Guidelines

The JFTC has issued a large number of guidelines. The major ones include merger guidelines, guidelines for distribution systems, guidelines for the licensing of intellectual property, and guidelines for patent pooling and standard setting.[149] Because the recent amendments to the AMA expanded the categories of conduct subject to administrative surcharges, the JFTC has also issued new guidelines directed at these areas, so as to prevent a chilling effect on business activities. The

[145] Art. 35(10).

[146] Secretary General's press conference on February 1, 2012, <http://www.jftc.go.jp/teirei/h24/kaikenkiroku120201.html> (in Japanese). According to the remarks by the Secretary General, the lawyers work in merger review, investigate alleged violations, or represent the JFTC in judicial review; the economists work on merger review or economic research.

[147] *See* statements of the Secretary General of the JFTC at a news conference on June 27, 2007, <http://www.jftc.go.jp/teirei/h19/kaikenkiroku070627.html> (in Japanese).

[148] Art. 56 (1). The word "investigator" should be interpreted to include JFTC officials engaged in criminal investigation and "examination" should be interpreted to include criminal investigation.

[149] There are also a number of guidelines for unfair business practices, including the setting of unfair low prices. English language versions of the Guidelines are available at <http://www.jftc.go.jp/en/legislation_guidelines/antimonopoly_guidelines.html>.

new guidelines thus cover exclusionary Private Monopolization, abuse of superior bargaining position, and a revision of the guidelines on unjust low price sales.

The JFTC's guidelines are an important tool for the JFTC to clarify its interpretation of the AMA. Such clarification is particularly important given the relative lack of judicial and administrative decisions construing the Act. The Tokyo High Court has indicated that the JFTC must respect an enterprise's reliance on the standards and rules established by past JFTC decisions, including guidelines,[150] and the JFTC's analyses and decisions generally adhere quite closely to its guidelines. Given the guidelines' importance, guidelines need to be established in a transparent way and reflect appropriate interpretations of the AMA.

In issuing guidelines the JFTC follows the requirements of the Administrative Procedure Act (Article 39(1)), posting the draft guidelines on its website for public comments and then posting responses to those comments on its website. In addition, courts reviewing the appropriateness of the guidelines seem to have respected their content.[151]

b) Decisions on private party complaints

The AMA provides that any person may report violations of the AMA to the JFTC and ask that appropriate measures be taken (Article 45(1)). If such a report presents specific facts in writing, the JFTC is required promptly to notify the reporter of its decision as to whether it will take measures regarding the reported fact (Article 45 (3)). In practice, however, the JFTC's notifications do not explain the reasons for its decision, nor does the party making the complaint have the right to demand that the JFTC actually take some measures as to the reported fact.[152]

In FY 2009, there were 11,773 reported violations and the JFTC made 6,862 notifications.[153] Chairman Takeshima recently disclosed that Microsoft and Rakuten, a major online shopping mall operator in Japan, made use of this reporting system in relation to the agreement between Google and Yahoo Japan pursuant to which Google would provide Yahoo with its search engine and search-advertising platform.[154]

[150] For past decisions, *Tokyo Mochi*, Tokyo High Court Judgment on March 29, 1996, Hanrei-Jihou vol. 1571, 48. The same consideration should also apply to companies' reliance on the content of the JFTC's guidelines.

[151] For example, *NTT East*, Supreme Court Judgment on December 17, 2010, Minshu vol. 64 no. 8 2067, seems to have just copied the content of JFTC's guidelines (Japan Fair Trade Commission, "The Guidelines for Exclusionary Private Monopolization under the Antimonopoly Act" October 28, 2009).

[152] *Ebisu Shokuhin Kigyo Kumiai*, Supreme Court Judgment on November 16, 1972, Minshu vol. 26, no. 9, 1573.

[153] JFTC Annual Report FY 2009, Part 2 Chapter 2 Section 1. The Commission does not classify the complaints by type of violation alleged.

[154] Chairman Takeshima's answer to questions at "the Shugiin Keizai Sangyo Iinnkai" (The House of Representatives Committee of Economy and Industry) on October 27, 2010.

c) Decisions not to proceed

Although there is no formal procedure for asking the JFTC to disclose details of its non-action decisions, the JFTC does disclose some details of these decisions. When a merger proposal receives a green light after getting into Phase 2, the JFTC "will explain in writing the result of the review including reasons" to the notifying parties.[155] The JFTC will also publicly release the reasons of those Phase 2 cases and selected Phase 1 cases.[156]

d) Public awareness of antimonopoly law and enforcement

The JFTC seeks opinions and requests regarding implementation of the AMA and competition policies from local experts, local economic associations, and consumer associations. For example, in FY 2009 it hosted "Antimonopoly Policy Cooperation Committee Meetings" in nine cities in Japan, at which JFTC Commissioners exchanged opinions with local experts, and held meetings with local officials of the "Advisory Panel on Antimonopoly Policy" in various cities in Japan.[157] The Commission also dispatched staff to speak on the role of competition in the economy and other issues at the request of junior high schools, high schools, and universities, and invites students to visit JFTC offices.[158] The JFTC has also produced and distributed various pamphlets, PR videos/DVDs, and email magazines.[159] The JFTC also provides copies of its press releases on its website, along with related information; some of these press releases are translated into English and are available on its English language website. The JFTC also publishes an annual report which contains extensive data about its operations.

JFTC Commissioners and high enforcement officials give public speeches regarding JFTC enforcement policy at professional legal and competition policy meetings around the world.[160] Perhaps the most valuable public speeches, however, are those given at the Secretary General's weekly press conference. At these press conferences (which generally last for twenty to thirty minutes), the Secretary General sometimes explains the progress of high-profile cases as well as the JFTC's general enforcement approaches. The content of the presentations and the Q&A sessions are available on the JFTC's Japanese-language website (but not in English).

155 JFTC Policies on Merger Review Procedures, Section 6 (3) A.

156 JFTC Policies on Merger Review Procedures, Section 6 (3) B. Even under the older regime of informal consultation, the JFTC released annual reports of selected merger cases.

157 JFTC Annual Report FY 2009, Part 2 Chapter 11 Section 2. For FY 2009 the JFTC reports giving lectures at 26 Junior high schools, 2 High schools and 19 Universities. *See* Annual Report at 7 (English version).

158 JFTC Annual Report FY 2009, Part 2 Chapter 11 Section 3.

159 JFTC Annual Report FY 2009, Part 2 Chapter 11 Section 1. The JFTC's video "Towards Fair and Free Competition" is available in an English-dubbed version at <http://www3.stream.co.jp/www11/jftc/090330/01_500k.asx>.

160 Speeches in English are posted on the JFTC's English version website at <http://www.jftc.go.jp/en/policy_enforcement/speeches/index.html>.

4. Accountability

The JFTC is accountable to the Diet in a number of important ways. First, its budget, which is part of the Government's budget as proposed by the Cabinet, must be approved by the Diet. The JFTC announces and discloses its budget and its policy-by-policy execution in its policy review protocol.[161] The JFTC drafts its budgetary request for the coming year considering its previous year's policy review.[162]

In March 2010, the JFTC established "The JFTC Budget Monitoring and Efficiency-Improving Team," aimed at improving the efficiency of the JFTC's execution of the budget.[163] Through this team, the JFTC promotes disclosure of the execution of the budget as well as an efficient budget execution plan.[164] In addition, the JFTC has established a "Budget Execution Opinion Box" and seeks opinions from citizens on the use of its budget resources.[165]

The Diet also exercises supervision over the JFTC through appointments and oversight. The consent of both Houses of the Diet is required for the Prime Minister's appointment of the Chairman and Commissioners.[166] The JFTC is also required to report to the Diet annually, through the Prime Minister, on the enforcement of the AMA.[167] In addition, Diet members can make use of parliamentary investigation rights provided in the Japanese Constitution to investigate the enforcement circumstances of the AMA.[168] Diet members sometimes take up high-profile cases for discussion, and the competent JFTC person, including the Chairman, will need to explain the Commission's decisions.[169]

The JFTC is also accountable to the courts, which have the power to review JFTC decisions. The extent to which courts cabin JFTC discretion, however, depends on whether parties take legal action to quash a JFTC decision. Because parties have often accepted JFTC orders without formally contesting them before the JFTC, JFTC quasi-judicial decisions have been relatively infrequent and appeals of those decisions consequently have been rare. This may mean that the JFTC has been very cautious in exercising its power, perhaps so as to avoid judicial control of its efforts.[170] With the increase in the surcharge power, however, the

161 e.g., *see* "Seisaku Hyoka Chosho" (Policy Review Protocol) drafted for the budgetary request for FY 2011, available at <http://www.jftc.go.jp/info/seisaku23.pdf>.

162 e.g., the Budgetary Request for FY 2011 is available at <http://www.jftc.go.jp/info/23sandan-hyou.pdf>.

163 *See* the JFTC's webpage of <http://www.jftc.go.jp/info/kanshiteam.html>.

164 Ibid., Article 2.

165 *See* the JFTC's webpage, <https://www.jftc.go.jp/yosan/index.html>.

166 Art. 29 (2).

167 Art. 44 (1).

168 The Constitution of Japan Article 62.

169 Recent examples include Seven Eleven Japan's Abuse of Superior Bargaining Position against its franchisees and Google's provisions of its search engine and search-advertising platform to Google's competitor, Yahoo Japan.

170 *See Antitrust Enforcement in Japan*, *supra* note 4, at 176–8.

JFTC may have less discretion to avoid imposing penalties for anticompetitive behavior, which may lead to more appeals to the courts to review its decisions.

Professional norms, as articulated in a wider competition law community, can also foster accountability. Although there are many academic commentators on the Antimonopoly Act and JFTC enforcement (mostly legal academics rather than economists), commentary from the bar and professional legal organizations has generally been weaker. Recently, however, lawyers have formed the Japan Competition Law Forum (JCLF), which now has about 200 lawyers as members (along with academics as "associate members").[171] Those involved in the JCLF are taking an active role in commenting on JFTC enforcement and reforms of its procedures, although this commentary has generally been from the point of view of lawyers representing potential targets of JFTC enforcement.

5. *Commitment to the rule of law*

We take the "rule of law" as requiring that decisions be made by applying previously stated rules and principles and not by whim or personal interest. Attributes of the rule of law include reasonable certainty of the governed as to what the law is, rights of review by an independent judiciary, and effective enforcement of the law.[172]

In many ways Japan measures up well on commitment to the rule of law. Formal actions are subject to judicial review; the JFTC publishes numerous guidelines to explain how it views the law and how it will exercise its discretion (although guidelines are often vague with regard to their application in specific settings, thereby leaving the JFTC with some discretion); and provides extensive formal and informal *ex ante* consultations with parties undertaking important commercial transactions. Nevertheless, because of the high number of unreported informal consultations, it is difficult to draw conclusions about how the JFTC makes many of its discretionary decisions.

Another important aspect of the rule of law is that changes in enforcement direction have often been made through amendments to the Antimonopoly Act rather than through bureaucratic redirection of enforcement policy. The Act has gone through substantial changes over time, but the changes since the mid-1990s have been particularly important, with the Diet reducing exemptions, increasing penalties, and altering JFTC internal processes.

Nevertheless, there has often been substantial concern that the JFTC has broad discretion in its internal decision-making, and particularly with regard to its investigative efforts, and that this discretion is not always exercised on a consistent basis. There has also been concern that the JFTC—like competition authorities

[171] E-mail to Tadashi Shiraishi from Kimitoshi Yabuki, secretary general of the Japan Competition Law Forum, March 28, 2011.

[172] *See*, e.g., Lon L. Fuller, *The Morality of Law* (rev. edn 1969); Joseph Raz, *The Rule of Law and its Virtue, in The Authority of Law: Essays of Law and Morality* 210 (1979).

elsewhere—may be subject to political pressure with regard to case selection.[173] Over the past two decades antitrust enforcement in Japan has had a relatively high level of political salience, having been tied first to the problems of barriers to import trade and subsequently to the problems of Japan's stagnant economy. As in other countries, competition law enforcement cannot be divorced from political values and support, but this can create a tension between political goals and specific enforcement policies and decisions.

C. Assessing the system

Japan's antitrust enforcement system is mostly an administrative one, under the control of the JFTC. There is some small amount of criminal enforcement, initiated by the JFTC and litigated by the PPO, and there is a modest amount of private litigation. As a general matter, however, it is the JFTC that articulates and enforces antitrust law in Japan. In this effort it has received some support from the Diet, which has made significant changes in the AMA, beginning with amendments in 1977, widening the coverage of the Act and increasing the Commission's powers.

Taking a broad view of the ten identified process areas, we see that over the past decade the Commission has taken many steps to provide greater substantive and procedural transparency, to increase awareness of competition law principles in Japan, and to reduce the potential for discriminatory treatment of non-Japanese firms involved in international licensing arrangements. It has also implemented a substantial leniency program, pursuant to a 2005 amendment to the AMA, receiving more than 300 leniency filings since the program began,[174] leading to a continuing increase in the amount of surcharges the Commission has imposed.

Our review also underscores some continuing issues in terms of the JFTC's processes. Most importantly, the Commission's adjudication processes have been under construction for the past five years, after the change in 2005 to a post-order hearing process under which the Commission now first enters an enforceable order and then holds a hearing on whether there is proof of a violation. The 2010 Bill focuses on placing the adjudicative step (the hearing on whether there is a violation) in the courts, thereby making a clearer separation between investigative/prosecutorial functions and adjudicative functions. The 2010 Bill also seeks to improve the due process of the pre-order hearing by requiring the JFTC to appoint a neutral hearing officer and to disclose some types of evidence to the addressee. Whether these legislative changes will actually improve due process in a substantial sense will

[173] For an example of JFTC decision-making affected by political corruption, *see* "Antitrust Enforcement in Japan," *supra* note 4, at 174–5, discussing the case of a bribe to the Minister of Construction to influence the JFTC not to refer a criminal bid-rigging case. The Minister was subsequently convicted for taking the bribe and successfully pressuring the Chairman of the JFTC. *See* Keizo Nabeshima, "Court Sends LDP A Message," Japan Times, January 26, 2003, <http://search.japantimes.co.jp/cgi-bin/eo20030128kn.html>.

[174] *See* statements of the Secretary General of the JFTC on January 6 2010, <http://www.jftc.go.jp/teirei/h22/kaikenkiroku100106.html#k100106_1>.

depend on the quality of the new pre-order hearing and the capability of the three-judge court that reviews the JFTC's decision. Nevertheless, the 2010 Bill is a good example of how due process norms are driving a major change in Japan's antitrust enforcement.

Developments in the JFTC's enforcement efforts might also raise renewed questions about non-discriminatory treatment of foreign firms. The JFTC is now engaged in an effort to increase its ability to handle international cases more efficiently, and there are several recent examples of the JFTC taking a proactive approach in enforcing the AMA against foreign companies in international cartels and merger cases.[175] In addition, in 2010 the JFTC established a permanent staff of investigators specialized in international cartels. The JFTC has also emphasized a desire to move Japan's competition law policies toward global standards, including increased cooperation with foreign competition authorities.[176] In the past, Japanese firms that have been members of international cartels have not been prosecuted by the JFTC even though the cartel likely affected markets in Japan.[177] If the Commission's new interest in international cartels is to meet non-discriminatory standards, future investigations will need to involve more cartels that include Japanese participants.

V. Evaluation and potential reforms

A. Process issues

1. Investigations

The 2010 Bill of the AMA made clear that due process in investigation is the next procedural issue for the Diet to consider.[178] Two areas are most prominently mentioned.

First are reforms of the JFTC's witness examination methods. The JFTC's investigation of a possible violation of the AMA frequently involves interrogations of individuals who allegedly engage in such violations. Either in administrative or criminal investigations, those individuals do not have the right to have their

[175] For an English language source, *see* Kawai Hirano Fujii Japan Chapter pp. 240–1. In *Marine Hose*, the JFTC, for the first time in its history, issued a cease-and-desist order to foreign companies located outside Japan in an international cartel case. In *Cathode Ray Tubes for Televisions*, the JFTC went further and ordered both a cease-and-desist order and an administrative surcharge order to foreign companies located outside Japan. In *BHPB-Rio Joint Venture*, the JFTC actively reviewed the merger plan between the parties and made a notice of problems to the parties telling that the proposed joint venture might be substantially to restrain competition in the field of the production and sale of certain types of iron ore in the worldwide seaborne market.

[176] *See* statements of the Secretary General of the JFTC at a news conference on 14 January 2009, <www.jftc.go.jp/teirei/h21/kaikenkiroku090114.html#k090114_1>.

[177] Of the eighty firms that the US has fined more than $10 million for antitrust violations, twenty-one were Japanese. *See* <http://www.justice.gov/atr/public/criminal/sherman10.xls>. None have been prosecuted in Japan. However, the cases brought against the Marine Hose and Cathode Ray Tubes cartels in 2008 and 2009, *see supra* note 175, did include Japanese firms as well as foreign companies.

[178] Art.16 of the Annex of 2010 Bill.

attorneys present during the interrogation. In the course of the interrogation, the JFTC's investigators draft and complete a written statement of what the individual disclosed, done in a narrative style. These written statements often become crucial evidence in the JFTC's quasi-judicial hearing or in a court hearing. Although the investigators require the individual to confirm the content of the drafted statement before finalizing it, many of those who sign such statements believe that the statements are strongly biased by the purpose and subjective view of the investigators whose mission is proving the violations.

Several proposals are currently being discussed to alter this system. Those proposals are: allowing the defense attorney to be present during the interrogations; recording the interrogation sessions; and changing the style of the written statements from a narrative format to a question-and-answer format.[179]

A second issue is the attorney-client privilege. Because the attorney-client privilege is not recognized in Japan, communications between the alleged violator and his or her attorney can be seized in investigations under warrants or are required to be submitted in the JFTC's administrative investigations under threat of criminal sanctions.[180] This can hamper joint defense efforts between Japanese defense attorneys and defense attorneys in other countries where the attorney-client privilege is recognized.[181] The business community has also argued that the lack of an attorney-client privilege may have a chilling effect on a company's internal investigations to detect or prevent violations of the AMA.[182]

On both issues, the investigative method of interrogations and the lack of attorney-client privilege, practice in Japan deviates (at least to some extent) from the practices of antitrust enforcement agencies in the United States and the European Union. Whether Japan can (or should) alter its procedures, however, is not perfectly clear. Both issues have deep roots in Japan's administrative enforcement system, including tax and financial investigations, as well as in Japan's criminal justice system. Changing the system regarding investigative methods and the attorney-client privilege in the ways that critics suggest will require discussions beyond the antitrust community.

2. *Transparency*

The JFTC has been putting more effort into publicizing its reasoning in a detailed manner so as to increase overall transparency.[183] Nevertheless, a substantial amount of the JFTC's work is done through informal consultations that are not published.

The JFTC is doing less well when it comes to transparency to the party subject to the investigation. Current practice is frequently criticized for insufficient disclosure

[179] *See*, e.g., Roundtable Discussion, 39 (comment by Toshiaki Tada).

[180] *See* Kawai Hirano Fujii Japan Chapter, 246.

[181] *See* Roundtable Discussion, 50 (comment by Toshiaki Tada).

[182] *See* Nippon Keidanren, "Proposal for Comprehensive Amendments to the Antimonopoly Act—To Establish International Parity in the Investigation and Appeals Process." (November 20, 2007), <http://www.keidanren.or.jp/english/policy/2007/091.html>.

[183] For the efforts on merger review, *see supra* notes 155–156 and accompanying text.

of evidence and reasoning on the part of the JFTC in the course of issuing administrative orders.

B. Institutional issues

1. Expertise

Most of the JFTC's staff consists of career employees who are expected to acquire their expertise in competition law and policy over the course of their career (which could include postings to other agencies). Except in very rare cases, they are not professionally trained either in law or economics. Hiring outside lawyers and economists would strengthen the JFTC's expertise, but would directly conflict with its normal personnel practices.

There is also a question of the qualifications and roles of JFTC Commissioners. The traditional tendency of appointing career bureaucrats of the Ministry of Finance as JFTC Chairmen has often been criticized as weakening the JFTC's commitment to a system of marketplace competition. Current Commissioners do have broader expertise in areas relevant to the Commission, but their role in making actual enforcement decisions is unclear. Changing the culture of appointment and role, of course, presents difficult challenges.

If the 2010 Bill is adopted, abolishing the post-order quasi-judicial JFTC hearing system and allowing those challenges to occur in court, the expertise on the part of judges who handle such becomes more important. The 2010 Amendment provides that the Tokyo District Court will have exclusive jurisdiction as the first instance to review the JFTC's order, but this will still require the courts system to increase the expertise of the judges who are assigned to such cases.

2. Use of resources

The JFTC makes an extremely large number of informal decisions. For example, it engages in extensive informal consultations (3,000 in FY 2009) and handles a very large number of complaints of violations of the AMA (more than 11,000 in FY 2009). In addition it has embarked on a vigorous program of enforcing various types of Unfair Trade Practices to protect small and medium sized business enterprises, including selling goods at "unfair" low prices (more than 3,000 cases in FY 2009) and using superior bargaining power to obtain discounts.

Nevertheless, if an antitrust enforcement agency allocates so much of its resources to this type of effort, it should at least pay some attention to the possibility that its efforts could prove anticompetitive and actually harm consumers.

VI. Conclusion

Japan's antitrust enforcement system has changed substantially since the original AMA was passed in 1947. Grafting a US-style FTC on to Japan's bureaucratic regulatory system has been more challenging than was likely thought at the time, although, even then, there were concerns about whether the JFTC could be an independent agency able to carry out a mission of opening Japan's markets to competition. The JFTC's recent history shows an agency attuned to the goals and processes of a modern competition authority, but sometimes struggling to be transparent in its decision-making and more frequently dealing with cases through consultations and guidance than through bringing direct enforcement actions. Better processes would likely bring a greater sense of fairness to JFTC decision-making. It might also increase the quality of that decision-making if it led the Commission to be more articulate in its decisions and goals.

7

South Africa
The Competition Law System and the Country's Norms

Dennis Davis and Lara Granville

South Africa's current competition regime is just over a decade old. It is based on the Competition Act, 1998, and is enforced by reasonably well-resourced and independent institutions. It has, since its inception, engaged robustly in both its merger review and law enforcement activities, with anti-cartel enforcement having moved to the top of the agenda over the last few years. South Africa has developed a strong competition culture, to the point of embracing it as a social movement.[1] The fight against exploitation by firms is seen by South Africans as an extension of the fight against poverty and inequality. There is thus enormous popular support for the competition authorities and the work performed by them.[2]

I. History and structure

A. History of competition enforcement in South Africa

The South African economy was shaped by the discovery of gold and diamonds in the late 19th century. Industry grew around the extraction of natural resources, and policies for economic development protected investors in these operations. In order to reduce heavy reliance on mining to drive the economy, the government adopted a number of policies such as the granting of monopoly concessions to certain industries. State monopolies dominated, with state-owned firms producing steel, fertilizer, oil, chemicals, and arms. The state-owned firms supplying steel and electricity kept prices low to customers, while protected from competition by high import tariffs. Labor costs were low, due to racial discriminatory policies.

[1] David Lewis, "Global Competition: Law, Markets and Globalization," (August 18, 2010), <http://lawprofessors.typepad.com/antitrustprof_blog/2010/08/david-lewis-on-global-competition-law-markets-and-globalization.html>.

[2] *See*, e.g., Joseph Stiglitz, Cape Times 13 December 2011 in which he emphasized the importance of competition law to the new economic strategy for South Africa developed by a ministerial team of which Professor Stiglitz was a member.

These features combined to shield white businesses against local and international competition.[3]

Through the years, the private sector diversified, as mining-based conglomerates extended their operations, and the government continued to extend support for agriculture and manufacturing in an effort to reduce reliance on mining. Given the relatively small local market, South Africa already had a predisposition for concentrated industry. This was aggravated in the 1980s, when import substitution increased in response to economic sanctions against apartheid. High market concentration extended from heavy industry to consumer products. By the 1990s, investment conglomerates with roots in the mining houses, accounted for 84 percent of the capitalization of the stock exchange.

The South African economy was thus defined by autarky, protection, government direction, and high concentration. However, it was also uniquely coupled with strong property rights and well-developed market institutions. These diverse elements produced an economy that is difficult to characterize: on the one hand it is largely well-developed, with sophisticated financial, legal, communications, and transport infrastructure. On the other hand, millions live in poverty, the unemployment rate has been estimated around 30 percent, and there is a severe bipolar distribution of income.[4] Apartheid divided the population in order to maintain this inequality.

Prior to 1994, there had been competition law statutes and agencies, but they were ultimately ineffective. Under legislation that was effective from 1923 to 1944, the Board of Trade and Industries could offer advice about competition policy problems. A report of the Board led to the promulgation of the first general competition law, the Regulation of Monopolistic Conditions Act, 1955. The law was generally permissive—no practices were prohibited per se and it provided for an administrative process to examine practices and recommend action. The Board of Trade and Industry, charged with enforcing the Act, had no independent powers —the Minister of Trade and Industry decided what was to be investigated and what relief would be applied. The law could only apply prospectively and was in any event rarely invoked. Over the twenty years of its existence, the Minister ordered only eighteen investigations. Most resulted in negotiated settlements.

A commission of inquiry in 1975 criticized this system. It called for a new competition body with more resources, stronger penalties against violations of orders, and an extension of the law to cover mergers. The new legislation, enacted in 1979,[5] created the Competition Board, appointed by the Minister of Trade and Industry. But in most respects, the new law looked like the old one—it contained no explicit prohibitions, the standard against which all practices were to be measured was the undefined "public interest," and decisions and orders were still

[3] OECD, OECD Peer Review: Competition Law and Policy in South Africa, (May 2003) at 9, <http://www.oecd.org/dataoecd/52/13/2958714.pdf>.

[4] OECD, OECD Peer Review: Competition Law and Policy in South Africa, (May 2003) at 10, <http://www.oecd.org/dataoecd/52/13/2958714.pdf>.

[5] Maintenance and Promotion of Competition Act 96 of 1979.

up to the Minister. The Board's membership was closely tied to the state, with six of its members being nominated by other ministries, and all the members except the chair serving part-time. The most noteworthy achievement of this period was a regulation by the Minister in 1984 which declared some practices per se prohibited: resale price maintenance, horizontal collusion, and bid rigging.[6] Violation of this regulation was a crime, but there were no prosecutions (bar one negotiated plea).[7] Ultimately, the Board was inefficient and not independent, as illustrated by the fact that in the Act's twenty-five year existence there had not been a single successful prosecution of anticompetitive conduct.[8]

Mounting opposition to apartheid led to the country's democratic transition in the 1990s and a new democratic government, led by the African National Congress, in 1994.[9] This was achieved through a constitutional transformation process which gave high priority to the redressing of economic imbalances.[10] The government chose competition law as one of the tools to achieve this. The new system promised to use competition policy to correct the faults of the old system and to promote the policy goals of employment and empowerment.

Interestingly, few expected that the new government would choose to control the economy through competition enforcement. In fact, the ANC had traditionally been left-of-centre and entered government in an alliance with the Communist Party and the powerful trade union movement. Its policy documents identified the leading role of the state in generating growth and overcoming poverty. Many expected a nationalization program to be the preferred means of regulating the economy.[11]

However, the ANC also had a long-held antipathy to monopolies,[12] rooted in the fact that such business was inevitably all-white owned and managed and seen as direct beneficiaries of apartheid. The ANC recognized that private concentrations of economic power did not signify effective democratic governance. It decided that competition law was the best means to ease entry into the private economy.[13]

6 Government Gazette GN 801 2 May 1986.

7 OECD, OECD Peer Review: Competition Law and Policy in South Africa, (May 2003) at 12, <http://www.oecd.org/dataoecd/52/13/2958714.pdf>.

8 Background document prepared for the OECD Global Forum on Competition, Challenges/Obstacles Faced by Competition Authorities in Achieving Greater Economic Development through the Promotion of Competition, (February 2004), <http://www.comptrib.co.za/Publications/Speeches/oecd_20oct.pdf>.

9 OECD, OECD Peer Review: Competition Law and Policy in South Africa, (May 2003) at 11, <http://www.oecd.org/dataoecd/52/13/2958714.pdf>.

10 OECD, OECD Peer Review: Competition Law and Policy in South Africa, (May 2003) at 4, <http://www.oecd.org/dataoecd/52/13/2958714.pdf>.

11 David Lewis, "Global Competition: Law, Markets and Globalization," (August 18, 2010), <http://lawprofessors.typepad.com/antitrustprof_blog/2010/08/david-lewis-on-global-competition-law-markets-and-globalization.html>.

12 Ibid.

13 Background document prepared for the OECD Global Forum on Competition, Challenges/Obstacles Faced by Competition Authorities in Achieving Greater Economic Development through

David Lewis (former chairperson of South Africa's Competition Tribunal) has noted that the ANC's choice was ironic—"an ideological standpoint that may, in different circumstances, have sought to replace the market with the state, saw the introduction, in the form of antitrust, of a robust defense of the market as the chosen instrument to discipline the powerful concentrations of private power that had been the product of apartheid."[14]

Lewis points out that these justifications may have given rise to a populist and punitive form of antitrust. And indeed the business sector was suspicious of the new government's intentions in introducing a robust competition law regime. However, the consensus that ended apartheid (through the negotiation of all major pieces of economic and social legislation) formally included participation by business in the process. The transition to democracy was facilitated through the introduction of a parliamentary democracy in which major social interests, including business, were given a voice, and a constitution which extended powerful protections to minorities. This ensured a more orthodox form of antitrust, although one in which the government was careful to insert broader social goals.[15]

An ambitious competition policy reform was part of the ANC's 1992 Policy Guidelines for a Democratic South Africa. The ANC's commitment to the rule of law was visible in these policy goals. The Guidelines noted that the proposed competition policy would embrace the principle of transparency and was to "assume that the resolution of competition law cases [would] be conducted in a procedurally fair manner, and that the new institutional arrangements for pursuing the policy [would] entail an appropriate division of labour within the relevant agency and independence."[16]

In 1995, the Department of Trade and Industry began a process of consultation to develop a competition framework. In 1997, it released its Proposed Guidelines for Competition Policy, which noted that dealing with the legacy of economic distortions in South Africa called for a unique approach. The promotion of competitiveness and efficiency would have to be married to the opening of the economy to those who had previously been denied access. This was followed by an extended consultation process which culminated in the promulgation of the Competition Act, 89 of 1997, which became effective on September 1, 1999.

the Promotion of Competition, (February 2004), <http://www.comptrib.co.za/Publications/Speeches/oecd_20oct.pdf>.

[14] David Lewis, "Global Competition: Law, Markets and Globalization," (August 18, 2010), <http://lawprofessors.typepad.com/antitrustprof_blog/2010/08/david-lewis-on-global-competition-law-markets-and-globalization.html>.

[15] Background document prepared for the OECD Global Forum on Competition, Challenges/Obstacles Faced by Competition Authorities in Achieving Greater Economic Development through the Promotion of Competition, (February 2004), <http://www.comptrib.co.za/Publications/Speeches/oecd_20oct.pdf>.

[16] OECD, OECD Peer Review: Competition Law and Policy in South Africa, (May 2003) at 14, <http://www.oecd.org/dataoecd/52/13/2958714.pdf>.

B. Influence of global forces

The influence of global forces in shaping this law cannot be denied. The Act and institutional structure draw heavily from developed-country practice. In respect of substantive law, the European Union has had the greatest influence, given its focus on preventing the frustration of access and entry into markets and its understanding that harm to competition should include harm to the competitive process. This is a relevant consideration for South Africa, given both its object to include the marginalized majority in the economic life of the country, and to manage the power of large, previously state-owned monopolies. As such, recourse to the EU became inevitable.[17] Moreover, the recognition of South Africa's place in a globalized world encourages the use of "international standards." This perspective is advanced primarily by business, which is concerned to create an attractive investment environment.

But at the same time, there has also been a conscious response to unique South African issues such as employment and black economic empowerment. In many ways, South Africa's approach to developing an appropriate regime for the country has been influential on the rest of the world. South Africa's approach in this regard is seen as a model for new competition jurisdictions.[18] Moreover, South Africa is a very active participant in global initiatives such as the ICN. In this regard, it has tried to highlight the concerns of developing countries that are embarking on new competition regimes. Lewis notes that from the first days of the ICN a number of young agencies from the developing world and the emerging market economies demanded a very active role in its work, thereby winning the respect and regard of counterpart agencies in the developed world.[19]

The outcome of this approach is robust antitrust, with a South African flavor.[20]

C. Structure of competition law institutions

The South African competition order comprises a statute—the Competition Act, and three institutions: the Competition Commission, the Competition Tribunal, and the Competition Appeal Court.

[17] Dennis Davis, "Reflecting on the Effectiveness of the Competition Authority: Prioritisation, Market Enquiries and Impact" (Speech, <www.comptrib.co.za>).

[18] *See* for instance Fox, who notes that a model on which to base a new competition law could include a "basket of laws, which would prominently include South African case law, which is the most developed body of developing country competition case law and which reflects the jurists' struggle to integrate feasible enforcement in view of scarce resources and well-endowed adversaries with the need to formulate and apply sound principles that promote competition." Eleanor Fox, "In search of a Competition Law Fit for Developing Countries," Law & Economics Research Paper Series, Working Paper no 11–04, <http://ssrn.com/abstract=1761619>.

[19] David Lewis, Introductory Address to ICN Conference—June 2009, <www.comptrib.co.za>.

[20] David Lewis, "Global Competition: Law, Markets and Globalization," (August 18, 2010) <http://lawprofessors.typepad.com/antitrustprof_blog/2010/08/david-lewis-on-global-competition-law-markets-and-globalization.html>.

The Commission is the investigative and prosecutorial authority. It is an executive administration with power vested principally in the Commissioner as its chief executive officer.

The Tribunal is an administrative tribunal composed of lay members drawn from a range of disciplines pertinent to competition law (economists, lawyers, and accountants, but not judges). It is considered a tribunal of record, although not a formal court.

The Competition Appeal Court is a special division of the High Court, which hears appeals from the decisions of the Tribunal. Only sitting judges can be appointed to the court.

The South African model is therefore a bifurcated model—a specialized competition investigation and enforcement authority brings enforcement proceedings before a specialized competition tribunal for adjudication. However, there are also elements of a bifurcated judicial model, since appeals from the Tribunal are heard by a division of the High Court, part of the general court structure. In addition, there are further appeals available to the Supreme Court of Appeal, and potentially the Constitutional Court, both part of the normal judicial hierarchy.[21]

II. Mandate of the competition authorities

A. Roles of the Commission and Tribunal

The Commission investigates complaints regarding alleged anticompetitive conduct. It can refer these complaints to the Tribunal for decision. It decides to approve or prohibit "intermediate mergers" (those mergers above the threshold that require notification, but below the threshold that deems the transaction "large") and it recommends action on large mergers. It is responsible for negotiating settlements with respondents to complaint proceedings; issuing advisory opinions; and granting exemptions from the Act. The Commission is also tasked with implementing measures to increase market transparency and develop public awareness of the provisions of the Act. Over time, it must review legislation and public regulations, and report to the relevant government ministry concerning any provision that permits uncompetitive behavior.[22]

Since 2004 (and updated in 2008), the Commission has adopted a policy in relation to the prosecution of cartels, known as the Corporate Leniency Policy (CLP). In terms of the CLP, a cartel member which comes forward and provides information to implicate its fellow cartelist will be entitled to leniency from the Commission—immunity from prosecution by the Commission. The Commission

[21] The Competition Act envisaged that the Court would, save for constitutional challenges to the Constitutional Court, be the highest court for competition matters. Unfortunately, the drafters failed to take account of section 168 (3) of the Constitution which makes the Supreme Court of Appeal the highest court *except* in constitutional matters. This position is the subject of present reconsideration.

[22] M Neuhoff et al., *A Practical Guide to the South African Competition Act*, at 19.

is responsible for engaging with leniency applicants, and granting conditional and final leniency, provided the applicant meets certain requirements.[23]

The Tribunal is in effect the court of first instance in all competition matters. It adjudicates on, and provides remedies in respect of, complaints against prohibited practices, and assesses and adjudicates large mergers referred to it by the Commission. On some occasions, it acts as an appeal body—in respect of issues over which the Commission has decision-making authority, such as the approval of intermediate mergers, and the granting of exemptions from the Act.[24] The Tribunal enjoys considerable powers of remedy, including prohibition of mergers, the imposition of injunctive relief, the levying of administrative penalties, and the ordering of divestiture.

Marketing practices and consumer protection issues are not included in the Competition Act nor in the responsibilities of the Commission or Tribunal. Complaints of unfair competition are matters for private dispute resolution under common law rules.[25] New legislation deals with consumer protection issues and grants separate administrative bodies authority over these issues[26] (although there are—as yet untested—areas of overlap between this new legislation and competition law, such as "unfair pricing" and "discriminatory pricing").[27] There is also no jurisdiction over adjacent policies such as intellectual property, or foreign direct investment issues. The Commission's involvement in these flanking issues is restricted to instances in which such policies raise competition law concerns, and the Commission will make submissions as part of the public comment procedure.

B. Objects enumerated in the Act

In keeping with the political objectives of the government when competition law was placed on the agenda the South African Competition Act has an extensive (and ambitious) list of goals. It calls on the authorities to balance both traditional competition concerns with public interest objectives. The Act embraces the goals of creating a free market and effective competition, but also incorporates uniquely South African elements, including addressing its exclusionary past by promoting participation of all citizens in the economy and promoting the fair distribution of ownership and control of the markets amongst different racial groups. The preamble to the Act promotes the pursuit of "an efficient, competitive economic

[23] The Commission's authority to grant leniency was challenged in the case of *Agri Wire (Pty) Ltd and Agri Wire Upington (Pty) Ltd v The Competition Commission and 12 Others (Case no: 7585/2010)*, on the basis that there was no provision in the Act enabling the granting of leniency. The High Court found that the Commission has authority to recommend to the Tribunal that no penalty be imposed on a respondent, but the immunity applicant is still a respondent to the referral proceedings and the Tribunal has discretion to impose a penalty or not.

[24] Ibid. 20.

[25] OECD, OECD Peer Review: Competition Law and Policy in South Africa (May 2003) at 16, <http://www.oecd.org/dataoecd/52/13/2958714.pdf>.

[26] Consumer Protection Act, 1998.

[27] Ibid. Sections 48(1)(a)(i) and 8(e).

environment, balancing the interests of workers, owners and consumers and focused on development."[28] Consistent with a rhetoric focused on equity, the preamble describes restrictions on competition as "unjust" rather than inefficient.[29]

The purposes of the Act, as further elaborated upon in the preamble and Section 2 of the Act are:

- To provide for markets in which consumers have access to, and can freely select, the quality and variety of goods and services they desire;
- To restrain particular trade practices which undermine a competitive economy;
- To establish independent institutions to monitor economic competition;
- To give effect to international law obligations of the Republic;
- To promote the efficiency, adaptability, and development of the economy;
- To expand opportunities for South African participation in world markets and recognize the role of foreign competition in the Republic;
- To ensure that all South Africans, including small and medium size enterprises, have an equitable opportunity to participate in the economy;
- To increase the ownership stakes of historically disadvantaged persons; and
- To promote employment and advance the social and economic welfare of South Africans.

The legislature has thus avoided assigning priorities and produced a law which seeks to achieve, and if possible, reconcile both greater competition and the promotion of public interest objectives. It has resisted a presumption that economic efficiency and the public interest will be in conflict.

Despite the prominence of equity and political economy concerns, they tend not to be the principal drivers of the law's application.[30] The authorities have noted that other statutory and regulatory bodies are specifically tasked with addressing the various public interest objectives.[31] Indeed, the OECD notes that the inclusion of such public interest goals allows the authorities to make direct reference to these concerns in a transparent manner rather than disingenuously

[28] Competition Act, Preamble.

[29] OECD, OECD Peer Review: Competition Law and Policy in South Africa, (May 2003) at 18, <http://www.oecd.org/dataoecd/52/13/2958714.pdf>.

[30] *Schumann (South Africa) (Pty) Ltd and Price's Daelite (Pty) Ltd* 10/CAC/Aug01; Eleanor Fox, "Equality, discrimination in competition law: lessons from and for South Africa and Indonesia" 2000 Harvard Comparative Law Journal 585, quoted in Philip Sutherland and Katherine Kemp, Competition Law of South Africa, at 4–3; *Shell South Africa (Pty) Ltd/Tepeco Petroleum (Pty) Ltd* 66/LM/Oct01.

[31] A decision which appears to have been primarily influenced by the public interest considerations is *ISCOR Limted and Saldanha Steel (Pty) Ltd* 67/LM/Dec01, although there are a number of decisions which incorporate conditions in order to address public interest concerns. (*Gold Fields Ltd and Harmony Gold Mining Company Ltd/Competition Commission* 93/LM/Nov04). Most recently the Tribunal upheld a public interest argument concerning a merger which had retrenchment implications in *Momentum Group Ltd and another v Competition Commission and another*104/CAC/Nov10 which decision is now subject of an appeal to the Competition Appeal Court.

justify actions on competition grounds when they are really responding to other considerations.[32]

Public interest considerations do play a significant role in mergers and exemptions.[33] In respect of mergers, an anticompetitive merger is allowed to be justified on public interest grounds, or a pro-competitive merger can be prohibited on public interest grounds.[34] As a result, a number of different interest groups have an interest in the competition law process. For instance trade unions have a formal role in the merger review process in that merger filing must be served on the unions, and they are entitled to make submissions regarding the proposed transaction and participate in the merger hearing.[35]

The Commission and Tribunal have increasingly taken their mandate to protect or consider employment considerations seriously, and often require merging parties to agree to conditions which alleviate some negative effects of certain mergers. The authorities have generally imposed short-term conditions in order to address the effects of mergers on employment, such as requiring merging parties to pay severance benefits calculated in accordance with the labor legislation, or placing a moratorium on retrenchments for a specified time period after the proposed transaction is implemented, or limiting the total number of retrenchments.

Recently, job losses have become a more common feature of proposed mergers as a result of the recession, and the Commission and Tribunal have adopted a more proactive stance to crafting conditions.[36] For example, the Commission has obliged merging parties to investigate and inform retrenched employees about alternative employment prospects and to identify opportunities for them to obtain career counseling and training, and to establish a skills fund which is available to all employees who are retrenched as a result of the merger for at least a year.[37]

The most expansive consideration of public interest issue has arisen in the recent Wal-mart/Massmart merger, which considered the effect of diminished local procurement on employment. As noted later in this chapter, trade unions and the government intervened in this large merger to request the imposition of conditions which protect employment and levels of local procurement. The intervening trade unions and government ministries were dissatisfied with the conditions imposed by the Tribunal to mitigate the potential public interest consequences of the merger, and thus took the matter on appeal and review to

[32] OECD, OECD Peer Review: Competition Law and Policy in South Africa (May 2003) at 18, <http://www.oecd.org/dataoecd/52/13/2958714.pdf>.

[33] In respect of exemptions, in terms of section 10 of the Act, the Commission is allowed to exempt prohibited agreements and practices which contribute towards the ability of small businesses or firms controlled by historically disadvantaged persons to become competitive.

[34] Section 12A(1)(a)(ii). Some mergers are permitted only after the parties accept conditions relating to employment, even where the transactions raise no competition concerns. *Telkom SA Ltd/ TPI Investments/Praysa* 81/LM/Aug00.

[35] Section 12A(3).

[36] *See* Heather Irvine, "Employment Concerns Delay Merger Clearance," <http://www.polity.org.za/article/employment-concerns-delay-merger-clearances-2010-02-01>.

[37] Heather Irvine, "Employment Concerns Delay Merger Clearance," <http://www.polity.org.za/article/employment-concerns-delay-merger-clearances-2010-02-01>. *See* also the *Momentum/Metropolitan* merger, footnote 29.

the CAC (Competition Appeal Court).[38] The Ministers sought an order referring the dispute to the Tribunal for rehearing primarily on the basis of allegations of unfairness of the initial hearing. The unions sought to prevent the approval of the merger, but in an alternative argument, it argued for the imposition of further conditions relating to the protection of small and medium sized businesses which were likely to be affected by the merger. The CAC approved the merger subject to the initial conditions which were designed to protect employees of the merged entity. It dealt with concerns raised about small business by way of a novel order which required the merged entity to commission a study to determine the most appropriate means by which local South African suppliers may be empowered to respond to the challenges posed by the merger. In particular, the study is to canvass the best means by which South African small and medium sized suppliers can participate in Wal-Mart's global value chain training programs that might be established to train local South African suppliers on how to conduct business with the merged entity. In addition, the CAC ordered the reinstatement of 503 retrenched employees, on the basis that the retrenchments were so closely linked to the merger and its timetable that they must have been merger-related (although the Tribunal had found they were not merger-related retrenchments). The CAC endorsed the Tribunal's order that there should be no retrenchments resulting from the merger for two years after the transaction and that the existing labor agreements and collective bargaining positions should be respected.

The ministries' role in the Wal-Mart matter has been criticized for using the competition process as a means to leverage concessions out of international investors. David Lewis commented that "such intervention made for bad law, bad competition law and bad industrial policy....There was no clarity, no transparency and a lack of urgency."[39] On the other hand, the government may be one of the few powerful litigants that demand the competition authorities properly consider the non-employment-related public interest issues. The Competition Commission had initially recommended the merger without any conditions which decision appeared to prompt the ministerial intervention.

C. Amendments to the Competition Act

Amendments to the Act will enhance the powers of the competition authorities particularly with respect to cartel activity. The amendments[40] have been signed into law, but have not yet come into effect.

[38] *The Minister of Economic Development and Others v The Competition Tribunal, The Competition Commission, Wal-Mart Stores Inc., Massmart Holdings Ltd and Others* (110/CAC/Jul11).

[39] "Broadside for Patel's 'competition meddling,'" Business Day 2012/04/05, <http://m.businessday.co.za/article.aspx?id=842767>.

[40] The Competition Amendment Act, 1 of 2009. It has now been three years since the law was signed but not promulgated, and there is no indication that the law will come into effect any time soon. This may be the result of the government considering the criticisms of the legislation's criminal provisions. However, the delay also affects all the other amendments to the Act described below.

The most significant aspect of the Amendment Act is the introduction of criminal liability for individual directors and managers who are personally responsible for—or who knowingly acquiesce in—collusive conduct. Although the criminal prosecutions will be pursued by the national prosecuting authority, the amendment does expand the scope of the Commission's powers, since the Amendment Act suggests that a finding by the Tribunal of collusive conduct by a firm will constitute "prima facie" evidence of the individual director or manager's contravention of competition law.[41]

The Amendment Act also enables the Commission to prosecute "conscious parallel" or coordinated conduct by competitors in highly concentrated markets ("complex monopoly conduct"). The Commission already has the power in terms of the Act to address written or oral agreements and "concerted practices" between competitors, as well as abuses of dominance. If the Commission has reason to believe that complex monopoly conduct exists, then it may investigate this conduct—without having received a complaint from parties like customers or competitors. Such conscious parallelism is not a violation alone. The Commission must first establish that at least one of the firms in the relevant market has at least 20 percent of the market and has engaged complex monopoly conduct, and this has resulted in conditions like high barriers to entry, exclusion of other firms, excessive pricing, or a refusal to supply other firms. Then the Commission may apply to the Tribunal for an order "reasonably requiring, prohibiting or setting conditions upon any particular conduct by the firm, to the extent justifiable to mitigate or ameliorate the effect of the complex monopoly conduct on the market." Contravening such an order is a prohibited practice.

The Commission is also given power under the amendments to conduct market inquiries. If the Commission "has reason to believe that any feature or combination of features of a market for any goods or services prevents, distorts or restricts competition within that market" it will be entitled to conduct "a formal study of the general state of competition in a market for particular goods or services, without exclusive reference to the conduct or activities of any particular named firm" at any time.

The Commission does not have to wait to receive complaints from customers or competitors—it can publish a notice in the government gazette announcing the commencement of a market inquiry, and invite members of the public to provide information. Such an inquiry may also be initiated in response to a request by the Minister.

These new provisions appear to extend the competition authorities' powers to conduct *ex ante* regulation to some extent. The new market study powers will enable the Commission to study the industry as a whole, and make recommendations to the Minister regarding legislative or regulatory changes needed to bolster competition. The complex monopoly provisions enable the Competition Commission, if it concludes that firms are engaged in complex monopoly conduct, to apply to the Tribunal for an order "reasonably requiring, prohibiting or setting conditions

[41] This provision is expected to be constitutionally challenged when it comes into force.

upon any particular conduct by the firm, to the extent justifiable to mitigate or ameliorate the effect of the complex monopoly conduct on the market."

These new provisions involve the competition authorities either setting conditions for proposed behavior in a market, or making recommendations on policy or legislation. Such *ex ante* roles tend to be assigned to sector specific regulators. And indeed, the Amendment Act also addresses issues of concurrent jurisdiction between the competition authorities and sector specific regulators and suggests that such regulators should have "primary authority" over *ex ante* regulatory roles.[42]

D. Competition authorities' jurisdiction in regulated industries

The Competition authorities have now been given jurisdiction to deal with "competition matters" in industries regulated by other regulators. The authorities' mandate in this regard has changed due to amendments to the Act over the years.

At first the Act applied to "all economic activity within, or having an effect within the Republic, except acts subject to or authorised by public regulation." This section was the subject of a decision[43] in which the Supreme Court of Appeal held that a literal reading of this section excluded any conduct to be regulated by other legislation.[44] The application of this precedent to other regulated industries such as the electronic communications sector would clearly have meant that the sector-specific legislation would exclude the application of the Competition Act in the sector, and as a result, the other regulator would enjoy exclusive jurisdiction to regulate even competition matters in the sector.[45] This was apparently an unintended outcome of the wording of the Act, and therefore the judgment prompted Parliament to amend section 3 of the Act to make it clear that the Act was intended to apply to sectors of the economy regulated by other legislation.[46] The Second

[42] H Irvine and L Granville, "Who to Call? Concurrent Competition Jurisdiction in the South African Electronic Communications Sector," Paper prepared for the Third Annual Competition Commission, Competition Tribunal and Mandela Institute Conference on Competition Law, Economics and Policy in South Africa and Celebration of 10 Years of the Competition Act and Competition Authorities.

[43] *Standard Bank Investment Corporation and The Competition Commission* (2000) 2 SA 797 (SCA).

[44] Schutz JA noted: "In the case before us there is no doubt that the proposed bank merger is an 'economic activity.' The question is whether it will be an 'act' (Afrikaans 'handeling') 'subject to or authorised by public regulation.' Read in the context of the Act the 'acts' envisaged form part of a confined class. That is so because the subject matter of the Act is what may broadly be described as actually or potentially monopolistic or anticompetitive agreements, practices or acts, which are grouped under the headings restrictive horizontal practices, restrictive vertical practices, abuse of dominant position and mergers. Entering into an agreement or abusing dominance may in themselves be 'acts' or 'handelinge.' Because of the frequency with which I will have to refer to the confined construction that I have placed on the word 'act,' and its importance, I shall refer to the word so construed as a 'monopolistic act.'"

[45] Willington Ngwepe, "Serving two masters: concurrent jurisdiction between the Competition Commission and the Independent Communications Authority of South Africa" (2003) 120 SALJ 243.

[46] Save for mergers in terms of the Banks Act, which were specifically carved out by provisions which allowed the Minister of Finance to remove bank mergers from scrutiny by the competition authorities Section 18(2) and (3) provide that:

> (2) Despite anything to the contrary in this Act, the Competition Commission may not make a decision in terms of section 13(5)(b) or 14(1)(b), and the Competition Tribunal may not make an order in terms of section 16(2), if the—

Amendment Act, 2000 stated that there should be concurrent jurisdiction between the competition authorities and sector-specific regulators, which concurrency must be managed with agreements between the regulators "to co-ordinate and harmonise the exercise of jurisdiction over competition matters within the relevant industry or sector, and to ensure the consistent application of the principles of the [Competition] Act."

Despite the clear intention to grant the competition authorities' concurrent jurisdiction in regulated sectors, the wording of the jurisdiction provision was ambiguous. This was thus the subject of a review application by the monopoly fixed line telecommunications operator in South Africa, Telkom. Telkom had been investigated by the Competition Commission for various abuses of a dominant position, and the Commission's findings were referred to the Tribunal. Telkom reviewed this conduct and argued that the telecommunications law required the issues to be dealt with by the sector specific regulator, the Independent Communications Authority of South Africa (ICASA), and that its telecommunications license permitted the conduct it engaged in.

Although the High Court found in favor of Telkom (on bases other than its jurisdiction argument) the decision was overturned by the Supreme Court of Appeal which definitively confirmed that the Competition authorities must be enabled to investigate anticompetitive practices in regulated industries.

Because of such ambiguity, the latest Amendment Act addresses issues of concurrent jurisdiction. The Amendment Act indicates that the Commission must continue to have concurrent jurisdiction with other sector specific regulators and that such concurrency is to be managed in terms of memoranda of understanding. In instances where the competition authorities and another regulator are *both* required to regulate competition, the Act attempts to clarify these roles by distinguishing between *ex ante* and *ex post* regulation. Whilst the sector specific regulator is tasked with exercising "primary authority to establish conditions within the industry that it regulates as required to give effect to the relevant legislation in terms of which that authority functions," the Commission will "exercise primary authority to detect and investigate alleged prohibited practices within any industry or sector, and to review mergers within any industry or sector, in terms of this Act."

The amendment will not entirely resolve the issue of concurrent jurisdiction and how it should be exercised because some legislation (such as the Electronic

(a) merger constitutes—
  (i) an acquisition of shares for which permission is required in terms of section 37 of the Banks Act, 1990 (Act No. 94 of 1990); or
  (ii) a transaction for which consent is required in terms of section 54 of the Banks Act, 1990 (Act No. 94 of 1990); and
(b) the Minister of Finance has, in the prescribed manner, issued a notice to the Commissioner specifying the names of the parties to the merger and certifying that—
  (i) the merger is a merger contemplated in paragraph (a)(i) or (ii); and
  (ii) it is in the public interest that the merger is subject to the jurisdiction of the Banks Act, 1990 (Act No. 94 of 1990) only.

(3) Sections 13(6) and 14(2) do not apply to a merger in respect of which the Minister of Finance has issued a certificate contemplated in subsection (2).

Communications Act) currently vests the sector-specific regulator with some capacity to regulate *ex post*,[47] while the Amendment Act itself seems to vest some *ex ante* regulatory power with the competition authorities. There is a further practical concern with handing over jurisdiction over competition matters to sector regulators: the competition authorities have better resources and experience compared to other sector regulators. For instance, in the case of ICASA, the electronic communications regulator, David Lewis has commented: "I am convinced that we are far better set up to deal with abusive conduct than is ICASA. We have the necessary investigatory powers, we have experience of abuse of dominance and an established jurisprudence. The Commission's investigatory powers, our inquisitorial powers, the adversarial nature or our proceedings, the extensive use of discovery and the transparency of our proceedings allows us to reduce the gravity of the problem suffered by all sector regulators, and certainly ICASA, namely the huge informational asymmetry between the regulated and the regulator. We also have an institutional structure—notably the strict separation of investigation from adjudication—that accords with some of our strict constitutional requirements of administrative fairness."[48]

The Commission still finds that government departments, in pursuit of their own objectives, do not take into account the competition law imperatives. David Lewis reflected that some "government policies and practices . . . demonstrate what, at best, is a tenuous regard for competition policy.... [T]he prevailing centrality of an interventionist industrial policy, the lack of concern for publicly erected entry barriers, a still powerful community of strong state-owned enterprises overseen by weak and captured regulators, all speak to an environment that has simultaneously managed to practice robust competition law in combination with a weak competition policy."[49]

However, it appears that sector regulators and other government agencies have become more aware of the competition law project than they were at first, and therefore more supportive of, and cooperative with, the Commission.[50]

[47] Section 67(1), (2), and (3) of the Electronic Communications Act 2005, in addition to its powers to regulate "ex ante" in Chapter 10. As ICASA noted in its submissions on the Bill, this *ex ante* regulatory competence granted to ICASA is consistent with the achievement of policy goals such as managed liberalization and the introduction of new and innovative services. However, its *ex post* regulatory competence concerns itself with the extent to which particular market conduct serves to subvert the promotion of effective competition, but in markets which are characterized by durable market failure, the structural disposition of such markets is usually the source of the market failure. As a result, ICASA was of the view that whilst exclusive *ex ante* regulatory jurisdiction ought to vest with ICASA, it was unnecessary for it to have *ex post* jurisdictional competence. As a result, ICASA proposed that sections 67(1), (2), and (3) of the ECA should be repealed. Unfortunately, the amendment does not do this.

[48] David Lewis, Speech for Neotel/Mail and Guardian Breakfast, 15 July 2009, <www.comptrib.co.za>.

[49] David Lewis, "Global Competition: Law, Markets and Globalization," (August 18, 2010), <http://lawprofessors.typepad.com/antitrustprof_blog/2010/08/david-lewis-on-global-competition-law-markets-and-globalization.html>.

[50] Telephone interview with Wendy Mkwanazi, Head of Legal Division, Competition Commission (December 8, 2010).

Maintaining consistent competition policy in regulated sectors will require reinforcing the relationship with sectoral regulators.[51] The initial MOUs (Memoranda of Understanding) concluded with other regulators tended to focus on strict procedural requirements of interaction. The Commission is in the process of updating its MOUs with sector regulators, particularly in light of the amendments to the Act which alter the manner in which concurrent jurisdiction is to be exercised. The new MOUs are apparently more flexible and attempt to encourage a spirit of cooperation, openness, and trust amongst the regulators.[52]

E. Carve-outs from the Act

Collective bargaining and collective agreements are specifically carved out from the application of the Act.[53] In addition, the Act's restrictions are balanced by exemptions that incorporate the policy considerations described above. The Commission is empowered to grant exemptions from a prohibited practice in the Act.[54] An exemption may be for a particular practice or agreement, or a category of practices or agreements. A firm may apply to the Commission to exempt it from a prohibited agreement or practice if that agreement or practice is required to attain one of the following objectives:[55]

- To maintain or promote exports;
- To promote the ability of small businesses, or firms controlled or owned by historically disadvantaged persons, to become competitive;
- To enable a change in productive capacity necessary to stop decline in the industry; or
- To enable the economic stability of any industries designated by the Minister, after consultation with the Minister responsible for that industry.

In theory, the Commission is not given a discretion to grant exemptions; if the conditions are met, then the exemption must be granted.[56] Designation of an industry for exemption to ensure "economic stability" was an intended avenue for ministerial input about matters of industrial policy. However, the designation itself does not confer an exemption: the Commission must still determine whether the restriction will achieve economic stability.[57]

[51] OECD, OECD Peer Review: Competition Law and Policy in South Africa, (May 2003), <http://www.oecd.org/dataoecd/52/13/2958714.pdf>.

[52] Telephone interview with Wendy Mkwanazi, Head of Legal Division, Competition Commission (December 8, 2010).

[53] Section 3 (a) and (b).

[54] OECD, OECD Peer Review: Competition Law and Policy in South Africa, (May 2003) at 22, <http://www.oecd.org/dataoecd/52/13/2958714.pdf>.

[55] Section 10(3)(b).

[56] Section 10(2)(a).

[57] OECD, OECD Peer Review: Competition Law and Policy in South Africa, (May 2003) at 22, <http://www.oecd.org/dataoecd/52/13/2958714.pdf>.

These exemptions illustrate the balancing act performed by the Act in its pursuit of the government's equity (and industrial policy) goals.

In addition, a professional association whose rules contain a restriction that has the effect of substantially preventing or lessening competition in a market may apply to the Commission for an exemption, if such a rule is reasonably required to maintain the professional standards or ordinary functions of the profession.[58]

While the Act does apply to the state itself in that government-owned entities are fully subject to it,[59] the Tribunal has refused jurisdiction over conduct by organs of state. In the case of *AECE/Department of Minerals and Energy (DME)*[60] the Tribunal drew a distinction between the wrongful exercise of market power, a matter over which the Tribunal has jurisdiction, and the wrongful exercise of public power, which falls within the purview of administrative law and over which it had no jurisdiction. The complaint related to the manner in which the DME had exercised its discretion as a regulator. AECE alleged that the DME's approval was required for it to sell its products to the industry and that such approval had been unfairly delayed. The Tribunal confirmed that it lacked the competence to instruct a state functionary exercising a public power to act in a particular manner or to desist from acting in a particular manner.

In *Dumpit Waste Removal (Pty) Ltd/the City of Johannesburg*, the applicants alleged that the City Council was excluding it from the market for the provision of waste delivery services. The Tribunal found that waste removal is a functional area regulated by statute and over which municipalities have the executive authority to make and administer bylaws. As such, the dispute fell outside of the ambit of the Competition Act and the Tribunal was accordingly an inappropriate forum to adjudicate them.

III. Procedural norms

A. Due process norms in case-by-case decision-making

South Africa has a well-developed legal culture, based on both Roman Dutch law brought by European settlers in the 17th century and on English law as part of the British Commonwealth. The Constitution, adopted during South Africa's transition to democracy in 1994, was designed to ensure that the state would be based on a legal, democratic foundation. Thus basing policy on law and implementing it

[58] Schedule 1, part A (1) and (2) of the Act. The General Council of the Bar of South Africa applied for an exemption on behalf of its constituent bar groups. The Commission exempted the bar groups' rules about recommended fees as a benchmark for adjudicating complaints about overcharging. The Commission objected to a rule requiring prior bar approval before entering a contingent fee agreement, and to the rule preventing advocates from dealing directly with clients.

[59] *See*, for instance, cases involving the behavior of state-owned entities include a predation complaint against South African Airlines (SAA), which is now wholly owned by the government after the failure of its private partner.

[60] *AEC Electronics (Pty) Ltd v The Department of Minerals and Energy* (48/CR/Jun09).

according to proper procedures are not only important aspects of the legal culture, but are also demanded by the Constitution.[61]

Prior to the adoption of the Constitution, South Africa had developed an administrative law through the common law. The fair process values developed over the years have now been constitutionalized through section 33 of the Constitution, which states that "everyone has a right to administrative action which is lawful, reasonable and procedurally fair." This has been expanded by national legislation mandated by the Constitution, the Promotion of Administrative Justice Act (PAJA), which elaborates on the meaning of administrative action, and the process which will make such action lawful and fair.

The competition authorities are administrative bodies and are thus mandated by law to conduct their procedures fairly and lawfully. Their conduct can be reviewed based on PAJA or on the constitutional right in section 33. In addition, section 1(2) of the Competition Act requires that the Act be interpreted in a manner consistent with the Constitution and accordingly the Bill of Rights.

But balancing the rights protected by the Constitution and PAJA with the goals of the Competition Act has been a difficult task. The designers of the South African competition law system wanted the institutions to reflect the goals of equality and accessibility espoused in the Act. This is a challenge given the legalistic nature of the South African law system, and the resources available to firms to use that system. In an attempt to avoid legalizing the competition process, the Act enjoins the Tribunal to conduct itself informally. The Tribunal is not required to follow High Court procedure and its restrictive rules regarding pleadings and evidence. The Tribunal is also granted inquisitorial powers. As discussed below, the Tribunal has reinforced its right to conduct a *sui generis* procedure.

However, the system also incorporates an extensive appeal process (discussed below), including appeals to the Competition Appeal Court (which in terms of the proposed Superior Court Bill will be regarded as a division of the High Court) and further to the Supreme Court of Appeal (the highest court in non-constitutional matters).[62] This has meant that the Tribunal has in fact been constrained by the expectations generated from its place in the generalist court structure. And it is in fact constrained by the requirements of the Constitution and the rule of law. But the difficulty inherent in trying to perform the public function of competition regulation in an expeditious manner, while prosecuting well-resourced and heavily lawyered firms, makes the task of applying the highest procedural fairness standards demanded difficult.

This is most clearly illustrated in respect of complaint proceedings. We first set out below the procedures adopted by the Commission in investigating and prosecuting complaints regarding prohibited practices.

[61] OECD, OECD Peer Review: Competition Law and Policy in South Africa, (May 2003) at 11, <http://www.oecd.org/dataoecd/52/13/2958714.pdf>.

[62] There is a proposal to amend the Constitution to abolish the right of appeal from the CAC to the SCA.

1. Complaint procedures

Chapter 5 of the Act sets out the general process for complaint proceedings. A complaint may be initiated either by the Commission (through the Commissioner) or by any person. Such person may either submit information concerning a prohibited practice in any manner or form, or may submit a complaint in the prescribed form (by filling in a Form CC1).[63] Typically a complaint initiated by the Commission will attach an "initiating statement" briefly setting out what the suspected prohibited practices are. Once a complaint is initiated, the Commissioner must direct an investigator to investigate the complaint as quickly as practicable.[64]

The investigation of the complaint by the Commission tends to proceed in a number of different ways. Typically, the Commission will send a questionnaire to the target of the investigation, briefly setting out the nature of the complaint against it, and requesting certain information or documentation. The explanation of the complaint contained in such a questionnaire is very often vague, occasionally not clearly describing the conduct under scrutiny. It is generally through reading the questions directed to the firm that one can guess at the nature of the complaint. The target of the investigation has a right to request the Form CC1—that is, the complaint itself—but the Commission does not always provide the initiating statement together with the CC1.[65]

Such questionnaires can be followed up with meetings with the investigating team, either at the request of the Commission or the request of the target of the investigation. Occasionally the Commission will not only request certain information or documentation, but will summon a person who is believed to be able to furnish any information on the subject of the investigation, or to have possession or control of documents bearing on the subject. That person can be summoned to appear before the Commission to be interrogated, or can be summoned to deliver or produce the relevant documentation.[66] Such an interrogation can be conducted under oath and the evidence can be used by the Commission in its prosecution. Sometimes a summons is the first indication to the target that it is being investigated. Sometimes, such a summons follows an earlier interaction with, or questionnaire from, the Commission. The Commission can also use its search and seizure powers (more fully described below) in the course of an investigation.

Targets of investigation are not always questioned by the Commission. The Commission regularly does not advise targets of a complaint of the case against them when it has a leniency applicant which provides the necessary evidence.[67]

[63] Section 49B.

[64] Section 49B.

[65] The Commission contends that this is restricted information in terms of Rule 14 of the Commission rules. This is supported in the *Loungefoam* decision, but the *Woodlands* decision may leave this up for challenge.

[66] No self-incriminating answer given or statement made to the Commission in terms of this provision of the Act is admissible as evidence in criminal proceedings (except for perjury) (Section 49A).

[67] Telephone interview with Wendy Mkwanazi, Head of Legal Division, Competition Commission (December 8, 2010).

In most of those cases, the respondents will first know of the case against them at referral stage.

At any time after the initiation of a complaint, the Commission is empowered to refer the complaint to the Tribunal for determination. If the complaint was lodged by a person other than the Commissioner, the Commission has one year in which to investigate the complaint, and choose to either refer it to the Tribunal or issue a "notice of non-referral." If after a year, there has been no notice of referral issued, then the Commission is deemed to have "non-referred" the complaint.

There are three instances in which the Commission has more than a year to investigate—firstly, if the complainant agrees with the Commission to extend the investigation period; secondly, if the Commission applies to the Tribunal to extend the period and the Tribunal grants that application; and thirdly, if the Commissioner is the initiator of the complaint.[68] The Tribunal decision of *Competition Commission and Clover Industries Ltd*[69] clarifies that a complaint initiated by the Commissioner is not subject to the time-period limitations contained in section 50 of the Act.

If the Commission chooses not to refer a complaint to the Tribunal, or is deemed to have non-referred a complaint, the complainant is entitled to refer the complaint to the Tribunal itself (in those instances where the complaint was initiated by the complainant and not the Commission).

The Commission generally welcomes settlement discussions with respondents. In terms of section 49D of the Act, if the respondent and Commission agree on the terms of an appropriate order (during, on, or after the completion of the investigation of a complaint), the Commission may apply to the Tribunal for confirmation of that order as a consent order. The Tribunal can make the order as proposed by the Commission and respondent or may indicate changes to be made to the draft order; or may refuse to make it an order. The Tribunal has also confirmed settlement agreements as orders after the referral of the complaint. The Commission views the conclusion of settlement agreements as successful prosecutions, since it tends to require the payment of hefty fines in terms of the agreement, and generally requires the respondent to admit to a contravention of the Act (particularly in collusion cases). Such admissions leave it open for complainants to pursue civil damages claims at the High Court against the respondent. Even if there is no admission in a consent order, a complainant may apply to the Tribunal to declare the conduct of a firm to be a prohibited practice.[70]

[68] Section 50.

[69] *Competition Commission and Clover Industries Ltd and others* 103/CR/Dec06.

[70] The Act's interim relief procedure is another way for complainants to pursue prohibited conduct before the referral of a complaint, or before the Tribunal's determination on an issue. Section 49C of the Act enables a complainant, at any time, whether or not a hearing has commenced into an alleged prohibited practice, to apply to the Tribunal for an interim order in respect of the alleged practice. The Tribunal must give the respondent an adequate opportunity to be heard, and may then grant an interim order, taking into account the evidence of a prohibited practice, the need to prevent serious or irreparable damage to the applicant, and the balance of convenience. This interim relief procedure was the means by which most prohibited practice complaints were pursued by complainants in the first years of the operation of the Act, and related primarily to abuse of dominance allegations.

Once a matter has been referred, the respondents are given a certain time to file answering affidavits to the referral (which acts as the founding affidavit in the matter) and the Commission/complainant is then given an opportunity to file a reply affidavit if it chooses to. Thereafter, dates for discovery are determined,[71] followed by dates for the filing of witness statements, which are aimed at addressing all the factual issues to be presented by the relevant witnesses. Thereafter, the hearing commences.

2. *Opportunity to be heard and full notice of allegations*

The firms that are the targets of competition enforcement and complainants are mostly represented by law firms and advocates well versed in traditional high court procedure. Competition law in South Africa has thus been largely "legalized" in that lawyers expect competition proceedings to run like High Court proceedings. This results in a conflict in expectations—the Competition Tribunal is not bound by the formalities observed in court proceedings, it is allowed to conduct its proceedings informally, and in an inquisitorial manner,[72] and the competition authorities aim to achieve administrative efficiency. On the other hand, the firms involved in competition proceedings are primarily concerned with the fair procedure protections to which they are accustomed in standard civil litigation.

Just as Trebilcock and Iacobucci[73] note in respect of Canadian proceedings, this has resulted in South Africa in the "judicialization" of the Tribunal's proceedings and a highly adversarial process, including days of hearing, voluminous documentary evidence, and days of evidence from industry and expert witnesses. Consequently, there has been significant substitution from Tribunal decision-making to Commission decision-making. Given protracted and costly adjudication proceedings, many firms choose to settle matters within the Commission. This is evident particularly in cartel proceedings, where the Tribunal has only made decisions in two cartel cases so far, and thus there is little case law or precedent. Moreover, process values, such as transparency, accountability, and reasoned public decision have certainly been diminished as a result.[74]

There is however some backlash to this trend. Although there are so far only a few Tribunal decisions involving section 4(1)(b)—the per se collusion provision—there have recently been a number of firms choosing to "fight" their cases in the Tribunal, rather than settle with the Commission. Some have even chosen to admit

The popularity of the procedure has worn off as the Commission has become more active in pursuing prohibited practice conduct itself, whereas its focus in the early years of the operation of the Act was on merger enforcement.

[71] The High Court discovery rules are adopted as the Commission and Tribunal Rules do not specifically provide for "discovery," although Rules 14 and 15 of the Commission Rules do allow for access to certain information.

[72] Section 52.

[73] Michael Trebilcock & Edward Iacobucci, "Designing Competition Law Institutions: Values, Structure, and Mandate," 41 Loyola Univ. Chic. L.J. 455 (2010).

[74] Ibid. at 461–2.

contraventions of section 4(1)(b) and pursue cases purely on mitigation arguments, thereby requesting the Tribunal to determine an appropriate penalty. Some practitioners suggest that this is a result of reduced transparency in Commission decisions regarding settlement, lack of clear guidelines regarding settlement, and inflexibility in settlement negotiations.[75]

The second consequence is that there is significant dissatisfaction on the part of targets of investigation in relation to the procedures followed by the Commission, and thus there are a number of procedural challenges in respect of almost all complaint proceedings. This is also a function of the need to develop and crystallize processes in a new and developing regime. At the same time, however, there is extreme frustration on the part of the Commission regarding the expectation that it must investigate and litigate to the standard of a civil process. The Commission contends that it is performing a public function, which requires a certain level of procedural flexibility so that it may proceed to explore any problematic conduct that arises in the course of its investigations.

Thus the issue of the application of procedural norms in the enforcement of the above complaint procedures is currently a lively issue in South Africa. There have been numerous statements by the authorities expressing frustration with the slow progress in prosecuting complaints/prohibited practices cases through the Tribunal. The authorities have expressed concerns that respondents use technical legal points to delay proceedings, thereby frustrating the authorities' attempts to "catch cartelists." However, the firms targeted by investigations and prosecutions and the practitioners defending them, contend that they are trying to protect the rule of law rather than cartelists.[76] A number of recent cases have addressed these issues and placed higher procedural burdens on the Commission, burdens it fears threaten to disable it in its work.

This string of recent decisions started with a judgment of the Supreme Court of Appeal (the *Woodlands* decision). That decision and reactions to it starkly illustrate this tension. The milk industry in South Africa has been under investigation by the Competition Commission for a range of anticompetitive practices, including collusion, since 2004. The *Woodlands* decision dealt with preliminary procedural points which were raised before the hearing of the complaint against firms in the milk industry. These procedural points related to the validity of summonses issued by the Commission against Woodlands and Milkwood (purchasers of raw milk from dairy farmers). After a series of appeals and cross appeals, these two firms were granted special leave to appeal to the Supreme Court of Appeal ("SCA").

In its decision, the SCA notes that Chapter 5 of the Act, dealing with complaint procedures, is not clear as to the sequence of steps that have to be followed in relation to the initiation of a complaint, the investigation, the use of power to

[75] Both the Tribunal and the CAC have noted that fining guidelines from the Commission would be desirable. In the CAC decision of *Southern Pipeline Contracts and Another v The Competition Commission* 106/CAC/Dec10 at para 16, the CAC notes that "*no set of guidelines has been provided in this country which does compound the problem of a consistent determination of fines.*"

[76] Andrew Smith, "Crying Over Spilt Milk," Sibergramme 5/2010 ISSN 1606–9986 5 October 2010.

summons witnesses, and the referral of complaints. The court concedes that this has given scope for delaying tactics through preliminary proceedings in cases before the Tribunal and CAC.

In this case, the Commissioner initiated a complaint in 2005 (arising from information submitted by a member of the public alleging price fixing of fresh milk). The complaint only mentioned three firms—Parmalat, Ladismith Cheese, and Clover—but purported to launch "a full investigation into the milk industry." On the basis of this complaint, the Commission issued summonses against representatives of Woodlands and Milkwood. The Woodlands summons stated it had been issued in connection with the investigation into the milk industry, based on the Commission's belief that there existed anticompetitive behavior in the industry, including price fixing, abuse of dominance, and restrictive vertical practices.

The Tribunal found these summonses to be void because they were overly broad and did not stipulate the prohibited practice alleged, and were not accompanied by any particularity as to the nature of the prohibited practice. However, the SCA's decision went further than confirming the voidness of the summonses and addressed the validity of the complaint initiation itself, even though this was not the basis of the case brought by the parties.

The SCA noted that a complaint must also contain particularity and clarity[77] and must be based on a reasonable suspicion of the existence of a prohibited practice. Without such information/reasonable suspicion, it states that an investigation would not be a rational exercise of power.[78] The SCA states that the far-reaching powers of summons and interrogation cannot "be used by the Commissioner for the purposes of a fishing expedition without first having initiated a valid complaint based on a reasonable suspicion."[79] The SCA decision reiterates that "a suspicion against some cannot be used as a springboard to investigate all and sundry."[80]

The SCA rejected a finding of the CAC—the court below—that because it is difficult to establish the existence of prohibited practices, a generous interpretation of the Commission's procedural rights is justified. The SCA states that the competition law must be interpreted consistently with the Constitution—particularly the rights to dignity, freedom, privacy, fair trial, and just administrative action. The actions of the Commission may lead to administrative penalties, which, the SCA suggests, bear a close resemblance to criminal penalties.[81] Thus it concludes that the CAC's approach would imply that the more difficult it is to prove a crime, the fewer procedural rights an accused would have.

[77] This was supported by a decision of the CAC in *Sappi Fine Paper (Pty) Ltd v Competition Commission of SA and Papercor cc* 23/CAC/SEP02 at paras 35 and 39 that a complaint can relate only to an alleged contravention of the Act as specifically contemplated by an applicable provision thereof by that complainant.

[78] *Woodlands Dairy (Pty) Ltd & Another v Competition Commission* [2010] ZASCA 104 (September 13, 2010) at paras 13 and 34–35.

[79] Ibid. at para 20.

[80] Ibid. at para 36.

[81] Ibid. at paras 10–11.

Ultimately, it was not the 2005 complaint which was referred to the Tribunal. The Commission initiated a number of later complaints in 2006, identifying the firms alleged to have engaged in collusive conduct. Some of those complaints named Woodlands and Milkwood. However, the SCA decided that all the evidence on which those new complaints were based was derived from the invalid 2005 complaint and the tainted interrogations in terms of the summonses.[82] Thus the SCA set aside the referral against these two respondents.

While the *Woodlands* decision was welcomed by some practitioners,[83] it elicited an angry response from the Commission and raised concerns that the prospects of any further success in cartel prosecutions will be considerably reduced by imposing "overly" strict procedural requirements on the Commission.[84] The reactions to *Woodlands* and the cases that followed it illustrate the problem of the competing expectations and objectives identified above—respondents' expectations to receive the same procedural protections they would in a civil or criminal case, and the authorities' desire to have the flexibility to root out anticompetitive conduct wherever and whenever they may find it. Some criticized the *Woodlands* decision as being inappropriate given the Competition Commission's public interest function, noting that, "what the SCA has succeeded in doing is impose the much tougher standards of criminal prosecutions on the competition authorities. In doing so it has set a standard of legality that is inappropriate for a competition enquiry."[85]

The Commissioner, Shan Ramburuth, in a hearing before Parliament, complained that the judgment by the SCA would encourage companies being investigated by the competition authorities to delay the implementation of any finding by pursuing technical legal points through the courts. He stated that "people with deep pockets have more access to the courts. If respondents in competition cases believe they can delay the outcome by pursuing technical legal points, then they will."[86] A report in a South African business newspaper suggested that "the chief beneficiary of the SCA ruling is the legal profession. The ruling provides scope for lawyers to generate even more legal fees as cartel cases get clogged up in technical legal challenges."[87]

[82] Ibid. at para 43.

[83] *See* Faaez Samadi, "SA court finds commission actions 'invalid,'" GCR Monday, 13 September 2010. The article quotes Martin Versfeld, at Webber Wentzel in Johannesburg: "The commission has often adopted too robust an approach to the procedural powers it enjoys when it exercises its right to summons individuals . . . It is hoped that the Supreme Court's decision will put an end to overly expansive requests which fall well outside of the parameters of the original complaint." Chris Charter, at DLA Cliffe Dekker Hofmeyr in Sandton stated: "It is clear that the [commission's] investigation procedure cannot be a free for all, and must be rooted in reasonable suspicion of actual anti-competitive conduct."

[84] Ann Crotty, "SCA Ruling on Watchdog Helps Cartels, Not Public," Business Report (September 22, 2010).

[85] Ibid.

[86] Ann Crotty, "Rich Firms will Use Courts to Drag Out Cases, Says Commission," Business Report (September 16, 2010).

[87] Ann Crotty, "SCA Ruling on Watchdog Helps Cartels, Not Public," Business Report (September 22, 2010). The judgment has also created further confusion in its apparent conflation of the requirements for a valid complaint and a summons issued by the Commission to secure evidence. In particular, the

The Commission initially applied to the Constitutional Court to appeal this decision, primarily on the basis that the SCA was wrong to compare competition prosecutions to criminal prosecutions and therefore apply the same procedural standards.[88] That appeal was subsequently withdrawn. It is not clear why the Commission withdrew the appeal, in light of its statements that the decision would hinder its public function, and in light of the fact that the decision would clearly impact on a number of other pending cases.

Firms currently under investigation by the Commission or respondents in cases before the Tribunal may take (and have already taken) this decision as an opportunity to revisit the Commission's initiation of the complaint against them and carefully study whether the initiating statement complies with the requirement set down by the SCA.[89] The Commission has for instance initiated industry-wide investigations in many areas including steel, fuel, food stores, airlines, furniture foam, and various chemical industries.[90] Three referrals have already been set aside following the *Woodlands* decision—two by the CAC (*Yara/Omnia*[91] and *Loungefoam*),[92] and one by the Tribunal (*SAB*).[93]

The *Yara/Omnia* case related to anticompetitive conduct in the fertilizer industry. A complainant, Nutri-Flo, lodged two complaints with the Commission, the first one was non-referred and the second was referred. On the face of it, both of these complaints alleged abuse of dominance by Sasol, a firm involved in the production of ammonia and fertilizer. The referral of the complaint by the Commission, however, alleged not only abuse of dominance by Sasol, but also collusion between Sasol, Omnia, and Yara (all firms involved in the manufacture of fertilizers). After a number of interlocutory applications, the proceedings progressed, and Sasol settled with the Commission (separately in respect of the collusion allegations against it and in respect of the abuse of dominance allegations). That left Omnia and Yara to defend the collusion allegations. The Commission proceeded to file witness statements, which the respondents complained addressed allegations which were not contained in the referral.

question arises as to the specificity now required of a complaint, particularly one brought by a member of the public.

88 Commission's Notice of Intention to Appeal filed with the Constitutional Court.

89 Ann Crotty, "Ruling Puts Cartel Cases in Jeopardy; Lawyers Embrace Loophole," Business Report (September 20, 2010).

90 The issue regarding the wide scope of initiation statements may become moot when the Amendment Act is promulgated as it will provide the Commission with more flexibility to conduct industry-wide investigations. The Amendment Act will empower the Commission to embark on market inquiries, being "a formal inquiry in respect of the general state of competition in a market for particular goods or services, without necessarily referring to the conduct of activities of any particular named firm." The Commission may conduct such an enquiry if "it has reason to believe that any feature or combination of features of a market for any goods or services prevents, distorts or restricts competition within that market" or, "to achieve the purposes of" the Competition Act. If it uncovers violations of the Act in the course of this inquiry, it can then refer them to the Competition Tribunal.

91 *Yara/Omnia and Competition Commission* (93/CAC/Mar10).

92 *Loungefoam and Others and Competition Commission* (102/CAC/Jun10).

93 *SAB and 13 Others and Competition Commission* (134/CR/Dec07).

The Commission applied to amend the complaint referral to accommodate the allegations contained in the witness statements. Both respondents opposed the application to amend. Yara and Omnia also brought counter-applications arguing that the Commission's referral was not permissible in law because the Nutri-Flo complaint was limited to abuse of dominance allegations against Sasol and not collusion allegations against all three firms. Yara and Omnia argued that if the Commission wished to refer collusion complaints, it ought to have initiated those complaints itself. The Tribunal found against Yara and Omnia by pointing out that the Act allows the Commission to "add further particulars to the complaint referral."

However, on appeal, the CAC (with reference to both *Woodlands* and the older case of *Glaxo*)[94] held that the Commission may only refer complaints to the Tribunal which have been submitted to it by a complainant, or which have been initiated by the Commission itself in the course of its investigations. Subsequent amendments by the Commission to add further transgressions to an existing complaint referral, where the particular conduct was not complained of by the complainant, are not permissible. The CAC accordingly declared that no complaint emanating from the Nutri-Flo complaint is pending against Omnia or Yara.

Similarly, in the *SAB* case, South African Breweries (SAB) and the other thirteen respondents (SAB's "appointed distributors") brought applications to dismiss the case which had been initiated in 2004, referred in 2007, and was nearing the end of hearing. The respondents contended that the initial complaint, lodged by an independent liquor wholesaler, conceived only of a margin-squeeze case against SAB. The complaint alleged that SAB sold beer to its downstream distribution arm at the same price at which it sold to retailers, and thus prevented independent wholesalers from earning a margin on the sale of beer. The case which was ultimately referred identified not only allegations of exclusionary conduct, but also price discrimination and resale price maintenance. In addition, the referral alleged that SAB's relationship with its "appointed distributors" (the thirteen other respondents) amounted to agreements to divide markets and alternatively were restrictive vertical practices. Such complaints had clearly not been conceived of in the initial complaint, and the appointed distributors had not been identified in the initial complaint.

The respondents thus contended that the Commission did not have jurisdiction to investigate or refer the other conduct and hence the Tribunal did not have jurisdiction to adjudicate on it. Based on the *Woodlands*, *Glaxo*, and *Yara* precedents, the Tribunal was bound to find in the respondents' favor. However, the Tribunal expressed disappointment and frustration with this outcome. It released a

[94] *Glaxo Wellcome (PTY) (Ltd) and Others v National Association of Pharmaceutical Wholesalers* (15/CAC/Feb 2002). That case stated: "While the complaint need not be drafted with precision or even a reference to the Act, the allegations or the conduct in the complaint must be cognisably linked to particular prohibited conduct or practices. There must be a rational or a recognisable link between the conduct referred to in a complaint and the prohibitions in the Act, otherwise it will not be possible to say what the complaint is about and what should be investigated."

press release at the time of issuing the order, which noted that the decision was "regrettable." It stated:

When we give reasons for our decision we will explain why the case law, which is binding upon us, has led us to this conclusion. We will also indicate why this case law may need re-consideration by superior courts in the future so that a complainant's rights of access to justice and the Commission's investigative powers are not unduly compromised.

We regret that this case has not been brought to finality so it could be decided on the evidence and not a point of jurisdiction. The complainant will not know whether its complaint was well founded and the respondents will not have an opportunity to clear their names from accusations of anticompetitive conduct.

The *SAB* decision was followed by a similar reaction to that which followed the *Woodlands* decision: that "technical" decisions were hindering the investigatory role of the Commission and bowing to the demands of well-resourced business. A business paper proclaimed that a "deliberately informal system has been clubbed over the head by a more traditionally legalistic approach."[95] The paper went on to report that by

taking into account legal and economic considerations, the tribunal system has offered a less formal, cheaper and accessible means to justice. But if legal arguments from higher courts are used to the extent that they render the tribunal system pointless, we could all be worse off, particularly in a country where access to justice is often hindered by social and economic inequalities. . . . The protection of rights enshrined in law is non-negotiable. . . . This means the system will sometimes be played by well-resourced companies to get themselves off the hook. The best defence against such cynical manipulation of constitutional rights will be for the commission to be more rigorous and disciplined; to leave as little scope as possible for claims based on technicalities.[96]

Despite the protestations of the Tribunal in the *SAB* case, a similar decision was made by the CAC a few weeks later, in the *Loungefoam* appeal. In that case the respondents opposed an application for amendment of the referral on the basis that the initiating complaint had not directed particular allegations against particular parties,[97] which allegations were sought to be introduced by the proposed amendments. Two of the respondents were joined to the proceedings only after referral.[98]

In its application for amendment of the referral, the Commission argued that it is only required to initiate a complaint against a prohibited practice and if it becomes clear during the course of the investigation or after referral that other entities were implicated in the illegal conduct, the Commission was entitled to seek an amendment to join those entities.[99] The Tribunal agreed with the Commission that an

[95] Michael Bleby, "SAB's win a blow to the little guy's day in court," Business Day, 8 April 2011.

[96] Michael Bleby, "Shot across the bows of the state: Competition watchdog on the wrong side of the law," Business Day, 11 April 2011.

[97] *Loungefoam (Pty) Ltd, Vitafoam (Pty) Ltd v Competition Commission* (103/CR/Sep08) at paras 21–22 and para 32.

[98] There are a number of similar referrals currently before the Tribunal. For instance, in a case involving the bicycle industry,[98] the majority of the twenty-eight respondents were only named at referral stage and did not know of the allegations against them until they received the referral. *See Competition Commission v Fritz Pienaar Cycles (Pty) Ltd & Others* 32/CR/Jun10.

[99] Ibid. at para 35.

initiation does not need to identify specified respondents.[100] It stated that "all that the Commission needs to demonstrate, . . . is that there is enough content in the act of initiation to make a cognizable or rational link with a subsequent referral. It cannot be expected to know at the stage of initiation what the process of investigation will reveal."[101] This decision was appealed to the CAC.

The CAC, in upholding the appeal, attempts to dispel the concern that has been expressed by the Commission that such court decisions hinder the Commission's ability to perform its tasks. Its justification is rooted securely in a commitment to the rule of law. It noted that the Act provides that the Commission's powers of investigation are triggered either by the initiation of a complaint by the Commissioner, or by the receipt of a complaint from a third party under section 49B. In *Woodlands* the SCA held that, in the case of the Commissioner, this requires that the Commissioner be in possession of information that gives rise to a reasonable suspicion that anticompetitive conduct, as defined in the Act, has been committed.[102] As anticompetitive conduct must involve a firm or firms it held that the firm or firms involved must be identified as being party to that conduct.[103]

The CAC in *Loungefoam* stated that it "is helpful in the light of the suggestion that the approach in *Woodlands* hampers the Commission in uncovering anticompetitive conduct" to compare the position under the Act with an investigation by the police. The police power to enter premises or seize documents is expressed in similar terms to the powers of an investigator under the Competition Act. However, the police have only a limited power, with judicial approval, to submit persons to interrogation. By contrast the Commission's investigator has such powers whenever the Commissioner decides to initiate a complaint.[104]

> The Commissioner is therefore both the gamekeeper striving to catch the perpetrators of anti-competitive conduct and the gatekeeper to the exercise by inspectors on the Commissioner's staff of the power of interrogation and some powers of entry, search and seizure . . . The investigator's powers are exercised without judicial oversight, other than judicial review, and are capable of being abused by the Commissioner as past experience has regrettably demonstrated.[105] *Woodlands* itself was also an example of such abuse. Had the police engaged in the same type of conduct as the Commission in *Woodlands* it would unequivocally have been unlawful and the courts would have constrained them from pursuing such an investigation. They would have failed in their duty to protect the targets of the investigation against a misuse of police powers had they not done so. The reason for circumscribing powers of investigation, whether by the police or the Commission, is to protect the rights of those subjected to investigation. That is a central pillar of our constitutional democracy. Quite rightly the Commission does not suggest in argument that these safeguards should be absent. It is for precisely that reason that the SCA held that the Commissioner must be in possession of information on which a reasonable suspicion of the Commission of unlawful anti-competitive conduct by a firm or firms can be based before initiating a complaint. In the same way the police are required to be in possession of information on the basis of which they suspect that a crime has been

[100] Ibid. at para 39. [101] Ibid. at para 56.
[102] *Woodlands* para 13. [103] *Loungefoam* para 42.
[104] Section 205 of the Criminal Procedure Act 51 of 1977.
[105] *Pretoria Portland Cement Co Ltd and Another v Competition Commission and Others* 2003 (2) SA 385 (SCA).

committed in order to exercise their powers of investigation. Any other approach is inimical to the protection of the rights guaranteed in the Bill of Rights.[106]

The CAC therefore illustrates that there are fundamental principled reasons to ensure that jurisdictional prerequisites are properly followed by the Commission. The Commission's complaint that such an approach is too formalistic "misses two fundamental points."[107] The first is that the initiation of a complaint affords the firm that is the target of the investigation an opportunity to engage with the Commission, dispel its concerns, and demonstrate that it has not engaged in conduct prohibited by the Act. As the Commission's own statistics show, many charges of anticompetitive conduct prove to be unfounded, and there are thus reasons to enable such firms to avoid the reputational and financial risks that arise with allegations of anticompetitive conduct.

Secondly, the CAC notes that section 67(1) of the Act, provides that prescription runs until the date of initiation of a complaint. A complaint in respect of a prohibited practice may not be initiated more than three years after the practice has ceased. In the absence of the initiation of a complaint, because the matter has been referred directly to the Tribunal without the complaint or the target firm having been the subject of a complaint initiation, the foundation for invoking section 67(1) is absent. In view of its importance in the application of the Act that cannot be correct. This illustrates the importance in every instance of every complaint against any firm of a proper initiation of that complaint in terms of section 49B.

Against these two important considerations, one must weigh the task of correctly filling out a complaint form. In a recent public symposium, a prominent senior counsel therefore noted that this debate is about "so little, and yet so much." He noted he was baffled by the controversy, since to address the problem, the Commission merely has to fill out a form (a CC1)—which cannot take longer than an hour to do—when it discovers new parties to prohibited conduct, or new forms of prohibited conduct during the course of its investigation. Yet the issue is about "so much" because it distinguishes between an instrumentalist view of the law, and a view of law which demands that certain regulatory powers be bounded.[108]

The authorities charged with enforcing the Act are thus clearly grappling with balancing the important public function of the Commission, against the procedural protections typically demanded in litigious environments. The Tribunal states that the "Commission is the guardian of the Act and while it is enjoined to enforce it so it is under a duty to ensure that competitors do not abuse the resources and procedures of the Commission and Tribunal."[109]

[106] *Loungefoam* paras 44–45.

[107] *Loungefoam* para 49.

[108] Speech by David Unterhalter, SC at a symposium organized by the Competition Committee of the Law Society of South Africa, 25 May 2011.

[109] *Competition Commission v Yara South Africa (Pty) Ltd and Omnia Fertilizer Ltd* (31/CR/May05, February 24, 2010) at para 35.

However, *Woodlands* and the other decisions have highlighted the controversy about whether the competition authorities, and the Commission in particular, consistently grant targets of investigation adequate notice of the allegations against them and thereby a proper opportunity to be heard.

Woodlands may also lead to a re-examination of the constitutional rights that are granted to targets of competition investigations. In the *Federal Mogul* case,[110] the parties sought to argue before the CAC that certain constitutional rights needed to be given effect during Competition Tribunal proceedings because of the criminal nature of the penalties imposed. In *Federal Mogul*, the CAC dismissed this argument.[111] According to Smith, the *Woodlands* decision here may suggest that respondents will attempt to revisit this issue, particularly when the Competition Amendment Act—which criminalizes cartel conduct—comes into force.[112] But even without the criminalization of cartel conduct, the observation of the SCA that administrative penalties bear a close resemblance to criminal penalties may encourage a constitutional re-examination of the entire scheme of administrative penalties.[113]

Prior to *Woodlands*, the Tribunal attempted to be permissive as a means to develop a substantive approach (as opposed to a formalistic attitude) to the procedural provisions of the Act, in order to ensure that cases brought are dealt with on the merits as quickly as possible.[114] However, as the *Omnia* and *Loungefoam* cases illustrate, *Woodlands* has had an impact on the CAC, and will restrict the Tribunal in its procedural decisions.

These concerns led the Commission to appeal a number of cases, including *SAB*, *Omnia/Yara*, and *Loungefoam*, directly to the Constitutional Court. In all three cases, the Constitutional Court refused to grant the Commission direct access to the Constitutional Court and dismissed the applications for leave to appeal. In *Loungefoam* (Case CCT 81/11, [2012] ZACC 14), the majority found that the circumstances of the case did not justify a direct approach to the Constitutional Court without seeking leave to appeal to the SCA from the CAC, in terms of section 63(2) of the Act. In *Yara/Omnia* (Case CCT 90/11 [2012] ZACC 15), the majority of the Constitutional Court found that the Commission's delay in lodging its application for leave to appeal was excessive and thus rejected the application for condonation for the late filing. Further, the Court found that it was preferable that

110 *Competition Commission of South Africa v Federal Mogul Aftermarket Southern Africa (Pty) Ltd and others* 08/CR/B/May01.

111 On the matter of procedural fairness, the Tribunal found the separation between the Commission and Tribunal as prosecutor and adjudicator as sufficient within the context of section 34 of the Constitution. Further, the Tribunal's operations are functionally independent of the executive. In sum, the Act contains adequate and appropriate procedural protections for the respondents to ensure fairness and even though the Tribunal is not an "ordinary court," it is an independent and impartial Tribunal for the purposes of section 34.

112 Andrew Smith, "Crying Over Spilt Milk," Sibergramme 5/2010 Issn 1606-9986 5 October 2010.

113 *Woodlands Dairy (Pty) Ltd & Another v Competition Commission* [2010] ZASCA 104 (September 13, 2010) at para 10.

114 Dennis Davis, "Reflecting on the Effectiveness of the Competition Authority: Prioritisation, Market Enquiries and Impact" (Speech, <www.comptrib.co.za>).

this matter should first be heard by the SCA if leave to appeal to that Court was granted. In *SAB*, the Court dismissed the application for leave to appeal without reasons. This does not signify the end of these cases: in the *Yara/Omnia* and *Loungefoam* cases, the Commission can seek leave to appeal from the CAC, and have the appeals heard by the SCA (and then perhaps one of the parties may appeal to the Constitutional Court thereafter). In *SAB*, the CAC will be hearing the Commission's appeal in September 2012 which in turn might be appealed to the SCA and Constitutional Court. The Constitutional Court in *Yara/Omnia* and *Loungefoam* have accepted that the cases raise constitutional issues and may well receive the Constitutional Court's attention in due course, *Yara* ([2012] ZACC), at para. 36. The Constitutional Court's comments on prospects of success and the minority decisions on the importance of the Commission's function in promoting competition may give some insight into the approach the Constitutional Court may take if it deals with these cases in the future.

Indeed, the recent Constitutional Court decision in *Senwes*[115] may also provide some clues (although it turned on different facts). In this matter, the Commission at first alleged that Senwes engaged in numerous exclusionary acts. The Tribunal found that Senwes was guilty of a "margin squeeze"—a particular type of exclusionary act which was not explicitly alleged in the papers, although it was raised in certain expert economist reports. While both the Tribunal and the CAC found that the evidence justified the finding of exclusionary conduct in terms of section 8(c) the SCA held that allegations of a margin squeeze had not formed part of the Commission's referral, which constituted the charge and hence the Tribunal and CAC had erred in upholding the Commission's case.

The Commission appealed the SCA decision, and the Constitutional Court found in its favor. In essence, the majority's holding is that the Tribunal can interrogate possible contraventions of the Act even where the complaint referred to it by the Commission did not cover the specific contravention. The Court's judgment gives the Tribunal flexibility, as long as the Commission has broadly identified what kind of anticompetitive practice it is pursuing and the respondent can understand the case it has to meet. In eschewing the formalistic approach to pleadings adopted by the SCA, the majority emphasized the Constitution's broad transformation goals, saying its purpose was to open up the economy "to enable all South Africans to have access to the control and ownership of the national economy."

The judgment in *Senwes* is no doubt a boost to the Commission, which now need not be so precise in how it formulates its referral.[116]

While the numerous procedural appeals have no doubt delayed these cases, it may be worthwhile to develop the procedural jurisprudence so that the Commission is aware of what its procedural obligations are, and so that, in the future, cases are no longer delayed by contentions of reduced procedural fairness.

115 *Competition Commission v Senwes Ltd* CCT 61/11 [2012] ZACC 6.

116 Franny Rabkin and Amanda Visser, "Court broadens scope for Competition Tribunal," Business Day, 13 April 2012.

3. *Adequate notice of evidence relied on*

A similar objection has also arisen in respect of the particularity of the referral itself. As noted above, in the *Omnia* case, there was an objection from one of the parties that the witness statements filed by the Commission, just before the commencement of the hearing, introduced allegations not contained in the referral. Similar concerns have been raised in a number of other cases, usually in the form of "exceptions" by respondents (a High Court interlocutory process which objects that the founding papers do not contain enough particularity to found a cause of action or to be able to meaningfully answer the allegations).[117]

In the matter of *Competition Commission v SAB and 14 Others*, South African Breweries (SAB), a beer manufacturer, applied for the dismissal of the referral on the basis that the witness statements filed after the close of pleadings and before the hearings introduced an entirely new case against SAB. In that case, the Tribunal encouraged the Commission to initiate a new complaint in respect of the new allegations, which it agreed to do.[118] The concern raised by SAB in this matter was that the Commission was conducting a "trial by ambush"—by not identifying the evidence to be relied on at an earlier stage of proceedings, it was accused of using the pleading process itself as a means of investigating.

The same allegation has been made, mostly in the context of requesting further particulars (or pursuing exceptions) after the filing of the Commission's founding affidavit/referral. There have been a number of applications for the Commission to more clearly identify the conduct that forms the basis of the contravention, or to make available documents evidencing the contraventions alleged in the referral.

There have been some attempts to acquire internal Commission notes and memoranda. In the *Astral*[119] case, the Tribunal was asked to consider whether to permit access to the Commission investigators' notes. The application was refused. The Tribunal pointed out that it was easier to conceive of cases justifying the Commission's concerns about the chilling disclosure of its investigators' notes than it was of the respondent's concerns about the suppression of exculpatory material. Similarly, in the context of mergers, in the *Netcare*[120] case, the Tribunal decided that the Commission was entitled to refuse access to its consultation notes. This is because, if informants were told that notes of their consultation were susceptible to discovery to merging parties, this would dampen the willingness of informants to be candid.

Respondents in cartel cases which have been initiated by the Commission upon submission of a leniency application tend to argue that access to the leniency application is needed in order to understand the nature of the allegations against

[117] *Competition Commission v Fritz Pienaar Cycles (Pty) Ltd & Others* (32/CR/Jun10); *Competition Commission v Yara South Africa (Pty) Ltd and Omnia Fertilizer Ltd* (31/CR/May05, February 24, 2010).

[118] *SAB and 13 Others v Competition Commission* (134/CR/Jun07).

[119] *Astral Operations Ltd, Elite Breeding Farms v The Competition Commission* (74/CR/Jun08).

[120] *Federal Mogul Aftermarket Southern Africa (Pty) Ltd v Competition Commission* [2003] SACAC 9; [2004] 1 CPLR 25 (CAC) (3 December 2003).

them. The Commission has invariably claimed that the leniency application is subject to "litigation privilege" and therefore not available either before the plea stage, or at discovery stage.

The basis for such requests is often founded in High Court rules. The Competition Act enables the Tribunal to apply High Court rules in instances in which its own rules do not provide for the particular procedure pursued. Respondents often use High Court Rule 35 as a basis to request documents. Rule 35(12) provides that, "Any party to any proceeding may at any time before the hearing thereof deliver a notice to any other party in whose pleadings or affidavits reference is made to any document . . . to produce such document for his inspection and to permit him to make a copy thereof."

This approach is generally unsuccessful. The Tribunal has on many occasions pointed out that its proceedings are *sui generis*[121] and thereby unconstrained by the rules regulating judicial proceedings. In the case of *Allens Mechco,*[122] the Tribunal made it clear that it is granted a discretion to adopt High Court rules but is not mandated to do so. It thus refused to adopt rule 35 formally, but notes that where a document is clearly relied upon to support a relevant allegation in the pleading, it should be provided to the respondent. An inference that a particular document is relied upon, however, is not sufficient to create an obligation to disclose such a document.

Other methods of accessing documents in order to understand the nature of the case against targets have been equally unsuccessful. In the recent case of *Arcelor Mittal and Others,*[123] Arcelor Mittal South Africa (AMSA) and Cape Gate, in separate applications on different grounds, requested a number of documents from the Commission prior to having to file a plea to the Commission's referral.

AMSA and Cape Gate (the applicants in this application, but respondents in the main case) are accused of collusion in respect of long-steel products. Both request the leniency application filed with the Commission, as well as other documents which appear to have formed the basis of the allegations in the Referral. In particular, the Referral attaches notes of telephone conversations, and emails, which appear to indicate collusive agreements prior to 2005. However, in respect of conduct post-2005, the referral alleges agreements on prices between the respondents reached "by telephone, emails and so forth" and notes that evidence, of the correspondence, discussions, and meetings, will be presented at the hearing.

AMSA based its case on Rules 14 and 15 of the Commission's Rules which state that anyone may inspect the Commission's record unless the information is "restricted information." A sub-rule in Rule 14 notes that "the description of conduct attached to a complaint, and any information received by the Commission during its investigation of the complaint, is restricted information, until the Commission issues a

[121] *See Competition Commission v American Natural Soda Ash CHG Global (Pty) Ltd* 49/CR/Apr00 at pp 14–15 and *National Association of Pharmaceutical Wholesalers (and Others) and Glaxo Wellcome (and Others)* 45/CR/Jul01 at para 55.

[122] *Allens Mechco (Pty) Ltd & Others v Competition Commission & Others* 63/CR/Sep09 (May 28, 2010).

[123] *Competition Commission v Arcelor Mittal South Africa Ltd & Others* 61/CR/Sep09 (September 3, 2010).

referral or notice of non referral in respect of that complaint." AMSA thus claimed that since a referral had been issued, AMSA should have been able to access the Commission's record. AMSA submitted that it would be inappropriate for the Commission to try and ambush respondents into committing themselves under oath, before affording them the opportunity to examine documents that are known to be in the Commission's possession and which will be used by the Commission for purposes of prosecution.

AMSA noted that South Africa's system of civil procedure is founded on the rule that the interests of justice are served if parties are obliged to disclose all documents in their possession in order to confine the case to be dealt with at trial. Denying a party access to relevant documents subjects that party to surprise.[124] Indeed, it seems that early disclosure is a policy contemplated by the Rules. AMSA noted that full disclosure will enable the respondents to consider properly the allegations made against them and conduct their internal investigation, and to respond to the fullest extent possible, rather than responding with tactical litigation.

However, the rule on which AMSA relied provides for a range of instances in which the Commission's record can remain "restricted information" even after referral, one of which is that the information must remain restricted if it is restricted in terms of the Promotion of Access to Information Act ("PAIA"). In this case, the commission relied on a provision in PAIA which states that a public body may refuse access to information when that information was supplied in confidence by a third party and the disclosure could prejudice the future supply of similar information.

The Tribunal agreed with the Commission in this regard. In respect of the leniency application for instance, and the documents and evidence attached to that leniency application, the Tribunal stated that the sources of the information relied on by the Commission must trust the Commission not to disclose information provided in the course of an investigation.[125] It concluded that leniency applicants would be more reluctant to come forward if they knew their leniency applications would be disclosed. In addition it concluded that the information (including documents attached to the leniency application) is privileged as the information is obtained by the Commission to conduct litigation in the Tribunal against members of a cartel.

Thus access by respondents to Commission documents, or a clear basis of the evidence against them, is difficult to secure. The Tribunal proceedings do not provide clear rules on what type of information one has a right to, and the Tribunal has rejected the application of High Court rules. In addition, the Competition Appeal Court has clearly held that the "right to a fair trial" which attaches to a criminal accused is not applicable to a party to competition proceedings.[126]

[124] *Ventoris v Mountain* [1991] 1 WLR 607; 611H at 45.

[125] *Competition Commission v Arcelor Mittal South Africa Ltd & Others* 61/CR/Sep09 (September 3, 2010) at para 21.

[126] *Federal Mogul Aftermarket Southern Africa (Pty) Ltd v Competition Commission* [2003] SACAC 9; [2004] 1 CPLR 25 (CAC) (3 December 2003).

The Tribunal implied, in the course of argument in the *Arcelor Mittal* case, that in certain circumstances the ambushing of respondents would be justified, particularly in light of the fact that respondents in competition proceedings do not enjoy the same rights afforded to an accused under criminal law.[127] Therefore the Tribunal implies that, since contraventions of section 4(1)(b) (collusive activity) are regarded as the most egregious form of competition contravention and are by their nature hardest to detect, they permit the bending on the ordinary rules of evidence, so that a respondent may be caught out on the stand.[128]

AMSA and Cape Gate took the Tribunal's decision on appeal to the CAC. The CAC disagreed with the Tribunal that the information could be restricted with reference to PAIA. It also found that the respondents required access to certain information in order to assess their position and understand the case made out against them before delivering its answering affidavit.[129] It did not rule on whether the information could be considered as privileged, but it concluded that the information was confidential. As such, it found that access thereto should have been applied for in terms of the rules governing access to confidential documents, and as such, the matter was remitted to the Tribunal.

In all of the above cases, the Tribunal has granted the objecting parties an opportunity to be heard in a hearing, and has on many occasions granted extensions of time to enable respondents to deal with allegations against them. While this may perpetuate the Commission's concern that these "technical" points are successful in delaying justice, practitioners contend that the resolution of these procedural issues (in addition to protecting the procedural rights of targets of investigation) can reduce the time to conclude proceedings, either through limiting the points or through dismissal.[130] In any event, both the Commission and Tribunal are accommodating in providing parties adequate time to prepare a defense.

4. *Independence of decision-makers*

The previous South African Competition regime was marked by a lack of independence. Under the Maintenance and Promotion of Competition Act, the decisions of the Competition Board were subject to review and approval by the Minister of Trade and Industry so that its decisions openly lacked political independence.[131]

[127] *See* the Tribunal record:

> CHAIR: But is ambushing always unfair in our law, or are there circumstances where you are looking at a balance of interest and the interest is naturally detecting the covert activity, may justify ambushing? Don't some of the discovery rules allow some discovery to be held back even at the time of trial in certain circumstances to do precisely that?

[128] Ann Boniwell, "Should an Old Dog Learn New Tricks? A Revision of the Rules of Evidence relevant to Competition Proceedings," COMPETITION LAW SIBERGRAMME, 20 December 2010 at p. 8.

[129] *Arcelor Mittal South Africa Ltd and Another v Competition Commission and Others* 103/CAC/Sep10 at para 36.

[130] Ibid. at 11: "in the absence of procedural irregularity, the need for protracted interlocutory or review proceedings would be nullified."

[131] Shan Ramburuth, Competition Commissioner, Independence and Accountability of Competition Authorities by South Africa, Address at Intergovernmental Group of Experts on Competition Law

Given that the Competition Act was drafted during the same period that the new Constitution came into effect, there was a very strong commitment to the constitutional principle of independence from political influence. As such, with the drafting of the Competition Act, parties were concerned to design a system institutionally and politically independent from the executive and private party stakeholders and the legislated independence of the authorities is clear from the provisions of the Act.[132]

The Act obliges the Commission to interact with government and regulatory authorities in certain instances. The Commission must for example:

- negotiate agreements with any regulatory authority to regulate and harmonize the exercise of jurisdiction in competition matters within various industries.
- advise, and receive advice, from any regulatory authority.
- consult with relevant government ministries where its input is needed.
- report to the minister on any matters relating to the application of the Act
- enquire into and report to the Minister on any matter concerning the purposes of the Act.
- review legislation and public regulation and report to the Minister concerning any provision that permits uncompetitive behavior.

To this extent the competition authorities do influence state policy through consultation with the executive. At the same time, the Minister, in consultation with the Commissioner, may prescribe regulations for matters relating to the functions of the Commission.

and Policy (July 16, 2008), <http://www.unctad.org/sections/wcmu/docs/c2clp_ige9p5South%20Africa_en.pdf>.

[132] Section 20(1) of the Competition Act states that the Competition Commission:

(a) is independent and subject only to the Constitution and the law; and
(b) must be impartial and must perform its functions without fear, favour or prejudice.

Section 20(2) places an obligation on each member of staff at the Competition Commission to not:-

(a) engage in any activity that may undermine the integrity of the Commission;
(b) participate in any investigation, hearing or decision concerning a matter in respect of which that person has a direct financial interest or any similar personal interest;
(c) make private use of, or profit from, any confidential information obtained as a result of per-forming that person's official functions in the Commission; or
(d) divulge any information referred to in paragraph 2(c) to any third party, except as required as part of that person's official functions within the Commission.

Section 20(3) of the Competition Act obliges each organ of state to assist the Commission to maintain its independence and impartiality, and to effectively carry out its powers and duties.

Section 70 of the Competition Act states that it is an offence to hinder, oppose, obstruct, or unduly influence any person who is exercising a power or performing a duty delegated, conferred or imposed on that person by the Act.

Section 73(2) states that a person commits an offence who:—

(a) does anything calculated to improperly influence the Competition Tribunal or Competition Commission concerning any matter connected with an investigation;
(b) anticipates any findings of the Tribunal or Commission concerning an investigation in a way that is calculated to influence the proceedings or findings.

It is submitted, however, that these interactions do not result in a lessening of the independence of the authorities. In respect of proceedings before the Commission, state officials participate in the proceedings in the same manner as members of the public and it is a matter of record that the Commission has in the past challenged ministries on uncompetitive or potentially uncompetitive legislation.[133]

The strict separation between the Tribunal and the Commission helps to shelter the system from constitutional and administrative challenge. The Commission is an autonomous statutory body with full control over its prosecutorial decisions. It is enjoined by statute to be "independent and subject only to the Constitution and the law," to be impartial and "perform its functions without fear, favour or prejudice." The Commissioner may only be removed for serious misconduct, permanent incapacity, or engaging in activity that may "undermine the integrity" of the Commission.[134] The decision of the Commission on whether to refer the complaint is independent of the Tribunal and when the Commission appears before the Tribunal as complainant, it does so on equal footing with the respondent in the matter. Such independence has been evidenced in cases where the Tribunal has made findings against the Commission, refused to confirm consent orders entered into by the Commission, and refused to confirm merger transactions approved by the Commission.

The Tribunal, like the Commission, is similarly enjoined to be independent and impartial and there have been no indications of any political effort to influence enforcement decisions.[135] Members of the Tribunal are experts in their fields, not representatives of interest groups. They may not be officials of political parties or movements. They may not be dismissed during their term of office (except for extremely serious offences), and their decisions are not subject to ministerial override. Remuneration and terms of employment, which are set by the Minister, may not be reduced during a member's term.

The CAC is a division of the High Court, and therefore brings with it all the independence implied by the judiciary.[136]

Finally, all competition proceedings are open to public scrutiny. Members of the public are entitled to attend the proceedings and may make representations where appropriate.

[133] Shan Ramburuth, Competition Commissioner, Independence and Accountability of Competition Authorities by South Africa, Address at Intergovernmental Group of Experts on Competition Law and Policy (July 16, 2008), <http://www.unctad.org/sections/wcmu/docs/c2clp_ige9p5South%20Africa_en.pdf>.

[134] OECD, OECD Peer Review: Competition Law and Policy in South Africa, (May 2003), <http://www.oecd.org/dataoecd/52/13/2958714.pdf>.

[135] Ibid.

[136] David Lewis, Chairperson Competition Tribunal, Competition Law Enforcement in South Africa, Paper presented to IBA Conference Cape Town (March 18, 2002), <http://www.comptrib.co.za/Publications/Speeches/lewis7.pdf>.

5. *Open-mindedness of first-level decision-makers*

The extent to which the Commission can be considered open-minded in its investigation stages is intricately tied up with the issues regarding the provision of adequate notice of the evidence that it is relying on. Thus, if parties are not provided with an indication of the evidence that the Commission is relying on, there is little opportunity for the targets of competition enforcement to engage with the Commission and explain their position.

Many practitioners have particular concerns with the Commission's approach to settlement discussions. They note that the Commission is reluctant to take into account particular circumstances of a respondent, such as their inability to pay a fine, or their limited engagement in a cartel, but prefers to set precedents for percentage-based fines that are consistent within a particular case. For instance, recent settlement agreements reached in a case regarding a plastic-pipe cartel[137] illustrates that the Commission requires parties to settle on the same percentage as other respondents in the same matter have settled. Respondent, Flo-Tek and Swan Plastics, both settled with the Commission on a 6 percent of total turnover basis, in line with a previous settlement with a company called Marley Pipe Systems. This is despite the fact that evidence revealed in the course of the trial indicated that Marley was a long-running member of the cartel for over two decades, but Flo-tek attended a single cartel meeting. A medium-sized player in the market also settled with the Commission for 6 percent of turnover. Its participation from the evidence led appeared to have been more extensive than Flo-Tek's but far less extensive than Marley. These parties were clearly penalized for settling with the Commission at a later stage than Marley did. Nevertheless, practitioners have noted that the delay in settling is often due to the Commission's refusal to acknowledge the particular circumstances of the defendant, and the mitigation claims made by the parties. The complaint is thus that the Commission appears concerned primarily with the precedent created by a particular settlement agreement, and the deterrent effect thereof, more than the application of particular facts in each circumstance.[138]

It is also not clear to what extent the first-level investigating team has an influence over the ultimate Commission decision-makers. The analysts allocated to cases report to senior officials within the Commission who then sign off on the final reports which result from a merger assessment or complaint investigation. All final reports and advisory opinions are presented to the EXCO (Executive Committee) of the Commission, which meets once every week. These reports and opinions are then interrogated at the applicable EXCO sitting, whereafter the Commission (the Commissioner and his deputy) makes the final decision.

EXCO apparently relies heavily on the assessment of the facts by the investigation team or case handler, but will often send a report back and ask for further

[137] *Competition Commission v Swan Plastics* (15/CR/Feb09).

[138] The same has happened with settlements in the scrap metal case, *see Competition Commission v National Scrap Metals (Pty) Ltd* (51/CR/Aug10).

issues to be addressed. It is not clear how often the EXCO rejects or accepts the investigating team's recommendations.[139]

6. *Equality before the law*

In terms of section 3 of the Act, the South African Competition Act applies to all economic activity occurring within or having an effect within South Africa. The extra-territorial reach of the law provided for in this section was dealt with in the *ANSAC* case. The matter concerned an export association based in the United States. Defendant American Soda Ash Corporation, a member of the association, pointed out that the matter challenged was a concerted low price, and claimed that the low price was pro-competitive. It argued that an anticompetitive effect was required to be shown before jurisdiction could be established. Both the Tribunal and the SCA rejected this argument and found that the provision did not require one to read in the words "harmful effect" in order to establish the jurisdiction of the Competition Authorities.

Thus, economic activity having an effect in South Africa, irrespective of the nature of such effect, may be subject to the Competition Act. Thus, an anti-competitive effect need not be shown at the jurisdictional state. South Africa has considered adopting an exemption from its Competition Act for export cartels whose effect is felt entirely outside the country,[140] although it is unclear why one would be needed, as the Act implies that external harms are excluded from the scope of the Act.

Nonetheless, the application of the law remains non-discriminatory with respect to location or status and there have been no formal complaints that it has been applied to foreign respondents differently than it is to domestic ones.[141]

A merger outside South Africa may have to be notified and approved if the parties' sales or assets in South Africa exceed the notification thresholds. Increased foreign investment and the concomitant expansion of South African business into global markets has resulted in an increase in the number of international transactions that have qualified for notification to the South African competition authorities and South African authorities have been tasked with an increasing number of multinational hostile takeover bids.

Sections 1(2) and 1(3) of the Act and the Constitution oblige the Competition Authorities to recognize and consider appropriate foreign and international law. Indeed, the South African competition authorities have previously relied upon decisions of the US, Canadian, and European competition authorities and the Commission has worked with the European Commission, Canada, Australia, and the US in merger matters.

[139] Telephone interview with Wendy Mkwanazi, Head of Legal Division, Competition Commission (December 8, 2010).

[140] Annual Report, Competition Commission, 2001, <http://www.compcom.co.za/assets/Files/annual-report-2000-2001.pdf>.

[141] OECD, OECD Peer Review: Competition Law and Policy in South Africa (May 2003), <http://www.oecd.org/dataoecd/52/13/2958714.pdf>.

Over time, the division has been building wider international networks to build its analytical capabilities through learning from international experience and drawing on international expertise.[142] Although the Commission has no formal cooperation agreements with other competition agencies, it has worked with the European Commission, Canada, Australia, and the US in merger matters. Ongoing relationships are maintained with other competition authorities in the region, notably in Zimbabwe, Zambia, and the other countries of the Southern African Development Community (SADC).[143] Significant effort has gone into hosting staff exchanges and fact-finding missions involving staff members from competition agencies on the continent. Current efforts to establish an African competition forum will focus on Africa-specific projects, activities, needs, and challenges in competition.

7. The right to challenge agency determinations

The Constitution requires that there be an avenue of appeal to an independent court. The Competition Act perhaps goes a little too far in accommodating this right as there are many layers of appeals and reviews open.

Firstly, decisions by the Commission may be appealed to the Tribunal. Thus, decisions in relation to exemptions or intermediate mergers can be taken to the Tribunal. Then the Tribunal's decisions in turn are appealable to the CAC. In the absence of the CAC, the ordinary course of appeal from actions applying the Competition Act would probably have been to a panel of High Court judges. All of the CAC's judges are High Court judges and thus what distinguishes the CAC is the fact that its members are appointed by the Judicial Service Commission, the constitutionally mandated body to conduct hearings and make judicial appointments, in this case on the basis of expertise and interest in competition matters. Therefore it is able to develop more perspective and expertise about competition issues.[144]

The CAC may review any decision of the Tribunal concerning legal error and jurisdiction. The CAC may consider an appeal concerning the substantive merits of any final decision of the Tribunal (except a consent order). It hears and decides cases in panels of three judges, although a single judge may decide interlocutory or procedural matters.[145]

[142] The Commission participates in the United Nations Conference on Trade and Development's (UNCTAD) annual intergovernmental expert meeting on competition law. The Commission is also focused on joint enforcement projects and ensuring the smooth and consistent review of international mergers. South Africa is a member of the Southern and Eastern Africa Competition Forum. The Commission chaired the second meeting of the SADC regional workshop on competition law and policy in Botswana in August 2009. The Competition Commission is also an active member of the International Competition Network (ICN) and the Commissioner is a member of its steering group. Staff members from relevant divisions participated in the ICN's cartels working group in October 2009 in Egypt.

[143] Annual Report, Competition Commission, 2001, <http://www.compcom.co.za/assets/Files/annual-report-2000-2001.pdf>.

[144] OECD, OECD Peer Review: Competition Law and Policy in South Africa (May 2003), <http://www.oecd.org/dataoecd/52/13/2958714.pdf>.

[145] Ibid.

The Act then creates a further appeal process to the Supreme Court of Appeal, and then possibly the Constitutional Court.[146] That further appeal is not a matter of right—special leave to appeal must be obtained from the CAC or from the higher court itself, and such leave may be conditioned on an order concerning security for the costs of appeal.[147] The Constitutional Court will only hear cases that involve a constitutional issue, and if the Court's hearing of the matter is in the interests of justice.

There is thus a bizarre four-stage appeal process available. In addition, as noted above, the Competition authorities exercise administrative power and are subject to the terms of the Promotion of Administrative Justice Act. As such, their exercise of administrative action is subject to review by the High Court[148] (which decision is itself appealable to the SCA, and then potentially the Constitutional Court).

There is thus an interesting balance created between generalist and specialist courts. In some ways, the generalist courts seem to restrict the ability of the specialist courts to create a unique procedural jurisprudence.

Members of the Tribunal however have expressed frustration with the willingness of the CAC to overturn its decisions, not only on issues of procedure (issues over which the generalist courts consider themselves to have greater expertise), but also on evidence assessment, and issues of fact and law. In the *Netstar*[149] matter for instance, the CAC was critical of the Tribunal's assessment of the facts, stating that the Tribunal had picked and chosen the evidence it liked. The CAC decision thus paints an entirely different factual matrix from the one the Tribunal discerned.[150]

On the one hand, the members of the Tribunal have minimal judicial experience, and thus the guidance of generalist courts is in many ways useful. On the other, there should be a consciousness on the part of superior courts regarding the need to be deferential to an expert body, which has directly heard the relevant evidence and made judgments on the credibility of witnesses. These differing considerations underlie a major tension between the Tribunal and the courts.

a) Proportionality of remedies to violations

The Act makes provision for the imposition of administrative penalties on firms which have engaged in the following prohibited conduct: direct or indirect price fixing,[151] market division,[152] collusive tendering,[153] resale price maintenance,[154] excessive pricing,[155] refusal of access to an essential facility,[156] inducing a customer not to buy from a competitor, refusing to buy scarce goods from a competitor, bundling of goods, selling goods below cost, and buying up scarce supply of intermediate goods or resources required by a competitor.[157]

[146] Section 62(4). [147] Section 63.

[148] *Competition Commission v Telkom SA Ltd, Competition Tribunal*, 623/2008.

[149] *Netstar (Pty) Ltd, Matrix Vehicle Tracking (Pty) Ltd and Tracker Network (Pty) Ltd v The Competition Commission and Tracetec (Pty) Ltd* (97/CAC/May10).

[150] *See*, for example, paras 48, 56, 59, and 61 of Netstar.

[151] Section 4(1)(b)(i). [152] Section 4(1)(b)(ii).

[153] Section 4(1)(b)(iii). [154] Section 5(2).

[155] Section 8(a). [156] Section 8(b). [157] Section 8(d).

Other prohibited conduct may also be subject to administrative penalty if it is repeated after the Tribunal orders it to stop. An administrative penalty may also be imposed if there is non-compliance with merger reporting requirements and processes. Divestiture can be required to undo a merger that contravenes the statutory requirements, or to remedy abuse of dominance if no other remedy would be adequate or if the respondent has repeated a previous violation. Divestiture orders must however be specifically confirmed by the CAC.[158]

Fines can be imposed on firms in two ways, either by way of a consent agreement[159] negotiated and concluded between the Commission and the firm, or by the unilateral imposition of a penalty by the Tribunal[160] at the conclusion of a hearing.

The Competition Tribunal has found that the main objective in the levying of these fines should be deterrent rather than punitive in nature. Section 59 of the Act governs the imposition of administrative penalties. In terms of this section, the penalty or fine imposed may not exceed 10 percent of the firm's annual turnover in the preceding financial year.[161] Section 59(3) provides that, in levying a penalty, the following factors "must" be taken into account:

- the nature, duration, gravity, and extent of the contravention;
- the loss or damage suffered as a result of the contravention;
- the behavior of the respondent;
- the market circumstances in which the contravention took place;
- the level of profit derived from the contravention;
- the degree to which the respondent has cooperated with the Competition Commission and the Competition Tribunal; and
- whether the respondent has previously been found in contravention of the Act.[162]

These factors were applied in the *Federal Mogul* case,[163] in which the Tribunal held that the maximum 10 percent should be used as a departure point when determining the amount of a fine. The Tribunal in the *SAA* case[164] allocated a percentage weighting, all adding up to 10 percent, to each of the factors mentioned in section 59 as follows: 3 percent attributed to the nature, duration, and extent of the contravention; 1 percent rating given to the loss or damage as a result of the contravention; 1 percent given to the behavior of the respondent; 1 percent attributed to the market circumstances; 0.5 percent given to the level of profit derived from the contravention; 1.5 percent attributed to the level of cooperation with the Commission and the Tribunal; and the remaining 2 percent allocated to any previous conduct.

[158] Section 60. [159] Section 49D.
[160] Section 59. [161] Section 59(2). [162] Section 59(3).
[163] *Competition Commission of South Africa and Federal Mogul Aftermarket Southern Africa (Pty) Ltd* 08/CR/Mar01.
[164] *Competition Commission and South African Airways (Pty) Ltd* 18/CR/Mar01.

The SAA formula has either been abandoned by the competition authorities or is not considered applicable in collusion cases. The Tribunal in its decision in *Pioneer Foods*[165] levied its largest fine in percentage terms on Pioneer Foods in the amount of R195 718 164.00 which constituted 10 percent of its affected turnover for the 2007 financial year. It also imposed a 10 percent fine on Southern Pipelines for its participation in a concrete-pipe cartel.[166]

The Tribunal has generally levied penalties on "the affected line of business" and not against the company's total turnover. It did so again in *Pioneer*, but noted that it is entitled to levy a penalty on total group turnover. The Commission appears to have taken a policy decision that all fines in collusion cases should be levied on the total turnover of the business, and thus it appealed the Tribunal's decision in *Pioneer* on the basis that the fine should have been levied on Pioneer's total group turnover, and not on the turnover of the bread division. This appeal has recently been abandoned. The Commission and Pioneer reached an innovative settlement in respect of a number of complaints in which Pioneer is implicated. The settlement included the creation of a fund (to be funded via the Treasury which receives the fine) to support small and medium businesses to enter the market as competitors, and a reduction of bread and flour prices for a period.

Southern Pipelines appealed the fine imposed on it to the CAC. The CAC's *Southern Pipelines* decision now constitutes the current precedent on administrative penalties. The CAC cleared up a number of areas of uncertainty: all factors listed in section 59(3) must be considered in determining the penalty; the base turnover against which those factors should be considered is the "affected" turnover; the 10 percent cap relates to the "total" turnover; and the preceding financial year against which the 10 percent cap relates is the year preceding the imposition of the fine. Commentators note that although "the CAC has provided a welcome framework for the determination of penalties, many areas of uncertainty remain, and it will take more time, or the introduction of fining guidelines before there is a predictable approach to fining guidelines."[167]

Most penalties have been determined through the conclusion of consent agreements with the Commission, rather than through the imposition of fines by the Tribunal. Pioneer is the only firm on which an administrative penalty was levied since the beginning of 2009 (and the only respondent in a section 4(1)(b) collusion case since the Act's inception). In sharp contrast, the Tribunal confirmed twenty consent/settlement orders during 2009, twenty-three in 2010, and twenty-six in 2012. A review of the consent agreements reached over the last ten years illustrates the increasing level of fines, in line with international trends.[168]

There may not be an express requirement on the Commission to consider the factors in section 59(3) of the Act when negotiating with settling parties, and in the

[165] *Competition Commission of South Africa v Pioneer Foods (Pty) Ltd* 15/CR/Feb07.

[166] *Competition Commission v Southern Pipeline Contractors Concrite Walls (Pty) Ltd* (23/CR/Feb09).

[167] Alan Wright, "It's a fine mess: The approach to administrative penalties under the Competition Act," POLITY, April 2, 2012.

[168] *See* confirmed consent orders, <http://www.comptrib.co.za/cases/consent-order/?start=0>.

absence of any fining guidelines, the SAA formula was used as a basis for settlement negotiations with the Commission for some time. However, since the *Pioneer* decision appears to have discarded this formula, settlement negotiations with the Commission are proceeding in a less formal manner.

Nevertheless, contrary to some of the Tribunal determinations, the section 59(3) factors are clearly considered by the Commission in reaching settlement agreements, as is illustrated by the Commission's references to these considerations in confirmation hearings at the Tribunal. Thus small firms have sometimes been treated leniently by the Commission, particularly in concentrated industries, where the Commission does not want to disadvantage such firms against their significantly more powerful competitors.[169] Firms that have provided the Commission with valuable information to assist in the prosecution of other respondents have also received lenient fines,[170] and firms that have engaged in collusive conduct in industries that directly affect the poor have been severely punished.[171]

Problems arise when factors not specifically mentioned in section 59(3) are present. For instance, both the Commission and respondents have no guidelines of how to approach penalties when there are financial restrictions on the respondent party and thus an inability to pay the fine. This issue has arisen in a number of cases recently, as a result of the recession.

The Commission has generally been unwilling to reduce penalties as a consequence of an inability to pay, because the consideration of this factor is not mandated by the Act. This has given rise to a trend in which firms admit to contraventions, but still go to the Tribunal to argue the matter on penalty, as they have been unable to afford the penalty offered by the Commission.[172]

In the case of mergers, fines for pre-implementation have been increasing over the years. In prior implementation cases, the Tribunal also applies the section 59(3) factors mentioned above. The parties' *bona fides* and rationale for non-notification are also almost always taken into account. In the *Structa Techology*[173] decision, the Tribunal imposed a symbolic fine of R1 on the parties as the contravention was based on a *bona fide* error, that had no negative consequences and the parties complied with their obligations as soon as they became aware of the error.

However, in the *Edgars*[174] decision the Tribunal levied a fine of R250,000 on the parties. Although this fine was significantly lower than the amount suggested by the Commission, the Tribunal still acknowledged the fact that a fine cannot be so low that a firm would deem it worthwhile to pay in order to expedite a deal going

[169] *Competition Commission v Safripol (Pty) Ltd* (48/CR/Aug10).

[170] *Competition Commission v Keystone Milling Co. (Pty)Ltd* (15/CR/Mar10).

[171] *Competition Commission of South Africa v Pioneer Foods (Pty) Ltd* 15/CR/Feb07.

[172] In 2008, the Commission settled with the New Reclamation Group in terms of which the group would pay the amount of R146 million representing 6 percent of its affected turnover over a three-year period. When the group struggled to pay its last instalment and approached the Tribunal for a revision of the payment terms, this application was opposed by the Commission because it undermines the underlying deterrent effect of penalties. *The Competition Commission v The New Reclamation Group (Pty) Ltd* (37/CR/Apr08).

[173] *Competition Commission and Structa Technology (Pty)* Ltd 83/LM/Nov02.

[174] *Competition Commission and Edgars Consolidated Stores Ltd* 95/FN/Dec02.

through. In 2008, the Tribunal confirmed a settlement agreement between the Commission, Bonheur General Trading, and Komatiland Forests[175] in which the respondents agreed to pay a fine of R500,000. The reasons given were *inter alia* that the respondents had not intended to evade the Act and were *bona fide* in their actions and intentions to comply with the Act. Another R500,000 fine was levied on Netcare, in an odd decision which implied that parties can be found to have failed to notify a merger and be guilty of collusion at the same time.[176]

Recently, the highest fine of R1.1 million for pre-implementation was levied on construction company WBHO, but that fine was part of a settlement agreement rather than Tribunal imposition.

A party that has suffered loss or damage from prohibited conduct may sue for damages in court, if damages were not already provided for in a consent order with the Commission. But that suit depends on a prior finding from the Tribunal or the CAC, which the plaintiff must file with its lawsuit. Damages could be awarded in excess of the 10 percent turnover limit of the administrative penalty determined in terms of the Act. Punitive damages are not awarded in South Africa, and thus the damages will reflect the amount of harm/damage suffered as proved by the plaintiff.

Recently, a number of consumer and trade union groups have tried to launch a class action suit against members of the bread cartel. They claim that the penalties paid to the state for price fixing by Pioneer Foods, Tiger Brands, and Premier Foods (which was granted leniency) do not do justice to compensate the ordinary people, in particular the poor, who suffered most. The High Court did not certify the claimants as a "class," but apparently the groups have in any event launched the claim.

In the ten years that the Act has been in effect, only one claim for civil damages in South Africa has reached trial stage, and it was finally settled out of court.[177]

B. Institutional performance norms

1. Timeliness of dispositions

There is significant disappointment with the pace of decision-making in competition cases.[178] Competition proceedings in South Africa have generally been lengthy and protracted (mostly in respect of complaint proceedings).

[175] *Competition Commission and Bonheur 50 General Trading (Pty) Ltd* 38/CR/Apr08.

[176] *Commission and Netcare & CHG* (27/CR/Mar07).

[177] *See* Malose Monama, "Price fixing cartels face consumer lawsuits," City Press Business 1 August 2009. Available at: <http://jv.news24.com/City_Press/Finance/0,186-246_2544284,00.html>. Last consulted: 03.08.2009. Florence de Vries, "Competition authority 'is a hammer seeking a nail'" Business Report 2 August 2009, <http://www.busrep.co.za/index.php?fArticleId=5109734>. Last consulted: 03.08.09.

[178] Speech by Tribunal chairperson Norman Manoim at annual Competition Committee breakfast on October 19, 2010.

a) Mergers

Deadlines and procedures differ according to the magnitude of the transaction. Mergers are classified as small, intermediate, or large depending on the turnover or assets of the merging parties. The thresholds have been increased substantially since 1998 to reduce the number of transactions that are subject to mandatory notification.

The Act gives the Commission twenty business days in which to decide whether or not to approve an intermediate merger (though this can be extended by forty business days if necessary). If the Commission does not act within the deadline, the merger is approved. The Commission has forty business days to consider a large merger, which can be extended by applying to the Tribunal, but the Tribunal may not grant an extension for more than fifteen business days at a time. (Therefore if the Commission requires further extension, it will have to make application for a further fifteen-day extension.) If the Commission misses its deadline in obtaining an extension, the parties can petition the Tribunal to proceed without a recommendation. The Commission's failure to act does not amount to an approval, because the Tribunal ultimately decides on all large mergers and the Commission's report amounts only to a recommendation to the Tribunal.

In March 2010, the Commission published new service standard commitments for merger notifications to replace the previous 2001 standards.[179] According to the Commission this was in line with its aim of being "a high performance regulatory agency with realistic, predictable and achievable service standards in finalising merger cases."[180]

In an effort to ensure predictable outcomes the new standards have created three categories of mergers according to the complexity of investigation needed. The categories include non-complex, complex, and very complex mergers:

Non-complex mergers (phase 1): Non-complex or phase 1 mergers are easily identifiable by the lack of competition concerns in that the parties do not compete in the same market or they have a small combined market share. Phase 1 mergers require the least amount of investigation before approval can be granted, and therefore there is minimal documentation and information required by the Commission. In line with its previous commitment to "fast track" non-complex mergers, the Commission aims to make a decision on phase 1 mergers within twenty business days following the filing in which to review the merger.

Complex mergers (phase 2): A complex merger is one in which there are not likely to be anticompetitive effects. However, due to the type of markets involved, a more detailed investigation is required. The Commission aims to review phase 2 mergers within forty-five business days.

Very complex mergers (phase 3): A very complex merger requires the most detailed investigation by the Commission due to the complexity of the transaction

[179] Available at <http://www.compcom.co.za/service-standards/>.

[180] Maarten van Hoven, "M&A Service Standards 2010" Competition News, Edition 35, <http://www.compcom.co.za/assets/Uploads/AttachedFiles/MyDocuments/June-2010-newsletter-Final-Draft.pdf>.

and the markets involved. Phase 3 transactions will necessitate a thorough investigation including obtaining specific documents and information from the merger parties and third-party industry participants. The Commission intends to complete phase 3 assessments after sixty business days.

The new service standards illustrate the Commission's commitment to keeping merger review timelines reasonable and predictable.

In 2010, the Commission also released its "Complete merger filing requirements."[181] This guideline sets out all the documents and information that the merging parties should submit when notifying a merger which meets the monetary thresholds, as well as comprehensive guidelines on the submission of any other documents and information which the Commission views as being relevant, necessary, and sufficient to constitute a complete filing. This document will hopefully reduce delays resulting from incomplete or insufficient merger filings.

The average turn-around time for mergers from the Act's inception in 1999 is thirty-one days. However, in the financial year ended March 31, 2010 and in terms of the then-applicable service standards, only 40 percent of phase 1 mergers, 13 percent of phase 2 mergers, and 14 percent of phase 3 mergers were completed in the requisite time period.[182]

As noted above, there have been some concerns that the requirement of providing extensive information on potential effects on employment, and agreeing on conditions to mitigate negative effects on employment have recently led to delays in the Commission's assessment of mergers.[183]

The Tribunal is not subject to statutory deadlines in merger cases, although it has generally moved expeditiously, convening hearings promptly (within ten days) after receiving Commission recommendations.[184] In its application to review the Tribunal's Wal-Mart/Massmart decision described above, the government intervenors argued that the Tribunal's imposition of a strict hearing and discovery schedule rendered the decision reviewable as it did not allow them to fully ventilate

[181] Practitioner Update Issue 6. <http://www.compcom.co.za/assets/Uploads/AttachedFiles/MyDocuments/Complete-filing-notice-Mch-2010.pdf>.

[182] Competition Commission, *Annual Report 2009/2010*, <http://www.compcom.co.za/assets/Publications/Annual-Reports/Annual-Report-2009-10-Final.pdf>.

[183] Heather Irvine, "Employment Concerns Delay Merger Clearance," <http://www.polity.org.za/article/employment-concerns-delay-merger-clearances-2010-02-01>. She refers to the transaction in which T-Systems South Africa acquired Arivia.com from Eskom and Transnet, where the relevant trade union failed to give notice of its intention to participate in the merger proceedings within the five day time period specified in the Act, and only approached the Commission to express concerns about the merger some six weeks after the filing was filed and served on them. The union then proceeded to raise concerns which were completely unrelated to the merger, such as the fact that the union was ideologically opposed to the privatization of state assets like Arivia, and the fact that two employees had been dismissed following internal disciplinary hearings some months before the merger agreement was signed. The Commission took about twelve weeks to investigate and approve the proposed transaction (although it eventually declined to impose any conditions). The recent *Metrolpolitan/Momentum* merger (footnote 29) has also been delayed since the Tribunal requested further information regarding employment effects, than those demanded by the Commission.

[184] OECD, OECD Peer Review: Competition Law and Policy in South Africa (May 2003), <http://www.oecd.org/dataoecd/52/13/2958714.pdf>.

all of their concerns. The CAC rejected this, and agreed with the Commission that the Act enables the Tribunal to play an active role in its proceedings to ensure that they are conducted as expeditiously as possible. The CAC stated:

> Indeed, at least part of the problem with merger hearings is that it appears that the Tribunal may adopt too passive an approach to the inquiry, arguably not giving sufficient effect to the provisions of s52 which, at the very least, allows the Tribunal to employ an informal or inquisitorial form of hearing. Thus, by ensuring that the key issues are defined as early as possible by the Tribunal, and that the parties are then immediately appraised thereof, the inquisitorial or informal form of hearing provided for in the Act, could ensure a far more satisfactory balance between expedition and natural justice. An adversarial form of hearing may prove both more helpful to the Tribunal and more conducive to the principles of natural justice in cases dealing with restrictive practices. But merger hearings are different. Here the Tribunal is mandated to engage in a statutorily defined inquiry, as opposed to a determination of a breach of a provision of the Act. This form of inquiry is therefore different to a determination about restrictive practices as defined in the Act. Merger hearings, the object of which is to determine whether a merger can be approved, should not be stultified by an excess of formalism or of procedures best suited to a trial. This observation is offered as guidance for the future.[185]

Contested merger cases tend to proceed much faster than complaint proceedings. Such hearings have tended to be concluded relatively expeditiously.

b) Complaint proceedings

Time periods in respect of complaint proceedings are governed by the Competition Act[186] as well as the Competition Tribunal Rules. In terms of Section 50 of the Act there is no set time period for a complaint initiated by the Commission to be referred to the Competition Tribunal.[187] However, in respect of a complaint initiated by a complainant, the Commission has one year within which to either refer the complaint to the Tribunal or to issue a notice of non-referral to the complainant.[188] This period may be extended by agreement between the Commission and the complainant or on application to the Tribunal.[189]

The issue of time periods in respect of initiation and referral of complaints was dealt with extensively in *Competition Commission and Clover Industries Ltd.*[190] In this matter Clover and another applicant raised a point *in limine* in terms of which they alleged that a one-year period had expired since the complaint had been initiated and that the complaint had therefore lapsed; alternatively that the Commission had not obtained the requisite extension in terms of Section 50(4) of the Act. The Tribunal noted that it is only a "complaint" by a complainant—other than the Commission—that is subject to the one-year prescriptive period. In this case, the Tribunal concluded that this was not a complaint by a complainant and

185 *The Minister of Economic Development and Others v The Competition Tribunal and Others* 110/CAC/Jun11 at para 85.

186 Act 98 of 1998.

187 Section 50(1) of the Act.

188 Section 50(2)(a) and (b) of the Act.

189 Section 50(4)(a) and (b) of the Act.

190 *Competition Commission and Clover Industries Ltd and others* 103/CR/Dec06.

was therefore not subject to the one year prescription period and consequently dismissed the point *in limine*.

The Tribunal Rules[191] set out the relevant time periods in terms of which the various papers and pleadings must be served in a complaint referral. Rule 14(2)(a) states that once a referral has been filed, it must be served on the respondent/s within three business days thereof. Within twenty business days of being served a complaint referral, respondents must serve and file an answering affidavit. Rule 17 provides that if an answering affidavit raises points that were not addressed in the complaint referral, then the complainant or the Commission (whoever filed the complaint referral) must serve and file a replying affidavit within fifteen business days of being served with the answering affidavit.

The reality in South Africa is that cases involving prohibited conduct seldom adhere to these time periods as respondents need time to investigate the allegations against them in order to respond to the complaint referral. All parties seem to delay proceedings to some extent—respondents take time to respond to the case against them (and occasionally launch interlocutory proceedings), while vague pleadings from the Commission and delays in completing investigations often contribute to the delays. The Tribunal Chair recently admitted that it is also taking too long for the Tribunal to issue its decisions.[192] Nevertheless, the Commission is reasonably accommodating in agreeing to grant parties extra time to prepare answers and collate any necessary supporting documents and therefore readily allows extensions. There have been few complaints that parties are given inadequate time to prepare.

It is clear that measures to expedite proceedings are needed. The Competition Tribunal has suggested that the Commission introduce fining guidelines which provide for a discount on a fine due to early settlement.[193] However, the Commission notes in its last Annual Report that even settlement discussions are lengthy. The Commission's experience has been that the settlement negotiations it engages in with respondents tend to be protracted and time-consuming, even in circumstances where a party does not dispute the Commission's findings. It notes that it has adopted a strategy that seeks to ensure that the prosecution of cases is not delayed due to protracted negotiations. It also plans to make the level of penalty imposed in settlements reflect the value that the Commission places on cooperation and early settlement. It is hoped that all these measures will yield an increase in the number of finalized consent and settlement agreements in the next financial year.[194]

[191] Available at: <http://www.comptrib.co.za/docs/Tribunal%20Rules.doc>.

[192] Speech by Tribunal chairperson Norman Manoim at annual Competition Committee breakfast on October 19, 2010.

[193] Ibid.

[194] Competition Commission, *Annual Report 2009/2010*, <http://www.compcom.co.za/assets/Publications/Annual-Reports/Annual-Report-2009-10-Final.pdf>.

2. *Expertise in determinations*

The Tribunal is an administrative body composed of representatives of the disciplines of law and economics and potentially chartered accountants. There are permanent and non-permanent members of the Tribunal. The current chair of the Tribunal, Norman Manoim, is a lawyer. The previous chair, David Lewis, is an economist. The Tribunal has the necessary expertise to perform its role. And indeed, the permanent members of the Tribunal are well respected.[195] Practitioners and members of the Bar note, however, that there appears to be little participation in hearings (in respect of questioning from the bench) from panel members besides the chair, and especially in the case of non-permanent members of the Tribunal. Most of the Tribunal's important decisions have been authored by the permanent members. One constraint on the members' qualifications is the need to include enough lawyers to assign at least one lawyer to each panel dealing with a case.

The CAC is composed of sitting members of the provincial divisions of the courts. The judges volunteer to serve on this court because of a particular interest or expertise in competition law. They serve in addition to their normal generalist duties on provincial benches. As noted, in order to serve on the CAC, they submit to full hearings before the Judicial Services Commission—the body which is responsible for nominating judicial appointments to the President.[196] But as the volume of appeals from the Tribunal increases, this "part-time" court may be overextended.

This process ensures that the pool of judges hear a relatively large number of competition cases and thus experience a critical mass to develop a working familiarity with this field of law. Lewis notes that they are in sufficient touch with the particularities of competition law to develop discerning regard for the expertise of the Tribunal, and in an appropriate position to become ambassadors for competition law among the judiciary.[197]

However, given the relative youth of the South African competition authorities, the Tribunal and CAC are also heavily reliant on the counsel that appears before them, and in this regard, they have been somewhat constrained. Firstly, the bar is primarily a defense bar, and secondly, there is still a paucity of competition expertise at the bar. This reduces the ability of the adjudicators to rely on assistance from the bar.

The adjudicators have also complained that they have at times been hamstrung by the absence of input from the Competition Commission. For instance, in the

[195] OECD, OECD Peer Review: Competition Law and Policy in South Africa (May 2003), <http://www.oecd.org/dataoecd/52/13/2958714.pdf>.

[196] OECD, OECD Peer Review: Competition Law and Policy in South Africa (May 2003), <http://www.oecd.org/dataoecd/52/13/2958714.pdf>.

[197] Background document prepared for the OECD Global Forum on Competition, Challenges/Obstacles Faced by Competition Authorities in Achieving Greater Economic Development through the Promotion of Competition, (February 2004), <http://www.comptrib.co.za/Publications/Speeches/oecd_20oct.pdf>.

Nationwide Poles v Sasol case, and in *Harmony Gold v Mittal Steel*, the Commission non-referred the complaints and the complainants pursued the matters themselves. This has disabled the Tribunal, because such complainants do not have the same resources that are available to the Commission. Davis commented for instance that in *Nationwide Poles*, "the small producer of treated wooden poles, who heroically litigated this case, was unable to put forward the kind of evidence that the Commission would have been able to procure to ensure that a different evidential matrix confronted the court." The Commission of course has limited resources and needs to make assessments of which cases are worthy pursuing. The fact that both *Mittal* and *Nationwide* were (at least partially)[198] successfully appealed may have vindicated the Commission's decisions in this regard.

In respect of the Commission's expertise, 51 percent of the employees in the Commission are lawyers or economists. 36 percent of the staff is support and administrative staff, and 4 percent of the staff is in management.[199] The four staff divisions at the Commission that are most directly responsible for substantive competition issues are the Mergers and Acquisitions Division; the Enforcement and Exemptions Division; the Policy and Research Division; and the Legal Services Division. The Commission sometimes retains outside counsel.

It has been a challenge to attract and retain professional staff who can deal effectively with the private sector's experienced and well-paid representatives. Thus, the Commission, like enforcement agencies everywhere, finds that either it cannot attract ambitious, bright, younger staff, or it cannot keep them after they have acquired enough experience to be most effective. While the Commission has enough funds to pay competitive salaries to entry-level people with only a few years of experience, there is difficulty in persuading those people to work with a government body rather than a private sector, which can promise larger rewards in the long run. There has thus been a high staff turnover. It has been reduced however from 26 percent in 2007/8 to 15 percent in 2009/10.[200]

The Commission's graduate program was designed to deal with this problem. At the end of the 2009/2010 financial year, eleven graduate trainees were recruited. The graduate trainees provide a pool of skilled and qualified people that the Commission can draw from for more permanent positions. In the 2009/2010 year, four graduate trainees were kept on as permanent staff.[201]

A concern is that the level of professionalism and expertise at the Commission is uneven. The top managers at the Commission are highly respected, but the skills,

[198] In *Mittal*, the CAC found that the Tribunal's decision in relation to excessive pricing did not accord with the Act. The case was remitted to the Tribunal, but the matter was settled before being heard by the Tribunal again.

[199] Competition Commission, *Annual Report 2009/2010*, <http://www.compcom.co.za/assets/Publications/Annual-Reports/Annual-Report-2009-10-Final.pdf>.

[200] Competition Commission, *Annual Report 2009/2010*, <http://www.compcom.co.za/assets/Publications/Annual-Reports/Annual-Report-2009-10-Final.pdf>.

[201] OECD, OECD Peer Review: Competition Law and Policy in South Africa (May 2003), <http://www.oecd.org/dataoecd/52/13/2958714.pdf>.

responsiveness, and professionalism of the case handlers at the Commission are variable.[202]

The Commission has also identified the tier of middle management as an area where there are severe resource constraints. The Commission claims that it undertook a number of initiatives, such as the creation of a management development program, to develop the capacity of middle management in 2009/2010.[203]

The Commission acknowledges the problems it has in maintaining qualified staff[204] and the critical need to improve the depth and strengthen the capacity of the professional staff. In particular, it notes that the success of the corporate leniency policy has created a backlog of applications and investigations that have to be completed, which has placed considerable strain on the resources of the division and the Commission. In addition, abuse of dominance cases are complex, involving a combination of legal, economic, and investigative skills. The Commission notes that this places considerable strain on the Commission's resources as these cases tend to take longer to investigate and often require larger teams with a wider set of skills and this is a further area where the Commission must continue to build capacity.

The Commission plans to develop a cartels unit into a stand-alone division specializing in cartel investigation and enforcement. It also plans to place emphasis on deepening capacity and expertise in the investigation of abuse of dominance and restrictive vertical and horizontal practices. This will involve hiring more staff and devoting more resources to training and development.[205]

3. *Sufficiency of investigative and sanctioning powers*

The Competition Commission has at its disposal powers to assist in its investigation which are usually available to criminal enforcement authorities.[206]

The Act allows the Commission to raid certain premises, and to search for and remove information if it reasonably believes an enterprise has contravened the Competition Act, or that someone within the enterprise is in possession of anything

[202] OECD, OECD Peer Review: Competition Law and Policy in South Africa (May 2003), <http://www.oecd.org/dataoecd/52/13/2958714.pdf>.

[203] Competition Commission, *Annual Report 2009/2010*, <http://www.compcom.co.za/assets/Publications/Annual-Reports/Annual-Report-2009-10-Final.pdf>.

[204] However, resources are limited and the workload has increased substantially. The mismatch between resources and the demand placed on the Commission resulted in a deficit in the financial year. This would have been bigger were it not for the financial support received from the Ministry of Economic Development (Competition Commission, *Annual Report 2009/2010*, <http://www.compcom.co.za/assets/Publications/Annual-Reports/Annual-Report-2009-10-Final.pdf>).

[205] Competition Commission, *Annual Report 2009/2010*, <http://www.compcom.co.za/assets/Publications/Annual-Reports/Annual-Report-2009-10-Final.pdf>.

[206] Criminal Procedure Act 51 of 1977. *See* chapter 2. Moodliyar, Reardon, and Theuerkauf, "The Relationship between Public and Private Enforcement in Competition Law," paper presented at Competition Commission, Tribunal and Wits Conference 10 Year Review, <http://www.compcom.co.za/assets/Uploads/events/10-year-review/parallel-3b/The-Relationship-between-Public-and-Private-Enforcement-of-Competition-Law-SA-EU-CH.pdf>.

connected to a matter that the Commission is investigating. Such a search requires a warrant, issued by a High Court judge or magistrate.[207]

The Commission may carry out a dawn raid with or without a warrant. To obtain a warrant, the Commission must show it reasonably believes that a prohibited practice has taken place, is taking place, or is likely to take place; or anything connected with an investigation in terms of the Act is in the possession of a person on the relevant premises.

The Commission may enter premises without a warrant if it gets permission from the persons on the relevant premises to do so, or if it reasonably believes the delay in obtaining one would defeat the object or purpose of the raid.

On gaining entry the Commission is entitled to

- examine all documents having a bearing on the relevant investigation;
- request further information on any item;
- take extracts of documents and make copies;
- use and if necessary remove computers; and
- remove any other information that has a bearing on the investigation.[208]

Police may accompany the investigators and overcome resistance with reasonable force, such as breaking a window to gain entry.[209]

In carrying out a dawn raid the Act requires those conducting the raid to do so with "strict regard for decency and order, and with regard for each person's right to dignity, freedom, security and privacy." The Act further regulates other matters of conduct the Commission must observe, such as advising those being raided of their right to be assisted by an attorney and issuing receipts for items removed.

The Commission has conducted a number of raids, including raids on companies in the scrap metal recycling industry, the freight industry, the tire manufacturing industry, the steel industry, and the concrete industry.

Beyond its "dawn raid" powers, the Commission also has extensive summons powers which can be utilized at any time during an investigation. In terms of section 49A of the Act, the Commissioners may summon any person who is believed to be able to furnish any information on the subject of the investigation, or to have possession or control of any document or other object that has a bearing on that subject. That person may either be summoned to appear at the Commission to be interrogated or to deliver the requested documents to the Commission.

A person being interrogated must answer each question truthfully and to the best of that person's ability, but the person is not obliged to answer any question if the answer is self-incriminating. No self-incriminating answer given or statement made in these circumstances is admissible as evidence against the person who gave the answer or made the statement in criminal proceedings.

[207] Section 46. [208] Section 48. [209] Section 49A.

The Commission's powers of investigation are relatively unrestricted. Cost awards are unlikely to restrict the Commission. In the *Omnia* case,[210] the Tribunal noted that although it has the power to make such costs awards, it is unlikely to do so in most circumstances, as this may restrict the Commission's public task.

In respect of sanctioning powers, the Commission has the power to enforce orders of the Tribunal as if they were an order of the High Court[211] and can institute proceedings in the High Court for recovery of an administrative penalty imposed by the Tribunal.[212] In addition, the Commission is entitled to make settlement agreements with respondents, and impose fines in terms of those agreements, which must then be confirmed by the Tribunal.[213]

For contraventions of the Act, the Tribunal can impose administrative penalties in terms of section 59 of the Act, and it can impose a range of other remedies, including:[214]

- interdicting any *prohibited practice*;
- ordering a party to supply or distribute goods or services to another party on terms reasonably required to end a *prohibited practice*;
- ordering divestiture;
- declaring the conduct of a *firm* to be a *prohibited practice*;
- declaring the whole or any part of an *agreement* to be void;
- ordering access to an *essential facility* on terms reasonably required; and
- condoning non-compliance with Commission or Tribunal rules.

In addition, criminal sanctions being introduced through the new Amendment Act will increase the scope of the Commission and Tribunal's sanctioning powers. Although the criminal prosecutions themselves are to be pursued by the National Prosecuting Authority, a finding of the Tribunal regarding the collusive conduct will constitute prima facie[215] proof that the individual engaged in the relevant conduct. In addition, the NPA and Commission will presumably cooperate closely in pursuing such criminal prosecutions.[216]

4. Reasonable predictability in application of law

The Commission's approach to its task is reasonably predictable in that it will investigate all complaints lodged with it and analyze all mergers that are notified.

210 *Competition Commission v Yara South Africa (Pty) Ltd and Omnia Fertilizer Ltd* 31/CR/May05 (February 24, 2010). A costs award was, however, made against the Tribunal, *see Yara and Omnia v Competition Commission* (93/CAC/Mar10) at para 43.

211 Section 64(1).

212 Section 64(2).

213 Section 49D.

214 Section 58.

215 This provision of the Amendment Act will almost certainly be constitutionally challenged when the Amendment Act comes into effect.

216 Competition Commission, *Annual Report 2009/2010*, <http://www.compcom.co.za/assets/Publications/Annual-Reports/Annual-Report-2009-10-Final.pdf> regarding the MOU to be agreed with the NPA.

Nevertheless, because of resource constraints, it has had to prioritize certain aspects of its work. The Commission regularly communicates these priorities to the public. It has noted that it prioritizes its work based on the potential and actual impact of anticompetitive conduct on low income consumers and it attempts to align its activities with government's economic policy. It notes that the investigation and prosecution of cartels are almost always a priority.[217]

In addition, the Commission has identified four broad sectors in which it will undertake proactive analysis of possible competition related problems. These are: food, agro-processing, and forestry; infrastructure and construction; intermediate industrial products; and financial services (banking).

The Commission's approach to settlements is slightly less predictable than its approach to investigations and prosecutions. There is very little clarity as to which considerations are applied by the Commission in determining what fine to offer respondents in settlement negotiations.

There is a severe dearth of guidelines issued by the Commission indicating how it will apply the law. The Commission has issued no substantive enforcement guidelines. The Commission used to issue so-called "Practice Notes,"[218] but have ceased doing so.

The Tribunal's application of the law is less predictable, especially since the bulk of its decisions relate to procedural issues and interim relief applications rather than final decisions on cartel and abuse of dominance conduct. There is thus little precedent to guide parties regarding these contraventions of the Act.

5. *Transparency in policy formulation or elaboration*

There are unfortunately very few guidelines released by the Commission regarding their approach to enforcement of the law. Although it released some practice notes in the first few years of its operation, these have dried up, except in respect of merger evaluations.

The Mergers and Acquisition team of the Commission released new service standards and guidelines for preparing merger notifications in March 2010.[219]

The Commission is very transparent in respect of developments in the law, new investigations, and prosecutions. A communications department of the Commission also regularly issues media statements regarding any of its activities which are of public interest. The Commission also publishes annual reports and quarterly bulletins, which also appear on the Commission's website. Those publications reveal its priorities and policies to some extent.[220]

[217] Competition Commission, *Annual Report 2009/2010*, <http://www.compcom.co.za/assets/Publications/Annual-Reports/Annual-Report-2009-10-Final.pdf>.

[218] The Commission issued Practice Notes on: Asset Securitisation Schemes, Risk Mitigation transactions, Trade unions, and Joint Ventures, <http://www.compcom.co.za/practice-notes/>.

[219] Available at <http://www.compcom.co.za/service-standards/>.

[220] In the year under review, outreach workshops were held in Johannesburg, Cape Town, and Durban with a total of thirty-four journalists who report on competition related issues. In the year under review, nineteen media releases were issued, and 181 radio and seventy-three television

The Commission uses various publications to communicate with external stakeholders. The Commission publishes Competition News on a quarterly basis. The aim of the journal is to highlight key cases and other key developments. This also serves as a vehicle for feedback from key stakeholders. The Commission launched its revamped website (<www.compcom.co.za>) in December 2009. The new website is more user-friendly and aims to cater for the needs of the frequent visitor.[221]

The Tribunal does not develop policies, but all basic statutory materials and decisions of the Tribunal and the CAC are available on clear and straightforward websites. The authorities furnish written reasons for their decisions which may then be taken on appeal.

6. Opportunities for public consultation and participation in policy formulation and elaboration

There is some opportunity for public participation in policy formulation. There are attempts by the Commission's Strategy and Stakeholder Relations team to raise awareness about the Competition Act and the role of the Commission and to mobilize civil society organizations' active participation in the Commission's processes, particularly through engagement with consumer groups, and the encouragement of the development of consumer advocacy.

It also appears that public concerns voiced through the media are taken into account by the Commission. Recently, as noted, the Commission proposed a range of innovative remedies in respect of a settlement between it and Pioneer Foods (a participant in a bread cartel) which aimed to address public concerns regarding the unforeseen consequences of the imposition of large administrative penalties.[222] Such remedies included the setting up of an "Agro-Processing Fund" (into which Pioneer would contribute R250 million) to assist small- and medium-sized enterprises in the industry in which the cartel operated, as well as price reductions by Pioneer, and a commitment not to reduce investments as a result of the fine. Some of these remedies were later amended due to concerns expressed by the National Treasury (since the Competition Act provides that all fines must be deposited into the National Revenue Fund). However, the Commission will still pursue the creation of the Agro Processing Fund, with the assistance and support of the National Treasury Department.

In addition, there is a Joint Working Committee between the Mergers and Acquisition division and the Competition Committee of the Law Society, and thus there is some interaction between competition laws and this division of the

interviews were conducted. Competition Commission, *Annual Report 2009/2010*, <http://www.compcom.co.za/assets/Publications/Annual-Reports/Annual-Report-2009-10-Final.pdf>.

[221] The number of hits to the Commission's website has grown considerably: in 2009/10 visits to the website trebled to 106,738 from 27,400 in 2008/09, and the number of visitors increased from 11,930 to 45,619. There was also an increase in the number of returning visitors, from 2,840 in 2008/09 to 11,630 in 2009/10. Most visitors are from South Africa (79 percent), and then from the United Kingdom, United States, Italy, Germany, and other countries.

[222] *Competition Commission of South Africa v Pioneer Foods (Pty) Ltd* 15/CR/Feb07.

Commission. This allows lawyers an opportunity to voice concerns and proposals regarding merger review. There is not, however, a similar working committee with the enforcements division of the Commission.

There is also extensive participation by the Commission in other policy and governmental processes in order to ensure synergy between the Competition Act and other policies and legislation. This includes commenting on all policies, legislation, and regulations that have a bearing on competition. The Commission in the last financial year has submitted several comments on issues of telecommunications regulation, and has also commented on the Department of Trade and Industry's new Industrial Policy Action Plan for 2010/11 to 2012/13. Analyses and reviews were done for the Department of Economic Development on the Eskom proposed electricity price increases, and on competition issues in food, infrastructure, and telecommunications. The Commission also engages government departments, sector regulators, and legislatures on its positions in relation to existing or proposed legislative amendments. Also, in the course of enforcement activities, policy issues arise and the aim of the Commission is to bring these to the attention of the relevant government department or sector regulator.[223]

In respect of new legislation, there is a constitutionally enshrined legislative process that incorporates significant public participation. For instance, there was public participation in respect of the development of the Amendment Bill, and there were a number of drafts of the Bill responding to public proposals. However, the legislative process was driven by the Department of Trade and Industry and not the competition authorities themselves.

In respect of public participation in the Tribunal, the Tribunal has sought to encourage participation by interested stakeholders. For instance, merger rules require notifying the relevant minister (previously the Minister of Trade and Industry and now the Minister of Economic Development) of the merger and the trade unions that represent a significant proportion of the employees of the merging parties. These parties then have a right to intervene in proceedings by submitting evidence and argument. Various government departments have recently intervened in the hearings related to the proposed merger of Massmart and Walmart. The ministries have argued, in particular, that the merger will have an adverse effect upon small, local suppliers of produce and clothing in that either the merged entity will import these goods or compel the local suppliers to sell at prices that, ultimately, will force them out of business. The trade unions have objected to the merger primarily because of the effect that they contend the merger will have for employment both in the merged entity and in respect of local suppliers.[224]

The Tribunal's rules allow for participation of consumer interests in its proceedings, but few consumer representatives have appeared. A notable exception is the Treatment Action Campaign (TAC), now known as Section 27, a very active civil

[223] Competition Commission, *Annual Report 2009/2010*, <http://www.compcom.co.za/assets/Publications/Annual-Reports/Annual-Report-2009-10-Final.pdf>.

[224] *See* the witness statements and transcripts, <http://www.comptrib.co.za/walmart-massmart-merger/>.

society organization involved in rights advocacy for persons infected and affected by HIV. In the consideration of the *Glaxo-SmithKline* merger,[225] the TAC participated in order to advocate accessible HIV/AIDS drugs.[226] Other consumer groups have however been less visible in the competition process. This may change if the opportunity for civil class actions develops. There is currently a civil action by a number of civil society organizations for damages against the bread cartel (although they were not certified as a "class" by the court).[227]

Interested parties can also intervene in other proceedings before the Tribunal[228]—they must however establish their interest, and such intervention application is frequently opposed by parties to the matter. Interventions are generally encouraged by the Tribunal when the intervener can demonstrate it has a significant interest in the matter.[229] The Tribunal's view appears to be that permitting wide-ranging participation in its proceedings improves the quality and breadth of evidence and argument, and assists in establishing a reputation for transparency and accessibility.[230] Moreover, the Tribunal has seldom refused intervention applications, but such applicants can be penalized with costs orders if the authorities consider that the intervention was vexatious rather than helpful.[231] The most significant recent intervention was by the trade union, NEHAWU, which persuaded the Tribunal to limit the number of job losses following a merger between Momentum Group Ltd and Metropolitan Holdings, two financial institutions which were allowed to merge but subject to conditions about job losses.

7. Transparency of reasons for decisions

Decision-making power is to a large extent *de facto* in the hands of the Commission due to the number of settlements ending competition litigation. The Commission publicizes settlement agreements widely in the media and publishes press releases on its website. In addition, the settlement agreements themselves have to be confirmed by the Tribunal and are accessible on the Tribunal's website once confirmed. As such, there is transparency on the part of the Commission in respect of settlement agreements. It is more difficult to obtain information regarding discontinuances, non-referrals, or decisions not to refer the matter. Notices of

225 *Glaxo Wellcome plc and Smithkline Beecham* (58/Am/May00).

226 OECD, OECD Peer Review: Competition Law and Policy in South Africa (May 2003) <http://www.oecd.org/dataoecd/52/13/2958714.pdf>.

227 *See* Bread price fixing cartel case dismissed at <http://www.sangonet.org.za/newsflash/bread-price-fixing-cartel-case-dismissed>.

228 Section 53.

229 *Barnes and Iskor*, 08/CR/JAN07.

230 Background document prepared for the OECD Global Forum on Competition, Challenges/Obstacles Faced by Competition Authorities in Achieving Greater Economic Development through the Promotion of Competition, (February 2004) <http://www.comptrib.co.za/Publications/Speeches/oecd_20oct.pdf>.

231 *Caxton, CTP Publishers and Printers Limited v Naspers Ltd, Electronic Media Network Ltd, Supersport International Holdings Ltd, The Competition Commission* (16/FN/Mar04).

non-referral are not publicized, but are generally provided only to the targets of the investigation.

The Tribunal's decisions and processes are extremely transparent. According to the Tribunal's own evaluation, it determined at an early stage that its principal roles in improving the competition culture resided in maximizing transparency in the decision-making process. In this way, it hoped to earn the respect of a suspicious business community, and inject a measure of realism into the expectations of the public.[232]

Tribunal hearings must be public, except to the extent necessary to protect confidential information,[233] but procedures may be flexible. The hearing may be conducted either informally or inquisitorially. Hearings are regularly announced in the media. Claims for confidentiality must meet the standards of the Act (in that it amounts to trade, business, or industrial information that belongs to a firm, has a particular economic value, and is not generally available to or known by others). All decisions of the Tribunal are fully reasoned and available on its website and are drafted so that they are easily understood. Representatives of the news media are welcome at hearings and considerable effort is made to ensure that decisions are widely available and understood. This approach seems to have raised the level of understanding of competition issues and has contributed to the Tribunal's reputation for fairness.

Reasons for intermediate merger decisions are not readily available, but they are provided to the parties, and presumably, subject to confidentiality protections, would be accessible to those who requested them.

The Commission also publishes its reasons for granting or refusing exemption applications in the Government Gazette, although these decisions are not available on the Commission's website. The Government Gazette notices in this regard also seem to be particularly thin in light of the complexity of exemption decisions, and the time it generally takes the Commission to make these decisions.[234]

8. *Public accountability mechanisms for general agency functioning*

According to Section 22 of the Competition Act, the relevant minister (now the Minister of Economic Development) appoints the Commissioner and Deputy Commissioner based on qualifications and experience in law, economics, commerce, industry, or public affairs. The Minister also sets their compensation

[232] Background document prepared for the OECD Global Forum on Competition, Challenges/Obstacles Faced by Competition Authorities in Achieving Greater Economic Development through the Promotion of Competition, (February 2004) <http://www.comptrib.co.za/Publications/Speeches/oecd_20oct.pdf>.

[233] Section 52.

[234] *See* for instance the Commission's reasoning for rejecting Spring Lights Gas, exemption application, which took over two years for the Commission to consider. *See* media release: Commission Rejects Spring Lights Gas Exemption Application, 27 February, 2012, <http://www.compcom.co.za/assets/Uploads/AttachedFiles/MyDocuments/FINAL-MEDIA-RELEASE-Spring-Lights-Gas.pdf>.

See also the reasons for granting a conditional exemption to SAPIA, which also involved approximately two years of consideration: Media Release, 10 October 2010, <http://www.compcom.co.za/assets/Uploads/AttachedFiles/MyDocuments/Final-Media-Release-SAPIA.pdf>.

and conditions of employment, in consultation with the Minister of Finance. The Commission has an annual performance agreement with the Department and is responsible to the Minister. The Department is also responsible for the budgets of the Commission and Tribunal.[235] Despite these ties, the decision-making independence of the Commission and the Tribunal is well established.[236]

Part D of the Competition Act requires that each year, the Commissioner of the Commission and/or Chairperson of the Tribunal must submit to the Minister a statement of estimated income and expenditure, and within six months after the end of each financial year, the Commissioner and Chairperson must prepare financial statements, and the Auditor General must audit the financial records of the Commission and the Tribunal.

Section 41 obliges the Commissioner and Chairperson to prepare and submit an annual report to the Minister. The annual report must include the audited financial statements, the auditor's report, and a report of activities undertaken in terms of the functions set out in the Act and a statement of progress achieved during the preceding year towards realization of the purposes of the Act. The Minister must table the annual report in Parliament. Further, the Minister requires that the Commission submit quarterly reports, which contain a detailed activity report for each Division within the Commission as well as a financial report.[237]

These tasks, and general oversight of the Commission, moved from the Department of Trade and Industry to the Department of Economic Development in the 2010/2011 financial year.

The Commissioner is also periodically called on to report directly to Parliament. As an example, on February 29, 2010 the Commissioner was called on to address Parliament on its major cartel investigations. Members of parliament, ordinary members of the public, and the media were present at the briefing. Moreover the Commission periodically hosts stakeholder participation forums where it informs stakeholders of the Commission's functions and receives feedback about the extent to which it is or is not fulfilling its mandate.[238]

In respect of internal review processes, the analysts allocated to cases report to senior officials within the Competition Commission who must sign off on the final reports which result from a merger assessment or complaint investigation. All final reports and advisory opinions are presented to the Executive Committee ("EXCO") of the Commission, which comprises the management of the Com-

[235] Competition Commission *Annual Report, 2002*, <http://www.compcom.co.za/assets/Files/annual-report-2001-2002.pdf>.

[236] OECD, OECD Peer Review: Competition Law and Policy in South Africa (May 2003) <http://www.oecd.org/dataoecd/52/13/2958714.pdf>.

[237] Shan Ramburuth, Competition Commissioner, Independence and Accountability of Competition Authorities by South Africa, Address at Intergovernmental Group of Experts on Competition Law and Policy (July 16, 2008), <http://www.unctad.org/sections/wcmu/docs/c2clp_ige9p5South%20Africa_en.pdf>.

[238] Ibid.

mission and meets once every week. These reports and opinions are then interrogated at the applicable EXCO sitting, whereafter the Commission makes the final decision.[239]

The Tribunal's members are nominated by the Minister, and appointed by the President of South Africa. The members' tenure, like that of the Commissioner, is five years.

The members of the Competition Appeal Court, who are High Court judges, are appointed by the President on the advice of the Judicial Service Commission, for a fixed but renewable term of 10 years.

IV. Critical evaluation

As the OECD reflected, the competition enforcement bodies are recognized in South Africa as competent and serious. It is generally accepted that the Commission has met the challenges of being a new body, with a new law, facing inevitable constraints of its capacities. The Commission and the Tribunal have listened to their critics and introduced improvements. The Commission has successfully prioritized cartel prosecutions, and cases in particular industries, in order to enable it to address issues that directly affect the poor. They are aware of resource constraints and are taking active steps to address these concerns. They are also striving to follow best practices from the experience of other enforcement agencies around the world.[240]

While the Commission and Tribunal's early years focused on creating an efficient merger review system, the latter years have focused on cartel enforcement. The Commission has been particularly successful in using the Corporate Leniency Program to detect and prosecute cartels and has managed to extract large fines which appear to be acting as a reasonable deterrent. Practitioners have found that clients have developed a greater awareness of competition law, and requests for competition audits and compliance programs have increased. It is expected that the introduction of criminal liability for directors will escalate such requests.

As Lewis notes, there is still much work to be done by the competition authorities in inculcating a regard for competition issues into government. "[I]f the beachhead established by strong antitrust enforcement is to elevate competition into a fundamental social value, then the competition authorities are going to have to give considerably more attention to the public restraints and the public policies

239 Ibid.

240 OECD, OECD Peer Review: Competition Law and Policy in South Africa, (May 2003), <http://www.oecd.org/dataoecd/52/13/2958714.pdf>.

that, sometimes purposefully, mostly inadvertently, threaten the place of competition in the dominant set of society's social values."[241]

There have been trade-offs between procedural fairness values and the Commission's moves to prosecute contraventions of the Act. The authorities are currently struggling to balance the need to investigate and prosecute contraventions expeditiously, and punish offenders in a manner which reflects the public's outrage, while at the same time protecting rights to procedural fairness and providing targets of enforcement with fair opportunities to be heard.

The South African law and procedures were designed to render a classically adversarial legal system more accessible to the general public. The Act frees the Tribunal from some of the more constraining elements of high court rules and grants in inquisitorial powers in an attempt to reduce the burden on poorly resourced complainants. As such, the Tribunal has shown some resistance to worrying too much over process detail. However, in South Africa's highly legalistic enforcement culture, overlooking process detail as mere technicalities has proven to be a risky course.

Therefore, the idea of an informal, approachable, expedient process has not come to fruition. The Commission and Tribunal's powers are in fact constrained by the Constitution and administrative law standards and thus enforcement initiatives are resisted by vigorous litigation over procedural and jurisdictional matters.[242]

Cases such as *Woodlands* and *SAB* have highlighted these tensions, disappointments, and frustrations. The authorities have expressed a real concern that the Commission's investigations and prosecutions are hampered more than necessary to accord with rights of defense. It is not clear whether *Woodlands*, *Yara/Omnia*, and *SAB* have unduly constrained the Commission. So far, the burden placed on the Commission by these decisions appears to be a relatively uncomplicated administrative one—the filling in of new complaint forms identifying the conduct that is being investigated as the process progresses. However, it is also not clear that an administrative obligation such as that should constrain the ability of the Commission to perform its public function.

On the one hand, it is appropriate to ensure that the law is observed in the process of applying it.[243] Lewis noted that the procedures of the Act were largely untested as were important aspects of the Constitution itself and it was inevitable that our early years would have been preoccupied with actions aimed at clarifying the parameters and procedures of a new Act in a new constitutional dispensation.[244]

[241] David Lewis, "Global Competition: Law, Markets and Globalization," (August 18, 2010) <http://lawprofessors.typepad.com/antitrustprof_blog/2010/08/david-lewis-on-global-competition-law-markets-and-globalization.html>.

[242] OECD, OECD Peer Review: Competition Law and Policy in South Africa (May 2003), <http://www.oecd.org/dataoecd/52/13/2958714.pdf>.

[243] OECD, OECD Peer Review: Competition Law and Policy in South Africa (May 2003), <http://www.oecd.org/dataoecd/52/13/2958714.pdf>.

[244] David Lewis, Chairperson Competition Tribunal, Competition Law Enforcement in South Africa, Paper presented to IBA Conference Cape Town (March 18, 2002), <http://www.comptrib.co.za/Publications/Speeches/lewis7.pdf>.

On the other hand, there is concern that claims under these principles can be deployed to thwart action completely.[245] Even in instances where such challenges seem appropriate, there is extreme disappointment with the fact that the process has not turned out to be as quick and accessible as it was planned. We will not know whether this has been an appropriate trade-off until the *Omnia* and *SAB* appeals have been decided and until the Commission begins to run its procedures in the way expected by *Woodlands* and *Yara/Omnia*. What is clear is that a number of the Commission's pending cases are at risk, and the procedural points will be taken by all respondents whose cases are affected.

When procedural challenges are used as delaying tactics, they should be punished by costs orders, and high administrative penalties on the firms, and perhaps even punitive civil damages in antitrust cases.[246]

To achieve the aim of creating an accessible and expedient means of enforcing competition, it may be necessary to take more drastic steps and re-evaluate the structure of the enforcement bodies. As noted above, a large amount of decision-making *de facto* occurs within the Commission. This reduces procedural protections which are supposed to be protected by the bifurcated model. Perhaps an integrated agency model, where a single agency is responsible for investigation, enforcement, and adjudicative functions, will enable enforcement to proceed quicker, and yet still protect procedural rights since procedural protection rules would be more carefully considered and explicit.[247]

Alternatively, the Tribunal could make more use of its flexible and inquisitorial process to expedite proceedings. Currently, the flexibility of the process appears to be taken advantage of by both the Commission and other parties to litigation, without the attendant constraints imposed by the Court in typical civil or criminal procedure. The Tribunal in complex cases may be able to assert its power to employ a more inquisitorial approach so as to ensure greater definition of issues and avoidance of repetitious and unnecessary evidence. Sometimes reports from economic experts contain as much law as economics, and the Tribunal could use the flexibility in its process to ensure that competing experts restrict evidence to those issues which are both in dispute and relevant to the issues before the Tribunal.[248]

[245] OECD, OECD Peer Review: Competition Law and Policy in South Africa (May 2003), <http://www.oecd.org/dataoecd/52/13/2958714.pdf>.

[246] David Lewis, Chairperson Competition Tribunal, Competition Law Enforcement in South Africa, Paper presented to IBA Conference Cape Town (March 18, 2002), <http://www.comptrib.co.za/Publications/Speeches/lewis7.pdf>.

[247] Telephone interview with Wendy Mkwananzi, Head of Legal Division, Competition Commission (December 8, 2010).

[248] By contrast *see* the approach adopted in Australia: Caron Beaton Nichols, *Proof of antitrust markets in Australia* (2003) at 287ff. In *SAA(Pty) Ltd v Comair Ltd and Nationwide (Pty) Ltd* 92/CAC/MAR10 the CAC was critical of the approach adopted by the Tribunal to expert evidence, part of which, in its view, proved entirely irrelevant to the determination of the case. The CAC suggested that the Tribunal consider adopting, at least, in part, an inquisitorial approach to expert evidence including the use of the hot tub (expert witnesses from both sides interact) in order to ensure that the expert evidence was germane to the key issues in dispute, which, in turn, would truncate proceedings and lend itself to more coherent records to be considered on appeal.

Attention is required as to the length and focus of hearings in order to achieve greater access to relief and expedition of hearing.

Either way, there is much work to be done to achieve the ambitious goals of South Africa's competition policy—the creation of a system that encourages efficiency and innovation; that addresses the inequality pervasive in the economy; that is accessible to the poor; and at the same time protects core Constitutional values.

8

The United States
The Competition Law System and the Country's Norms

Harry First, Eleanor M. Fox, and Daniel E. Hemli

I. The history of antitrust enforcement

A. Federal enforcement

Three major federal antitrust statutes—the Sherman Act, the Clayton Act, and the Federal Trade Commission Act—set out the basic substantive provisions of US antitrust law and its enforcement structure. Although each statute has been amended over time, sometimes in important ways (penalties have been increased substantially, for example), judicial interpretation and enforcement practice have been more significant for the development of US antitrust law than has legislative action.

One of the most important innovations of the original Sherman Act was to create a system of public enforcement. Prior to the Act's passage in 1890, enforcement was a common law enterprise, invoked by private litigants seeking to avoid contractual obligations by arguing that enforcement of a particular contract would restrain trade and should therefore be void as against "public policy." Important substantive antitrust doctrines were developed in litigation framed this way, particularly the basic ideas behind what types of restraints might be considered "unreasonable." Sporadic private contract litigation, however, was not adequate to deal with the increasing power of large business enterprises (often formed through the legal vehicle of a "trust"). This led Congress to provide for government enforcement of the Sherman Act's prohibitions, through suits in equity to enjoin violations and through criminal prosecutions.

Government enforcement of the Act developed slowly. It was not until 1903 that a special division in the Department of Justice ("DOJ" or "Justice Department") was funded to deal with antitrust enforcement, and the modest number of cases the Department filed in the early years led many to view it as an ineffective enforcement agency. Judicial interpretation of the Act during this time was also thought to have compromised the Act's effectiveness. Particularly important was the Supreme Court's 1911 decision in *Standard Oil*,[1] adopting a general "rule of

[1] Standard Oil Company v. United States, 221 U.S. 1 (1911).

reason" approach to the Sherman Act which critics believed launched judges on a "sea of doubt," leaving the legality of any particular restraint to be determined more by a judge's predilections than by clear legal rules.[2]

The Clayton Act and Federal Trade Commission Act were passed in 1914 to correct these perceived substantive and institutional weaknesses. The Clayton Act added certain specific prohibitions to federal antitrust law, dealing, for example, with mergers, tying, and exclusive dealing contracts. The Federal Trade Commission Act established a new administrative agency, the Federal Trade Commission ("FTC" or "Commission"), and gave it authority to prevent "unfair methods of competition" (not otherwise defined). Congress also gave both the FTC and the Justice Department authority to enforce the new Clayton Act's prohibitions.

Passage of the FTC Act and the Clayton Act set up the possibility that the Justice Department and the FTC would have overlapping enforcement authority. At the time the statutes were enacted, however, Congress apparently saw the two agencies as focusing on competition problems in different ways and using different procedures. The Justice Department would continue to deal with monopoly "as established fact," litigating in court the legality of a company's practices. The new FTC would engage in preventive regulation, checking monopoly "in the embryo" by stopping unfair methods of competition by a corporation of "no conspicuous size."[3] Nevertheless, the statutory language did not clearly set out these different roles and Congress paid no attention to the potential for conflict between the agencies, being more concerned with adding a new enforcement authority to strengthen government antitrust enforcement.

Whatever the possibilities for conflict, the two federal enforcement agencies developed along the lines that Congress apparently anticipated in 1914, generally dividing their responsibilities and sharing enforcement burdens.[4] Prior to 1950, for example, the Justice Department rarely filed suit under the Clayton Act provisions dealing with mergers or exclusive dealing while the FTC filed a substantial number of complaints. On the other hand, during this period the Justice Department handled all Sherman Act criminal prosecutions, given its exclusive authority over criminal enforcement, and both agencies handled non-criminal pricing conspiracies, with the FTC being slightly more active.[5]

It was not until 1938 that the FTC and the Justice Department entered into an informal agreement to determine which agency should handle a particular investi-

[2] *See* United States v. Addyston Pipe & Steel Co., 85 F. 271, 283–4 (6th Cir. 1898) (referring to some common law judges deciding "how much restraint of competition is in the public interest, and how much is not").

[3] *See* Marc Winerman, "The Origins of the FTC: Concentration, Cooperation, Control, and Competition," 71 ANTITRUST L.J. 1, 68, 74 (2003).

[4] We note that our discussion generally refers to the Justice Department Antitrust Division and the FTC as "agencies." As a technical matter, only the FTC is an independent agency; the Justice Department is part of the executive branch of government. For further description, *see* text at notes 26–45 *infra*.

[5] *See* Gilbert H. Montague, "The Commission's Jurisdiction Over Practices in Restraint of Trade: A Large-Scale Method of Mass Enforcement of the Antitrust Laws," 8 GEO. WASH. L. REV. 365 (1940) (FTC and Justice Department enforcement data).

gation, an agreement not formalized until 1948.[6] After a change in the Clayton Act's antimerger provision in 1950, the Justice Department became active in merger enforcement, leading to some conflict over case selection and the development of a "clearance" process for merger enforcement that has reduced, but not eliminated, conflicts in particular cases.[7]

The two agencies' policy views have sometimes differed over time and each has been criticized for somewhat different reasons. The FTC, perhaps true to the vision that it should engage in preventive regulation of "unfair" conduct, has at times been criticized for being overly regulatory, for focusing on matters of small consequence, and for being unduly protective of small business.[8] During the late 1970s and 1980s it came under intense criticism from Congress for its enforcement policies, leading to a period when Congress refused to pass annual appropriations bills for the agency and to an eventual restriction of its "unfairness" jurisdiction.[9] The Justice Department, on the other hand, has often been criticized for lax enforcement policies, with periods of perceived reduced enforcement often followed by increased enforcement efforts when national elections bring a change of administration.[10]

Although the Justice Department and the FTC are the major federal antitrust enforcement agencies, Congress has often given concurrent or exclusive jurisdiction over competition matters to sectoral regulatory agencies. For example, the Interstate Commerce Commission was given exclusive jurisdiction over railroad and trucking mergers under a broad "public interest" standard when those industries were regulated; the Commission's replacement, the Surface Transportation Board, still has exclusive jurisdiction over railroad mergers.[11] Even though the airline industry has been virtually deregulated, the Department of Transportation continues to have jurisdiction over unfair methods of competition[12] and has the power to exempt international airline alliances, including code-sharing agreements.[13] Telecommunications and broadcasting mergers are reviewed by the Federal Communications Commission as well as by the Justice Department and the FTC.[14]

[6] *See* Report of The Attorney General's National Committee to Study the Antitrust Laws 376 & n.53 (1955).

[7] For further discussion of the clearance process, *see infra* notes 167–172.

[8] For critical studies, *see*, e.g., Robert A. Katzmann, *Regulatory Bureaucracy: The Federal Trade Commission and Antitrust Policy* (1980); "Report of the American Bar Association Section of Antitrust Law Special Committee to Study the Role of the Federal Trade Commission," ANTITRUST L. J. 53 (1989).

[9] *See* Federal Trade Commission Act Amendments of 1994, 108 Stat.1695, codified at 15 U.S.C. § 45 (n) (narrowing unfairness jurisdiction). The FTC went without a budgetary reauthorization from 1982 to 1994. *See* Hearing Before the Sen. Subcomm. on Consumer of the Comm. on Comm., Science, and Transp., 103d Cong. 2 (1993) (statement of Sen. Hollings).

[10] For critical studies, *see*, e.g., Suzanne Weaver, *Decision to Prosecute: Organization and Public Policy in the Antitrust Division* (1977); Mark J. Green, Beverly C. Moore, & Bruce Wasserstein, *The Closed Enterprise System* (1972).

[11] *See* 49 U.S.C. § 11324.

[12] *See* 49 U.S.C. § 41712.

[13] *See* 49 U.S.C. §§ 41308, 41309.

[14] *See* 47 U.S.C. §§ 214(a), 310(d) (FCC jurisdiction).

Banking mergers are reviewed under a competition standard by bank regulatory agencies and by the Department of Justice under antitrust law.[15] As with the original Congressional decision to create two antitrust enforcement agencies, the decision to give sectoral regulators concurrent or exclusive jurisdiction over competition matters has been more a matter of the political and policy concerns of the time and less a matter of a conscious plan for creating an optimal structure for government antitrust enforcement.

B. State enforcement

States have enacted their own antitrust laws, some of which precede the passage of the Sherman Act.[16] The states were relatively vigorous enforcers of their antitrust laws in the period between 1890 and 1914, often bringing suit against the major trusts of the day and sometimes bringing such suits before the federal government did.[17] Although the importance of state antitrust law enforcement subsequently declined, states continue to enforce their laws, bringing both criminal and civil cases, the latter for injunctions or damages incurred by state agencies or consumers.

States can also enforce the Sherman and Clayton Acts in federal court. In 1945 the Supreme Court recognized the power of the states to bring suit as *parens patriae* on behalf of their citizens for injunctive relief for a violation of the federal antitrust laws.[18] In 1976 Congress passed the Hart-Scott-Rodino Antitrust Improvements Act giving state attorneys general the right to bring suit in federal court as *parens patriae* for treble the damages that "natural persons" residing in their respective states incurred by virtue of a Sherman Act violation.[19] As a result, state antitrust enforcers have brought federal suits challenging mergers, monopolization, and cartel agreements, often obtaining large monetary recoveries to be distributed to injured consumers.[20] Critics have argued that state enforcement is duplicative of federal efforts at best, and potentially in conflict with federal policies at worst, but in 2007 the congressionally-mandated Antitrust Modern-

[15] *See* 12 U.S.C. § 1828(c).

[16] Early state antitrust legislation and judicial interpretations are discussed in, e.g., James May, "Antitrust Practice and Procedure in the Formative Era: The Constitutional and Conceptual Reach of State Antitrust Law," 1880–1918, 135 U. Pa. L. Rev. 495 (1987); David Millon, "The First Antitrust Statutes," 29 Washburn L. J. 141 (1990).

[17] *See* United States v. Int'l Harvester Co., 214 F. 987 (D. Minn. 1914) (federal suit filed after suits brought by Kentucky and Missouri), appeal dismissed, 248 U.S. 587 (1918).

[18] *See* Georgia v. Pa. R.R. Co., 324 U.S. 439 (1945).

[19] *See* 15 U.S.C. §§ 15c-15h.

[20] *See*, e.g., United States v. Microsoft Corp., 253 F.3d 34 (D.C. Cir.), cert. denied, 534 U.S. 952 (2001) (monopolization case; separate suit filed by twenty-one states, consolidated for trial with Justice Department litigation); New York v. Kraft Gen'l Foods, Inc., 926 F. Supp. 321 (S.D.N.Y. 1995) (state suit challenging merger); Harry First, "Delivering Remedies: The Role of the States in Antitrust Enforcement," 69 Geo. Wash. L. Rev. 1701, 1718–20 (2001) (describing vitamins litigation; US $250 million state settlement).

ization Commission decided against recommending any substantial changes to the current system.[21]

C. Private enforcement

The Sherman Act as passed in 1890 provided that anyone injured in their "business or property" by a violation of the Act could bring suit in federal court to recover treble their damages plus attorneys' fees. The reason for including a private action was to provide compensation to those victimized by antitrust violations; damages were trebled to give plaintiffs adequate incentive to bring suit for what might otherwise have been small damages.[22] As with federal government enforcement, however, the number of private cases brought in the period immediately following passage of the Sherman Act was modest (somewhat less than the number brought by the federal government). When Congress passed the Clayton Act in 1914 it added some important procedural provisions to make it easier to bring private suits (for example, making government settlements prima facie evidence of a violation). Congressional debate over the Clayton Act also stressed the important role that private suits might have in deterring antitrust violations, and private litigants have subsequently been referred to as "private attorneys general" to emphasize this role.[23]

Views of the effectiveness and wisdom of the private action have varied over time. Prior to 1950, commentators judged the private suit as ineffective, based on the relatively small numbers of cases brought. Increased federal government enforcement in the 1940s helped fuel a dramatic post-war increase in private litigation, with the result that the number of private cases brought since the 1950s has substantially exceeded the number of cases that the federal agencies have filed.[24] The increased number of filings, coupled with the development of the class action device and liberal pretrial discovery rules, then brought criticism of the private action as leading to unwarranted recoveries against defendants. Recent Supreme Court cases have tended to accept this criticism and have restricted the use of the private action in significant ways.[25]

[21] *See* Antitrust Modernization Comm'n, Report And Recommendations (2007) (hereinafter AMC Report), <http://govinfo.library.unt.edu/amc/>. For criticism of state antitrust enforcement, *see*, e.g., Richard A. Posner, "Antitrust in the New Economy," 68 ANTITRUST L.J. 925 (2001).

[22] *See* Harry First, "Lost in Conversation: The Compensatory Function of Antitrust Law," <http://papers.ssrn.com/sol3/papers.cfm?abstract_id=1579343>.

[23] *See* Perma Life Mufflers v. International Parts Corp., 392 U.S. 134, 147 (1968) (Fortas, J., concurring).

[24] For statistics on private and government enforcement, *see*, e.g., L. White, "The Georgetown Study of Private Antitrust Litigation," 54 ANTITRUST L.J. 59 (1985); B. Zorina Kahn, "Symposium on Antitrust," 9 CORNELL J. LAW & PUB. POL. 133, 137 (1999) (Figure 1); Richard A. Posner, "A Statistical Study of Antitrust Enforcement," 13 J.L. & ECON. 365, 373 (Figure II) (1970). For a mid-century view of the private action, *see* Homer Clark, "The Treble Damage Bonanza: New Doctrines of Damages in Private Antitrust Suits," 52 MICH. L. REV. 363 (1954).

[25] *See*, e.g., Bell Atlantic Corp. v. Twombly, 550 U.S. 544 (2007) (requiring plaintiff to plead "enough factual matter" to show "plausible grounds" to infer illegal agreement; dismissing complaint); Verizon Comm'ns Inc. v. Law Offices of Curtis V. Trinko LL.P, 540 U.S. 398 (2004) (disallowing

II. Institutional structure

A. Federal enforcement

1. Department of Justice

The Department of Justice is part of the Executive Branch and has the responsibility for representing the United States in court proceedings. The Department is divided into divisions that are given specific responsibilities. The Antitrust Division is responsible for civil and criminal antitrust enforcement, even though federal criminal prosecutions are generally the responsibility of the Justice Department's Criminal Division and the ninety-three US Attorneys' Offices located throughout the United States. Supreme Court antitrust litigation is handled by the Office of the Solicitor General, which is part of the Justice Department, working closely with the Antitrust Division. The head of the Justice Department (the Attorney General) and the head of the Antitrust Division (Assistant Attorney General) are appointed by the President and are subject to Senate confirmation.[26]

Antitrust enforcement by the Antitrust Division follows the bifurcated judicial model. That is, with rare exception,[27] the Division investigates cases, using legally available processes, makes its own internal determination whether to charge a violation of the antitrust laws, and then files suit in federal court where it is required to prove its case. The determination of whether there has been a violation of the antitrust laws is made by a federal district court judge of ordinary jurisdiction, not by a specialized court. In criminal matters, defendants have a constitutional right to trial by jury, but in civil suits for injunctive relief, decisions are made solely by a judge. District court antitrust decisions in government cases are subject to appellate review under the same processes as other federal litigation, with appeal as of right to a circuit court of appeals and discretionary review by the US Supreme Court.[28]

Government civil enforcement often ends in settlement, generally agreed to prior to the filing of litigation. By custom, these settlements have been incorporated into "consent decrees," judicial decrees entered by district court judges, whose violation can be enforced through civil or criminal contempt proceedings.[29] Consent decrees are an important part of antitrust enforcement and their use has a long and controversial history.[30]

Sherman Act Section 2 private damages claim arising out of failure of monopoly local exchange carrier to provide adequate interconnection service to rival).

[26] *See* 28 U.S.C. §§ 503, 506.

[27] *See* 28 C.F.R. § 48.1 et seq. (allowing Attorney General to appoint an Administrative Law Judge to hold fact-finding hearings to determine whether a joint newspaper operating agreement qualifies for an exemption under the Newspaper Preservation Act).

[28] *See* 15 U.S.C. § 29.

[29] *See*, e.g., United States v. Microsoft Corp., 980 F. Supp. 2d 537 (D.D.C. 1997) (refusing government petition for criminal contempt, but entering injunction restraining bundling practices that violated decree), *rev'd*, 147 F. 3d 935 (D.C. Cir. 1998) (injunction improperly issued).

[30] Settlements of important cases were often believed to reflect political deals and grant inadequate relief. For a history of consent decree practice, *see*, e.g., John J. Flynn, "Consent Decrees in Antitrust

2. Federal Trade Commission

The Federal Trade Commission is an independent regulatory Commission consisting of five Commissioners appointed for seven-year terms by the President, subject to Senate confirmation.[31] To help assure political independence, no more than three can be from the same political party and Commissioners can be removed by the President only for cause.[32] The President chooses the chairman of the FTC, with a new chairman being selected when presidential administrations change.

As originally envisioned, the FTC's structure follows the integrated agency model where the agency investigates and adjudicates all violations internally.[33] FTC staff in the Bureau of Competition undertake the investigation into potential violations and decide whether to recommend to the Commission that formal charges be brought.[34] If the Commission determines that there is "reason to believe" a violation has occurred, it will issue a complaint, which will then be tried before an Administrative Law Judge ("ALJ") under procedural rules similar to those used in federal court litigation.[35] An appeal of the ALJ's decision can then be taken (either by staff "complaint counsel" or by the respondent) to the full Commission.[36] The Commission, after briefing and argument, will issue a written decision, entering a cease-and-desist order (and other appropriate relief) if it finds a violation. The respondent can then appeal to a federal circuit court of appeals, with subsequent discretionary review in the Supreme Court.[37] At any time in the process the Commission can also decide to settle a case with a "consent order" analogous to the Antitrust Division's consent decree except that it is not entered in court.[38]

As Commission practice has developed, however, important parts of its enforcement mission are now undertaken in a way that more nearly resembles the bifurcated judicial model. In 1973 Congress added Section 13 (b) to the FTC Act, giving the Commission the power to seek temporary and permanent injunctions in federal district court for violations of the FTC Act.[39] The Commission has

Enforcement," 53 Iowa L. Rev. 983 (1968). The consent decree process is now governed by the Tunney Act, *see infra* notes 232–242 and accompanying text.

[31] *See* 15 U.S.C. § 41.

[32] *See id.*

[33] The FTC also has "notice and comment" rule-making authority, *see* 15 U.S.C. § 57a. The aggressive use of this rule-making authority provoked considerable controversy in the 1970s and the Commission has not recently used this authority in competition matters.

[34] *See* 15 U.S.C. § 49 (FTC investigative powers); Federal Trade Comm'n, Nonadjudicative Proceedings, 16 C.F.R. § 2.1 et seq.

[35] *See* 15 U.S.C. § 45 (b); Federal Trade Comm'n, Rules of Practice for Adjudicative Proceedings, 16 C.F.R. § 3.1 et seq. ("Part 3 proceedings").

[36] *See* FTC Rules, §§ 3.52, 3.54.

[37] *See* 15 U.S.C. § 45 (c). Since 1975 the Commission has had the power to represent itself before the Supreme Court, rather than be represented by the Justice Department's Solicitor General's office, *see* 15 U.S.C. § 56 (a) (3), but the FTC has only invoked this provision three times. *See* Office of Gen'l Counsel, A Brief Overview of the Federal Trade Commission's Investigative And Law Enforcement Authority n.7 (rev. 2008), <http://ftc.gov/ogc/brfovrvw.shtm#N_7_>.

[38] *See* FTC Rules, §§ 2.31–2.34, 3.25.

[39] *See* P.L. 93–153, 87 Stat. 592, codified at 15 U.S.C. § 53 (b).

subsequently argued that this provision not only gives it the power to bring suit in federal court for any violation of the FTC Act, but also to obtain any equitable relief, including orders of restitution which require defendants to pay to consumers the damages their anticompetitive conduct has caused.[40]

More critically for the FTC's enforcement mission, the Commission has made use of Section 13 (b) to seek preliminary injunctions to stop mergers that it believes violate Section 7 of the Clayton Act and/or Section 5 of the FTC Act, with the result that the FTC now litigates most of its merger challenges in federal court. In 1995 the Commission adopted a general practice of not continuing with administrative litigation if it lost its court motion for a preliminary injunction.[41] The practice of litigating merger cases exclusively in court, however, is not required by the FTC Act and the Commission has more recently indicated that it may decide to litigate at least some merger cases under its "Part 3" procedures[42] even if it loses its preliminary injunction motion in federal court.[43] Because the standard for granting preliminary relief under Section 13 (b) is arguably more favorable to the FTC than the general common law standard for preliminary injunctions applied in Justice Department cases,[44] some critics argue that Section 13 (b) produces inconsistent merger results that depend on which federal agency brings suit.[45]

B. State and private enforcement

1. State enforcement

Each US state, plus each of the five additional federal jurisdictions—the District of Columbia, the Commonwealth of Puerto Rico, and the three US territories of

[40] *See* FTC v. Mylan Labs, Inc., 62 F. Supp. 2d 25, 36 (D.D.C. 1999) (upholding FTC legal claim).

[41] *See* Statement of the Federal Trade Commission Policy Regarding Administrative Merger Litigation Following the Denial of a Preliminary Injunction, 60 Fed. Reg. 39,741, 39,743 (1995). Technically, the Commission said it would make the decision on a case-by-case basis, using five specific factors: (i) the factual findings and legal conclusions of the district court or any appellate court; (ii) any new evidence developed during the course of the preliminary injunction proceeding; (iii) whether the transaction raises important issues of fact, law, or merger policy that need resolution in administrative litigation; (iv) an overall assessment of the costs and benefits of further proceedings; and (v) any other matter that bears on whether it would be in the public interest to proceed with the merger challenge. *Id.* at 39,743.

[42] "Part 3" procedures are so named because the FTC's rules for adjudicative procedures are Part 3 of the FTC's general rules of procedure.

[43] In 2009 the Commission changed its rules to make it clear that it will not automatically withdraw from administratively adjudicating cases that it loses on preliminary injunction. *See* 74 Fed. Reg. 1811–12 (January 13, 2009). For further discussion of the 2009 amendments to the FTC's procedures, *see* text at notes 183-187 *infra*.

[44] Section 13(b) states that a court may grant preliminary relief "[u]pon a proper showing that, weighing the equities and considering the Commission's likelihood of ultimate success, such action would be in the public interest." 15 U.S.C. § 53(b). By contrast, the DOJ, like any other plaintiff, must establish (i) a likelihood of success on the merits; (ii) that it faces a substantial threat of irreparable harm if the injunction is not granted; (iii) that the balance of harms weighs in the DOJ's favor; and (iv) that the grant of an injunction would serve the public interest.

[45] *See*, e.g., AMC Report, *supra* note 21, at 130–32 (recommending change in § 13(b) to conform it to the same standard as applies to Justice Department cases).

Guam, Northern Mariana Islands, and the Virgin Islands—has some form of antitrust legislation.[46] Enforcement in these jurisdictions, whether accomplished through suit under federal antitrust law or under state antitrust law, is handled by the state Attorney General. State Attorney General Offices usually have a specialized division or bureau responsible for antitrust enforcement. Enforcement conforms to the bifurcated judicial model, taking place exclusively through court litigation.

A critical aspect of the institution of state enforcement is the mechanisms employed to coordinate the activities of state enforcement agencies. Although state antitrust enforcers bring many of their cases on an individual state basis, they also investigate and file cases jointly. As a general matter, the most significant state antitrust cases since the 1980s have been brought as multistate cases involving a varying number of state enforcement agencies, depending on the interest of each individual state in the particular matter as well as the resources that individual states have available at the time. Joint state effort can also occur in coordination with the federal enforcement agency investigating the same matter.[47] If the federal agency files suit in federal court, participating states will most often join the litigation rather than filing a separate suit.[48]

The key organizational vehicle for cooperation among the fifty-five state jurisdictions is the National Association of Attorneys General ("NAAG"). Through its central office in Washington, DC, NAAG has helped coordinate the states' efforts in investigation, litigation, lobbying, and training.[49] In addition, the states, through NAAG, have put together a number of agreements formalizing some of the relationships that have evolved to handle multistate merger enforcement, joint state and federal merger enforcement, and joint state and federal criminal investigations.[50]

Nearly all state attorneys general are elected officials.[51] This direct political accountability to the electorate is perhaps unique in the world for antitrust enforcers; certainly it is different from the more indirect political accountability mech-

[46] We refer to these jurisdictions collectively as "states."

[47] Nearly all *parens patriae* cases have been brought by the states without federal participation; cases seeking some form of injunctive relief have most often been brought in conjunction with one of the federal Agencies.

[48] *See*, e.g., United States v. Oracle Corp., 331 F. Supp. 2d 1098 (N.D. Cal. 2004) (Justice Department and ten states). The Microsoft monopolization litigation, in which the states filed a separate complaint, is a rare exception to this pattern.

[49] *See* <http://www.naag.org/about_naag.php> (describing organization of NAAG).

[50] *See*, e.g., Nat'l Ass'n of Attorneys Gen., Voluntary Pre-Merger Disclosure Compact, *reprinted in* 4 Trade Reg. Rep. (CCH) ¶ 13,410 (March 21, 1994); Antitrust Div., U.S. Dep't of Justice, Protocol For Coordination In Merger Investigations Between the Federal Enforcement Agencies and State Attorneys General, reprinted in John J. Flynn et al., *Antitrust: Statutes, Treaties, Regulations, Guidelines, Policies* 535–43 (2011) (governing confidentiality of information, sharing of information, and guidelines for joint investigations and settlements); U.S. Dep't of Justice, Protocol for Increased State Prosecution of Criminal Antitrust Offenses, reprinted in 70 ANTITRUST & TRADE REG. REP. (BNA) 362 (March 28, 1996).

[51] *See* <http://www.naag.org/about_naag.php> (attorneys general are popularly elected in 43 states; remaining states have a variety of selection mechanisms).

anisms that constrain federal antitrust enforcement officials.[52] It is unclear how this institutional position affects enforcement decisions. It may be that, as elected officials, state attorneys general are more interested in obtaining monetary recoveries on behalf of their citizens (voters) than are federal antitrust enforcers, which would align antitrust enforcement with consumer welfare. On the other hand, some have criticized state enforcement as being influenced by improper political considerations, for example, favoring in-state business interests over out-of-state interests.[53] Although political concerns could theoretically lead state attorneys general to favor their constituents in this way, there is no empirical support for this proposition.[54] This is not to say that interest groups do not attempt to influence state attorneys general when making antitrust enforcement decisions. As with the federal government, business interests may try to pressure state enforcers not to bring suit and labor groups may try to pressure the attorney general to consider the effect on jobs of bringing an antitrust case.[55] Whether state attorneys general are more amenable to this political pressure than federal enforcers is difficult to say.

2. *Private enforcement*

Private antitrust enforcement is pursued through litigation in federal and state court. Such litigation is conducted in courts of general jurisdiction, under procedural rules that do not distinguish antitrust cases from other types of cases. To the extent that these cases involve multidistrict or complex litigation, the special federal provisions applicable to such litigation also apply.

Private party litigation is often filed after the government has investigated the matter and brought suit (such private cases being called "follow-on" or "complementary" litigation), but not all private litigation is complementary to government litigation.[56] Business firms often bring antitrust suits in the normal course of business dealings without regard to prior government actions (for example, in contract or patent disputes, or for exclusionary business conduct) and all the most important recent Supreme Court antitrust cases have been decided in the context of private suits rather than government litigation.

[52] For further discussion of these accountability mechanisms, *see* text at notes 250–266 *infra*.

[53] *See*, e.g., Posner, "Antitrust in the New Economy," *supra* note 21, at 940–41.

[54] *See* First, "Delivering Remedies," *supra* note 20, at 1726–27.

[55] For example, Texas did not file suit against Microsoft, reportedly after Dell met with the state Attorney General, and the State of Washington, Microsoft's home state, was conspicuously absent from the state Microsoft litigation.

[56] *See* Donald W. Hawthorne, "Recent Trends in Federal Antitrust Class Action Cases," 24 Antitrust 58 (Summer 2010) (reporting that nearly 60 percent of antitrust class actions arose out of prior government enforcement, including government cases outside the United States; but this does not include cases filed by individual litigants). For an earlier study, *see* Marvel, Netter, & Robinson, "Price Fixing and Civil Damages: An Economic Analysis," 40 Stan.L.Rev. 561, 572 (1988) (of 117 government criminal cases filed between 1972 and 1979, only about one-half resulted in follow-on civil suits, despite the fact that all but three of the cases resulted in convictions).

Private parties also attempt to convince government enforcers to bring cases. Critics have been concerned that such approaches can lead to a form of capture, where the agency ends up protecting a complaining business firm rather than advancing competition policy. On the other hand, it has been argued that business firms often possess information about anticompetitive practices that is unavailable to government enforcers and that consumers are generally not in a position to complain about antitrust violations because they are usually unaware that they are victims of anticompetitive practices. This need for private-party information is true both in exclusionary practices cases and in cartel cases (where the government offers amnesty to incentivize private parties to provide information) and government enforcers indicate that they are aware of the possibility of self-serving complaints.

C. International enforcement

Informal ("networked") coordination occurs between and among authorities and it sometimes influences enforcement decisions. As discussed above, coordination occurs between the two federal agencies (Justice Department and the Federal Trade Commission), between the Justice Department or the FTC and the states, and among the states. Internationally, networking occurs between the federal agencies and the European Union Competition Directorate and between US authorities and many national authorities. Canada probably leads the list of frequent contacts with national authorities. Many of these contacts are made pursuant to bilateral cooperation agreements.[57] In addition, the US authorities take a major role in the International Competition Network, the virtual network of more than 100 competition authorities from more than ninety jurisdictions around the world.[58]

The US Agencies' most intense coordination is with the Competition Directorate of the European Union, especially on merger enforcement. Under the aegis of the US-EU Merger Working Group, the parties have agreed to best practices on cooperation in merger investigations.[59] They exchange, on a day-to-day basis, ideas and analyses of particular mergers that have been filed in both jurisdictions. Often they investigate in close cooperation with one another. Despite two well-known cases to the contrary,[60] the jurisdictions usually reach the same conclusions as to anticompetitive effects. On occasion, the jurisdictions coordinate their remedies so

[57] *See,* e.g., Christine A. Varney, Assistant Att'y Gen., Antitrust Div., U.S. Dep't of Justice, International Cooperation: Preparing for the Future, Remarks prepared for the Fourth Annual Georgetown Law Global Antitrust Enforcement Symposium 3 (Washington, D.C., September 21, 2010), <http://www.justice.gov/atr/public/speeches/262606.htm>.

[58] *See* ICN Factsheet and Key Messages, <http://www.internationalcompetitionnetwork.org/uploads/library/doc608.pdf>. For further discussion of the international aspects of competition coordination, *see* International Institutions, *infra* Ch. 10.

[59] *See* <http://ec.europa.eu/competition/mergers/legislation/eu_us.pdf>.

[60] *See* Boeing/McDonnell Douglas, Statement of FTC Commissioners on Decision of July 1, 1997 to Close Investigation, CCH Trade Reg. Rep. [1997–2001 Transfer Binder] ¶ 24,295; European Commission Case IV/M877, O.J. L 336/16 (1997); GE/Honeywell, General Electric Co. v. Commission, Case T-210/01, [2005] ECR II-5575.

as to take substantially the same action at the same time on both sides of the ocean.[61] A good example of the extent of this cooperation is the 2010 merger of Cisco Systems and Tandberg ASA where the Justice Department was satisfied that the relief offered and accepted in the EU also cured the competition problems in the United States.[62] The Department accordingly closed its investigation with no challenge, concluding that "the proposed deal is not likely to be anticompetitive due to the evolving nature of the videoconferencing market and the commitments that Cisco has made to the European Commission (EC) to facilitate interoperability."[63]

III. Competition mandate

A. Federal agencies

1. Department of Justice Antitrust Division

The Justice Department's Antitrust Division, in enforcing the provisions of the Sherman and Clayton Acts, has a mandate to consider the entire range of competition issues: agreements in restraint of trade, single-firm monopolizing conduct, and mergers whose effect may be to lessen competition. Although as a constitutional and statutory matter this mandate is limited to acts that affect interstate commerce, the Supreme Court has taken a sufficiently expansive approach to the interstate commerce requirement that the Justice Department is able to reach fairly localized behavior if it so chooses.[64] Because of the way the Justice Department is organized, the Antitrust Division has responsibility both for civil and criminal antitrust enforcement; prosecutors outside the Antitrust Division are not used for criminal antitrust investigations or prosecutions.

In addition to its antitrust enforcement mandate, the Division pursues an active competition advocacy role within the federal government. This role most often involves providing its views on the competitive effects of decisions that sectoral regulators are considering, including rule making proceedings and merger approvals, but it can also involve providing advice on antitrust analysis of specific cases that sectoral regulators are considering.[65] The Division has used its advocacy role to

[61] *See, e.g.*, Joel I. Klein, Assistant Att'y Gen., Antitrust Div., U.S. Dep't of Justice, Time for a Global Competition Initiative?, Remarks prepared for the EC Merger Control 10th Anniversary Conference 3–4 (Brussels, Belgium, September 14, 2000), <http://www.justice.gov/atr/public/speeches/6486.pdf>, citing the Halliburton-Dresser merger.

[62] *See*, e.g., the matter of Tandberg/Cisco, <http://europa.eu/rapid/pressReleasesAction.do?reference=IP/10/377&format=HTML&aged=0&language=EN&guiLanguage=en>.

[63] <http://www.justice.gov/atr/public/press_releases/2010/257173.htm>.

[64] *See*, e.g. Summit Health, Ltd. v. Pinhas, 500 U.S. 322 (1991) (conspiracy to exclude a single ophthalmological surgeon from "the Los Angeles market" met the Sherman Act's jurisdictional requirement).

[65] For the comments that the Division has filed with various federal agencies, *see* <http://www.justice.gov/atr/public/comments/comments.htm> (posting comments involving ten federal agencies). For an example of providing antitrust advice to other federal agencies on a less formal basis, *see* Sarah N. Lynch, Brent Kendall, & Jacob Bunge, "CME Inquiry Gets an Assist," Wall St. J., August 28–29,

prod regulatory agencies to take greater account of competition when making their decisions, advice that regulators have not always heeded.

One important gap in the Division's mandate is in the area of trade policy. Although there are occasions when trade policy and antitrust policy are aligned (for example, the effort to end non-tariff barriers that block market access for US exports),[66] more often trade policy runs counter to basic antitrust concepts. Thus, the Division appears to have had little influence over most aspects of US-negotiated trade agreements.[67] Similarly, the Division has no involvement with the statutory process for reviewing foreign acquisitions of domestic companies that the President has authority to block on national security grounds.[68]

2. *Federal Trade Commission*

The FTC's mandate is similar to the Antitrust Division's, in that the Commission can consider the same range of competition issues that the Division can. Likewise, the FTC plays an important role in competition policy advocacy, not only at the federal level but also at the state level.[69] Nevertheless, there are two major differences between the FTC's mandate and the Antitrust Division's.

The first is that the FTC has no power to bring criminal proceedings. As an independent administrative agency it cannot represent the United States in a criminal proceeding. Also, the statutes that the FTC enforces—the Federal Trade Commission Act and the Clayton Act—contain no criminal penalties.

The second major difference is that the FTC has a consumer protection mandate under the FTC Act to prevent "unfair or deceptive acts or practices," as well as its competition mandate to prevent "unfair methods of competition." This consumer protection mandate involves practices that do not necessarily have a connection

2010, at B3 (reporting "informal talks" between Commodities Futures Trading Commission and Justice Department lawyers concerning a futures exchange's refusal to open its market to competition) ("It isn't unusual for the Justice Department's antitrust experts to help other agencies that are looking into competition issues.").

66 *See* Mitsuo Matsushita, "The Structural Impediments Initiative: An Example of Bilateral Trade Negotiation," 12 Mich. J. Intl. L. 436 (1991) (discussing US efforts to get Japan to increase its antitrust enforcement as a way of opening Japan's markets to imports).

67 The Division indicates that "from time to time" it "participates in U.S. Government delegations negotiating agreements with other governments"; that it "occasionally" advises the United States Trade Representative of the antitrust implications of trade policy options; and that it "usually" represents the Justice Department in the interagency Trade Policy Group. *See* U.S. Dep't of Justice, Antitrust Division Manual, at VII-38 (4th edn 2008), <http://www.justice.gov/atr/public/divisionmanual/index.htm> (hereinafter Antitrust Division Manual).

68 Under the Exon-Florio Amendment to the Defense Production Act, the Committee on Foreign Investment in the United States ("CFIUS") makes recommendations to the President regarding foreign-firm acquisitions that affect national security. *See* 50 U.S.C. App. § 2170 (k). The Attorney General is a member of the CFIUS, but the National Security Division of the Justice Department, not the Antitrust Division, serves as the Attorney General's representative. *See* U.S. Dep't of Justice, Nat'l Security Div., FY 2009 Performance Budget, Congressional Submission, at 6, <http://www.justice.gov/jmd/2009justification/pdf/fy09-nsd.pdf>.

69 The FTC's state and federal level "Advocacy Filings" since 1983 are posted at <http://ftc.gov/opp/advocacy_date.shtm>.

with competition issues. For example, in the exercise of its consumer protection authority the Commission has promulgated its extremely popular "Do Not Call" regulation of telemarketers, a regulation that is not based on remedying an adverse effect on competition. Nevertheless, there are ways in which the consumer protection mandate can overlap with, and inform, the competition mandate. Consumer protection often deals with information asymmetries, opportunism, and information failures, all of which might not only harm consumers directly but also lead to less transparent and less efficient markets.[70]

Even though the Antitrust Division's and the FTC's mandates are otherwise similar, the two agencies have often been interested in somewhat different matters. A recent example of this different focus is the Commission's concern for the granting and exercise of intellectual property rights, leading the Commission, for example, to issue a study highly critical of the patent granting policies of the US Patent and Trademark Office.[71] By contrast, during this same period the Antitrust Division was not very concerned about the anticompetitive potential of broad intellectual property protection.[72] Another example is the FTC's historic interest in enforcing the anti-price discrimination provisions of the Clayton Act; the Justice Department, on the other hand, believed that enforcement of these provisions had the potential for dampening price competition. In recent years, however, the Commission's views changed, becoming more like the Antitrust Division's, and its enforcement of the anti-price discrimination law has almost completely ended.[73]

B. States and private enforcement

Although state enforcers have statutory mandates that are at least as broad as federal enforcers, they have traditionally exercised their mandates in somewhat different ways. For example, state enforcers have long emphasized their role in obtaining damages on behalf of their citizens injured as a result of antitrust violations.[74] Federal enforcers could, in theory, also undertake such actions, but neither the

[70] *See* Timothy J. Muris, Chairman, Fed'l Trade Comm'n, "The Federal Trade Commission and the Future Development of U.S. Consumer Protection Policy," Prepared Remarks, August 19, 2003 ("the core of modern consumer protection policy is to protect consumer sovereignty by attacking practices that impede consumers' ability to make informed choices, such as fraud, unilateral breach of contract, and unauthorized billing").

[71] *See* Fed'l Trade Comm'n, To Promote Innovation: The Proper Balance Of Competition And Patent Law And Policy (2003), <http://www.ftc.gov/os/2003/10/innovationrpt.pdf> (critiquing the patent system).

[72] *See* Thomas O. Barnett, Ass't Att'y Gen., Dep't of Justice, Antitrust Div., Presentation to the George Mason University School of Law Symposium: Interoperability Between Antitrust and Intellectual Property 3–4 (September 13, 2006), <http://www.usdoj.gov/atr/public/speeches/218316.pdf> (arguing for a "Schumpeterian view" of antitrust law and for "strong intellectual property protection," because "properly applied, strong intellectual property protection creates the competitive environment necessary to permit firms to profit from their inventions, which encourages innovation effort and improves dynamic efficiency").

[73] *See* William E. Kovacic, "The Modern Evolution Of U.S. Competition Policy Enforcement Norms," 71 Antitrust L.J. 377 (2003) (discussing change in FTC enforcement norms between 1961 and 2000).

[74] The statutory basis for such suits is discussed *supra* notes 18–19 and accompanying text.

FTC nor the Justice Department has shown much interest in allocating their enforcement resources in this way.[75] Similarly, the states' concern for consumer injuries has led the states to be more active than federal enforcers in the area of minimum resale price maintenance agreements, again obtaining monetary relief on behalf of retail consumers when prices are increased as a result of such agreements.[76]

There is also an important area in which the states' enforcement mandate is broader than the mandates of federal enforcers. Following the Supreme Court's decision in *Illinois Brick*[77] that indirect purchasers lack standing to sue for their damages, many states enacted indirect purchaser laws to allow their citizens to sue for such damages under state antitrust law.[78] After the Supreme Court upheld the states' power to pass such laws,[79] state enforcers aggressively used these indirect purchaser laws in broad multistate efforts to obtain large recoveries on behalf of end-user consumers who lack standing to sue under federal antitrust law.[80]

Private litigants take their competition "mandate" from the private right of action under federal and state law. Various procedural doctrines, such as standing requirements and strict pleading rules, limit this mandate in ways that do not affect government enforcers. For example, whereas government enforcers can bring suit for any violation of the antitrust laws without needing to prove harm, private litigants must show that their injury is of the type that the antitrust laws were designed to remedy, that their injuries were "direct" rather than "remote," that their damages would not be duplicative of others and not complex to determine, and that there are not more direct victims available to bring suit.[81] Similarly, class actions under Rule 23 of the Federal Rules of Civil Procedure are constrained by the need to show numerosity, common issues of fact or law, typicality, and adequacy of representation, whereas state *parens patriae* suits under Section 4A of the Clayton Act have no such constraints. The result is that private enforcers effectively have a narrower mandate to enforce federal antitrust law than might otherwise appear from the Clayton Act provision creating a private right of action.

[75] For a rare example of the FTC seeking restitution on behalf of consumers, *see Mylan*, *supra* note 40 and accompanying text.

[76] *See*, e.g., In Re Compact Disc Minimum Advertised Price Antitrust Litigation, 216 F.R.D. 197 (D. Me. 2003) (approving US$143 million settlement for retail pricing overcharges of 3.5 million consumers who purchased CDs at retail over a five year period). For data on state litigation against resale price maintenance between 1995 and 2004, *see* Statement of Harry First, "Before the Antitrust Modernization Commission," at 22 (Table 5) (October 26, 2005), <http://govinfo.library.unt.edu/amc/commission_hearings/pdf/Statement-First.pdf>.

[77] Illinois Brick Co. v. Illinois, 431 U.S. 720 (1977).

[78] *See* Kevin J. O'Connor, "Is The Illinois Brick Wall Crumbling?," 15 Antitrust 34 (Summer 2001) (discussing indirect purchaser statutes in various states).

[79] *See* California v. Arc America, 490 U.S. 93 (1989).

[80] *See* O'Connor, *supra* note 76 (detailing settlements). For more recent information, *see* Harry First, "Modernizing State Antitrust Enforcement: Making the Best of a Good Situation," 54 Antitrust Bull. 281, 300–1 (2009).

[81] *See* Associated Gen'l Contractors v. California State Council of Carpenters, 459 U.S. 519 (1983).

IV. Procedural characteristics of the US enforcement system

A. Introduction

The purpose of this section is to describe the procedural characteristics of the US enforcement system. As indicated above, the US "system" is highly fragmented, consisting of numerous competition enforcement agencies with the legal authority to act completely independently of each other. Rather than analyze the procedural characteristics of each agency in this loosely networked environment, we have chosen to concentrate on the two main federal government enforcement agencies, the Justice Department's Antitrust Division and the Federal Trade Commission. These agencies do the bulk of public antitrust enforcement in the United States. A description of their very different procedures should provide a sufficient (albeit not complete) understanding of the extent to which the identified norms are followed in US antitrust enforcement.

This Section is organized as follows. We divide the procedural characteristics into two broad categories, case-by-case decision-making and overall institutional performance. Within the case-by-case category, we describe three aspects of the process—the decision to proceed, adjudication, and appeals—and two broad due process norms relevant to individual case decision-making—non-discrimination and proportionality of remedies. Within the institutional performance category, we describe five broad norms—operational efficiency, expertise, transparency, accountability, and the rule of law. With regard to each of these ten areas, we describe the two agencies separately. The Section concludes with a brief overall assessment of the two agencies viewed together.

B. Case-by-case decision-making: due process norms

1. *The decision to proceed*

a) Department of Justice

Antitrust Division enforcement decisions are made after investigation by staff attorneys and economists. Recommendations to proceed are made to the Division's "Front Office" and all litigation, whether civil or criminal, is approved by the Assistant Attorney General in charge of the Antitrust Division. Although the Division needs no further approval to commence an enforcement action, there are times when the Attorney General or the White House might be notified before suit is filed.[82]

One consequence of the Antitrust Division's dual civil and criminal enforcement powers is that while some matters (for example, merger investigations) are by their

[82] For example, in 1998 in the Clinton Administration, the White House Counsel's Office and Council of Economic Advisors were informed prior to the Justice Department's filing of its suit against Microsoft. *See* Harry First & Andrew I. Gavil, "Reframing Windows: The Durable Meaning of the *Microsoft* Antitrust Litigation," 2006 Utah L. Rev. 641, 688 n.207.

very nature civil investigations, in other matters a choice must be made to proceed by either criminal or civil investigation and, if necessary, prosecution. In general, the nature of the investigation is determined by the type of suspected underlying conduct. The Division currently reserves criminal investigation and prosecution for cases involving per se unlawful agreements among competitors in violation of Section 1 of the Sherman Act, such as price fixing, bid rigging, and customer and territorial allocations,[83] although even here it reserves the possibility of initiating civil rather than criminal proceedings notwithstanding the apparent per se nature of the suspected conduct.[84] All other antitrust violations are handled through civil process, although in recent years the Division has filed very few non-criminal Section 1 cases, either of a per se or rule of reason nature.[85]

In both civil and criminal matters, the parties are afforded an opportunity to present their views to the investigating staff before the staff makes its formal recommendation. This generally occurs through one or more face-to-face meetings and often includes the presentation of a "White Paper" setting out the parties' views of the case. In civil matters, the staff informs the parties in advance of its competitive concerns and the basis for those concerns, although the degree of specificity of the explanation provided by the staff is within its discretion and can vary from case to case. Where the staff recommends bringing a case, the parties usually will request and be granted the opportunity to meet with the reviewing officials at each successive level within the DOJ, including the appropriate chief of section, the Director of Operations, the relevant Deputy Assistant Attorney General, and, in some cases, the Assistant Attorney General.[86] The Division treats criminal cases more circumspectly. Although the Director of Criminal Enforcement and the Deputy Assistant Attorney General for criminal enforcement will "ordinarily" provide an opportunity for counsel to present arguments against indictment, a meeting with the Assistant Attorney General will occur only in "very unusual circumstances."[87]

[83] *See* Antitrust Division Manual, *supra* note 67, at III-20.

[84] These situations may include cases in which (1) the case law is unsettled or uncertain; (2) there are truly novel issues of law or fact presented; (3) confusion reasonably may have been caused by past prosecutorial decisions; or (4) there is clear evidence that the subjects of the investigation were not aware of, or did not appreciate, the consequences of their action. *Id.*

[85] For a recent civil case, *see* United States v. KeySpan Corporation, No. 10-cv-1415 (S.D.N.Y. February 22, 2010) (civil complaint challenging financial swap agreement for its effect on electricity prices), <http://www.justice.gov/atr/cases/f255500/255507.htm>. The case was simultaneously settled with an agreement under which KeySpan disgorged US$12 million in profits to the United States Treasury. *See* Competitive Impact Statement, <http://www.justice.gov/atr/cases/f255500/255578.htm>. The Justice Department subsequently entered into a similar agreement with Morgan Stanley for facilitating the anticompetitive agreement. *See* United States v. Morgan Stanley, No. 11-cv-6875 (S.D.N.Y. September 30, 2011), Competitive Impact Statement, <http://www.justice.gov/atr/cases/f275800/275857.pdf> (disgorgement of US$4.8 million in profits).

[86] *See* Christine A. Varney, Ass't Attorney Gen., Antitrust Div., Procedural Fairness, Speech to 13th Annual Competition Conference of the International Bar Association (September 12, 2009) (describing opportunities for counsel to be heard during the investigation of civil cases and emphasizing the importance of procedural fairness in the Division's internal processes), <http://www.justice.gov/atr/public/speeches/249974.htm>.

[87] *See* Antitrust Division Manual, *supra* note 67, at III-124. The Division provides no information on how often such meetings are actually held.

The decision to proceed in criminal cases is also affected by two formalized procedural steps not applicable to civil investigations: the grand jury process and the amnesty (or "leniency") program. The grand jury process imposes special rules of secrecy that are not applicable in civil matters and which prevent Justice Department attorneys from sharing certain information with potential defendants.[88] Rules relating to grand jury procedures may also prevent the Division from using information gained through the grand jury process in a subsequent civil suit.[89] The Division's leniency program provides a well-publicized process that corporations and corporate employees can use to convince the Division not to bring charges against them in return for their cooperation in the investigation and prosecution of others.[90] Leniency grants are made on the recommendation of staff lawyers to the Deputy Assistant Attorney General for criminal enforcement and then to the Assistant Attorney General for the Antitrust Division.[91] Counsel are "generally afforded" an opportunity to meet with the Deputy Assistant Attorney General when an initial decision to grant leniency is being considered.[92]

b) Federal Trade Commission

FTC competition matters are investigated by staff in the Bureau of Competition and the Bureau of Economics.[93] Compulsory process to obtain information in such investigations must be approved by the Commission (most often acting through a single "moving Commissioner").[94] Current FTC procedures assume that staff will be in contact with the parties during the investigation and that the parties will make efforts to convince the staff not to recommend action, but current rules do not formally provide for such meetings.

When the investigation is complete, the Bureau of Competition and the Bureau of Economics file separate memoranda with the Commission giving their recommendations as to whether the Commission should vote out a complaint. It is not uncommon for the opinions of the two Bureaus to diverge.[95] The parties will be informed that recommendations have been forwarded to the Commission and will be told to contact the Commission. Because the federal "Sunshine Act" forbids agencies from holding closed-door meetings on official agency matters at which a quorum of commissioners is present, the parties will meet individually with each of the five Commissioners. Although the Commission's formal procedures leave it

88 *See* Fed. R. Crim. P. 6(e).

89 *See*, e.g., United States v. Sells Engineering, Inc., 463 U.S. 418 (1983) (government attorneys involved in grand jury investigation cannot disclose evidence brought before the grand jury to attorneys not involved in the investigation without a court order based on a "particularlized need" for the evidence).

90 The leniency process is described at text at notes 192–197 *infra*.

91 *See* Antitrust Division Manual, *supra* note 67, at III-107.

92 *See id.* (conditional grant of leniency).

93 "Large-scale" or industry-wide investigations requiring substantial expenditures require prior approval by the full Commission. *See* Federal Trade Comm'n, Operating Manual, ch.3, § .1.2.4.1 (hereinafter FTC Operating Manual), <http://www.ftc.gov/foia/adminstaffmanuals.shtm>.

94 *See id.* at § .3.6.7.3.

95 *See* Darren S. Tucker & Amanda P. Reeves, "Effective Advocacy Before the Commission," 24 Antitrust 52, 54 (Summer 2010).

within the discretion of each Commissioner as to whether to meet with the parties,[96] current practice is to provide this opportunity. Parties will take this opportunity to submit White Papers to the Commissioners, as well as to tailor their arguments to the particular interests of individual Commissioners.[97] A majority vote of the eligible Commissioners is necessary to issue a complaint.[98]

2. Adjudicating the charge

a) Department of Justice

The Antitrust Division can act only through the federal judicial system; that is, through trial-type proceedings decided in non-specialized law courts. This is true for both civil and criminal cases.

The Division exercises its enforcement authority in civil matters by seeking injunctions to prevent antitrust violations, pursuant to Section 15 of the Clayton Act[99] for mergers and Section 4 of the Sherman Act[100] for non-merger conduct. When seeking injunctive relief, the Division will request both a preliminary and final injunction, sometimes litigating both requests in the same proceeding. Merger cases tend to proceed more quickly than non-merger civil cases. This is usually at the behest of the merging parties, as prolonged delay in reaching a final outcome can erode the economic benefits of the merger. Complex monopolization cases, on the other hand, carry the potential for highly protracted litigation. The monopolization case brought against IBM in 1969, for example, continued in trial until 1982, when the Justice Department decided to obtain dismissal of its complaint.[101] More recent cases have been tried more expeditiously, as judges and the government have become concerned about the costs of delay. The trial in the Microsoft case, the most recent major Justice Department monopolization suit, was tried in sixteen months, from the filing of the complaint to the close of the evidence.

A significant percentage of litigated Antitrust Division cases are brought as criminal cases, mostly for alleged cartel activity in violation of Section 1 of the Sherman Act. Judicial process in federal criminal cases is governed by the Federal Rules of Criminal Procedure, the Federal Rules of Evidence, and the local rules of court. These rules cover the entire process, from summoning a grand jury and returning an indictment, to arraignment, pretrial discovery and motions, and trial and sentencing.

US criminal procedure provides heightened protections for defendants. These include Fourth Amendment protections against unreasonable searches and seizures,

[96] *See* FTC Operating Manual, *supra* note 93, at § .3.6.1.

[97] *See* Tucker & Reeves, *supra* note 95, at 54–6 (describing advocacy process). The authors, who are attorney-advisors to FTC Commissioner Rosch, conclude that "[t]o outsiders, the decision-making process at the Commission may seem like a black box." *Id.* at 56.

[98] *See* 16 C.F.R. § 3.11(a).

[99] 15 U.S.C. § 25.

[100] 15 U.S.C. § 4.

[101] *See* Barnaby J. Feder, "End Of Action On I.B.M. Follows Erosion Of Its Dominant Position," N.Y. Times, January 9, 1982, at 1.

the Fifth Amendment privilege against self-incrimination,[102] the Sixth Amendment right to a speedy trial by jury,[103] and the due process right to have guilt proved beyond a reasonable doubt (as compared with a "preponderance of the evidence" standard for liability in civil antitrust cases).[104] On the other hand, the defendant's right to discover evidence in criminal cases is more limited than in civil cases,[105] while the government's ability to use the powers of the grand jury gives the government a powerful weapon for investigating criminal antitrust offenses.[106]

b) Federal Trade Commission

As discussed above, the FTC has statutory authority to seek preliminary and permanent injunctions in federal court to stop parties from violating the FTC Act.[107] When the Commission proceeds under this authority, it is subject to the same adjudicatory process as is the Antitrust Division when it seeks injunctive relief in federal court.

In addition, section 5(b) of the FTC Act[108] empowers the FTC to commence an administrative adjudicatory proceeding challenging alleged "unfair methods of competition," which includes any conduct that would violate the Sherman Act or the "spirit" of the Act. Section 11 of the Clayton Act parallels Section 5(b) of the FTC Act in authorizing FTC administrative enforcement of alleged Clayton Act violations, including potentially anticompetitive mergers.[109]

Several aspects of FTC administrative enforcement have caused significant controversy. These include the identity and choice of Administrative Law Judges, the FTC's dual roles as both prosecutor and appellate tribunal, and the speed (or lack thereof) of administrative proceedings. Some of these issues implicate due process norms.

The Administrative Procedure Act ("APA"), which governs the rulemaking process of federal administrative agencies, allows the Commission itself to preside over a hearing or to designate one of its members to preside over the hearing.[110] The FTC Act and its Rules of Practice also authorize such a practice.[111] The FTC has exercised this right from time to time, appointing a Commissioner as

[102] "No person . . . shall be compelled in any criminal case to be a witness against himself." U.S. Const. amend. V.

[103] "In all criminal prosecutions, the accused shall enjoy the right to a speedy and public trial, by an impartial jury of the State and district wherein the crime shall have been committed, which district shall have been previously ascertained by law, and to be informed of the nature and cause of the accusation; to be confronted with the witnesses against him; to have compulsory process for obtaining witnesses in his favor, and to have the Assistance of Counsel for his defence." U.S. Const. amend. VI.

[104] *See* In re Winship, 397 U.S. 358 (1970).

[105] *See* F.R.Crim. P. 16.

[106] These powers were established in an early Sherman Act criminal prosecution, Hale v. Henkel, 201 U.S. 43 (1906).

[107] *See supra* notes 39–45 and accompanying text.

[108] 15 U.S.C. § 45(b).

[109] 15 U.S.C. § 21.

[110] 5 U.S.C. § 556(b).

[111] *See* 15 U.S.C. § 49; 16 C.F.R. § 3.42(a).

the ALJ to handle discovery and fact-finding in the administrative trial. The FTC typically justifies such action as a means of expediting the administrative process, pointing to the antitrust expertise and litigation experience of the chosen Commissioner.[112]

The practice of appointing a Commissioner to serve in the capacity of an ALJ, although permitted as a matter of the FTC's discretion, calls into question the impartiality of the decision-maker. This concern is especially acute if the Commissioner serving as the ALJ in a particular case participated in the FTC's decision to vote out the complaint, but it may also be problematic if the Commissioner had learned about the case in connection with a Commission decision to issue compulsory process or if the Commissioner had received periodic updates on the case from the Bureau of Competition.[113] For a Commissioner to then preside over an administrative hearing can therefore create an appearance of impropriety beyond the usual concern that arises when the Commission both approves complaints (the prosecutorial function) and reviews ALJ findings and decisions (the adjudicative function).[114] This, of course, is a problem inherent in the integrated agency model. Respondents have, in some cases, sought recusal or disqualification of individual Commissioners from acting as the ALJ. Such motions, which are heard by the FTC itself, have generally been unsuccessful.[115]

Several changes in FTC practice may make the issues surrounding its administrative hearings more significant. As noted above, in 2009 the FTC changed its rules of practice to make it more likely that it will pursue cases using its administrative hearing procedures even where it first loses a motion for a preliminary injunction in federal district court.[116] The Commission has also taken the position that the commencement of Part 3 administrative litigation obviates the need for separate discovery or an evidentiary hearing in federal court.[117] The FTC's recent approach signals its intent to utilize fully its administrative enforcement powers, perhaps largely supplanting the role of federal district courts as the first-level arbiter in disputed cases and returning to its earlier practice of continuing with an administrative hearing even after losing a preliminary injunction.

[112] *See*, e.g., Press Release, FTC, FTC Designates Commissioner J. Thomas Rosch as ALJ in Case Challenging Inova Health System Foundation's Acquisition of Prince William Health System, Inc. (May 9, 2008), <http://www.ftc.gov/opa/2008/05/inovafyi.shtm>.

[113] *See* Tucker & Reeves, *supra* note 95, at 53 (describing such contacts).

[114] *See* J. Thomas Rosch, So I Serve as Both a Prosecutor and a Judge—What's the Big Deal?, Remarks before the American Bar Ass'n, August, 2010, at 12–16 (discussion of due process issue by FTC Commissioner who has served as an ALJ), <http://ftc.gov/speeches/rosch/100805abaspeech.pdf>.

[115] *See*, e.g., In the Matter of Whole Foods Market, Inc., and Wild Oats Markets, Inc., File No. 0710114, Docket No. 9324, *Order Denying Respondent's Motion To Disqualify The Commission* (September 5, 2008), available at <http://www.ftc.gov/os/adjpro/d9324/080905order.pdf>; In the Matter of Inova Health System Foundation, and Prince William Health System, Inc., File No. 0610166, Docket No. 9326, *Statement of Commissioner J. Thomas Rosch Accompanying Order Certifying Respondents' Motion to Recuse* (May 29, 2008), available at <http://www.ftc.gov/os/adjpro/d9326/080529ordercert.pdf>.

[116] *See supra* notes 41–45 and accompanying text.

[117] *See*, e.g., *FTC v. Inova Health Sys. Found.*, No. 1:08-cv-460 (E.D. Va. 2008).

3. *Appeals*

a) Decision not to proceed

No appeal lies from an allegedly inappropriate decision not to proceed, either by the FTC or by the Justice Department. In this respect, US law differs from European law. In the European Union, an interested party may appeal from a European Commission decision not to bring proceedings.[118] A fortiori, no appeal lies from insufficient explanation of a decision not to proceed. Indeed in the US, unlike the EU, the authorities are not required to give reasons for not challenging a merger, although both US agencies have done so from time to time.[119] In this respect the US has opted for flexibility and efficiency in enforcement decisions, and to some extent protection of confidentiality, in preference to greater transparency.

b) Department of Justice

From 1903 to 1974 appeals of Justice Department civil cases went directly from the district court to the Supreme Court. Congress changed this practice in 1974 and civil appeals are now taken to the relevant federal circuit court of appeals, with the losing party able to petition the Supreme Court for discretionary review.[120]

Appeals in criminal cases have always been taken to the court of appeals and then, through discretionary review, to the Supreme Court. Convicted defendants have numerous grounds on which they can base an appeal, including the imposition of an improper sentence and the refusal of a court to allow the defendant to enter a plea of nolo contendere (no contest). The government's rights to appeal are much more limited. Most importantly, because of the constitutional protection against double jeopardy, the government may not appeal a judgment of acquittal. The government may, however, appeal a trial judge's sentence if it feels that the sentence was improperly low.[121]

Appellate procedures are governed by detailed federal court rules that apply both to civil and criminal appeals. Appellate courts are required to provide a fair and timely opportunity to be heard, with adequate notice of the evidence to be relied on and adequate time to prepare a defense. The courts themselves are composed of independent decision-makers. Federal court judges are nominated by the President

[118] *See* Impala v. Commission (Sony/BMG,), Case T-464/04, [2006] ECR II-2289.

[119] *See*, e.g., Boeing/McDonnell Douglas, Statement of FTC Commissioners on Decision of July 1, 1997 to Close Investigation, CCH Trade Reg. Rep. [1997–2001 Transfer Binder] ¶ 24,295; Whirlpool Corporation and Maytag Corporation, Statement of Department of Justice on Decision of March 29, 2006 to Close Investigation, 7 CCH Trade Reg. Rep. ¶ 50, 209; XM Satellite Radio Holdings and Sirius Satellite Radio, Statement of Department of Justice on Decision of March 25, 2008 to Close Investigation, 7 CCH Trade Reg. Rep. ¶ 50, 277.

[120] Antitrust Procedures and Penalties Act, 88 Stat. 1709, Pub. L. 93–528, sec. 4, 15 U.S.C. § 29 (December 21, 1974). Direct Supreme Court review is still possible, but only for cases "of general public importance in the administration of justice." Since the passage of the 1974 Act, the Supreme Court has only reviewed two such cases, both of which involved the Justice Department's 1982 settlement decree with AT&T. *See* California v. United States, 464 U.S. 1013 (1983); Maryland v. United States, 460 U.S. 1001 (1983).

[121] 18 U.S.C. § 3742(b).

and confirmed by the Senate after a usually thorough screening process. Judges are required to avoid conflicts of interest. For example, they may not sit on cases involving a party in which they have stock holdings. These rules are self-policed in the courts,[122] but the Supreme Court and courts of appeals are often called on to disqualify judges not only for actual conflicts of interest that show bias but also for conduct that may appear to show bias.[123]

Standing rules for filing appeals are rigorous. For example, non-parties directly interested in the outcome do not automatically have standing to appeal from a judgment,[124] as they do in Europe. Notwithstanding these limitations on access to courts, there appears to be nothing in the appeals process that might suggest a systemic lack of due process. Any arguable denial of due process would arise in a particular litigation, and is subject to challenge in court.

c) FTC

Appeals from the Commission's final order, entered after an administrative trial, may be taken to a federal circuit court of appeals.[125] A party can file an appeal in

[122] *See,* e.g., the statement of Chief Justice Rehnquist in Microsoft v. United States, 530 U.S. 1301 (2000), denying petition for direct appeal from the district court. Chief Justice Rehnquist disclosed that Microsoft had retained his son's law firm as local counsel in Boston in private antitrust litigation and explained why in his opinion his participation in the *Microsoft* appeal would create neither a conflict nor the appearance of one.

Perhaps the most famous case of recusal is United States v. Aluminum Co. of America (*Alcoa*), 148 F.2d 416 (2d Cir. 1945). On appeal from a district court decision dismissing the complaint, four justices recused themselves because of their involvement with the defendant and thus a quorum of six could not be mustered. Accordingly, the Supreme Court, pursuant to a specially enacted statute, referred the case to an ad hoc panel of the Court of Appeals to decide the case in its stead. *See Alcoa* at 421.

[123] *See,* e.g., United States v. Microsoft Corp., 56 F.3d 1448, 1463–65 (D.C. Cir. 1995), where the Justice Department and Microsoft appealed the district court's refusal to enter a proposed consent decree. The court of appeals, observing that the district court judge, Judge Sporkin, had apparently been influenced by reading a book outside of the record and had made comments evidencing his distrust of Microsoft's lawyers and his poor view of Microsoft's practices, concluded that a reasonable observer would question the judge's impartiality. It accordingly remanded the case for assignment to another district court judge, with instructions to enter the decree.

An issue of disqualification also arose in the later monopolization case against Microsoft, involving different conduct. In the final stages of the trial, the district court judge, Judge Thomas Penfield Jackson, gave secret interviews to selected reporters, obtaining promises that the interviews would be embargoed until after final judgment was entered, disclosing his view on the facts, the law, and the appropriate remedy and offering "contemporaneous impressions of testimony"—including his disbelief in the credibility of key Microsoft witnesses. The appellate court found that the judge had breached his duty of appearance of impartiality. While affirming most of the case on the liability issues, and dismissing and remanding other claims, the appellate court disqualified the judge retroactive to the date that he had ordered a breakup of Microsoft. *See* United States v. Microsoft Corp., 253 F. 3d at 107–18.

[124] In some cases, however, particularly where the appellant withdraws from a case of public importance, courts have allowed an intervenor or an amicus to step into the appellant's place. *See,* e.g., California Retail Liquor Dealers Ass'n v. Midcal Aluminum, Inc., 445 U.S. 97 (1980) (intervenor); Utah Pub. Service Comm'n v. El Paso Nat'l Gas Co., 395 U.S. 464 (1969) (amicus). *See also* Massachusetts v. Microsoft Corp., 373 F.3d 1199 (D.C. Cir. 2004), allowing two amici industry associations to intervene in Massachusetts' appeal from entry of a proposed consent decree where the amici had raised additional considerations, were abreast of the issues, and would not need more time to prepare.

[125] *See* 15 U.S.C. §§ 21(c), 45(c).

any district in which the party resides or does business or where any act that was a subject of the proceeding took place.[126] The Federal Rules of Appellate Procedure, and where relevant, local federal circuit rules, apply.

Cases in which the FTC has sought injunctive relief in district court may be appealed to the relevant federal circuit courts of appeal. To challenge a federal circuit court opinion, the party must petition the US Supreme Court for a writ of certiorari. Writs of certiorari are seldom granted, absent significant questions of law or policy, or a conflict among the federal circuits.

The FTC is an expert body charged with both finding the facts and interpreting and applying the law. Normally in the United States, both the findings of fact and the policy/law judgments of the expert commission are entitled to deference by the appellate courts.[127] At least, findings of fact should not be overturned when they are supported by substantial evidence.[128] Accordingly, the opinions of expert commissions are not frequently overturned. Notwithstanding the deference that courts often accord administrative findings, several important FTC decisions have been reversed on interpretations of law and mixed questions of law and fact[129] and critics have expressed concern that FTC decisions are not accorded adequate deference in the courts.[130]

4. *Equality and non-discrimination*

When can discrimination on the basis of nationality undermine markets and offend the spirit of antitrust? There are two major points of concern. One is in connection with the treatment of foreign goods and persons who are selling into the US; the other is in connection with a possible nationalistic motivation to bless "national champions" at the expense of out-of-country rivals and consumers. There is no indication, however, that in either regard US antitrust enforcement fails to treat similarly placed persons equally or discriminates on the basis of nationality. Indeed, US antitrust officials normally pride themselves on supporting competition, whatever its source. Competition is nation blind.

[126] For an indication that before filing a complaint the Commissioners may consider the circuit court to which the case might be appealed, *see* Tucker & Reeves, *supra* note 95, at 53.

[127] *See* Chevron U.S.A., Inc. v. Natural Resource Defense Council, Inc., 467 U.S. 837 (1984); Hospital Corp. of America v. FTC, 807 F.2d 1381 (7th Cir. 1986).

[128] *See,* e.g., Fall River Dyeing & Finishing Corp. v. NLRB, 482 US 27, 42 (1987).

[129] *See,* e.g., California Dental Association v. FTC, 526 U.S. 756 (1999). In Indiana Fed'n of Dentists, the Supreme Court held that the FTC's deferential standard is coextensive with the APA's requirement that a court defer to an agency's factual findings so long as they are supported by "substantial evidence." 5 U.S.C. § 706(2)(E); FTC v. Ind. Fed'n of Dentists, 476 U.S. 447, 454 (1986) (holding that the standard of review under § 5(c) is "essentially identical" to the substantial evidence test). *See also Rambus Inc. v. FTC,* 522 F.3d 456 (D.C. Cir. 2008); Schering-Plough Corp. v. FTC, 402 F.3d 1056, 1062 (11th Cir. 2005). For a description of FTC process and appellate review, *see* William C. MacLeod, The Federal Trade Commission and the Federal Trade Commission Act §§ 9:40–9:57, in Antitrust Advisor (Irving Scher, ed., 4th edn 2009).

[130] *See,* e.g., Stephen Calkins, "*California Dental Association*: Not a Quick Look But Not The Full Monty," 67 ANTITRUST L.J. 495, 555 (2000).

A particularly good example is the Japanese electronics antitrust case, Matsushita Electronics Indus. v. Zenith Radio Corp.[131] The Japanese electronics industry had been damaging the US electronics industry by charging significantly lower prices in the US market than the American firms. The US producers sued the Japanese firms, alleging that they had entered into a predatory-pricing cartel. This was a time of American paranoia that Japanese competition was making dangerous inroads into American markets.[132] After extensive discovery, the defendants moved to dismiss the complaint on grounds that the Americans had no plausible evidence of a low price conspiracy, and that a below-cost conspiracy would not have made sense because it would have cost more than it could have returned in profits. When the Japanese firms lost in the court of appeals, the Justice Department supported their petition for review in the Supreme Court and, after the Court decided to take the case, filed an amicus brief in support of their position. The Supreme Court held for the Japanese firms. It took the occasion to articulate the importance of freedom of low pricing, the implausibility of a low price conspiracy, and the double implausibility that a cartel engaged in price predation could ultimately obtain high prices. The Court's opinion has been much criticized for the presumptions underlying its economic analysis and its inattention to cultural detail (it has also been praised), but it could never be criticized on grounds of protecting the Americans against the Japanese.

We know of no US antitrust case that leans in the opposite direction—that is, one that condemns conduct of foreign competitors under standards looser than courts would apply to the same conduct by American firms. A matter criticized as nationalistic, whether fairly or unfairly, is the US closure of investigation of the Boeing/McDonnell Douglas merger. Boeing was the largest manufacturer of commercial jet aircraft, accounting for about 64 percent of the world market. The European consortium Airbus Industrie was second with about 30 percent. Boeing wished to acquire the only other competitor, McDonnell Douglas, with about 6 percent. The US Department of Defense strongly supported the merger because it would consolidate assets for building military jets (military jets were not part of the contested relevant market). The FTC opened an investigation and later closed it, announcing that there was no antitrust problem; McDonnell Douglas had failed to invest in current technology and could no longer compete for new orders of commercial jet aircraft. The FTC (unusually) issued a closing statement noting—and vehemently denying—speculation that the merger was actually anticompetitive and that the FTC was merely supporting a national champion.[133] In a parallel investigation, the European Competition Directorate investigated the merger and concluded that it was anticompetitive. It ultimately allowed the transaction but only with stringent and elaborate conditions.[134]

131 475 U.S. 574 (1986).

132 *See*, e.g., Michael Crichton, Rising Sun (1992).

133 *See* Statement of FTC Commissioners on Decision of July 1, 1997 to Close Investigation, CCH Trade Reg. Rep. [1997–2001 Transfer Binder] ¶ 24,295.

134 Case IV/M877, O.J. L 336/16 (European Commission 1997).

One area in which it might appear that antitrust enforcement is stronger against foreign firms than domestic enterprises is criminal prosecutions. Many of the recent major cartel prosecutions have involved international cartels composed almost entirely of non-US participants.[135] The Justice Department has prosecuted these cartels vigorously and non-US executives of these firms have served sentences of imprisonment in US jails.[136] Nevertheless, it is difficult to make out a claim that these cartels were discriminatorily prosecuted, particularly given their simultaneous prosecution by enforcement agencies around the world. There is also no evidence that US enforcement authorities fail to investigate or prosecute US firms or their executives for price-fixing activities.

The cosmopolitan approach that US antitrust enforcement authorities normally take, welcoming open markets and competition on the merits without regard to nationality, sometimes contrasts with Congressional attitudes and pressures. For example, US Congressional opposition defeated the 2005 bid by China's CNOOC for Unocal and the 2006 bid by Dubai Ports World of United Arab Emirates for contracts to operate six US ports.[137] US statutes outside of the antitrust area, such as the antidumping and tariff laws and the Defense Production Act, which sets rules for clearance of foreign investment, may also facilitate nationalism and protectionism.[138]

5. *Proportionality of remedies*

The US antitrust agencies and the courts are generally attentive to remedies. They seek a remedy tailored to the violation and likely to cure the competition problem. In the merger context, the Antitrust Division of the Department of Justice has been particularly clear on this point. The Department of Justice Antitrust Division's Policy Guide to Merger Remedies states:[139]

[135] As of March 5, 2012, eighty of the ninety-three firms that had been fined US$10 million or more were non-U.S. firms (86 percent); eighteen of the twenty firms that had been fined US$100 million or more were non-U.S. firms (90 percent). *See* Antitrust Division, Sherman Act Violations Yielding a Corporate Fine of US$10 Million or More, <http://www.justice.gov/atr/public/criminal/sherman10.html>.

[136] *See* Scott D. Hammond, Dept'y Ass't Att'ny Genl., "The Evolution of Criminal Antitrust Enforcement Over the Last Two Decades," Speech to The 24th Annual National Institute On White Collar Crime at 7–8 (February 25, 2010) ("Since May 1999, more than 40 foreign defendants have served, or are serving, prison sentences in the United States for participating in an international cartel or for obstructing an investigation of an international cartel. Foreign nationals from France, Germany, Japan, Korea, Norway, the Netherlands, Sweden, Switzerland, Taiwan and the United Kingdom are among those defendants."), <http://www.justice.gov/atr/public/speeches/255515.pdf>.

[137] *See* Up to 8 companies vie for Dubai's US port assets, Reuters, September 1, 2006; C. Fred Bergsten, op-ed., "Avoiding Another Dubai," Washington Post, February 28, 2006 at A15; "US Lawmakers Meddle in CNOOC's Unocal Bid," China Daily, July 6, 2005; Edward M. Graham, op-ed., "No Reason to Block the Deal," Far Eastern Economic Rev., July/Aug 2005 at 24.

[138] *See supra* note 68 and accompanying text. CNOOC and Dubai Ports, *see supra* note 137, were aired as CFIUS matters.

[139] *See* <http://www.justice.gov/atr/public/guidelines/272350.pdf>.

Before the Division will conclude that a proposed remedy is acceptable, the relief must effectively address each of the Division's competitive concerns. There should be a close, logical nexus between the proposed remedy and the alleged violation—and the remedy should fit the violation and flow from the theory or theories of competitive harm.[140]

When relief has no reasonable relationship to the violations found, it must be set aside. Indeed, courts have set aside remedies that are not related to competition concerns even if the remedy might be regarded as good social policy.[141]

Although the US Supreme Court has not specified proportionality as a goal of antitrust remedies,[142] commentators have argued that proportionality is important in crafting them.[143] But proportionality is not a self-executing goal. Moreover, what qualifies as appropriate relief is often a matter of contention and may vary with time. For example, in the 1974 *Ford/Autolite* merger case, relied on by the Department of Justice Policy Guide to Merger Remedies discussed above, the Supreme Court held that a ten-year injunction against Ford's entry into the auto spark plug market, in addition to divestiture, was appropriate to remedy Ford's vertical acquisition of the number three spark plug company. One may confidently speculate that these obligations would be regarded as gargantuan when judged by 21st century measures.

In the *Microsoft* monopolization case, the court of appeals explicitly required the district court to enter a decree "tailored to the harm" that the plaintiffs had proved. Although the final settlement that the district court approved closely tracked the exact conduct shown to be illegal, that settlement has been criticized by many as having fallen far short of the relief necessary to cure the effects of Microsoft's anticompetitive behavior.[144] Indeed, some have argued that excessive focus on

[140] Footnote 6 of the guide collects the authorities thus: Ford Motor Co. [v. United States], 405 U.S. 562, 575 (1972) (In a Section 7 action, relief "necessarily must 'fit the exigencies of the particular case.'"); [Massachusetts v.] Microsoft Corp., 373 F.3d 1199, 1228 (D.C. Cir. 2004) ("[T]he court carefully considered the 'causal connection' between Microsoft's anticompetitive conduct and its dominance of the market...."); [United States v.] Microsoft Corp., 253 F.3d 34, 105–7 (D.C. Cir. 2001) (Relief "should be tailored to fit the wrong creating the occasion for the remedy.").

[141] *See* Wal-Mart Stores Inc. v. Rodriguez, 238 F. Supp. 2d 423 (D.P.R.) (preliminarily enjoining Puerto Rican government minister from imposing buy-national and employee-retention obligations on Wal-Mart as a condition of acquiring Supermercados grocery chain; conditions violated the Commerce and Equal Protection clauses of the Constitution), *vacatur granted*, 322 F.3d 747 (1st Cir. 2003).

[142] *See* Ford Motor Co. v. United States, 405 U.S. 562, 577 (1972) (purpose of remedial decree is to "unfetter a market from anticompetitive conduct"); United States v. United Shoe Mach. Corp., 391 U.S. 244, 250 (1968) (decree should "terminate the illegal monopoly" and "ensure that there remain no practices likely to result in monopolization in the future"). *See* also E. Thomas Sullivan, "Antitrust Remedies in the U.S. and EU: Advancing a Standard Of Proportionality," 48 ANTITRUST BULL. 377, 378, 423 (2003) (observing that "proportionality" is a term not normally employed in the United States).

[143] *See*, e.g., William E. Kovacic, "Designing Antitrust Remedies for Dominant Firm Misconduct," 31 CONN. L. REV. 1285, 1312–1313 (1999) ("Remedies should be proportional in the sense that they reflect the dangers of the conduct by which a firm has achieved or sustained a position of dominance"); John E. Lopatka & William H. Page, "A (Cautionary) Note on Remedies in the Microsoft Case," 13 ANTITRUST 25, 26 (1999) ("Indeed, one of our principal points is that a remedy should be proportionate to the violation."). *See* also Philip E. Areeda & Herbert Hovenkamp, II ANTITRUST LAW 303 at 37 (3rd edn 2007).

[144] Carl Shapiro, "Microsoft: A Remedial Failure," 75 ANTITRUST L.J. 739 (2009); Herbert Hovenkamp, *The Antitrust Enterprise* 300 (2005). Not all commentators are critical, of course. *See*, e.g., William

"tailoring" can produce inadequacies where the defendant's conduct is systemic.[145] Further, in a globalized economy, there may be a misfit between national remedies and global harms, leading to remedies that are insufficiently robust to counter transnational violations.[146]

In the criminal area, maximum penalties are set by statute, but the penalties in specific cases are governed by the federal Sentencing Guidelines, which apply to all criminal cases in federal court. Because current Justice Department policy is to criminally prosecute only price fixing, bid rigging, or market allocations, criminal penalties in antitrust cases are imposed only in a limited range of offenses, and, most importantly, not in monopolization cases.[147]

Under the Sentencing Guidelines, fines are explicitly keyed to monetary harm. The base corporate fine for price-fixing cases is set at 20 percent of the volume of commerce affected, an amount that the US Sentencing Commission believes represents an average overcharge of 10 percent of the selling price plus a welfare loss of 10 percent.[148] The total amount of the fine is also capped, either at the Sherman Act's US$100 million maximum fine or at a fine of twice the gain or loss, whichever is larger.[149]

There has been a number of very substantial fines imposed in international cartel cases and some have argued that the combination of high fines in the United States and in other jurisdictions, plus private treble-damages recoveries in the United States, could result in excessively high penalties.[150] Other commentators criticize the fine structure as producing fines that are too low, leading to under-deterrence because "average" cartel overcharges are, it is estimated, more than 20 percent and because the fines fail to account adequately for the fact that not all cartels are discovered or prosecuted.[151] Because fines in cartel cases have been accepted under negotiated plea agreements rather than litigated in court, it is difficult to tell how close the fines come to an accurate measure of harm, or whether the parties have

H. Page, "Mandatory Contracting Remedies in the American and European Microsoft Cases," 75 ANTITRUST L.J. 787 (2009); John E. Lopatka, "Assessing Microsoft from a Distance," 75 ANTITRUST L.J. 811 (2009).

[145] *See*, e.g., Harry First, "Netscape is Dead: Remedy Lessons from the Microsoft Litigation" (2008), <http://papers.ssrn.com/sol3/papers.cfm?abstract_id=1260803>.

[146] *See* Eleanor Fox, "Remedies and the Courage of Convictions in a Globalized World: How Globalization Corrupts Relief, " 80 TULANE L. REV. 571 (2005).

[147] Under the Sherman Act fines can be imposed only in the context of a criminal prosecution. There is no provision for "civil fines," although it has been argued that the law should be changed to allow for the imposition of civil fines at least in monopolization cases. *See* Harry First, "The Case for Antitrust Civil Penalties," 76 ANTITRUST L. J. 127 (2009).

[148] *See* U.S. Sentencing Guidelines Manual § 2R.1.1(d) and Application Note 3 (2010), <http://www.ussc.gov/Guidelines/2010_guidelines/Manual_HTML/2r1_1.htm>.

[149] *See* 18 U.S.C. § 3571 (c), (d).

[150] *See*, e.g., Michael L. Denger & D. Jarrett Arp, "Criminal And Civil Cartel Victim Compensation: Does Our Multifaceted Enforcement System Promote Sound Competition Policy?," 15 ANTITRUST 41 (Summer 2001).

[151] *See*, e.g., John M. Connor & Robert H. Lande, "The Size of Cartel Overcharges: Implications for U.S. and EU fining policies," 51 ANTITRUST 983 (2006) (surveying prior studies showing a range of average overcharges between 18 and 37 percent; concludes that fines are "far too low").

agreed to consider the impact of non-US effects, or whether there has been some multiplier applied to take account of the likelihood of detection.[152]

Sentences of imprisonment under the Sherman Act are also subject to the Sentencing Guidelines.[153] As with fines, the term of imprisonment for price-fixing is keyed to monetary harm, with the length increasing with the volume of commerce involved. Unlike fines, however, there is no metric for correlating economic harm to the severity of the sentence. It is difficult to say how much a year in prison is "worth" to an offender or to society, making it hard to assess whether offenders are being punished too severely or not severely enough. When the Sentencing Guidelines were initially promulgated in 1987, the Sentencing Commission made an explicit effort to increase prison sentences for all white-collar offenders, responding to a general feeling that such sentences were too low.[154] In recent years Congress has also increased statutory maxima in a number of white-collar crimes, including an increase in antitrust penalties in 2004 from a three-year maximum to a ten-year maximum.[155] Indeed, enforcers often stress the importance of imprisonment for attaining adequate deterrence.[156] Nevertheless, most prison sentences in cartel cases have been agreed to in plea negotiations and do not come anywhere close to the statutory maximum.[157] Whether they are disproportionate to the harm caused cannot be determined, but at least the sentences are transparent so

[152] The Division currently takes the view that non-US commerce can be relevant to a defendant's culpability (both individual and corporate) but that it will not include non-US commerce in calculating the "volume of commerce" under the Sentencing Guidelines. *See* Scott D. Hammond, Dept'y Ass't Attny. Gen'l, U.S. Dept. of Justice, "Charting New Waters In International Cartel Prosecutions," at 14 n.28 (March 2, 2006) (noting two corporate plea agreements in which sales outside the United States were considered), <http://www.justice.gov/atr/public/speeches/214861.pdf>. The Sentencing Guidelines are silent on the issue.

[153] Since 2005 the Guidelines have been discretionary, rather than mandatory, *see* United States v. Booker, 543 U.S. 220 (2005), but courts still impose "within Guidelines" sentences in a majority of all cases. *See* U.S. Sentencing Comm'n Sourcebook of Federal Sentencing Statistics Tbl. N (2009) (for FY 2009, 56.8 percent of sentences within Guidelines range; 15.9 percent below Guidelines range; 25.3 percent Government-sponsored below Guidelines range; 2 percent above Guidelines range), <http://www.ussc.gov/ANNRPT/2009/TableN.pdf>.

[154] *See* U.S. Sentencing Guidelines Manual ch. 1 § 4(d), 52 Fed. Reg. 18,046 (May 13, 1987) ("Under present sentencing practice, courts sentence to probation an inappropriately high percentage of offenders guilty of certain economic crimes, such as theft, tax evasion, antitrust offenses, insider trading, fraud, and embezzlement, that in the Commission's view are 'serious.' If the guidelines were to permit courts to impose probation instead of prison in many or all such cases, the present sentences would continue to be ineffective.").

[155] Antitrust Criminal Penalty Enhancement and Reform Act of 2004, Pub. L. No. 108–237, § 215, 118 Stat. 661 (2004) (codified as amended in scattered sections of 15 U.S.C.) (increasing imprisonment from three-year maximum to ten-year maximum).

[156] *See* Hammond, *supra* note 136, at 11 ("The Antitrust Division has long emphasized that the most effective way to deter and punish cartel activity is to hold culpable individuals accountable by seeking jail sentences.").

[157] In 2007, the average prison sentence for cases prosecuted by the Antitrust Division was 31 months; this was an historic high, but it includes non-antitrust offenses as well as antitrust violations. *See id.* at 9. As of 2010, the longest prison sentence that a foreign national has agreed to serve in an antitrust case is thirty months. *See* United States v. Whittle, Crim. No. H-07-487-03, S.D. Tex. (12/3/07) (Plea Agreement) (to be reduced by amount of time served in the United Kingdom for same cartel activities), <http://www.justice.gov/atr/cases/f228500/228582.htm>.

that an offender can argue over whether a particular sentence is out of line with sentences in similar cases.[158]

The principle of proportionality of remedies requires that the remedy must be proportionate to the aims of the statute in condemning the conduct; that is, reasonably related and not excessive in view of the aims. In antitrust the aims are several: to restore competition, to deter, to compensate, and for criminal violations, also to punish. It does not appear that US remedies are disproportionate, or that they otherwise raise concerns of due process.

C. Institutional performance norms

1. *Operational efficiency*

a) Setting enforcement priorities

It is not clear how the Agencies set enforcement priorities.[159] To some extent enforcement agendas at both Agencies are determined by external events that are not within their control. The announcement of a merger can trigger immediate review; private parties can bring complaints of antitrust violations to the Agencies that may lead to an extended investigation and, possibly, litigation; decrees from past cases need to be policed and enforced.[160] To a large extent, however, both Agencies have a great deal of discretion in setting their enforcement agendas. For the Antitrust Division, discretionary enforcement policies have been a blend of the overall political goals of the national administration and the specific policies that the Assistant Attorney General in charge of the Antitrust Division wants to pursue. For the FTC, discretionary enforcement generally reflects the priorities of the Chairman. Given that the Chairman is politically appointed by the President, these priorities have been a blend of the national administration's goals and the Chairman's policy preferences. In addition, individual Commissioners may identify specific policy areas in which they are interested. Their interest may, in turn, provide support to staff to pursue enforcement in these areas.

b) Agency merger review

The Hart-Scott-Rodino Antitrust Improvements Act of 1976 ("HSR Act")[161] requires parties to mergers exceeding certain size-of-company and size-of-transac-

[158] All plea agreements are public records and the Justice Department posts all agreements on its website. Note that inequality between co-defendants or among similar defendants is not formally accounted for in the Sentencing Guidelines, although judges do sometimes make an effort to compare sentences in similar cases. *See* United States v. Parris, 573 F. Supp. 2d 744 (E.D.N.Y. 2008) (comparing sentences in fraud cases).

[159] The FTC formally reports some of its enforcement agenda on a semi-annual basis. *See*, e.g., FTC, Statement of Regulatory Priorities, 75 Fed. Reg. 79695 (December 20, 2010); Federal Trade Comm'n Act, § 22 (d), 15 U.S.C. § 57b-3(d) (requiring semi-annual publication of regulatory agenda listing rules FTC intends to propose or promulgate in the following twelve months).

[160] *See*, e.g., Federal Trade Comm'n, Press Release, "Toys 'R' Us to Pay $1.3 Million Penalty for Violating FTC Order (March 29, 2011) (civil penalty for violating FTC order entered in 1998 at conclusion of litigation for conduct that occurred between 1999 and 2010), <http://ftc.gov/opa/2011/03/toysrus.shtm>.

[161] 15 U.S.C. § 18a.

tion thresholds and having a sufficient nexus to US commerce to file a notification form with the FTC and the Antitrust Division and observe a waiting period prior to consummating the merger. For most HSR-reportable transactions, the initial waiting period is thirty calendar days.[162] This period provides the government time to determine whether to allow the transaction to proceed or to conduct a more extensive investigation. The initial waiting period may be terminated early if the parties so request and the government determines there are no material competitive issues, or it may simply be allowed to expire.[163] In either case, the parties may then close their transaction. Alternatively, the government can extend the waiting period by issuing a request for additional information and documentary material, known as a "second request."[164] If a second request is issued, the waiting period during which the parties cannot close their transaction is extended, in most instances until thirty days after both parties have "substantially complied" with the second request.[165] A second request is usually very burdensome, often taking weeks or months and costing the merger parties millions of dollars. Only a small percentage of reported transactions receive second requests.[166] Before the end of the second waiting period, the FTC or DOJ must decide whether to allow the transaction to close without conditions, seek to block the transaction, or negotiate a consent decree with the merger parties allowing the transaction to proceed subject to conditions resolving competitive concerns.

There are several aspects of the HSR merger review process that are not a formal part of the statutory regime (that is, are not included in the HSR Act or regulations) and yet can have a significant impact on the efficiency of the process and the timeliness of decisions.

Following an HSR filing, if staff at either the FTC or the DOJ determine that an investigation is warranted, the transaction is assigned to one of the agencies through a process known as "clearance."[167] In most cases, generally involving industries in which one agency has an established record of expertise and experience, only that agency requests clearance, which the other agency grants quickly.[168] In instances where both agencies seek clearance or one agency objects to the other's request for

[162] 15 U.S.C. § 18a(b); 16 C.F.R. § 803.10(b). For cash tender offers and acquisitions involving a party in bankruptcy, the initial waiting period is fifteen calendar days. Any waiting period scheduled to expire on a weekend or federal holiday is automatically extended to the next business day. *Id.*

[163] 15 U.S.C. § 18a(b)(2).

[164] 15 U.S.C. § 18a(e); 16 C.F.R. § 803.20.

[165] 15 U.S.C. § 18a(e)(2); 16 C.F.R. §§ 803.10(b)(2), 803.20(c). For cash tender offers and acquisitions involving a party in bankruptcy, a second request extends the waiting period for ten calendar days, and the waiting period restarts upon compliance by the acquiring party. *Id.*

[166] From fiscal year 2002 to fiscal year 2011, the number of second requests issued as a percentage of the total number of transactions reported under the HSR Act ranged from 2.5 percent to 4.5 percent. *See* Federal Trade Comm'n & U.S. Dep't of Justice, Hart-Scott-Rodino Annual Report, Fiscal Year 2011, at 5, <http://www.ftc.gov/os/2012/06/2011hsrreport.pdf>. In fiscal year 2011 the number of reported transactions increased, from 1166 to 1450, but the percentage of second requests remained the same, at 4.1 percent. *See* Federal Trade Comm'n & U.S. Dep't of Justice, Hart-Scott-Rodino Annual Report, Fiscal Year 2011, at 1, 5, <http://www.ftc.gov/os/2012/06/2011hsrreport.pdf>.

[167] This is not to be confused with clearance of a transaction following an investigation.

[168] *See* Federal Trade Comm'n & U.S. Dep't of Justice, "FTC/DOJ Clearance Procedures for Investigations" (December 1993), reprinted in 65 ANTITRUST & TRADE REG. REP. (BNA) 746 (1993).

clearance, the agencies must determine jointly which will conduct the investigation. Neither agency can (formally) investigate a transaction until clearance has been agreed. While some clearance disputes are resolved fairly rapidly, others can escalate all the way up to the Chairman of the FTC and the Assistant Attorney General at the DOJ.

Although clearance disputes are relatively infrequent, when they occur they can consume a significant portion of the initial HSR waiting period and can even result in a situation where the staff lack sufficient time to complete the initial competitive assessment within the initial waiting period. This may force the parties to withdraw and refile their HSR notifications, thereby restarting the waiting period, or to accept a second request that otherwise might have been avoided.[169] In either case, clearance disputes often cause material delay in the review of proposed transactions and impose additional costs and burdens on the transaction parties, with potentially significant consequences for time-sensitive transactions, as well as postponing the pro-competitive benefits of transactions.

The FTC and DOJ attempted to address the clearance problem in 2002 by formalizing an agreement allocating primary areas of responsibility on an industry-specific basis.[170] They abandoned the agreement, however, after strong opposition from some members of Congress.[171] Although there have since been repeated calls for the FTC and DOJ to implement a new clearance agreement, the Agencies continue to operate under the pre-2002 procedures.[172]

The second request procedure has also been the subject of concern. In 2006 the FTC and the DOJ adopted separate, non-identical procedures aimed at streamlining and reducing the costs and burden of second request compliance.[173] These reforms focused primarily on reducing the volume of documents parties must produce in response to a second request, as this is usually the most costly and inconvenient component of second request compliance. To obtain the benefits of these reforms, however, the parties must, *inter alia*, agree to certain provisions extending the length of the investigation and providing for a minimum stipulated

[169] An acquiring party may withdraw its HSR notification and refile within two business days without paying an additional filing fee, thereby restarting the initial waiting period and allowing for further discussion with agency staff. This procedure, which may be used only once without another filing fee, introduces valuable flexibility into the process and is sometimes utilized by merger parties to provide additional time to attempt to resolve competitive concerns and avoid the issuance of a second request.

[170] *See* Memorandum of Agreement Between The Federal Trade Commission and The Antitrust Division of The United States Department of Justice Concerning Clearance Procedures for Investigations (March 5, 2002), <http://www.ftc.gov/opa/2002/02/clearance/ftcdojagree.pdf>.

[171] *See* Press Release, DOJ, Statement by Charles A. James Regarding DOJ/FTC Clearance Agreement (May 20, 2002), <http://www.justice.gov/atr/public/press_releases/2002/11178.htm>. For further discussion of this incident, *see infra* notes 257–263 and accompanying text.

[172] *See*, for example, AMC Report, *supra* note 21, at 134–7.

[173] *See* Fed. Trade Comm'n, Reforms to the Merger Review Process (February 16, 2006), <http://www.ftc.gov/os/2006/02/mergerreviewprocess.pdf> (hereinafter FTC Merger Process Reforms); U.S. Dep't of Justice, Background Information on the 2006 Amendments to the Merger Review Process Initiative (December 14, 2006), <http://www.justice.gov/atr/public/220241.htm> (hereinafter DOJ Background on Merger Process Amendments) and U.S. Dept's of Justice, Merger Review Process Initiative (December 14, 2006), <http://www.justice.gov/atr/public/220237.htm> (hereinafter DOJ Merger Process Initiative).

discovery period in the event of litigation.[174] It has been suggested that these conditions effectively amount to an administrative amendment of the statutory waiting periods and circumvent the court's authority and discretion to set an appropriate period for litigation discovery.[175]

In HSR-reportable transactions that receive a second request, it is common practice for the transaction parties "voluntarily" to delay the closing to permit additional time for discussions with the investigating agency. Such discussions may focus on negotiating the details of a consent decree with staff who, in the absence of additional time, may need to switch to "litigation preparation" mode, leaving little or no time for further settlement negotiations. Alternatively, the extra time may be used to make presentations to senior management, including ultimately the Assistant Attorney General at the DOJ or the Commissioners at the FTC, in an effort to dissuade them from bringing an action to block the merger. A refusal by the transaction parties to delay the closing can cause staff to terminate settlement negotiations (or at least threaten to do so) or may limit meetings with the decision-makers. Such timing agreements can take several forms and range in duration from an extra few days to several weeks.[176]

Mergers are also reviewed outside the HSR notification procedures. Each year the FTC and DOJ investigate and challenge a small number of consummated mergers that were not reportable under the HSR Act but are later discovered by the agencies, typically due to industry complaints of anticompetitive conduct, such as a post-consummation price increase.[177] Investigations of mergers not subject to the HSR statutory deadlines can last for considerable periods of time. This creates uncertainty for the merged company, which may face the prospect of eventually being required to divest all or a substantial portion of the acquired business, assuming such a remedy is feasible.[178] The company may also have an incentive to use stalling tactics in the hope that the investigation will eventually "run out of steam" and close.[179] It has been recommended that the FTC and DOJ create flexible timelines or roadmaps for non-HSR investigations.[180]

[174] The FTC requires the parties to delay certifying substantial compliance until thirty days after producing responsive documents and data or to agree to a "rolling" production, and to agree to a joint scheduling order containing at least a sixty-day pretrial discovery period. FTC Merger Process Reforms, at 10, 15–19. The DOJ envisages a negotiated schedule for the investigation and requires that the parties agree to provide sufficient time for post-complaint discovery, noting that "four to six months is generally necessary." DOJ Background on Merger Process Amendments, at 11; DOJ Merger Process Initiative, at 5–7.

[175] *See* AMC Report, *supra* note 21, at 170.

[176] For a more detailed discussion of the strategic implications of timing agreements in merger reviews, *see* ABA Section of Antitrust Law, *The Merger Review Process: A Step-by-Step Guide to U.S. and Foreign Merger Review,* 4th edn, at 379 (2012).

[177] Technically, the Antitrust Division and the FTC are legally free to re-investigate and challenge consummated mergers that already cleared HSR review. For a rare example of such a challenge, *see* Chicago Bridge & Iron Co. v. FTC, 534 F.3d 410, 421 n.2 (5th Cir. 2008).

[178] Once the acquired business has been fully integrated into the combined company, it can be extremely difficult to "unscramble the eggs" and return to the pre-merger position.

[179] American Bar Association Section of Antitrust Law, Transition Report on the Current State of Federal Antitrust and Consumer Protection Enforcement, at 9–10 (November 2008), available at <http://www.abanet.org/antitrust/at-comments/2008/11-08/comments-obamabiden.pdf> (hereinafter ABA Transition Report).

[180] *Id.* at 9–10. This suggestion applies not only to non-HSR reportable mergers but also to investigations of anticompetitive conduct.

c) FTC procedures

A common criticism of FTC administrative adjudication is that it is too slow, thereby undermining its effectiveness.[181] In merger cases, for example, the prospect of lengthy proceedings has caused parties to abandon transactions before the antitrust merits could be adjudicated.[182] The FTC's increasing tendency to use the administrative process has brought this concern to the fore.

The FTC's 2009 amendments to Parts 3 and 4 of its Rules of Practice are intended, in part, to expedite its proceedings. The new rules provide that, unless a different date is determined by the FTC, an evidentiary hearing must be commenced within five months from the date of the complaint where the FTC is seeking a preliminary injunction (primarily, unconsummated merger cases) and within eight months in all other cases.[183] The revised rules also set deadlines for the ALJ's decision[184] and for the FTC's decision if there is an appeal.[185] The amended Part 3 also shortens various other deadlines, some of which apply to the respondents as well as to FTC complaint counsel.[186] Despite these changes, commentators have called for an even faster timetable in unconsummated merger cases, to bring the FTC's administrative proceedings in line with the typical timeline in federal district court proceedings initiated by the DOJ and to reduce the period of uncertainty for pending transactions (as well as the instances of merging parties abandoning transactions rather than facing the prospect of lengthy administrative litigation with an uncertain outcome).[187]

The revised rules further attempt to expedite administrative litigation by providing for earlier Commission involvement in administrative proceedings, such as in

[181] Federal Trade Commission, The Federal Trade Commission at 100: Into Our 2nd Century—The Continuing Pursuit of Better Practice, 43 (January 2009), <http://www.ftc.gov/ftc/workshops/ftc100/docs/ftc100rpt.pdf> (hereinafter FTC at 100 Report).

[182] In fiscal year 2009, for example, the FTC commenced simultaneous administrative proceedings and federal district court preliminary injunction challenges to block CCS Corporation's acquisition of Newpark Environmental Services; the merger of CCC Information Services and Mitchell International Inc.; and Oldcastle Architectural Inc.'s acquisition of Pavestone Companies. In two of these challenges—*CCS/Newpark* and *Oldcastle/Pavestone*—the parties abandoned their transaction after the FTC filed its complaints initiating litigation. *See* <http://www.ftc.gov/os/adjpro/d9333/081210redskycmpt.pdf> (CCS/Newpark, Commission order dismissing complaint); <http://www.ftc.gov/opa/2009/01/pavestone.shtm> (Oldcastle/Pavestone, FTC statement).

[183] 16 C.F.R. § 3.11(b).

[184] The ALJ must file an initial decision within seventy days after the last-filed proposed findings of fact and conclusions of law, or eighty-five days after the closing of the hearing record if the parties waive filing proposed findings. The ALJ can extend these deadlines by 30 days "for good cause." The previous rule required that the initial decision be filed within ninety days of the close of the hearing record and permitted the ALJ to grant consecutive sixty day extensions. *See* 16 C.F.R. § 3.51(a).

[185] For cases in which the FTC has sought preliminary relief under Section 13(b) of the FTC Act, it will issue a final decision within forty-five days of oral argument; i.e., within 100 days of the filing of the initial decision by the ALJ. For all other cases, the FTC will issue a final decision within 100 days after oral argument; i.e., within six months after the initial decision. *See* 16 C.F.R. § 3.52.

[186] For example, the respondents' deadline for filing an answer was shortened from 20 days to 14 days. 16 C.F.R. § 3.12(a).

[187] ABA Transition Report, *supra* note 179, at 31; Comments of the ABA Section of Antitrust Law In Response to the Federal Trade Commission's Request For Public Comment Regarding Parts 3 and 4 Rules of Practice Rulemaking—P072104, at 16 (November 6, 2008), <http://www.abanet.org/antitrust/at-comments/2008/11-08/comments-3and4.pdf> (hereinafter ABA Comments).

resolving dispositive motions, for example, motions for summary decision and prehearing motions to dismiss.[188] These changes were premised on the desirability of the Commission applying its antitrust expertise at an earlier stage and avoiding the potential cost and delay to the litigants that an erroneous ALJ decision might cause. On the other hand, commentators have criticized the rule change as likely to impact negatively the perception of the fairness and impartiality of administrative proceedings by permitting the Commission to adjudicate dispositive issues shortly after it has voted out the decision to bring a challenge in the first place.[189] This highlights the inherent tension that can exist between enabling a more efficient enforcement procedure and upholding due process norms.

d) Department of Justice procedures

As a general matter, the Antitrust Division has no internal rules imposing time constraints on its investigations. Nevertheless, some time constraints on its activities are imposed either by federal statute or by other agencies' processes. For example, the Antitrust Division operates under the same HSR time constraints in considering notified mergers as does the FTC. When the Division engages in competition advocacy before federal regulatory agencies it must take care to comply with regulatory deadlines and so endeavors to prepare pleadings "promptly."[190]

Antitrust Division civil litigation in federal court is subject to the same time constraints as any other civil litigation. As discussed above, earlier criticism of the slowness of the Division's civil litigation efforts has generally abated.[191] In part, however, this lack of criticism reflects the fact that the Division did not file any monopolization cases from 2001 through 2010 (monopolization cases tend to be the most complex to litigate) and that nearly all of the rest of its civil litigation during this period involved merger cases which have generally been litigated quickly under a single preliminary and permanent injunction hearing. The Department publishes no statistics on the length of time it takes to investigate or litigate cases.

The Division is more constrained in investigating and litigating criminal cases. Some of the constraints are self-imposed; others are the result of federal statutes and the US Constitution.

Today, nearly all criminal cases begin with amnesty (or leniency) applications in which corporations come forward with evidence of their own participation in illegal cartel activity. The leniency process is one the Antitrust Division adopted internally in the exercise of its prosecutorial discretion and is available both to organizations and individuals. The Division's extensive efforts to publicize the program and the benefits available to applicants have made it into an extremely useful prosecutorial tool, one that has been adopted by other enforcement agencies around the world.[192] The Division posts its formal policy on its website, along with other

[188] 16 C.F.R. § 3.22(a).

[189] ABA Comments, *supra* note 187, at 3–4, 11.

[190] *See* Antitrust Division Manual, *supra* note 67, at V-7.

[191] *See supra* text accompanying note 101.

[192] *See*, e.g., Hammond, *supra* note 136, at 15 (noting "proliferation of effective leniency programs" in "multiple jurisdictions").

relevant information.[193] In addition, the Division's Manual explains the procedures it follows when considering amnesty applications,[194] in particular its procedure for granting an applicant a "marker" preserving its place in line for leniency pending further investigation of the quality of its disclosures.[195]

There has been little criticism of the leniency process in practice.[196] As of 2011 there had been only one case in which the courts reviewed the Division's conduct under the program. The case involved a decision by the Division to revoke a grant of conditional leniency which had required the company to cease its illegal conduct. The Division believed it had evidence demonstrating that the company had not stopped its illegal price fixing conduct after its general counsel brought the conduct to the attention of upper management, even though the company had told prosecutors otherwise. The company, however, vigorously resisted the Division's efforts to revoke its amnesty. A district court eventually dismissed the indictment brought against the company and its executives, holding that the Division had no reasonable basis to revoke the leniency agreement because it had not demonstrated any breach of the agreement.[197]

Outside of the leniency process, the Division's main tool for criminal investigation is the grand jury, which is subject to the process and time constraints of Rule 6 of the Federal Rules of Criminal Procedure. Although prosecutors have great control over the grand jury, judges still retain a degree of supervision over the grand jury's processes, sometimes reviewing their subpoenas before the trial and sometimes reviewing the conduct of prosecutors before the grand jury after an indictment has been handed down. Trials are subject to the time constraints of the Speedy Trial Clause of the Sixth Amendment as well as the Speedy Trial Act.

2. *Expertise*

a) Staff

As the two oldest and best-established antitrust agencies in the world, the FTC and the DOJ each have substantial staffs consisting of attorneys, economists, paralegals, and administrative personnel. A particularly noteworthy feature of both agencies' functional organization and internal expertise is the considerable number of PhD-level economists employed by the Agencies and the significant degree of integration of those economists into the Agencies' workings.[198]

193 *See* <http://www.justice.gov/atr/public/criminal/leniency.htm>.

194 *See* Antitrust Division Manual, *supra* note 67, at III-102–8.

195 *See id.* at III-106.

196 The AMC's Report, for example, does not criticize the program or offer any suggestions for improvement.

197 *See* United States v. Stolt-Nielsen S.A., 524 F. Supp. 2d 586, 609 (E.D. Pa., 2007). The Division chose not to appeal. *See* Press Release, December 21, 2007, <http://www.justice.gov/atr/public/press_releases/2007/228788.htm>.

198 *See* Fed'l Trade Comm'n, The FTC in 2010 at 9 ("more than 70 Ph.D. economists" in the Bureau of Economics), <http://www.ftc.gov/os/2010/04/2010ChairmansReport.pdf>.

The FTC's PhD economists are mostly organized together in the Bureau of Economics, which has a Director who reports directly to the FTC Chairman. Similarly, most of the DOJ's economists are part of the Economic Analysis Group which consists of three sections, the Economic Litigation Section, the Economic Regulatory Section, and the Competition Policy Section. These three economic sections report to the Deputy Assistant Attorney General for Economic Analysis, who in turn reports to the Assistant Attorney General. As a matter of practice, both the Director of the Bureau of Economics and the Deputy Assistant Attorney General for Economic Analysis have been outside academic economists of distinguished reputation.

The housing of Agency economists in organizationally distinct groups within the FTC and DOJ reflects the important role of economic analysis across all facets of the Agencies' activities. The Agencies' economists perform a wide range of functions, including analyzing the competitive effects of mergers and alleged anti-competitive practices (sometimes involving sophisticated econometric analysis), assessing proposed regulatory changes, participating in the Agencies' competition advocacy efforts, engaging in policy-related research, and international outreach.[199] Economists participate fully in civil enforcement matters from the initial investigative stage to their final resolution, including the assessment of proposed enforcement measures and remedies.[200]

Staff economists at the FTC and DOJ not only play an important attorney support function in merger and civil non-merger investigations, they also participate in internal case strategy meetings and meetings with the parties and usually are afforded an opportunity to influence directly the key decision-makers at the Agencies. While staff attorneys and economists assigned to an investigation work closely together, input by economists is not merely subsumed into recommendations controlled by attorneys. Rather, staff economists typically prepare a separate recommendation memorandum that follows a parallel review track to the staff attorneys' recommendation, ultimately reaching the Assistant Attorney General at the DOJ or the Commissioners at the FTC. It is not unheard of for staff attorneys and economists to offer conflicting recommendations to senior management.

One role that Agency economists are unlikely to play is that of testifying in court (or in an administrative trial before the FTC). Testifying economists need to be shielded from the general investigation of a case so that they will not be forced to testify about matters that the Agency views as irrelevant (or potentially harmful) to its case.[201] Thus, although the Agencies hold open the possibility that an inside

[199] Economists at the FTC also support its consumer protection activities.

[200] For a more detailed description, *see* Michael Salinger and Paul A. Pautler, "The Bureau of Economics at the US Federal Trade Commission" (2006), <http://www.ftc.gov/be/recruit/06beover.pdf>; Antitrust Division Manual, *supra* note 67, at VI-6–8.

[201] *See* Antitrust Division Manual, *supra* note 67, at VI-8 ("The materials provided to the 'outside' economist will depend upon the needs of the case and must be monitored so that an appropriate record is maintained for use later in discovery. The testifying expert's participation in strategy and enforcement decision meetings is severely curtailed.").

economist could perform the role of testifying economist, the general practice has been to hire an outside economist to perform this role.

In recent years the Agencies have occasionally found the need to hire outside lawyers to take the role of lead counsel in high-profile civil litigation. The best-known example is the Microsoft monopolization litigation, where the Antitrust Division hired David Boies, a highly experienced litigator, to try the case.[202] In April 2012, the FTC hired Beth Wilkinson, a former Justice Department prosecutor, to lead its investigation of Google's business practices. Hiring outside counsel may reflect the fact that government civil antitrust litigation has become rare over the course of successive administrations, which have emphasized criminal enforcement and merger reviews but have filed few civil cases. Hiring an experienced litigator can thus make up for a lack of staff civil trial experience, but the practice does have the potential of damaging staff morale.[203]

b) Agency leadership

The statutory provisions regarding the appointment of the five FTC Commissioners and the Assistant Attorney General for the Antitrust Division do not specify minimum or preferred qualifications. The fact that they are political appointees, however, means that considerations other than expertise in the fields relevant to the Agencies' jurisdiction play a role in their appointments. Such considerations may include, for example, a desire to select individuals who will promote the White House's policy preferences or to reward loyal political operatives. The fact that these appointments are subject to Senate confirmation means that Congressional political concerns must also be taken into account.

The quality of FTC Commissioner appointments in particular has attracted scrutiny and criticism.[204] This scrutiny is particularly appropriate, given the fact that Congress, in establishing the FTC and granting it broad discretion, expected federal judges to defer to FTC decisions because of the FTC's anticipated expertise in understanding business matters. The Commissioners were to be an important component of the FTC's capability and Congress intended the FTC to be comprised not only of eminent lawyers but also of distinguished economists and business executives.[205] Over time, however, economists and business executives have been sparsely represented among the Commissioners. Since the FTC's

[202] *See* also "DOJ Hires Axinn as a Consultant for Its Review of MCI WorldCom/Sprint Deal," 77 Antitrust & Trade Reg. Rep. (BNA) 658 (Dec.16, 1999) ("The last time the division retained an outside lawyer of Axinn's standing was when it hired David Boies to work on the government's case against Microsoft Corp., DOJ noted.").

[203] *See* ABA Transition Report, *supra* note 179, at 15 (recommending employing outside trial counsel "[i]n exceptional circumstances and on a case-by-case basis").

[204] *See*, e.g., William E. Kovacic, "The Quality of Appointments and the Capability of the Federal Trade Commission," 49 Admin. L. Rev. 915 (1997). Kovacic argues that one of the reasons a lack of suitable qualifications has been more of an issue at the FTC than at the DOJ is the FTC's multi-member structure, which "may reduce the inclination of the executive branch and Congress to insist that each appointee possess outstanding qualifications." *Id.* at 948.

[205] *See id.* at 917–20. For oral histories of the careers of eight of the FTC's Commissioners, *see* <http://www.ftc.gov/ftc/history/oralhistory.shtm>.

founding, only three professional economists have been appointed as Commissioners, despite the substantial economic dimension of the FTC's mission, although the professional diversity of FTC Commissioners has increased somewhat since the 1980s.[206]

c) Expertise of ALJs

Another controversial expertise-related issue involves the selection process for ALJs in FTC administrative proceedings. The ALJ selection process is dictated by government-wide requirements, not by FTC rules or policy,[207] and the FTC's rule of practice on presiding officials is silent regarding the necessary or desirable qualifications of ALJs.[208] Commentators have expressed concern that familiarity with antitrust or consumer protection law is not a factor in the choice of the ALJ, which results in situations where the initial decision-maker in administrative litigation has little or no expertise in the areas of FTC enforcement.[209] Thus the ALJ tends to resemble more a district court judge of general jurisdiction than an expert decision-maker, except where a Commissioner acts as ALJ, raising the impartiality concerns previously described.[210]

3. Transparency

Transparency has both *ex ante* and *ex post* elements. The former refers to the process by which the Agencies develop and explain policy. The latter refers to transparency of actual enforcement decisions made by the Agencies in specific cases, including decisions to challenge, not to challenge, or to settle. Both aspects of transparency assist lawyers, businesses, judges, and the general public in understanding how the competition laws are administered. This in turn enhances public confidence in, and the credibility of, the competition agencies, and can enable more informed and efficient decision-making by those inside and outside the Agencies.

Transparency is not without costs, of course. For one, statements of policy may cabin discretion. Despite disclaimers that the Agencies place on any *ex ante* statements of policy, courts may take the Agency at its word and hold it to its written statements even though the Agency would prefer to do something different. For another, explanation of policy, whether *ex ante* or *ex post*, takes time and resources. Agencies must consider carefully whether their resources could be better devoted to actual enforcement rather than to the explanation of their policies, particularly *ex post* explanations of their reasons for failing to bring a particular case.

[206] Kovacic, *supra* note 204, at 935–6; FTC at 100 Report, *supra* note 181, at 28. The Assistant Attorney General in charge of the Antitrust Division must be a lawyer.

[207] *See* 5 U.S.C. §§ 556, 3105; 5 CFR § 930.204 (regulation of Office of Personnel Management); FTC at 100 Report, *supra* note 181, at 45 ("It bears noting, however, that the ALJ selection process is dictated by government-wide requirements and not by FTC rules or policy.").

[208] 16 C.F.R. § 3.42.

[209] FTC at 100 Report, *supra* note 181, at 44.

[210] *See supra* notes 110–115 and accompanying text.

a) ***Ex ante* transparency**

The Justice Department and the FTC practice *ex ante* transparency through several means. Perhaps the most influential method is the issuance of guidelines, policy statements, and reports (collectively referred to here as guidelines) describing the Agencies' approach in applying the antitrust laws. In recent years guidelines have typically been issued jointly by the FTC and DOJ, although there have also been several notable examples where the Agencies were unwilling to act together.[211] Current guidelines explain competition policy in horizontal merger review,[212] collaborations among competitors including joint ventures,[213] intellectual property licensing,[214] and health care.[215]

Enforcement guidelines outline the Agencies' decision-making criteria and can also serve as an ongoing commentary on the law from the antitrust regulators' perspective. As such, guidelines are relied upon not only by businesses and their counsel but also by the courts.[216] The degree of deference given to the guidelines in the courts varies, however. The guidelines are not formally adopted as "notice and comment" agency regulations and thus do not receive the level of deference that such agency rules would receive.[217] Although courts often acknowledge that the Agencies have embodied their expertise in the guidelines, judges have also pointed out that the guidelines do not have the force of law and do not bind the courts.[218]

Although the US antitrust Agencies have been increasingly willing to issue guidelines, there are some problems in their use. These problems include ensuring that guidelines accurately reflect current Agency thinking given the practical

[211] One such example was the disagreement between the Justice Department and the FTC during the George W. Bush Administration over a report analyzing single-firm conduct under Section 2 of the Sherman Act. *See infra* notes 272–274 and accompanying text.

[212] *See* U.S. Dep't of Justice & Federal Trade Comm'n, Horizontal Merger Guidelines (August 19, 2010), <http://www.ftc.gov/os/2010/08/100819hmg.pdf>. Prior to the 2010 revision, the FTC and DOJ had issued a commentary on how the Agencies apply the Horizontal Merger Guidelines in particular investigations. *See* Fed. Trade Comm'n & U.S. Dep't of Justice, Commentary on the Horizontal Merger Guidelines (2006), <http://www.ftc.gov/os/2006/03/CommentaryontheHorizontalMergerGuidelinesMarch2006.pdf>.

[213] *See* Fed. Trade Comm'n & U.S. Dep't of Justice, Antitrust Guidelines for Collaborations Among Competitors (2000), <http://www.ftc.gov/os/2000/04/ftcdojguidelines.pdf>.

[214] *See* U.S. Dep't of Justice & Fed. Trade Comm'n, Antitrust Guidelines for the Licensing of Intellectual Property (1995), available at <http://www.ftc.gov/bc/0558.pdf>; U.S. Dep't of Justice & Fed. Trade Comm'n, Antitrust Enforcement and Intellectual Property Rights: Promoting Innovation and Competition (2007), <http://www.justice.gov/atr/public/hearings/ip/222655.pdf>.

[215] *See* U.S. Dep't of Justice & Fed. Trade Comm'n, Statements of Enforcement Policy in Health Care (1996), <http://www.ftc.gov/bc/healthcare/industryguide/policy/hlth3s.pdf>.

[216] FTC at 100 Report, *supra* note 181, at 128.

[217] Before issuing the 2010 revision of the Horizontal Merger Guidelines, the Agencies first held joint "workshops" seeking comments on the then-current guidelines. The FTC subsequently posted on its website a draft of a new version of the guidelines, seeking public comment. Four months later the FTC and the Antitrust Division issued a revised version of the draft, but sought no further comments. No hearings were held on either the draft or final guidelines.

[218] *See*, e.g., State of New York v. Kraft Gen. Foods, Inc., 926 F.Supp. 321, 359 (S.D.N.Y. 1995); FTC v. PPG Industries, Inc., 798 F.2d 1500, 1503 (D.C.Cir. 1986).

difficulty in updating guidelines on a frequent basis;[219] the perception that because guidelines represent the collective views of members and staff at one or more of the Agencies, the inevitable compromises to reach consensus lead to a watered-down document that may not be truly informative; and a concern, at least from the Agencies' perspective, that although guidelines do not have the force of law, they may nevertheless be used against the agencies, especially during litigation.[220]

Apart from issuing guidelines, the FTC and DOJ host a variety of events that are open to the public, including conferences and workshops designed to bring together government and members of the business and legal communities to discuss timely topics in competition (and also, in the FTC's case, consumer protection) policy. For example, the DOJ recently held a series of joint workshops with the US Department of Agriculture to explore competition issues in the agriculture industry[221] and held joint workshops with the FTC to review and explore the possibility of updating the Horizontal Merger Guidelines.[222] In addition to affording members of the public an opportunity to participate in the proceedings themselves, the Agencies provided public website access to transcripts of the workshops and hearings, any public comments submitted, and any resulting Agency reports.

Senior officials at the FTC and the DOJ speak regularly at conferences and seminars, both in the US and abroad. Transcripts of speeches are published on the agencies' websites and, despite the oft-used disclaimer that the speaker's comments do not necessarily represent the views of the speaker's agency, these speeches can provide insight into topics of particular interest to the agencies at any given time. As useful as these speeches are, some are skeptical about statements of "luncheon law," which might more reflect what the agency would like the law to be rather than what it is.

Another *ex ante* transparency tool is the issuance of advisory opinions by the FTC[223] and business review letters by the DOJ.[224] The advisory opinion/business review procedure allows persons concerned about the legality of proposed business conduct to seek a statement from the FTC or the DOJ of its current enforcement intentions with respect to that conduct.[225] There are no

[219] For example, with the exception of a new section on efficiencies added in 1997, the FTC/DOJ Horizontal Merger Guidelines remained unchanged from 1992 until a major revision in 2010, and some believed that their usefulness in describing how the Agencies analyze horizontal mergers diminished during that period. *See*, e.g., William Blumenthal, "Scope and Specificity in the 2010 Guidelines: A Pretty Good Balance," 25 Antitrust 10, 12 (Fall 2010) ("We have known for many years that the 1992 Guidelines . . . were only a blurry depiction of actual Agency practices. . . .").

[220] *See* FTC at 100 Report, *supra* note 181, at 129.

[221] *See* DOJ & USDA, Agriculture and Antitrust Enforcement Issues in Our 21st Century Economy, at <http://www.justice.gov/atr/public/workshops/ag2010/index.htm>.

[222] *See* FTC & DOJ, Horizontal Merger Guidelines Review Project, at <http://www.ftc.gov/bc/workshops/hmg/index.shtml>; *supra* note 217.

[223] *See* 16 C.F.R. §§ 1.1–1.4.

[224] *See* 28 C.F.R. § 50.6.

[225] There are two types of FTC advisory opinions: (1) Commission advisory opinions, and (2) advisory opinions provided by FTC staff. Most advisory opinions are issued by FTC staff. Commission

limitations on the industries or subject areas that may be considered for an advisory opinion or business review letter.[226] Advisory opinions and business review letters are not legally binding—the FTC and DOJ both make clear that they remain free to bring whatever action they subsequently determine to be required. Moreover, not all forms of proposed conduct are suitable for advisory opinions and business review letters.[227] Although in practice these letters are infrequently sought, in appropriate circumstances they can offer substantial comfort to the requesting person(s), provided there is a full and true disclosure of the pertinent facts regarding the proposed conduct. Advisory opinions and business review letters are posted on the Agencies' websites (after confidential business information is redacted), enabling the broader business community to benefit from their guidance regarding the application of the antitrust laws to specific proposed conduct.[228] The FTC and DOJ maintain a clearance procedure for assigning requests for advisory opinions and business review letters to either agency.[229]

From a procedural perspective, the Antitrust Division Manual and the FTC's Operating Manual provide detailed guidance to agency staff regarding internal practices and procedures for investigating and litigating matters.[230] Although not binding and intended for internal advisory purposes, these documents offer a window into the day-to-day workings of the agencies and can be useful to businesses and their counsel in determining how best to navigate the investigatory waters.

b) *Ex post* transparency

The FTC and DOJ also utilize *ex post* mechanisms to shed light on specific matters after an investigation has concluded. The majority of filed civil cases are settled by consent decree. At both agencies, the consent decree process involves publishing the proposed complaint, the consent agreement and any related documents, and information about the merits of the proposed consent decree, and then inviting public comments before the consent decree is made final. This process is observed

advisory opinions are intended to address substantial or novel questions of fact or law or subjects of significant public interest. *See* 16 C.F.R. § 1.1(a).

[226] In practice, most FTC advisory opinions have involved the health care sector, while the subject matter of DOJ business review letters has been more varied.

[227] For example, advisory opinions and business review letters may be inappropriate where the same or substantially the same course of action is presently under investigation, or where an informed opinion cannot be made without extensive investigation going beyond the facts presented by the person(s) requesting the opinion/letter. *See* 16 C.F.R. § 1.1(b).

[228] *See* <http://www.ftc.gov/ftc/opinions.shtm>; <http://www.justice.gov/atr/public/busreview/index.htm>. Parties can seek to have certain information treated as confidential and redacted from the public version. *See* 16 C.F.R. § 1.4, 28 C.F.R. § 50.6.

[229] For additional information, *see* FTC, Guidance From Staff of the Bureau of Competition's Health Care Division on Requesting and Obtaining an Advisory Opinion, at 2 (May 2010), <http://www.ftc.gov/bc/healthcare/industryguide/adv-opinionguidance.pdf>; DOJ, Business Reviews, <http://www.justice.gov/atr/public/busreview/201659a.htm>.

[230] *See* Antitrust Division Manual, *supra* note 67; FTC Operating Manual, *supra* note 93.

for every matter settled by consent decree, although the specific procedures differ between the agencies.[231]

The DOJ's consent decree procedure is governed by the 1974 Antitrust Procedures and Penalties Act, also known as the Tunney Act.[232] The Tunney Act requires that all DOJ settlements of civil antitrust actions be approved by a federal district court judge as being in the public interest, following a minimum sixty-day public comment period that commences when the proposed consent judgment is filed with the court and published in the Federal Register.[233] The DOJ must file, together with the proposed consent decree, a Competitive Impact Statement that explains the nature of the proceeding and why the proposed judgment is appropriate under the circumstances.[234] In making the public interest finding, courts have recognized that their inquiry is limited and have accorded substantial deference to the DOJ, in order to preserve the practical benefits of settlement through the consent decree process as an alternative to the cost and burden of litigation.[235] If the court does conclude that a consent decree is not in the public interest, the court only has the power to reject the decree. The Tunney Act does not give the court the power to modify the decree according to its view of what constitutes appropriate relief, although, in practice, courts have suggested modifications that the parties have then accepted.[236]

Some critics, particularly those who disagreed with the DOJ's settlement of the much-publicized Microsoft litigation in 2001, view the courts as excessively deferential to the Justice Department and have called for a more thorough review process.[237] Although the Tunney Act was amended in 2004, the changes were relatively modest.[238] The amended Tunney Act sets out certain factors that the court must consider in making the public interest determination, but it also expressly states that the court is not required to conduct an evidentiary hearing or to permit third parties to intervene.[239] In a very lengthy proceeding under the

[231] In merger cases, the merging parties are generally allowed to consummate the transaction once the consent decree has been filed or published and before the public comment period, subject to appropriate hold separate orders for assets to be divested. *See* ABA Merger Review Process, *supra* note 176, at 410, 417.

[232] 15 U.S.C. § 16.

[233] 15 U.S.C. §§ 16(b), (d), (e). The Tunney Act does not apply to the dismissal of an enforcement action. In the merger context, the Tunney Act does not apply to the decision not to challenge a merger, nor does it apply to negotiated "fix-it-first" divestitures that do not involve the filing of a judicial complaint and consent decree.

[234] The Tunney Act sets out six specific topics that the competitive impact statement must cover. *See* 15 U.S.C. § 16(b).

[235] *See*, for example, United States v. Microsoft Corp., 56 F. 3d 1448, 1461–2 (D.C. Cir. 1995).

[236] *See* United States v. Microsoft Corp., 56 F. 3d 1448, 1458–59 (D.C. Cir. 1995) (review power). For an example of party acceptance of suggested judicial modifications, *see* United States v. Thomson Corp., 1997–1 Trade Cas. (CCH) ¶ 71,735 (D.D.C. 1997) (entering decree after parties conformed it to meet judge's concerns).

[237] For criticism of the application of the Tunney Act to post-trial settlements, *see* John J. Flynn & Darren Bush, "The Misuse and Abuse of the Tunney Act: The Adverse Consequences of the 'Microsoft Fallacies,'" 34 Loy. U. Chi. L.J. 749 (2003).

[238] *See* ABA Merger Review Process, *supra* note 176, at 418.

[239] 15 U.S.C. § 16(e).

amended Tunney Act involving two mergers of four of the country's largest telecommunications companies, SBC/AT&T and Verizon/MCI, a federal district court concluded that its "scope of review remains sharply proscribed by precedent and the nature of Tunney Act proceedings,"[240] that it "must accord deference to the government's predictions about the efficacy of its remedies,"[241] and that the government "need only provide a factual basis for concluding that the settlements are reasonably adequate remedies for the alleged harms."[242]

The FTC's consent order procedure is governed by Part 2 Subpart C of the FTC's Rules of Practice.[243] There is no court involvement in FTC consent decrees. The FTC publishes the proposed complaint, the consent agreement, and an Analysis to Aid Public Comment (similar to the DOJ's Competitive Impact Statement) on the FTC website and in the Federal Register. There is a thirty-day public comment period, following which the FTC decides whether to withdraw from the proposed consent agreement, modify it, or make the order final.[244] In practice, it is rare for the FTC to withdraw or modify its proposed order based on public comments received.

The FTC and Antitrust Division also occasionally issue public statements in connection with the decision to close an antitrust investigation. Such closing statements describe the reasons for not bringing an action in particular cases. This practice, which was adopted from the European Commission, is entirely within the agencies' discretion and remains sporadic.

The Antitrust Division has a formal policy on the issuance of closing statements.[245] This policy provides that the Division will consider issuing a closing statement only if the investigation has previously been publicly confirmed, and that in deciding whether to issue a statement in a particular case it will evaluate whether the matter has received substantial publicity and consider the value to the public in receiving information regarding the reasons for non-enforcement (including public trust in the Division's enforcement and the value of the analysis to other enforcers, businesses and consumers). Issued statements have been relatively brief, sketching out the markets the Division reviewed and the basic theories it applied.[246]

By contrast, the FTC has no formal policy on closing statements. Sometimes the Commission issues a statement; sometimes individual Commissioners issue state-

240 United States v. SBC Commc'ns, Inc., 489 F. Supp. 2d 1, 11 (D.D.C. 2007). The court issued its opinion and order entering the consent decrees almost seventeen months after the proposed decrees were first filed by the DOJ.

241 *Id.* at 17.

242 Ibid.

243 16 C.F.R. §§ 2.31–2.34.

244 16 C.F.R. § 2.34.

245 Antitrust Div., Dep't of Justice, Issuance of Public Statements Upon Closing of Investigations (n.d.), <http://www.justice.gov/atr/public/guidelines/201888.htm>.

246 *See*, e.g., Dep't of Justice, Press Release, Statement By Assistant Attorney General Thomas O. Barnett Regarding The Closing Of The Investigation Of At&T's Acquisition Of Bellsouth (October 11, 2006) (includes two-page "background" regarding the closing of the investigation), <http://www.justice.gov/atr/public/press_releases/2006/218904.pdf>; Dep't of Justice, Press Release, Background To Closing Of Investigation Of United Health Group's Acquisition Of Oxford Health Plans (July 20, 2004), <http://www.justice.gov/atr/public/press_releases/2004/204676.htm>.

ments; and generally the dissenting Commissioners will issue statements.[247] On the other hand, the FTC's statements typically provide greater detail than the Justice Department's. Having multiple independent Commissioners provides an opportunity to air policy differences publicly, whereas the Antitrust Division's single decision-maker structure means that all policy differences are ironed out internally and not disclosed. This diminishes the incentive for the Division to be open about the problems in a particular case and to disclose the counter-arguments to those that eventually convinced the Assistant Attorney General not to take action.

Consent decrees, Competitive Impact Statements, Analyses to Aid Public Comment, and closing statements are scrutinized carefully by industry and the private bar for guidance as to the agencies' enforcement stance in a given area. They provide the most tangible and up-to-date insight into the manner in which the FTC and DOJ exercise prosecutorial discretion. There is nevertheless some debate regarding the effectiveness of these processes in achieving full disclosure and whether the agencies could provide more information and explanation than they currently do, while still maintaining appropriate confidentiality protections.[248]

Many of the efforts undertaken by the FTC and DOJ to promote transparency also serve to enhance the degree of predictability in their application of the antitrust laws. Understanding the agencies' enforcement policies and priorities, and their reasons for decisions in specific matters, can enable better predictions of how new situations are likely to be treated. That said, the norms of transparency and predictability are not always positively correlated. For example, the new Horizontal Merger Guidelines released by the FTC and DOJ in draft form in April 2010 and finalized in August 2010 set out a more detailed but also more open-ended approach to merger analysis than the previous guidelines, which may reduce rather than facilitate predictability in merger review.[249]

4. Accountability

The FTC and DOJ observe internal processes that facilitate accountability. Both agencies publish extensive information and data regarding their enforcement decisions. The FTC has an online Competition Enforcement Database that catalogs its competition enforcement actions, both merger and non-merger, including a short description of each action and links to related documents.[250] The DOJ publishes

[247] For examples, *see* Press Release, FTC Closes its Investigation of Genzyme Corporation's 2001 Acquisition of Novazyme Pharmaceuticals, Inc. (January 13, 2004), <http://www.ftc.gov/opa/2004/01/genzyme.shtm> (with links to statements by Chairman Muris and Commissioner Harbour, and dissenting statement of Commissioner Thompson); In the Matter of Royal Caribbean Cruises, Ltd./P&O Princess Cruises plc and Carnival Corporation/P&O Princess Cruises plc (October 4, 2002), <http://www.ftc.gov/os/caselist/0210041.shtm> (with links to FTC Statement and dissenting statement of Commissioners Anthony and Thompson).

[248] FTC at 100 Report, *supra* note 181, at 119.

[249] *See* David S. Neill, Nelson O. Fitts and Daniel E. Hemli, "U.S. Antitrust Agencies Unveil Proposed New Horizontal Merger Guidelines," 44(5) Bank and Corporate Governance Law Reporter, July 2010.

[250] *See* <http://www.ftc.gov/bc/caselist/index.shtml>. The Competition Enforcement Database, which replaced the FTC's annual Antitrust Enforcement Activities reports, covers the period from fiscal year 1996 to the present. Each fiscal year commences October 1 and ends September 30.

workload statistics for its civil and criminal enforcement activities as well as an annual update newsletter.[251] The agencies also file joint annual reports to Congress regarding the HSR pre-merger notification regime; these reports provide a statistical summary of the operation of the HSR Act and summarize the agencies' merger enforcement activities, with descriptions of specific matters.[252]

These data and statistics, while interesting, are at best a crude measure of the quality of agency performance. A more direct method of reviewing agency effectiveness and increasing public confidence in government competition enforcement involves empirical studies of past decisions to assess whether the agencies achieved the intended outcome and enhanced consumer welfare in specific instances. Most of the discussion regarding such retrospective studies has centered around mergers, although very little empirical work has been performed to date.[253] It has been suggested that the agencies also develop metrics to evaluate the degree of success of civil non-merger challenges in advancing their mandates.[254] There are, however, difficulties in conducting retrospectives and interpreting their results.[255]

At the macro level, the FTC recently conducted a comprehensive self-assessment, spearheaded by then-FTC Chairman William E. Kovacic. The initiative, titled "FTC at 100: Into Our Second Century," involved internal deliberations and external consultations, including a series of public roundtables held in various cities around the world.[256] The project's stated goals were to encourage acceptance of a norm of periodic self-assessment, to create a template for the agency to engage regularly in an analysis of its performance, and to identify approaches for improvement over both the short and long term.

The Executive Branch has some power to hold the agencies accountable for their enforcement policies. To the extent that accountability is an *ex post* exercise, the Executive can remove politically appointed agency leaders, but the removal power is not significant (it is legally circumscribed with regard to the FTC)[257] and has not been overtly exercised. The Executive maintains budgetary controls over the Justice Department through which it can constrain (or reward) the agencies' activities.

[251] *See* <http://www.justice.gov/atr/public/division_operations.htm>.

[252] *See* <http://www.ftc.gov/bc/anncompreports.shtm>.

[253] One noteworthy example involved an analysis carried out by the DOJ's Economic Analysis Group, at the direction of then Assistant Attorney General Tom Barnett, of the effect of the 2005 merger of Whirlpool Corporation and Maytag Corporation on the prices of residential laundry machines sold in the United States (Barnett's decision not to challenge the merger was one of the most controversial of his tenure as Assistant Attorney General). Comparing the pre-merger and post-merger periods, the study showed that there was no apparent increase in price for washers of comparable quality. *See* Thomas O. Barnett, *Current Issues in Merger Enforcement: Thoughts on Theory, Litigation Practice, and Retrospectives* (June 26, 2008), <http://www.justice.gov/atr/public/speeches/234537.pdf>.

[254] ABA Transition Report, *supra* note 179, at 28.

[255] For a useful discussion in the merger context, *see* Barnett, "Current Issues in Merger Enforcement," *supra* note 253, at 19–21; Dennis W. Carlton, "The Need to Measure the Effect of Merger Policy and How to Do It" (U.S. Dep't of Justice, Paper No. EAG 07–15, December 2007), <http://www.justice.gov/atr/public/eag/228687.pdf>.

[256] *See supra* note 181.

[257] 15 U.S.C. § 41 ("Any Commissioner may be removed by the President for inefficiency, neglect of duty, or malfeasance in office").

The FTC and the Antitrust Division are also accountable to the United States Congress in three important ways. First, Congress can pass a law to narrow an agency's jurisdiction or regulatory authority, an approach it has taken in the past with regard to the FTC.[258] Second, Congress can try to influence the agency through the budget process. For example, for several years Congress specifically refused to allow the Justice Department to expend funds to argue in the Supreme Court against the per se rule in resale price maintenance cases.[259] In another well-known case, Microsoft unsuccessfully lobbied Congress to cut the Justice Department's budget after the Department filed its monopolization suit against Microsoft.[260] A third recent example occurred in 2002 when Senator Ernest F. Hollings, then Chairman of the Senate Appropriations Subcommittee on Commerce, Justice, and State,[261] publicly objected to the proposed FTC/DOJ merger clearance agreement and threatened to cut the agencies' funding.[262] After a few months of behind-the-scenes maneuvering, the agencies abandoned the agreement in response to Senator Hollings' opposition.[263] Third, Congress exercises oversight power with regard to the executive branch and independent regulatory agencies. Congressional oversight comprises a variety of activities, such as holding investigative hearings and imposing reporting obligations on federal agencies.[264] The FTC's Office of Congressional Relations and the DOJ's Legal Policy Section are responsible for coordinating the agencies' respective relations with Congress and for responding to Congressional requests and inquiries.

[258] *See supra* note 9 and accompanying text.

[259] *See* Pub. L. No. 98–166, § 510 ("None of the funds appropriated in title I and title II of this Act may be used for any activity, the purpose of which is to overturn or alter the per se prohibition on resale price maintenance in effect under Federal antitrust laws...."). The bill was enacted less than a month before oral argument in Monsanto v. Spray-Rite Service Corp. 465 U.S. 752 (1984) in which the per se rule was potentially an issue.

[260] *See* Dan Morgan & Juliet Eilperin, "Microsoft Targets Funding for Antitrust Office," Wash. Post, October 15, 1999, at A1 (describing efforts of Microsoft and its allies to cut Antitrust Division funding by US$9 million).

[261] This subcommittee is now known as the U.S. Senate Appropriations Subcommittee on Commerce, Justice, Science, and Related Agencies.

[262] Brent Shearer, "Merger Clearance Accord Turns Nasty," Mergers & Acquisitions J. (June 1, 2002). Senator Hollings was concerned about the potential ramifications of formally allocating review of all mergers in certain industries to the Justice Department, an executive branch agency answerable directly to the President.

[263] *See* Press Release, DOJ, *Statement by Charles A. James Regarding DOJ/FTC Clearance Agreement* (May 20, 2002), <http://www.justice.gov/atr/public/press_releases/2002/11178.htm> ("... in view of the opposition expressed by Senator Hollings... to the agreement and the prospect of budgetary consequences for the entire Justice Department if we stood by the agreement, the Department will no longer be adhering to the agreement."). This event also highlights the potential for conflict between different Congressional committees—Senators Herb Kohl and Mike DeWine, then Chairman and Ranking Member, respectively, of the Senate subcommittee with responsibility for overseeing competition matters, supported the proposed clearance agreement. *See* Letter from Senator Herb Kohl, Chairman, Subcommittee on Antitrust, Bus. Rights, & Competition, & Senator Mike DeWine, Ranking Member, Subcommittee on Antitrust, Bus. Rights, & Competition, to John Ashcroft, Attorney General, Charles James, Assistant Attorney General for Antitrust, & Timothy Muris, Chairman, Fed. Trade Comm'n (March 1, 2002), <http://www.ftc.gov/opa/2002/03/clearance/kohldewine.pdf>.

[264] For example, the FTC submits to Congress annual Performance and Accountability Reports providing the results of the FTC's program and financial performance. *See* <http://www.ftc.gov/par>.

The third formal accountability constraint on the Agencies is the judiciary, particularly when they decide to file suit (declinations of prosecution, whether civil, criminal, or administrative, are not reviewable under US law). In a sense, the Agencies are always acting in the shadow of the law, i.e., apart from the courts' ability to overturn Agency decisions, the mere prospect of ending up in court, and the uncertainty of a litigated outcome, can constrain the Agencies' behavior. For FTC matters, the path to court can be more circuitous, because the FTC has the option of pursuing administrative proceedings rather than suing in district court, thereby precluding respondents from having their day in court until the appeals stage. The practical influence of judicial constraints on the functioning of the FTC is thus somewhat diminished compared to the DOJ, although in issuing a complaint the Commission may consider the circuit court in which the potential respondent might seek review.[265]

Finally, to some extent the Agencies are constrained by professional norms—"consensus views of what public competition authorities ought to do."[266] There is a long tradition in the United States of developing these consensus views through professional debate involving academic commentators and the private bar. Particularly important in this debate has been the role played by the Antitrust Section of the American Bar Association. Its more than 8000 members include attorneys from private law firms that represent defendants and plaintiffs, in-house counsel, non-profit organizations, consulting firms, federal and state government agencies, judges, professors, and law students. The Section publishes three important journals devoted to antitrust law and policy and provides continuing institutional support for a system of antitrust law.

5. *Commitment to the rule of law*

The rule of law connotes a bundle of values, perhaps none so important as rule by application of previously stated rules and principles and not by whim or personal interest. If the decision-maker must have discretion, the rule of law connotes bounded discretion, for unbounded discretion invites unpredictability, unequal treatment, and the intrusion of personal and vested interests and other biases into the process. Attributes of the rule of law include reasonable certainty of the governed as to what the law is, rights of review by an independent judiciary, and effective enforcement of the law.[267]

We have already considered equal treatment and right to appeals, above. We will limit our inquiry here to the following set of questions: is US antitrust law rule by law, not by personal interest or whim?; is the decision-makers' discretion appropriately cabined?; does the law give sufficient notice of what the law is and how it will be applied?; thus, is it sufficiently clear and predictable?

[265] *See* Tucker & Reeves, *supra* note 95, at 53.

[266] Kovacic, "Enforcement Norms," *supra* note 73, at 380.

[267] *See*, e.g., Lon L. Fuller, *The Morality of Law* (rev. edn 1969); Joseph Raz, *The Rule of Law and its Virtue, in The Authority of Law: Essays of Law and Morality* 210 (1979).

First, as background, the US Constitution requires a degree of clarity of law. This is particularly so as to criminal law: "To satisfy due process, a penal statute [must] define the criminal offense [1] with sufficient definiteness that ordinary people can understand what conduct is prohibited and [2] in a manner that does not encourage arbitrary and discriminatory enforcement."[268] Applying this standard, the Supreme Court recently held that the "honest services" mail fraud statute could constitutionally reach only offenses that were clear (such as bribery and kickbacks).[269] Nevertheless, we do not believe that this holding calls into question the constitutionality of criminal prosecutions under the Sherman Act—vague though the statutory language is. In recent years the Justice Department has limited its criminal prosecutions to price fixing, which is at least as clear an offense as bribery or kickbacks. Indeed, over the course of a century, the Supreme Court has explicitly and implicitly upheld the constitutionality of the criminal provisions of the Sherman Act.[270]

In its civil applications, antitrust law has a greater margin of flexibility. Antitrust law is economic law and its application requires a mixed law-and-economic analysis applied to particular facts of an industry. We address here whether US antitrust law, civilly applied, is sufficiently clear and predictable, and whether the litigant can expect its conduct or transaction to be analyzed on the basis of the relevant competition facts and conditions rather than on the basis of extraneous considerations.[271]

Robert Bork, in his 1978 book *The Antitrust Paradox*, argued that antitrust law was "mush"—filled with non-economic considerations, and unpredictable. Beginning in the 1980s, US antitrust law became rationalized along lines of an economic model. The Supreme Court overturned many earlier decisions and honed the law. Still, there is a margin of flexibility, with some antitrust enforcers and jurists more willing than others to find persistent market power, for example, and some more concerned than others about the costs of antitrust interventions.

The margin of flexibility is illustrated by the story of the Sherman Act Section 2 Report. In the George W. Bush Administration, the Antitrust Division and the Federal Trade Commission undertook a study of the appropriate standards for analysis of conduct that might violate Section 2 of the Sherman Act, which prohibits monopolization. The study was concluded, but the FTC refused to join or endorse the report—in fact, a majority of the Commissioners openly criticized its conclusions.[272] As a result, in September 2008 the Justice Department released the

[268] Skilling v. United States, 130 S. Ct. 2896, 2904 (2010) (internal quotation marks omitted).

[269] *See id.* at 2906.

[270] *See*, e.g., Nash v. United States, 229 U.S. 373 (1913) (upholding Sherman Act against vagueness claim) (Holmes, J.); cf. United States v. U.S. Gypsum Co., 438 U.S. 422 (1978) (imposing intent requirement in criminal prosecution and rejecting mistake of law defense).

[271] The antitrust case law rules out consideration of non-competition values; there is no "public interest" defense. The failing company defense to an otherwise anticompetitive merger is a rare exception and hardly visible in practice, because the conditions to its use are so stringent that it is virtually not available.

[272] *See* Press Release, FTC, FTC Commissioners React to Department of Justice Report, "Competition and Monopoly: Single-Firm Conduct Under Section 2 of the Sherman Act" (September 8, 2008), available at <http://www.ftc.gov/opa/2008/09/section2.shtm>.

Report on its own, expressing its concern that antitrust lawsuits challenging dominant firms' strategies tend to chill competition and innovation from those firms, and taking the view that conduct should not violate Section 2 unless the anticompetitive effects disproportionately outweigh the pro-competitive benefits.[273]

Eight months later, Christine Varney, President Obama's newly appointed Assistant Attorney General, withdrew the Report. She characterized it as having "an excessive concern with the risks of over-deterrence and a resulting preference for an overly lenient approach to enforcement."[274]

The recommendations of the Report in general stand on the conservative side of the antitrust spectrum—a position compatible in spirit with several recent Supreme Court decisions. Varney's perspective is more sympathetic to antitrust enforcement; a perspective that also finds grounding in the sometimes disparate case law. The two perspectives frame an on-going debate about the appropriate scope and limits of anti-monopoly enforcement.

Subject to the margin of difference in perspective and to the tension between predictability and complex analysis, practitioners and thus their clients have a substantial basis on which to predict legality or illegality of particular conduct.[275]

The 2010 Horizontal Merger Guidelines provide an illustration of a different sort—the balance between transparency, predictability, and analytical clarity. The new merger guidelines have fewer bright line standards than the predecessor guidelines, yet they reveal more accurately the analytical criteria that the Agencies in fact use in assessing mergers. The Guidelines' revision thus reflects the "predictability/flexibility" problem of antitrust, especially in a common law jurisdiction. There is a tension between bright lines (and thus predictability), on the one hand, and the best analysis to evaluate complex anticompetitive effects, on the other. At present in the United States, the tension tends to be resolved against bright line rules.

Thus far we have considered the uncertainties of antitrust law even when the decision-maker takes account only of competition factors. For the most part, the litigant can be assured that the authorities and courts will not smuggle into the analysis factors unrelated to competition concerns,[276] but the intrusion of other factors cannot be ruled out.

[273] *See* U.S. Dep't of Justice, Competition and Monopoly: Single–Firm Conduct Under Section 2 of the Sherman Act (2008), reprinted at 7 CCH Trade Reg. Rep. ¶ 50, 231.

[274] Christine A. Varney, Assistant Att'y Gen., Antitrust Div., U.S. Dep't of Justice, Vigorous Antitrust Enforcement in this Challenging Era, Remarks prepared for the Center of American Progress 8 (May 11, 2009), <http://www.usdoj.gov/atr/public/speeches/245711.pdf>.

[275] Treatises, frequently updated, set forth the law and report when, for example, there are conflicting interpretations of law among the circuits. *See*, e.g., ABA Section of Antitrust Law, *Antitrust Law Developments* (7th edn 2012), and annual review of developments for each subsequent year; Phillip Areeda and Herbert Hovenkamp, *Fundamentals of Antitrust Law* (3rd edn, loose leaf, as supplemented 2010). But *see* Edwin S. Rockefeller, *The Antitrust Religion* (2007) (arguing that antitrust law is incoherent). Compare Maruice E. Stucke, "Does the Rule of Reason Violate the Rule of Law?," 42 U.C. Davis L. Rev. 1375 (2009) (arguing that the rule of reason in U.S. antitrust law has deficiencies from a rule-of-law perspective, but they can be cured).

[276] *See*, e.g., Wal-Mart Stores, Inc. v. Rodriguez, *supra* note 141.

Within these parameters, we think it fair to say that the US Agencies and courts are strongly committed to the rule of law.

D. Assessing the system

The US antitrust enforcement system is complex. It features two federal enforcement agencies, following different organizational forms but with similar enforcement mandates. Added into the mix are state enforcers and private actions. The system is further split between civil enforcement and criminal enforcement, each of which has its own process demands. The federal Agencies themselves do not have complete control over the process of antitrust enforcement, much of which is pursued through litigation in courts of general jurisdiction under rules applicable to all federal litigation.

Looking at the ten identified process areas in broad terms, however, this complex system performs well. In the area of individual case decisions, investigated parties are given opportunities to present arguments to the Agencies prior to official action; initial adjudications and appeals test the legal and factual validity of enforcement agency charges; there are no claims of discriminatory treatment; and remedies are closely tied to the claimed illegal behavior. In the area of institutional performance, the Agencies have made efforts to reach decisions more quickly (although these efforts are not always successful); their staffs and managers are professional; there is a high degree of transparency; there are mechanisms at work that provide political accountability (although law enforcement also requires a level of independence from political actors to assure impartiality); and all the identified factors foster the commitment to the rule of law.

Nevertheless, there are tensions inherent in the enforcement structure that affect due process norms as conventionally conceived. Probably the most significant are the tensions within the FTC between its prosecutorial and adjudicatory roles, tensions most apparent when FTC Commissioners vote on complaints and then sit as administrative law judges. In addition, the dictates of confidentiality in the criminal process necessarily reduce procedural transparency and the tradition of prosecutorial discretion in the US makes review of agency decisions to decline prosecution less subject to outside control than in other systems. Finally, the Agencies must often decide between the identified process norms and the overall goal of effective and appropriate enforcement. Recent behavior, particularly the adoption of the revised Horizontal Merger Guidelines, indicates that the Agencies today may be inclined to give greater weight to the latter than the former. Whether this weighting is appropriate, and whether the Agencies could improve on process norms without sacrificing effectiveness, are subjects to which we turn in the next Section.

V. Evaluation

The US antitrust enforcement system described in Section IV shows a high degree of adherence to the identified process norms. Of course, adherence does not imply that improvements cannot be made. Indeed, there is a rich history in the United States of organized efforts to study and suggest improvements to the institutions of antitrust enforcement, dating from Gerard Henderson's 1924 study of the Federal Trade Commission[277] to the Antitrust Modernization Commission's broad study of antitrust enforcement agencies and doctrine completed in 2007. Some of the issues that our study has highlighted have long been discussed as potentially problematic—particularly the lack of separation of adjudicatory and prosecutorial functions in the FTC—while others, such as transparency and review of decisions not to bring cases, are newer.

We focus our evaluation on two major categories: institutional design and transparency.

A. Institutional design

The two US federal enforcement Agencies combine certain functions in ways that enforcement agencies elsewhere do not: the FTC combines prosecutorial and adjudicative functions; the Antitrust Division combines civil and criminal enforcement. Certainly, other arrangements could be chosen. The FTC could present its cases to a separate competition tribunal, for example; the Justice Department could reassign the Antitrust Division's criminal responsibilities to the Department's Criminal Division and to the US Attorneys' offices.

Based on our study, however, it is hard to make an argument that either alteration would enhance process norms. With regard to the FTC, the concern for unfairness arising out of the lack of separation of functions does not seem to have been realized. One reason may be that, as a practical matter, the FTC's merger enforcement today generally takes place in federal court litigation rather than in administrative trials (although this may be changing). Another reason may be that federal appellate court review of FTC decisions casts a critical shadow over FTC decision-making. The FTC has come a long way from the days when "the FTC's trial examiners [predecessors to ALJs] simply presided over hearings and sent the transcript to the commission, whose members reached their decision in secret and left it to the lawyers to justify the result after the fact."[278] Today, Commissioners anxious about appellate review have every incentive to conform their processes more closely to judicial norms of fair procedures and reasoned decision-making. Hostile courts are unlikely to look kindly on FTC decisions.

With regard to the Justice Department's structure, having both civil and criminal enforcement authority in one "shop" does not appear to have adversely affected any of the process norms, perhaps because of the many legal restrictions that US law

[277] Gerard C. Henderson, *The Federal Trade Commission: A Study in Administrative Law and Procedure* (1924). For discussion of the book's "vivisection of a faltering federal agency" and its impact on the debate regarding proper administrative procedures, *see* Daniel R. Ernst, "Ernst Freund, Felix Frankfurter and the American Rechtsstaat: A Transatlantic Shipwreck, 1894–1932" at 23–5 (2009), <http://scholarship.law.georgetown.edu/cgi/viewcontent.cgi?article=1017&context=facpub>.

[278] Daniel Ernst, "Morgan and the New Dealers," 20 J. Pol'y Hist. 447, 471 (2008) (discussing views of the FTC in the 1930s).

places on the investigation and prosecution of criminal offenses.[279] If anything, the integration of enforcement responsibilities likely permits the Antitrust Division to carry out its mandate more efficiently. It can see antitrust policy (and optimal deterrence) as an integrated whole and the Division has no institutional incentives to advantage one set of enforcement tools (civil enforcement) over another (criminal). Arguably, the integration of functions has helped the Antitrust Division to be a formidable advocate for the use of criminal penalties to deter cartel behavior.

Another critical issue for institutional design is the question whether there should be two general federal antitrust enforcement agencies with overlapping jurisdiction. This has been a long-standing topic of debate in the antitrust community. Some have argued that a unified federal agency would produce consistent policy decisions and perform more efficiently; others have argued that having two federal agencies has an important back-stopping function in terms of vigorous antitrust enforcement and that unification would be unlikely to produce significant efficiency gains.[280] The Antitrust Modernization Commission considered this issue in its 2007 Report, concluding that "[a]lthough concentrating enforcement authority in a single agency generally would be a superior institutional structure, the significant costs and disruption of moving to a single-agency system at this point in time would likely exceed the benefits."[281] The Modernization Commission also pointed out that there was no consensus on which agency would retain antitrust enforcement authority.[282] More recently, the question of dual enforcement was visibly raised by reports of jurisdictional disagreements between the Agencies over merger clearances, health-care antitrust enforcement, and potential major monopolization investigations.[283]

Eliminating dual federal enforcement might have some impact on due process and institutional norms, but it is hard to say whether the impact would be a net positive or negative because that would depend, in part, on how the new enforcement agency were designed. This makes it difficult to recommend unification based on the enhancement of process or institutional norms alone. Rather, the question of

[279] Note that any potential for unfairness in using criminal enforcement tools in civil litigation is mitigated by legal doctrine and Justice Department practice. *See supra* notes 86–87 and accompanying text.

[280] Compare Ernest Gelhorn et al., "Has Antitrust Outgrown Dual Enforcement? A Proposal for Rationalization," 35 ANTITRUST BULL. 695 (1990) (favoring single enforcement) with Report Of The American Bar Association Section Of Antitrust Law Special Committee To Study The Role Of The Federal Trade Commission, 58 ANTITRUST L.J. 53 (1989) (after reviewing virtues and disadvantages of multiple agencies, majority concludes, on balance, not to recommend consolidating antitrust enforcement in a single agency).

[281] *See* AMC Report, *supra* note 21, at 129–30.

[282] *See id.* at 130. The Commission instead made recommendations aimed at specific areas in which it believed dual enforcement has had negative consequences, including the merger clearance process and the different avenues available to the FTC and DOJ in HSR Act merger challenges. *See id.* at 130–1.

[283] *See* Thomas Catan, "This Takeover Battle Pits Bureaucrat vs. Bureaucrat," WALL ST. J., April 12, 2011, p.A1 (describing current disagreements between the Agencies and reporting that FTC Commissioner Kovacic "said his agency had a better working relationship with the European Union than it did with the Justice Department, just two blocks away").

unification will likely depend more on a prediction of its effect on antitrust policy outcomes, an area that lies beyond the scope of this study.

B. Transparency

Increasing the transparency of government decision-making has been an important goal of administrative law. Transparency has many virtues. It can increase political accountability; it can increase law observance and improve deterrence; it can reduce the chances of arbitrary government action. Transparency has costs as well. By cabining discretion, transparency may hamper the ability of policy-makers to change directions or to experiment. Forcing decisions into public view may also make debate less robust by making policy-makers cautious about how they articulate their decisions. And mechanisms to increase transparency can take resources away from an agency's positive enforcement agenda.

The main transparency issue our study has identified centers around decisions not to bring cases. Explanation of such decisions would be consistent with the goals of transparency, particularly in cases where the decision not to go forward is controversial, but there is no formal mechanism in the US system for requiring either the Antitrust Division or the FTC to justify failures to act.

The major proposal advanced for dealing with declinations is the closing statement. Both Agencies have moved toward greater use of these statements, but only in major merger investigations and on a discretionary basis. Recent reviews of both Agencies have urged greater use of such statements, although these recommendations have focused on the merger area and not discussed a broader use of these statements.[284] Nor have these recommendations urged the adoption of a statutory requirement for such statements, one that might be similar to the requirements for the entry of consent decrees in Justice Department cases.[285]

It is hard to fault a recommendation for greater use of closing statements, although it is much more difficult to assess whether a statutory obligation would be wise. Indeed, it is not necessarily the case that requiring closing statements will provide substantially greater transparency. Much depends on the willingness of the agency to discuss its reasons honestly and fully. In this regard, the FTC may have an institutional comparative advantage over the Justice Department. Dissenting Commissioners have incentives to make their conflicting policy views known, which, in turn, can force majority Commissioners to provide fuller explanations of their own views. The Assistant Attorney General in charge of the Antitrust Division has no similar incentives. It is difficult to know how a statutory obligation could much alter these incentives.

Mechanisms other than closing statements may exist that could provide some of the benefits of transparency, particularly political accountability. The United States has a broad system of public and private enforcement that, in part, back-stops and

[284] *See* FTC at 100 Report, *supra* note 181, at 119–20 (testimony generally approving such statements); AMC Report, *supra* note 21, at 64–5 (Recommendation 11a).

[285] *See supra* notes 232–242 and accompanying text.

checks federal agency decisions not to bring cases. Providing more information about federal investigations (not just the Agencies' conclusions) might enable other enforcers to make more informed judgments about the Agencies' decisions not to prosecute and, perhaps, to decide to bring suit on their own. Such transparency, of course, involves costs to the parties and risks to confidentiality of business information, and would require significant changes in federal law governing merger and criminal investigations.[286]

VI. Conclusion

This chapter's review of the US antitrust enforcement system describes a system that measures up well in terms of the due process and institutional performance norms that are the focus of this study. Although major structural changes in the system appear to be both unnecessary and unlikely, there is still room for incremental changes that increase transparency and accountability throughout the decision-making process. Whether such changes are warranted will depend on how the enforcement agencies weigh the values embodied in the norm against the effects that such changes might have on the Agencies' ability to carry out their mandate to effectively enforce US antitrust law.

[286] For restrictions on disclosure of documents, *see*, e.g., 15 U.S.C. § 18a(h) (pre-merger notification documents); Fed. R. Crim. P. 6(e) (documents produced to grand jury).

9

The European Union

The Competition Law System and the Union's Norms

Ioannis Lianos and Arianna Andreangeli

I. Institutional structure and institutional performance norms

A. Overview of the main competition law provisions

Established by the Treaty of Coal and Steel in 1951 and the Treaty of Rome on the European Economic Community in 1957, the competition law provisions of the EU Treaties have remained largely unchanged since that time. At the time of the enactment of the Treaty of Rome, Germany was the only member state of the Union with a proper competition law enforced by an independent administrative authority, the *Bundesskartellamt*, established in 1958, the other five Member States at the time having only provisions on unfair competition and regulating prices in large parts of their economy.[1] The main provisions of EU competition law are the following:

Article 101 (1) of the TFEU[2] prohibits agreements, concerted practices, and decisions of associations of undertakings that have as their object or effect to restrict competition and affect trade between Member States. The different elements of Article 101(1) have been defined by an extensive case law of the European courts. Article 101(3) provides that practices falling within the scope of Article 101(1) may not be found illegal under Article 101 and thus not subject to the prohibition principle if they fulfill some conditions. They have to contribute to improving the production or distribution of goods or promoting technical or economic progress, while allowing consumers a fair share of the resulting benefit and not imposing on the undertakings concerned restrictions which are not indispensable to the attainment of these objectives or do not afford such undertakings the possibility of eliminating competition in respect of a substantial part of the products in question. Article 101(2) TFEU deals with some of the civil law effects of Article 101(1)'s prohibition.

[1] For an historical overview of the evolution of the competition law idea in Europe, *see* Gerber, *Law and Competition in Twentieth Century Europe: Protecting Prometheus* (1998, OUP).

[2] Treaty on the Functioning of the European Union, <http://eur-lex.europa.eu/LexUriServ/LexUriServ.do?uri=OJ:C:2008:115:0047:0199:EN:PDF>.

Article 102 prohibits the abuse by one or more undertakings of a dominant position within the internal market or in a substantial part of it in so far as it may affect trade between Member States. Both Articles 101 and 102 provide examples of prohibited or abusive conduct. However, this list is not exhaustive and the case law of the European courts as well as the decisional practice of the Commission show an extensive interpretation of these provisions, leading, for example, to the expansion of the application of Article 102 to situations where the dominant position is maintained by more than one undertaking (collective dominant position)[3] or to situations where the abuse and the dominant position are not in the same relevant market.[4] The scope of Article 101 TFEU does not extend to situations of tacit collusion if there is no evidence of some degree of concertation between the undertakings: parallel behavior does not constitute evidence of an illegal concerted practice or agreement.[5]

An important issue that has been examined from time to time in the case law of the European Courts and the decisional practice of the European Commission is whether competition law and policy is an objective of EU law or is it also a means to further other objectives of EU Law. Initially, competition law and policy have been conceived as means to enhance the objective of establishing a common (internal) market. This "outer" aim of competition policy might explain the teleological and extensive interpretation of the competition law provisions of the Treaty that the European courts have followed in a number of cases against private or public practices that raise barriers to trade and restrict competition.[6] The objective of market integration has influenced the Courts in the interpretation of the competition law provisions of the Treaty.[7]

All Member States have adopted competition law statutes that are heavily inspired by EU competition law. In particular, Regulation 1/2003 has fostered a process of convergence across Europe of the substantive competition law provisions of several Member States with a specific provision mandating convergence in the context of the application of national provisions equivalent to Article 101, ensuring

[3] *See* Case C-395/96P & C-396/96 P, *Compagnie Maritime Belge v. Commission* [2000] ECR I-1365.

[4] *See* Case C-333/94, *Tetra Pak II* [1996] ECR I-I-5951.

[5] Case 48/69, *ICI v. Commission* [1972] ECR 619.

[6] Cf. Case 56 & 58/64, *Consten&Grundig v Commission* [1966] ECR 299 applying Article 85 of the EC Treaty (now Art. 101 TFEU) to distribution practices establishing vertical restraints to competition.

[7] Cf. Joined Cases C-501/06 P, C-513/06 P, C-515/06 P, and C-519/06 P *GlaxoSmithKline Services Unlimited v. Commission* [2009] ECR I-929 (finding that a dual pricing system restricting the opportunities of parallel trade constituted a restriction of competition by its object under Article 101 TFEU); *see* also, Joined cases C-468/06 to 478/06, *Sot. LeloskaiSia v GlaxoSmithKline* [2008] ECR (where the Court examined the compatibility to Article 102 TFEU of a refusal to supply wholesalers engaging in parallel exports. The Court implicitly recognized that certain types of conduct, such as a restriction of parallel trade are presumptively anticompetitive, because they frustrate the objective of the Treaty to achieve the integration of national markets through the establishment of a single market); Case 13/77, *INNO/ATAB* (1977) ECR 2115 (extending the application of the competition law provisions of the Treaty to state restrictions of competition).

a level playing field with regard to the scope of competition law in Europe.[8] However, according to the last sentence of Article 3(2) of Regulation 1/2003, Member States are not precluded from adopting and applying stricter national laws prohibiting or sanctioning unilateral conduct. Unilateral behavior capable of affecting trade between Member States can thus be prohibited by national law, even if it occurs below the level of dominance or is not considered abusive within the meaning of Article 102.[9]

Regulation 17 of 1962[10] governed how the EC Treaty's provisions on anti-competitive agreements and abuses of dominant position were enforced, until the "modernization" of the EU competition policy[11] with the implementation of Regulation 1/2003.[12] Regulation 1/2003 transformed the previous legal authorization system into a legal exception regime, where practices are found illegal only after a thorough analysis of their possible negative and positive effects to competition by the competition authorities and courts. Regulation 1/2003 decentralized the European system of competition law enforcement, as it abolished the practice of notifying illegal agreements to the European Commission and empowered national competition authorities and national courts to apply fully the competition law provisions of the Treaty.

There was no effective system of merger control in the European Communities,[13] at least until the first EC Merger regulation (ECMR) was implemented in 1989.[14] The regulation established a centralized preventive and one-stop shop merger control system with a suspensory effect. The competence for the examination and the decision in merger cases with a Community dimension lies exclu-

[8] Article 3(2) of Regulation 1/2003.

[9] Countries with statutes on the abuse of economic dependence or equivalent provisions include Germany, France, Portugal, Greece, Italy, Spain, Ireland, Latvia, Hungary, and Slovakia.

[10] Council Regulation No 17 (EEC): First Regulation implementing Articles 85 and 86 of the Treaty [1962] OJ P 13, 204.

[11] On the process of modernization *see* White Paper on the Modernisation of the Rules implementing Articles 85 and 86 of the EC Treaty (1999) OJ C 132/1; Wesseling, *The Modernisation of EC Antitrust Law* (2010, Hart Publishing); Ehlermann & Atanasiu (eds), *European Competition Law Annual 2000: The Modernisation of EC Antitrust Policy* (Hart 2001); Ehlermann & Atanasiu (eds), *European Competition Law Annual 2002: Constructing the EU Network of Competition Authorities* (Hart 2004); Cahill & Cooke (eds), *The Modernisation of EU Competition Law Enforcement in the EU* (FIDE 2004); and my own *Principles of European Antitrust Enforcement* (Hart 2005).

[12] Council Regulation (EC) No 1/2003 of 16 December 2002 on the implementation of the rules on competition laid down in Articles 81 and 82 of the Treaty (2003) OJ L 1/.1, as amended by Council Regulation (EC) No 411/2004 of 26 February 2004 repealing Regulation (EEC) No 3975/87 and amending Regulations (EEC) No 3976/87 and (EC) No 1/2003, in connection with air transport between the Community and third countries (2004) OJ L 68/1 and Council Regulation (EC) No 1419/2006 of 25 September 2006 repealing Regulation (EEC) No 4056/86 laying down detailed rules for the application of Articles 85 and 86 of the Treaty to maritime transport, and amending Regulation (EC) No 1/2003 as regards the extension of its scope to include cabotage and international tramp services (2006) OJ L 269/1.

[13] Neither the Treaty of Rome nor the German GWB provided any specific provision for controlling mergers, with the exception of Art. 66(1)–(6) of the European Coal and Steel Community (ECSC) Treaty, which established an exclusive competence for the High Authority of the ECSC without any residual competence to Member States for establishing national merger control and without the requirement of an effect on trade between Member States.

[14] Council Regulation (EEC) No 4064/89 of 21 December 1989 on the control of concentrations between undertakings [1989] L 395/1. The case law of the European Court of Justice had however extended the scope of application of Articles 101 TFEU (Joined Cases 142 and 156/84 *BAT* and *Reynolds v. Commission* [1987] ECR) and 102 TFEU to economic concentrations.

sively with the European Commission. Member States are free to develop their own merger control systems for mergers without a Community dimension. The concept of "Community dimension" is defined by Article 1 of the ECMR, which refers to specific quantitative thresholds of the turnover of the undertakings concerned and the cross-national influence of the transaction.[15]

The revised Merger Regulation 139/2004 included mergers that create a significant impediment to effective competition, and not just mergers that create or reinforce a dominant position, as was the case with the previous merger regulation.[16] The new framework also explicitly recognized the role of efficiency gains in the competition assessment of mergers under Regulation 139/2004,[17] thus increasing the discretion of the European Commission in applying its merger control policy to different types of mergers. The inquisitorial administrative procedure of the Merger Regulation is different from the adversarial procedure developed by some national systems of merger control, where prohibition decisions can only be made by courts or court-like institutions.[18] It also differs from the administrative procedure systems of merger control in some Member States, as the prohibition decisions are not adopted by a specialized competition agency,[19] but by the college of the European Commission that is the "executive power" or "government" of the EU.[20]

Article 106 TFEU extends the application of the competition law provisions of the Treaty to public undertakings and undertakings to which Member States grant special or exclusive rights. In this regard, Article 106(2) TFEU introduces an exception to the application of the rules of the Treaty when the latter would obstruct the provision of services of general economic interest in so far as the application of the competition law rules would not obstruct the performance, in law or in fact, of the particular tasks assigned to them.

State aids are prohibited under Article 107 TFEU. It is a unique characteristic of the European system of the protection of competition to include a control of state subsidies to undertakings. The main reason is the effort to curtail the development of protectionist industrial policies that could compromise the objective of market integration. Nevertheless, some exceptions authorize aid justified by common

[15] Article 1 ECMR contains a general threshold which is relevant to most concentrations reviewed by the Commission (Art. 1(2)) and a special threshold which is brought into consideration if the quantitative thresholds in Art. 1(2) are not met (Art. 1(3)).

[16] Recital 24 and Art. 2(2) of Council Regulation (EC) No 139/2004 of 20 January 2004 on the control of concentrations between undertakings [2004] OJ L 24/1.

[17] Recital 29 and Art. 2(1)b of Council Regulation (EC) No 139/2004 of 20 January 2004 on the control of concentrations between undertakings [2004] OJ L 24/1. *See* also, Guidelines on the assessment of horizontal mergers under the Council Regulation on the control of concentrations between undertakings [2004] OJ C 31/5, Part VII.

[18] *See*, for instance, in Austria.

[19] *See*, for instance, in Germany and France.

[20] Because of the large number of merger cases, the European Commission has empowered one of its Members to take management or administrative measures if these are not of fundamental importance: *see*, Art. 13 of the Commission's Rules of Procedures [2000] OJ L 308. This task is often delegated to the Director General of DG Competition who also communicates with the other Directorates-General of the European Commission. However, other Members of the Commission have the right to involve the President of the Commission, for politically sensitive cases.

interest objectives, that is, for services of general economic interest, as long as they do not distort competition in such a way as to be contrary to the public interest. The monitoring of state aid is carried out by the European Commission.

B. Institutional design

1. *An administrative-centered enforcement system: The central role of the European Commission*

a) The European Commission and the EU integrated agency model

The EU Treaty (Article 105 TFEU) entrusts the European Commission with the power to apply Articles 101, 102, and 106 to individual cases, either directly, or following a regulation or directive adopted by the Council (Article 103 TFEU). Under Council Regulation 139/2004, the Commission enjoys powers to review and authorize concentrations having a "Community dimension." Although there are significant differences between antitrust and merger proceedings, certain procedural features are by and large common to both areas, such as the rules governing access to the file and some of the administrative practices developed to establish a "dialogue" between the case-handling officials and the undertakings concerned.

The Commission has an important array of powers in the area of competition law. It performs a "supervisory task," which includes "the duty to investigate and punish individual infringements as well as the duty to pursue a general policy designed to apply, in competition matters, the principles laid down by the Treaty."[21] It is composed of twenty-seven members, appointed for a renewable period of five years by the Council of the European Union, after being nominated by their Member States and approved by the European Parliament. They should be independent in performing their duties and should not receive instructions from their respective governments. Each member of the Commission has responsibility over a specific policy area. The Commission is organized in a number of Directorates General, one of those being the Directorate General for Competition (DG Comp) with responsibility over the enforcement of competition law. Other DGs, such as the Directorate General for Enterprise and Industry, may also be involved in the broader issues of competition policy.

DG Comp is headed by a Director General, working under the authority of the Commissioner responsible for competition policy. The Director General is assisted by three deputy Directors General (one on antitrust and mergers, one on operations, and one on state aids) and a number of directorates dealing with specific industries or more general operational issues (policy and strategy, registry and resources). Since September 2003, there is also a Chief Competition Economist (CCE) office, comprising ten specialized economists and headed by a Chief economist who is appointed by the European Commission. To fulfill its institutional mandate, the Commission benefits from a broad regulatory competence in

[21] Cases C-189/02, 202/02, 208/02 & 213/02, *Dansk Rørindustri A/S & others v. Commission* [2005] ECR I-5425, para 170.

adopting measures of general application. According to Article 105(3), it can adopt regulations and directives on certain categories of agreements[22] along with other normative measures designed to implement the competition law provisions of the Treaty.[23] These texts are completed by an array of guidelines, Communications, notices, priority guidance, best practices, annual reports, oral statements, press releases, guidance letters, expert reports, and third-party studies, which provide valuable information on the enforcement of competition law.

Having regard especially to its competence to apply the competition rules to individual alleged infringements, it should be emphasized that the framework through which this power is exercised has undergone significant reforms in the past ten years. According to the first Implementing Regulation, namely Council Regulation No 17/62, the Commission was structured as an "integrated agency" responsible for the investigation of alleged infringements, for the adoption of a decision as to whether that infringement has indeed occurred and for the imposition of sanctions on the undertakings responsible for it. The choice of this "centralized" enforcement model, which relies predominantly on the action of one administrative agency and little (if at all) on private lawsuits, was dictated by a specific legal, economic, and political context. The context included the need for market integration,[24] together with a perceived weakness if not absence of a competition culture in Europe, with the exception of Germany.

In addition, the influence of the civil law tradition of "inquisitorial" as opposed to more "adversarial" modes of decision-making was decisive for the creation of an

[22] Commission Regulation (EU) 330/2010 of 20 April 2010 on the application of Article 101(3) of the Treaty on the Functioning of the European Union to categories of vertical agreements and concerted practices, [2010] OJ L 102/1; Commission Regulation (EU) 461/2010 on the application of Article 101(3) of the Treaty on the Functioning of the European Union to categories of vertical agreements and concerted practices in the motor vehicle sector, [2010] OJ L 129/52; Commission Regulation (EC) No 2658/2000 of 29 November 2000 on the application of Article 81(3) of the Treaty to categories of specialisation agreements, [2000] OJ L 304/3; Commission Regulation (EC) No 2659/2000 of 29 November 2000 on the application of Article 81(3) of the Treaty to categories of research and development agreements, [2000] OJ L 304/7; Commission Regulation (EC) No 772/2004 of 27 April 2004 on the application of Article 81(3) of the Treaty to categories of technology transfer agreements, [2004] OJ L 123/11; Commission Regulation (EC) of 24 March 2010 on the application of Article 101(3) of the Treaty to certain categories of agreements, decisions, and concerted practices in the insurance, [2010] OJ L 83/1; Commission Regulation (EC) No 906/2009 of 28 September 2009 on the application of Article 81(3) of the Treaty to certain categories of agreements, decisions, and concerted practices between liner shipping companies (consortia), [2009] OJ L 256/31.

[23] Commission Regulation (EC) No 773/2004 of 7 April 2004 relating to the conduct of proceedings by the Commission pursuant to Articles 81 and 82 of the EC Treaty, [2004] OJ L 123/18. On merger control, *see* Commission Regulation (EC) No.802/2004 implementing Council Regulation (EC) No 139/2004 (The "Implementing Regulation") and its annexes (Form CO, Short Form CO and Form RS), [2004] OJ L 133/1, as amended by Commission Regulation (EC) No 1033/2008 of 20 October 2008 amending Regulation (EC) No 802/2004 implementing Council Regulation (EC) No 139/2004 on the control of concentrations between undertakings, [2008] OJ L 279/3; on the settlement procedure for cartels, *see* Commission Regulation (EC) No 622/2008 of 30 June 2008 amending Regulation (EC) No 773/2004, as regards the conduct of settlement procedures in cartel cases (Text with EEA relevance), [2008] OJ L 171/3.

[24] Evans, "Why different jurisdictions do not (and should not) adopt the same antitrust rules," (2009) 10 Chi. J. Int'l L. 161 at 168–9.

integrated agency as the authority responsible for the implementation of competition policy in the newfound EEC.[25] Within this framework, the Commission was primarily responsible for the investigation and the sanctioning of competition infringements, thus acting in each case as "police, prosecutor and judge": its decisions were liable to judicial challenge before the EU Courts.[26] Also, the Court of Justice of the EU (formerly the European Court of Justice) and the General Court (formerly the Court of First Instance) were not "appeal courts," in the sense of being empowered to re-examine each decision in their merits, but were only courts of limited review, and in that context they have traditionally shown significant deference to the Commission's evaluation of individual cases.[27]

A similar framework was also established by the first Merger Regulation in 1989 and was left substantially unaltered by the 2004 second Merger Regulation.[28] Although in this context proceedings are initiated via a notification of the proposed transaction to the Commission, the process follows a similar pattern, with the Commission acting as an "integrated" agency and the EU Courts responsible only for the review of the decisions.[29] Nonetheless, merger proceedings present ad hoc features, such as the sharp partition between "phase one" and "phase two" proceedings and the presence of tight deadlines;[30] they are also characterized by the close involvement of the parties affected by the concentration and by the presence of "negotiations" of those modifications that are regarded by the Commission as necessary to secure the approval of individual deals.[31]

The enforcement framework was not affected in its essential characteristics by the Modernisation Regulation; that is, Council Regulation No 1/2003. The 2003 reforms sought to respond to new challenges and to the needs and features of a changing political and economic landscape. The increase in the number of Member States from six to twelve and again to fifteen at the time the White Paper on Modernisation was launched meant that, according to the Commission, the centralized notification system was no longer sustainable and prevented it from engaging in investigations concerning "serious" antitrust infringements.[32] For these reasons, the regulation not only strengthened the Commission's investigative and decision-making powers. It also, and perhaps most importantly, proposed a "decentralization agenda" by abolishing the "notification system" for prima facie anti-competitive agreements that could qualify for an exemption from the sanction of

[25] *See* Fox, "Antitrust and institutions: design and change" (2009) 41 Loy. U. Chi. L J 473 at 475.

[26] Council Regulation No 17 of 6 February 1962, [1959–62] OJ Spec Ed 57, *see*, e.g., Articles 3, 9, and 11 et seq.

[27] *See id.*, e.g. Article 17; cf. Article 262 TFEU (formerly Article 230 EC Treaty).

[28] Council Regulation No 4064/89 of 21 December 1989, [1989] OJ L395/1. This Regulation was replaced by Council Regulation No 139/2004 of 209 January 2004, [2004] OJ L24/1.

[29] *See*, e.g., Articles 2 and 6 of the 1989 Merger Regulation and Articles 2, 4 and 6 of the 2004 Regulation.

[30] *See* Articles 6 and 8 of the 2004 Merger Regulation.

[31] *See*, e.g., Articles 6(2) and 8(2) of the 2004 Merger Regulation.

[32] *See* White Paper on the modernization of the rules implementing Articles 85 and 86 of the EC Treaty, [1999] OJ C132/1 (hereinafter referred to as Modernisation White Paper), p. 3–5.

nullity under Article 101(3) TFEU, by encouraging private antitrust claims before the national courts and by drawing the national competition authorities (hereinafter referred to as NCAs) "closer" to itself within the European Competition Network.

In this specific context, the 2003 Regulation provides an express legal basis for various forms of cooperation between the Commission and the NCAs as well as among the NCAs themselves, including an obligation to notify the Commission and hence the ECN of new cases and of decisions adopted or contemplated that involve the application of the EU competition rules, the power to exchange and use as evidence information obtained by authorities having jurisdiction in another Member State, and the power to request and carry out investigative measures on behalf of another agency. Accordingly, it is suggested that, on the one hand, the framework established by Council Regulation No 17/62 was the "by-product" of a specific context characterized by a "small" Community, consisting predominantly of member states having a civil law tradition and an embryonic competition culture. The 2003 reforms, on the other hand, were the result of a changed landscape in which a larger and more diverse membership and a deeper and more rooted competition culture and experience feature prominently.[33]

b) Proceedings before the European Commission in competition and merger cases

As was anticipated, the European Commission's institutional structure is inspired by the "integrated agency" model: the Commission acts as "police, prosecutor and judge" in respect to individual allegations of anti-competitive behavior as well as to concentrations notified to it and its administrative decisions are open to review on the part of the European Union Courts, namely the General Court, and, on a point of law, the Court of Justice of the EU. The procedure for the application of Articles 101 and 102 TFEU before the Commission is set out in Regulation 1/2003, Regulation 774/2003, and other administrative statements.[34] In merger cases, the EU Merger Regulation[35] and its implementing instruments provide a distinct procedural framework for the assessment of notified transactions.[36]

According to Article 7 of Council Regulation No 1/2003 the Commission can initiate competition investigations either *proprio motu* or upon a complaint lodged by a third party. The proceedings are articulated in a preliminary and a more "formal" phase. In the former, the necessary fact-finding tasks are carried out to

[33] Modernisation White Paper, paras 4, 8–10.

[34] Commission Notice on the rules for access to the Commission file in cases pursuant to Articles 81 and 82 of the EC Treaty, Articles 53, 54 and 57 of the EEA Agreement and Council Regulation (EC) No 139/2004 (hereafter Access to File Notice).

[35] Council Regulation (EC) No 139/2004 on the control of concentrations between undertakings, [2004] OJ L 24/1 (Merger Regulation).

[36] Art 18(1) of the Merger Regulation and Art 13 of the Implementing Regulation (Commission Regulation (EC) 802/2004 implementing Council Regulation (EC) 139/2004 on the control of concentrations between undertakings, [2004] OJ L133/1). *See* also Best Practices on the Conduct of EC Merger Control Proceedings (2004) (hereinafter, "Best Practices"), <http://ec.europa.eu/competition/mergers/legislation/proceedings.pdf>.

ascertain whether the investigated parties have "a case to answer" in respect of the allegations made against them. The latter instead is opened via a written statement of the "objections" raised by the case-handling officials, and involves a formal hearing, in writing and orally, before the adoption of a decision.[37]

Having regard to the investigative phase, the Commission according to Arts 17 to 21 of Council Regulation No 1/2003 can carry out market inquiries and studies of specific economic sectors[38] and ask individual undertakings for specific information via a simple request, setting out the subject matter and purpose of the measure and the time limit within which to comply with it. If the undertakings do not submit the required information, the Commission can issue a binding formal decision, compliance with which is ensured through the threat of monetary penalties according to Arts 23 and 24 of the Regulation.[39] The Commission can also take statements from any person that consents to be so interviewed by the case-handling officials[40] and conduct inspections of the premises, land, and means of transport of individual firms.[41] The officials can inspect books or records, extract copies, and seal the inspected premises for the duration of the investigations; they can also ask any member of staff to provide on the spot explanations "on facts or documents related to the subject matter and purpose of the investigation and to record their answers."[42]

Article 20 draws a distinction between inspections conducted solely on the basis of a written authorization, specifying the subject matter and the purpose of the investigation and the sanctions that can be inflicted on the parties if they fail to cooperate with the officials—for example, by giving "incorrect or misleading answers" or by failing to produce "complete" records—and those carried out upon a formal decision of the Commission: whereas undertakings may oppose the former, they "are required to submit" to the latter, on pain of financial penalties being imposed on them according to Articles 23 and 24 of the Regulation.[43]

Furthermore, Article 21 allows the Commission to inspect "other premises," including the homes of the undertakings' employees, if a "reasonable suspicion" exists that relevant documents are kept there. This type of inspection can only be carried out via a formal decision indicating the subject matter, the date, and place of the investigation and that the parties have a right to appeal before the Court of Justice and upon prior authorization of the judicial authority in whose jurisdiction it is to be executed. The domestic court must be satisfied that the Commission decision is authentic and that the measure is not arbitrary or excessive given the seriousness of the allegations, the involvement of the undertaking in the infringe-

[37] *See*, *inter alia*, case 374/87, *Orkem v Commission*, [1989] ECR 3283, especially paras 20–25.

[38] Council Regulation No 1/2003, Article 17.

[39] Council Regulation No 1/2003, Article 18. *See*, e.g., case 136/79, *National Panasonic (UK) v Commission*, [1980] ECR 2033, para 11.

[40] Council Regulation No 1/2003, Article 19.

[41] Council Regulation No 1/2003, Article 20.

[42] Article 20(1) and (2).

[43] Article 20(3). *See* also Explanatory note to an authorization to conduct an inspection in execution of a Commission decision under Article 20(4) of Council Regulation No 1/2003, <http://ec.europa.eu/competition/antitrust/legislation/explanatory_note.pdf>, section 6.

ment, and the importance of the evidence sought and the "reasonable likelihood" that the records being sought are kept at the premises in question. However, the Regulation states clearly that the national court cannot question the "necessity of the inspection" or "demand" access to evidence kept on the Commission's file; it can only ask the Commission to provide "detailed explanations" solely for the purpose of assessing the "proportionality" of the investigative measure, whose validity is subject to scrutiny only on the part of the Court of Justice.[44]

After the preliminary investigations, the Commission may decide that there are no grounds to proceed further; in this case, if the case originated from a third-party complaint, in accordance with Article 7 of the Commission Regulation No 773/2004, it is obliged to notify the complainant of its decision and to allow him or her to express their views.[45] Or it could take the view that the allegations are prima facie capable of founding a prohibition decision; in this case, the Commission will issue the parties with a statement of objections, that is, a formal account of the allegations made against them, thereby leading to a formal hearing and to the disclosure of evidence to the investigated parties. The latter can also offer commitments, according to Article 9 of Council Regulation No 1/2003.[46]

The statement of objections reflects the duty of the Commission to investigate each case in accordance with principles of impartiality and objectivity and the resulting obligation to consider both exculpatory and inculpatory evidence.[47] It ensures that the right to be heard is appropriately exercised and therefore must spell out not only all the facts and legal arguments supporting its allegations[48] but also explain the inferences which it has drawn from the evidence collected during the proceedings and on which it relies against the investigated undertakings.[49] Further-

[44] Article 21(3). *See* case C-94/00, *Roquette Frères SA v Directeur général de la concurrence, de la consommation et de la répression des fraudes, and Commission of the European Communities*, [2002] ECR I-9011, especially paras 31–32, 52, 54–62; also, mutatis mutandis, case C-198/01, *Consorzio Italiano Fiammiferi (CIF) v Autorita' Garante della Concorrenza e del Mercato*, [2003] ECR I-8055, paras 45–46, 49.

[45] Article 7, Commission Regulation No 2842/98 of 22 December 1998 on the hearing of parties in certain proceedings under Articles 85 and 86 of the EC Treaty, [1998] OJ L354/18; Article 6, Commission Regulation No 773/2004 of 7 April 2004 relating to the conduct of proceedings by the Commission pursuant to Articles 81 and 82 of the EC Treaty, [2004] OJ L123/18; case T-24/90, *Automec v Commission*, [1992] ECR I-222, paras 79, 85; *see* also case T-114/92, *BEMIM v Commission*, [1995] ECR II-147, paras 80 and 86. *See, inter alia*, European Commission, White Paper on Modernisation of the rules implementing Articles 85 and 86 [now 81 and 82] of the EC Treaty, April 28, 1999, [1999] O.J. L123/1.

[46] *See* Articles 5 and 9 of Council Regulation No 1/2003; *see* also Article 10, Commission Regulation No 773/2004.

[47] *See* Recital 32, Preamble to Council Regulation No 1/2003; for commentary, *see*, e.g., Paulis, "Checks and balances in the EU antitrust enforcement system," in Hawk (ed), Proceedings from the Fordham Corporate International Law Institute 2002 Antitrust Law and Policy Conference, 2003: New York, 381 at 383–5.

[48] *Inter alia*, case T-191/98, *Atlantic Container Line AB and others v Commission*, [2003] ECR II 3275, para 113.

[49] *Id.*, para 162. *See* also case T-48/00, *Corus UK v Commission*, [2004] ECR II-2325, paras 144–146; cf. with e.g. case 45/69, *Boehringer Mannheim v Commission*, [1970] ECR 769, para 9; case 51/69, *Bayer v Commission of the European Communities*, [1972] ECR 745, para 11; Cases 142 & 156/84, *BAT & Reynolds v Commission*, [1986] ECR 1899, para 27; case T-40/92, *Groupement CB & Europay International SA v Commission*, [1994] ECR II-49, paras 57–58; case T-67/01, *JCB Service v*

more, if the Commission wishes to impose financial penalties on the undertakings, it must also provide a brief assessment of the nature, the severity, and the duration of the breach to allow the investigated party to foresee the dimension of the penalty that is likely to be inflicted on them and to challenge it in its submissions.[50] In addition, according to the forthcoming revised Best Practices Guidelines, this section will be extended to comprise an indication of other factual elements, such as the value of the profits that the Commission estimates have been accrued to the firm as a result of its unlawful activity and whether the Commission envisages applying the aggravating circumstance of recidivism and with what effects.[51]

A key factor for the "meaningful participation" of the parties in the proceedings is their ability to access the evidence that the Commission has gathered and on which basis it has made inferences against them.[52] The investigated parties must be entitled to access all the evidence that is "relevant for the case," with only limited exceptions justified by the need to protect the confidentiality of "business secrets, internal documents and other confidential information,"[53] in accordance with the principle of "equality of arms": thus, it is not for the case-handling officials to assess the relevance of individual pieces of evidence with a view to disclosing them to the parties but for the parties themselves, with appropriate legal assistance.[54]

If the Commission wishes to withhold knowledge of any evidence on grounds of confidentiality, it is obliged to include it in the list of the relevant evidence that is annexed to the statement of objections, so that the parties can object to its non-disclosure.[55] Also, it cannot rely on "secret" evidence against them unless, acting with "due diligence," it has made available to the parties a "non-confidential version" of the documents concerned or provided for access via alternative means, for example, by allowing the parties to peruse the documents at the Commission's premises.[56]

Having regard to the formal hearing of the parties, Commission Regulation No 773/2004 states that this will take place primarily in writing, for reasons of

Commission, [2004] ECR II-49, paras 50–51. Also case T-109/02, *Bollore SA and others v Commission*, [2007] ECR II-947, paras 80–81.

50 Case T-48/00, *Corus UK v Commission*,[2004] ECR II-2325, paras 144, 146; *see* also case C-328/05, *SGL Carbon v Commission*, [2007] ECR I-3921, para 56.

51 Joaquim Almunia, "Fair process in EU competition proceedings," speech given at the European Competition Day, Budapest, 30 May 2011, SPEECH/11/396.

52 Article 27(2), Council Regulation No 1/2003; *see* also Commission Notice on the rules for access to the Commission file in cases pursuant to Articles 81 and 82 of the EC Treaty, Articles 53, 54 and 57 of the EEA Agreement and Council Regulation (EC) No 139/2004 (hereinafter referred to as Commission Notice on Access to the File), [2005] OJ C325/7. *See*, Commission notice on best practices for the conduct of proceedings concerning Articles 101 and 102, OJ [2011] C308/6; § 85.

53 *See*, e.g., case T-30/91, *Solvay SA v Commission*, [1995] ECR II-1175, paras 81, 83; also Commission notice on access to the file, para 1.

54 *Id.*, paras 83 and 89; *see* also case T-175/95, *BASF Coating v Commission*, [1999] ECR II-1581, paras 46–50.

55 e.g. case 85/76, *Hoffmann LaRoche v Commission*, [1979] ECR 461, para 13–14.

56 *See* Commission Notice on access to the file, paras 24, 31 et seq.; *see* also case 53/85, *AKZO Chemie BV and AKZO Chemie UK Ltd v Commission* [1986] ECR 1965, para 29; also case C-310/93 P, *BPB Industries plc and British Gypsum ltd v Commission*, [1995] ECR I-865, paras 25–26; case T-30/91, *Solvay SA v Commission*, [1995] ECR II-1175 at para 89.

"procedural economy";[57] however, the investigated undertakings are all afforded the opportunity to make their case at an oral hearing, which supplements the written submissions.[58] The formal hearing is conducted by the Hearing Officer, who can be appointed even from outside the Commission[59] and is charged with ensuring that the procedure is fair and objective.[60] The function of "Hearing Officer" was established in 1982, in order to enhance impartiality and objectivity in competition proceedings before the Commission. According to their most recent Mandate,[61] Hearing Officers are independent from DG Competition and are attached to the Commissioner to whom they report. The Hearing Officers have the mandate to ensure that the effective exercise of the right to be heard is respected in competition proceedings before the Commission for any of Articles 101, 102, 106, and merger control proceedings.

The Officer chairs the oral hearing and is empowered to check that the investigated parties are fully informed of the allegations made against them[62] and to decide as to the admissibility of third parties to the hearing itself.[63] She is also entitled to be kept informed as to the development of individual proceedings up to

[57] *See* Article 10(3), Commission Regulation (EC) No 773/2004 of 7 April 2004 relating to the conduct of proceedings by the Commission pursuant to Articles 81 and 82 of the EC Treaty, [2004] OJ L123/18; Article 13(3), Commission Regulation (EC) No 802/2004 of 7 April 2004 implementing Council Regulation (EC) No 139/2004 on the control of concentrations between undertakings, [2004] OJ L133/1.

[58] *See inter alia* Commission of the European Communities, *Dealing with the Commission: Competition Enforcement*, 1997, Brussels: Official Publication Centre, 46; for commentary, e.g. Kerse, "Procedures in EC Competition Cases: The Oral Hearing," (1994) 15 ECLR 40. *See* more recently, Wils, "The oral hearing in competition proceedings before the European Commission", (2012) 35(3) W. Comp. 397, especially pp. 400–402.

[59] Articles 1–2, Commission Decision 2001/462/EC, ECSC, on the terms of reference of Hearing Officers in certain competition proceedings, [2001] OJ L162/21, revised by Decision 2011/695 of the President of the European Commission of 13 October 2011 on the function and terms of reference of the Hearing Officer in certain competition proceedings [2011] OJ L 275/29.

[60] Commission of the European Communities, *XII Report on Competition Policy*, 1983: Brussels, 31. For a discussion of the role of the Hearing Officer up to the 2001 Mandate, *see* House of Lords Select Committee on the European Union, *XIX Report: Strengthening the role of the Hearing Officer*, sess. 1999/2000. *See* Commission of the European Communities, Brussels: 1994, 116–17; also, Decision 2011/695 of the President of the European Commission of 13 October 2011 on the function and terms of reference of the Hearing Officer in certain competition proceedings [2011] OJ L 275/29.

[61] Decision 2011/695 of the President of the European Commission of 13 October 2011 on the function and terms of reference of the Hearing Officer in certain competition proceedings [2011] OJ L 275/29.

[62] Article 4, Decision 2011/695 of the President of the European Commission of 13 October 2011 on the function and terms of reference of the Hearing Officer in certain competition proceedings [2011] OJ L 275/29.

[63] Articles 5 & 6, Decision 2011/695 of the President of the European Commission of 13 October 2011 on the function and terms of reference of the Hearing Officer in certain competition proceedings [2011] OJ L 275/29 For the position of third parties, *see* also, Article 7, Commission Regulation No 2842/98 of 22 December 1998 on the hearing of parties in certain proceedings under Articles 85 and 86 of the EC Treaty, [1998] OJ L354/18; Article 6, Commission Regulation No 773/2004 of 7 April 2004 relating to the conduct of proceedings by the Commission pursuant to Articles 81 and 82 of the EC Treaty, [2004] OJ L123/18; case T-24/90, *Automec v Commission*, [1992] ECR I-222, paras 79, 85; *see* also case T-114/92, *BEMIM v Commission*, [1995] ECR II-147, paras 80 and 86. *See*, *inter alia*, European Commission, White Paper on Modernisation of the rules implementing Articles 85 and 86 [now 81 and 82] of the EC Treaty, April 28, 1999, [1999] O.J. L123/1.

the stage at which a draft decision is adopted,[64] to submit observations to the College of Commissioners at any stage of the case, and is charged with producing a report on the hearing.[65] The Hearing Officer operates as "an independent arbiter" between the parties concerned, other involved parties, complainants, or interested third persons in order to resolve issues affecting the effective exercise of their procedural rights, when these issues could not be resolved through prior contacts with the Commission: her report is made public and therefore fosters the ability of the parties to seek the judicial scrutiny of the final decision on matters of procedure.[66] The Hearing Officer is also competent to decide on the admissibility of requests for access to the file and on the admission to the hearing of "fresh" documents, that is, documents related to the allegations already notified to the parties in the statement of objections, subject to the parties being allowed a reasonable opportunity to peruse the material and to comment on it.[67] Since the last reform of its mandate in 2011, the Hearing Officer also became responsible for solving "privilege-based issues," namely disputes between the investigated parties and the Commission as to the nature—whether privileged or otherwise—of the evidence gathered during an investigation.[68] However, the decisions adopted by the Hearing Officer cannot be challenged before the General Court[69] on grounds of their "preparatory" and thus soft law and non-definitive nature.[70]

If a competition law infringement is found, the Commission has extensive powers to impose sanctions (fines and periodic penalties),[71] including penalties of up to 10 percent of the annual worldwide turnover of an undertaking[72] and has discretion to set the amount of fines for each infringement, also taking into account the need to ensure deterrence.[73] The total amount of fines has increased consider-

[64] Article 3.

[65] Articles 16-17.

[66] Recital 8, Decision 2011/695 of the President of the European Commission of 13 October 2011 on the function and terms of reference of the Hearing Officer in certain competition proceedings [2011] OJ L 275/29Hearing Officer. *See* House of Lords Select Committee on the European Union, *XIX Report: Strengthening the role of the Hearing Officer*, sess. 1999/2000 at para 37.

[67] Article 7, Decision 2011/695 of the President of the European Commission of 13 October 2011 on the function and terms of reference of the Hearing Officer in certain competition proceedings [2011] OJ L 275/29. *Inter alia,* case 45/69, *Boehringer Mannheim v Commission,* [1970] ECR 769, para 9. For a more recent examination of these issues, *see* Wils, "The role of the Hearing Officer in competition proceedings before the European Commission", (2012) 35(3) W. Comp. 431, especially pp. 433–435.

[68] Article 8, Decision 2011/695 of the President of the European Commission of 13 October 2011 on the function and terms of reference of the Hearing Officer in certain competition proceedings [2011] OJ L 275/29; *see* also, Joaquim Almunia, "Fair process in EU competition proceedings," speech given at the European Competition Day, Budapest, 30 May 2011, SPEECH/11/396.

[69] Cases T-10-12/92 & 15/92, *Cimenteries CBR SA and others v EC Commission,* [1992] ECR II-2667 at para 47.

[70] *Id. See* also case T-90/96, *Automobiles Peugeot SA v Commission,* [1997] ECR II-663, paras 32, 34, 37; also case T-216/01, *Reisebank AG v Commission,* [2001] ECR II-3481, paras 46–47. Confirmed in T-219/01, *Commerzbank AG v Commission,* [2001] ECR II-3501, para 38–39–40; mutatis mutandis, case T-198/03 P, *Bank Austria Creditanstalt AG v Commission,* [2003] ECR II-4879, paras 31–32, 34; *see* also, more recently, case T-213/01, *OsterreicischePostsparkasse AG v Commission,* [2006] ECR II-1601, paras 142, 151.

[71] Article 23, Regulation 1/2003 (fines); Article 24, Regulation 1/2003 (periodic penalty payments).

[72] The fines have been steadily increasing, with the largest single penalty being that of €1.06 billion imposed on Intel in 2009 for having abused its dominant position.

[73] *See*, e.g., Joined Cases 100–103/80, *MDF v Commission,* [1983] ECR 1825, para 109; also case C-209/04, *Showa Denko v Commission,* [2006] ECR I-5859, para 23. *See* however Guidelines on the

ably since 2004, indicating a "clear shift towards a more aggressive fining practice."[74] The Commission can also impose conduct or structural remedies.[75] Furthermore, the Commission can initiate general inquiries into a sector of the economy, which can give rise to fines and penalties (excluding, however, remedies).[76]

Following the modernization of EU competition law enforcement with Regulation 1/2003, the previous system of notification of illegal agreements to the Commission was abandoned in favor of a legal exception regime. Regulation 1/2003 allows, however, the Commission to adopt decisions of inapplicability of Article 101 or 102[77] or to issue "guidance letters" for novel questions concerning Articles 102 and 102 TFEU[78] that arise in individual cases. Regulation 1/2003 confers on the Commission a privileged position, at least in so far as it does not formally grant NCAs the power to adopt positive decisions or publish individual guidance with regard to the enforcement of EU competition law. Where on the basis of the information in their possession the conditions for a prohibition are not met, NCAs cannot adopt a non-infringement decision but, according to Article 5 Regulation 1/2003, must simply decide that there are "no grounds for action on their part."[79]

An exception is cartel enforcement, where the Commission has recently adopted a regulation establishing a settlement procedure for cartel cases in order to enable the Commission to handle cartel cases faster and more efficiently by rewarding cooperation in the conduct of proceedings commenced in view of the application of Article 101 TFEU, by reducing the fine imposed on the undertaking by 10 percent. The parties should acknowledge their participation to a cartel violating Article 101 TFEU and thus accept liability.[80] The Commission enjoys discretion in deciding to explore the settlement procedure or to adopt a commitment decision. In principle, both commitment decisions and settlements constitute voluntary procedures which cannot be imposed on the parties. The Commission retains a broad margin of discretion to determine which cases may be suitable to explore the parties' interest to engage in them (the Commission can enter into bilateral and confidential

method of setting fines imposed pursuant to Article 23(2)(a) of Regulation No 1/2003, [2006] OJ C210/2.

[74] *See*, the statistics compiled by Schwarze and Bechtold, *Deficiencies in European Community Competition Law—Critical analysis of Current Practice and Proposals for Change*, Gleiss Lutz, September 2008, at 11–12.

[75] Article 7(1), Regulation 1/2003.

[76] Article 17, Regulation 1/2003.

[77] Article 10, Regulation 1/2003.

[78] Recital 38, Regulation 1/2003, which specifically contemplates the possibility that parties should be able to seek and obtain informal guidance from the Commission in cases giving rise to genuine uncertainty because they present novel or unresolved questions; *see* also Notice on informal guidance relating to novel questions concerning Articles 81 and 82 of the EC Treaty that arise in individual cases (guidance letters, [2004] OJ C 101/78, hereinafter "Notice on informal guidance.").

[79] *See*, Notice on informal guidance, para 41.

[80] Commission Regulation (EC) No 622/2008 of 30 June 2008 amending Regulation (EC) No 773/2004, as regards the conduct of settlement procedures in cartel cases, [2008] L 171/3; Commission Notice on the conduct of settlement procedures in view of the adoption of Decisions pursuant to Article 7 and Article 23 of Council Regulation (EC) No 1/2003 in cartel cases, [2008] C 167/1.

settlement discussions with the undertakings), or to discontinue them, or to definitively settle. Without the undertaking's consent the Commission will not transmit settlement submissions to national courts. The undertaking maintains the right to appeal against the Commission's decision before the General Court.

The Commission has also established a procedure rewarding voluntary production of evidence to trigger or advance the Commission's investigations (leniency policy), operating since 1996.[81] The leniency reduction can be cumulated to the settlement reduction, at the discretion of the Commission. According to the current Notice,[82] full immunity will be granted to the first undertaking to provide information that the Commission considers will justify a targeted inspection or will allow it to find a competition breach provided that at the time the Commission lacked sufficient evidence to take such action.[83] A reduction in the applicable fines may also be granted to those undertakings that agree to end their involvement in the cartel and to collaborate with the investigating officials and provide "significant added value" to the existing inquiries.[84]

In addition, when the investigation has uncovered reliable and relatively uncontroversial evidence of an infringement, it is open to undertakings to approach the Commission and ask, before the issuing of a statement of objections, to "settle the matter" under investigation.[85] The investigated parties are required to provide a statement in which they acknowledge liability for the breach and indicate the maximum amount of fine that they are prepared to pay.[86] The Commission can accept or reject the settlement proposal: if it accepts it, it will adopt a decision without proceeding to an oral hearing.[87] If it rejects it, the procedure will resume according to its normal course.[88]

Having regard to merger control, the EU Courts have consistently indicated that these proceedings are governed by the same due process standards as for antitrust cases.[89] Nonetheless, their structure differs from that of competition investigations in a number of ways. First of all, merger proceedings are characterized by a two pronged structure, with the more "formal" set of proceedings taking place only if "serious doubts" exist as to the compatibility of the concentration with the common market.[90] Second, the parties have a right to be heard in writing and to make observations at an oral hearing.[91] However, the "formal phase" of the

[81] Commission Notice on Immunity from fines and reduction of fines in cartel cases, [2006] OJ C-298/17.

[82] Ibid.

[83] *Id.*, para 10.

[84] *Id.*, paras 24–25.

[85] Commission Notice on the conduct of settlement procedures in view of the adoption of decisions pursuant to Articles 7 and 23 of Council Regulation No 1/2003 in cartel cases, [2008] OJ C167/01; *see* paras 2, 9.

[86] *Id.*, para 12; *see* also paras 20–21.

[87] *Id.*, paras 22, 28–29.

[88] *Id.*, para 24.

[89] Case T-221/98, *Endemol Entertainment Holding BV v Commission of the European Communities*, [1999] ECR II-1299, para 50.

[90] Council Regulation No 139/2004, *see* especially Arts 6, 8, and 10.

[91] Article 18.

procedure is not the only forum in which the parties can raise arguments and concerns relating to the Commission's case. To allow the notifying parties "ample opportunity for full and frank discussion" at all stages of the procedure[92] the 2004 Best Practice Guidelines envisage voluntary "state of play" and "triangular" meetings (the latter involving not only the parties concerned by the transaction, but also third parties having an interest in the concentration) to allow them to exchange information on the notified transaction as well as to negotiate any commitments that the parties may wish to offer to secure the approval of the transaction.[93] And finally merger proceedings are subject to tight time limits for the adoption of a final decision; that is, twenty-five working days for the conclusion of Phase I, and ninety working days for Phase II.[94]

This tight time frame may be contrasted with proceedings relating to the application of Articles 101 and 102 TFEU, which are not subject to any binding deadlines. Although the Commission is bound to deal with individual cases "within a reasonable time,"[95] no statutory time limit is fixed: in its Notice on the Handling of Complaints, the Commission states that it "will in principle endeavour to inform complainants of the action that it proposes to take on a complaint within an indicative time frame of four months from the reception of the complaint".[96] However, this is not a "binding deadline": the Commission is therefore free to take action outside this time frame if it considers it appropriate in light of the nature of the individual case.[97]

c) Judicial involvement and control of legality in the EU administrative competition law enforcement system

In *Les Verts v. European Parliament*, the Court of Justice (ECJ) emphasized that the European Community is a community based on the rule of law, inasmuch as neither its Member states nor its institutions can avoid judicial review of their actions to determine whether those actions are in conformity with the Treaty.[98] The control of legality exercised by the European judiciary of the measures adopted by the European institutions constitutes the cornerstone of this institutional framework.[99]

[92] Commission of the European Communities, DG Competition, *Best Practices on the conduct of EC merger control proceedings*, <http://ec.europa.eu/competition/mergers/legislation/proceedings.pdf>, para 29.

[93] *See*, respectively, *id.*, paras 30–34 and 38–39.

[94] Article 10, Council Regulation No 139/2004. But *see* the "stop the clock clause": Article 10(3) and (4), Council Regulation No 139/2004.

[95] *See*, e.g., case C-282/95 P, *Guérin Automobiles v Commission of the European Communities*, [1997] ECR I-1503, para 37; also Case T-58/01, *Solvay SA v Commission*, paras 100, 112–114.

[96] Commission Notice on the handling of complaints under articles 101 and 102 TFEU, [2004] OJ C101/65, paras 61–62.

[97] *Id.*, para 60.

[98] Case C-294/83, *Les Verts v. Parliament* [1986] ECR 1357, para 23.

[99] The General Court was called Court of First Instance, before the entry into force of the Treaty of Lisbon in December 2009. It was originally set up in 1989. The Court of Justice (ECJ) is assisted by Advocates General who deliver an opinion on a case prior to the judgment of the ECJ.

There are two routes to contest the legality of the acts of the EU institutions. First, Article 263 TFEU provides that the Court may review the legality of the decisions or acts of the Commission that are capable of affecting the interests of individuals. Challenges are made at first instance to the General Court[100] and appeals on points of law can be made from the General Court to the ECJ. Second, national courts can request the ECJ to make a preliminary ruling on the interpretation of EU law, where such ruling is necessary to enable that court to give judgment. Only courts or tribunals, not competition authorities, have access to this preliminary rulings procedure.[101] The interpretation of the EU law may indirectly raise the issue of the legality of the act of an EU institution under primary EU law and thus lead to an indirect control of the legality of the act.

With respect to challenging competition decisions, those to which the latter are directly addressed, together with third parties who can demonstrate "direct and individual concern" (such as, *inter alia*, competitors), can file an appeal with the General Court. The grounds of review are lack of competence, infringement of an essential procedural requirement, infringement of the Treaty or any rule of law relating to its application, and misuse of powers. The standard of review under Article 263 TFEU is a limited one: the General Court cannot "remake" the Commission's decision or inquire on the merits of it, but it can only verify whether the Commission has produced sufficiently precise and coherent proof to support its case, whether it has misinterpreted or misapplied the law, or has made a "manifest error of appraisal" in the statement of the facts or the assessment of the evidence before it, so that the latter cannot support its conclusions as to the nature—whether unlawful or otherwise—of the practice.[102]

Since its creation in 1989, the General Court has intensified the judicial control of the Commission's decisions as it is now possible to conduct a systematic examination of the factual basis of the decision of the Commission, the European Court of Justice focusing more on questions of law than questions of facts. However, the General Court does not interfere with the exercise by the Commission of economic and technical complex appraisals and limits its control to the observance of the rules of procedure, or the statement by the Commission of the reasons for its decisions, which is mostly a formal rather than a substantive investigation of the Commission's reasoning.[103] The position of the General Court varies across the judicial control exercised in applications of Articles 101(1), 101(3), 102, or merger control. In some recent cases, the review has been "rigorous" (in particular for mergers and Article 101(3)),[104] while in other recent cases the European Court of

[100] A fast-track procedure is available in certain cases. *See* codified rules of the General Court, Art. 76a.

[101] *See* the refusal by the Court to rule on a reference from the Greek competition authority, the authority being not a court or a tribunal: Case C-53/03, *Syfait v. GlaxoSmithKline* [2005] ECR I-4609.

[102] *See*, e.g., case 42/84, *Remia and others v Commission*, [1985] ECR 2545, para 26.

[103] Case T-201/04, *Microsoft v. Commission* [2007] ECR II-3601, paras 87–89. *See*, however, Case C-368/10 P *Chalkor AE Epexergasias Metallon v European Commission*, December 8, 2011, not yet officially published.

[104] *See*, Case C-12/03P, *Commission v. Tetra Laval* [2005] ECR I-987 (mergers); Case T-168/01, *GlaxoSmithKline Services v. Commission* [2006] ECR II-2969, confirmed by case C-501/06P, *Commission v. GlaxosmithKline Services Unlimited* [2009] ECR I-9291.

Justice has supported and emphasized the wide degree of discretion of the European Commission, for example, in the adoption of commitment decisions under Article 9 of Regulation 1/2003 (negotiated remedies) by applying differently the principle of proportionality in this context than for decisions adopted under Article 7 (imposed remedies).[105] Upon annulment, the case is remitted to the Commission for a fresh examination of the issues or evidence.

The judicial control of the appropriateness of the amounts of fines is more intensive, following the interplay of Article 261 TFEU and of Article 31 of Regulation 1/2003. Pursuant to these provisions, the Court of Justice is endowed with *unlimited jurisdiction* to assess the appropriateness of, and if necessary to vary, downward or upward, the amount of the fine imposed by the Commission. The Court is not able to impose a different fine but to rule on existing fines set by decisions of the Commission.[106]

In a recent wide-ranging statistical analysis of the judicial review of the Commission's decisions before the European Court of Justice and the General Court in the period 2001–2005, TRIDIMAS and GARI observe that out of 344 actions for annulment launched before the General court (then named CFI) during the period 2001–2005, ninety-eight were contested competition decisions (28.8 percent) and 57 (16.8 percent) contested state aids.[107] According to the authors, "(a)ctions lodged against competition measures are the most likely to succeed with a rate of success of 44.9 per cent," the measure of success being the total or partial annulment of the decision or the revision of the fine.[108] These findings may indicate that judicial oversight of the European Commission's decisions in competition law has an impact on competition law enforcement and does not constitute a mere formal rubber stamping exercise, despite the considerable discretion given the Commission in complex economic and technical appraisals.[109]

A specific concern is also the speed of judicial review, which is of particular importance for merger cases.[110] It was reported that the average time for proceedings under the normal procedure from lodging of the action to final judgment stood

[105] *See*, more recently case C-441/07, *Commission v. Alrosa* [2010, June 29], nyr.

[106] Case T-275/94, *Groupement des cartes bancaires "CB"/Commission* [1995] ECR II-2169, paras 59 & 60. *See*, e.g., Gerard, "EU cartel law and the shaking foundations of judicial review" (July 10, 2010). <http://ssrn.com/abstract=1675451> at 4.

[107] Tridimas and Gari, "Winners and Losers in Luxembourg: A statistical analysis of judicial review before the European court of Justice and the Court of First Instance (2001–2005)" 2010 35(2) European Law Review, 131–173, at 160.

[108] *Id.*, at 161. The rate of success of actions of annulment against state aids decisions, agriculture, the law governing institutions, and commercial policy are significantly lower.

[109] *See*, however, Geradin and Petit, "Judicial Review in European Union Competition Law: A Quantitative and Qualitative Assessment" (October 26, 2010). <http://ssrn.com/abstract=1698342>, noting the lack of effective judicial review of the decisions of the Commission in the enforcement of Article 102 TFEU, as opposed to Article 101 TFEU and merger control.

[110] Fifteenth Report of the Select Committee on European Union of the House of Lords, <http://www.publications.parliament.uk/pa/ld200607/ldselect/ldeucom/75/7502.htm>, citing (at footnote 2) the Confederation of British Industries brief added as an annex to the report which stated that: "CBI members have made it clear that if parties to a merger cannot obtain a final decision within six months they are likely to abandon the merger because the costs and uncertainty of delay become unacceptable."

at 29.5 months in 2007.[111] Following the criticism by the business community, the General Court (previously CFI) introduced in 2007 an "expedited procedure" for cases that are given priority within the Court's timetable. The Court does not have to give reasons and decisions are taken having regard to the particular urgency and the circumstances of the case. The procedure involves some degree of case management by the judge-rapporteur, who can arrange informal meetings between the parties as the case progresses,[112] the objective being to reduce the time between the lodging of action and the final judgment, although no time frame is explicitly provided. The benefit of the "expedited procedure" may be requested by the applicants or the defendant.

2. *Modernization of EU competition law and the limited role of national courts*

The previous section illustrated the manner in which NCAs and the Commission cooperate with each other in the context of the European Competition Network (ECN), a network formed by national competition authorities and the European Commission, and in that context emphasized the central role of the Commission itself as the "lead" in the setting and implementing of a "quasi-common" enforcement agenda. However, it is also clear that Regulation No 1/2003 calls for a deeper involvement of national courts in the application of the EU competition rules and to that end provides for a number of devices designed to assist domestic judges in fulfilling their functions in competition cases.

National courts are bound to apply directly effective Treaty provisions and give them precedence over conflicting national law norms. Both Articles 101 and 102 TFEU are directly effective. A litigant may enforce the competition law provisions of the Treaty by requesting the nullity of an agreement that is found to infringe these rules, or the termination of a conduct incompatible with competition rules before a national court. He may also seek some form of redress in respect of the breach of the competition law provisions of the Treaty (such as damages, restitution, or an injunction to put an immediate end to the violation and to prevent future breaches of the rules). The enforcement of EU law is dependent on the procedural, evidential, and substantive rules applicable in each Member State, subject to the principles of equivalence (national rules must not be less favorable for EU law-based claims than those relating to similar claims based on domestic law) and effectiveness (national rules must not make it virtually impossible or excessively difficult to exercise the rights that the national courts are obliged to protect).

According to Article 15 of Council Regulation No 1/2003 the Commission can appear as *amicus curiae* before domestic courts, either *proprio motu* or upon request, to provide expert opinion on matters of law or fact concerning pending cases. On

[111] Fountoukakos, "Judicial review and EC Merger Control: Reflections on the effectiveness of the system with regard to the standard of review and speed", Ch. 5 in 10 *Cambridge Yearbook of European Legal Studies* 2007–2008 (Hart Publishing, 2009), 133–66, at 153.

[112] Article 76(a) 10 of the Rules of procedure of the Court of First Instance.

this point, the 2004 Notice on Cooperation with national courts states that the Commission is likely to intervene in domestic proceedings only when necessary for the coherent application of Articles 101 and 102 TFEU and "will limit its observations to an economic and legal analysis of the facts underlying the case pending before the national court."[113] It was suggested that this approach is consistent with the necessity to reconcile the need to preserve the unity and consistency of EU competition law with more general principles of a constitutional nature, such as the right to a fair trial and the overall independence of the judiciary.[114] A similarly cautious approach was adopted by the EU legislature in respect to the existence of conflicts between Commission decisions and judgments, either adopted or contemplated, by the domestic courts. According to Article 16 of Council Regulation No 1/2003, national courts cannot adopt judgments inconsistent with Commission decisions concerning the same case, that is, the same sets of facts and the same parties. Thus, although the Regulation leaves intact the possibility of a reference to the Court of Justice, domestic judges must abide by the "Commission's precedent" so long as there is identity of subject matter between, respectively, the domestic court case and the EU administrative proceedings.[115]

By contrast, the decisions adopted by the Commission in proceedings other than those pending before national courts that present "elements of analogy" with the subject matter of previous administrative decisions constitute merely "significant information for reaching a judgment"[116] and provide only non-binding "guidance" to the domestic judge. The national court, therefore, remains free to assess their content as part of the available evidence and may depart from them when required.[117] Accordingly, it appears that the duty of "sincere cooperation" which underscores the relationship between the Commission and the national courts has been fashioned by both the EU legislature and the Commission itself in a manner that seeks to reconcile the constitutional principles of impartiality, due process, and judicial independence with the need to maintain uniformity in the application of Articles 101 and 102 TFEU.

The jurisprudence of the EU courts has also added an array of tools to the remedial toolbox of national judges, according to certain specific circumstances: for example, the European Court of Justice (ECJ) has pronounced that the full effectiveness of the EU antitrust rules would be put at risk if it were not open to

[113] Commission Notice on the cooperation between the Commission and the Courts of the EU Member States in the application of Articles 81 and 82 EC Treaty, [2004] OJ C101/4, para 32.

[114] *See*, e.g., Lenaerts and Gerard, "Decentralisation of EC competition law enforcement: judges in the frontline," (2004) 27 W. Comp. 313 at 332.

[115] *See* Article 16, Council Regulation NO 1/2003; *see* also case C-344/98, *Masterfoods Ltd v HB Ice Cream Ltd*, [2000] ECR I-11369, per AG Cosmas, para 16.

[116] Commission Notice on the cooperation between the Commission and the Courts of the EU Member States in the application of Articles 81 and 82 EC Treaty, [2004] OJ C101/4, para 8: "[W]ithout prejudice to the ultimate interpretation of the EC Treaty by the court of Justice, national courts may find guidance in Commission regulations and decisions which present elements of analogy with the case they are dealing with, as well as in Commission notices and guidelines relating to the application of Articles 81 and 82 EC (...)."

[117] *Inntrepreneur Pub Company (CPC) and others v Crehan*, [2006] UKHL 23, judgment of 19 July 2006, per Lord Hoffmann, para 52.

any individual to claim damages for harm caused by infringements of these rules.[118] Despite this possibility of private enforcement of competition law, there is very little private enforcement of EU competition law.[119] Assessing the application of Articles 101 and 102 TFEU by national courts is a daunting and frustrating task. Due to a well-functioning and systematic Europe-wide collection and publication system, the access to such case law is difficult. In accordance with Article 15(2) of Regulation 1/2003 Member States are to forward to the Commission a copy of any written judgment of national courts deciding on the application of Articles 101 and 102 of the Treaty. These judgments are then posted on the website of the Commission's Directorate-General for competition.[120] Unfortunately, as deplored by the Staff Working Paper,[121] this system of transmission of information—which should be the primary source of information—does not function effectively. The judgments posted on the Commission's website only represent a fraction of the judgments of the national courts applying Articles 101 and 102. This is because most national courts do not systematically forward these judgments to their national authority and a large number of Member States lack a collection system. At the national level, it is difficult to collect relevant case law of the courts. A second problem is that a number of the judgments which are indeed forwarded to the Commission and can be found on the website are of little relevance (for example, cases where an Article 101 TFEU argument is incidentally made in a commercial dispute, without being actually dealt with by the court). Third, the judgments are published in their national language, which creates an additional barrier.

The European Commission has been encouraging the development of private actions for damages. The Commission's 2005 Green Paper identified the main obstacles to effective enforcement and launched a public debate on various options to overcome them.[122] The Commission's 2008 White Paper made concrete suggestions in order to promote private enforcement of competition law.[123] Most recently, the Commissioner for Competition Policy, Mr Almunia, has announced the launch of a public consultation on collective redress in Europe.[124] Private actions for the enforcement of competition law are thus likely to rise in the future, thus challenging the administrative-centered nature of EU competition law enforcement.

Private enforcement of competition law is also encouraged at the national level. In the UK, it is possible for direct or indirect consumers, competitors, or parties to

[118] Joined Cases C-295/04 to C-298/04 *Manfredi* [2006] ECR I-6619. *See* also Case C-453/99 *Courage v. Crehan* [2001] ECR I-6297.

[119] *See*, for the same conclusion, European Commission, Staff Working document, Report from the Commission on Competition Policy 2009, COM(2010)282 final, para 87.

[120] <http://ec.europa.eu/competition/elojade/antitrust/nationalcourts>.

[121] At pt 291.

[122] COM(2005) 672 final, *see* <http://ec.europa.eu/competition/antitrust/actionsdamages/index.html>.

[123] COM(2008) 165 final, *see* <http://ec.europa.eu/competition/antitrust/actionsdamages/index.html>.

[124] *See*, <http://europa.eu/rapid/pressReleasesAction.do?reference=SPEECH/10/554>.

an unlawful agreement to bring an action for damages on the basis of a competition law infringement found by the OFT (follow-on actions), either under Section 47A or under Section 47B of the Competition Act (for consumer claims brought by a "specified body" appointed by the Secretary of State). Standalone actions, where the alleged breach of competition law is not already the subject of an infringement decision by the European Commission or OFT are brought to the High Court.[125] Very few standalone private actions for damages are brought, although an important number of settlements have been reported.[126]

II. Mandate

Importantly, unlike in several other jurisdictions, DG Competition lacks a specific competence in other areas, such as, for instance, consumer policy. However, in individual cases its action has touched upon other important policy areas, thus "testing the limits" of the area of applicability of Articles 101 and 102 TFEU.[127] In this specific respect, the underlying question is which ultimate goal the application of the competition rules should pursue. According to the original text of Article 3(i) of the EC Treaty, competition policy was regarded as one of the many tools designed to achieve the overarching objective of market integration, a reading that was supported by earlier case law, such as, *inter alia*, *Consten & Grundig v Commission*.[128] However, the development of the "European project," while not casting doubt on the central role of the goal of integration, has highlighted the importance of other policy objectives, such as enhancing consumer welfare and encouraging research and development. It would appear that the increasing importance of economic analysis and evidence in decision-making has actually encouraged the consideration of these non-integrationist factors, among others. For instance, in *Glaxo*[129] the General Court expressly referred to the concept of consumer welfare as relevant in the interpretation and application of Article 101 TFEU. Although the judgment was overturned on appeal, it is suggested that this statement constitutes evidence of the growing

[125] *See*, for a description, OFT Guide to Private Litigation in Competition Cases, March 2010, <http://www.oft.gov.uk/shared_oft/business_leaflets/private-litigation.pdf>.

[126] *See*, Rodger, "Competition law litigation in the UK courts: a study of all cases 2005–2008 Part I" (2009) Global Competition Litigation Review 93–114; Rodger, "Competition law litigation in the UK courts: a study of all cases 2005–2008 Part II" (2009) 3 Global Competition Litigation Review 136–47. *See*, e.g., *Emerald Supplies Lts v British Airways Plc*, [2010] EWCA Civ 1284; cf., *inter alia*, mutatis mutandis, *Duke of Bedford v Ellis*, [1900] AC 1. *See* Section 47A and 47B, Competition Act 1998; *see* also, e.g. *Consumers' Association v JJb Sports Plc*, [2009] CAT 2; *see* also, generally, Civil Justice Council, "Improving access to justice through collective actions," report to the Lord Chancellor's Office, July 2008, especially parts 2 and 4.

[127] *See*, e.g., case C-67/96, *Albany International BV v StichtingBedrijfspensioenfondsTextielindustrie* [1999] ECR I-5751.

[128] Cases 56 and 58/64, [1966] ECR 299.

[129] Case T-168/01, *GlaxoSmithKline Unlimited v Commission* [2006] ECR II-2969, para 118 (the protection of the welfare of final consumers constitutes the objective of Article 101(1) TFEU).

concern for this objective, albeit not on a par with that of strengthening the working of the internal market.[130]

The role and importance of competition law also sparked discussion during the drafting and signing of the Treaty of Lisbon in 2009: the debate was precipitated by the attempt of the president of France, Nicolas Sarkozy, to abolish any reference to competition law as an objective of the Union and eventually led to the abolition, in the Treaty of Lisbon's final version, of the old Article 3. According to the new Article 3 no reference is made to the principle of "undistorted competition." Article 3(3) provides only that the Union shall establish an internal market that shall work for "a highly competitive social market economy," aiming at full employment and social progress.

Competition law in the EU therefore remains strictly linked to the objective of the internal market. This link becomes even more explicit in Protocol No. 27 concerning "the internal market and competition," which provides that "the internal market as set out in Article 3 TEU includes a system ensuring that competition is not distorted," but does not include any reference to the concept of "social market economy." Article 3(c) TFEU states that competition policy is, as before, one of the EU's exclusive competences, which is confined to the establishment of competition rules "necessary for the functioning of the internal market."

The structure of Article 3 TFEU raises also the issue of the rank of competition law and its relation to other provisions of the Treaty, in case of conflict, or, more generally, the importance of undistorted competition as an interpretative principle for the European Courts. In terms of legal effect, pursuant to Article 51 TEU, the Protocol has clearly the same legal status as the TEU and the TFEU. The Courts thus maintain their ability to ensure the "*effet utile*" of this provision, as was previously the case with Article 3(1)g. The inclusion in Article 3(3) of the concept of "social market economy" might, however, influence the Courts when they decide on the interaction of competition law with other objectives and public policies.

This is particularly important as the Lisbon Treaty has also added broader horizontal integration provisions in Article 9 of the TFEU stating that "(i)n defining and implementing its policies and activities, the Union shall take into account requirements linked to the promotion of a high level of employment, the guarantee of adequate social protection, the fight against social exclusion, and a high level of education, training and protection of human health."[131] Such broad policy integration provisions did not exist in the previous Treaties, except in some specific areas, such as environmental protection.[132] The inclusion of these provisions will inevitably lead the Commission and arguably the Courts to grant more

[130] Joined Cases C-468/06 to 478/06, *Sot LeloskaiSia v GlaxoSmithKline* [2008] ECR I-7139, paras 56–57; Cases C-501, 513, 515, & 519/06P, *GlaxoSmithKline Services Unlimited v Commission*, [October 6, 2009], para 63.

[131] Article 9 TFEU.

[132] Article 6 TEC, now Article 11 TFEU.

importance to broader public interest concerns than the principle of "undistorted competition."

The broad mandate that the European Commission has in enforcing EU competition law in conformity with other policies and objectives pursued by the European Union is an illustration of a broader trend in Europe to adopt a more holistic perspective in defining the scope of competition law in order to include broader public policy considerations that are of relevance to the action of public authorities. There are various sectors that are exempted from the application of competition law or that benefit from a special regime, such as, *inter alia*, some aspects of the functioning of the agricultural sector and, in as much as this may have an impact on Member States' security, the trade in weapons.[133] Also, although some activities do not benefit from a blanket exemption from the scope of competition law, they might be excluded after a case-by-case analysis.

Of particular interest is the interaction between competition law and regulation in the area of regulated utilities. Following the dismantling of national legal monopolies and the liberalization of transport, telecommunications, energy, and most recently the post sector, the EU legislator has enacted a number of regulations and directives putting in place an EU framework for these regulated industries. The enactment of this sector specific discipline, designed to create competitive markets in these areas, has not however prevented the application of general competition law, thus boosting the role of the EU Commission alongside the national sector regulatory agencies.[134]

III. Due process norms in case-by-case decision-making

A. Introduction: the notion of "due process" in EU competition enforcement

Due to its limited purview, this report cannot provide a detailed account of the development of the concept of "due process" in EU law. It is acknowledged that although certain rules of procedure had been provided by EU law in certain areas, no generally applicable concept of "fair administrative procedure" had been dictated either by the Treaty or by the legislature. It is suggested that the silence of the

[133] Council Regulation 1184/2006 applying certain rules of competition to the production of, and trade in, agricultural products, [2006] OJ L 214/7, Art. 2.

[134] *See*, e.g., in the field of telecommunications, Directive 2009/140/EC of the European Parliament and of the Council of 25 November 2009 amending Directives 2002/21/EC on a common regulatory framework for electronic communications networks and services, 2002/19/EC on access to, and interconnection of, electronic communications networks and associated facilities, and 2002/20/EC on the authorization of electronic communications networks and services [2009] OJ L 337/37; Regulation (EC) No 1211/2009 of the European Parliament and of the Council of 25 November 2009 establishing the Body of European Regulators for Electronic Communications (BEREC) and the Office [2009] OJ L 337/1; *see*, e.g., Case T-271/03, *Deutsche Telekom/Commission* [2008] ECR II-477; COMP/38.784—*Telefonica SA* (broadband) 4 July 2007, <http://ec.europa.eu/competition/antitrust/cases/dec_docs/38784/38784_311_10.pdf> [appeals pending T-336/07 (*Telefonica*), T-398/07].

Founding Treaty on these matters should be seen against the more general background of the issues arising from the lack, during the first decades of the European project, of express standards of human rights protection within the EEC/EC/EU.[135] As is well known, the Court of Justice recognized that certain standards of human rights protection belonged to the general principles of Community law, largely as a response to criticism and concerns raised by a number of domestic courts.[136] Against this background, it is not surprising that the recognition of certain rules of "fair procedure" stemmed from the same work of judicial creation.[137]

The Court of Justice sought to reconcile two different legal traditions: on the one hand, the English tradition, grounded in the two principles of natural justice of *nemo judex in causa sua* and *audi alteram partem*,[138] and, on the other hand, the dominant "continental" French tradition, which instead aims at achieving goals of efficiency in the interest of the common good.[139] In addition, the Court was mindful of the need to secure the "*effet utile*" of the Treaty itself and especially the efficacy of the action of the (then) Community institutions.[140] As a result, the Court came to recognize the existence in the general principles of Community law of the rule of *audi alteram partem*, applicable to all administrative proceedings whose outcome could affect the legal position of private parties, as an expression of "good administration" and in the interest of "sound justice."[141]

In light of these principles, the Court acknowledged the existence of the right to adequate notice, prior to an opportunity to be heard in the context of administrative action.[142] Although the scope of individuals' right to be heard is flexible and

[135] Weiler, "Eurocracy and distrust: some questions concerning the role of the European Court of Justice in the protection of fundamental human rights within the legal order of the European Communities," (1986) 61 WASH. LAW REV. 1103 at 1111; Dauses, "The Protection of Fundamental Rights in the Community Legal Order," (1985) 10 ELREV 398 at 400. *See*, e.g., case 11/70, *InternationaleHandelsgesellschaft v Einfuhr und Vorratstelle fur Getreide und Futtermittel*, [1970] ECR 1125; cf. the adverse position of the German Constitutional Court, described, *inter alia*, in Crossland, "Three major decisions given by the Bunderverfassungsgericht (Federal Constitutional Court)," (1994) 19 ELREV 202, and reversed only in case 69/85, *WunscheHandelsgesellschaft*, [1986] ECR 947.

[136] *See*, e.g., case 11/70, *InternationaleHandelsgesellschaft v Einfuhr und Vorratstelle fur Getreide und Futtermittel*, [1970] ECR 1125.

[137] Schwarze, "Tendencies towards a common administrative law in Europe," (1991) 16 ELREV 3 at 5.

[138] Joshua, "The right to be heard in EEC Competition procedures," (1991–1992) 15 FORDHAM INT'L L. J. 16 at 21.

[139] Schwarze, "Tendencies towards a common administrative law in Europe," (1991) 16 ELREV 3 at 6. For commentary on the concept of "procedural due process" in the Common law and especially in the North-American legal tradition *see* generally MacDonald, "Judicial review and procedural fairness in administrative law," (1979–80) 25 McGILL L J 520, (1980) 26 McGILL L J 1.

[140] *Id. See* also Andreangeli, *EU Competition Enforcement and Human Rights* (E. Elgar Publishing Ltd, 2008), 37 et seq.

[141] *See*, e.g., case 32/62, *Alvis v Council*, [1963] ECR 49, 55; also Case 17/74, *Transocean Marine Paint Association v Commission*, [1974] ECR 1063, para 15 of the judgment and per AG Warner; case C-135/92, *Fiskano v Commission of the European Communities*, [1994] ECR I-2885, para 39.

[142] *Inter alia, Franklin v Minister of Town and Country Planning*, House of Lords, [1948] AC 87.

must be determined in relation to the context in which it must be exercised,[143] at a minimum it must confer a right to know the case against them, to be acquainted with the relevant evidence, and to be given an opportunity to refute it.[144] Seen in this light, the right to be heard in EU law emerges as an "*absolute* or *objective standard of good administration*"[145] which serves a twofold purpose: "it contributes to the accuracy of the *substantive* outcome of the decision-making"[146] and at the same time "it constitutes a *process* right designed to protect individual substantive rights and interests,"[147] thus conferring on the EU agencies administrative functions legitimacy vis-à-vis affected parties.

However, it should be emphasized that the concept of "due process" does not appear as such in the Treaties or indeed in the case law of the EU Courts[148] which, instead, refers to the more descriptive concept of "rights of defence," probably in translation from the French term of "*droits de la défense.*" It should also be noted that over time the Courts have repeatedly recognized the importance of the rule of law as a founding principle of the EU legal system. In the already cited *Les Verts* case, it was held that, as a result of the application of that principle, neither the Member states nor the European institutions can avoid judicial scrutiny of their actions in light of the Treaty.[149] Their actions should therefore find a basis in law and the latter should conform to principles of clarity, accessibility and foreseeability;[150] in addition, any expression of public power should be proportionate and

[143] *Alfred ThangarajahDurayappah of Chundikuly, Mayor of Jaffna v. W.J. Fernando and Others*, Privy Council, [1967] 2 AC 337, per Lord Upjohn at 349.

[144] *Kanda v Government of Malaya*, House of Lords, [1962] AC 322, per Lord Denning at 337.

[145] NEHL, *Principles of Administrative Procedure in EC Law* (1999, Hart Publishing), 96 (emphasis in the original text).

[146] *Id.*, 97.

[147] *Id.* For the consequences of a violation of the "due process" rules *see*, *inter alia*, joined cases 209–215 and 218/78, *Heintz van Landewyck v Commission*, [1980] ECR 3125.

[148] Case 27/76, *United Brands Company and United Brands Continentaal BV v Commission* [1978] 207, para 269. In the French text of the Court's judgment, "due process" is referred to as "droits de la défense." *See* also Joined cases 60 and 190/81 R, Order of the President of the Court of 7 July 1981, *International Business Machines Corporation v Commission*, [1981] ECR 1857, para 5; Case C-142/87, *Kingdom of Belgium v Commission*, [1990] ECR I-959, para 45; Case T-352/94, *Mo OchDomsjö AB v Commission* [1998] ECR II- II-1989, para 381; Case T-198/01, *TechnischeGlaswerkeIlmenau GmbH v Commission* [2004] II-2717, para 194; Case C-289/04, *Showa Denko KK v Commission*, [2007] ECR I-5859, paras 64–78 (the expression "due process" employed in order to describe a cluster of rights); Case T-43/02, *Jungbunzlauer AG v Commission*, [2006] ECR II-3435; Case C-426/05, Opinion of Mr Advocate General Poiares Maduro, [2008] ECR I-685, para 42; *see* also, Commission Notice on Case Referral in respect of concentrations [2005] OJ C 56/2, especially para 58; also, mutatis mutandis, Directive 2009/140/EC of the European Parliament and of the Council of 25 November 2009 amending Directives 2002/21/EC on a common regulatory framework for electronic communications networks and services, [2009] OJ L 337/37.

[149] Case C-294/83, *Les Verts v. Parliament* [1986] ECR 1357, para 23.

[150] On the principle of the "Rule of law" in the European legal system *see* Pech, "The Rule of Law as a Constitutional Principle of the European Union" (April 28, 2009), *Jean Monnet Working Paper Series* No. 4/2009 <http://ssrn.com/abstract=1463242>. On the elusive nature of the expression "rule of law" *see* Tamanaha, *On the Rule of Law. History, Politics, Theory* (2004, Cambridge University Press); Fallon, "The rule of law as a concept in constitutional discourse," (1997) 91(1) COLUM L REV 1. *See* also, within the European context, Emberland, *The human rights of companies* (2004, Oxford University Press), 45.

not arbitrary and seek the attainment of the goal of the public interest for which that power was envisaged.[151]

In this specific context, it is clear that although not all of the components of the rule of law are directly enforceable before the Courts,[152] this "cluster" of values is strictly dependent on the presence of an independent judiciary and provides strong justification for the existence of a number of "procedural," fully enforceable rights, such as the right of access to an independent and impartial court, the right to "due process" and to a "fair trial," all of which aim at constraining the exercise of public powers within precise confines.[153] The emergence of a notion of due process in EU law could therefore be regarded as a means through which to provide analytical coherence to a set of rights progressively recognized by the European courts, which include, among others, the right to be heard, to have access to the evidence concerning allegations made against individuals or firms, to obtain a decision within a reasonable time, and to challenge it before a court of law.[154]

The principle of proportionality has also been consistently regarded as forming part of the general principles of EU law by the Court of Justice,[155] which has relied on it in reviewing a number of Union measures, especially in the area of economic regulation; the principle is now expressly recognized in Article 3 TFEU.[156] In the light of the above it is suggested that the cluster of principles enshrined in the rule of law encompasses in the European legal tradition both formal and substantive elements: among the former are found the principle of legality of action of the public authorities as well as a set of justiciable "due process" rights, centered on the idea of "fairness" of the action of public authorities. The latter point to the principles of "purposefulness," necessity, and proportionality, thus contributing to ensure that individual measures are not "arbitrary" or "capricious."

The importance of the due process principles in the EU legal order is now established as part of the EU acquis as well as of the rights enshrined in the EU Charter of Fundamental Rights. According to Article 41 of the Charter, every person enjoys a "right to good administration," namely the right "to have his or her affairs handled impartially, fairly and within a reasonable time by the institutions and bodies of the Union." As a result, she is entitled to be heard, to have access to the case made against her, and to the supporting evidence and the corresponding

[151] *See* Emberland, op. cit., 157, 160–1.

[152] *See*, e.g., Waldron, "The concept and the rule of law," (2008) 43(1) GA. L. REV 1 at 6 et seq.

[153] Emberland, op. cit., 44; also Neuman, "The US Constitutional conception of the rule of law and the Rechstaatsprinzip of the Grundgesetz," *Columbia Law School, Public Law and Legal Theory Working Paper Group*, Paper No 5, 1999, 2–4.

[154] Emberland, op. cit., 44; also Neuman, "The US Constitutional conception of the rule of law and the Rechstaatsprinzip of the Grundgesetz," *Columbia Law School, Public Law and Legal Theory Working Paper Group*, Paper No 5, 1999, 2–4.

[155] *See*, e.g., case 11/70, *Internationale Handelsgesellschaft*, [1970] ECR 1125, para 2 and 16. For a discussion, De Burca, "The principle of proportionality and its application in EC law," (1993) 13 *Yearbook of European Law* 105–50; Tridimas, *The General Principles of EU Law* (2006, OUP); Hartley, *The Foundations of European Union Law* (7th edn, 2010, OUP), 164–5.

[156] *See*, e.g., case C-343/09, *Afton Chemical Ltd v Secretary of State for Transport*, judgment of 8 July 2010, para 45.

obligation on the part of the competent institution to give reasons for its decisions. Also, Article 47 of the Charter now enshrines an express right to an effective remedy against decisions affecting the legal position of an individual and to a fair trial.[157]

These principles are therefore uniformly applicable to all administrative action, including in areas covered by legislation, such as competition enforcement. In the *Transocean Marine Paint* judgment[158] the Court of Justice took the view that even when the applicable legislation did not expressly require it, "a person whose interests are perceptibly affected by a decision taken by a public authority must be given the opportunity to make his point of view known"[159] before the adoption of that decision, to acquaint herself with the allegations made against them,[160] and to obtain a reasoned decision which can be challenged before the EU Courts.[161]

It can be concluded that the notion of due process is now consolidated in the EU legal system as an overarching cluster of rights, applicable across the spectrum of the action of the Union institutions. At the same time, it is clear that this principle applies in different ways and has a different intensity depending on the nature of the agencies' power in specific policy areas and on the importance of the goals being pursued. The next sections will discuss the extent to which this principle applies to competition enforcement and the features and attributes that the individual rights, identified above, assume in that context.

B. Due process and EU competition law enforcement design: criticism of the status quo

It was anticipated in the previous sections that the choice of institutional design made at EU level for the European Commission was that of an integrated agency, whose decisions were open to challenge before the EU Courts. It was also noted that according to the current Implementing Regulation 1/2003 the Commission enjoys very extensive investigative powers as well as the power to impose substantial financial penalties. This section will consider criticism and defense of process in enforcement proceedings, that is, both the "preliminary" phase of the case handling and its more "formal" stage, leading to the adoption of the final decision as to the existence or otherwise of the infringement.

As we begin, we note three points. First, much of the criticism has been raised by litigants in the system, although also by others, and much of the criticism is based on comparison with and a preference for an adversarial over an administrative and

157 For commentary, *see* Lord Millett, "The right to good administration in European Law," (2002) Public Law 309.

158 Case 17/74, *Transocean Marine Paint Association v Commission*, [1974] ECR 1063.

159 *Id.*, para 15 of the judgment.

160 Case T-30/91, *Solvay SA v Commission*, [1995] ECR II-1175, para 59; also joined cases 100–103/80, *SA Musique Diffusion Francaise and Others v Commission*, [1983] ECR 1825, at para 29; case T-5/02, *Tetra Laval BV v Commission*, [2002] ECR II-4381, para 89.

161 *See*, e.g., case T-22/97, *KeskoOy v EC Commission*, [1999] ECR II-3775 at para 57; joined cases T-374, 375, 384, 388/94, *European Night Services and others v Commission,* [1998] ECR II-3141 at para 61; also, case 222/84, *Johnston v Chief Constable of the Royal Ulster Constabulary*, [1986] ECR 1651 at paras 18–19.

inquisitorial system. Second, the Competition Directorate and the Commission have listened to the critiques and have responded to them, introducing various reforms into the EU system, as we note below. Third, litigants in the EU and similar systems have challenged administrative/inquisitorial procedures and combinations of prosecutorial and judicial functions as systemically not conforming to the requirements of fundamental rights. These challenges have been made in the European Court of Justice and in the European Court of Human Rights and thus far have not succeeded. Rather, the courts have thus far been satisfied with greater intensity of court review.

The passage that follows first puts forward the critical arguments, many of which were made before the more recent reforms. Following that, we put forward the counter arguments in defense of the system.

The arguments by the critics: the Commission acts as "police, prosecutor, and judge" in individual cases. It is argued that this conflation does not respect basic standards of "fairness," and that such standards of fairness should bind not just judicial but also administrative authorities whose action is capable of directly affecting the rights and obligations of individuals or firms.[162] It was argued that adoption of a decision by the full college of Commissioners after a procedure managed by the DG Competition officials is not compatible with the requirements of a "fair and public hearing" and that decision-making is not fair when the decision-maker is the same body that heard the evidence against the investigated parties.[163] Critics noted that the level of fines for violation of EU competition law has increased considerably ("threefold and more") over the two decades in view of the Commission's increasing quest for deterrence,[164] and it is urged that these very high fines constitute penalties of a "criminal nature"[165] and thus should lead to the

[162] *See*, Montag, "The Case for a Radical Reform of the Infringement Procedure under Regulation 17", (1996) 8 ECLR 428; Hofmann, "Good governance in European merger control: due process and checks and balances under review", (2003) 24(3) ECLR 114–131; Schwarze and Bechtold, "Deficiencies in European Community Competition Law—Critical analysis of current practice and proposals for change" (Gleiss Lutz, September 2008); ICC (International Chamber of Commerce) Commission on Competition, "Due process in EU antitrust proceedings" Policy statement, March 8, 2010; American Chamber of Commerce, "Explaining AMCham EU's position on Due Process in EU Competition Cases", Information paper, March 3, 2010; Forrester, "Due process in EC competition cases: a distinguished institution with flawed procedures", (2009) 34(6) ELRev. 817–43; Slater, Thomas, and Waelbroeck, "Competition Law Proceedings before the European Commission and the right to a fair trial: no need for reform?," Global Competition Law Centre Working Paper 04/08; Andreangeli et al., "Enforcement by the Commission—the decisional and enforcement structure in antitrust cases and the Commission's fining system," in Merola and Waelbroeck (eds), *Towards an optimal enforcement of competition rules in Europe*, Chapter 3 (2010, Bruylant).

[163] ICC, "Due process in EU antitrust proceedings", op. cit., at 1. For the criticism levelled in the past, e.g. in respect to the proposal for a European cartel office, *see* Resolution on the 10th Report of the Commission of the European Communities on Competition Policy [1982] OJ C 11/78. For a critical analysis, *see* Wilks and McGowan, "Disarming the Commission: the Debate over a European Cartel Office", (1995) 32(2) Journal of Common Market Studies 259–73; Van Miert, "The Proposal for a European competition agency", (1996) 2 EC Competition Policy Newsletter, <http://ec.europa.eu/competition/speeches/text/sp1996_023_en.html>; also Ehlermann, "Reflections on a European Cartel Office", (1995) 32 CMLRev 471–86.

[164] Schwarze and Bechtold, op. cit., at 5 and figures at 11–12.

[165] *See*, e.g., series A No 43, *LeCompte, Van Leuven and de Meyere v Belgium*, [1982] 4 EHRR 1, paras 45–47.

elevation of standards of due process to the rigorous standards of a criminal procedure.[166]

Those who view the high-fine cases as akin to criminal cases also make a point of the fact that the Commissioners are not judges, the Commission does not constitute a tribunal, there is no right to cross-examine witnesses, and there is no opportunity to be heard on the amount of the fine.[167] Although an oral hearing may take place before a Hearing Officer, this is not mandatory (being merely an option for defendants) and not conducive to a proper trial.[168] The Hearing Officer settles procedural disputes between the parties. Although the powers and responsibilities of this office have increased to include supervision of the disclosure of documents and access to the file, the Hearing Officer "remains, controversially, a Commission employee and member of the Directorate General for Competition."[169] For example, she has no power to halt proceedings if the Commission's procedure has been inadequate or unfair. Nevertheless, the Hearing Officer writes a report after the event and can express her views.

Further complaints have been directed towards the fines.[170] Litigants claim that they desire more legal certainty, and note that the fining guidelines are only soft law and that they are less precise than the US Sentencing Guidelines, which impose, however, only criminal sanctions.[171]

The Commission decision is of course subject to the judicial scrutiny of the EU courts, but critics argue that the right of appeal is not sufficient to meet the requirements of a "fair hearing." The Court has limited power of review, especially in respect to the complex economic evaluations carried out by the Commission. For cases that are akin to criminal, full judicial appraisal, extending to all matters of fact and of law, may be required.[172] Other critics noted that, contrary to other adminis-

[166] *See*, Forrester, op. cit., at 825; ICC, op. cit., at 2–3.

[167] *See*, e.g., Merola and Waelbroeck (eds), *Towards an optimal enforcement of competition rules in Europe* (2010, Bruylant), 199 et seq.

[168] It has been noted that oral hearings are requested in around 75 percent of all cases for which a statement of objections ("SO") has been issued, this figure being 90 percent for cartel cases: *see*, Albers and Williams, "Oral Hearing - Neither a Trial Nor a State of Play Meeting", (2010) 3(1) The Antitrust Chronicle, accessible at <https://www.competitionpolicyinternational.com/oral-hearings-neither-a-trial-nor-a-state-of-play-meeting/>.

[169] House of Lords Select Committee on the European Union, *XIXth Report*, session 1999–2000, 21/11/2000, para 2.

[170] *See*, ICC, op. cit., at 5–7, noting that (i) the level of the review of the General Court (GC) does not meet ECHR standards, in particular as the GC does not have the power to quash in all respects, on questions of fact and law, the decision of the European Commission, (ii) the GC does not use its unlimited jurisdiction on fines but only on rare occasions (the Report cites three), and (iii) appeals before the GC have no suspensory effect in general. For a different view, *see*, most recently, Wils, cit. (fn. 66), pp. 443–445.

[171] Schwarze and Bechtold, op. cit., at 16–17 and 26–7.

[172] *See* Appl. Nos 7299/75 and 7496/76, *Albert & LeCompte v Belgium*, [1983] 5 EHRR 533, para 29; also, *inter alia*, Appl. No 19178/91, *Bryan v United Kingdom*, [1996] 21 EHRR 342, para 46 of the judgment; *see* also Commission Opinion, separate concurring Opinion of Mr N. Bratza, 354. For commentary, *see*, e.g., Boyle, "Administrative justice, judicial review and the right to a fair hearing under the European Convention on Human Rights," (1984) PL 89 at 100; also Andreangeli, *EU Competition enforcement and human rights* (2008, Cheltenham, E Elgar). Cf. Merola and Waelbroeck (eds), Comments to Chapter 3, in *Toward an optimal enforcement of the competition rules in Europe* (2010, Bruylant), 467 at 474–5.

trative law systems (for example, Germany), the legal effects of the contested Commission's decision are not suspended, as it is the case in Germany during the so-called "administrative self-regulation" procedure (a mandatory review step taking place before an aggrieved party files a court action), and that filing an action for annulment does not have any suspensory effect; that is, an aggrieved party can only request the suspension of the Commission's decision after filing an action for annulment and only after satisfying prima facie on both factual and legal grounds the General Court that the suspension of the decision is necessary in order to avoid serious and irreparable damage, following a balance of interests.[173] Fines are thus payable upon the publication of the Commission's decision.

In defense of the system, the criticisms addressed to the primary role played by the European Commission in the EU competition law process take a very narrow perspective on the optimal institutional structure for competition law enforcement. The EU system is an administrative and inquisitorial system, one of the well-tried and accepted institutional systems of competition law enforcement in the world and perhaps even more common than the adversarial system. It is a system of administrative adjudication, where the investigation is done by a specialized authority, the European Commission, not with the aim to prosecute but to discover the truth about the existence, or not, of a possible infringement. Hence, the Commission not only investigates inculpatory elements for the undertaking concerned, but also exculpatory ones.[174] The system also enables a specialized public authority to adopt a holistic perspective, combining competition law enforcement and competition advocacy, and to ensure consistency in the enforcement of EU competition law in various economic sectors. The absence of a court trial-focused adversarial process can thus be understood by the emphasis given to the specialized expertise of DG Comp at the European Commission and on the importance of documentary, as opposed to oral, evidence. The expertise and experience of the public competition authority is thus essential for the elucidation of the complex economic and technical facts involved in competition cases. This combination of legal, economic, and technical expertise is unmatched: a generalist court can only provide it with difficulty by recourse to expensive outside experts, thus raising the cost of competition law enforcement.[175] The proponents of the system point to the multitudes of safeguards built into it, through the multifarious vetting of the facts; the overall role of the coordination unit providing case support during the proceedings; the existence of devil's advocate panels set up in complex cases in order to provide a fresh pair of eyes; the input of the legal service and the chief economist's team; the consultation of the Advisory Committee composed by national experts; cross-examination by the Director General, or the possibility for a Deputy-Director General to attend the oral hearings; the fact that the decision is made by the College

[173] Macgregor & Gecic, "Due process in EU Competition Cases Following the Introduction of the New Best Practices Guidelines on Antitrust Proceedings", forthcoming (2012) Journal of European Competition Law & Practice, 1–44.

[174] *See*, e.g., Paulis, cit. (fn. 47), 382–383.

[175] Ibid. 387.

of Commissioners, etc. These safeguards are constantly increasing. A combination of functions may be justified by efficiency and effective enforcement reasons. Even with the combination of functions, rights of defense can be protected: undertakings subject to competition law proceedings benefit from the right not to self-incriminate, the right to be heard, once the investigation phase is completed, the right to have access to the Commission's investigation file in order to prepare their written and oral defense, the right to a formal Oral hearing, chaired by the independent hearing officer, and the right to appeal the decision of the Commission to a specialized European Court (the general Court). The critics like to confine their arguments to the large fine cases, because that is where they can call the action akin to criminal, but so far the European Court of Human Rights (ECtHR) has not challenged the legality, from the point of view of the protection of human rights, of the EU system. In its recent case law, the ECtHR has confirmed, apropos of the Italian Competition authority, another integrated agency subject to a two-tier judicial control; that an administrative system where the integrated agency imposes sanctions, subject to full review by an independent court, complies with the provisions of the ECHR.[176]

It has been noted that although fines have increased in aggregate, some recent studies on the European Commission's cartel fines found that these were considerably less than provided for in the 2006 Guidelines and that the average fine per firm has declined significantly since 2007.[177] Concerning the alleged "criminal nature" of the fines, this is explicitly excluded by Article 23(5) of Regulation 1/2003.[178] On this point, it was argued that the European Court of Human Rights, which developed the "substantive approach" to the determination of the nature—criminal or civil—of penalties, drew a distinction between "criminal offences" that belong to the "hard core of criminal law" and those infringements which do not meet the same degree of gravity and therefore lie outside that "core."[179] Thus, it was suggested that in cases concerning infringements of the latter kind the safeguards enshrined in Article 6 of the Convention and expressly applicable to "criminal" cases should not apply with the same stringency as in proceedings affecting natural persons accused of "hard core" criminal offences.[180]

This view was also considered compatible with the "relative" nature of the concept of "fair trial" contained in the ECHR, as a result of which, while no-one can be denied this basic safeguard in its essence, its elements can vary in light of

[176] Judgment of the ECtHR, September 27, 2011, *A. Meranini Diagnostics S.R.L. v. Italy*, Appl. No. 43509/08.

[177] *See*, Veljanovski, "European Cartel Fines Under the 2006 Penalty Guidelines—A Statistical Analysis" (December 10, 2010). <http://ssrn.com/abstract=1723843>.

[178] However, this article does not constitute a limit to the Commission's power to impose fines. *See* Schwarze and Bechtold, op. cit., at 23.

[179] *See*, e.g., Appl. No. 73053/01, *Jussila v Finland*, judgment of 23 November 2003, <http://cmiskp.echr.coe.int/tkp197/view.asp?item=1&portal=hbkm&action=html&highlight=JUSSILA&-sessionid=70158786&skin=hudoc-en>, *see* especially paras 35–37 and 43–44. For commentary *see*, e.g., Wils, "EU antitrust enforcement powers and procedural rights and guarantees: the interplay between EU law, national law, the Charter of Fundamental Rights of the EU and the European Convention on Human Rights," (2011) 34(2) World Competition, 189–213.

[180] Ibid.

the circumstances of individual cases, such as, *inter alia*, the intensity of the investigative powers exercised by the authorities and the nature of the consequences attached to each offence.[181] It was also emphasized that the Human Rights Court itself read the ECHR as expressly allowing for the adoption of non-judicial decisions by a public authority imposing penalties for deterring and punishing infringements of laws enacted in the public interest and having general application by non-judicial authorities, which fell outside the "core of criminal law" discussed above. According to the Strasbourg Court, providing that their decision was open to the scrutiny of a full court of law in respect to all matters of fact and law,[182] administrative bodies could pursue and punish those responsible of these "penal" infringements.[183] As a result, it is argued that the existence of the jurisdiction of the General Court to review the Commission's decisions could make the EU system fully compatible with Article 6.[184]

Thus, with regard to the administrative stage of competition cases, it is undeniable that EU competition law procedures have undergone significant evolution aimed at safeguarding the principle of due process. The existence and the function of the Hearing Officer aims to ensure that the case is heard with full respect for the parties' rights of defense and that all the evidence gathered by the Commission either in favor or against the investigated parties is properly disclosed and assessed. The Hearing Officer's report, coupled with her power to chair the oral hearing and, more generally, with her duties of independence and impartiality, have been regarded as a key check on the case-handling officers' powers of investigation. Furthermore, this "guarantee" function is likely to be strengthened by the recent revisions to the Hearing Officer's mandate.[185] Although previously the Hearing Officer could intervene only after the adoption of the statement of objections, his role has now been extended to the entirety of the Commission's proceedings, the investigative phase, and for any type of decisions, including commitment decisions. The Hearing Officer is now allowed to resolve legal professional privilege issues and has been given a new role with regard to disputes about extensions of the deadline to reply to decisions requiring information in antitrust investigations.

[181] *See*, *inter alia*, mutatis mutandis, Appl. No. 39665/98 and 40086/98, *Ezehand Connors v UK*, judgment of 9 October 2003, <http://cmiskp.echr.coe.int/tkp197/view.asp?item=1&portal=hbkm&action=html&highlight=EZEH&sessionid=70158786&skin=hudoc-en>, *see* especially para 83.

[182] Wils, "The Increased Level of EU Antitrust Fines, Judicial Review and the European Convention on Human Rights", (2010) 33(1) World Competition 1 at 21–2; also, Merola and Waelbroeck (eds), cit. (fn. 179) at 476–80.

[183] *See*, e.g., Appl. Nos 7299/75 and 7496/76, *Albert & LeCompte v Belgium*, [1983] 5 EHRR 533, para 29; also more recently, Appl. Nos 15809/02 and 25624/02, *O'Halloran and Francis v UK*, judgment of 29 June 2007, available in [2008] 46 EHRR 21, especially paras 56–57.

[184] House of Lords Select Committee on the European Union, *XIXth Report*, session 1999–2000, 21/11/2000, para 56. Cf. evidence given by Sir Christopher Bellamy, ibid. para 56 in respect to decisions not imposing penalties, e.g. decisions imposing commitments. *See* also, Judgment of the ECtHR, September 27, 2011, *A. Menarini Diagnostics S.R.L. v. Italy*, Appl. No. 43509/08.

[185] Decision 2011/695 of the President of the European Commission of 13 October 2011 on the function and terms of reference of the Hearing Officer in certain competition proceedings [2011] OJ L 275/29. Joaquim Almunia, "Fair process in EU competition proceedings," speech given at the European Competition Day, Budapest, 30 May 2011, SPEECH/11/396.

The Commission has adopted extensive Best Practices Guidelines and has recently published online, following the admonition of the European Ombudsman, a summarized version of its internal manual on antitrust procedure (ManProc) containing detailed guidance to Commission's officials on how to conduct antitrust proceedings.[186] The new Best Practices Notice clearly divides the Commission's procedure into two broad phases: the investigative phase, and should the Commission decide to issue a Statement of Objections ("SO"), a second phase of the procedure leading to a prohibition decision, during which an Oral Hearing may be organized. The investigative phase is also divided into two stages: the initial assessment and case allocation and the opening of the proceedings. State of Play meetings, which are not conducive to a formal Oral Hearing but a voluntary opportunity for communication between the DG Comp staff and the parties subject to the proceedings, are now offered at several key stages of the proceedings, also in the context of the investigation phase, shortly after the opening of proceedings. This is also now possible for cartel cases (it was only possible for dominance cases in the past), but only after the oral hearing stage. Besides these internal mechanisms, some authors have also suggested that the very fact that the final decisions are adopted by the College of Commissioners upon consultation with the Advisory Committee (a committee bringing together competition experts from the Member States) strengthens the transparency and fairness standards governing competition enforcement proceedings.[187] It is suggested that the involvement of all the Commissioners in the final adoption of the decision, together with their ability to participate in the hearing and to be consulted, in the person of their Directorates' officials, throughout the proceedings, constitutes a positive check on the case-handling officers' discretion.[188]

Perhaps stronger arguments in favor of the current system were developed in light of the features of the judicial scrutiny mechanisms established by the EU Treaties. It was argued that since its establishment the General Court has acted as a scrupulous judge of the legality of competition decisions: despite not being empowered to "remake" the impugned measures, by substituting its own assessment of the facts and evidence for that of the Commission, the Court has closely monitored its decisions.[189] Although it is acknowledged that its review powers are limited to a "manifest error" type of review, it is emphasized that the Court has held the Commission to a high standard in respect to the statement and the appraisal of the facts, the sufficiency and soundness of the evidence, and to the quality of its reasoning.[190] In its most recent case law, the Court of Justice prescribed rigorous

186 Commission notice on best practices for the conduct of proceedings concerning Articles 101 and 102, OJ [2011] C 308 /6; Best Practices for the submission of economic evidence [2011], available at <http://ec.europa.eu/competition/antitrust/legislation/legislation.html>. For the ManProc *see*, Antitrust Manual of Procedures, March 2012, <http://ec.europa.eu/competition/antitrust/information_en.html>.

187 *See*, e.g., Paulis, cit. (fn. 47), 390–1.

188 *Id.*, 391; *see* also 398.

189 *See*, e.g., case 42/84, *Remia v Commission*, [1985] ECR 2545, para 34; for commentary, *see* Paulis, cit. (fn. 47), 388–90; also Wils, cit. (fn. 182), 8.

190 *See*, e.g., Paulis, cit. (fn. 47), 389.

standards of judicial review for the decisions of the Commission by the General Court and established its full jurisdiction to review decisions in which the Commission imposes fines. In particular, the Court held that "the Courts cannot use the Commission's margin of discretion—either as regards the choice of factors taken into account in the application of the criteria mentioned in the Guidelines (of the Commission) or as regards the assessment of those factors—as a basis for dispensing with the conduct of an in-depth review of the law and of the facts".[191] To this stage of judicial scrutiny, one should also add the increasing involvement of the ECtHR in various competition law matters, such as searches and seizures, for the time being in the context of the enforcement of the national competition statutes of the EU Member States, but, once the Union adheres to the ECHR, certainly also in the context of EU competition law enforcement.[192]

Having outlined some of the most frequent criticisms made against the existing EU competition enforcement structure, but also its defense, the remainder of this study will discuss the question of whether these concerns are warranted and suggest, where appropriate, options for improvement. This concern will be considered in relation to specific issues, that is, the right to remain silent, the confidentiality of lawyer–client communications, and the extent to which the Commission's power to devise antitrust remedies responds to principles of proportionality.

C. Due process issues I: the preliminary investigations

The Commission enjoys significant fact-finding powers in competition cases. It can ask the investigated undertakings for information, to inspect their premises, land and means of transport, as well as, in certain cases, the homes of their staff members and to ask "on the spot" explanations as to specific documents. Importantly, the parties concerned are obliged to submit to the exercise of these investigative powers if the Commission officials are acting upon a formal decision, on pain of the imposition of financial penalties.[193] Against this background, the situation may be envisaged of case-handling officials seeking to obtain potentially incriminating information or to access documents detailing advice obtained by a legal advisor. On this point, the EU Courts acknowledge that the investigative powers of the Commission, necessary though they may be to protect genuine competition in the internal market and thereby protect the interests of firms and of consumers, are

[191] *See*, Case C-368/10 *P Chalkor AE Epexergasias Metallon v European Commission*, December 8, 2011, not yet officially published, para 62. *See* also, Case C-389/10 P *KME Germany AG, KME France SAS and KME Italy SpA v. European Commission*, December 8, 2011, not yet officially published; Case C-272/09 P *KME Germany AG, KME France SAS and KME Italy SpA v. European Commission*, December 8, 2011, not yet officially published.

[192] *See*, e.g., Judgment of the ECtHR, December 21, 2010, *Gaz de Pétrole Primagaz v. France*, Appl. No. 29613/08; Judgment of the ECtHR, December 21, 2010, *Groupe Canal Plus and Sport Plus v. France*, Appl. No. 29408/08. *See*, Vogel, "When the European Court of Human Rights mingles with competition law: national search and seizures found unacceptable for lack of effective judicial review", (2011) 2(3) Journal of Competition Law & Practice 229.

[193] *See* Articles 17–21, Council Regulation No 1/2003; *see*, also, e.g., case 136/79, *National Panasonic (UK) v Commission*, [1980] ECR 2033, especially paras 11–13.

not unlimited but must be subject to constraints aimed at protecting the integrity of the investigated parties' rights of defense from being irremediably impaired even at the preliminary stage of the investigation.[194]

As a result, the Court of Justice has held that investigated undertakings could claim a limited right not to incriminate themselves during the preliminary stages of a case. This right is not however absolute but must be reconciled with the duty, imposed on the investigated parties, to cooperate with the Commission in the investigations and thereby to avoid jeopardizing the effectiveness of the Commission's functions.[195] It was held, therefore, that the Commission could "compel an undertaking to provide all necessary information concerning such facts as may be known to it and to disclose to it, if necessary, such documents (. . .) even if the latter may be used to establish, against it (. . .), the existence of anti-competitive conduct."[196]

However, the Court expressly denied that the Commission could coerce the undertaking into "providing it with answers which might involve an admission (. . .) of the existence of an infringement which it is incumbent upon the Commission to prove."[197] To claim the applicability of the privilege, the applicant would have to demonstrate "first, the exercise of coercion against the suspect in order to obtain information from him and second establishment of the existence of an actual interference" with the rights of the defense.[198] Thus, the privilege would only be available in respect to prima facie self-incriminating information requested by way of a formal decision or in the context of an inspection ordered pursuant to Article 20(4) of Regulation No 1/2003.[199] The applicant would also have to establish that the validity of the final decision was affected by him or her responding to a potentially self-incriminating question asked under coercion.[200]

Furthermore, in the *A.M. & S.* case the Court of Justice took the view that investigated undertakings could rely on a limited degree of protection of the confidentiality of their communications with a lawyer, subject to strict conditions[201] inspired by the need to reconcile the differing principles and concepts relating to the protection of the privilege in individual Member States. Therefore, lawyer–client communications "exchanged after the initiation of the administrative procedure under Regulation no 17,"[202] including "earlier written communications which have a relationship to the subject-matter of that procedure,"[203] would be privileged provided that they "are made for the purposes and in the interests of the

[194] *See*, e.g., case 374/87, *Orkem v Commission*, [1989] ECR 3283, para 33; also, mutatis mutandis, case T-30/91, *Solvay SA v Commission*, [1995] ECR II-1775, para 83.

[195] Case 374/87, *Orkem v Commission*, [1989] ECR 3283, para 27. Also, case T-112/98, *Mannesmannrohren Werke v Commission*, [2001] ECR II-729, para 66.

[196] Case 374/87, *Orkem v Commission*, [1989] ECR 3283, para 34.

[197] *Id.*, para 35.

[198] Case C-238/99, *LVM NV and others v Commission*, [2002] ECR I-8375, para 275.

[199] *Id.*; *see* also para 279.

[200] *Id.*; *see* also para 282. Also *see* case 301/04, *Commission v SGL Carbon AG*, [2006] ECR I-5915, paras 40–43.

[201] Case 155/79, *AM & S Europe Limited v Commission of the European Communities*, [1982] ECR 1575, para 18.

[202] *Id.*, para 23.

[203] *Id.*

client's rights of defense and . . . emanate from independent lawyers, that is to say, lawyers who are not bound to the client by a relationship of employment"[204] and are entitled to "practise [their] profession in one of the Member States, regardless of the Member State in which the client lives."[205]

The General Court added in *Akzo Nobel and Ackros Chemicals v Commission* that an undertaking wishing to claim that evidence is covered by privilege, while not being obliged to disclose its contents, would be bound to produce sufficient and relevant material to support its claim.[206] If the Commission considered that the information adduced is not sufficient to ground a claim for privilege, it would be entitled to order the production of the actual documents and to take a "cursory look" at them to establish whether they are privileged or not on the basis of external indicia such as the "layout, heading, title or other superficial features."[207]

However, the Court made clear that when even a "cursory glance" at the document is likely to prejudice the investigated parties' rights of defense, the Commission should place the documents in a sealed envelope with a view to it being reopened at a later stage for the purpose of resolving the matter[208] and should not read the documents in question until the undertaking concerned has had the opportunity to challenge the decision in Court and, if an action is brought, until the General Court has handed down a judgment.[209] It was held that the decision by which the Commission officials determine whether the documents seized from the investigated parties should be protected by the legal professional privilege constitutes a "reviewable act" for the purpose of bringing an action for annulment,[210] since it brings to an end an "ad hoc segment" of the investigation carried out by the case-handling officials. Moreover, it was emphasized that this measure, regardless of whether the decision had been adopted expressly or tacitly, that is, by seizing the document and placing it on the investigation file without taking a formal decision on its nature,[211] is capable of producing irreversible and potentially adverse legal consequences for the undertakings' rights of defense that cannot be made good by a later challenge to (and annulment of) the final decision.[212] On this point, it should be emphasized that, as was anticipated above, these decisions will fall within the purview of the Hearing Officer, according to the revisions to the current Best Practices Guidelines.[213] Thus, it could be argued that, unlike the decisions adopted

[204] *Id.*, para 21.

[205] *Id. See* also, more recently, case C-7/04 P (R), *Commission v AKZO Nobel and Ackros Chemicals*, [2004] ECR I-8739, para 43; also joined cases T-125/03 and 253/03, [2007] ECR II-2753, paras 167–168, 171–173; cf. case T-125/03, *AKZO Nobel Chemicals Ltd and Ackros Chemicals Ltd v Commission*, [2003] ECR II-4771, paras 126–127. For the procedure to follow in case of allegations that evidence is privileged, *see*, e.g., Commission Draft Best Practices on the conduct of proceedings concerning Articles 101 and 102 TFEU, <http://ec.europa.eu/competition/consultations/2010_best_practices/best_practice_articles.pdf>, paras 47–52.

[206] Joined cases T-125/03 and 253/03, *AKZO Nobel Ltd and Ackros Chemicals Ltd v Commission*, [2005] ECR II-3523, para 79.

[207] *Id.* para 81.

[208] *Id.* para 83.

[209] *Id.* para 88.

[210] *Id.* paras 45, 48.

[211] *Id.* para 49.

[212] *Id.* para 46.

[213] Article 8, Decision 2011/695 of the President of the European Commission of 13 October 2011 on the function and terms of reference of the Hearing Officer in certain competition proceedings [2011] OJ L 275/29. *See* also Wils, cit. (fn. 66), pp. 448–449.

by the Officer on other evidentiary matters, these decisions should be open to challenge before the EU courts, in order to comply with the *AKZO* ruling.[214]

It seems that, due to the "creative jurisprudence" of the Court of Justice of the EU, ad hoc limits have been built into the otherwise pervasive investigative powers enjoyed by the European Commission. It is clear that the right to silence and to the confidentiality of lawyer–client communications remain important safeguards against the Commission's otherwise extensive fact-finding powers. However, it is undoubted that they are confined within rather narrow boundaries, which, in turn, are the expression of a very clear "trade-off" between the demands of due process and the need to allow the Commission to accomplish its institutional objectives. Consequently, the question that emerges from the current standards of the "rights of defence" enjoyed in the preliminary investigation is whether the existing trade-off meets the requirements of "proportionality" that are required by a legal system based on the rule of law.

Some commentators argue that competition infringements do not belong to the "core" of the criminal offences to which the Convention refers, and consequently applying the "full guarantees" attending court criminal proceedings are not justified.[215] Other authors take a different view that, although a more nuanced interpretation of these guarantees may indeed be consistent with the principles governing the application of the Convention to "commercial matters,"[216] a more generous interpretation of the scope of the safeguards attending competition proceedings may be required to strike a "fair balance" between the protection of the rights of the investigated parties and their effective functioning.[217] In respect especially to the "preliminary" phase of the procedure (that is, the investigative stage), it is clear that Council Regulation No 1/2003 conferred stronger investigative powers to the Commission. Against this background, it could be questioned whether the current level of protection of the investigated parties' right to silence is actually capable of counterbalancing these more extensive powers. Nevertheless, despite repeated calls for its expansion,[218] the EU Courts have declined to reconsider the remit of the privilege against self-incrimination.[219]

[214] *See*, e.g., Andreangeli, "The protection of legal professional privilege in EU law and the impact of the rules on the exchange of information within the European Competition Network on the secrecy of communications between lawyer and client: one step forward, two steps back?" (2005) 2(1) Comp L Rev 31 at 44 ff.

[215] Wils, "The increased level of EU antitrust fines, judicial review and the European Convention on Human Rights," (2010) 33(1) World Competition 5 at 12 et seq.

[216] *See*, e.g., Appl. No. 10572/83, *Markt Intern Verlag GmbH and Klaus Bermann v Germany*, judgment of 20 November 1989, Ser. A No 165, [1990] 12 EHRR 161, paras 26, 35 et seq.

[217] *Inter alia*, Appl. No. 58478/00, *Rupa v Romania*, [2010] 50 EHRR 10, para 222 et seq.

[218] *See*, e.g., Riley, "*Saunders* and the power to obtain information in Community and United Kingdom competition law," (2000) 25 ELRev 264; also, Andreangeli et al., "Enforcement by the Commission—the decisional and enforcement structure in antitrust cases and the Commissions fining system," report presented at the 5th Annual Conference of the Global Administrative Law Centre, 11–12 June 2009, especially 40 et seq. Cf. Wils, cit. (fn. 182), 24–6.

[219] Case T-112/98, *MannesmannrohrenWerke v Commission*, [2001] ECR II-729, para 66; also, case C-238/99, *LVM NV and others v Commission*, [2002] ECR I-8375, paras 275, 279–282. Also *see* case 301/04, *Commission v SGL Carbon AG*, [2006] ECR I-5915, paras 40–43.

As for the Commission's practice, in the current Best Practices Guidelines it is noted that "in the context of requests for information [the investigated parties] will (...) be reminded of the privilege against providing self-incriminating information", which suggests that the Commission officials are now committed to serving a "Miranda-type" warning at the start of the investigations.[220]

However, it is not clear whether a similar warning should be made during an inspection, if the officials wish to ask questions "on the spot" to those present at the premises. More generally, doubts remain as to whether a simple "administrative commitment" to serving these warnings will be sufficient to meet the requirements of legal certainty enshrined in European human rights instruments, such as the European Convention on Human Rights.

The General Court's *AKZO Nobel* judgment emphasizes the importance of the role of the EU Courts as a "check" over otherwise extremely pervasive investigative powers enjoyed by the Commission and contributes to the overall fairness of the preliminary phase of the competition proceedings.[221] Conferring on the Hearing Officer the power to decide on a first instance whether a specific item of evidence should be regarded as "privileged," as was recently envisaged by Commissioner Almunia, should contribute to strengthening these checks on the case-handling officials' powers.[222] Without going as far as extending the remit of the privilege to employed counsel's advice, the current notion of privilege as it arises from the more recent developments constitutes an attempt to ensure a "fairer balance" between the need to uphold the very essence of the privilege as a means for every person to be "able without constraint, to consul a lawyer" in the interest of the sound administration of justice[223] and the legitimate interest to the effective enforcement of the competition rules of the Treaty.[224]

This brief examination of the issues arising from the protection of, respectively, the right to silence and that to the confidentiality of lawyer–client communications provides an important example of the way in which the EU Courts and the Commission have gradually fashioned the "balance" between the needs of "due process" and the demands of effective competition enforcement in individual cases. We will address in the next section a few of the questions arising from the final stage of the procedure, that is, the adoption of a decision on the merits of a specific complaint or allegation, more specifically, issues relating to the judicial scrutiny to which the decision is open and the "proportionality" of the fines and remedies.

[220] Commission notice on best practices for the conduct of proceedings concerning Articles 101 and 102, OJ [2011] C 308/6, para 36.

[221] *See, inter alia*, Appl. No. 27052/95, *Jasper v United Kingdom*, [2000] 30 EHRR 441, para 52. Cf., mutatis mutandis, cases T-10–12/92 & 15/92, *Cimenteries CBR SA and others v EC Commission*, [1992] ECR II-2667, para 47; case T-90/96, *Automobiles Peugeot SA v Commission*, [1997] ECR II-663, paras 32, 34, 37.

[222] Joaquim Almunia, "Fair process in EU competition proceedings," speech given at the European Competition Day, Budapest, 30 May 2011, SPEECH/11/396.

[223] *Id.*, para 121.

[224] *See* also, mutatis mutandis, case T-30/89, *Hilti AG v Commission* (interim order), [1990] ECR II-163, paras 17–18.

D. Due process issues II: competition law sanctions/remedies and proportionality

Competition law remedies are adopted with the principal aim of restoring competition in the market.[225] This includes first the goal of putting the infringement to an end, compensating the victims,[226] and curing the particular problem for competition, but also the goal of putting incentives in place "so as to minimize the recurrence of just such anticompetitive conduct."[227] Remedies may thus take different forms. In some cases, they will be specific to the nature of the competition law violation and will impose injunctions, conduct remedies, and structural measures. In other cases, the duty imposed on the violator will entail a substitutionary (pecuniary) remedy, such as damages or fines, often when it is difficult or impossible to cure all the negative effects of the practice with specific conduct or structural remedies.

Article 7 of the Regulation 1/2003 confers an express legal basis on the European Commission to impose antitrust remedies on undertakings responsible for unlawful behavior, with a view to restoring effective competition in relevant markets.[228] The principle of proportionality constitutes an important limit to the European Commission's discretion in imposing remedies.[229] It is explicitly provided in Article 7 of Regulation 1/2003 that the Commission may impose on undertakings any behavioral or structural remedies which are proportionate to the infringement committed and necessary to bring the infringement effectively to an end. This provision mainly codifies previous case law of the Court relying on Article 3(1) of Regulation 17/62 that the remedies imposed should "not exceed what is appropriate" and should be "necessary to attain the objective sought, namely to restore compliance with the rules infringed."[230] Structural remedies are generally not favored unless there is no

[225] *See* Melamed, "Afterword: The Purposes of Antitrust Remedies" (2009) 76 Antitrust Law Journal 359.

[226] Taking illegal gains away from the law violators and "restor[ing] the monies to the victims" constitutes a principal goal of competition law remedies: *see* Pitofsky, "Antitrust at the Turn of the Twenty-First Century: the Matter of Remedies" (2002) 91 Georgetown Law Journal 169, 170.

[227] Fox, "Remedies and the Courage of Convictions in a Globalized World: How Globalization Corrupts Relief" (2005) 80 Tulane L Rev 571, 573.

[228] On the distinction between remedies and sanctions *see*, e.g., OECD, Remedies and Sanctions in Abuse of Dominance Cases, DAF/COMP(2006), May 2007, <http://www.oecd.org/dataoecd/20/17/38623413.pdf>, at 18 "(t)ypically, remedies aim to stop a violator's unlawful conduct, its anti-competitive effects, and their recurrence, as well as to restore competition. Sanctions are usually meant to deter unlawful conduct in the future, to compensate victims, and to force violators to disgorge their illegal gains." For commentary, *see* Melamed, "Afterword: The Purposes of Antitrust Remedies" (2009) 76 Antitrust Law Journal 359; *see* also Pitofsky, "Antitrust at the Turn of the Twenty-First Century: the Matter of Remedies" (2002) 91 Georgetown Law Journal 169, 170.

[229] *See*, Lianos, "Competition Law Remedies: In Search of a Theory" in Lianos and Sokol (eds.), *The Global Limits of Competition Law* (2012, Stanford University Press).

[230] *See* Case T-170/06, *Alrosa Co. Ltd v Commission* [2007] ECR II-2601, para 102; Case T-338/94, *Finnboard* [1998] ECR II-1617, para 242; Case T-76/89, *RTE and ITP v Commission* [1991] ECR Ii-757, para 93; Case T-7/93 *Langnese-Iglo v Commission* [1995] ECR II-1533, para 209; Case T-9/93 *Schöller v Commission* [1995] ECR II-1611, para 163.

equally effective behavioral remedy or where any equally effective behavioral remedy would be more burdensome for the undertaking concerned.

In accordance with Article 23 of Council Regulation No 1/2003, the Commission is also empowered to impose financial penalties for competition infringements. The principle of proportionality takes an arithmetic form in Article 23(2) of the Regulation, which provides that the Commission may not impose fines on undertakings that exceed 10 per cent of the value of the investigated firms' annual worldwide turnover in the preceding business year. This indicates an attempt by the legislator to draw a rough balance between the anticompetitive harm and the harm to the undertaking's financial position. In addition, in fixing the amount of the fine, regard shall be had both to the gravity and to the duration of the infringement as well as to the effect of the competition law infringement on the market.[231]

As to the review of competition decisions, it was anticipated that the General Court and, on appeal on points of law, the Court of Justice of the EU, would exercise powers of scrutiny over the Commission's findings and the size of the fines imposed on the investigated parties. However as was previously explained, the nature and intensity of this power differs significantly in respect to the subject matter of the appeal: according to Article 261 TFEU, the General Court enjoys full jurisdiction when it comes to assessing the lawfulness of the fine imposed on the applicant by the Commission; thus, it can reduce or increase its size, to reflect the gravity and duration of the infringement and the nature of involvement of the concerned party. By contrast, in accordance with Article 263 TFEU its powers of review are confined to a "manifest error"-type review when the appeal relates to the economic and legal assessment of the findings made by the Commission as to the nature and impact of the alleged infringement.[232] The General Court has explained in a number of judgments that the limited nature of this scrutiny is justified by the need to preserve the "inter-institutional balance" within the Union and especially to prevent the Courts from encroaching upon the discretionary powers of the Commission in the area of competition policy.[233] Having regard to the review of merger decisions, the EU Courts had initially adopted an approach to the breadth of their scrutiny which was largely consistent with that applicable to Article 101 and 102 decisions.[234]

However, in other cases, that is, the *Airtours*, *Schneider*, and *Tetra Laval* appeals, the EU Courts signaled a move toward a more exacting and intensive standard of

[231] *See* Joined Cases C-189/02 P, C-202 P, C-205–208/02 P, C-213/02 P, *Dansk Rørindustri and others* [2005] ECR I-5425, para 243.

[232] *Inter alia*, case T-112/99, *Metropole Television and others v Commission*, [2001] ECR II-2459, para 114.

[233] e.g. joined cases T-68, 77–78/89, *SocietàItalianaVetroSpA and Others v Commission*, [1992] ECR II-1403, paras 319–320; also case T-65/98, *Van den Bergh v Commission*, [2003] ECR II-4653, para 135; more recently, case C-194/99 P, *Thyssen Stahl AG v Commission of the European Communities*, [2003] ECR I-10821, para 73; case T-168/01, *GlaxoSmithKline Services Unlimited v Commission of the European Communities*, [2006] ECR II-2969, para 57.

[234] *Inter alia*, case T-102/96, *Gencor v Commission*, [1999] ECR II-753 at para 165.

review.[235] It was held in *Tetra Laval* that although the Commission enjoyed a relatively wide margin of appreciation when reviewing notified concentrations, this did not mean that the EU Courts did not possess the power to scrutinize carefully its decisions.[236] Instead, the Court emphasized that, due to the "forward looking nature" of the merger assessment, its scrutiny would have to encompass an exhaustive judgment of the reliability and sufficiency of the evidence, and of its ability to support the Commission's conclusions.[237]

Similarly limited powers of review are also exercised in respect to antitrust remedies imposed on the parties found to be responsible for unlawful practices. It was anticipated that, in light of Article 7 of Council Regulation No 1/2003, the primary objective of competition remedies is the recreation of the "status quo ante" in the relevant market, that is, the conditions of competition that would have prevailed absent the infringement.[238] Consequently, any remedies should "not exceed what is appropriate" and should be "necessary to attain the objective sought, namely to restore compliance with the rules infringed."[239] On this point, the case law indicates that the rules enshrined in Article 7 constitute an expression of the general principle of proportionality, which should govern the action of the EU institutions as a whole and which has been given an express legal sanction in Article 3b of the TFEU.[240] According to the EU Courts this principle should be read as meaning that "measures adopted by Community institutions [should] not exceed the limits of what is appropriate and necessary in order to attain the legitimate objectives pursued by the legislation in question; when there is a choice between several appropriate measures, recourse must be had to the least onerous, and the disadvantages caused must not be disproportionate to the aims pursued."[241]

It could be argued that the General Court, despite being able to consider the extent to which the Commission provided a sufficiently clear and exhaustive statement of reasons in respect to the "necessity" of the remedy in each case, remains constrained in its ability to appraise its suitability in light of the nature of the infringement and especially of the "theory of harm" advanced by the

[235] Case T-342/99, *Airtours v. Commission* [2002] ECR II-2585, paras 127, 167, 210; Case T-310/01, *Schneider Electric v. Commission* [2002] ECR II-4071; Case C-12/03, *Commission v. Tetra Laval* [2005] ECR I-987, paras 39, 42–44.

[236] Case C-12/03, *Commission v Tetra Laval*, [2005] ECR I-987, para 39.

[237] *Id.*, para 44.

[238] *See*, e.g., mutatis mutandis *US v Microsoft Corp.*, 253 F.3d 34, 103 (DC Cir. 2001); on this issue, *see* generally Economides and Lianos, "A Critical Appraisal of Remedies in the EU Antitrust Microsoft Cases," (2010) (2) Columbia Business Law Review 346; Economides and Lianos, "The Quest for Appropriate Remedies in the Microsoft Antitrust EU Cases: A Comparative Appraisal," in Rubini (ed.), *Microsoft on Trial: Legal and Economic Analysis of a Transatlantic Antitrust Case* (Edward Elgar, 2010), 393–463; Andreangeli, "Between economic freedom and effective competition enforcement: the impact of the antitrust remedies provided by the Modernisation Regulation on the investigated parties' freedom to contract and to enjoy property," (2010) 6(2) Comp L Rev 225.

[239] *See* Case T-170/06, *Alrosa Co. Ltd v Commission* [2007] ECR II-2601, para 102; Case T-338/94, *Finnboard*[1998] ECR II-1617, para 242; Case T-76/89, *RTE and ITP v Commission* [1991] ECR Ii-757, para 93; Case T-7/93 *Langnese-Iglo v Commission* [1995] ECR II-1533, para 209; Case T-9/93 *Schöller v Commission* [1995] ECR II-1611, para 163.

[240] Case T-260/94, *Air Inter v Commission* [1997] ECR II-997; Case T-65/98, *Van den Bergh Foods v Commission* [2003] ECR II-4653, para 201; Case T-170/06, *Alrosa v Commission*, para 98.

[241] Opinion of Advocate General Kokkott in Case C-441/07 P, *European Commission v. Alrosa Company Ltd* [29 June 2010], nyr, para 46; *see* also, mutatis mutandis, paras 38, 48 of the judgment.

Commission in its decision. While it could be suggested that this position is broadly consistent with the "manifest error" standard of review applied to the "complex assessments" made in individual cases, it could be questioned whether it is sufficiently exacting as to ensure that the economic freedom of the applicant is not hindered beyond what is "necessary" to achieve the objectives of competition policy in individual cases.[242]

It would appear that the analysis conducted so far has highlighted a more general question as to the extent to which the role of the EU courts and especially the nature or intensity of their powers is sufficient to meet the requirements of "fairness" that should govern competition enforcement procedures. While it could be argued that the nature of the control exercised in merger cases is overall consistent with the demands of a "forward-looking," administrative framework for the assessment of "civil" transactions, that is, transactions affecting the rights and obligations of the merging parties, it has been doubted whether the limited type of scrutiny exercised in respect to Articles 101 and 102 TFEU decisions complies with the same principles.[243]

It has been argued that given the broadly "criminal nature" of these infringements the EU Courts should be empowered to exert more stringent control over the lawfulness of antitrust decisions, so as to encompass all matters of law and fact concerning each case and, therefore, to take a "fresh look" at the case.[244] On this point, it is acknowledged that similar concerns prompted domestic legislators, such as the British Parliament, to create "specialized jurisdictions" for the hearing of competition appeals and to confer on them powers of review on the merits.[245] However, it should be emphasized that similar proposals have so far encountered significant opposition at EU level, largely for the consequences that they would entail for the institutional structure of the EU as a whole.[246]

E. Decentralization of the EU public competition law enforcement and due process: the role of national competition authorities

This brief examination of the due process issues arising from the enforcement of the EU competition rules would not be complete without a brief review of the role of

[242] For the position in, e.g. UK competition law *see inter alia Tesco Plc v Competition Commission*, [2009] CAT 6, at paras 136–139; also *Barclays Bank Plc v Competition Commission* [2009] CAT 27, paras 21–23 and 26–28; *BAA Limited v Competition Commission* [2009] CAT 35, para 261.

[243] *See*, e.g., Appl. Nos 7299/75 and 7496/76, *Albert & LeCompte v Belgium*, [1983] 5 EHRR 533, para 29. See also Boyle, "Administrative justice, judicial review and the right to a fair hearing under the European Convention on Human Rights," (1984) PL 89 at 100; Andreangeli, *EU Competition enforcement and Human Rights*, 2008: Cheltenham, E Elgar, pp. 210 ff.

[244] See Appl. No. 19178/91, *Bryan v United Kingdom*, [1996] 21 EHRR 342, para 46 of the judgment; see also Commission Opinion, separate concurring Opinion of Mr N. Bratza, p. 354.

[245] *See* Appl. Nos 7299/75 and 7496/76, *Albert & LeCompte v Belgium*, [1983] 5 EHRR 533, para 29; also, *inter alia*, Appl. No. 19178/91, *Bryan v United Kingdom*, [1996] 21 EHRR 342, para 46 of the judgment; *see* also Commission Opinion, separate concurring Opinion of Mr N. Bratza, 354.

[246] *See* Sections 47 and 48, UK Competition Act 1998; *see* also Section 3, Schedule 8 to the Act. For a discussion of the nature of this jurisdiction, *see inter alia NAPP Pharmaceuticals v Director General of Fair Trading*, [2002] ECC 13.

the national competition authorities and of national courts in the "decentralized" landscape established by Council Regulation No 1/2003. Since the enactment of Regulation 1/2003, NCAs have been more directly involved in the enforcement of EU competition law than under Regulation 17/62, in particular with regard to the application of Article 101(3) TFEU, which has now direct effect and can thus be enforced by national competition authorities and courts.

The new legal exception regime adopted by Regulation 1/2003 establishes a system where the burden of competition law enforcement is shared between the Commission and national competition authorities. National competition authorities act on their own initiative or following a complaint and have the power to require that the infringement is brought to an end, order interim measures, accept commitments, impose fines, periodic penalty payments, or any other penalty provided for in their national law.[247] The Member States are free to determine which body will enforce the EU competition law provisions and the procedure and mechanisms for investigations and for the enforcement of the decisions reached.[248] The Member States may allocate different powers and functions to those different national authorities, whether administrative or judicial.[249]

There is a considerable variety of institutional structures across the EU and although the trend is towards some degree of convergence with the EU administrative-centered model, Member States remain free to choose the institutional format for their national competition agencies, which could also be judicial organs. One could distinguish between (i) the purely administrative enforcement system, the dominant enforcement system in Europe, which involves either a single independent administrative authority that conducts both the investigation and the adjudicatory function,[250] or an administrative enforcement system with a dual structure, where the investigation and adjudicatory functions are more or less separated from each other and exercised by different bodies within the same NCA, most often involving for the adjudicatory function a college of commissioners,[251] the decisions being also subject to some form of judicial control, and (ii) the mixed enforcement system, where the investigation and adjudicatory functions are shared between the administration (a competition authority or a government

[247] Article 5, Regulation 1/2003.

[248] Article 35, Regulation 1/2003.

[249] Commission Notice on cooperation within the Network of Competition Authorities, [2004] OJ C 101/43, para 2.

[250] This is the institutional enforcement system chosen by Bulgaria, Cyprus, Germany, Hungary, Italy, Latvia, Lithuania, Malta, the Netherlands, Poland, Portugal, Czech Republic, Romania, United Kingdom (but not for merger decisions), Slovakia, and Slovenia.

[251] This is the institutional enforcement system chosen by France, Luxembourg, and Spain. One could also add to some degree Greece, Hungary, Romania and Italy where the final decision is taken by a college of commissioners, after the conduct of the investigation by the directors of the competition authority, but, contrary to France, Luxembourg and Spain, there is no complete separation between the two organs, as the college exercises some degree of higher authority over the investigation teams of the authority.

department), which conducts the investigation and a judicial organ (of an administrative,[252] civil,[253] or criminal[254] nature) which exercises the adjudicative function.

The nature of the proceedings can be administrative, civil, or criminal (or some combination). In some Member States, sectoral regulators are empowered to enforce the EU competition rules in specific sectors; for example, telecommunications, postal services, energy. Some Member States have adopted a dual administrative enforcement structure uniquely for merger control, while applying a single structure for all other cases.[255] Some Member States have created specific authorities with the aim to supervise the level of concentration across national markets, although the powers granted vary significantly, some authorities exercising merely a reporting function to the government,[256] others being granted the power to conduct sector-specific investigations and impose remedies.[257] Finally, one should also take into account the federal structure of some Member States, and thus the additional layer of competition law enforcement at the state level.[258]

The decisions of the competition authorities are subject to judicial control,[259] either before courts, which can be a generalist court with exclusive competence to hear all competition appeals[260] or before a specialized tribunal in competition or

[252] This is the institutional enforcement system chosen by Belgium (the investigation is conducted by the ministry of Economics, but the final decision taken by the college of the Conseil de la concurrence which has the statute of an administrative judicial body), and Finland (where the Ministry of Economics conducts the investigation and the final decision is taken by the Kilpailuvirasto or Market tribunal—an administrative judicial organ).

[253] This is the institutional model chosen by Austria (where the federal ministry of economics conducts the investigation phase, the Federal cartel Attorney, "Bundeskartellanwalt," is entrusted with the representation of the public interests in competition matters and brings proceedings to the Kartellgericht or Cartel court, which exercises the adjudicatory function) and Sweden (the investigation being at the hands of the konkurrenvertsket and the adjudicatory function being exercised by the Tribunal of Stockholm).

[254] This is the institutional model chosen by Denmark (where the "konkurrencestyrel" or Ministry of economics is the investigating body but the final decision is taken by a criminal judge), Estonia (where the investigation is conducted by the Estonian Institute of competition, which is part of the Ministry of Economics, the final decision being taken by a criminal judge), and Ireland (where the investigation is conducted by the Irish Competition Authority, the final decision being taken by either the High Court—for civil court cases—or for hardcore restrictions by the Central Criminal Court, after the case has been presented to the Director of public prosecutions). The same system is also chosen by the UK, when enforcing the cartel offence under the Enterprise Act 2002 with the OFT investigating, the Serious Fraud Office acting as the prosecutor, and the magistrates' court (summary trial) or the Crown Court (trial on indictment) adjudicating.

[255] *See*, for example, the UK, with the first phase of the merger investigation being conducted by the OFT, the second one by the Competition Commission.

[256] *See*, for example, in Germany, the Monopolkommission.

[257] *See*, for example, in the UK, the Competition Commission.

[258] *See*, for instance, in Germany, when the Länder have jurisdiction to apply their own competition laws. For an analysis, *see* Petit, "How much discretion do, and should, competition authorities enjoy in the course of their enforcement activities? A multi-jurisdictional assessment," 2010 (1) CONCURRENCES 44–62.

[259] For a useful summary *see*, Roseau, "Panorama des procédures d'appel contre les décisions des ANC en Europe," (2007) 2 CONCURRENCES 209–18.

[260] *See*, for instance, in Belgium (the Court of Appeal of Brussels for the decisions of the *Conseil de la concurrence* and the Council of State for Ministerial decisions in case of mergers), Bulgaria (the Supreme administrative court), Cyprus (the Supreme court), Czech Republic (Regional Court of Brno), France (the Court of Appeal of Paris), Germany (the judicial control of federal competition

economic litigation.[261] The judicial control might take different forms: it might be a limited judicial review of the legality of the decision[262] or involve a full jurisdiction (appeal) process.[263] An additional layer of judicial control of the review or appeal decisions may occur at a higher jurisdiction, which in some cases comprises a specialized chamber in competition litigation.[264]

The NCAs' role in the enforcement of EU competition law has been steadily rising,[265] following the Commission's relative disinvestment from active competition law enforcement in certain specific areas (vertical restraints) in order to focus on cartel investigations,[266] following the decentralization of competition law enforcement in 2004. The empowerment of NCAs to enforce EU competition law was followed by the establishment of close cooperation mechanisms between the Commission and the NCAs, founded on equality, respect, and solidarity[267] and especially on the idea that Member States accept that their enforcement systems differ but nonetheless mutually recognize the standards of each other's system as a basis for cooperation. This mutual recognition depends on the agreement of all Member States involved on a number of core principles[268] and remains subject to

decisions takes place at the Higher Regional Court of Düsseldorf), Greece (the Administrative Appeal court of Athens), Estonia (The Administrative Court of Talin), Latvia (the Administrative court of Riga), Lithuania (the Administrative Court of Vilnius), the Netherlands (the Court of Rotterdam), Slovenia (the Administrative Court but only in specific circumstances as the decision of the NCA is final), Slovakia (the Regional Court of Appeal of Bratislava), Luxembourg (the Administrative Tribunal of Luxembourg), Greece (the Administrative Appeal Court of Athens), Hungary (the Metropolitan Tribunal of Budapest), Italy (the Regional Administrative Court of Lazio), Ireland (the High Court), Portugal (the Commercial Court of Lisbon), Romania (the Court of appeal of Bucharest), Slovenia (the Administrative Court).

261 *See*, for instance, Austria (Antitrust Court of Appeal), Denmark (Competition Court of appeal), Finland (Market Court), Spain (Defence of Competition Tribunal for the decisions of the Service for the protection of competition and the *Audiencanacional* for the decisions of the Defence of Competition Tribunal), Sweden (the Market Court for the decisions of the konkurrensverket and the Court of Stockholm for the decisions of the Market Court), Poland (Competition and Consumer Protection Court), UK (the Competition Appeal Tribunal).

262 *See*, for instance, Austria, Estonia, Latvia, Lithuania, Slovakia.

263 *See*, for instance, Belgium (with the exception of the ministerial decisions for mergers where the Council of State exercises a control of legality), Bulgaria, Cyprus, Czech Republic, Denmark, Finland, Germany, Greece, Italy, Netherlands, Slovenia Sweden, UK (with the exception of merger decisions where it is a judicial review), Portugal.

264 *See*, for instance, in Germany (where the Federal Court of Justice comprises a specialized chamber in antitrust litigation), and in the Netherlands (the Dutch Trade and Industry Appeals Tribunal).

265 *See* also, Commission Staff Working Paper, Report on the Functioning of Regulation 1/2003, COM(2009)206 final documenting more than 1000 cases initiated between 2004 and 2009 by NCAs on the enforcement of EU competition law.

266 The re-centralization of the Commission's activity on cartel investigations constituted one of the principal aims of the reform: *see* "Report on the functioning of Regulation 1/2003," Communication from the Commission to the European Parliament and the Council, COM (2009) 206 of 29.4.2009; Commission Staff Working Paper, SEC (2009) 574.

267 Available at <http://ec.europa.eu/competition/ecn/joint_statement_en.pdf>.

268 *See*, Commission Notice on cooperation within the Network of Competition Authorities, [2004] OJ C 101/43, para 72, "The principles set out in this notice will also be abided by those Member States' competition authorities which have signed a statement in the form of the Annex to this Notice. In this statement they acknowledge the principles of this notice, including the principles relating to the protection of applicants claiming the benefit of a leniency programme and declare that

the Commission's overarching power to set the goals of EU competition policy that are to be attained in close liaison with its national partners.[269]

The European Competition Network (ECN) was established with the aim to promote cooperation between the NCAs and in order to guarantee that the Commission would, as the coordinator of the network, monitor the enforcement of Articles 101 and 102 TFEU by the NCAs. The network is "a forum for discussion and cooperation" in the application and enforcement of EU competition policy, "provides a framework for the cooperation of European competition authorities" in cases where Articles 101 and 102 TFEU are applied, and "is the basis for the creation and maintenance of a common competition culture in Europe."[270]

The ECN is intended to ensure the effectiveness of the enforcement of EU competition law and seeks to maintain the consistency in its interpretation.[271] Importantly, in its context each agency enjoys parallel competence to deal with individual cases, subject only to the Commission's power to "relieve" them with jurisdiction to deal with individual cases.[272] Thus, it could be argued that it is more appropriate to refer only to the relationship between domestic agencies as "parallel" and "egalitarian": as was aptly put by the General Court in a recent case, each NCA enjoys a merely "contingent" jurisdiction to deal with alleged EU competition infringements, given the Commission's power to take action whenever the "Union interest" so requires.[273]

The shared nature of the task performed by the ECN gives rise to important questions as to the extent to which investigated parties are afforded sufficiently strong safeguards in the course of competition proceedings, especially bearing in mind the extensive powers of cooperation enjoyed by the network members, that is, the power to exchange and use as evidence documents and other information collected in the course of domestic investigations, to transmit information related to new cases, and to carry out fact-finding measures on behalf of other authorities and to transmit the findings in a different jurisdiction.[274] It has been argued that

they will abide by them." On the NCAs that have signed this Statement, *see* <http://ec.europa.eu/competition/antitrust/legislation/list_of_authorities_joint_statement.pdf>.

[269] Joint Statement of the Council and the Commission on the functioning of the network of competition authorities, Recital 9. The Commission can intervene if there is a serious risk of incoherence, by relieving the national competition authority of its competence to act (Art. 11(6) Regulation 1/2003). NCAs have also the obligation to inform the Commission at the latest 30 calendar days before an envisaged decision is adopted (Art. 11(4) Regulation 1/2003).

[270] Commission Notice on cooperation within the Network of Competition Authorities, [2004] OJ C 101/43, para 1.

[271] *See*, e.g., Commission Staff Working Paper, Report on the Functioning of Regulation 1/2003, COM(2009)206 final, para 200 ff.; *see* especially paras 268–269; *see* also, Article 11(3) of Regulation 1/2003 regarding the information requirements for NCAs to the Commission, once they commenced a formal investigative measure. The principles of case allocation were endorsed by the General Court in Joined Cases T- 339/04 and T-340/04, *France Télécom v. Commission*, [2007] ECR II-521.

[272] Article 11(6), Council Regulation No 1/2003; *see* also Joined Cases T- 339/04 and T-340/04, France Télécom v. Commission, [2007] ECR II-521, paras 277, 281.

[273] *See* cases T-340/03, *France Télécom v. Commission*, [2007] ECR II-107 and 343/03, cit., (fn. 286), para 248.

[274] *See* Articles 11, 12 and 22, Council Regulation No 1/2003; for the approach taken by NCAs *see* the example of the Office of Fair Trading: Powers of investigation—draft competition guidelines, OFT404a (2004).

the absence of a "common standard" as to the protection of the rights of defense enjoyed by individual firms in each national jurisdiction could lead to a gradual erosion of their protection.[275] In particular, some commentators argue that the current extensive cooperation obligations and powers could allow individual agencies to circumvent any higher standard of safeguard of these rights existing within their own jurisdiction, by seeking to obtain evidence from abroad which it would not have otherwise been able to acquire itself.[276]

Further concerns have been raised in respect to the "parallel" nature of the jurisdiction exercised by the ECN members: whether the powers and obligations established by Council Regulation No 1/2003 in respect to addressing allegations of anti-competitive conduct could lead to outcomes that are incompatible with the principle of *ne bis in idem*, that is, the right of "everyone" (guaranteed within the Union, according to the EU Charter of Fundamental Rights) not to be prosecuted and sanctioned twice for the same law infringement.[277] It has been argued that the powers of each of the network members to investigate and punish breaches having a significant impact within their territory may be incompatible with this principle.[278] Differences existing across the Member States' jurisdictions may also weaken the effectiveness of individual leniency programs as well as jeopardize legal certainty more generally due to the lack of rigid case allocation rules.[279] Commentators have suggested that since the lodging of an application for, or even the grant of, leniency does not prejudice the application of the principle of parallel jurisdiction within the Network and although the information supplied to the Network as regards new proceedings initiated following a leniency application cannot be used as a "direct"

[275] *See*, e.g., Van der Woude, "Exchange of information within the European Competition Network: scope and limits," in Ehlermann and Atanasiu (eds), *European Competition Law Annual 2002: constructing the EU network of competition authorities*, (2004, Hart Publishing) 369 at 387; also Andreangeli, "The impact of the Modernisation Regulation on the guarantees of due process in competition proceedings," (2006) 31(3) ELRev 342 at 352–4; cf. Wils, cit. (fn. 182), 26–30.

[276] *See*, e.g., Merola and Waelbroeck, cit. (fn. 167), 465 at 470 ff. Cf. Bloom, "Exchange of confidential information among members of the EU network of competition authorities: possible consequences of a relatively broad scope for the exchange of confidential information," in Ehlermann and Atanasiu, cit. (fn. 248), 403–4.

[277] *See*, e.g., mutatis mutandis, Appl. No. 37/950/97, *Franz Fischer v Austria*, judgment of 29 May 2001, not yet reported, paras 22, 25, 29; Appl. No. 15963/90, *Gradinger v Austria*, judgment of 23 October 1995, Ser. A, no 328-C (HUDOC Reference No 33/1994/480/562), paras 53–54–55. *See* also, *inter alia*, case C-436/04, *VanEsbroeck*, [2006] ECR I-2033, paras 27–28, 30–32; cf. case C-204/00, *AalborgPortlandandothers v Commission*, [2004] ECR I-123, para 338. For commentary, *see*, *inter alia*, Wils, *Principles of European Antitrust enforcement* (2005, Hart Publishing), 96.

[278] *See inter alia* Merola and Waelbroeck (eds), cit. (fn. 167), 472–3.

[279] For commentary, *see*, e.g., Wils, "The EU network of competition authorities, the European Convention on Human Rights and the Charter of Fundamental Rights of the EU," in Ehlermann and Atanasiu (eds), *European Competition Law Annual 2002, constructing the EU network of competition authorities*, (2004, Hart Publishing) 433 at 449; Dekeyser and Dalheimer, "Cooperation within the European Competition Network—taking stock after 10 months of case practice," paper presented at the International Bar Association 2005 Conference: "Decentralisation of EC Competition Law, a year in practice," *see* especially 8 et seq.; *see* also, more recently, Wils, cit. (fn. 182), 29–30. Cf. Andreangeli, cit. (fn. 289), 348–9; *see* also Merola and Waelbroeck, cit. (fn. 167), 483; more recently, Forrester, "Due process in EC competition cases: a distinguished institution with flawed procedures," (2009) 34(6) ELRev 817.

basis for filing a new case in a different European jurisdiction,[280] a separate set of proceedings may be initiated in respect of the same set of facts if the authority concerned has received a "tip off" from a different source—save when the Commission itself has taken action, in accordance with Article 11(6).[281] Consequently, unless applicants make multiple applications across the EU and are successful in all cases, there would be no real certainty of EU-wide immunity.[282]

IV. Administrative performance norms

Good administration, including the fair, impartial and timely handling of one's case, is a fundamental right protected by Article 41 of the Charter of Fundamental Rights.[283] There are several mechanisms to ensure good administration in the EU competition law administrative enforcement system.

The European Commission is subject to an external mechanism of administrative control, ensuring the quality of its decisions, its political accountability, and its compliance with principles of good administration.

In respect to the "scientific input" into the decision-making process and to other "performance control" mechanisms, the Commission officials are assisted by the Chief Competition Economist (CCE)[284] who is responsible for giving economic guidance to case teams from the early stages of the proceedings and for acting as a check on the adoption of individual decisions.[285] She provides the Director General with an internal opinion on any case and meets regularly with the Commissioner, the DG Competition officials, the Hearing Officer, and the Legal Service to discuss current cases.[286] Also, upon request from or with the agreement of the DG, the CCE provides the College of Commissioners with an independent opinion as to formal proposals that are submitted for the final decision to the

[280] Network Notice, para 39.

[281] *Id. See* Henry, "Leniency programmes: an anaemic carrot for cartels in France, Germany and the UK," (2005) 26(1) ECLR 13 at 22.

[282] In respect to the consequences of Article 12 for information submitted with a leniency application, *see* Network Notice, para 40–41; for commentary, *see inter alia* Garzaniti, Gudofsky, and Moffat, "Dawn of a new era? Powers of investigation and enforcement under Regulation 1/2003," (2004–2005) 72 Antitrust L J 159 at 200.

[283] According to Article 41 of the Charter, "the right includes:

- the right of every person to be heard, before any individual measure which would affect him or her adversely is taken;
- the right of every person to have access to his or her file, while respecting the legitimate interests of confidentiality and of professional and business secrecy;
- the obligation of the administration to give reasons for its decisions."

[284] *See* Mario Monti, "EU Competition Policy," speech given at the Fordham annual conference on International Antitrust Law and Policy, New York, 31 October 2002; also, Ryan, "Reform of the EU Merger Control System—a comprehensive package of proposals," (2003) *EC Competition Policy Newsletter*, Issue 1, 9, at 12.

[285] *See* Roller and Buigues, "The office of the Chief Competition Economist at the European Commission," May 2005, <http://ec.europa.eu/dgs/competition/officechiefecon_ec.pdf> (last accessed 1 July 2010), 5 et seq.

[286] *Id.*, 6–7.

College.[287] In addition, the CCE fulfills a more general role as the impetus for capacity building by acting as a focus for economic debate, by contributing to the Commission's own training plan in economic matters, and by providing advice and assistance, as well as proposing the initiation of market studies[288] and for contributing economic insight in the drafting of notices, guidelines, and block exemption regulations.[289]

Having regard to the control of the "quality" of individual decisions, the Commission has also established an informal "peer review" mechanism as a result of which "panels" of DG Competition and Legal Service officials, meeting in private, oversee draft decisions.[290] In light of the above, it appears that the Commission provides a number of instruments to assess the efficacy of its own enforcement, policy making, and capacity building activity[291] as well as more generally to guarantee effective performance in discharging its investigation and decision-making functions in respect to allegations of anti-competitive behavior.[292]

In respect of the assessment of the efficacy of its enforcement action,[293] the Commission has developed mechanisms aimed at setting up goals for future action and at evaluating the extent to which its activity has achieved the objectives that it had set out to fulfill. Its Annual Management Plan sets the priorities for the year ahead and allocates resources for each of these objectives and in each policy area, in relation to enforcement, policy making and capacity building and advocacy.[294] The Commission reports to the European Parliament every year as to the outcomes of its competition policy and enforcement activities. The Report allows a review of whether the objectives identified in the Plan have been attained.[295]

Increasing the transparency of the Commission and the NCAs' decision-making processes was regarded as one of the objectives at the forefront of the Modernisation agenda. According to the Commission 1999 White Paper, the publication of Notices and Guidelines designed to assist the national courts would be indispensable to secure the unity and consistency of EU competition rules. It would also be essential to support individual undertakings in the self-assessment of their commercial practices and ultimately in ensuring self-compliance with the Treaty's antitrust laws.[296] This

287 *Id.*, 8–9.

288 *Id.*, 13–14. *See* CCE Mandate, in *id.*, 20 et seq.

289 *Id.*, 16–17.

290 *See*, *inter alia*, most recently, Forrester, "Due process in EC competition cases: a distinguished institution with flawed procedures?" (2009) 4(6) ELRev 817, 823.

291 *Inter alia*, Kovacic, "Rating the competition agencies: what constitutes good performance?" (2009) 16 Geo Mason L Rev 903, 923–4.

292 On this point, *see*, e.g., ICN Competition policy implementation working group, sub-group 1, "Agency effectiveness project," Kyoto, April 2008, especially 5–8.

293 *See*, e.g., ICN Competition policy implementation working group, sub-group 1, "Agency effectiveness project," Kyoto, April 2008; Kovacic and Eversley, "An assessment of institutional machinery," ICN Competition policy implementation working group, subgroup 2, report submitted on May 23. 2007.

294 *See*, e.g., European Commission DG Competition, Annual Management Plan 2009, <http://ec.europa.eu/competition/publications/annual_management_plan/amp_2009_en.pdf>, 13 et seq.

295 *See* Report on competition policy 2009, published on 3 June 2010, <http://ec.europa.eu/competition/publications/annual_report/2009/en.pdf>.

296 *Inter alia*, Gilliams, "Modernisation: from policy to practice," (2003) 28(4) ELRev 451, 466–7.

drive toward enhancing transparency and predictability in its decision-making, however, was not entirely new. For several years the Commission had been criticized for the perceived lack of predictability of its fining policy[297] and for that reason, it adopted its first Notice on the setting of fines in 1996: the Notice was later revised in 2002 and 2006, thus contributing at least in part to a better understanding of the processes and factors that the Commission would consider in determining sanctions in individual cases.[298]

The drive toward enhancing transparency and therefore improving the legitimacy of its decision-making function has been boosted by the increasing number of consultations initiated (especially recently) by the Commission in respect to key aspects of its enforcement activity as well as to more general aspects of its competition policy.[299] Although this move should clearly be welcomed as a sign of the Commission's willingness to "open up" its decision-making activity to wider scrutiny and involve those affected by it more closely in the setting of the administrative standards that should govern it, the pool of stakeholders involved in these processes seems to be rather limited.[300]

The publication by the Commission of a number of block exemption regulations in the context of the enforcement of Article 101(3) simplifies enforcement and increases legal certainty for companies in the context of a system of legal exception.[301] By including clear market share thresholds as criteria for the applicability of the exemption and a list of hard-core restrictions that exclude this benefit, the block exemption regulations provide an important tool for competition law compliance and reduce the Commission's margin of discretion in individual decisions. Although the possibility for adopting detailed rules for the application of Article 101 (3) is explicitly mentioned in Article 103(2)b of the TFEU, it is submitted that the Commission could rely on the broad mandate conferred by Article 103(2) to adopt detailed regulations on the scope of Article 102 TFEU, in particular with regard to the concept of dominant position and the possible efficiency defenses that dominant firms may raise to allegations that they are abusing their dominant position.

As for ensuring the political accountability of the Commission, advisory committees allow for the involvement of Member States in the development of EU competition law. An Advisory Committee on Restrictive Practices and Dominant Positions, composed of representatives of national competition authorities, is consulted on all draft decisions of the European Commission and prepares an

297 Joaquim Almunia, "Fair process in EU competition proceedings," speech given at the European Competition Day, Budapest, 30 May 2011, SPEECH/11/396.

298 *See*, e.g., Gilliams, "Modernisation: from policy to practice," (2003) 28(4) ELRev 451, 471–2.

299 *See*, e.g., <http://ec.europa.eu/competition/consultations/2009_vertical_agreements/index.html#contributions> for a full list of contributions to the consultation on new rules for the assessment of vertical agreements; *see* also <http://ec.europa.eu/competition/consultations/2009_horizontal_agreements/index.html> for information about the consultation on new rules for the assessment of horizontal practices.

300 *See*, e.g., <http://ec.europa.eu/competition/antitrust/actionsdamages/green_paper_comments.html> for a full list of contributions to the consultation on the Commission's Green Paper on Antitrust Damages (COM(2005) 672).

301 Paulis, cit. (fn. 47), 396–7.

opinion on the draft decision, which is not, however, binding on the Commission and which is disclosed to the parties concerned by the Commission's investigation. The Committee attends oral hearings and is also consulted on legislative proposals in the area of antitrust law and merger control (in the last case the advice is issued by the Advisory Committee on Concentrations).[302]

In addition, the Economic and Social Committee, an advisory body representing various societal groups, such as employers, trade unions, consumers, and small and medium undertakings, comprises a specific Section dealing with "Single Market, Production and Consumption," which deals with competition policy.[303] The Committee may be consulted on legislative proposals by the Commission, the Council, and the European Parliament or may issue an opinion on its own initiative. The Committee also issues an opinion every year on the Commission's Annual Report on Competition Policy. Article 228 TFEU also empowers the European Ombudsman to receive complaints on alleged instances of maladministration and to open an inquiry if the complainant has advanced sufficient evidence on facts that have not been or are not the subject of legal proceedings.[304] The concept of maladministration has a broader scope than the principle of legality. The Ombudsman has recently examined in *Intel* the scope of the European Commission's discretion in not taking minutes of meetings with third parties where inculpatory or exculpatory evidence might have been collected. It found that the Commission's failure to take notes of a meeting with a senior Dell representative (the complainant) was an act of "maladministration" and could also be considered a breach of Intel's rights of defense, in case that evidence was not previously at the disposal of the Commission and the Commission made use of it in its eventual decision.[305]

Finally, one should note the role of the Council of the European Union and of the European Parliament in the design of EU competition policy and indirectly the activity of the European Commission in this area. Both have adopted legislation of paramount importance for the enforcement of EU competition law (for example, Regulation 1/2003, Block exemption regulations, the Merger regulation). The Committee of Permanent Representatives (COREPER) at the Council follows up the activity of the European Commission. Established in 2002, the "Competitiveness Council" is a formation of the Council of the EU. Depending on the items on the agenda, this Council is composed of European Affairs Ministers, Industry Ministers, Research Ministers, etc. It meets about five or six times a year. The Competitiveness Council assumes a horizontal role in ensuring an integrated

[302] For commentary on the Advisory Committee and its role in the proceedings, *see*, e.g., Paulis, cit. (fn. 47), 387–8.

[303] *See*, <http://www.eesc.europa.eu/?i=portal.en.int-section>.

[304] For an analysis, *see* Diamandouros, "Improving EU Competition Law Procedures by Applying Principles of Good Administration: The Role of the Ombudsman", (2010) 1(5) Journal of European Competition Law & Practice 379–396.

[305] Decision of the European Ombudsman, Case 1935/2008/FOR, <http://www.ombudsman.europa.eu/cases/summary.faces/en/4399/html.bookmark>. *See* also, for examples of other decisions of the Ombudsman in competition cases: Case 2953/2008/FOR, <http://www.ombudsman.europa.eu/cases/summary.faces/en/5416/html.bookmark>; Case 3699/2006/ELB, <http://www.ombudsman.europa.eu/cases/decision.faces/en/4752/html.bookmark>.

approach to the enhancement of competitiveness and growth in Europe, by reviewing horizontal and sectoral competitiveness issues, ensuring that competitiveness is integrated in all actions, and legislative proposals. Two Committees at the European Parliament oversee the Commission's activities in the area of competition policy: the Committee on Internal Market and Consumer Protection and the Committee on Economic and Monetary Affairs. The European Parliament also adopts each year a resolution on the Commission's Annual Report on Competition Policy and comments on all proposals of the European Commission.

V. Conclusions: suggestions for reform and improvement

This study has reviewed the central features of the EU framework for competition enforcement and illustrated a number of controversial areas relating to the way in which the EU legal system sought to reconcile the need to ensure the *effet utile* of the competition rules Articles 101 and 102 TFEU and the respect for basic principles of administrative performance and due process. Our conclusions will consider a number of possible suggestions for reform and improvement of the existing system with a view to ensuring that the outcome of the trade-off between these two apparently competing values is compatible with the paramount objective of guaranteeing a "fair procedure" to investigated undertakings.

With regard to administrative performance norms, the EU enforcement system has made considerable progress over the last twenty years and, in the opinion of the authors of this study, gets high marks. As far as transparency is concerned, DG Competition has been a leader in publicizing draft guidelines and guidance, asking for and posting comments and holding hearings on such documents. With regard to the quality of decision-making this has steadily improved under the dual influence of the reinforcement of evidentiary standards following more intensive judicial scrutiny by the General Court and the extensive integration of economics in the normative texts and individual decisions adopted by the Commission. The Commission's appointment of a Chief Economist reflects its responsiveness to changes in intellectual climate and economic theory. Its internal re-organization with the reinforcement of checks and balances, the establishment of the position of Hearing Officers, and the publication of best practices for merger and antitrust proceedings illustrate also its commitment to impartiality in competition law proceedings.

The decentralization of EU competition law enforcement offers also the opportunity to integrate different institutional cultures and to establish a terrain for experimentation that has the potential to improve the quality of the enforcement system. The coherence of the EU competition enforcement system is preserved by the active role recognized for the European Competition Network (ECN) and the various working groups that compose it. Although timeliness of proceedings is still a matter of concern, there have been important steps towards simplification and reduction of the length of the competition law proceedings with a more formalized and extensive use of the expedited procedure before the General Court, which is particularly important for merger cases.

The current system has been widely criticized on the ground of the choice of enforcement "model" made at EU level.[306] Although, at least in principle, the "integrated agency model" created in the EU legal framework fulfills basic due process requirements,[307] a closer examination reveals a number of concerns at least in the perception of stakeholders relating to an insufficient protection of due process, such as the lack of a public hearing before the decision-making authority (that is, the college of commissioners), the restrictive view of key rights of defense such as the right not to incriminate oneself, the lack of judicial supervision over the disclosure of the evidence gathered in the case file and, in the judicial phase of the proceedings, the "limited review" exercised by the EU Courts over the economic assessment contained in antitrust decisions.[308]

The previous subsections highlighted a number of improvements that have been made in the structure of the Commission's proceedings, such as the strengthening of the role of the Hearing Officer, the publication of notices and guidelines relating to, *inter alia*, fines and access to the file, informal "peer review panels" to "vet" contemplated decisions before their adoption, and the enhanced contact with the investigated parties through "state of play" meetings.[309] However, it may be argued that these changes, while not "cosmetic," are not in themselves sufficient to meet the criticism attracted by the current trade-off between effective enforcement and "due process," in view of the high standard of protection of rights of defense contemplated by the ECHR, should competition law sanctions be considered as "core" criminal sanctions.[310]

Adopting a wider definition of the right not to incriminate oneself and of legal professional privilege, together with some form of judicial supervision over decisions affecting their scope in individual cases, could ensure better protection of the investigated parties vis-à-vis prima facie disproportionate exercise of investigative powers. Although entrusting the Hearing Officer with the function of arbitrating disputes on the nature—whether privileged or not—of the evidence gathered in the course of an investigation, may go some way toward restraining the powers of the

[306] e.g. Appl. Nos 7299/75 and 7496/76, *Albert & LeCompte v Belgium*, [1983] 5 EHRR 533, para 29.

Cf. case T-156/94, *SiderurgicaAristrain Madrid SL v Commission*, [1999] ECR II-645, paras 102 and 109.

[307] *Inter alia*, case 17/74, *Transocean Marine Paint Association v Commission*, [1974] ECR 1063; also case T-156/94, *SiderurgicaAristrain Madrid SL v Commission*, [1999] ECR II-645, paras 102 and 109.

[308] Case C-7/95 P, *John Deere Ltd v Commission*, [1998] ECR I-3111, para 21; also case C-2/01, *BAI and Commission v Bayer*, [2004] ECR I-23, para 47.

[309] *See inter alia* Andreangeli, *EU Competition enforcement and Human Rights*, op. cit., 230 et seq.

[310] *See*, e.g., Slater, Thomas and Waelbroeck, "Competition law proceedings before the European Commission and the right to a fair trial: no need for reform?," College of Europe, Global Competition Law Centre Working Paper Series, paper no 04/08, <http://www.coleurope.eu/content/gclc/documents/GCLC%20WP%2004–08.pdf>, especially 26 et seq.; also, Andreangeli et al., "Enforcement by the Commission—the decisional and enforcement structure in antitrust cases and the Commission's fining system," report presented at the 5th Annual Conference of the Global Administrative Law Centre, 11–12 June 2009, especially 18 et seq.

case-handling officials,[311] there does not seem to be very much support for a move in the direction of expanding the scope of the privilege itself.[312]

In respect of the "judicial" stage of EU competition proceedings, the "limited" review powers exercised by the EU courts may not be sufficiently stringent to ensure that the Commission is kept in "check" as to its investigation and decision-making functions. The options are either to adopt a system close to the plenary jurisdiction control exercised in France by the Paris Court of Appeal or a system that will involve the creation of a specialized tribunal, like the Competition Appeal Tribunal (CAT) in the UK, able to perform a more extensive review of the complex economic assessments entailed in the decisions of the European Commission.[313] The UK Enterprise Act 2002 has indeed established an independent specialized judicial body, the Competition Appeal Tribunal (CAT), with cross-disciplinary expertise in law, economics, business, and accountancy, in order to hear appeals and review the decisions of the OFT, the Competition Commission, and the sector-specific regulators that have concurrent powers.[314] The CAT can also hear actions for damages and monetary claims made under the Competition Act for infringement of the EU and the UK competition law as well as appeals against certain decisions made by OFCOM and/or the Secretary of State on infringements of the Communications Act 2003 or under the Mobile EU Roaming Regulations 2007. The intensity of judicial control varies according to the decisions brought to the attention of the CAT: for infringements of Articles 101 and 102 TFEU and their national equivalents it is appeal on the merits, the CAT being able to confirm, set aside, revoke, or vary the OFT's/sector-specific regulator's decision, penalty, or any finding of fact on which the decision is based, or remit the matter to the OFT/ sector-specific regulator, or make any other decision that the OFT/sector-specific regulator could have made. In contrast, the intensity of CAT's judicial control is more limited for the review of mergers and market investigation references, where it takes the form of judicial review.

It could be questioned whether either conferring on the General Court jurisdiction on the merits or creating a specialized court, according to Article 257 TFEU, endowed with these powers, would constitute an appropriate solution to this problem.[315] New Article 257 TFEU enables the European Parliament and the Council, acting in accordance with the ordinary legislative procedure (co-decision),

[311] *See* Joaquim Almunia, "Fair process in EU competition proceedings," speech given at the European Competition Day, Budapest, 30 May 2011, SPEECH/11/396.

[312] *Inter alia*, case C-238/99, *LVM NV and others v Commission*, [2002] ECR I-8375, para 275; *see* also case C-550/07, *AKZO Nobel Chemicals and another v Commission*, Opinion of AG Kokott, 29 April 2010, not yet reported, paras 46–48, 70–72.

[313] The Competition Appeals Tribunal enjoys powers of "review on the merits," for the purpose of satisfying the requirements of "fair process" enshrined in the Human Rights Act 1998: Schedule 8, para 3(2), Competition Act 1998; *see*, e.g., *NAPP Pharmaceuticals v Director General of Fair Trading*, [2002] ECC 13, paras 93, 117.

[314] The CAT was, under the Competition Act 1998, forming part of the Competition Commission but became an independent judicial body with the Enterprise Act 2002.

[315] Appl. Nos 7299/75 and 7496/76, *Albert & LeCompte v Belgium*, [1983] 5 EHRR 533 at para 29. Also Marion Simmons, Chair of the CAT, speech given at the British Institute of International and Comparative Law conference on "Antitrust Litigation: Where do we stand?" on February 3, 2006.

to establish specialized courts attached to the General Court to hear and determine at first instance certain classes of action or proceedings brought in specific areas. The decisions by specialized courts may be subject to a right of appeal on points of law only or, when provided for in the regulation establishing the specialized court, a right of appeal also on matters of fact, before the General Court.

However, the option of a specialized tribunal[316] must be reconciled with the existing judicial structure.[317] Giving evidence before the House of Lords Select Committee on the EU, a number of experts pointed out that creating a judicial body endowed with powers of review on the merits would be incompatible with the "inter-institutional balance" existing within the EU and especially between the Commission and the Union judiciary for two main reasons: first of all, because such an extensive power of review would be difficult to reconcile with the limited nature of the EU Courts' powers enshrined in the Treaty, although there is room for a more expansive interpretation of these powers, and secondly, because it could entail a significant shift of power from the Commission to the newly established specialized court as regards the determination of the objectives of competition policy.[318] In the course of the same inquiry it was added that a similar proposal would be unlikely to find support among the Member States[319] due to its far-reaching consequences for the carefully crafted institutional balance resulting from the Treaty.[320] It is submitted that although these concerns cannot be easily dismissed, the needs of due process may over time come to justify more extensive reforms of the EU judicial and institutional architecture to accommodate the human rights consequences of the Lisbon Treaty and for a more effective competition law enforcement system overall, which would have capabilities to enforce a more economic evidence-oriented EU competition law.[321]

The option of a specialized tribunal has the potential to provide an adequate institutional response to the increasing integration of economic evidence in competition law proceedings and the need to provide some form of judicial scrutiny of

[316] There has been some discussion on the need to create a specialized competition court in the EU, following the proposals made by the Confederation of British Industries in 2006 and a discussion at the House of Lords Select Committee. *See*, CBI Brief, "The need for an EU Competition Court," 15 June 2006. House of Lords Select Committee, *XV Report: an EU Competition Court*, session 2006–07, 23 April 2007 (hereinafter referred to as *XV Report*).

[317] There has been some discussion on the need to create of a specialized competition court in the EU, following the proposals made by the Confederation of British Industries in 2006 and a discussion at the House of Lords Select Committee. *See*, CBI Brief, "The need for an EU Competition Court," 15 June 2006. House of Lords Select Committee, *XV Report: an EU Competition Court*, session 2006–07, 23 April 2007 (hereinafter referred to as *XV Report*).

[318] *See*, e.g., written evidence submitted to the inquiry re: *XV Report* by the Office of Fair Trading, 6.

[319] *Inter alia*, joined cases T-68, 77–78/89, *SocietàItalianaVetroSpA and Others v Commission*, [1992] ECR II-1403 at para 319. Also, written submission made by the OFT to Subcommittee E, *supra*, fn. 317, 6 (para 24). Cf. House of Lords Select Committee on the European Union, *XV Report*, op. cit., paras 78–79.

[320] Minutes of Evidence given before Subcommittee E during the inquiry leading to the publication of the XV Report by Judge Bo Vesterdorf, 99.

[321] *See* also, mutatis mutandis, Minutes of Evidence given before Subcommittee E by Sir Christopher Bellamy, 41.

the economic assessments made by competition law enforcers.[322] However, its creation could raise important questions as to the extent to which its extensive powers may be consistent with the overall institutional framework established by the Treaty.[323] In addition, it should be recognized that the General Court has exercised its limited powers of scrutiny in a remarkably effective way since its institution, as its case law in many landmark competition and merger cases demonstrates.[324] Although it could be argued that timeliness of review still remains an issue, especially in the field of the control of concentrations,[325] it is undeniable that the Court has, by means of its review of individual decisions,[326] managed to hold the Commission to rather strict standards of proof and sound reasoning.[327]

It can be questioned whether totally separating the investigation from the decision-making functions and entrusting each of them to distinct authorities would go some way to assuaging the due process concerns.[328] It is noteworthy that a similar proposal, advanced in the mid-1990s, envisaged the creation of an independent European Cartel Office,[329] endowed with "exclusive jurisdiction" to apply the antitrust and the merger rules to individual cases, under the review of the Commission and subject to further judicial appeal before the General Court.[330] However, this proposal did not attract significant support.[331] Consequently, radical reforms whereby an independent agency vis-à-vis the Commission is created and entrusted with investigative powers, while the Commission retains decision-making functions, despite being perhaps the most appropriate solution for the "due process versus effective enforcement trade-off," would remain very controversial.[332]

Nonetheless, it is submitted that these are by no means the only options that could be envisaged. It is argued that the fairness concerns arising from the structure of the EU competition framework could be dealt with through an "internal

[322] For an analysis, *see* Lianos, "'Judging Economists': Economic expertise in competition litigation: a European view," in Lianos and Kokkoris (eds), *The Reform of EC Competition Law: Towards an Optimal Enforcement System* (2009, The Hague), 185–320.

[323] *See*, e.g., written evidence submitted to the inquiry re: *XV Report* by the Office of Fair Trading, 6.

[324] *See*, e.g., case T-342/99, *Airtours plc v Commission*, [2002] ECR II-2585; also case 12/03 P, *Tetra Laval v Commission*, [2005] ECR I-987; for commentary, *inter alia*, Vesterdorf, "Standard of proof in merger cases: reflections in the light of recent case law of the Community Courts," (2005) 1(1) CLJ 3.

[325] *See*, e.g., the example of Case T-342/99, *Airtours*, cit.

[326] *See inter alia* case 15/02 P, *Tetra Laval*, cit. (fn 352), paras 42–44.

[327] *See*, e.g., case T-201/04, *Microsoft Corp v Commission*, [2004] ECR II-3601; *see* Wils, "The increased level of EU antitrust fines, judicial review and the ECHR," (2010) 33(1) World Competition 5 at 27–8. *See* also, generally, Joaquim Almunia, "Fair process in EU competition proceedings," speech given at the European Competition Day, Budapest, 30 May 2011, SPEECH/11/396.

[328] *See*, *inter alia*, Meade, "Modelling a European Competition Authority," (1996) 46 Duke L J 153.

[329] For an examination of the proposal, *see*, *inter alia*, Riley, "The European Cartel Office: a guardian without weapons," (1997) 18 ECLR 3.

[330] *Id.*, 4–5, 7.

[331] Meade, "Modelling a European Competition Authority," (1996) 46 Duke L J 153 at 194.

[332] *See inter alia* Andreangeli, *EU Competition enforcement and Human Rights*, cit. (fn. 8), 235 et seq. Cf. Wils, "The combination of the investigative and prosecutorial function and the adjudicative function in EC antitrust enforcement: a legal and economic analysis", (2004) 27(2) W. Comp. 201 at 210 et seq.

reorganization" of the Commission's DG for Competition.[333] The investigation and the decision-making phases of the proceedings could be separated and entrusted each to a different unit within the Directorate,[334] perhaps along the lines of the structure of the European Anti-Fraud Office (OLAF).[335] OLAF, whilst not having decision-making powers, exercises wide ranging powers of investigation into allegations of fraud, corruption, and other professional misconduct threatening the EU's financial interests, not dissimilar to those enjoyed by the Commission in competition investigations.[336] In doing so it enjoys significant independence from the other EU institutions and bodies and is subject to the supervision of a "Surveillance Committee," which exercises its function in conditions of operational independence.[337] Adopting this internal restructuring option could secure more efficient and fairer competition enforcement.[338] Provided that sufficiently robust "Chinese walls" are in place between the units responsible for the investigation and for the decision-making functions, this option would go a considerable way toward meeting due process concerns and would not require an amendment of the EU Treaty.[339]

Another option would be to add some adversarial dimension in the decision-making process by offering more representation to stakeholders (for example, consumer groups) in the decision-making process (for example by establishing a consumer panel within the DG Competition, as it is the case with some national regulatory agencies[340]) and increased procedural safeguards to parties involved,

[333] *See* Andreangeli et al., "Enforcement by the Commission—the decisional and enforcement structure in antitrust cases and the Commissions fining system," report presented at the 5th Annual Conference of the Global Administrative Law Centre, 11–12 June 2009, especially 26 et seq.

[334] *See Id.*, especially 35 et seq.

[335] Commission Decision 1999/352/EC, ECSC, Euratom of 28 April 1999, [1999] OJ L136/20; Regulation 1073/1999 of 25 May 1999 of the Council and the European Parliament, concerning investigations conducted by the European Anti-Fraud Office (OLAF), [1999] L136/1. *See* also the case of state aids: Council Regulation No 659/1999 of 22 March 1999 laying down detailed rules for the application of Article 87 EC Treaty [now Article 107 TFEU]; for commentary, *see*, e.g., Arnull et al., *Wyatt and Dashwood's European Union Law*, (2006, Sweet & Maxwell), 1176 ff.

[336] *See* Reader, "Moving forward, never backwards: preventing fraud in the European Union and defining European Central Bank independence," (2004) 27 FORDHAM INT'L L J 1509 at 1529–1530.

[337] Case C-11/00, *Commission v European Central Bank*, [2003] ECR I-7147, paras 138–141; *see* also Opinion of AG Jacob, para 165. *See*, e.g., Reader, cit. (fn. 336), 551–2; also Odudu, Case comment to C-11/00, *Commission v European Central Bank*, judgment of 10 July 2003, (2004) 41 CMLREV 1073 at 1081–2.

[338] *See*, e.g., House of Lords Select Committee on the EU, *XV Report*, para 155.

[339] *See inter alia* Andreangeli, *EU Competition enforcement and Human Rights*, cit. (fn. 8), 238 et seq.; also Andreangeli et al., "Enforcement by the Commission—the decisional and enforcement structure in antitrust cases and the Commissions fining system," report presented at the 5th Annual Conference of the Global Administrative Law Centre, 11–12 June 2009, especially 25 et seq. *See* also, mutatis mutandis, the example of France: Article 95, Economy Modernisation Act 2008; for commentary, *see*, e.g., "Reform of the French competition regulatory system," <http://www.autoritedelaconcurrence.fr/user/standard.php?id_rub=317>. For commentary, *see*, e.g., Lasserre, "The new French Competition Authority: mission, priorities and strategies for the coming five years," <http://www.autoritedelaconcurrence.fr/doc/intervention_bl_autorite_trustubusters_09.pdf> 2–3.

[340] *See*, for instance, the Communications consumer panel established by the British Communications Act 2003 within OFCOM, the UK communications regulator: <http://www.communicationsconsumerpanel.org.uk/>.

while preserving at the same time the flexibility and consistency offered by the integrated agency inquisitorial model. It is submitted that this could be achieved by the enactment of a European Administrative Procedure Act,[341] which, as in the case of the Administrative Procedure Act in US law,[342] would codify existing procedural constraints for the exercise of rule-making and adjudication and would provide for core administrative process rights, such as more extensive oral hearings, certain adversarial rights, including the right for the parties to present oral testimony by witnesses and party experts and to cross-examine experts and witnesses during the oral hearings, thus providing more opportunities to the European Commission to test its factual record,[343] a duty for the competition authorities to establish an evidentiary record, with an obligation to indicate clearly the studies used or the chosen methodology and a duty to detail reasons for adopting the specific decision (involving for instance the integration of an impact assessment for every decision made that could facilitate the review by the General Court or a specialized EU court[344]). One could further distinguish between the administrative process standards for rule-making (regulatory measures) and for adjudication (adopting individual decisions), which could emphasize different dimensions: more extensive oral hearings and a duty to provide, more extensively than now, reasons for regulatory measures, and more extensive adversarial rights for individual decisions. As has been shown by some recent studies, the adoption of a European APA is "perfectly imaginable in the context of existing provisions of the Treaty and of secondary legislation."[345]

Finally, in respect of the impact of the principles at the basis of the European Competition Network on the protection of due process rights, the absence of a minimum standard of procedural harmonization across the Union and, more generally, the lack of clear case allocation criteria, may expose investigated undertakings to significant legal uncertainty as to the available safeguards and to the risk that any existing domestic procedural rights may be compromised, due to the

[341] *See* for an analysis of this option, Lianos and Korah, *Competition Law: Cases and Materials* (2011, Hart Publishing), chap. 10.

[342] U.S.C. §§ 551–9.

[343] Contrary to what some authors argue (*see*, Bouquet, Comments, in Merola and Waelbroeck (eds), *Towards an optimal enforcement of competition rules in Europe*, Chapter 3 (2010, Bruylant), 467–94), this will not amount to a fully adversarial hearing as the decision will be ultimately taken by the Commission and not by an independent judge.

[344] *See*, Opinion of AG Sharpston, Case C-310/04, *Spain v. Council* [2006] ECR I-7285, para 82–96 considering that the failure of the European Commission to rely on an impact study constituted a breach of the principle of proportionality, thus affecting the legality of the regulation on the agricultural support scheme in question. It is submitted that a similar conclusion may be reached with regard to individual decisions (not only regulatory texts), although the requirement of a duty to provide reasons should be adjusted to the individual and ad hoc nature of the decisions in this case.

[345] Yataganas, "Delegation of regulatory authority in the European Union; the relevance of the American model of independent agencies," Jean Monnet Working Paper 3/01, Jean Monnet Programme, New York University School of Law, 50–1; *see* also the analysis of Meuwese, Schuurmans, and Voermans, "Towards a European Administrative Procedure Act," (2009) 2(2) Review of European Administrative Law 3.

overriding obligation of members to cooperate within the Network.[346] Consequently, the decisions by which a case is "re-allocated" from the Commission to another enforcement agency or any evidence is transmitted from Brussels to a different domestic jurisdiction should be open to challenge before the General Court.[347]

However, it is clear that the operation of the ECN discloses a more general problem stemming directly from the possible conflict between the parallel jurisdiction enjoyed by the Network members and the right not to be prosecuted or sanctioned twice in respect to the same offence, which is now part of the EU Charter of Fundamental Rights.[348] An NCA, or indeed the Commission itself, should not be permitted to take action against undertakings in respect of practices that have already formed the subject matter of a "definitive decision" as to their lawfulness or otherwise in light of the EU competition rules. This rule should, however, find an exception as regards allegations that have been "dropped" in a specific jurisdiction without any detailed examination of their merits, perhaps due to resource constraints or to a lack of "Union interest."[349] It should be noted, however, that the ECN has put in place a working group on cooperation and due process, meeting four times a year, with the mandate to reflect on due process issues raised in the discussions on the convergence of enforcement procedures between the different Member States.[350]

[346] *See*, e.g., Andreangeli, "The impact of the Modernisation Regulation on the guarantees of due process in competition proceedings," (2006) 31 ELRev 342 at 355–6; also Perrin, "Challenges facing the EU network of competition authorities: insights from a comparative criminal law perspective," (2006) 31 ELRev 540 at 556–7.

[347] Case 60/81, *International Business Machines Corporation v Commission*, [1981] ECR 2639 at para 9; *see inter alia* Van der Woude, "Exchange of information within the European Competition Network: scope and limits," in Ehlermann and Atanasiu (eds), *European Competition Law Annual 2002*, op. cit., 369 at 382.

[348] Waelbroeck, "'Twelve feet dangling down and six necks exceeding long.' The EU network of competition authorities and the European Convention on Fundamental Rights," in Ehlermann and Atanasiu (eds), *European Competition Law Annual 2002*, op. cit., 465 at 470 ff.

[349] *See*, e.g., Article 54, Schengen Implementing Convention between 22 EU Member States on the gradual abolition checks at their common borders, [2000] OJ L239/19; for a consideration of this provision *see inter alia*, joined cases C-187/01 and C-385/01, *criminal proceedings against HuseinGozutok and Klaus Brugge*, [2003] ECR I-1345, para 38; also case C-150/05, *Van Straaten v Staat der Nederlanden und Republiek Italie*, [2006] ECR I-9327, para 4445. Cf. e.g., case C-328/05, *SGL Carbon v Commission*, [2007] ECR I-3921, para 29. Also, Commission of the European Communities, *Green Paper on conflicts of jurisdiction and the principle of ne bis in idem in criminal proceedings*, 23 December 2005, SEC(2005) 1767, COM(2005) final 696, 8–9.

[350] *See*, ECN, "A Look Inside the ECN, its Members and its Work," ECN Special Issue, December 2010, <http://ec.europa.eu/competition/ecn/brief/05_2010/brief_special.pdf>, 8; "Chile, The Private Competition Enforcement Review," Ilene Knable Gotts (ed.), 3rd edn, *Law Business Research*, 2010, 31.

10

The International Institutions of Competition Law

The Systems' Norms

*Eleanor M. Fox and Amedeo Arena**

I. Introduction

This book on global process norms in competition law has thus far focused on eight selected nations and one regional jurisdiction; namely, Australia, Canada, Chile, China, Japan, New Zealand, South Africa, the United States, and the European Union. Experts from each of the countries have identified the process and procedure norms embedded in their systems. They report various degrees of protected transparency, predictability, accountability, expertise, quality of performance, and rights of defense, and various trade-offs among norms. Yet there emerges a strikingly similar understanding of norms that govern and should govern procedure and process in competition law systems.

There are now more than 120 national competition law systems in the world. Increasingly, transactions and conduct are cross-border. Multinational corporations are larger than nations themselves. Walmart, for example, has revenues of approximately $408 billion per year while South African GDP is $354 billion. Books are written on global markets and the "hollowed-out" state; business surmounts borders, and in some regulatory respects the state may retreat from regulation in the interest of competitiveness of "its" business. Should we expect that governance of competition will move to a higher level, to obtain a coherent view of global competition, to discipline cross-border harms, to count costs wherever in the world they fall, and to capture worldwide benefits? Should we at least expect coordination

* Eleanor Fox is Walter J. Derenberg Professor of Trade Regulation at New York University School of Law. Amedeo Arena is Assistant Professor of International and European Union Law at the University of Naples "Federico II" School of Law. The authors thank Russell Pitman and Andreas Reindl, as well as the participants to the GAL Competition Workshop held at New York University School of Law on February 4 and 5, 2011 for their most helpful comments. Professor Fox thanks the Filomen D'Agostino and Max E. Greenberg Foundation for generous research support. Dr Arena thanks the US-Italy Fulbright Commission for its generous support in the initial stages of this project.

This chapter is the result of the joint work and research of both authors. Professor Fox wrote sections I and III; Dr Arena wrote sections II and IV.

among the multitudinous state players in the system, to achieve harmony, dissipate disputes, and bridge gaps? And to the extent that supranational systems operate, how can we assure their accountability, responsiveness, and flexibility to adapt to change?

The dilemma of global antitrust has been pondered, and vigorously so for the last two decades. Indeed, the prospect of global antitrust dates back to the late 1940s when, in the aftermath of World War II, world trading partners negotiated for an International Trade Organization and its Havana Charter, which would have required members to take appropriate measures "to prevent on the part of public or private commercial enterprises, business practices affecting international trade which restrain competition, limit access to markets, or foster monopolistic control."

The Havana Charter was never adopted. The United States feared loss of sovereignty and withdrew its support. The project gave way to the more focused General Agreement on Tariffs and Trade (1947), later elaborated and brought under the umbrella of the World Trade Organization (1994), both of which (GATT and WTO) fostered freer trade and thus freer competition.

The 1990s were a decade of soul-searching regarding international antitrust. The case was made—and carried forward particularly by the European Union—that international competition required an international framework. The EU concluded that the WTO was the logical home for an international competition competence. A group of experts convened by the European Competition Directorate proposed a system, beginning with building blocks of cooperation, comity, and capacity building, proceeding to minimum substantive rules, with norms of non-discrimination, due process, and transparency. In 1996, largely at the behest of the European Union, the WTO Singapore Ministerial resolved to establish a working group on competition (along with working groups on three other issues). Thus was born the Working Group on the Interaction between Trade and Competition Policy, whose task was to study issues that could merit further consideration in the WTO framework.

Proposals for a WTO competition competence drew criticism from the United States, which feared a process that would result in overly aggressive competition rules and loss of sovereignty, and also skepticism from most developing countries, which feared loss of domestic policy space and a sweeping takeover of their markets by foreign and multinational enterprises.

In response the European Union reduced the scope of its proposal. The revised plan called for only one substantive item—a requirement to adopt and maintain law against hard-core cartels. Also, it called for dispute resolution limited to breach of clear obligations such as the promise to adopt a law against hard-core cartels; principles of transparency, due process and non-discrimination; and capacity-building. This proposal was offered for the new trade round, launched by a ministerial conference in 2001 at Doha, Qatar. The United States agreed not to object to the Doha competition agenda item, as did most developing countries. Japan, Korea, and Canada were affirmative supporters, along with the EU. Thus, the proposal appeared on the Doha Ministerial Declaration of 14 November 2001, in paragraphs 23–25.

The Doha round, however, was ill-fated almost from the start. Initial negotiations on the core agricultural mandate, at Cancun in 2003, floundered at the outset because developed jurisdictions, particularly the United States and the EU, offered insufficient concessions for reducing their massive cotton subsidies, and the developing countries offered no concessions in return. To save the round, the competition and three other Singapore issues were jettisoned. Shortly thereafter, the WTO Working Group on Trade and Competition was disbanded.[1]

Meanwhile, however, cross-border coordination on competition law issues was robust and becoming even more so. Nations or their competition authorities entered into bilateral cooperation agreements. These were designed largely to advise one another of investigations and cases affecting them and to apply negative or positive comity (deference or assistance when interests were sufficiently aligned). Some jurisdictions undertook deeper one-on-one cooperation as did the US and EU with a merger working group. Coordination, cooperation, and cross-fertilization also took place at meetings of international organizations such as the OECD and UNCTAD. And in 2001, antitrust agencies launched the International Competition Network (ICN), which, in contrast with the WTO, started from roots-up, not top down, and was totally voluntary with no rules or dispute resolution. ICN became a vibrant forum for cross-fertilization and soft convergence. In addition, regional organizations with competition policy dimensions, such as the North American Free Trade Association and a number of such organizations in Latin America, Africa, and Asia, were formed.

More and deeper coordination through regional and world systems may lie ahead for antitrust. Do and will the supporting institutions apply global norms of procedure, process, and performance? Who will monitor them?

This chapter is intended to play a role in highlighting these issues of norms and accountability. We examine four institutions that have or prospectively may have a significant role to play in global competition law or policy: the World Trade Organization (WTO), the Organisation for Economic Cooperation and Development (OECD), the United Nations Conference on Trade and Development (UNCTAD), and the International Competition Network (ICN).

As for antitrust in the WTO, the GATS Annex on Telecommunications and the Reference Paper set out a clear-cut enforceable antitrust discipline. Several other WTO agreements contain antitrust law references. More generally, virtually all WTO instruments, and obligations such as non-discrimination and most favored

[1] *See* generally for the history and proposals regarding world antitrust, Aditya Bhattacharjea, *Trade and Competition Policy*, ICRIER Working Paper No. 146 (2004), available at <http://www.icrier.org/pdf/wp146.pdf>; Eleanor M. Fox, "Competition Law and the Millennium Round," 2 J.Int'l Econ. L. 665 (1999); Eleanor M. Fox, "Toward World Antitrust and Market Access," 91 A.J.I.L. 1 (1997); Jurgita Malinauskaite, "Harmonisation in Competition Law in the Context of Globalisation," 2010 E.B.L.Rev. 369; David Gerber, *Global Competition: Law, Markets and Globalization* (2010); Michael J. Trebilcock and Edward M. Iacobucci, "National Treatment and Extraterritoriality: Defining the Domains of Trade and Antitrust Policy," in Richard A. Epstein and Michael S. Greve, eds, *Competition Laws in Conflict: Antitrust Jurisdiction in the Global Economy* (2004, AEI Press) 169–71; Michael Trebilcock and Robert Howse, *The Regulation of International Trade* (2005, Routledge), 608–9.

nations clauses, are infused with competition policy, for the WTO is largely devoted to freeing markets from state restraints, which invariably limit both trade and competition. Moreover, it is possible that support for a general antitrust competence in the WTO might resurface in the future.

The other three intergovernmental organizations we treat (OECD, UNCTAD, and ICN) all have important mandates in antitrust law and policy. Although none of them have rule-making, decision-making, or enforcement powers, they all have significant influence on the development of antitrust norms, particularly at the national level.

Since the WTO is the one of the four that has decision-making, rule-making, and enforcement powers, it is the most obvious candidate for investigation of both due process and institutional performance norms. Accordingly, we devote most of this chapter to the WTO.

In all cases our modus operandi is to describe the institutional system to the extent necessary to report what process norms are implied or express in the inputs and outputs of the system. (Complaints and agenda-setting are examples of inputs; decisions and recommended practices are examples of outputs.) We then examine the norms against notional international standards. Finally, we offer a critical evaluation and recommendations.

II. The World Trade Organization

A. Institutional design

The WTO institutional structure does not encompass a functional equivalent to an antitrust "agency" or "authority." Therefore, none of the three models described in the template is applicable to the WTO. Rather, the WTO institutional structure could be described as akin to a pure private enforcement model, in that it relies upon the harmed entity to initiate enforcement. It is for each WTO member to monitor compliance by other members with WTO rules and, upon detection of a violation that harms that member's commercial interests, to invoke the dispute resolution mechanism governed by the Dispute Settlement Understanding (DSU). If a report establishes that a member has infringed a provision of a WTO agreement, it is for the winning WTO member to activate the enforcement procedures set out in the DSU to ensure that recommendations are ultimately complied with by the offending member.

1. WTO's tripartite governance structure

The WTO has a tripartite governance structure. Its legislative functions are concentrated in ministerial conferences. Its administrative functions are carried out by the secretariat, a number of councils and committees, and the Trade Policy Review Body. Its adjudicatory functions are entrusted to the Dispute Settlement Body

(DSB), which in turn relies upon ad hoc panels and a standing Appellate Body (AB).

Distribution of decision-making authority within the WTO is concentrated in the legislative and adjudicative branches, since Members have been traditionally reluctant to confer independent decisional authority on the administrative bodies. The case-by-case application and interpretation of WTO rules rests with the adjudicative or dispute resolution branch. The WTO legislative branch adopts the rules that the dispute settlement branch applies. According to most scholarly commentators, the WTO legislative branch lacks transparency and accountability. Negotiations during the Uruguay Round were opaque and secretive.[2] Against this background, the Doha mandate encouraged active participation of all members, and limited access to non-members.[3] This resulted in the establishment of trade negotiations committees on specific topics. Still, a significant share of the real negotiations shifted from the committees to informal meetings organized by a core group of WTO members, usually Brazil, the European Union, India, Japan, and the US.[4] The General Council entrusted the WTO secretariat with the task of managing direct contact with NGOs.[5] In spite of the manifold initiatives organized by the secretariat,[6] certain commentators[7] argue that many of the elements of the "club" model that characterized the GATT[8] system are still inherent in the WTO legislative process.[9]

2. *Dispute resolution in the WTO: the bodies*

Three bodies administer the WTO dispute settlement system: the DSB, the AB, and panels.

The DSB establishes panels, appoints AB members, adopts panel and AB reports, supervises their implementation, and authorizes sanctions for failure to

[2] *See*, e.g., Ernst-Ulrich Petersmann, "Challenges to the legitimacy and efficiency of the World Trading System: democratic governance and competition culture in the WTO—Introduction and Summary," 7 J.Int'l Econ.L. 585 (2004); Richard Blackhurst and David Hartridge, "Improving the Capacity of WTO Institutions to Fulfill their Mandate," 7 J.Int'l Econ.L. 705 (2004).

[3] Doha Ministerial Declaration, WT/MIN(01)/DEC/1, adopted on 14 November 2001, para 49 ("The negotiations shall be conducted in a transparent manner among participants, in order to facilitate the effective participation of all. They shall be conducted with a view to ensuring benefits to all participants and to achieving an overall balance in the outcome of the negotiations.").

[4] *See* generally Gregory Shaffer, "The role of Director-general and Secretariat: Chapter IX and Sutherland Report," 4 World Trade Rev. 429 (2005).

[5] Guidelines For Arrangements on Relations With Non-Governmental Organizations, WT/L/162 (adopted on 18 July 1996). *See* Article V:2 of the Marrakesh Agreement.

[6] For a comprehensive account, *see* Secretariat Note "WTO Secretariat Activities with NGOs," WT/INF/30 (adopted on April 12, 2001).

[7] J.L. Dunoff, "The Misguided Debate Over NGO Participation at the WTO," 1 J.Int'l Econ. L. 433 (1998); Daniel C. Esty, "Non-governmental Organizations at the World Trade Organization: Cooperation, Competition, or Exclusion," 1 J.Int'l Econ.L. 123 (1998).

[8] General Agreement on Tariffs and Trade.

[9] Richard B. Stewart, "Multiple Dimensions of Global Administrative Law," I.I.L.J. International Legal Theory Colloquium Discussion Draft (2009) <http://www.iilj.org/courses/documents/2010Colloquium.Stewart.pdf>, 6.

comply with those rulings. The general council of the WTO serves as the DSB, which is composed of representatives of all WTO Members. It has its own chairman and procedures.

The AB is a standing body comprising seven individuals with a high level of trade expertise who are appointed by the DSB for four-year terms, renewable once, cannot be affiliated with any government (unlike panel members), and must be "broadly representative" of WTO membership. (Article 17.3 DSU.) The Appellate Body sits in randomly selected divisions of three, although non-sitting AB members must "stay abreast of dispute settlement activities." (Article 17.3 DSU.)

Panels are composed of three (occasionally five) members, well-qualified governmental or non-governmental individuals, including persons who have served on or presented a case to a panel. The WTO secretariat proposes nominations drawing from an indicative list of individuals possessing the qualifications. The parties may oppose nominations for "compelling reasons." (Article 8.6 DSU.)

3. Panel stage

At the request of the complaining party and after consultations, a panel must be established, unless the DSB decides by consensus not to establish a panel. The panel receives evidence and argumentation from both sides through two rounds of written submissions and two hearings ("substantive meetings"). The DSU provides that each panel has the right to seek information and technical advice from any individual or body, and to consult experts to obtain their opinion on certain aspects of the matter. With respect to factual issues involving complex scientific or technical matters, a panel may request an advisory report in writing from an expert review group.

The panel must issue its report within six months (three for urgent matters) from the date of establishment of the panel. The period can be exceptionally extended to nine months. The panel first must submit a draft report including only descriptive sections to the parties, who may submit written observations. Thereafter the panel must submit to the parties an interim report, including both the descriptive sections and the panel's findings and conclusions. The parties may request the panel to review specific aspects of that document prior to its circulation to the other WTO members. Within sixty days after the date of circulation of a panel report to the members, the report must be adopted by the DSB unless: i) the DSB decides by consensus not to adopt the report, or ii) one of the parties to the dispute formally notifies the DSB of its intention to appeal the panel report before the AB.

4. Appellate body stage

Only parties to the dispute may appeal a panel report. Third parties having a substantial interest in the matter may make written submissions to the AB and be given an opportunity to be heard. Appeals must be limited to issues of law covered in the panel report and legal interpretations developed by the panel, which the AB may uphold, modify or reverse; the AB may not remand. Opinions expressed in the

AB reports are anonymous. No dissenting or concurring opinions are allowed. The parties have the right to submit written observations and the right to a hearing before the AB. The AB report is usually issued and circulated within sixty days after the appeal is lodged; ninety days in exceptional circumstances. AB reports are adopted by the DSB and must be "unconditionally accepted by the parties to the dispute" (Article 17.14 DSU) unless the DSB decides by consensus not to adopt the AB report. Members may, however, express their views on AB reports.

5. Implementation and enforcement of DSB reports

When a panel or the AB concludes that a measure is inconsistent with a covered agreement, it recommends that the member concerned bring the measure into line with that agreement and may suggest ways in which those recommendations can be implemented. As per Article 21.3 DSU, the member concerned must inform the DSB of its intentions in respect of implementation of the recommendations and rulings of the DSB within thirty days of the date of the adoption of a panel or AB report.

If it is impracticable to comply immediately with the DSB recommendations and rulings, the member concerned must be afforded a "reasonable period of time" in which to do so. According to Article 21.3 DSU, the length of that period can be: i) set by the DSB on the basis of a proposal by the member concerned; ii) agreed upon by the parties; or iii) determined through binding arbitration within ninety days after the adoption of the report by the DSB. Once the latter arbitration process has started, the parties may still negotiate to reach a mutual agreement on the length of the "reasonable period of time."[10]

Failure to comply with DSB rulings may trigger both a tender of compensation by the losing party in the form of additional trade concessions or the right of retaliation by the winning party entailing the suspension of concessions. Where there is disagreement as to the existence or consistency with a covered agreement of measures taken to comply with DSB recommendations and rulings, the matter can be referred to a compliance panel, which is usually the same as the merits panel, under Article 21.5 DSU. Moreover, if the losing party fails to bring its offending measures into line with the agreement within twenty days of the "reasonable period of time" set in accordance with Article 21.3 DSU, the winning party may request authorization from the DSB to retaliate by suspending trade concessions. The DSB must either grant such authorization within thirty days or refer the matter to arbitration, under Article 22.6 DSU.

[10] For example, in *United States—Final Dumping Determination on Softwood Lumber from Canada*, WT/DS264/12, 8 December 2004, Canada and the US reached a mutual agreement on a time period of seven and a half months, and requested the arbitrator to terminate the arbitration proceedings.

B. Mandate

1. Introduction

The general mandate of the WTO is to remove trade restraints and increase the flow of the trade (trade liberalization), through the periodic bargaining by members, and enforcement as described above.

We pause at this point to show the tight interaction between trade and competition, for increasing trade entails increasing competition and, although the specific antitrust provisions in WTO agreements are limited, we observe that virtually all pro-trade elements are also pro-competition and therefore relevant to an inquiry as to process/procedure/performance norms in the world's competition systems. Thereafter, we engage with the specific WTO provisions that either are or are adjacent to antitrust.

Trade liberalization and competition policy are two sides of the same coin.[11] They both have as a goal the establishment of an economic system based on a market economy as a means to increase economic welfare.[12] Although no WTO agreement on competition is currently in place, the basic principles of national treatment, most-favored-nation treatment, and transparency that underpin WTO agreements support the operation of impartial competition policy regimes.[13]

Competition law deals with the prohibition of anticompetitive conduct and transactions by market actors, both governmental and private.[14] It is well-established that private anticompetitive conduct may offset the benefits accruing from the removal or reduction of governmental barriers.[15] International cartels can limit the cross-border movement of goods and services by limiting output or allocating markets between competitors, as shown by antitrust challenges brought in the United States in *National Lead*,[16] *ICI*,[17] and the *Uranium* cartel[18] and in the European Union in the *Sugar* cartel,[19] the *Quinine* cartel,[20] and *Wood Pulp*.[21] The

[11] *See* generally Michael Trebilcock, "Competition Policy and Trade Policy: Mediating the Interface," 31 J. World Trade 71 (1996); Michael Trebilcock and Robert Howse, *The Regulation of International Trade* (2005, Routledge), 588–91.

[12] Mitsuo Matsushita, Thomas J. Schoenbaum, and Petros C. Mavroidis, *The World Trade Organization: Law, Practice, and Policy* (2006, Oxford University Press), 541.

[13] International Competition Policy Advisory Committee, U.S. Dep't of Justice, Final Report (2000) (available at <www.usdoj.gov/atr/icpac/finalreport.htm>). See also Report of the Working Group on the Interaction between Trade and Competition Policy to the General Council, WT/WGTCP/4 (November 30, 2000), paras 11–15.

[14] Cf. Bernard Hoekman and Petros C. Mavroidis, "Economic Development, Competition Policy and the World Trade Organization," 37 J.World Trade 1 (2003), 4 (defining "competition policy" as a discipline that constrains both private and government actions and "antitrust rules" as pertaining only to the behavior of private entities).

[15] *Id.* at 4–5.

[16] *See* United States v. National Lead Co., 63 F. Supp. 513 (S.D.N.Y. 1945).

[17] *See* United States v. Imperial Chemical Indus., 100 F. Supp. 504 (S.D.N.Y. 1951).

[18] *See* In re Uranium Antitrust Litigation, 480 F. Supp. 1138 (N.D. Ill. 1979).

[19] *See* Coöperatieve Vereniging "Suiker Unie" UA v. Commission, of the European Communities, Joined cases 40–48, 50, 54–56, 111, 113 and 114/73, 1975 ECR 1663 (ECJ 1975).

[20] *See* ACF Chemiefarma NV v. Commission, Case 41/69, 1970 ECR 661 (ECJ 1970).

[21] *See* A. Ahlström Osakeyhtiö v. Commission of the European Communities, Joined cases C-89/85, C-104/85, C-114/85, C-116/85, C-117/85 and C-125/85-C-129/85, 1993 ECR I-1307 (ECJ 1993).

harm caused by export and import cartels on transnational trade is even more obvious, as shown by the *Soda Ash*[22] and *Tanner Crab*[23] cases. Vertical agreements also can be harmful, for instance by granting a given distributor absolute protection from intra-brand competition in a specified territory. For the European Union, tight territorial restraints at member state lines can frustrate the establishment of the EU internal market and thereby violate EU competition law.[24] Cross-border mergers may impede import competition, as in the *Gillette*[25] and *Brunswick*[26] cases, and domestic mergers of world leaders can mimic export cartels.[27]

The line between governmental barriers to competition and private anticompetitive conduct becomes increasingly blurred when anticompetitive restraints are "hybrid": mixed public and private.[28] Domestic industrial policy may pursue the protection of national champions and the preservation of employment levels by requiring or encouraging firms to enter into anticompetitive arrangements. Moreover, sovereign states may wish to achieve indirectly through public or private firms the protectionist goals they cannot pursue directly, thus circumventing their WTO obligations. This phenomenon, known as "privatizing protection", is well-known in WTO circles—especially since the panel report in *Japan—Fuji Film*[29]—and was recently an important issue in the first WTO panel report finding an antitrust violation (*Mexico—Telecoms*).[30] As hybrid restraints often lie outside the scope of national competition laws by virtue of the so-called State action defense or similar

[22] *See* In re Asahi Glass Co., Decision of Japan Fair Trade Commission of Japan, 31 March 1983, 29 Shinketsushu 104.

[23] *See* United States v. C. Itoh & Co., 1982–83 Trade Cas. (CCH) para 65,010 (W.D. Wash. 1982).

[24] *See, e.g.*, Établissements Consten S.à.R.L. and Grundig-Verkaufs-GmbH v. Commission, Joined cases 56 and 58/64, 1966 ECR (English Special Edition) 299 (ECJ 1966) para 8; IAZ International Belgium and Others v Commission, Joined cases 96/82 to 102/82, 104/82, 105/82, 108/82 and 110/82, 1983 ECR 3369, paras 23–27; Javico, Case C–306/96, 1998 ECR I–1983, paras 13 and 14; P. General Motors v. Commission, Case C–551/03, 2006 ECR I–3173, paras 67 to 69; Sot. Lélos kai Sia EE and Others v. GlaxoSmithKline AEVE Farmakeftikon Proïonton, Joined cases C-468/06 to C-478/06, 2008 ECR I-07139, para 65.

[25] *See* United States v. Gillette Co., 406 F. Supp. 713 (D. Mass. 1975).

[26] *See* Brunswick Corp., 94 F.T.C. 1174 (1979), aff'd as modified sub. nom; Yamaha Motor Co. v. FTC., 657 F.2d 971 (8th Cir. 1981).

[27] *See* Gencor Ltd v. Commission, Case T-102/96, 1999 ECR II-753 (CFI 1999).

[28] Eleanor M. Fox, "The WTO's First Antitrust Case—*Mexican Telecoms*: A Sleeping Victory for Trade and Competition," 9 J.Int'l Econ.L. 2, at 272–92 (2006).

[29] *See* Panel Report, Japan—Measures Affecting Consumer Photographic Film and Paper (United States v Japan), WT/DS44/R, adopted 22 April 1998.

[30] *See* Panel Report, *Mexico—Measures Affecting Telecommunications Services*, T/DS204/R, adopted 1 June 2004. Mexico did not appeal. *See* WT/DS204/9/Add.8, acknowledged 19 August 2005. For commentaries, *see* Chan-Mo Chung, "Interpretation of 'Interconnection' by the WTO *Mexico—Telecommunications* Panel: A Critique," 41 J. World Trade 4, 783–98 (2007); Eleanor M. Fox, *supra* note 28; Carol George, "WTO Panel Condemns Anti-Competitive Behavior in International Telecoms Case: Mexico-Measures Affecting Telecommunications Services—WT/DS204/R," 10 Int'l Trade L.Reg. (2004); Philip Marsden, "Trade and Competition: WTO Decides First Competition Case—With Disappointing Results," 3 Comp.L. Insight (2004); Antonio Ortiz Mena L.N. and Ricardo Rodriguez, "Mexico's international telecommunications policy: Origins, the WTO dispute, and future challenges," 29 Telecommunications Policy 429–48 (2005); Damien J. Neven and Petros C. Mavroidis, "El mess in Telmex: a comment on Mexico—Measures Affecting Telecommunications Services," 5 World Trade Rev. 271 (2006).

doctrines, applicability of WTO law to those restraints becomes increasingly relevant.

Presently there is no comprehensive WTO framework on antitrust matters.[31] Proposals to that effect from academic and diplomatic circles have been met with varying degrees of opposition.[32] The experts convened by the European Competition Directorate put forward a proposal comprising minimum substantive rules and process norms. The European Commission endorsed such proposal and put it on the world agenda. The United States, however, strongly opposed that proposal, which was perceived as a threat to United States sovereignty. Moreover, several developing countries were opposed to the proposal as it could have constrained their autonomy in the industrial policy domain and could have facilitated takeover of their markets from abroad.

Subsequently, on the run-up to the launch of the Doha Round, the European Union put forward a significantly less ambitious proposal. It only set out one substantive obligation for WTO members, that is, to adopt and maintain a ban on hard-core cartels. That proposal also envisaged a system of dispute resolution limited to clear-cut infringements of that obligation, such as failing to adopt the ban above. Other provisions reaffirmed the principles of transparency, due process and non-discrimination, and capacity-building.

This time, neither the United States nor developing countries objected to the proposal. In fact, Korea, Japan, and Canada openly supported it. The proposal appeared on the Doha Ministerial Declaration of 14 November 2001. When, however, initial negotiations at Cancun in 2003 on the core agricultural mandate crippled the round, the competition and three other issues (the Singapore issues) were jettisoned. Shortly after, the WTO Working Group on Trade and Competition was disbanded.

The principal mandate of the WTO is to engage negotiations of the members to lower trade barriers and to provide the enforcement framework to resolve disputes regarding application of the negotiated commitments. There is no general antitrust competence. However, several provisions in the WTO agreements deal with

[31] For a recent stocktaking of the competition policy debate between the WTO and other multilateral fora, *see* Jurgita Malinauskaite, "Harmonisation in Competition Law in the Context of Globalisation," 21 E.B.L.Rev. 369, 384–6 (2010). *See* also Mitsuo Matsushita, Thomas J. Schoenbaum, and Petros C. Mavroidis, *supra* note 12, at 577–84.

[32] In support of a global framework and strategy to get there, *see* David Gerber, *Global Competition: Law, Markets and Globalization* (2010, Oxford University Press), at 304 et seq.; Eleanor Fox, *supra* note 1, at 125; Andrew T. Guzman, "Antitrust and International Regulatory Federalism," 76 N.Y.U.L. Rev. 1142 (2001); European Commission (1995), "Competition Policy in the New Trade Order: Strengthening International Cooperation and Rules" (Van Miert report) (Brussels: European Commission). But *see* Michael J. Trebilcock and Edward M. Iacobucci, "National Treatment and Extraterritoriality: Defining the Domains of Trade and Antitrust Policy," in Richard A. Epstein and Michael S. Greve, *Competition Laws in Conflict: Antitrust Jurisdiction in the Global Economy* (2004, AEI Press) at 152 et seq.; Michael Trebilcock and Robert Howse, *supra* note 1, at 609–10; Alan L. Winters, *Doha and the World Poverty Targets*, mimeo (2002, Sussex University); J. Klein, "International Antitrust: A Justice Department Perspective," speech at Fordham Corporate Law Institute, New York City, 26 October 1995; John Hilary et al., "A Genuine Development Agenda for the Doha Round of WTO Negotiations, joint statement by ten development NGOs," (January 2002).

antitrust law. The core WTO antitrust provisions can be divided into three groups:[33] i) *positive obligations*, which require WTO members to ensure that firms carry out a specific pro-competitive behavior; ii) *negative obligations*, which require WTO members to prevent undertakings from engaging in a specified anticompetitive conduct; iii) *exhortative or permissive provisions*, which highlight certain potentially anticompetitive practices and allow WTO members to prohibit them.

Of particular interest are the provisions set out in the GATS Annex on Telecommunications. Those provisions respond to the fact that telecoms have traditionally been owned by the state; many telecom State-owned enterprises have been recently privatized but in ways that carry on their monopoly status; and the maintenance of monopolized national telecommunications threatens significant impairment of cross-border communications and thus of cross-border business. We deal with telecommunications in point 2 below.

Hereafter, we set forth the competition-related provisions of the WTO, starting with the GATT.

2. The General Agreement on Tariffs and Trade (GATT)

Article XI GATT sets out a negative obligation concerning import and export cartels:

> *No prohibitions or restrictions* other than duties, taxes, or other charges, whether made effective through quotas, import or export licences or other measures, *shall be instituted or maintained by any contracting party on the importation* of any product on the territory of any other contracting party *or on the exportation or sale for export of any product* destined for the territory of any other contracting party.[34]

Thus, states may not institute or maintain import and export cartels. The scope of such prohibition is relatively broad: most recently, in *China—Exportation of Raw Materials,* the panel concluded that China had acted in breach of Article XI:1 GATT by imposing a Minimum Export Price (MEP) requirement on exporters of certain raw materials through a "system of self-discipline" based on "informal statements and oral agreements between traders and export regulators".[35] The

[33] Cf. Alberto Alvarez-Jiménez, "Merging WTO Competition Jurisprudence and its Possibilities for Future Development," 24 Nw. J. Int'l L. & Bus. 441, 488–92 (2004) (suggesting a tripartite classification of WTO antitrust provisions encompassing (i) pro-competition provisions, (ii) mandatory anti-restrictive business practices precepts, and (iii) exhortatory anti-restrictive business practices norms).

[34] Emphasis added.

[35] Panel Report, *China—Measures Related to the Exportation of Various Raw Materials*, WT/DS394/R, WT/DS395/R, WT/DS398/R, adopted 5 July 2011, para 7.1082. On appeal, the AB found that the Panel erred under DSU Article 6.2 in making findings regarding the MEP requirement claims, and it therefore declared the Panel's substantive findings on these issues to be "moot and of no legal effect". *See* AB Report, *China—Measures Related to the Exportation of Various Raw Materials*, WT/DS394/AB/R, WT/DS395/AB/R, WT/DS398/AB/R, adopted 30 January 2012, paras 234–235. *See* also Marek Martyniszyn, "Export Cartels: is it Legal to Target Your Neighbour? Analysis in Light of Recent Case Law," 15 J.Int'l Econ.L. 181–222, 215 (2012) (noting that although the AB report stripped the

prohibition set out in Article XI:1 GATT, possibly, also implies that state-owned or controlled firms may not be party to import or export cartels.[36] Does the mere tolerance of a private cartel amount to a "restriction" within the meaning of Article XI:1 GATT? Some commentators have argued that it does,[37] relying upon the GATT panel's dictum in *Japan–Semiconductors* that the term "restriction" invites a wider reading than the terms "law", "regulation", or "requirement" appearing in other GATT provisions such as Article III:4.[38] However, the Panel in *Argentina—Hides and Leather* squarely held that Article XI GATT does not require WTO members "to assume a full 'due diligence' burden to investigate and prevent cartels from functioning as private export restrictions."[39]

Article XVII:1 GATT requires WTO members to ensure that their State Trading Enterprises (STEs), in their purchases or sales involving either imports or exports, act in a manner consistent with the general principles of non-discriminatory treatment and, in particular, that STEs make such purchases or sales "solely in accordance with commercial considerations". In the context of the *Canada—Wheat* dispute, the United States had argued before the Panel that the latter clause must be interpreted as prohibiting STEs from using their exclusive or special privileges to the disadvantage of commercial actors. The Panel rejected this argument.[40] On appeal, the AB clarified that the disciplines of Article XVII:1 seek to prevent certain types of discriminatory behavior, not to impose "comprehensive competition-law-type obligations on STEs" as the United States had contended.[41]

3. General Agreement on Trade in Services (GATS)

The WTO framework on trade in services contains both positive and negative obligations concerning antitrust matters. Article VIII GATS is an instance of the latter type. It requires each member to ensure that its monopoly or exclusive service suppliers do not act in a manner inconsistent with that member's specific commitments and MFN obligations both inside the scope of their monopoly rights, and, through abuse of their monopoly position, outside that ambit.

Section 5(a) of the GATS Annex on Telecommunications constitutes a positive obligation. It requires each member to ensure that any telecom service supplier of

panel report of its legal effects, "the reasoning offered by the panelists reinforces a view advocating a greater role to be played by the trade regime in addressing transnational anticompetitive arrangements").

[36] GATT Annex I, *Ad* Articles XI, XII, XIII, XIV and XVIII ("Throughout Articles XI, XII, XIII, XIV, and XVIII, the terms "import restrictions" or "export restrictions" include restrictions made effective through state-trading operations.")

[37] *See* Hoekman and Mavroidis, *supra* note 14, 13.

[38] GATT Panel Report, *Japan—Trade in Semi-conductors*, L/6309, adopted on 4 May 1988, 35S/116, 153–5, paras 104–109.

[39] Panel report, *Argentina—Measures Affecting the Export of Bovine Hides and The Import of Finished Leather*, WT/DS155/R, adopted on 19 December 2000, para 11.52.

[40] Panel report, *Canada—Measures Relating to Exports of Wheat and Treatment of Imported Grain*, WT/DS276/R, adopted 6 April 2004, para 6.106.

[41] AB Report, *Canada—Measures Relating to Exports of Wheat and Treatment of Imported Grain*, WT/DS276/AB/R, adopted 30 August 2004, para 145.

any other member is accorded "access to and use" of public telecommunications transport networks and services on "reasonable"[42] and "non-discriminatory"[43] terms and conditions for the supply of a service included in that member's schedule of commitment.

When the Annex was adopted, telecommunication services and networks in most WTO members were managed by state-owned or controlled companies.[44] WTO members could thus take advantage of those connections to place foreign suppliers of services at a competitive disadvantage without breaching their national treatment or market access commitments.[45] The aim of the Annex on Telecommunications is, therefore, not so much to further liberalize public telecommunication networks and services but to ensure "a level playing field for services suppliers who depend on the access to telecommunications."[46]

The core provisions of the Telecommunications Reference Paper, which have been incorporated in whole or part by 89 WTO members into their GATS schedules, do not apply to all telecoms operators but only to "major suppliers,"[47] that is, those who can "materially affect the terms of participation . . . in the relevant market for basic telecommunications services as a result of: (a) control over essential facilities;[48] or (b) use of its position in the market."[49]

Section 1(1) of the Reference Paper sets out a negative obligation requiring the scheduling WTO member to prevent its major suppliers from engaging in "anticompetitive practices" such as those listed in paragraph 2 thereof.[50] The panel in *Mexico—Telecoms* clarified that the list is not exclusive[51] and also that anticompetitive horizontal agreements fall within the ban.[52] Interestingly, in reaching that

[42] *See* Panel Report, *Mexico—Telecoms*, para 7.334.

[43] "Non-discriminatory" is defined in footnote 15 of the Annex on Telecommunications.

[44] *See* Bobjoseph Mathew, *The WTO Agreements on Telecommunications* (2003, Peter Lang), 77.

[45] *See* Kelly Cameron, "Telecommunications and Audio-Visual Services in the Context of the WTO: Today and Tomorrow," in Damien Geradin and David Luff (eds), *The WTO Agreements on Telecommunications* (2004, Cambridge University Press), 21 et seq.

[46] *See* Bobjoseph Mathew, *supra* note 44.

[47] In contrast, other provisions of the Reference Paper make no reference to the competitive situation of suppliers. *See* Section 5 thereof (requiring that "Independent regulators" be "separate from, and not accountable to, *any* supplier of basic telecommunications services") (emphasis added).

[48] For the definition of "essential facilities", *see* para 2 of the "Definitions" section of the model Reference Paper.

[49] In order to establish whether the Mexican incumbent operator Telmex constituted a "major supplier" they examined: (i) the "relevant market"; (ii) whether Telmex had "the ability to materially affect the terms of participation" in that market; and (iii) whether this ability resulted from "control over essential facilities" or "use of its position in the market." *See* Panel Report, *Mexico—Telecoms,* para 4.178.

[50] *See* Section 1(2) of the Reference Paper (referring to anticompetitive cross-subsidization, use of information obtained from competitors with anticompetitive results, and not making available to other services suppliers technical information about essential facilities and commercially relevant information which are necessary for them to provide services).

[51] *See* Panel Report, *Mexico—Telecoms,* para 7.232 (noting that the list in Section 1(2) of the Reference Paper only includes the most relevant unilateral practices to the telecommunications sector).

[52] *Id.*, para 7.234.

conclusion, the panel referred to WTO members' antitrust legislation and international instruments that address competition policy.[53]

Section 2(2) of the Reference Paper sets out a positive obligation for the scheduling WTO member to ensure that its major suppliers enable interconnection under non-discriminatory terms, in a timely fashion at cost-oriented rates[54] (having regard to economic feasibility),[55] and upon request, at points in addition to the network termination points offered to the majority of users. The following paragraphs of Section 2 of the Reference Paper lay down procedural requirements related to interconnection, including availability of dispute settlement before an "independent domestic body."

4. The Agreement on Technical Barriers to Trade (TBT Agreement)

Article 8.1 of the TBT Agreement sets out a positive and a negative obligation:

> Members shall take such reasonable measures as may be available to them to ensure that *non-governmental bodies within their territories* which operate conformity assessment procedures *comply with the provisions of Articles 5 and 6,* with the exception of the obligation to notify proposed conformity assessment procedures. In addition, *Members shall not take measures which have the effect of, directly or indirectly, requiring or encouraging such bodies to act in a manner inconsistent with the provisions of Articles 5 and 6.*[56]

Articles 5 and 6 of the TBT Agreement deal with, respectively, procedures for assessment of conformity by central government bodies and recognition of conformity assessment carried out by those bodies. In short, those provisions stipulate that national treatment must be observed vis-à-vis foreign products, technical regulations must not be more trade restrictive than necessary, and mutual recognition of technical regulations must be promoted.[57]

Trade associations involving traders of a certain country may have incentives to discriminate against imported products.[58] For instance, the allegation that Japanese trade associations applied testing procedures in a protectionist manner prompted the Japanese Fair Trade Commission to revise its Guidelines on the Activities of Trade Associations in the framework of the US–Japan Structural Impediments Initiative.[59]

53 *Id.*, paras 7.235–7.236.

54 *Id.*, para 7.177 (employing incremental cost methodologies to assess the "cost-oriented" requirement).

55 *Id.*, para 7.183 (interpreting "having regard to economic feasibility" as allowing the major supplier to derive a "reasonable rate of return" from interconnection fees).

56 Emphasis added.

57 Mitsuo Matsushita, Thomas J. Schoenbaum and Petros C. Mavroidis, *supra* note 12, 546.

58 *See,* e.g., National Macaroni Manufacturers Ass'n v. FTC, 345 F.2d 421 (7th Cir. 1965); United States v. Automobile Mfrs. Ass'n, Inc., 307 F. Supp. 617, 1969 Trade Cas. (CCH) paras 721, 907 (C.D. Cal. 1969).

59 Japan Fair Trade Commission, Guidelines Concerning the Activities of Trade Associations under the Antimonopoly Act, October 30, 1995, <www.jftc.go.jp/e-page/legislation/ama/tradeassociation.pdf>.

The goal of Article 8.1 of the TBT Agreement is thus twofold: on the one hand, to ensure that the restraints placed on governmental action by Articles 5 and 6 thereof are not nullified by private conduct of non-governmental bodies entrusted with conformity assessment procedures and, on the other hand, to prohibit "privatizing protection" scenarios, thus preventing WTO members from circumventing their TBT obligations by recourse to non-governmental actors.

The relevance of this provision to competition policy—albeit not competition law—is that discriminatory action by firms is often anticompetitive. Member states must insure that these discriminations by private firms and bodies do not occur.

5. *The Agreement on Safeguards*

Article 11.1(b) of the Agreement on Safeguards stipulates: "a Member shall not seek, take or maintain any voluntary export restraints, orderly marketing arrangements or any other similar measures on the export or the import side." Footnote 4 to that provision provides examples of similar measures: "export moderation, export-price or import-price monitoring systems, export or import surveillance, compulsory import cartels and discretionary export or import licensing schemes, any of which afford protection."

As in the case of Article 8.1 of the TBT Agreement, the direct ban on anticompetitive governmental action laid down in Article 11.1(b) is backed by an anticircumvention provision, set out in Article 11.3, requiring WTO Members not to "encourage or support the adoption or maintenance by public and private enterprises of non-governmental measures equivalent to" the ones above.

The purpose of these provisions of the Agreement on Safeguards is to prohibit voluntary export restraints (VERs); viz., agreements between an exporting country and an importing one where the former agrees to limit or to discontinue its export of a given product at a request of the latter. VERs, which were popular prior to the Uruguay round (thus prior to the establishment of the WTO), are anticompetitive and are often lacking in terms of transparency.

Following the outright ban on VERs introduced by the Agreement on Safeguards, some VERs have "gone underground" and have taken the form of international cartels sponsored or tolerated by governments.[60] As with Article XI GATT, the interpretive question arises as to whether state toleration of private import/export restraints falls within the prohibition.

6. *The Agreement on Trade-Related Aspects of Intellectual Property Rights (TRIPS)*

Article 40.1 of the TRIPS Agreement states that some licensing practices or conditions pertaining to intellectual property rights may restrain competition. Article 40.2 of the TRIPS Agreement provides:

[60] *See* Matsushita, Schoenbaum, and Mavroidis, *supra* note 12, at 211.

Nothing in this Agreement shall prevent Members from specifying in their legislation licensing practices or conditions that may in particular cases constitute an abuse of intellectual property rights having an adverse effect on competition in the relevant market. As provided above, a Member may adopt, consistently with the other provisions of this Agreement, appropriate measures to prevent or control such practices, which may include for example exclusive grantback conditions, conditions preventing challenges to validity and coercive package licensing, in the light of the relevant laws and regulations of that Member.[61]

The list of potential anticompetitive licensing practices that members may control is not exhaustive. Other potential candidates for proscription by domestic antitrust laws include excessive royalties, tie-in arrangements, resale price maintenance,[62] and parallel import bans,[63] although in some member states these practices are not, or are not presumptively, anticompetitive.

Article 40.3 sets out a consultation mechanism whereby if an IPR holder residing in a WTO member state is alleged to have acted in a manner inconsistent with another member's (antitrust) legislation, the former must consult with the latter and supply "publicly available non-confidential information of relevance to the matter in question" as well as "other information available."[64] The goal of this consultation process is to facilitate the provision of the necessary information to the investigating authorities or antitrust agencies of WTO Members in cross-border licensing cases involving anticompetitive restrictions. This consultation mechanism is "without prejudice to any action under the law and to the full freedom of an ultimate decision of either Member."

Article 40.4 complements the "offensive" consultation mechanism laid down in Article 40.3 with a "defensive" one, extending the right to request consultations to the WTO member where the respondent IPR holder resides.

7. Agreement on Trade-Related Investment Measures (TRIMs)

Article 9 TRIMs sets out a negotiation mandate for the Council for Trade in Goods which, within five years from the entry into force of the WTO Agreement, must review the operation of the TRIMs Agreement and may propose amendments to the Ministerial Conference amendments. In particular, the Council for Trade in Goods must "consider whether the Agreement should be complemented with provisions on investment policy and competition policy."

[61] Emphasis added.

[62] *See* Matsushita, Schoenbaum, and Mavroidis, *supra* note 12, at 549. *See*, for a discussion of TRIPs and its relationship to competition law, Eleanor M. Fox, "Trade, Competition, and Intellectual Property—TRIPS and its Antitrust Counterparts," 29 Vand. J. Transnat'l L. 481 (1996).

[63] *See* Hoekman and Mavroidis, *supra* note 14, at 15 (noting that some WTO members call for harmonized rules at the WTO level on this issue, although recent research suggests that the case for harmonization is in fact weak).

[64] Article 40.3 TRIPS.

Pursuant to Article 9 TRIMs, the Council for Trade in Goods launched the review of the operation of the TRIMs Agreement in 1999.[65] Even though the review process has not yet resulted in the incorporation of competition policy provisions in the TRIMs Agreement, Article 9 is commonly regarded as evidence of the awareness by the framers of the close link existing between competition policy and the matters governed by the TRIMs Agreement.[66]

8. Agreement on Government Procurement

The aim of the WTO Agreement on Government Procurement is to increase the openness and transparency of laws, regulations, procedures, and practices regarding government procurement with a view to prevent protectionist or discriminatory practices against foreign products or suppliers. To this end, that agreement sets out a comprehensive set of rules on several aspects of the tendering procedures.

It has been observed that the framework set forth in the Agreement on Government Procurement may also contribute to prevent anticompetitive practices such as collusive tendering or bid rigging,[67] which tend to occur more frequently in settings where competitive and transparent bidding procedures are not in place.[68]

C. Due process norms

1. Opportunity to be heard

Direct access to the dispute settlement system is restricted to WTO member governments. This section will deal with WTO members' opportunity to be heard, both as parties to a dispute and as third parties. Participation of non-state actors is addressed in the section on transparency below.

At the consultation stage, each member undertakes to accord sympathetic consideration to, and afford adequate opportunity for consultation regarding any representations made by another member concerning measures affecting the operation of any covered agreement taken within the territory of the former (Article 4.2 DSU). In particular, problems and interests of developing country members should be given special attention (Article 4.10 DSU). Members having a substantial trade interest in consultations other than the consulting members may notify the latter and the DSB of their desire to be joined in the consultations. Such member will be joined in the consultations if the member to whom the request for consultations was addressed agrees that the claim of substantial interest is well-founded.

During the panel phase, parties are involved in the establishment of the panel and in the determination of the latter's term of reference. The merits phase consists of two rounds of written submissions and two hearings ("substantive meetings")

[65] Council for Trade in Goods, Minutes of the Meeting held in the Centre William Rappard on 15 October 1999, G/C/M/41, p. 10–11.

[66] Matsushita, Schoenbaum, and Mavroidis, *supra* note 12, 550.

[67] Trebilcock and Howse, *supra* note 1, at 594.

[68] Hoekman and Mavroidis, *supra* note 14, at 16–17.

before the panel. The panel may put questions to the parties at any time and may ask them for explanations either in the course of a substantive meeting or in writing. During the interim review stage, parties may submit to the panel their written comments on the draft report (which will include only the descriptive part), and later on the interim report (which will include the panel's findings), and they may request the panel to hold a further meeting on the issues identified in the written comments.

Third parties having a substantial interest in a matter before a panel may notify their interest to the DSB. This entitles them to be heard by the panel and to submit written observations, which are accounted for in the panel report. Third parties are also entitled to receive the parties' written submissions.

At the appellate review stage, parties (which at this stage are referred to as "participants") and third parties ("third participants") are entitled to present written submissions and to attend one oral hearing.[69] At any time during the appellate proceeding, including, in particular, during the oral hearing, the AB division may address questions orally or in writing to the parties and to third participants. WTO members that have not been a third party at the panel stage cannot take part in the appellate review stage. They may submit *amicus curiae* briefs, which the AB may take into account but is under no obligation to do so.[70]

We conclude that parties and third parties to WTO disputes have ample opportunity to be heard during all stages of the dispute settlement procedure. As noted below, however, the significance accorded to the need to hear parties and third parties comes at a price: a non-negligible increase in the duration of the dispute settlement process.

2. *Full notice of allegations*

The DSU sets out several procedural arrangements to ensure that the respondent party in a WTO dispute settlement procedure is informed in detail of the complainant's claim. This section will show how i) the request for consultations, ii) the request for establishment of a panel, and iii) the notice of appeal contribute to provide the respondent with full notice of the complainant's allegations.

The mandatory consultations phase precedes the establishment of a panel. Pursuant to Article 4.4 DSU, requests for consultations must be submitted in writing and give the reasons for the request, including identification of the measures at issue and an indication of the legal basis for the complaint. Although such requests are often very brief (usually they consist of no more than two pages), they must be sufficiently precise to achieve the objective of consultations; that is, to give the parties an opportunity to discuss the matter and to find a satisfactory solution

[69] Following revision of the AB Working Procedures, third participants are not required to file a third participants' submission in order to be entitled to attend the oral hearing before the AB, but should notify the AB Secretariat in writing of the intention to appear at the oral hearing.

[70] *See* AB Report, *European Communities—Trade Description of Sardines*, WT/DS231/AB/R, adopted 23 October 2002 paras 161–167 (accepting an *amicus curiae* brief submitted by Morocco).

without resorting to litigation. Even when consultations are not successful, they serve an important function: that of providing the respondent with a sufficiently clear picture of the complainant's claims and to clarify the subject of the dispute.[71]

The request for establishment of a panel also contributes to providing a full notice of the complainant's allegations. Under Article 6.2 DSU, that request must identify the specific measures at issue, and provide a brief but sufficiently clear summary of the legal basis of the complaint. The content of the request for establishment of the panel determines the standard terms of reference for the panel's examination of the matter (Article 7.1 DSU), thus defining the subject and scope of the dispute and the extent of the panel's jurisdiction.

The AB in *EC—Bananas III* recognized that the request for establishment of the panel has the function of informing the respondent (and third parties) of the basis for the complaint,[72] allowing the latter to exercise its right of defense. In *Chile—Price Band System* the AB expressly linked the duty to clearly state the claims in the request for the establishment of the panel to the "requirements of due process and orderly procedure."[73] Moreover, in *EC—Bananas III*, the AB held that if a given claim is not included in the initial request, it cannot be introduced at a later stage (for example, in the complainant's written submissions or in oral statements to the panel).[74]

Drafting the request for the establishment of a panel with sufficient precision is thus of the essence. In *Korea—Diary*, for instance, the AB carefully considered whether the respondent's ability to defend itself was prejudiced by the fact that the complainant's request for establishment of the panel merely set out a list of provisions allegedly infringed by the respondent.[75] Most recently, in *China—Exportation of Raw Materials*—a case involving multiple claims concerning *inter alia* the endorsement of an export cartel for certain raw materials—the AB ruled that the panel request failed to provide "sufficiently clear linkages" between the broad range of obligations contained in the WTO provisions claimed to have been infringed and the thirty-seven Chinese measures challenged by the complainants.[76]

[71] Picone and Ligustro, *Diritto dell'Organizzazione Mondiale del Commercio* (Cedam, 2002) 584.

[72] AB Report, *European Communities—Regime for the Importation, Sale and Distribution of Bananas*, WT/DS27/AB/R, adopted 25 September 1997, DSR 1997:II, 591, para 142.

[73] AB Report, *Chile—Price Band System and Safeguard Measures Relating to Certain Agricultural Products*, WT/DS207/AB/R, adopted 23 September 2002, para 164.

[74] *See* AB Report, *European Communities—Regime for the Importation, Sale and Distribution of Bananas*, WT/DS27/AB/R, adopted 25 September 1997, DSR 1997:II, 591, para 143 (holding that only if claims are clearly stated the panel, other parties, and third parties may understand that "a specific claim has been made, be aware of its dimensions, and have an adequate opportunity to address and respond to it").

[75] AB Report, *Korea—Definitive Safeguard Measure on Imports of Certain Dairy Products*, WT/DS98/AB/R, adopted 14 December 1999, para 127. *See* also AB Report, *Thailand—Anti-Dumping Duties on Angles, Shapes and Sections of Iron or Non-Alloy Steel and H-Beams from Poland*, WT/DS122/AB/R, adopted 5 April 2001, para 95.

[76] AB Report, *China—Measures Related to the Exportation of Various Raw Materials*, WT/DS394/AB/R, WT/DS395/AB/R, WT/DS398/AB/R, adopted 30 January 2012, paras 234–235.

The principles governing the notices of appeal are similar to those concerning the request for establishment of a panel. According to Rule 20(2)(d) of the AB Working Procedures, notices of appeal must contain a brief statement of the nature of the appeal, including: i) the allegations of errors in the issues of law covered in the panel report and legal interpretations developed by the panel; ii) a list of the legal provisions of the covered agreements that the panel is alleged to have erred in interpreting or applying; and iii) an indicative list of the paragraphs of the panel report containing the alleged errors.

The degree of detail required for notices of appeal is somewhat controversial. In *US—Shrimp* the AB held that notices of appeal are not intended to be a summary or outline of the arguments of the appellant, which must be laid down in the latter's written submission.[77] In a similar vein, in *EC Bananas III* the AB ruled that it was acceptable for a notice of appeal not to cite the numbered paragraphs of the panel report containing the findings appealed as long as it clearly identified which panel findings or interpretations the AB was requested to review.[78] However, in the same report the AB stated that the notice of appeal serves to give the appellee notice of the findings appealed so that it can prepare its defense, and it refused to review a finding that was not mentioned in the notice of appeal.[79] Similarly, in a subsequent report, the AB dismissed a claim of error that was not included in the notice of appeal.[80]

Therefore, in spite of the uncertainties concerning the required level of detail of the request for consultations, the request for establishment of a panel, and the notice of appeal, it can be argued that those three acts contribute significantly to ensuring that the respondent receives full notice of the complainant's allegations. In particular, those acts serve the function of protecting the respondent against surprise claims, allowing that party to fully exercise its right of defense. Both in respect of the request for establishment of a panel and of the notice of appeal, the AB has been adamant in rejecting claims that were not laid down, albeit perfunctorily, in those two documents.

3. *Reasonable time to prepare*

The principle that parties must be afforded sufficient time to prepare is expressly recognized in Article 12.4 DSU, which requires panels to take that element into account when determining the timetable for the panel process under Article 12.3 DSU. A proposed timetable for panel work is set out in paragraph 12 of Appendix 3 to the DSU: the complainant is given three to six weeks to submit its complaint; the respondent has two to three weeks to submit its written observations; both parties

[77] *See* AB Report, *United States—Import Prohibition of Certain Shrimp and Shrimp Products*, WT/DS58/AB/R, adopted 6 November 1998, DSR 1998:VII, 2755, para 95.

[78] *See* AB Report, *European Communities—Regime for the Importation, Sale and Distribution of Bananas*, WT/DS27/AB/R, adopted 25 September 1997, DSR 1997:II, 591, para 96.

[79] *Id.* at para 152.

[80] *See* AB Report, *United States—Import Measures on Certain Products from the European Communities*, WT/DS165/AB/R, adopted 10 January 2001, paras 75–77.

are granted one to two weeks to prepare for the first substantive meetings; after that the parties can submit their written rebuttals in two to three weeks; again they have one to two weeks to prepare for the second substantive meeting.

The DSU offers a degree of flexibility. Article 12.1 DSU and paragraph 11 of Appendix 3 explicitly state that the panel can follow different procedures after consulting the parties. In practice, panels have taken full advantage of that opportunity to grant the parties additional time to prepare above and beyond the DSU requirements. For instance, it has become standard practice for panels to grant one to two weeks for third parties' submissions before the first substantive meeting, up to two weeks to reply to panel questions after both substantive meetings, and a final opportunity to comment on those replies.[81]

In sum, parties are generally afforded adequate time to prepare their submissions, often even beyond the time frames set out in the DSU timetable. While this certainly promotes due process and the exercise of right of defense, it inevitably slows down the dispute settlement system, thus undermining its institutional performance record, as clarified in the section on timeliness below.

4. *Right to appeal*

One of the most significant improvements relative to the pre-WTO dispute settlement system is the introduction of an appeal stage. Other interstate free trade agreements, such as the NAFTA and the CAFTA, provide for procedures similar to the WTO interim review but do not allow for appeal.

Only the parties to a dispute—not third parties—can appeal a panel report (Article 16.4 DSU). Both the winning and the losing party are granted this right. They may seek appellate review of different findings of the panel, as well as of the same findings but for different reasons. It is not uncommon for parties to appeal panel findings that support that party's position in a specific dispute but may be harmful on a general level. For instance, in *Japan—Alcoholic Beverages II* the US government appealed the panel report, even though the panel had upheld its claim that Japan had infringed Article III:2 GATT, because the US government objected to the panel's interpretation of Article III.[82]

Multiple appeals can be filed in two ways. First, more than one party may exercise its right of appeal under Article 16.4 DSU. In that event, the AB handles those appeals jointly (Rule 23(5) of the Working Procedures). Second, a party to the dispute other than the original appellant (i.e. the party that initiated the appeal under Article 16.4 DSU) may join in that appeal. Such an appeal, usually referred to as "other appeal" or "cross-appeal," broadens the scope of appellate review so as to cover other errors of law alleged by the cross-appellant (Rule 23(1) of the Working Procedures).

[81] Matthew Kennedy, "Why are WTO panels taking longer? And what can be done about it?", 45 J. World Trade 221, 231 (2011).

[82] *See* AB Report, *Japan—Taxes on Alcoholic Beverages*, WT/DS8/AB/R, WT/DS10/AB/R, WT/DS11/AB/R, adopted 1 November 1996, DSR 1996:I, 97.

Appellate review is restricted to issues of law covered in the panel report and to legal interpretation developed by the panel, which the AB may uphold, modify, or reverse (Articles 17.6 and 17.13 DSU). The AB case law provides some guidance in differentiating between issues of law, which are subject to appellate review, and issues of fact, which are excluded from review. In *Korea—Alcoholic Beverages* the AB held that the establishment of factual circumstances as well as the examination and weighing of evidence falls within the panel's discretion and is not subject to appeal.[83] However, in *EC—Hormones* the AB ruled that establishing the "consistency or inconsistency of a given fact or set of facts with the requirements of a given treaty provision" is a legal characterization issue, subject to appellate review.[84] In a similar vein, in *US—Wheat Gluten* the AB asserted its competence to review compliance by the panel with the legal limits to its discretion,[85] especially where the panel allegedly disregarded, distorted, or misrepresented evidence or committed "egregious errors" in evaluating it.[86]

In sum, the WTO dispute resolution system fully recognizes the parties' right to appeal from panel reports and provides for an institutional structure that enables a comprehensive appellate review, especially by intergovernmental standards. Moreover, as clarified in the timeliness section below, the appellate review phase is usually carried out expeditiously.

5. *Independence of decision-makers*

In terms of the independence of panel and AB members, a distinction must be drawn between the external and the internal dimension. External independence implies that decision-makers are protected from undue pressure from outside parties, such as lobby groups, NGOs, and multinational undertakings. Internal independence, more readily understood as "impartiality," implies equal and unbiased treatment of the parties to a dispute.

Article 8.2 DSU states that panel members must be selected with a view to ensuring their independence. Article 8.3 DSU stipulates that citizens of members whose governments are parties to a dispute or third parties cannot serve on a panel concerned with that dispute unless the parties agree otherwise. If customs unions or common markets are parties to a dispute, that provision applies to citizens of all member countries of the customs unions or common markets. Since panel members (unlike AB members) can be affiliated with governments of a WTO member, Article 8.9 DSU specifies that panel members must serve "in

[83] *See* AB Report, *Korea—Taxes on Alcoholic Beverages*, WT/DS75/AB/R, WT/DS84/AB/R, adopted 17 February 1999, DSR 1999:I, 3, para 161.

[84] *See* AB Report, *EC Measures Concerning Meat and Meat Products (Hormones)*, WT/DS26/AB/R, WT/DS48/AB/R, adopted 13 February 1998, DSR 1998:I, 135, para 132.

[85] *See* AB Report, *United States—Definitive Safeguard Measures on Imports of Wheat Gluten from the European Communities*, WT/DS166/AB/R, adopted 19 January 2001, para 151.

[86] *See* AB Report, *EC Measures Concerning Meat and Meat Products (Hormones)*, WT/DS26/AB/R, WT/DS48/AB/R, adopted 13 February 1998, DSR 1998:I, 135, para 133.

their individual capacities and not as government representatives, nor as representatives of any organization" and that members must not "give them instructions nor seek to influence them as individuals" with regard to matters before a panel.

Those statements of principle are reflected in the procedure set out in the DSU governing the composition of panels. The Secretariat usually proposes nominations to the parties, drawing from an indicative list of people that meet certain expertise and independence requirements. Names proposed by WTO Members are almost *de plano* included in that list, subject to a limited number of peremptory challenges. Although parties are constrained not to oppose nominations except for compelling reasons (Article 8.6), in fact they object to nominations rather frequently, providing reasons that are not subject to review. When this occurs, the Secretariat draws other names from the list.

As for AB members, Article 17.3 DSU stipulates that they must not be affiliated with any government and they must not participate in the consideration of any disputes that would create a direct or indirect conflict of interest. Rule 2 of the AB Working Procedures requires AB members not to accept employment or professional activities inconsistent with their duties and to refrain from accepting or seeking instructions from any international, governmental, or non-governmental organization or any private source.

These principles are fleshed out by a self-disclosure procedure set out in Section VI of Annex II attached to the Working Procedures for Appellate Review. Upon the filing of a Notice of Appeal, each AB member (as well as the professional staff of the AB Secretariat) must complete a form whereby he or she undertakes to disclose any information likely to affect his or her independence or impartiality or which could give rise to justifiable doubts as to the integrity and impartiality of the dispute settlement mechanism. Moreover, any party to a dispute who comes into possession of evidence of a material violation of the obligations of independence, impartiality, or confidentiality or the avoidance of direct or indirect conflicts of interest that may impair the integrity, impartiality, or confidentiality of the dispute settlement mechanism must submit such evidence to the Chair of the DSB, the Director General, or the Standing Appellate Body.

In sum, the WTO dispute resolution system appears to be designed in a manner that ensures the impartiality of panel and AB members vis-à-vis the parties to a dispute. This is achieved essentially by granting the parties significant powers in the appointment of panel members and in reporting evidence of possible conflicts of interest on the part of AB members. The concentration of those powers in the parties' hands, however, is not necessarily conducive to the independence of panel and AB members from external influences and special interests, which may be unbeknown to or tolerated by the parties. This, nonetheless, is a reflection of the intergovernmental character of the WTO dispute settlement system, which relies extensively on WTO members as qualified—yet potentially imperfect—representatives of the interests of their nationals and of stakeholders at large.

6. *Rules of evidence*

The DSU does not include any express rule concerning the burden of proof in panel proceedings. The AB has attempted to remedy that shortcoming by ruling that the concept of a burden of proof is implicit in the WTO dispute settlement system. In *US—Wool Shirts and Blouses* the AB endorsed the traditional maxim *onus probandi incumbit ei qui dicit,* according to which it is for the party which asserts a fact, whether complainant or respondent, to provide proof thereof.[87] Accordingly, the complainant must state and provide evidence that the respondent has infringed a given provision of a WTO agreement,[88] while the respondent bears the burden of proving that the requirements set out in an exception or affirmative defense have been met. A review of the precedents on the burden of proof issue seems to reveal that the AB has consistently followed the rule established by *US—Wool Shirts and Blouses.*[89]

The required level of proof is unclear. The AB has affirmed that if the party bearing the burden of proof is able to put forward evidence sufficient to make a prima facie case (a presumption), the *onus* shifts to the other party, who will fail unless it submits sufficient evidence to disprove the claim (thus rebutting the presumption). Precisely how much and what kind of evidence will establish a prima facie case varies from measure to measure, provision to provision, and case to case.

Moreover, the WTO dispute settlement system's epistemic legitimacy in the handling of economic evidence has been recently questioned.[90] Although most WTO rules are based on economic concepts or involve economic evaluations, panels and the AB have been generally unwilling to engage rigorously with economic evidence and argument and have often refused to turn to experts for assistance.[91] For instance, some commentators criticized the panel and AB reports in *US—Offset Act (Byrd Amendment)*[92] in that they ruled on the effects on competition of the challenged US legislation without performing an economic analysis based on empirical verification.[93] In *US—Upland Cotton 21.5,* the AB

[87] *See* AB Report, *United States—Measure Affecting Imports of Woven Wool Shirts and Blouses from India*, WT/DS33/AB/R and Corr.1, adopted 23 May 1997, DSR 1997:I, 323.

[88] *See,* e.g., AB Report, *EC Measures Concerning Meat and Meat Products (Hormones)*, WT/DS26/AB/R, WT/DS48/AB/R, adopted 13 February 1998, DSR 1998:I, 135, para 104.

[89] Matsushita, Schoenbaum, and Mavroidis, *supra* note 12, 39. *See* also Michelle Grando, *Evidence, Proof, and Fact-Finding in WTO Dispute Settlement* (Oxford University Press, 2009).

[90] *See* C.A. Thomas, "Of Facts and Phantoms: Economics, Epistemic Legitimacy, and WTO Dispute Settlement," 14 J.Int'l Econ.L. 295–328 (2011).

[91] Ibid., 305–12.

[92] Panel Report, *US—Continued Dumping and Subsidy Offset Act of 2000*, WT/DS234/R, adopted 27 January 2003; AB Report, *US—Continued Dumping and Subsidy Offset Act of 2000 (US—Offset Act (Byrd Amendment))*, WT/DS234/AB/R, adopted 27 January 2003.

[93] Horn and Mavroidis, "United States—Continued Dumping and Subsidy Offset Act of 2000" in Horn and Mavroidis (eds), *The American Law Institute Reporters' Studies on WTO Case Law: Legal and Economic Analysis* (2007, Cambridge University Press) 622–56, 629, 633.

itself vehemently condemned the panel's perfunctory assessment of the economic models presented by the parties.[94]

The absence of rules of evidence and epistemic legitimacy in decision-making can undermine the principle of due process in the context of the WTO dispute resolution system. Those shortcomings would especially be a problem if antitrust should become a core WTO competence, because antitrust law often requires complex economic assessments that may significantly affect the outcome of a dispute.

D. Institutional performance morms

1. Transparency

Transparency of the WTO institutional architecture in general, and of WTO dispute settlement in particular, is hotly debated. For reasons of space, regard will be had to two aspects only: i) the interim review procedure and ii) NGOs participation in WTO dispute settlement procedures.

The balance between transparency and confidentiality struck in the DSU is generally in favor of the latter. Consultations are confidential (Article 4.6 DSU), as are panel deliberations (Article 14.1 DSU), and proceedings of the AB (Article 17.10 DSU). Documents submitted to panels and to the AB are confidential, although parties are entitled to disclose statements of their own position; parties are requested to submit, along with their confidential submissions, a non-confidential summary that can be disclosed to the public (Article 18.2 DSU and paragraph 3 of the Working Procedures in Appendix 3 to the DSU).

Against this background, the publication of reports is one of the bulwarks of the transparency of the WTO dispute settlement system and has certainly contributed to transforming that process from one of diplomatic facilitation to one of reasoned adjudication of a high quality.[95] The interim review procedure laid down in the DSU, however, may be perceived as undermining that safeguard, insofar as it encourages the parties to find a mutually agreed solution before the final panel report is circulated to other WTO members and made accessible to the public.[96] So long as a WTO member can grant compensatory trade concessions regarded as adequate by the other party, it can prevent anticompetitive conduct from ever being publicly established.

However, it must be recalled that, in spite of the adjudicative character of the WTO dispute settlement procedure, the drafters clearly envisaged that WTO members remain in control of the dominant features of dispute settlement, includ-

[94] AB Report, *US—Subsidies on Upland Cotton—Recourse to Article 21.5 by Brazil (US—Upland Cotton 21.5)*, WT/DS267/AB/RW, adopted 20 June 2008, paras 357–358 ("The relative complexity of a model and its parameters is not a reason for a panel to remain agnostic about them. . . . the Panel could have gone further in its evaluation and comparative analysis of the economic simulations and the particular parameters used.").

[95] Richard B. Stewart, *supra* note 9, at 6.

[96] Terence P. Stewart and Amy A. Karpel, "Review of the Dispute Settlement Understanding: Operation of Panels," 31 L. Policy Int'l Bus. 593, 640 (2000).

ing the possibility of reaching a mutually agreed solution.[97] In fact, Article 3.7 DSU provides that "a solution mutually acceptable to the parties to a dispute and consistent with the covered agreements is clearly to be preferred." As in the context of the implementation of DSB rulings and recommendations, therefore, the political dimension of the WTO dispute settlement system is paramount.

Moreover, statistical data suggest that concerns over the impact of the interim review stage on the transparency of the WTO dispute settlement system are overrated. Of the 181 disputes started with a consultation request before 1 July 2002, eighteen cases were settled or dropped after establishment of the panel,[98] ten of which followed the achievement of a mutually agreed solution.[99] However, in only one of those cases an understanding was reached *during* the interim review stage; that is, after issuance of the interim report but prior to the issuance of the panel's final report.[100] In another case, a mutually agreed solution was reached *after* the final report was submitted to the parties, but prior to circulation to other WTO members and public disclosure.[101] In fact, mutually agreed solutions are in most cases reached after the conclusion of panel proceedings.[102]

Another bulwark of the transparency of the WTO dispute settlement system is participation of non-state actors in panel and AB proceedings. Following repeated calls for greater NGO involvement in the dispute resolution process, the AB affirmed that both panels and the AB have discretion to consider unsolicited amicus briefs (respectively in the *US—Shrimp*[103] and *US—Lead and Bismuth*[104] cases).

[97] Armin Steinbach, "The DSU Interim Review—Need For Its Elimination or Extension to the Appellate Body Stage?" 12 J.INT'L ECON.L. 417, 422 (2009).

[98] William Davey, "The WTO Dispute Settlement System: How Have Developing Countries Fared?" Illinois Public Law Research Paper No. 05–17, 15, <http://ssrn.com/abstract=862804>.

[99] Steinbach, *supra* note 97, 12 J. INT'L ECON. L. 417, 422 (2009).

[100] *See* Panel Report, *European Communities—Trade Description of Scallops—Request by Canada*, WT/DS7/R, 5 August 1996, unadopted, DSR 1996:I, 89, Notification of Mutually Agreed Solution on 19 July 1996 and *see* Panel Report, *European Communities—Trade Description of Scallops—Requests by Peru and Chile*, WT/DS12/R, WT/DS14/R, 5 August 1996, unadopted, DSR 1996:I, 93, Notification of Mutually Agreed Solution on 19 July 1996.

[101] *See* Panel Report, *European Communities—Measures Affecting Butter Products*, WT/DS72/R, 24 November 1999, unadopted, Notification of Mutually Agreed Solution on 18 November 1999.

[102] *See* Panel Report, *United States—Anti-Dumping Duty on Dynamic Random Access Memory Semiconductors (DRAMS) of One Megabit or Above from Korea—Recourse to Article 21.5 of the DSU by Korea*, WT/DS99/RW, 7 November 2000, unadopted, Notification of Mutually Agreed Solution on 20 October 2000; *see* Panel Report, *Canada—Measures Affecting the Importation of Milk and the Exportation of Dairy Products—Second Recourse to Article 21.5 of the DSU by New Zealand and the United States*, WT/DS103/RW2, WT/DS113/RW2, adopted 17 January 2003, modified by Appellate Body Report, WT/DS103/AB/RW2, WT/DS113/AB/RW2, DSR2003:I, 255, Notification of Mutually Agreed Solution on 15 May 2003; *see* Panel Report, *Japan—Measures Affecting the Importation of Apples—Recourse to Article 21.5 of the DSU by the United States*, WT/DS245/RW, adopted 20 July 2005, Notification of Mutually Agreed Solution on 2 September 2005.

[103] *See* AB Report, *United States—Import Prohibition of Certain Shrimp and Shrimp Products*, WT/DS58/AB/R, adopted 6 November 1998, DSR 1998:VII, 2755, paras 105–108.

[104] *See* AB Report, *United States—Imposition of Countervailing Duties on Certain Hot-Rolled Lead and Bismuth Carbon Steel Products Originating in the United Kingdom*, WT/DS138/AB/R, adopted 7 June 2000, DSR 2000:V, 2601.

In *Asbestos*, the AB set out a special procedure to that end, pursuant to Rule 16(1) of the Working Procedures.[105]

The AB has been adamant in stating that the entity filing the brief has no enforceable right to have it considered.[106] Indeed, in *Asbestos* the AB eventually rejected all *amicus curiae* submissions. The situation is different, however, when *amicus curiae* briefs are attached to the submission of a party to the proceedings, for instance, as exhibits. The AB has regarded such briefs as an integral part of the submission of the party, who assumes responsibility for their contents.[107] However, this solution entrusts to the parties the role of gatekeepers to NGOs participation in dispute settlement proceedings.

Greater involvement of NGOs in WTO activities, particularly dispute settlement, is an extremely controversial issue. Following the adoption of the additional procedures for *amicus curiae* submissions in *Asbestos*, at a special meeting of the General Council, a majority of WTO members objected to AB discretion to accept and consider *amicus curiae* briefs.[108] By and large, WTO members that are developing countries object to greater NGO participation because they perceive most NGOs, and in particular those dealing with environmental and labor issues, as inimical to their interests at their current level of economic development.[109] Others fear that NGO involvement may lead the WTO decision-making process to be captured by special interests,[110] since NGOs may lack accountability and legitimacy.[111] In contrast, advocates of greater NGO involvement argue that their involvement would enhance WTO decision-making[112] and legitimacy[113] and would allow for interests and concerns not adequately represented by national governments (especially undemocratic governments) to be taken into account.[114]

[105] *See* AB Report, *European Communities—Measures Affecting Asbestos and Asbestos-Containing Products*, WT/DS135/AB/R, adopted 5 April 2001, paras 52–55.

[106] *See* AB Report, *US—Lead and Bismuth II, supra* note 104, paras 40–41.

[107] *See* AB Report, *US—Shrimp, supra* note 103, paras 89 and 91.

[108] *See* General Council, Minutes of the Meeting of 22 November 2000, WT/GC/M/60 (January 23, 2001).

[109] *See,* e.g., Decision by the Appellate Body Concerning Amicus Curiae Briefs, Statement by Uruguay at the General Council on 22 November 2000, WT/GC/38 (December 4, 2000); Dispute Settlement Body—Special Session—Negotiations on the Dispute Settlement Understanding—Proposal by the African Group, TN/DS/W/15 (September 25, 2002).

[110] *See* Jeffrey L. Dunoff, "The Misguided Debate over NGO Participation at the WTO," 1 J.Int'l Econ.L. 437 (1998).

[111] *See* Peter Van den Bossche, "NGO Involvement in the WTO: a Comparative Perspective," 11 J.Int'l Econ.L. 717, 721 (2008).

[112] *See* Daniel Esty, "Non-Governmental Organizations at the World Trade Organization: Cooperation, Competition, or Exclusion," 1 J.Int'l Econ.L. 136 (1998) (arguing that NGOs should function as "intellectual competitors" to governments in the quest for optimal decision-making at the WTO level).

[113] *See* Markus Krajewski, "Democratic Legitimacy and Constitutional Perspectives of WTO Law," 35 J.World Trade 167 (2001).

[114] *See* Robert Howse, "Membership and its Privileges: the WTO, Civil Society, and the Amicus Brief Controversy," 9 Eur.L.J. 496, 509 (2003) (arguing that corporate interests, thanks to their privileged access to politicians, delegates, ambassadors, and lawyers, already have effective and non-transparent means of making their point of view known to WTO judicial bodies; thus, allowing NGO participation would contribute to putting previously under-represented actors on equal footing, enhancing the legitimacy of the WTO).

In sum, the WTO dispute settlement system, albeit more open and accessible than its GATT predecessor, still favors confidentiality over transparency. While the ongoing transition from a system of diplomatic facilitation to one of reasoned adjudication governed by the rule of law is undeniable, the political dimension of WTO dispute settlement is still of paramount significance as is its emphasis on the role of WTO members as the only actors in that system. This is apparent from the favor that the DSU accords to mutually agreed solutions between WTO members as an alternative to judicially-centered dispute resolution leading to publicly accessible reports. Even so, mutually agreed solutions occur in only approximately 10 percent of the disputes, and the interim review stage contributes only minimally to the achievement of those informal understandings. The limited participation of non-state actors in panel and AB proceedings also reflects the state-centered dimension of WTO dispute settlement, insofar as the AB does not recognize an enforceable right to have one's *amicus curiae* brief considered by a panel or by the AB unless one of the parties expressly consents to its incorporation in its own submissions.

2. *Predictability*

Although "providing security and predictability to the multilateral trading system" is one of the goals of the WTO dispute settlement system (Article 3.2 DSU), the latter's predictability is undermined by the absence of a *stare decisis* doctrine.

Panel and AB reports do not formally constitute binding precedents for other disputes, whether between the same parties on different matters or different parties on the same or other matters.[115] A panel is not obliged to follow previous AB reports dealing with identical matters, nor is the AB bound to maintain the legal interpretations of a given WTO provision it has developed in past cases.

Those who support the view that there is no *stare decisis* rule in WTO law usually rely on the last sentence of Article 3(2) DSU, according to which DSB rulings "cannot add to or diminish the rights and obligations in the covered agreement," and on Article IX:2 of the WTO Agreement, whereby the Ministerial Conference and the General Council are granted the "exclusive authority" to adopt interpretations of WTO agreements.[116] It has been observed, however, that neither of those provisions preclude the development of a *stare decisis* doctrine. The requirement to stand by precedent merely consists in the "clarification" of existing WTO rules by reference to earlier reports, not in the "authoritative interpretation" of WTO rules within the meaning of Article IX:2 of the WTO Agreement, an activity which "adds to" or "diminishes" the scope of existing rules and is, accordingly, entrusted exclusively to the Ministerial Conference and the General Council.[117]

[115] *See* D. Palmeter and P. Mavroidis, "The WTO Legal System: Sources of Law," 92 AM.J.INT'L. L. 398, 404 (1998).

[116] *Id.*

[117] Anne Scully-Hill and Hans Mahncke, "The Emergence of the Doctrine of Stare Decisis in the World Trade Organization Dispute Settlement System," 36 LEG.ISSUES EUROP.INTEGR. 133, 147–50 (2011).

If the reasoning developed in a given report is particularly compelling, it is very likely that the panel or the AB will follow it in a similar case. The AB in *Japan—Alcoholic Beverages* ruled that adopted GATT and WTO panel reports "create legitimate expectations among WTO Members, and, therefore, should be taken into account where they are relevant to any dispute."[118] This also holds true for AB reports, as clarified in *US—Shrimp*.[119] In *US—Oil* the AB went so far as to state that "following the Appellate Body's conclusion in earlier disputes is not only appropriate, but is what would be expected from panels, especially where issues are the same."[120] In *US—Stainless Steel*, the AB held that a panel's "failure to follow previously adopted Appellate Body reports addressing the same issues undermines the development of a coherent and predictable body of jurisprudence."[121]

Of particular interest is the recent Panel report in *US—Orange Juice from Brazil*, dealing with the use of the "zeroing" methodology during administrative reviews of an anti-dumping measures.[122] That issue has been the subject of almost a decade of conflicting panel and AB rulings. Although the panel expressly stated that it found the AB line of reasoning "difficult to accept",[123] it eventually considered that "our function under Article 11 of the DSU, and the integrity and effectiveness of the WTO dispute settlement system, are best served in the present instance by following the Appellate Body."[124] This passage seems to suggest that an *opinio iuris* might be developing around the necessity of following AB rulings not so much because of their persuasiveness, but rather for the sake of the overall consistency and predictability of the dispute settlement system.[125]

Unadopted panel reports have no formal legal status in the GATT or WTO system because they have not been endorsed through decisions by GATT or WTO members.[126] In the GATT system, where unanimity was required to adopt panel reports, non-adoption was usually the result of a strategic decision by the losing party rather than of a negative assessment of the panel's work.[127] Not surprisingly, both the panel and the AB in *Japan—Alcoholic Beverages* found that the reasoning contained in an unadopted panel report could provide useful guidance in a subsequent case involving the same legal questions.[128]

[118] *See* AB Report, *Japan—Alcoholic Beverages*, II DSR 1996:I, 97 at p.107–8.

[119] *See* AB Report, *US—Shrimp (Article 21.5—Malaysia)*, para 109.

[120] *See* AB Report, *United States—Sunset Reviews of Anti-Dumping Measures on Oil Country Tubular Goods from Argentina*, WT/DS268/AB/R, 17 December 2004, para 188.

[121] *See* AB Report, *US—Final Anti-Dumping Measures on Stainless Steel from Mexico*, WT/DS344/AB/R, 20 May 2008, para 160.

[122] AB Report, *United States—Anti-Dumping Administrative Reviews and Other Measures Related to Imports of Certain Orange Juice from Brazil*, WT/DS382/R, 25 March 2011.

[123] *Id.* para 7.131.

[124] *Id.* para 7.135.

[125] Cf. *id.* para 7.134 ("we firmly believe that all Members have a strong systemic interest in seeing that a lasting resolution to the 'zeroing' controversy is found sooner rather than later").

[126] *See* Panel Report *Japan—Alcoholic Beverages*, WT/DS8, 10, 11/AB/R, 1 July 1996, para 6.10.

[127] Anne Scully-Hill and Hans Mahncke, *supra* note 117, at 150.

[128] *See* Panel Report, *Japan—Alcoholic Beverages II*, para 6.10; *see* AB Report, *Japan—Alcoholic Beverages* II DSR 1996:I, 97 at 108.

Therefore, it is fair to say that, while the development of a *stare decisis* doctrine would certainly add to the predictability of the WTO dispute settlement system, the current status of AB reports as persuasive sources of guidance and the consistent pattern of deference by panels to AB interpretations indicate that, by and large, the dispute settlement system does not suffer from a major predictability deficit.

3. Timeliness

The timeliness of WTO dispute settlement procedures is a source of increasing concern.[129] During the last five years, significant delays have occurred at the panel stage.[130] While Articles 12.8 and 12.9 DSU provide that the panel must conduct its examination in six months, which can be extended to nine months following a reasoned notice to the DSB, the annual median time for panel proceedings since 2005 has ranged from eleven to fifteen months,[131] with five disputes taking more than two years.[132]

In contrast, the AB generally complies with the (extended) ninety-day time frame laid down in Article 17.5 DSU. So far, only about one-tenth of AB reports have exceeded that deadline.[133] Of course, the AB's task in each dispute is more limited than that of the panel, as the AB only reviews the issues of law raised by the parties on appeal. Moreover, AB reports, unlike panel reports, are not subject to review by a higher-ranking body.

Why do panels not comply with the time frames set out in the DSU? One reason is that most panels liberally grant parties' requests for additional time for submissions, even in cases where no provision for extension of time is made in the DSB.[134] For instance, it has become standard practice for panels to allow one or two weeks for third parties' submissions before the first substantive meeting, two weeks to reply to panel questions after both substantive meetings, and a final opportunity to

[129] *See,* e.g., William Davey, "Expediting the Panel Process in WTO Dispute Settlement," in M. Janow et al., eds, *The WTO: Governance, Dispute Settlement and Developing Countries* (New York: Juris Publishing 2008), 409–40, 440; Pilita Clark, "Airbus Fears WTO Delay on Boeing Report Could Hurt Contract Hopes," *Financial Times,* December 20, 2009.

[130] Also the implementation stage has recently given rise to timeliness concerns. For an exhaustive analysis of the possible abuses arising in the determination of the "reasonable period of time" accorded by Article 21:3 DSU to the losing party to comply with DSB rulings and recommendations, *see* MA Qian, "'Reasonable Period Of Time' in the WTO Dispute Settlement System," 15 J.INT'L.ECON. L. 257–85, 264–74 (2012).

[131] Kennedy, *supra* note 81, figure 1, at 223.

[132] *Id.*, 221, footnote 3 (referring to the following disputes: *EC—Biotech (GMOs)*, WT/DS291, DS292, DS293; *US/Canada—Continued Suspension of Obligations in the EC-Harmony Dispute*, WT/DS320, DS321; *EC and certain Member States—Large Civil Aircraft*, WT/DS316; *US—Large Civil Aircraft (2nd complaint)*,WT/DS353; *Australia—Apples*, WT/DS367).

[133] *Id.* 228, footnote 40 (referring to the following disputes: *EC—Hormones*, WT/DS26 and WT/DS48 (114 days); *Thailand—H-Beams*, WT/DS122 (140 days); *EC Asbestos*, WT/DS135 (140 days); *US—Lead and Bismuth II*, WT/DS138 (104 days); *EC—Sugar*, WT/DS265 (105 days); *US—Upland Cotton*, WT/DS 267 (136 days); *Mexico—Antidumping Measures on Rice*, WT/DS295 (132 days); *US—Upland Cotton* (Article 21.5), WT/DS267 (111 days); *US/Canada—Continued Suspension of Obligations in the EC-Harmony Dispute*, WT/DS320 and WT/DS321 (140 days)).

[134] Matthew Kennedy, *supra* note 81, at 231.

comment on those replies. If the length of those additional procedures is added to the maximum time frames set out in the DSU, the expected duration of panel proceedings exceeds nine months, thus making compliance with the ordinary six-month time frame set out in Article 12.8 DSU impossible.

Another major cause of delay in panel proceedings is the scope or complexity of the issues raised in each dispute. Complainants may broaden the scope of disputes and increase their complexity by including weak, consequential, and speculative claims in their panel requests. Respondents, in turn, may mount unsubstantiated but time-consuming defenses, raise procedural issues, and engage in dilatory tactics.[135] Panels themselves contribute to expanding the scope of disputes by submitting sometimes unnecessary written questions, which may give rise to multiple responses and many rebuttal arguments, as in *EC—Biotech (GMOs)*.[136]

Possibly, the most evident reason for delays is the length of panel reports. In *Mexico—Corn Syrup*, the AB stated the reasons underlying the requirement that panel reports set out "the basic rationale behind any findings and recommendations"[137] (Article 12.7 DSU). The first reason is to ensure that respondents are informed of the reasons why their measure has been found inconsistent with WTO agreements. Panels have interpreted this dictum as requiring that all arguments raised by the parties be addressed in their reports, even though the AB has consistently held that panels are not under such obligation.[138] The second reason behind the duty for panels to state the "basic rationale" of their findings is to assist the losing party in implementing the DSB rulings and recommendations and in making an informed decision as to whether to appeal the panel report before the AB. In fact, panels appear to be willing to go to great lengths to render rulings that may be regarded as persuasive, if not by the parties, at least by the AB upon review. This creates an upward pressure on the length of panel reports and, accordingly, slows down proceedings at the panel stage.[139]

4. Implementation and remedies

Implementation and remedies in the WTO dispute settlement system confront two major and very different problems: the ambiguity of the procedural arrangements and the disparate bargaining power of WTO members.

As to the first aspect, one of the most evident shortcomings in the language of the DSU is the lack of coordination between Articles 21.5 and 22.6 thereof. If the losing party fails to comply with DSB rulings and recommendations, the winning party may either request the establishment of a compliance panel under Article 21.5 DSU or request authorization from the DSB to retaliate by suspending trade

[135] *Id.* at 240.

[136] *EC—Biotech (GMOs)*, WT/DS291/R, paras 7.14 and 7.39.

[137] *See* AB report in *Mexico—Corn Syrup (Article 21.5)*, WT/DS132/AB/R, para 107.

[138] *See*, e.g., AB report in *US—Lead and Bismuth II*, para 71; *Canada—Autos*, paras 112–114.

[139] Cf. AB report in *China—Audiovisual Services*, WT/DS363/AB/R, paras 213—215 (criticizing the panel's decision not to resolve an issue, even though neither party requested the panel to rule on that issue nor was a ruling to that effect necessary to resolve the dispute).

concessions, a matter which may be referred to arbitration under Article 22.6 DSU. However, nothing in the DSU prevents the compliance procedure under Article 21.5 and arbitration under Article 22.6 from running in parallel, possibly with conflicting outcomes. This is known as the "sequencing problem."[140] In *EC—Bananas,* for instance, the matter of compliance was referred both to a compliance panel[141] and to arbitration.[142] It has been observed that allowing arbitrators to rule on permissible retaliatory measures before the compliance panel has determined whether the losing party has complied with the DSB's recommendations or rulings can amount to an encroachment on the losing party's right of defense.[143] In current practice, however, arbitration under Article 22.6 DSU is suspended until the compliance panel has handed down its report.[144]

The problem of unequal bargaining power must be seen in the following context. If DSB rulings and recommendations are not complied with, the DSU envisages two types of sanctions: compensation and retaliation. Compensation usually consists in additional trade concessions, offered by the losing party to the winning one, which are equivalent to the benefit that the offending conduct has nullified or impaired. Retaliation consists of punishment through erecting new trade barriers equivalent in value to the loss of benefits as a result of the offending conduct. It may consist in a suspension of concessions by the winning party i) in the same economic sector in which the nullification or impairment of benefits has taken place (parallel retaliation), ii) in a different sector, but in the framework of the same agreement (cross-sector retaliation), or iii) in connection with a different agreement (cross-agreement retaliation). Parallel retaliation is generally preferred over cross-sector and cross-agreement retaliation.[145]

The coercion and deterrence effects of those sanctions can vary significantly depending on the bargaining power of the parties concerned.[146] The inequality of bargaining power may affect the content and scope of compensation, which, unlike those of retaliatory measures, are determined by the parties. Retaliatory measures, which usually take the form of additional customs duties on the goods originating

140 *See* Cherise M. Valles and Brendan P. McGivern, "The right to retaliate under the WTO Agreement: the 'Sequencing' Problem," 34 J. World Trade 63 (2000).

141 Article 21.5 Panel Report, *European Communities—Bananas, Recourse to Article 21.5 by Ecuador,* WT/DS27/RW/ECU, 12 April 1999.

142 Arbitration Report, *European Communities—Bananas, Recourse to Arbitration by the European Communities under Article 22.6 of the DSU,* Decision by the Arbitrators, WT/DS27/ARB.

143 *See* M. Distefano, "Certezza del diritto ed esecuzione delle decisioni OMC alla luce dei primi arbitrati," in 2000 Rivista di Diritto Internazionale privato e processuale 579.

144 Matsushita, Schoenbaum, and Mavroidis, *supra* note 12, at 32.

145 As per Article 22.3(e) DSU, if a WTO member seeks to obtain authorization to engage in cross-sector and cross-agreement retaliation, it must state the reasons for its choice in its request. There is no similar requirement if that member applies for parallel retaliation.

146 *See* Benjamin L. Brimeyer, "Bananas, Beef, and Compliance in the World Trade Organization: The Inability of the WTO Dispute Settlement Process to Achieve Compliance from Superpower Nations," 10 Minn. J. Global Trade 133 (2001). But see Chad P. Bown, Bernard M. Hoekman, "Developing Countries and Enforcement of Trade Agreements: Why Dispute Settlement is Not Enough," 42 J. World Trade 177 (2008) (noting that developing countries are rarely challenged in formal trade disputes for failing to live up to commitments, reducing the benefits of their participation in international trade agreements).

in the territory of the losing WTO member, can prove ineffective if they are put into place by a weak bargaining party against a stronger one. Besides, not all WTO members have the same practical ability to resort to the suspension of obligations, as nationals of the winning member will have to bear additional import duties and may have to switch to suboptimal supply sources.[147] Although Article 22.1 DSU states that "neither compensation nor the suspension of concessions is preferred to full implementation of a recommendation to bring a measure into conformity with the covered agreements," in fact a strong bargaining party may offer a wide range of trade concessions to persuade a weaker party to allow the former party to maintain measures at variance with WTO agreements.

In sum, while the record by WTO members in complying with adverse panel and AB rulings is generally positive,[148] the leeway accorded to the winning party in the implementation phase and the absence of modalities to address the unequal bargaining power of WTO members may undermine the legitimacy of the WTO dispute settlement system.

III. The other international institutions

In addition to the WTO, three world institutions play a significant role in competition policy and indirectly in competition law. They are the OECD, UNCTAD, and ICN. A number of other arrangements of less than global scope also play a role. These include regional agreements, such as in South America, Africa, and Australia/New Zealand; collaborations such as the BRIC Competition Conference (among Brazil, Russia, India, China); and bilateral agreements among growing numbers of nation pairs. Regional agreements range in their ambitions from free trade areas and customs unions with a competition dimension to looser cooperations. Bilateral agreements for antitrust cooperation normally include provisions to notify one another before pursuing litigation that affects the important interests of the other and to consider positive and negative comity; that is, refraining from proceedings while the other is pursuing the matter and thus positively aiding both parties (positive comity), or refraining from proceedings where the other has superior interests in not challenging the conduct (negative comity). The United States has such agreements with the European Union, Canada, Japan, Australia, Mexico, Israel, and Chile. The European Union has cooperation, partnership, or association agreements with a very large number of countries in addition to the United States, from Albania to Ukraine. Relatively few bilateral cooperation agreements are between developed and developing countries in view of lack of symmetrical

[147] Reto Malacrida, "Towards Sounder and Fairer WTO Retaliation: Suggestions for Possible Additional Procedural Rules Governing Members' Preparation and Adoption of Retaliatory Measures," 42 J. World Trade 3, 11–12 (2008).

[148] Bruce Wilson, "Compliance by WTO Members with Adverse WTO Dispute Settlement Rulings: The Record to Date," 10 J.Int'l Econ.L. 397 (2007) (noting that in virtually all cases of adverse rulings the WTO member concerned indicated its intention to bring itself into compliance and that in most cases it had already done so).

interests and thus of scope for equal mutual benefit. Developing countries, therefore, get fewer advantages of cooperation.[149]

We proceed here to consider the three international organizations: the OECD, UNCTAD, and ICN. These institutions have no decision-making, rule-making, or enforcement powers. All three are designed to be catalysts for conveyance of knowledge, increasing understanding, cross-fertilization, facilitating soft convergence of national laws, and, to a greater or lesser extent, offering constructive criticism, technical assistance, and capacity building. Despite lack of powers of the three organizations, it is worth asking to what extent the work and outputs of each influence the shaping of laws and procedures in the world; for example, what is their influence on notional "international standards"? Moreover, the institutions may have an effect on modalities of developing countries; that is, influence on developing countries' framework and perspective in drafting and implementing their laws and deciding on their priorities. Therefore, as we treat each of the three institutions, we will consider the following norms: access to agenda setting and decision-making, such as formulation of recommendations and guidelines; transparency; expertise in general; expertise and neutrality in peer reviews and technical assistance; effectiveness in satisfying their own mandates; and accountability including periodic reviews of their outputs.

A. OECD competition law committee

The OECD was established in 1961, a child of the OEEC—the (former) Organization for European Cooperation, which was formed in 1947 to administer the Marshall Plan. Its members are states. It has a secretariat and is headquartered in Paris. The OECD's mandate is to bring together governments around the world committed to democracy and a market economy "to help its member countries to achieve sustainable economic growth and employment and to raise the standard of living in member countries while maintaining financial stability—all this in order to contribute to the development of the world economy." Its members, now numbering thirty-three with Estonia soon to join as thirty-four, are the more developed countries. The OECD also cooperates with more than seventy developing and emerging market economies. It organizes Global Forums to address transboundary issues that involve non-OECD members.

The OECD has a Council comprised of a representative of each member nation and the European Union. It operates through committees, which number about 250. Through the committees it collects data, organizes discussions, writes research reports, conducts peer reviews, and issues publications. Discussions may culminate in agreements, standards, and recommendations.

149 *See* generally D. Daniel Sokol, "International Antitrust Institutions," Chapter 10 in Andrew Guzman, ed., *Cooperation, Comity, and Competition Policy* (2011, Oxford University Press), 187 et seq.; Maher M. Dabbah, "Future Directions in Bilateral Cooperation, A Policy Perspective," Chapter 10 in Guzman, *supra*, at 287; Michal S. Gal, "Regional Competition Law Agreements: An Important Step for Antitrust Enforcement," 60 U.Toronto L.J. 239 (2010).

The Competition Committee is one of the committees. It has a highly qualified professional secretariat, most of whose members were senior staff members of national competition authorities.

The Competition Committee brings together the top officials of the competition agencies and certain other policymakers, and observers from non-OECD countries. Global Forums bring together leaders from competition authorities in developing and transitional countries. The chair of the Competition Committee is elected by the members. This position has been held for more than ten years by Frédéric Jenny, who is one of the most respected and outstanding members of the world competition community. The Committee Bureau, a steering group, is composed of a small group of elected committee members. Under the leadership of the Chair and the Bureau, the Committee sets an agenda of issues to be pursued, which are often the cutting-edge issues of the time including critical and sometimes controversial issues of law. Outside experts may be invited to contribute to the discussion. Numerous countries make submissions on point. Research reports, best practices, or guidelines may result. The Committee may submit recommendations for adoption by the OECD Council. The Competition Committee sponsors peer reviews of competition authorities of member countries, at their request. The reviews are undertaken by recognized experts and are in general careful and thoughtful. The reviews contain recommendations, some of which may be used by the officials of the subject authority to seek support for legislative reforms. Adoption of work product is by consensus.

The Business and Industry Advisory Committee to the OECD (BIAC) represents the views of the business community at all Competition Committee meetings. It regularly contributes to discussions and may also comment on drafts of more formal instruments such as recommendations. NGO participation is on an ad hoc basis. At the annual Global Forum for Competition, for example, certain NGOs are normally invited to participate.

Two OECD recommendations in the field of competition are normally regarded as most important. These are: 1) The 1995 Recommendation concerning cooperation between member countries on anticompetitive practices affecting international trade. This Recommendation has, for many years, set the framework for cooperation in competition matters in the absence of bilateral agreements. 2) The 1998 Recommendation concerning effective action against hard-core cartels. This Recommendation advises prohibition of hard-core cartels, calls upon competition authorities to review and ratchet back their exemptions from the anti-cartel law, and calls for transparency of any new exemptions.

Other OECD recommendations and best practices include: Guidelines for combatting bid rigging in public procurement, Recommendation on competition assessment, Guiding principles for regulatory quality and performance, Best practices for the formal exchange of information between competition authorities in hard-core cartel investigations, Recommendation on merger review, Recommendation concerning structural separation in regulated industries, and Recommendation on competition policy and exempted or regulated sectors.

The OECD held three roundtable discussions on transparency and procedural fairness in 2010 and 2011, and published a report summarizing the discussions.[150]

1. *Analysis regarding application of norms*

Do OECD Council Recommendations and Competition Committee outputs influence national competition law and norms? Council Recommendations have been used on numerous occasions, sometimes in conjunction with instruments of other institutions such as the ICN, to support changes in national competition laws. Committee outputs, such as publications of roundtable discussions, may also have an influence on the day-to-day work of competition authorities and policy-makers. The nature of the influence is that which results from increased knowledge, including benchmarking.

Regarding access and transparency: access of members is good. All members are invited to contribute, and their suggestions are seriously considered. All members have a right to nominate the chair of the Committee and members of the Committee Bureau. Transparency is excellent. Communications and committee documents or their links are sent to all members. Submissions for some sessions, such as policy roundtables, are eventually made public by the OECD. Accountability to members seems good. Output is evaluated by the committee members every other year. The OECD Council allocates financial resources to the committee for each succeeding bi-annual budget period based on how the evaluation of the performance of the Competition Committee compares with the evaluations of the other committees, thus assuring accountability not only to participants in the committee meetings and projects but also to the OECD member governments. Over the past decade, competition from the ICN, which we discuss below, seems to have improved the responsiveness and level of activity of the OECD Competition Committee in functioning on the major competition issues of the day.

B. UNCTAD

The United Nations Conference on Trade and Development (UNCTAD) was founded in 1964 as the principal arm of the United Nations General Assembly dealing with issues of trade, investment, and development. Like the OECD, the UNCTAD is a body whose members are states, not competition agencies.

The aim of UNCTAD is to improve trade, investment, and development opportunities of developing countries "with a particular focus on ensuring that domestic policies and international action are mutually supportive in bringing about sustainable development." UNCTAD is a forum for intergovernmental deliberations, aimed at building consensus, especially for the benefit of the least developed countries. It also undertakes research, policy analysis and data collection.

[150] See Procedural Fairness and Transparency—2012 (OECD), available at <http://www.oecd.org/document/20/0,3746,en_2649_37463_50235668_1_1_1_37463,00.html>.

UNCTAD has 193 members. It has a Secretary General. Its headquarters are in Geneva.

Many countries are represented at UNCTAD meetings by members of their permanent mission to the UN, and these representatives usually do not have familiarity with competition issues.

UNCTAD carries out its work through branches. One of these is the Competition and Consumer Policies Branch. The CCPB has a small team located in Geneva. It hosts development-focused fora addressing issues of practical and policy concern. It sponsors peer reviews of developing and transitional countries, at their request. It provides technical assistance and capacity building, often by stand-alone seminars that may be staffed by outside speakers (not always fully conversant with the context of the country).

Much of the work of the CCPB is centered around the Set of Multilaterally Agreed Equitable Principles and Rules for the Control of Restrictive Business Practices, adopted in 1980 by the United Nations General Assembly, and now better known as the UN Set on Competition Policy. Albeit voluntary, it is the only multilaterally agreed set of principles governing competition. The Sixth Review Conference, held in November 2010, marked the thirtieth anniversary of the adoption of the Set, and reaffirmed it.

At the time of adoption of the Set, UNCTAD had positioned itself as a champion of the developing countries against the multinationals of the developed world. UNCTAD now takes a more mainstream approach, aligning itself as a multilateral organization along with OECD and ICN, and aims to collaborate with them in advancing the national, regional, and multinational dimensions of antitrust.

CCPB has prepared a Model Law on Competition, based on the Set, for the guidance of developing countries in adopting and amending their antitrust laws. It has prepared commentaries for each chapter, which have recently been revised. It publishes various related research and assessment documents.

CCPB engages in self-assessment, as indicated by its recently published document on "Assessment of the application and implementation of the set" and "Review of capacity-building and technical assistance on competition law and policy."

The CCPB faces a hurdle as it helps developing countries to adopt and modernize their competition laws. The language of the Set is somewhat outdated, and reopening the project for revision would risk the chance that no consensus would form. This means that, with regard to the Set and the periodic work programs for its renewal, there may be a gap between recommended principles (the Set) and best applications. This gap may implicate transparency, accountability, and relevance.

The CCPB has recently launched a research platform with twenty-five research institutes, universities, and corporate affiliates, through which it is tackling major research questions that underlie the formulation and implementation of good competition rules and standards.

Do the UNCTAD outputs influence national law and norms? To some extent they do. Developing countries often pay regard to the Set, the Model Law, and the commentaries reflecting developing nations' formulation and implementation of their own laws. Because the "black letter" of the Set is not formulated in the most modern language and the commentaries until revised in November 2010 were confusing and inconsistent, these outputs may have had limited influence. Nonetheless, they have always had influence at least as a referent for developing countries. The November 2010 updating of the commentaries is promising, as is the sponsorship of a research agenda with platform partners. Moreover, the CCPB conferences and programs have a significant impact in bringing together leading officials in the competition authorities of most developing countries (and developed countries), who share experiences, perceptions, problems, and solutions, and profit from personal contacts and benchmarking. The projects directed at helping particular members and regions, such as the voluntary peer reviews and a program of capacity building in Latin America (Competition and Consumer Protection for Latin America or "COMPAL"), have particularized impact.

1. Analysis regarding application of norms

Do members have access to the agenda? Members may suggest agenda items. The work of UNCTAD is largely steered by the secretariat.

Is UNCTAD's CCPB transparent and accountable? The studies and reports are transparent. The agenda generally responds to developing countries' needs.

Is the work done with expertise? The work product increasingly reflects expertise. Some important work such as peer reviews is assisted by experts from member countries. The peer reviews reflect a very high level of expertise. A program of capacity building in Latin America (COMPAL) has been designed and implemented with high expertise and sensitivity to context.

C. ICN

The International Competition Network was founded in 2001. It was created to fill a gap that could not be filled by the OECD, UNCTAD, or the WTO. The OECD is an organization of developed countries. The UNCTAD is an organization of all UN members but devoted to developing countries. The WTO is a trade organization; and the competition authorities take a second seat—even on competition issues—to the trade representative. Moreover, the WTO members negotiate trade rules which are then subject to dispute resolution—a framework that is not always sympathetic with antitrust.

The competition authorities needed a "room" of their own. They wanted and designed an organization of the competition authorities—not of the states. The organization is without rule-making or administrative or adjudicatory power; it creates an informal environment conducive to solving actual problems and to converging law "on the ground." According to the original Memorandum on the Establishment and Operation of the ICN, the mission of the ICN is to "address antitrust enforcement and policy issues of common interest and formulate proposals for procedural and substantive convergence" and "encourage the dissemination of antitrust experience and best practices, promote the advocacy role of antitrust agencies and seek to facilitate international cooperation."[151]

The ICN now has more than 100 members—all national competition authorities. It has generated an immense and useful work product. It hosts annual conferences and periodic workshops. It convenes working groups of volunteers—including non-governmental advisors—from numerous jurisdictions, whose work ranges from coordination of jurisdictions' rules on pre-merger process, to informal technical assistance, to attempts to understand the abuse of dominance laws of all of the members and to tease out the common principles on which recommended practices or guidelines can be built. It has ongoing projects on anti-cartel leniency programs, agency effectiveness, and development of a curriculum for competition authorities.

The ICN has no secretariat. Policy and agenda-setting are done by the steering group, which currently has fifteen members. The steering group is selected by the ICN membership. Members of the ICN may volunteer for service on the group. The steering group makes recommendations on which the members vote. The steering group maintains as a priority a principle of inclusiveness, so that all voices may be heard; although, as may be expected, developing countries have less time and fewer resources than developed countries and frequently have a less confident voice.

Non-governmental advisors (NGAs) participate in ICN in a major way. NGAs are drawn from the business community, defense lawyers, plaintiffs' lawyers, academics, and consumer and competition think tanks. NGAs are designated by each member authority and, we believe, virtually all who wish to participate are invited to do so. NGA participation is especially sought in the working groups—from which all recommendations, guidelines, and other work product originate.

As noted, ICN has no formal powers. However, the leaders of ICN work hard to get ICN recommended practices and guidelines implemented in the member jurisdictions. The ICN keeps records of which jurisdictions have, for example, made legislative changes to conform with recommended practices. Speeches at annual conferences chart this progress. This is not a matter of coercion. Normally, national authorities seek to conform their law and practice to ICN recommendations except when there is a reason for divergence; for example, when their law or practice is different because of their statutes, objectives, and contexts. Member nation agencies sometimes rely on the authority of the ICN when seeking a change of law before their legislatures. ICN recommendations may be seen as soft world standards.

The ICN, now more than ten years old, is normally regarded as a success in moving law and process towards convergence. Its success is in large part attributed to the fact that it is comprised of the competition law community, not the trade community, and that, since it has no formal powers, little seems to be at stake in agreeing to (for example) recommended practices or principles. Moreover, because

[151] See <www.internationalcompetitionnetwork.org>.

the agencies' agreements in ICN do not bind their governments, no higher governmental authorization is needed, thus facilitating agreement.

It has been argued that more is at stake than meets the eye; that agreed standards become soft international law and may influence development of hard law. This argument is often made in connection with an observation that the developed countries tend to control the agenda and to write the drafts, if only because they have the time, money, people, and expertise to do so, and that the rules that emerge are likely to be those that fit the developed countries and may not be the most appropriate for the developing world.

1. *Analysis regarding application of norms*

Do all stakeholders have access to ICN? The answer is yes. Since ICN is an organization of competition authorities, members of those authorities have the greatest access.

If access is not complete, it is because of lack of resources and other more urgent priorities especially of less-well resourced authorities.

Is the work of the ICN transparent? Yes. All competition authorities and NGAs involved in any particular project are invited to be part of the working communications, usually done by telephone calls and supporting email. Work product—which will have been made public beforehand—is adopted at annual conferences. Comments are invited in advance and discussion is invited from the floor. Adoption is by consensus.

Are the outputs crafted with expertise? Yes.

Is the ICN accountable? The ICN is accountable to its members. In recent initiatives, the steering group surveyed and personally interviewed all members of the ICN and surveyed all NGAs to determine their level of satisfaction, the extent to which the ICN is meeting their needs, what criticisms they have, and what proposals they suggest for the ICN's future. The results of these surveys and interviews are posted on the ICN website.[152] The feedback from the members indicates satisfaction with the original mission statement and support for continuing on the course. Feedback further indicates: ICN should continue to aim for convergence, continue to encourage dissemination of antitrust experience, continue to support agencies' advocacy efforts, and continue to facilitate international cooperation. For new or deeper work, members suggested more training and educating agency staff and work on economic analysis, among other things.[153]

The NGA feedback, which was pursuant to a questionnaire, may be summarized as follows: 66.7 percent of NGAs surveyed agreed that the ICN is sufficiently transparent, 51.3 percent agreed that there are adequate opportunities for NGAs to

[152] The results of the interviews with members are summarized in the Note from the Chair, 2 September 2010, <http://www.internationalcompetitionnetwork.org/uploads/2010-2011/chairnote 8.9.10.pdf>. The responses to the August 2010 NGA Survey are available at: <www.internationalcompetitionnetwork.org/uploads/2010-2011/responses%20nga%20survey%208.10.pdf>.

[153] *See* Note from the Chair, *supra*.

contribute to the ICN, 34.6 percent agreed that there is sufficient diversity of NGA's professional background, while 38.5 percent disagreed that there is sufficient geographical distribution of NGAs.[154] The steering committee is taking account of the results of the surveys and interviews in mapping the future of ICN.

IV. Findings and critical evaluation

As this chapter reveals, compliance with institutional performance and due process norms varies considerably among the four international institutions concerned, as do their institutional design and mandate.

Due process norms are not applicable to antitrust in the OECD, UNCTAD, and ICN, for those organizations have no rule making, decision-making, or enforcement powers. With reference to the WTO, our analysis on due process norms focused on dispute settlement, for there is no WTO antitrust agency or authority.

Our analysis of due process norms in the WTO dispute settlement system showed that parties and third parties to WTO disputes have, by and large, ample opportunity to be heard during all stages of the WTO dispute settlement procedure. Moreover, the Appellate Body (AB) jurisprudence on the elements of three key procedural steps (that is, the request for consultations, the request for establishment of a panel, and the notice of appeal) seem to ensure that respondents receive full notice of the complainant's allegations and are not exposed to surprise claims. The AB and panels contribute to assure that parties are generally afforded adequate time to prepare their submissions—often more time than the DSU itself requires. The WTO dispute resolution system recognizes the parties' right to appeal panel reports and features an institutional structure that enables a comprehensive and expeditious appellate review. The impartiality of panel and AB members vis-à-vis the parties to a dispute is assured by granting the parties significant powers in the appointment of panel members and in requiring the reporting of possible conflicts of interest on the part of AB members. Still, this arrangement could leave the backdoor open to influence by external actors and special interests (which may be unknown to or tolerated by the parties). A possible deficiency in respect of due process norms is the absence of rules of evidence and the lack of epistemic legitimacy in the handling of economic data. This shortcoming would especially be a problem if antitrust, which often requires complex factual assessments, should become a core WTO competence.

As for institutional performance norms, we will address the OECD, UNCTAD, ICN, and the WTO seriatim.

In the OECD competition committee, access is good; all members are invited to contribute and are listened to, and all have a right to nominate the chair of the committee and members of the Committee Bureau. Transparency is excellent: communications and committee documents or their links are sent to all members;

[154] *Id.*, at 5–6.

submissions for some sessions, such as policy roundtables, are made public. Accountability to members seems good; the committee members evaluate output every other year. The OECD Council (the overall governing body) allocates financial resources to each of its committees for each succeeding bi-annual budget period based on how the evaluation of the performance of that committee compares with the evaluations of all of the other committees, thus assuring accountability not only to participants in the committee meetings and projects but also to the OECD member governments. The research outputs are excellent.

In the UNCTAD competition branch, agenda-setting is open to members; they may suggest agenda items, but the work is largely steered by the secretariat, which has a small staff. UNCTAD studies and reports are transparent. The agenda focuses on developing countries' needs. The mission and ambition have been of limited range, but the work product increasingly reflects expertise. Experts from member countries assist some important work, such as peer reviews. The peer reviews reflect a very high level of expertise.

Regarding ICN, this "virtual" organization of competition authorities is a success story. Access is excellent. If smaller or developing country competition agencies do not experience complete access, it is because of their lack of resources and the pressure of their other priorities. ICN's work is transparent. All competition authorities and NGAs involved in any particular project are invited to be part of the working communications. Outputs are crafted with expertise. The ICN is accountable to its members. In recent initiatives, the steering group has surveyed all members of the ICN and NGAs to determine their level of satisfaction.

More serious problems inhere in the WTO. Transparency is often sacrificed in the name of confidentiality. The publication of panel reports has contributed to increased transparency, albeit a degree of opaqueness is still inherent in the interim review stage. NGO participation could also be a means to promote transparency, but the AB has allowed it only in part. The predictability of the WTO dispute settlement system is affected by the absence of a *stare decisis* doctrine, although in fact panels consistently follow AB reports. The lack of timeliness of WTO dispute settlement procedures has become a source of concern, especially at the panel stage. Implementation and remedies in the WTO dispute settlement system are not always clearly regulated and suitable to take into account the inequality of WTO members' bargaining power.

The reasons underlying these deficiencies are manifold. Independence of decision-makers is recognized in WTO law, but is ensured by concentrating powers in the parties, which might be unable to detect or prevent external influence. Rules of evidence are not laid down in the DSU, although the AB jurisprudence has acknowledged the need for such rules and has tried to fill the gap by way of interpretation. The epistemic legitimacy deficit, instead, stems largely from the AB and the panel's unwillingness to rely upon existing DSU provisions, such as the right to seek technical advice from experts enshrined in Article 13 thereof. Transparency, in turn, is recognized in some WTO documents as a matter of principle, but its development into a full-blown doctrine is impeded by the intergovernmental nature of the WTO and the contrary will of its members. Predictability is expressly recognized as a desideratum by the DSU, although that document does not contain any reference to the *stare decisis* doctrine. As mentioned above, however, the AB jurisprudence and the consistent panel practice of following AB reports have substantially remedied that shortcoming. As far as timeliness is concerned, delays are chiefly attributable to a trade-off with due process norms, notably the parties' right to be heard and to be granted time to prepare their cases. Implementation and remedies are also a reflection of the intergovernmental and member-driven character of the WTO, which in spite of a number of "special and differential treatment" provisions cannot remedy the inequality of bargaining power among its members. The implementation record, however, is generally positive.

The potential for improvement varies according to the specific reason underlying the shortcomings outlined above. Deficiencies attributable to the intergovernmental character of the WTO (that is, insufficient guarantees of external independence of decision-makers; lack of transparency; failure to address inequality of bargaining power in the implementation phase) are the most difficult to rectify, for doing so would require amending the WTO agreements and the necessary political consensus appears to be lacking. Broadening the participation of non-state actors in panel and AB proceedings would certainly add to the transparency of the WTO dispute resolution system and would bring to the fore the need for broader guarantees of the external independence of decision-makers. Still, the negative reaction by many WTO members to the opening of floodgates to unsolicited *amicus curiae* briefs in *Asbestos* suggests that such changes are unlikely to take place in the short-to-medium run. Shortcomings linked to the lack of express recognition of certain due process norms by the DSU (that is, on *stare decisis* and on evidence) can be remedied by the AB jurisprudence without recourse to amendment of the WTO Agreements. AB case law has contributed significantly to enhancing the predictability of the dispute resolution system by establishing the current status of AB reports as persuasive sources of guidance. It might be hoped that the AB jurisprudence will reach a comparable level of clarity and consistency in respect of evidentiary principles and that it will be more willing to rely upon independent experts in the context of its economic evaluations. Finally, the current trade-off between timeliness and the parties' right to be heard and to be granted time to prepare their cases can be addressed by streamlining the application of the existing procedural arrangements, for instance by relying more extensively on the principle of judicial economy, by avoiding clearly redundant or duplicative questions by panels to the parties, and by limiting the additional time the panel accords to parties beyond the DSU requirements.[155]

The resulting picture is extremely heterogeneous. Compliance with institutional performance norms appears to be higher in the case of international organizations, such as OECD, UNCTAD, and ICN, which have no case-by-case decision-making and enforcement powers in antitrust matters. The only international organization

[155] *See* Matthew Kennedy, *supra* note 81, at 241–2.

whose mandate includes such powers, the WTO, faces shortcomings in terms both of due process and institutional performance. The institutional design of WTO as a member-driven, intergovernmental organization is directly linked to some of those deficiencies. At the same time, the provision of a comprehensive dispute settlement system and of a standing AB allowed the WTO to autonomously overcome some of the imperfections in the original design by its drafters.

Index

The manufacturer's authorised representative in the EU for product safety is Oxford University Press España S.A. of El Parque Empresarial San Fernando de Henares, Avenida de Castilla, 2 - 28830 Madrid (www.oup.es/en or product.safety@oup.com). OUP España S.A. also acts as importer into Spain of products made by the manufacturer.
Printed and bound by CPI Group (UK) Ltd, Croydon, CR0 4YY
14/09/2026
02216304-0015